D0151683

A CULTURE FOR DEMOCRACY

A Culture for Democracy

*Mass Communication and the Cultivated Mind
in Britain Between the Wars*

by
D. L. LeMahieu

CLARENDON PRESS·OXFORD

1988

Oxford University Press, Walton Street, Oxford OX2 6DP
Oxford New York Toronto
Delhi Bombay Calcutta Madras Karachi
Petaling Jaya Singapore Hong Kong Tokyo
Nairobi Dar es Salaam Cape Town
Melbourne Auckland
and associated companies in
Berlin Ibadan

Oxford is a trade mark of Oxford University Press

Published in the United States
by Oxford University Press, New York

British Library Cataloguing in Publication Data
LeMahieu, D. L.
A culture for democracy: mass communication
and the cultivated mind in Britain
between the wars.
1. Mass media – Great Britain – History
I. Title
302.2′ 34′ 0941   P92.G7
ISBN 0-19-820137-0

Library of Congress Cataloging in Publication Data
LeMahieu, D. L., 1945-
A culture for democracy.
Bibliography: p.   Includes index.
1. Mass media – Great Britain – History – 20th
century. 2. Great Britain – Popular culture – History –
20th century. I. Title.
P92.G7L46 1988   001.51′ 0941   87–31510
ISBN 0-19-820137-0

Phototypeset by Dobbie Typesetting Service,
Plymouth, Devon
Printed in Great Britain by
Biddles Ltd., Guildford and King's Lynn

To
Mary Hummel

ACKNOWLEDGEMENTS

I WOULD like to express my gratitude to a number of individuals and institutions. In 1977, a summer seminar sponsored by the National Endowment for the Humanities introduced me to the issues explored in this book. A year later, my research was generously assisted by a Rockefeller Foundation Humanities Fellowship. Throughout the project, Lake Forest College supported my efforts in many constructive ways.

The staffs of libraries and archives in both Great Britain and the United States greatly eased my task. My thanks to the British Library, BBC Written Archives Centre, British Film Institute, National Film Archive, Public Record Office, House of Lords Record Office, General Post Office Library, Cambridge University Library, the Institute of Historical Research, University of London Library, St Bride's Library, John Grierson Archive at the University of Sterling, Harry Ransom Humanities Research Center at the University of Texas at Austin, University of Michigan at Ann Arbor, University of Illinois at Chicago, Art Institute of Chicago, Center for Research Libraries in Chicago, University of Illinois at Urbana-Champaign, Northwestern University, Newberry Library, University of California at Los Angeles, New York Public Library, and the University of South Carolina. I owe a particular debt of gratitude to the librarians of the University of Chicago and Lake Forest College.

For permission to quote copyright sources, I would like to thank the BBC Written Archives Centre, the House of Lords Record Office, the Post Office Archives in London, and Mrs J. B. Priestley. E. McKnight Kauffer's *Soaring to Success* appears by courtesy of the Board of Trustees of the Victoria and Albert Museum.

Charles Miller and Arthur Zilversmit read the entire manuscript and offered valuable, detailed suggestions for improvement. I would also like to thank Elizabeth Eisenstein and James Turner for their perceptive suggestions on individual chapters.

My wife, Mary Hummel, often interrupted her own work as a molecular biologist to support me in this project. She listened to my ideas, travelled with me to distant archives, read every version of the manuscript, and encouraged me whenever the enterprise floundered. I dedicate the book to her.

D.L.LeM.

March 1987
Chicago, Illinois

CONTENTS

LIST OF ILLUSTRATIONS

Introduction

IN Arnold Bennett's drama *What the Public Wants*, first produced in 1909, a newspaper proprietor, clearly modelled on Lord Northcliffe, controls over forty different publications and enjoys reminding acquaintances that he revolutionized journalism. Sir Charles Worgan believes enthusiastically in one principle, reiterated throughout the play: 'Give the public what it wants.' As a merchant of culture, Worgan never questions the inherent justice of the market-place, where business serves its sovereign master, the consumer. He considers himself 'a man of the people' because his success as a journalist hinges upon the public's willingness to purchase his publications. He is a press lord precisely because he is a cultural democrat.

Yet, though Worgan may be invited to exclusive clubs, gentlemen ignore him. Oxford grants him an honorary degree, but only in exchange for a substantial contribution. In a society where wealth alone cannot assure social status, Worgan feels isolated. 'Your superior people won't have anything to do with me', he laments. To gain respect, he decides to underwrite a failing theatre whose manager, Holt St John, is 'a man of the finest artistic taste'. St John despises trade and ignores all commercial considerations in the production of his plays. Grateful for the subsidy and yet passionately committed to retaining complete artistic control, St John soon clashes with his benefactor.

ST JOHN. My scheme is to produce masterpieces.
WORGAN. And if the public won't come to see them?
ST JOHN. So much the worse for the public! The loss is theirs!
WORGAN. It seems to me the loss will also be ours.

Worgan believes that the box office measures success. St John argues that aesthetic excellence must be measured by other, more enduring standards. What the public wants is not what the public ought to have. Worgan eventually dismisses St John and rescues the theatre from bankruptcy by introducing a more popular repertoire. 'You've saved a fine enterprise,' St John remarks bitterly, 'and ruined it at the same time.'[1]

---

[1] Arnold Bennett, *What the Public Wants* (London: Duckworth, 1909), 7, 17, 23, 27, 31. Bennett first saw Northcliffe in London in 1896 and conceived the idea for the

Bennett's drama eschewed one-dimensional characters. Brusque, callow, and shamelessly materialistic, Worgan embodied personal traits which a West End audience expected of a press baron. Yet he was also generous to his employees, full of infectious vitality, and not without personal charm. The aesthete St John, on the other hand, championed a number of admirable cultural ideals, but was arrogant, self-indulgent, and in one episode needlessly cruel to an aspiring actress. St John revelled in his alienation from common humanity. As a writer from the provinces who often suffered the patronizing slurs of London critics, Arnold Bennett understood the pretensions and insensitivities of the conventionally sophisticated. Though he expressed reservations about the popular press, he refused to condemn its underlying democratic tendencies, just as he could never completely endorse the upper classes' view of their own cultural superiority.[2]

Bennett's play dramatized an important issue in modern British cultural history. In the late nineteenth and early twentieth centuries, the development of popular national daily newspapers, the cinema, the gramophone, and other forms of mass entertainment threatened to upset traditional patterns of British culture. Attracting an audience of unprecedented size, this 'mass' or 'commercial' culture—no single term unambiguously defines the phenomenon[3]—was created for profit, dependent upon new technologies, and often dominated by individuals outside the mainstream of British cultural life. Writers, artists, musicians, critics, and their numerous sympathizers responded in a variety of ways. Some retreated

play in Paris in 1908. See Arnold Bennett, *The Journals of Arnold Bennett, 1896–1910*, ed. Newman Flower (London: Cassell, 1932), 19, 299, 317. See also Arnold Bennett, *Letters of Arnold Bennett*, ed. James Hepburn, vol. 1 (London: Oxford University Press, 1966), 108, and vol. 2 (London: Oxford University Press, 1968), 252.

[2] On Bennett's life, see Margaret Drabble, *Arnold Bennett* (London: Weidenfeld and Nicolson, 1974).

[3] The problems of definition in cultural studies are notorious and need not be rehearsed at length here. Virtually every major descriptive term, including most notably 'culture', 'mass media', and 'mass communications', raises difficulties not easily mitigated by either elaborate attempts at more precise definition or the substitution of new, more idiosyncratic terminology. For good discussions of these problems, see, among others, Raymond Williams, *Keywords: A Vocabulary of Culture and Society* (n.p.: Fontana / Croom Helm, 1976); and C. W. E. Bigsby, 'The Politics of Popular Culture', in *Approaches to Popular Culture*, ed. C. W. E. Bigsby (Bowling Green, OH: Bowling Green University Press, 1976), 3–25. During the inter-war period, many observers used the words 'highbrow', 'middlebrow', and 'lowbrow' to describe various features of culture. I have tried to avoid these terms, in part because of the obvious bias within the spatial metaphor, and in part because it was not always clear to what the terms referred: the medium, the message, the communicator, or the relevant social class. My own descriptive shorthand, such as 'commercial culture' and 'cultivated élites', has obvious problems of its own, but seeks, perhaps naïvely, to provide more neutral terminology. For a good example of a pluralistic approach to various 'taste cultures', see Herbert J. Gans, *Popular Culture and High Culture: An Analysis and Evaluation of Taste* (New York: Basic Books, 1974).

into self-conscious isolation from the popular and the profane. Others engaged in detailed polemics against the mass media. Still others embraced new technology and sought to uplift tastes. All these groups struggled against a culture that measured success by popularity rather than aesthetic merit. With the significant extensions of the franchise in 1918 and 1928, Britain finally approached full parliamentary democracy. What culture was appropriate for that democracy became a question pitting the forces of the market-place against the influence of an articulate minority.

The following study analyses, selectively rather than comprehensively, the relations between commercial and élite culture in Britain during the inter-war period. Part One, 'The Rise of Modern Commercial Culture, 1890–1930', focuses on two closely related themes. First, it examines in detail the cultural relationship between supply and demand in the commercialized mass media. With more discretionary income, fewer working hours, and limited educational opportunities, audiences in the late nineteenth and early twentieth centuries responded eagerly to the attempts of entrepreneurs to meet their cultural needs. These entrepreneurs tapped new markets and devised new strategies in their attempt to entertain the public. A crucial element of these strategies, and the second theme of Part One, concerns how the press, cinema, and recording industries adapted new technologies to evolving cultural traditions. The development of film narrative, combined with a more visually oriented layout in newspapers, helped make images, as well as words, a central mode of communication. The gramophone, dominated like cinema by American influences, affected British popular music in complex, sometimes para-doxical ways.

Part Two begins by analysing the critique of commercial culture by intellectuals in the 1920s. Drawing upon the social psychology of crowds developed earlier in the century, a number of critics linked the popular press, cinema, and jazz to the lower instincts and sensations. They feared that American influences would buttress materialistic and egalitarian values which they argued were inimical to British culture and society. Some defended their élitism by claiming that art, like religion, transcended the ephemeral and the profane. Others sought a more scientific explanation for the superiority of their own tastes. Yet, despite pervasive hostility to the commercialized mass media in some circles, a surprising number of individuals refused to withdraw into cultural pessimism and sought instead to uplift tastes. These figures, here deemed 'progressives', faced two major problems. First, they needed to find sources of patronage which would shield them from the often harsh realities of the box office. In its attempt to raise standards, the BBC secured from government the right to monopolize an entire medium. Then too, a number of artists, typographers, and film-makers fostered good design by working for advertisers and government agencies committed to better public relations. Even with assured patronage, however, these progressives confronted a second problem. They felt the need to justify and make legitimate their embrace of new and often suspect technologies. In its hiring practices, official publications, and especially in its programming, the BBC conducted an extensive campaign to enhance its own respectability. Commercial artists and the early documentary film-makers helped gain legitimacy by borrowing heavily from artistic techniques on the Continent.

Part Three argues that the 1930s proved a crucial decade in the emergence of a culture that transcended the usual boundaries of class, region, and other determinants of aesthetic taste. The economic slump of the early 1930s made a number of intellectuals more sensitive to the needs of the general public. At the same time, marked improvements in technology combined with an infusion of creative talent raised the aesthetic standards of the commercialized mass media. Sight, sound, and the written word manifested these changes. Like Chaplin before them, gifted film-makers engaged audiences of all classes and backgrounds. Newspapers incorporated elements of layout and design once integral to the progressive agenda. After a series of quiet accommodations, the BBC became an important component of a genuinely national culture. Literary figures on the Left and Right formulated a critique of mass communications that implicitly acknowledged its hold over all social ranks. By the outbreak of the Second World War, Britain was still a nation profoundly divided by class. Yet an emerging common culture provided a shared frame of reference among widely divergent groups. Individuals, not unlike those from Bennett's play, could find common ground.

PART ONE

The Rise of Modern Commercial Culture
1890–1930

1

Producers and Consumers

BY making the market-place the most important arbiter of success, the mass media circumvented the authority of traditional cultural élites, accelerating a process begun centuries before in Britain. In a culture made explicitly for commerce, economic factors superseded aesthetic judgement as the central standard of merit. The producers of commercial culture treated popular newspapers, films, and gramophone records as commodities to be sold for profit rather than objects of intrinsic value or special moral worth. Unlike artists, writers, critics, and other creators of élite culture, those who marketed the commercialized mass media rarely claimed to be guardians of enduring values. They were businessmen who pursued their economic self-interest in a competitive market-place.

Yet the questions of who controlled the market-place and the cultural implications of such control remain highly controversial. To some observers, the consumer exercised ultimate sovereignty in an open market. The economic success of the commercialized mass media hinged upon their ability to entertain and instruct a diverse public. Press lords and movie moguls did indeed give the public what it wanted, and capitalism, for all its sins, satisfied the individual cultural desires of the general population. To other observers, ownership of the media carried with it the power to set agendas and manipulate audiences. The proprietors of mass communications exercised sovereignty over the market and, in a variety of ways, imposed their views on a public who lacked access to the same means of production. To still other observers, neither the producer nor the consumer reigned supreme. The mass media evolved through a complex interaction among many groups and interests, all of whom shared responsibility for commercial culture.

What was the relationship between supply and demand in the commercialized mass media? Who ultimately exercised sovereignty in the cultural market-place? What was the relationship between the producer and consumer of such things as a popular newspaper or a Hollywood film? By their nature, these questions invite speculation and resist definitive answers. No single theory encompasses fully the complex realities of an evolving culture, and persuasive historical evidence on many fundamental issues remains intrinsically difficult to find. For purposes here, however, these questions will be confronted by first examining the nature of supply and demand in the late nineteenth and early twentieth centuries. Then, after briefly examining the arguments of other commentators, it will be possible to suggest and provide detailed examples of an alternative means of understanding the elusive relationship between the producers and consumers of commercial culture.

A. COMMERCIAL CULTURE AND THE MARKET MECHANISM

From 1890 to 1930, the structure of demand for commercial culture altered considerably. The public which streamed into the cinemas and purchased daily newspapers by the millions differed substantially from the popular audience of the nineteenth century. First, the lower middle class burgeoned in size and changed in composition. Often despised and rarely studied in Britain, this class traditionally consisted of such groups as shopkeepers and small businessmen.[1] In the late nineteenth and early twentieth centuries, however, a marked increase in clerks, commercial travellers, and other white-collar occupations greatly enhanced the cultural power of this neglected class. Though, as usual, statistics involve considerable ambiguities, the total number of male white-collar employees over the age of fifteen increased from over 262,000 in 1871 to over 918,000 in 1911.[2] By 1911, the clerical profession, which included over 124,000 women, comprised one of the largest and most rapidly expanding occupational groups in Britain. This growth persisted throughout the inter-war period. Taking salaried workers as a whole, the number rose from 1.67 million in 1911 to 3.84 million in 1938.[3] Though frequently from impoverished backgrounds and often living within working-class neighbourhoods, the lower middle class identified strongly with the more affluent middle class. Intensely preoccupied with social status, clerks and other recruits to more 'respectable' occupations sought guidance about middle-class life from newspapers such as the *Daily Mail* and *Daily Express*. Northcliffe directed his journalists to write for an audience eager to keep up appearances.[4]

---

[1] See Michael J. Winstanley, *The Shopkeeper's World, 1830–1914* (Manchester: Manchester University Press, 1983), 2–104.

[2] Geoffrey Crossick, 'The Emergence of the Lower Middle Class in Britain: A Discussion', in *The Lower Middle Class in Britain, 1870–1914*, ed. Geoffrey Crossick (New York: St Martin's Press, 1977), 12, 19.

[3] G. L. Anderson, 'The Social Economy of Late-Victorian Clerks', in ibid., 113; Derek H. Aldcroft, *The Inter-War Economy in Britain, 1919–1939* (New York: Columbia University Press, 1970), 357–8.

[4] Richard N. Price, 'Society, Status and Jingoism: The Social Roots of Lower-Middle-Class Patriotism, 1870–1900', in Crossick, op. cit., 96; Tom Clarke, *My Northcliffe Diary* (New York: Cosmopolitan Book Corporation, 1931), 37, 39.

The rise in disposable incomes during the early decades of the twentieth century also affected demand for the commercialized mass media. Though statistical averages conceal substantial differences in wages among varying occupations and regions, the general trend was unmistakable. In 1938, average real wage-earnings were 30 per cent higher than in 1913, and real income per capita had risen by 31 per cent.[5] Working-class families began to retain more discretionary income. In 1904, for example, an average working-class household devoted 60 per cent of its income to food and 16 per cent to rent and local taxes. By 1938, these figures dropped to only 35 per cent spent on food and 9 per cent on rent and rates. Though a considerable minority of the British population still endured poverty, most wage-earners found themselves with more to spend on pleasurable diversions. A daily newspaper became easily affordable, and the cinema, with its low admission prices, rapid turnover of films, and often lavish surroundings, entertained entire families.[6]

An increase in leisure time also contributed to a greater demand for newspapers, films, and other mass media. Shortly after the First World War, the average working week dropped from 55 to 48 hours. This reduction followed a pattern of other decreases in the working week during the previous hundred years. As M. A. Bienefeld has demonstrated, adjustments occurred simultaneously throughout the economy during periods of relative prosperity. Workers believed that these reductions enhanced their job security.[7] Of course, more leisure time need not be synonymous with sharper demand for novel forms of entertainment. Many workers no doubt chose to sleep longer, engage in other forms of recreation, or simply remain idle.[8] Still, more free time made it easier to read a newspaper or attend a cinema.

Although a growing lower middle class, greater discretionary income, and more leisure time helped transform the structure of cultural demand, a vital constant remained the relatively low level of educational opportunity in Britain. At the turn of the century, authorities exempted around 40 per cent of all children from the school-leaving age of fourteen; only in 1922

[5] Aldcroft, op. cit., 363. See also A. L. Chapman and Rose Knight, *Wages and Salaries in the United Kingdom, 1920–1938* (Cambridge: Cambridge University Press, 1953), 30–3.

[6] Sidney Pollard, *The Development of the British Economy, 1914–1950* (London: Edward Arnold, 1962), 177, 290–1. On the relationship of price to the elasticity of demand, see H. G. Jones, 'Consumer Behaviour', in *The Economic System in the United Kingdom*, ed. Derek Morris (Oxford: Oxford University Press, 1977), 29–48.

[7] Arthur Marwick, 'After the Deluge', in *Twentieth-Century Britain: National Power and Social Welfare*, ed. Henry R. Winkler (New York and London: New Viewpoints, 1976), 27; M. A. Bienefeld, *Working Hours in British Industry: An Economic History* (London: Weidenfeld and Nicolson, 1972), 3–6, 224–5.

[8] R. W. Vickerman, *The Economics of Leisure and Recreation* (London: Macmillan, 1975), 6–7.

were such exemptions finally removed.[9] Kenneth Lindsay was shocked to report in 1926 that, of over a half-million children who left elementary schools each year, less than 10 per cent proceeded to secondary schools and only one in a thousand ever reached the university. Four years earlier, R. H. Tawney complained that, even among exceptionally intelligent students, only one-third were granted formal education beyond the age of fourteen.[10] Education remained a perquisite of wealth and social standing. 'The people of the upper classes and middle classes . . . get the best education for their children', one trade unionist remarked bitterly in 1920, '. . . then they turn around and twit us with our lack of educational culture.'[11] Attempts at reform during the inter-war period encountered formidable opposition. The Conservative Party clung to existing privileges, and the Labour Party often deferred to traditional notions of pedagogy. Above all, politicians agreed that the country could not afford a more equitable educational system.[12]

The result was a population whose formal education rarely extended beyond basic skills. Though generalizations about the curricula of primary schools prove hazardous,[13] most students acquainted themselves only fleetingly, if at all, with works which the élites deemed 'culture'. Moreover, since classes in many elementary schools enrolled as many as sixty children in often dilapidated surroundings, mere exposure to selections from the humanistic tradition hardly assured lifelong assimilation. For the working class especially, school often seemed a burdensome preliminary to the more authentic experience of work.[14] Even among the expanding lower middle classes, the limited opportunities for a respectable secondary education and university training separated them from the élites they sought to emulate. A good education, of course, did not assure allegiance to the cultivated arts. Young gentlemen in public schools and universities often squandered opportunities which others, including many women,

---

[9] Noreen Branson, *Britain in the Nineteen-Twenties* (London: Weidenfeld and Nicolson, 1975), 118–21. See also Charles Loch Mowat, *Britain Between the Wars, 1918–1940* (Chicago: University of Chicago Press, 1955), 206–11; and J. J. Curtis, *Education in Britain Since 1900* (London: Andrew Dakers, 1952).

[10] Kenneth Lindsay, *Social Progress and Educational Waste* (London: George Routledge and Sons, 1926), 7; R. H. Tawney, *Secondary Education for All: A Policy for Labour* (London: George Allen and Unwin [1922]), 67.

[11] Quoted in Brian Simon, *The Politics of Educational Reform, 1920–1940* (London: Lawrence and Wishart, 1974), 26.

[12] D. W. Dean, 'Conservatism and the National Education System, 1922–40', *Journal of Contemporary History* 6, 2 (1971): 150–65; Rodney Barker, *Education and Politics, 1900–1951: A Study of the Labour Party* (Oxford: Clarendon Press, 1972), 158–9.

[13] Peter Gordon and Denis Lawton, *Curriculum Change in the Nineteenth and Twentieth Centuries* (London: Hodder and Stoughton, 1978), 5.

[14] Standish Meacham, *A Life Apart: The English Working Class, 1890–1914* (Cambridge: Harvard University Press, 1977), 170–81.

would have sacrificed much to attain. Still, as recent studies demonstrate, educational background remains a crucial variable in determining cultural preferences.[15] Confronted with a public with rudimentary formal training, the commercial mass media refused to shoulder a responsibility which politicians largely ignored. Commercial culture entertained a public that the government claimed it could not afford to educate.

Much remains uncertain about the structure of demand for the commercial mass media, particularly in the early decades of the twentieth century. Though some British advertisers engaged in audience research after the First World War, extensive statistical data became available only in the 1930s, and much of this material lacked sophistication. Even if good evidence existed for earlier decades, however, knowledge of the age, sex, class, region, and occupation of the audience for newspapers, films, and music would reveal only part of the story. A young housewife from Slough who read the women's page of the *Daily Mail* might also appreciate the music of Chopin, just as a businessman who read *The Times* might faithfully attend the films of Douglas Fairbanks. Moreover, participation in a cultural activity ought not be equated with acquiescence to its values. Not all readers of the *Daily Express* shared Beaverbrook's idiosyncratic political views any more than a Queens Hall concert audience included only enthusiasts for Bach. Finally, even a sophisticated questionnaire cannot probe the deeper reasons for individual tastes, which often relate intimately to notions of personal identity. The 'masses' consisted of individuals whose distinctiveness statistical aggregates easily obscured. The essential nature of demand for the mass media, particularly in earlier eras, will always remain largely unknown.

The elusiveness of demand may help explain why most interested historians and sociologists prefer to concentrate on supply. Here evidence proves more abundant and less intractable. Newspapers, films, and other mass media were produced by a limited number of institutions which prospered by practising economies of scale. The greatest costs were incurred in creating the first copy of a newspaper or master print of a film. For this reason, large companies exercised a number of advantages over smaller competitors. Because they could afford the latest, most efficient technology, larger firms could create a technically superior product at less cost per unit. Large companies also enjoyed a more sophisticated division of labour, thus increasing both efficiency and quality. Moreover, they raised more money, spread their financial risk, and profited from other advantages as well.[16] As many scholars

---

[15] Colin Seymour-Ure, *The Press, Politics and the Public: An Essay on the Role of the National Press in the British Political System* (London: Methuen, 1968), 40–1.

[16] On economies of scale, see E. A. G. Robinson, *The Structure of Competitive Industry* (Cambridge: Cambridge University Press, 1935); C. F. Pratten and R. M. Dean,

have noted, the ownership of the mass media in the twentieth century concentrated into fewer hands.

The press offers the most closely studied illustration. In the nineteenth century, the British press remained a small-scale operation. A great many daily, Sunday, weekly, and provincial newspapers survived with comparatively few readers. With the coming of the popular national daily press at the turn of the century, however, advertisers flocked to papers with large circulations. Improvements in printing technology, an expanding urban population, and the entrepreneurial skills of men such as Alfred Harmsworth contributed to the rapid expansion of the popular daily press. The entry price into this market increased dramatically. Whereas in 1850 it cost £25,000 to establish a daily newspaper, by 1900 the price rose to over £500,000. By 1910, three companies controlled over a third of the morning circulation and four-fifths of the evening circulation in London.[17]

These trends continued during the inter-war period. In 1918, national dailies sold 3.1 million copies; eight years later the figure climbed to 4.7 million. By 1939, 10.6 million copies of daily newspapers sold each day. Moreover, the number of provincial morning dailies declined from 41 in 1921 to 25 in 1937, many controlled by large newspaper chains based in London. Trusts owned 40 per cent of the provincial evening papers in 1934 and half the Sunday newspapers.[18] By the 1930s, the press constituted a major British industry, with net output surpassing that of shipbuilding and chemicals.[19]

The film industry underwent a similar evolution towards greater concentration of power. The story is complicated, since the industry was divided into three interrrelated operations—production, distribution, and exhibition—each with its own history. Moreover, unlike the newspaper business, British film suffered from intense foreign competition. During

The Economies of Large-Scale Production in British Industry: An Introductory Study (Cambridge: Cambridge University Press, 1965); and C. F. Pratten, *Economies of Scale in Manufacturing Industry* (Cambridge: Cambridge University Press, 1971).

[17] Alan Lee, 'The Structure, Ownership and Control of the Press, 1855–1914', in *Newspaper History: From the Seventeenth Century to the Present Day*, eds. George Boyce, James Curran, and Pauline Wingate (London: Constable; Beverly Hills: Sage, 1978), 127.

[18] Graham Murdock and Peter Golding, 'The Structure, Ownership and Control of the Press, 1914–76', in ibid., 130; Colin Seymour-Ure, 'National Daily Papers and the Party System', in Oliver Boyd-Bennett, Colin Seymour-Ure, and Jeremy Tunstall, *Studies on the Press*, Royal Commission on the Press (London: HMSO, 1977), 189–90. On newspaper trusts, see aso Viscount Camrose, *British Newspapers and Their Controllers* (London: Cassell, 1947); and J. Cranfeld Hicks, *Newspaper Finance* (London: General Press, n.d.)

[19] Political and Economic Planning, *Report on the British Press: A Survey of its Current Operations and Problems* (London: Political and Economic Planning, 1938), 44. On the press as an industry, see also H. A. Innis, *The Press: A Neglected Factor in the Economic History of the Twentieth Century* (London: Oxford University Press, 1949).

the First World War and throughout much of the inter-war period, American companies dominated the production and distribution of the movies. In 1926, less than 5 per cent of the films shown in British cinemas were domestically produced.[20] The exhibition of films, however, was largely controlled by the British. As the presentation of films moved from music halls, fairgrounds, and rented rooms into more permanent structures, the number of exhibiting companies skyrocketed from only three in 1908 to an astounding 1,833 in 1914. The American control of production and, through their subsidiaries, distribution as well, accelerated the formation of exhibiting circuits. These circuits could bargain more effectively with producers and practice economies of scale. Often well-financed and with a guaranteed distribution, some circuits began to produce films of their own. Three circuits set the standards for exhibition in the 1930s. Gaumont British, founded in 1927, acquired the largest circuit of exhibitors from Lord Beaverbrook in 1929, and by 1931 owned well over 300 cinemas.[21] With Michael Balcon in charge of operations, Gaumont British also produced films at Shepherd's Bush. One of their rivals, Associated British Cinemas, operated over 300 cinemas by the mid-1930s and, like Gaumont British, produced its own films. The third major circuit, Odeon, became famous for the modern design of its conveniently situated cinemas. By 1937, over 200 Odeons, many with enormous seating capacities, served the British public. Though these three circuits controlled only a fraction of all cinema seats in Britain, they often exhibited the most popular films at the best locations.[22]

The history of the gramophone industry in Britain remains less well documented. Though in the early days of acoustic recording a variety of small firms cut records and produced phonographs, two companies quickly emerged as the industry's leaders. Formed in the late 1890s, the Gramophone Company quickly prospered and within a decade included branches throughout Europe. In 1908, it began pressing records at its giant plant at Hayes, Middlesex. Though predictably the company lost much of its European business during the First World War, it rebounded

---

[20] On the American domination of the film in Britain, see, among others, Rachael Low, *The History of the British Film, 1918–1929* (London: George Allen and Unwin, 1971), 71–106; and Robert Sklar, *Movie-Made America* (New York: Vintage, 1975), 215–27.

[21] Political and Economic Planning, *The British Film Industry* (London: Political and Economic Planning, 1952), 17–44; Board of Trade, *Tendencies to Monopoly in the Cinematograph Film Industry* (London: HMSO, 1944), 19.

[22] Perhaps the most pronounced concentration of the film business in England occurred in the 1940s, when J. Arthur Rank consolidated a large share of the industry under his own command. See Alan Wood, *Mr. Rank: A Study of J. Arthur Rank and British Films* (London: Hodder and Stoughton, 1952), 50–7, 81 ff.; and F. D. Klingender and Stuart Legg, *Money Behind the Screen* (London: Lawrence and Wishart, 1937), 14–23. Klingender and Legg should be used with care.

sufficiently in the 1920s to expand into radio, telephones, and film. Its chief competitor, Columbia, began as an American operation which opened its first office in London in 1900. By 1903, Columbia manufactured 50,000 records a month for the European market. In a reversal of the usual pattern, the American parent industry performed considerably less well than its English subsidiary. In 1923, a British consortium bought out the American branch. The company flourished in the 1920s and purchased a number of its European rivals. The world depression, however, severely affected sales. In 1931, Columbia and the Gramophone Company merged into Electrical and Musical Industries—EMI—a gigantic firm which dominated the English market in the 1930s to a degree unmatched in either the film or newspaper industries. Only Decca provided real competition.[23]

The cultural implications of this concentration of economic power within various media remains a contentious topic. To commentators on the British Left—an extraordinarily diverse group who in recent times have dominated the relevant historical and theoretical research[24]—the trend towards monopoly ownership rendered meaningless any unqualified claims to consumer sovereignty. Some Marxist scholars equated economic control of the mass media with cultural authority over its audience. These observers replaced the doctrine of consumer sovereignty, where demand generated supply, with the opposing orthodoxy of producer sovereignty, where supply created demand.[25] Others among the Left strongly criticized

[23] Oliver Read and Walter L. Welch, *From Tin Foil to Stereo: Evolution of the Phonograph*, 2nd edn. (Indianapolis: Howard W. Sams, 1977), 506–10. See also Roland Gelatt, *The Fabulous Phonograph, 1877–1977*, 2nd rev. edn. (London: Cassell, 1977), 245–77; Ogilvie Mitchell, *The Talking Machine Industry* (London: Sir Isaac Pitman and Sons [1922]); and Geoffrey Jones, 'The Gramophone Company: An Anglo-American Multinational, 1898–1931', *Business History Review* 59 (1985): 76–100.

[24] In general, this brief analysis does not include discussion of those Marxist writers in Britain heavily influenced by French theorists such as Metz, Lacan, and Althusser. This tradition, prominent especially in the 1970s, sustained its most severe criticism from other Marxists who charged that its implicit philosophical idealism ignored or distorted the historical experience of actual individuals. See, among others, E. P. Thompson, *The Poverty of Theory and Other Essays* (New York and London: Monthly Review Press, 1978), 1–210; Nicholas Garnham, 'Subjectivity, Ideology, Class and Historical Materialism', *Screen* 20, 1 (1979): 121–34; Stuart Hall, 'Recent Developments in Theories of Language and Ideology: A Critical Note', in *Culture, Media, Language: Working Papers in Cultural Studies*, ed. Stuart Hall *et al.* (London: Hutchinson in association with the Centre for Contemporary Cultural Studies, University of Birmingham, 1980), 157–62; and Kevin McDonnell and Kevin Robins, 'Marxist Cultural Theory: the Althusserian Smokescreen', in *One-Dimensional Marxism: Althusser and the Politics of Culture*, ed. Simon Clarke *et al.* (London: Allison and Busby, 1980), 157–231. For a recent attempt to reformulate the Left's relationship to popular culture, see Colin MacCabe, ed., *High Theory/Low Culture: Analysing Popular Television and Film* (New York: St Martin's Press, 1986).

[25] See, for example, Stuart Holland, 'Countervailing Press Power', in *The British Press: A Manifesto*, ed. James Curran (London: Macmillan, 1978), 94–113; Graham Murdock and Peter Golding, 'Confronting the Market: Public Intervention and Press Diversity',

this 'economic reductionism'. Borrowing their analytic categories from Gramsci and others, they maintained that élites sustained their cultural hegemony over society in complex ways, including tolerance of opposing political philosophies and a pious but essentially hollow commitment to liberal-democratic principles. Though in this view producers still remained ultimately sovereign, the working class consented to its own domination and thereby bore some responsibility for its cultural plight.[26] Although the notion of 'hegemony', if carefully defined, might be applied usefully to interpret commercial culture in the early twentieth century, Gramsci's analytical concept was not without serious limitations.[27]

in ibid., 75–93; eid., 'Ideology and Mass Media: The Question of Determination', in *Ideology and Cultural Production*, ed. Michelle Bennett *et al.* (New York: St Martin's Press, 1979), 198 ff.; and eid., 'Capitalism, Communications and Class Relations', in *Mass Communication and Society*, ed. James Curran, Michael Gurevitch, and Janet Woollacott (London: Edward Arnold, 1977), 12–43.

[26] The literature on hegemony and culture in Britain remains immense. For two good general discussions, see Raymond Williams, *Marxism and Literature* (Oxford: Oxford University Press, 1977), 75–141; and Stuart Hall, 'Culture, the Media, and the "Ideological Effect"', in *Mass Communication and Society*, 315–48. See also Geoff Eley, 'Reading Gramsci in English: Some Observations on the Reception of Antonio Gramsci in the English-Speaking World, 1957–1982', CRSO Working Paper 314, Center for Research and Social Organization, University of Michigan; and Robert Bocock, *Hegemony* (Chichester: Ellis Horwood; London and New York: Tavistock, 1986). For studies of specific media that employ the concept with varying degrees of sophistication, see, among many others, Alan Lee, *The Origins of the Popular Press in England, 1855–1914* (London: Croom Helm; Totowa, NJ: Rowman and Littlefield, 1976); James Curran and Jean Seaton, *Power Without Responsibility: The Press and Broadcasting in Britain* (n.p.: Fontana Paperbacks, 1981); James Curran and Vincent Porter, eds., *British Cinema History* (London: Weidenfeld and Nicolson, 1983); Michael Chanan, *The Dream That Kicks: The Prehistory and Early Years of Cinema in Britain* (London: Routledge and Kegan Paul, 1980); and Jerry Palmer, *Thrillers: Genesis and Structure of a Popular Genre* (London: Edward Arnold; New York: St Martin's Press, 1979). For some particularly controversial applications of the notion, see Glasgow University Media Group, *Bad News* and *More Bad News* (London: Routledge and Kegan Paul, 1976 and 1980). See also Greg Philo *et al.*, *Really Bad News* (London: Writers and Readers, 1982).

[27] Two criticisms might be emphasized. First, for some (though certainly not all) of its proponents, the theory of hegemony became almost always self-verifying. For example, some practitioners of the concept argued that a society ensured its own stability by maintaining a consensus of values to which virtually all elements of culture contributed. Once this essentially tautological argument had been asserted, what remained was to show how specific institutions and cultural norms functioned as part of a larger social consensus. Yet the notion of hegemony proved elastic enough to explain apparent deviations from the norm as well. Thus, if a liberal-democratic society occasionally became subject to intense criticism, these attacks reinforced 'bourgeois capitalism' because they were encompassed in the widely accepted norm of 'freedom of speech'. This logic made every exception part of the rule. Even evidence adduced to break out of the argument's fundamental circularity often depended upon essentially oracular judgements. What constituted 'hegemonic' and 'counter-hegemonic' behaviour became easy to assert in theory; far more arbitrary, controversial, and problematic to determine in practice. What are the specific criteria, and who decides what is 'hegemonic' and what 'counter-hegemonic'? Second, even the more sophisticated applications of the theory presumed an understanding of self-interest distinct from and superior to the historical figures or groups under discussion. Though

Marxist arguments embodied an important corrective to the naïve doctrine of consumer sovereignty. The growing concentration of ownership of the mass media in the twentieth century unquestionably carried with it power to help set cultural agendas, shape tastes, and mould political opinions. Press lords, for example, used their newspapers to disseminate their personal views on a number of controversial issues. Beaverbrook's 'Empire Free Trade Campaign' in the late 1920s and early 1930s was an especially blatant attempt to manipulate the political views of his readers.[28] There were also far more subtle ways of promoting self-interest and relegating opposing or threatening views to the political margins. Clearly, ownership of a major branch of communications carried with it the power to generate favourable publicity for self-serving causes and, often less overtly, for the interests of the dominant social classes.

Yet, significant economic and cultural restraints limited this power. Press lords and movie moguls often faced intense competition from within their own medium and from other media. Edison's attempt to monopolize the American film industry was broken, in part, by independents who refused to be excluded from a lucrative market. When these independents themselves gained control of the industry, their dominance, like that of the Motion Picture Patents Company earlier, proved short-lived.[29] Moreover, the economies of scale which gave large enterprises an advantage over their smaller competitors existed in part because the public was often unpredictable in its tastes. In the film and recording industries,

its adherents often disavowed the connection, the doctrine of hegemony represented a more subtle version of the Marxist concept of 'false consciousness'. It assumed but rarely made explicit the view that by consenting to mass culture, the working class departed from more authentic responsibility to itself and to its historical mission. Historians and sociologists became, in effect, arbiters of the self-interest of their subjects. They quietly patronized the cultural tastes and political convictions of the average individuals whose 'real' interests they claimed to understand and sought to promote. Though such often unintended condescension drew upon a long tradition among radical intellectuals in Britain, it undermined the democratic and populist elements in socialism which many Marxists so eloquently defended. For some recent critiques of the notion of hegemony, see Nicholas Abercrombie, Stephen Hill, and Bryan S. Turner, *The Dominant Ideology Thesis* (London: George Allen and Unwin, 1980); and, mainly on American examples, T. J. Jackson Lears, 'The Concept of Cultural Hegemony: Problems and Possibilities', *American Historical Review* 90, 3 (1985): 567–93.

[28] A. J. P. Taylor, *Beaverbrook* (New York: Simon and Schuster, 1972), 246–326. For an example of a campaign by Northcliffe, see Reginald Pound and Geoffrey Harmsworth, *Northcliffe* (London: Cassell, 1959), 404.

[29] Sklar, *Movie-Made America*, 33–47, 141–60, 269–85; Ralph Cassady, Jun., 'Monopoly in Motion Picture Production and Distribution: 1908–1915', in *The American Movie Industry: The Business of Motion Pictures*, ed. Gorham Kindem (Carbondale: Southern Illinois University Press, 1982), 25–68; Jeanne Thomas Allen, 'The Decay of the Motion Pictures Patents Company', in *The American Film Industry*, ed. Tino Balio (Madison: University of Wisconsin Press, 1976), 119–34. See also Mae Huettig, *Economic Control of the Motion Picture Industry* (Philadelphia: University of Pennsylvania Press, 1944).

particularly, owners needed to create their products in quantity, since most records and films failed or barely broke even. For every hit record, scores languished unsold. For every successful film, others attracted only the compulsive movie-goer. Though film producers often overstated their dependence on the changing tastes of the paying customer, few could portend what films would prove successful.[30] The fickleness of demand limited the powers of supply. Those who championed notions of producer sovereignty never explained how a newspaper or a film could be forced upon an unwilling public, or why it was that only producers pursued their own self-interest. Newspapers, films, and popular music were not necessities of life. Even a complete monopoly could not assure sales of an item no one wanted to purchase. The doctrine of producer sovereignty, like that of consumer sovereignty, simplified the relationship between producer and consumer.

A preoccupation with the ownership and economic control of the commercialized mass media easily led to a belief in the doctrine of producer sovereignty or to its more sophisticated counterpart, the notion of hegemonic domination. Conversely, an analysis which stressed the sovereignty of the consumer reduced the producers to passive servants of the public and ignored the ability of powerful economic interests to manipulate the market to the own advantage. In either case, discussion about the mass media often quickly became a commentary upon the fairness or inequities of capitalism itself. Such arguments proved difficult to resolve empirically and summoned convictions beyond the reach of dispassionate analysis. Nevertheless, the cultural relationship between producer and consumer, between performer and public, lay at the heart of modern commercial culture in Britain.

B. MASS MEDIA AND AUDIENCE IDENTIFICATION

In the past thirty years, sociologists have proposed a number of models which describe the relationship between mass communicators and their audiences in liberal-democratic societies. These models range greatly in complexity. The simplest, or 'one-step flow theories', claim that messages proceed directly from the media to the public— a variation of the notion of producer sovereignty. The more complicated theories, often portrayed

---

[30] 'If we knew in advance when we made any picture how it was going to be taken by the public, we'd have to hire a hall to hold the money.' Quoted in Jay Leyda, ed., *Voices of Film Experience* (New York: Macmillan; London: Collier Macmillan, 1977), 523. See also Mel Gussow, *Don't Say Yes Until I Finish Talking: A Biography of Darryl F. Zanuck* (New York: Doubleday, 1971), 97–8; and Jack L. Warner, *My First Hundred Years in Hollywood* (New York: Random House, 1964), 125, 326–7.

with the help of elaborate charts and diagrams, argue in favour of a complex interrelationship between communicators and the audience. These 'multi-cycle, multi-step' flow models reject the view that any single group or factor determines the nature of mass communication.[31] Though the models differ substantially, they share the notion that mass communication always involves some degree of 'feedback'. This inelegant and now pervasive term refers, of course, to the way in which a system regulates itself in response to changing conditions.[32] In the study of mass media, the term usually encompasses opinion polls, market surveys, letters, and other means of discovering audience reaction. The communicator employs this information to modify his product in response to changing public demands.

In the late nineteenth century and early twentieth centuries, the most significant measure of audience response for the commercial mass media was found in the market-place. Producers measured approval by sales. 'A daily paper which does not receive significant support from readers and advertisers to pay its own way', one of Northcliffe's best editors proclaimed, 'cannot be said to represent the opinions of any substantial section of the people.' Northcliffe himself put it more succinctly. 'A newspaper is to be made to pay. Let it deal with what interests the mass of people.'[33] This belief that profitability measured public support was not always disputed by the more traditional editors of the quality press. In his memoirs, J. A. Spender, the former editor of the bankrupted *Westminster Gazette*, admitted disarmingly that 'had we been put in charge of a really popular paper with an up-to-date circulation, we could have been relied upon to kill it in about a fortnight.'[34] Garvin of the *Observer*

[31] For a brief summary of recent theories, with diagrams, see Phillip Emmert and William Donaghy, *Human Communications: Elements and Contexts* (Reading, MA: Addison Wesley, 1981), 351–9. On the sociology of mass communications, see Melvin L. DeFleur, *Theories of Mass Communication* (New York: David McKay, 1966), 118–40; Denis McQuail, *Towards a Sociology of Mass Communications* (London: Collier Macmillan, 1969), 36–57; Jeremy Tunstall, 'Introduction', in *Media Sociology: A Reader*, ed. Jeremy Tunstall (Urbana: University of Illinois Press, 1970), 1–38; David Chaney, *Processes of Mass Communications* (London: Macmillan, 1972); and W. Phillips Davison and Frederick T. C. Yu, eds., *Mass Communications Research: Major Issues and Future Directions* (New York: Praeger, 1974).

[32] F. Craig Johnson and George R. Klare, 'Feedback: Principles and Analogies', *Journal of Communication* 12, 1 (1962): 150–9; Theodore Clevenger, jun. and Jack Matthews, 'Feedback', in *Basic Readings in Communication Theory*, ed. C. David Mortensen (New York: Harper and Row, 1973), 153–60. The term was popularized in the cybernetics of Norbert Wiener. See Stephen Littlejohn, *Theories of Human Communication* (Columbus, Ohio: Charles E. Merrill, 1978), 37–41.

[33] Kennedy Jones, *Fleet Street and Downing Street* (London: Hutchinson [1920]), 323. Northcliffe quoted in Hamilton Fyfe, *Northcliffe: An Intimate Biography* (New York: Macmillan, 1930), 83.

[34] J. A. Spender, *Life, Journalism and Politics*, vol. 2 (London: Cassell, 1927), 136. On the failure of the *Gazette*, he wrote: 'The appeal, therefore, was deliberately to the few. The trouble was that they were so very few, as newspapers reckon numbers.' Ibid., 134.

was equally indifferent to mass appeal. 'I mean to give the public what they don't want,' he declared.[35] Editors like Spender and Garvin measured their success by such intangibles as political influence and reputation among the cultivated élite.[36] Films and popular newspapers relied upon a quantifiable and far more certain indication of approval.

The feedback mechanism of sales and box-office receipts was only one means whereby consumers helped shape the content of commercial culture. A more important and less obvious bond between producer and consumer occurred whenever either, or both, identified with the other. On the one hand, producers shaped their products in expectation of audience response. As a number of recent studies of the mass media have demonstrated, communicators constantly accommodated their often self-serving messages to fit what they believed the public expected. Newspaper editors frequently pondered the views of 'imaginary interlocutors' from their intended audience and adjusted their journalism accordingly. The script writers of films created movies that identified with the views of their targeted public.[37] On the other hand, audiences purchased newspapers and selected films which best met their expectations about entertainment and information. They too pursued their self-interest in the market-place. The economic power of press lords, movie moguls, and their counterparts in other areas of commercial culture remained contingent upon the approval of the audience they sought to inform and amuse. Far from dictating the cultural preferences of their public, producers needed to bind themselves to the tastes of a diverse audience.

In describing their business, the creators of British commercial culture often affirmed the need to identify with their intended audience. 'In order to purvey successfully to any section of a public "what it wants",' Northcliffe believed, 'the purveyor must be in sympathy with his customers.' James Drawbell, who became editor of the *Sunday Chronicle* in

[35] Quoted in Linton Andrews and H. A. Taylor, *Lords and Laborers of the Press: Men Who Fashioned the Modern British Newspaper* (Carbondale: Southern Illinois University Press; London: Feffer and Simons, 1970), 83.

[36] Thus, for example, in evaluating the performance of the *Observer*, the historian Alfred Gollin remarks: 'Although the paper was failing as a business institution, men like Edward Dicey, H. D. Trail and Justin Huntley McCarthy had established its reputation as a thoughtful, high-class journal of opinion.' Alfred M. Gollin, *The* Observer *and J. L. Garvin, 1908–1914: A Study in a Great Editorship* (London: Oxford University Press, 1960), 6.

[37] Ithiel de Sola Pool and Irwin Shulman, 'Newsmen's Fantasies, Audiences, and Newswriting', in *People, Society and Mass Communications*, ed. Lewis Anthony Dexter and David Manning White (New York: Free Press, 1964), 141–58; Paul Espinosa, 'The Audience in the Text: Ethnographic Observations of a Hollywood Story Conference', *Media, Culture and Society* 4 (1982): 77–86. See also Denis McQuail, 'Uncertainty About the Audience and the Organization of Mass Communications', in *Mass Communications: Selected Readings for Librarians*, ed. K. J. McGarry (London: Clive Bingley, 1972), 178–86.

1925, put it another way. 'All must spring from the editor's identification
with the reader. . . . An editor must first and last know people, the great
mass of people, happy and unhappy, who work for a living.'[38] This
process of identification meant that communicators needed to approach
their public as individuals worthy of close attention. 'The man who buys
this paper in the street may have as clear a head and as sound a judgement
as the man who sits in the editorial chair,' the *Daily Express* declared
on its first day of publication in 1900. 'We do not think that because
we print our thoughts and you speak only yours, our thoughts are
necessarily better than yours.' Even allowing for rhetorical exaggeration,
this view marked a departure from the approach of the élite press, where
editors sometimes considered themselves enlightened arbiters of political
opinion.[39]

   This need to identify with the average reader helps explain why many
popular journalists lacked more than a minimum of formal education.
'Highly educated men, I find as a rule, have no sense of news,' the editor
of the *Daily Mirror* complained to Northcliffe in 1911. 'We have Oxford
men here and Eton men,' he continued, '. . . and they are woefully ignorant
of any thing that has happened since BC 42.'[40] London popular dailies
recruited most journalists from the provinces, and few were educated
beyond the school-leaving age of fourteen. 'The truth is', Arthur Lawrence
wrote in his *Journalism as a Profession*, published in 1903, 'that certain
writers are commonplace people who perceive and reflect in a very
commonplace fashion, and therefore make a direct appeal to average
people.' One of Northcliffe's best editors, Kennedy Jones, freely admitted
the truth behind Salisbury's sneer that the *Daily Mail* was written for
and by office boys.[41] The success of a popular newspaper hinged upon
its ability to engage a public at its own level of understanding.

   Within the commercial mass media, many individuals privately expressed
contempt for the general public. Critics of Hollywood, in particular,
exposed the greed and cynicism which permeated the 'democratic art'.
It might therefore seem naïve to argue that the media identified strongly
with their public. Yet it is crucial to distinguish between private opinions

---

[38] Fyfe, *Northcliffe*, 37; James Drawbell, *The Sun Within Us* (London: Collins, 1963), 276.

[39] *Daily Express*, 24 Apr. 1900. On the élite press, see Stephen Koss, *The Rise and Fall of the Political Press in Britain*, 2 vols. (Chapel Hill: University of North Carolina Press, 1981, 1984).

[40] Alex Kenealy to Northcliffe, 12 Mar. 1911, Northcliffe MSS, British Library Deposit 4890, vol. 82. The same statement is slightly misquoted in Pound and Harmsworth, *Northcliffe*, 416.

[41] Arthur Lawrence, ed., *Journalism as a Profession* (London: Hodder and Stoughton, 1903), 14–15; Jones, *Fleet Street*, 202. There are a number of versions of Salisbury's famous remark.

and professional roles. As private individuals, journalists, film-makers, song writers, and other creators of commercial culture might indeed have been cynical about their craft and contemptuous of the public. As professional communicators, however, these same people could not afford to alienate their audience. The creators of the media needed the good will of the public to survive. They needed to engage their audience. Private attitudes could not be allowed to cloud professional responsibilities.

It could be argued that members of the public also played roles in the process of mass communication. As members of an audience in a cinema, for example, they willingly suspended disbelief in order to be entertained. They accepted fantasies which as private individuals they rejected in their daily lives. Men and women who recognized life to be tragic often demanded happy endings as members of an audience. Individuals who knew evil could prevail in actual circumstances often demanded moral order to be restored in films and fiction. Professional communicators responded to these desires. Although they often understood little about the actual individuals who purchased newspapers or attended films, they knew a great deal about the expectations of members of the audience. In commercial culture, it could be argued, the key relationship was often that between the 'communicator' and the 'audience member', not between the two private individuals who happened to be filling those roles.[42]

By identifying pragmatically with the needs of their audience, and then measuring success by actual sales, commercial culture evolved through a process of trial and error. 'His hits were so numerous that his misses were soon forgotten,' a colleague of Northcliffe wrote, 'but if anyone cared to compile a record of them, their total would be surprising.'[43] In general, Northcliffe, like other press lords in Britain and the film studios of Hollywood, tended to play it safe. They adopted the techniques which had proved successful over time. Film-makers, for example, borrowed from the literary formulas of nineteenth-century popular culture and adapted them to the new medium. The Western, for example, drew for its early development from a popular literary tradition that began with James Fenimore Cooper and included the dime novels of the late nineteenth century. Hollywood producers could always rely on a relatively small but dependable audience for the simple adventure stories of conventional Western films. If a film producer sought a mass audience, however, he

---

[42] These types of distinction are sometimes employed in reader-response criticism. For an early and instructive discussion of this separation between individual and author, and individual and reader, see Walker Gibson, 'Authors, Speakers, Readers, and Mock Readers', in *Reader-Response Criticism: From Formalism to Post-Structuralism*, ed. Jane P. Tompkins (Baltimore: Johns Hopkins University Press, 1980), 1–6.

[43] J. A. Hammerton, *With Northcliffe in Fleet Street* (London: Hutchinson [1932]), 145.

needed to alter the formula to anticipate the demands of a more diverse public. Once a new variation became successful, imitators quickly exhausted the market until yet another departure invigorated the old themes and stereotyped characters. This preference for refurbishing established formulas rather than experimenting with new genres often exasperated critics, but Hollywood claimed that it could not afford to be radically innovative.[44]

Less studied by scholars than formulas and genre films, the 'human-interest story' was another example of how the commercial mass media engaged their audience by borrowing from the traditions of nineteenth-century popular culture. Easy to recognize and difficult to define, the human-interest story gained prominence in the American 'penny press' of the 1830s. The *New York Sun* (1833), *New York Evening Transcript* (1833), and *New York Herald* (1835) rapidly increased their circulations by filling their pages with reports of crime, animal stories, anecdotes about bizarre occurrences, and other entertaining bits of information.[45] In the Yellow Press of late nineteenth century America, Pulitzer and Hearst specialized in exposing scandals and corruption among the rich and powerful. Their newspapers became self-proclaimed champions of populist causes.[46] In Britain, the popular Sunday press of the nineteenth century carried detailed accounts of lurid crimes, but it was not until the 'New Journalism' of the 1880s that the human-interest story began to penetrate the journalism of the daily press.[47] Drawing upon these traditions and also his own experience as founder and editor of a successful imitator of *Tit-Bits*, Northcliffe created a daily popular press in England which

[44] John G. Cawelti, *Adventure, Mystery and Romance: Formulaic Stories as Art and Popular Culture* (Chicago: University of Chicago Press, 1976), 192–259 and esp. 231–2. See also his *The Six-Gun Mystique* (Bowling Green, OH: Bowling Green University Press, 1971). On Westerns, see also James K. Folson, *The American Western Novel* (New Haven: College and University Press, 1966); and Phillip French, *Westerns* (Bloomington: Indiana University Press, 1973). There are also a number of books on individual writers of Westerns and on directors of Western films. On the conservatism of genre films, see Thomas Schatz, *Hollywood Genres: Formulas, Film-making and the Studio System* (Philadelphia: Temple University Press, 1981), 5–6.

[45] Helen MacGill Hughes, *News and the Human-Interest Story* (Chicago: University of Chicago Press, 1940), 7. I have learned much from this perceptive and original study.

[46] Julian S. Rammelkamp, *Pulitzer's* Post-Dispatch, *1878–1883* (Princeton: Princeton University Press, 1967), 165–7; George Juergens, *Joseph Pulitzer and the New York* World (Princeton: Princeton University Press, 1966), esp. ch. 10. See also W. A. Swanberg, *Pulitzer* (New York: Charles Scribner's Sons, 1967); and id., *Citizen Hearst: A Biography of William Randolph Hearst* (New York: Charles Scribner's Sons, 1961).

[47] Raymond L. Schults, *Crusader in Babylon: W. T. Stead and the* Pall Mall Gazette (Lincoln: University of Nebraska Press, 1972), 29–65; Lee, *Origins of Popular Press*, 117–30. See also Richard D. Altick, *Deadly Encounters: Two Victorian Sensations* (Philadelphia: University of Pennsylvania Press, 1986), 3–10.

sought to create a personal relationship with its readers. 'A newspaper makes its way in the world', Kennedy Jones wrote, 'and stands highest in the graces of its readers which establishes a reputation for the human qualities we seek in our friends.'[48]

Human-interest stories engaged their audience on a number of levels. First, by extending the definition of news beyond its customary preoccupations with politics and business, such stories underscored the significance of commonplace events.[49] Though the general population could become intensely involved with such issues as peace and war, politics remained the preserve of an élite, remote from the daily life of most citizens. Then too, although economic news might retain its objective importance, a vast majority of people lacked the disposable income to be concerned with investments and shifting business fortunes. Human-interest stories permitted newspapers to reflect a broader mosaic of English society. Northcliffe maintained that in the nineteenth century 'journalism dealt with only a few aspects of life. What we did was to extend its purview to life as a whole.'[50] In the *Daily Mail*, *Daily Express*, and other popular dailies, journalism divorced itself from prevailing notions of historical significance. News no longer concentrated exclusively on the public lives of powerful élites. The everyday life of the common man acquired more importance. Human-interest stories engaged their audience because they allowed a large public to read about a world they recognized.

Second, human-interest stories often dignified common existence by transforming it into a form of literature. On any given day, reporters and editors confronted a variety of factual incidents from which they created their 'stories'. These narratives often borrowed from the conventions of nineteenth-century popular literature. Newspapers became filled with Mystery, Adventure, and Romance. There were mysteries of unsolved robberies, kidnappings, and murders; adventure stories of aviators, mountaineers, and race-car drivers; romances about devotion, sacrifice, and love. Journalists often portrayed the protagonists of these dramas in stereotyped terms as either heroes or villains. Editors found particularly attractive stories that involved sudden changes in wealth and power.[51] Sometimes, as in the following story from the *Daily Express* of 3 February 1905, fiction provided the framework for understanding facts.

[48] Jones, *Fleet Street*, 201.
[49] Michael Schudson, *Discovering the News: A Social History of American Newspapers* (New York: Beacon Books, 1978), 26–7; Hughes, *Human-Interest Story*, 55.
[50] Quoted in Fyfe, *Northcliffe*, 82.
[51] For a brief analysis of the types of human-interest stories in the American press, see Carroll Dewitt Clark, 'News: A Sociological Study' (Ph.D. diss., University of Chicago, 1931), 433–5.

STOPPED AT THE ALTAR
Dramatic Interruption to a Love Romance

The romance, though happily not the tragedy of Romeo and Juliet, has just been re-enacted in real life in the small East Lancashire town of Darwen.

Both Romeo and Juliet were members of families of equal status and having made up their minds to be quietly married at Holy Trinity Church, the banns were put up and published the required number of times.

As no one came forward on any of the three legal opportunities on the invitation of the clergyman, the Rev. L. Savafard, to put forward any 'cause or just impediment', all was assumed to be well and the young couple made all the preparations for married life.

Then a bolt fell from the blue. The heads of the two families quarrelled. Montague and Capulet were at feud.

The young couple deemed it no quarrel of theirs, and went on with their preparations resolving, however, to keep the date of their prospective wedding a secret. Romeo would wed, no matter what the obstacle and Juliet, like Barkis, was 'willin'.'

One day this week, abjuring wedding finery and wearing their everyday clothes, they each went secretly to church.

Alas! The wedding ceremony which united the real Romeo and Juliet was destined to be interrupted in this case.

They had reached the altar and the wedding service had begun, when a commotion at the church door heralded the dramatic arrival of the bridegroom's father.

'I forbid the ceremony,' he cried. The clergyman was astonished, and asked for an explanation.

'My son' he said 'shall not marry the daughter of a man with whom I am not on friendly terms. My son is a minor, and without my consent he cannot marry.'

The clergyman sought to move him, the young couple made tearful appeals, but the father refused to yield, though his son will be of age in a few months. The ceremony was abandoned.

This tale embodied a number of characteristics typical of the genre. First, the self-conscious comparison with one of Shakespeare's most famous plays provided the narrative with a formulaic structure of wide familiarity. The reporter selected details—the couple's mutual love, the quarrel between their families, a secret wedding ceremony—which fit the formula and wrote in the clichéd language of popular romantic fiction. The reporter even felt free to create dialogue. At the same time, however, the reader presumes the story to be true, even though the couple remains anonymous and no dates are given. Yet, the actual facts deviated sufficiently from the formulaic theme to make the story unique. The lovers did not kill themselves and would be allowed to marry legally within a few months. Finally, the story has no discernable social or historical significance. The tale's real importance may be symbolic. A couple from East Lancashire

became, like Romeo and Juliet, 'star-crossed lovers'. A reporter transformed a routine factual incident into a story of universal meaning.

Human-interest stories engaged their readers because they drew upon
the emotions of private life. Like the popular novelists they often imitated,
reporters presented recognizable people undergoing difficult experiences
which required no special expertise or formal training to grasp. It was
not difficult to understand why a mother grieved over the loss of a son,
or how a clerk brought himself to ruin by embezzling company funds.
Nor was it difficult to comprehend the triumph of the first flight over
the English Channel or the grim irony of a zoo-keeper trapping himself
in a cage of wild animals. 'The fundamental element of human interest',
Helen McGill Hughes wrote in her pioneering study of the subject, 'is
a curiosity to know what it is like to undergo those common personal
crises and visitations of good and bad luck . . . suffered by persons who
are shown to have essentially one's own nature. In the end, human interest
approaches the interest every man has in himself.'[52] When critics accused
the popular press of triviality, they underestimated how even minor
incidents aroused important human emotions. A missing child in Cornwall
might engage the sympathy of parents throughout England. Human-
interest stories invited vicarious participation in distant events. They
provided endless variations on the constant themes of human existence.

The human-interest story, like the use of formulaic plots in the cinema,
were both means of engaging an audience which the mass media borrowed
directly from the nineteenth century. Both were examples of cultural
conservatism engendered by a preoccupation with commercial success.
At the same time, however, the media developed more novel means of
anticipating and responding to the demands of a large public. None
of these means were without precedent within the rich traditions of
nineteenth-century popular culture, but a number of approaches and
techniques became more insistent and widely diffused by the
commercialized mass media in the early twentieth century. Not all of these
techniques will be discussed here. The creation and development of the
sports pages, for example, represented one editorial response to the
changing patterns of leisure among male readers. Then, too, imposing
and luxurious cinemas attracted and flattered a public concerned with
keeping up appearances.[53] Other examples might have been selected.
Instead, the cultural relationship of pragmatic identification between
producer and consumer in commercial culture will be illustrated by

[52] Hughes, *Human-Interest Story*, 216.
[53] On picture palaces, see Audrey Field, *Picture Palace: A Social History of the Cinema*
(London: Gentry Books, 1974); G. J. Mellor, *Picture Pioneers: The Story of the Northern
Cinema, 1896–1921* (Newcastle: Frank Graham, 1971); and Denis Sharp, *The Picture
Palace and Other Buildings for the Movies* (London: Hugh Evelyn, 1969).

examining the language of the press, the intense efforts by popular journalists to attract female readers, and the rise of film stars and other celebrities of the media.

1.   *Language and the Press*

The popular press engaged its readers by writing concise, vivid prose. Northcliffe often complained of the 'dreary word spinning' and 'tedious leading articles' of the élite press. He claimed that 'the success of the *Daily Mail* has been mainly due to its compactness and brevity.'[54] He envisaged his readers as active individuals with neither the leisure nor inclination to tolerate lengthy, ornate articles. Northcliffe associated modernity with speed and became fascinated by anything which quickened the pace of life. He loved aeroplanes, racing cars, dictaphones, and typewriters.[55] He bought the fastest machines to print his papers and hired the most rapid trains to distribute them. He ate, walked, and talked quickly. He intimidated subordinates by making decisions rapidly. The *Daily Mail* and later other popular national dailies reflected this hectic pace. They were not written to be read at a club. They were designed to be scanned quickly by people in a hurry. The slogan of the *Daily Mail* was 'The Busy Man's Paper'.[56]

Editors stressed the need to write in simple language familiar to most readers. Before launching the *Daily Mail* in 1896, Northcliffe trained his personnel in the use of the vernacular and discouraged the use of foreign phrases which might perplex his readers. A *'fait accompli'* became an 'accomplished fact'. In one of the early books on British journalism, published in 1903, Arthur Lawrence claimed that 'I have never yet seen the manuscript of a beginner which erred in the direction of excessive colloquialism.' He recommended that a young reporter should 'endeavour to write pretty much as he speaks'.[57] Compared to the 'Tabloid English' of the *Daily Mirror* in the late 1930s, early efforts to imitate in print the language of oral communication now appear quite tame. Before the 1920s,

---

[54] Alfred C. Harmsworth, 'The Making of a Newspaper', in Lawrence, *Journalism*, 170; Alfred C. Harmsworth, *The Romance of the* Daily Mail (London: Carmelite House, 1903), 12.

[55] See, for example, Alfred C. Harmsworth, ed., *Motors and Motor-Driving* (London: Longmans, Green and Co., 1902), 41–71; Russell Stannard, *With the Dictators of Fleet Street: The Autobiography of an Ignorant Journalist* (London: Hutchinson, 1934), 67; and Tom Clarke, *Northcliffe in History: An Intimate Study of Press Power* (London: Hutchinson, n.d.), 18.

[56] Pound and Harmsworth, *Northcliffe*, 190, 202, 205–6, 260. See also Max Pemberton, *Lord Northcliffe: A Memoir* (London: Hodder and Stoughton, n.d.), 75; and Tom Clarke, *My Northcliffe Diary* (New York: Cosmopolitan Book Corporation, 1931), xii and throughout.

[57] Ibid., 196, 200; Lawrence, *Profession*, 59.

editors tolerated very little slang and reporters wrote complete sentences. Still, the short, crisp paragraphs and vivid diction of the popular press in the early twentieth century came closer to spoken English than the often ponderous formal prose of the élite dailies. Tabloid English did not arrive upon the scene wholly unanticipated.[58]

This attempt to write concise prose in familiar language demanded constant attention. As late as 1918, Northcliffe reminded one of his editors: 'We have got to train our writers to write short articles. They do not seem to understand it.'[59] Some newspapers distributed specific rules of composition. In his 'Do's and Don'ts for Reporters and Sub-Editors', R. D. Blumenfeld defined the house style of the *Daily Express*, a paper he helped edit from 1904 to 1932. 'The newspaper-reading public appreciate good, clear English,' he instructed his writers: '*Simplicity, accuracy, conciseness,* and *purity of style* are the surest signposts of success.' Articles ought to 'keep to the POINT' and sentences should be 'short, sharp, clear-cut. . . . Give the gist of the story in the first paragraph and build upon that foundation.' Diction should be familiar, concrete, and lively. A 'BRIGHT STYLE' meant 'SHORT WORDS in preference to long ones' and the frequent use of 'EMPHATIC words like MUST, WILL'. Since headlines should 'leave the reader with a desire to read the story itself', writers should try to employ words such as 'MYSTERY, SECRET, TRAGEDY, DRAMA, COMEDY, SCANDAL and HUMAN'. Verbs were usually more 'newsy' than adjectives.[60] Some words were prohibited. Blumenfeld objected to such 'slang' terms as *middie, taxi,* and *tram*. Though eventually some of these prohibitions were dropped, the *Daily Express*, like the *Daily Mail*, remained alert to the linguistic proprieties of its middle-class readers.[61]

How effective were these rules? How and in what ways did the style and presentation of the popular daily press differ from that of the élite press? A definitive answer to these questions would demand a thorough linguistic analysis of the British press over an extended period. A tentative answer can be found by comparing the *Daily Mail* and the *Daily Express*

---

[58] On 'tabloid English', see Keith Waterhouse, Daily Mirror *Style* (London: Mirror Books, 1981). Waterhouse claims that the attempt to write in a language people could understand began in the 1930s (see p. 9). There is a good overview of tabloid English in a perceptive review of Waterhouse's book by Roy Harris, 'The Dialect of Fleet Street', *TLS*, 22 May 1981, 559–60.

[59] Northcliffe to Marlowe, 10 May 1918, Northcliffe MSS, British Library Deposit 4890, vol. 47.

[60] R. D. Blumenfeld, *What is a Journalist?* (London: World's Press New Library, n.d.), 11–17.

[61] Clarke, *Northcliffe Diary*, 39. See also Northcliffe's comment: 'I am decidedly averse to any deliberate attempt to appeal to a lower class of readers.' Northcliffe to Marlowe, n.d., Northcliffe MSS, British Library Deposit 4890, vol. 46.

with *The Times* during selected weeks over a 35-year period.[62] Several factors make even a limited comparison subject to qualification. The popular press covered a wider range of stories than did *The Times*, and to compare only those items covered by both would often obscure important and obvious distinctions among them. Then too, Northcliffe bought *The Times* in 1908 and retained control until 1922. Though he usually detached himself from daily operations, his suggestions no doubt contributed to making the paper more lively. Finally, even within the bounds of my limited comparison, it has been necessary to be highly selective. Others might choose different examples. Still, granting these qualifications, some clear differences and trends emerge.

One clear early difference between the popular daily press and *The Times* lay in their approach to headlines. Quite apart from size—an important consideration discussed later—headlines functioned in the popular press as both a summary and invitation to what lay below. They embodied a language which, as Heinrich Straumann pointed out in his remarkable work on the subject, came closest to the 'ellipsis' of everyday speech.[63] The differences between the popular and quality press were most pronounced before the First World War. Thus, for example, the *Daily Mail* of 2 October 1905 carried among its headlines the following:

(*a*) CONVICT'S AMAZING STORY
COURTSHIP AND FORGERY
LOVE AS AN AID TO CRIME
ROMANCE OF A PLOT

(*b*) WORSHIP OF THE BABY
GROWING EXTRAVAGANCE OF
CHRISTENING GIFTS

(*c*) FREAKS OF A HIGH TIDE
VESSELS RIDING ABOVE THE
LEVEL OF THE LAND

On the same day, *The Times* was more circumspect:

(*a*) CHINESE STUDENTS IN JAPAN.
(*b*) THE LAUNCH OF THE NETAL.
(*c*) OPENING OF A BRIDGE BY THE KING.

For a story on political unrest in Poland, the *Daily Express* of 1 February 1905 announced:

---

[62] In comparing the *Daily Mail* and *The Times*, I selected the first week in October, 1896, 1900, and every five years thereafter to 1930. For the comparison of the *Daily Express* and *The Times*, I selected the first week in February in 1905, and every five years thereafter to 1930. I also looked at selected weeks from other years.

[63] Heinrich Straumann, *Newspaper Headlines: A Study in Linguistic Method* (London: George Allen and Unwin, 1935), 21.

TERROR IN POLAND

WARSAW LIKE A CITY
OF THE DEAD

PEOPLE AFRAID TO
VENTURE OUT OF
THEIR HOMES

SILENT STREETS

FAMINE PRICES

MIDNIGHT BURIAL OF
THE VICTIMS.

The headline for the same story in *The Times* was:

THE RIOTING AT WARSAW.
OFFICIAL ACCOUNT.

and, in another story:

POLISH FEELING

It was not simply that the headlines of the popular press were more 'sensational' than those of *The Times*. The headlines on Poland from the *Daily Express*, for example, dramatized but did not contradict the 'official account' presented in *The Times*. After extensive rioting by strikers, Polish troops killed or injured 169 people and imposed a strict curfew. Food shortages created inflated prices. The headlines of the *Daily Express* sought to draw the reader into the drama of these events, whereas *The Times* self-consciously distanced itself from any emotive reaction. Moreover, by conveying the story in the linguistic shorthand of a telegram, the *Daily Express* allowed the reader to grasp the story in a few seconds. The reader of *The Times* needed to pore through thirteen paragraphs of 'official' prose to obtain a more complete, but less focused, version of events.

Ten years later, during the First World War, the headlines of the popular press and *The Times* became less distinguishable.

LATE WAR NEWS
RUSSIANS ATTACK.
GENERAL POSITION BETTER.
DVINSK DEFENCES STILL FIRM.
ENEMY CONVOYS TAKEN.

(*Daily Mail*, 2 October 1915)

LATE WAR NEWS
VIGOROUS RUSSIAN ATTACKS.
CAVALRY CHARGE ON A CONVOY.
TOWN CARRIED BY ASSAULT.
(*The Times*, 2 October 1915)

On the same day, *The Times* also proclaimed:

(*a*) DAUNTLESS FRENCH AIRMEN.
STORIES FROM THE FRONT.
(*b*) ALLIES FIGHT FOR LIBERTY.
IMPASSIONED TRIBUTE BY AN AMERICAN.

The understandable passions of wartime were not completely abandoned by *The Times* after the Armistice. For a story of the conflict between Russia and Poland, the *Daily Mail* of 7 October 1920 announced:

DRAMATIC CHANGE OF FORTUNES.
BOLSHEVIKS EAGER FOR ARMISTICE.

The same story in *The Times* became:

REDS FORCED TO YIELD.
POLAND'S DEMANDS ACCEPTED.
THE NEW FRONTIER.
SOVIET TROUBLES INCREASING.

The day before the two papers carried the following:

BIGGEST LINER BURNED.
MYSTERY OF THE BISMARCK.
ALLIES' LOSS.
LONG LIST OF GERMAN SHIP CRIMES.
(*Daily Mail*, 6 October 1920)

GERMAN GIANT LINER DESTROYED.
MYSTERIOUS DOCKYARD FIRE.
BRITISH OWNERS AND THE BISMARCK.
PROBLEMS OF MONSTER SHIP.
(*The Times*, 6 October 1920)

This limited evidence indicates that *The Times* first adopted the practices of popular press during the First World War. Headlines more clearly summarized stories and contained emotive, hyperbolic language. This practice continued in the years immediately following the armistice, when *The Times* sometimes became more heated in its language than the *Daily Mail*.

Yet it would be misleading to overstate this convergence of journalistic practices. During the 1920s, the popular press began to shed its prohibitions against slang and, especially in feature stories and in sports, accentuated its commitment to the vernacular.

LEFT HOOKS FOR THE BRIGHT YOUNG THINGS.
(*Daily Mail*, 2 October 1930)
(*a*) TOO KEEN
CHELSEA WIN BUT DO NOT PLEASE.
(*b*) VICTORY AT LAST!
SWINDON OUTPLAYED.
(*c*) CHANCES WASTED.
NOT THE OLD BRENTFORD.
(*Daily Mail*, 6 October 1930)

By 1930, some headlines in the popular press reflected the colloquial informality of a conversation among friends. Abandoning traditional grammar, newspapers used clichés to mimic the patterns of speech.

Editorials were another area in which the popular press sought brevity and conciseness. Northcliffe was never convinced that even politicians read the long, involved leaders of *The Times* and other élite newspapers. He was determined to make his own paper's opinions brief and to the point. On the first day of its publication, 4 May 1896, the *Daily Mail* devoted only 17 column-inches to its leaders; *The Times* provided 81 column-inches and the *Morning Post* 53.[64] In general, specific leaders in the *Daily Mail* ran to about half the length of comparable ones in *The Times*. Thus, for example, on 6 October 1910 *The Times* devoted a leader to 'The Revolution in Portugal' which ran to three paragraphs and 1,103 words. On the same day, the *Daily Mail* addressed the same subject in three paragraphs, but only 483 words. More important, the *Daily Mail* managed to convey the same amount of substance in fewer words. In a section concerning the destination of the fleeing king, for example, *The Times* took five sentences and 155 words to say what the *Daily Mail* communicated in two sentences and 42 words. The *Daily Mail* began its leader with a direct sentence and throughout the first paragraph relied on uncomplicated grammatical constructions. Compared to the overstuffed language of *The Times*, the *Daily Mail* embodied the efficiency of the modern machines Northcliffe so much admired.

Over the next twenty years, *The Times* continued to devote about twice as much space to its individual leaders as did the *Daily Mail*. Yet by the 1920s, the editorial writers of *The Times* were beginning to adopt the tauter prose characteristic of the popular press. Sentences, for example, were often shorter and more to the point.

[64] Pound and Harmsworth, *Northcliffe*, 199.

But these resolutions do not end the matter. They are rather the point of a new departure. They are declarations to indicate the necessity for prompt and continuous action outside.

The Liverpool Conference has enunciated a principle. So far, so good. A policy must follow. Communism must not only be condemned; it must be cast out.[65]

This leader on the Labour Party Conference of 1925 contained ten sentences of fewer than ten words. Two sentences were, strictly speaking, not sentences at all. In the leader on the revolution in Portugal fifteen years before, not a single sentence included fewer than ten words and all were grammatically impeccable. Writers on *The Times* were beginning to appreciate that simple sentences could express complex thoughts.

By training their journalists to write concise prose in familiar language, the popular press hoped to gain readers by identifying itself with its mass audience. Language was not employed as a weapon of social hierarchy. The popular press 'spoke' to its readers without a recognizable accent. 'He must keep on the level of common, everyday people,' an early text said of the journalist, 'and must remember he is writing for a newspapaer and not for fame.'[66] The hyperbolic, the emotive, the 'sensational'—all were elements of private conversation which the popular press adopted as means to engage a wider public in familiar, personal terms. Unlike *The Times*, the *Daily Mail* and *Daily Express* rarely spoke from on high. Through familiar, colloquial language, they levelled the relationship between producer and consumer. Though traditionalists might deplore such liberties with the written word, even *The Times* was not immune from innovation. The popular daily press in London established trends which the élite press assimilated over time. The style and vocabulary of headlines in *The Times* of 1920 would have fitted unobtrusively into the *Daily Express* of 1900. By 1920, however, the *Daily Express* had moved on to other experiments yet to be made legitimate by more traditional editors. Vivid, colloquial language in daily journalism was one of many scandals of the popular press that eventually made their way into respectable circles.

2. The Women's Page

Politics and business dominated the nineteenth-century daily press. With increasing sophistication, speed, and accuracy, journalists reported on

---

[65] *The Times*, 1 Oct. 1925.

[66] H. F. Harrington and T. T. Frankenberg, *Essentials in Journalism* (Boston and London: Ginn, 1912), p. vii. For modern studies of the relationship of language and class, see B. Bernstein, 'Some Sociological Determinants of Perception: An Inquiry into Sub-Cultural Differences', *British Journal of Sociology* 9 (1958): 159–74; and Leonard Schatzman and Anselm Strauss, 'Social Class and Modes of Communication', *American Journal of Sociology* 60, 4 (1955): 329–38. For a historical perspective, see K. C. Phillips, *Language and Class in Victorian England* (Oxford: Basil Blackwell, 1984).

concerns which males controlled with unquestioned authority. Newspapers reflected the public world of commerce and politics; the private sphere of home and family remained hidden, obscured by custom and Victorian propriety. Although the popular Sunday papers carried items which entertained the entire family and the 'New Journalism' of the 1880s prospered on human interest stories, few newspaper editors considered the female reader worthy of attention until Northcliffe arrived on Fleet Street. Still in his twenties, Northcliffe, then Alfred Harmsworth, first tapped the market for women's journalism when he launched *Forget-Me-Not* in 1891. Within three years, this inexpensive weekly magazine, featuring pictures and stories intended for a middle-class audience, boasted a circulation of over 140,000, and paved the way for one of Northcliffe's most enduring successes.[67] *Home Chat* covered virtually all aspects of a woman's domestic responsibilities and helped persuade Northcliffe that a huge audience awaited attention in the daily press.

When Northcliffe began the *Daily Mail* in 1896, he applied what he had learned from his successful women's magazines to the daily newspaper. Over the objections of his best editor, he insisted upon two columns of articles devoted especially to women's concerns. Within a short period, this feature had grown to a full page, and eventually expanded even further. Northcliffe constantly reminded his editors to include items which might fascinate women readers. 'The "Daily Mail" is ceasing to be the women's paper,' he warned his editor Marlowe in 1911. 'We must be very watchful about this.' Two years earlier he was even more alarmed. 'I notice that while the "Express" . . . is trying to take away our women readers, one of the main sources of strength for advertising, the "Daily Mail" magazine page is less and less feminine. I wrote from America saying that it ought to be almost entirely feminine.'[68]

Northcliffe's motive in attracting female readers to the *Daily Mail* astonished no one. 'Our object was purely commercial,' Kennedy Jones later acknowledged. 'We realized that women are by nature more loyal and conservative than men, and that if we . . . got a firm footing in their homes, the value of our papers from the advertiser's point of view would be greatly enhanced.'[69] This strategy derived from two related considerations. As a significant percentage of the population, women represented an enormous potential for gains in circulation. More important, they often controlled the budgets of family households. In working-class homes it was women who shopped for food, bought clothes, paid the

---

[67] Cynthia L. White, *Women's Magazines, 1693–1968* (London: Michael Joseph, 1970), 75–7; Pound and Harmsworth, *Northcliffe*, 128–9, 179–80.

[68] Northcliffe to Marlowe, 12 Dec. 1911 and 10 Mar. 1909, Northcliffe MSS, British Library Deposit 4890, vol. 46; Pound and Harmsworth, op. cit., 200–2.

[69] Jones, *Fleet Street*, 331.

rent, and made the daily financial decisions. It was women, as well, who often made the important choices about consumption in middle-class families.[70] 'Women are the holders of the domestic purse-strings,' Northcliffe once said. 'They are the real buyers. Men buy what women tell them to.'[71] By attracting female readers to the *Daily Mail*, Northcliffe and eventually other press barons provided advertisers with an irresistible target.

Newspapers and advertising became inextricably linked. 'The newspaper is the backbone of the advertising business,' an executive of *The Times* wrote in 1911, 'and advertisements are the backbone of the newspaper business.' Thomas Russell, a leading writer on British advertising, was more specific. 'London daily papers', he wrote in one of his textbooks, 'are the most powerful media for advertising in this country.'[72] As a business, advertising experienced marked growth in the late nineteenth century. Though no reliable statistics cover the country as a whole, the advertising budget for one firm, Beecham's, rose from £22,000 in 1884 to £120,000 in 1891. At the same time, the role of the advertising agent changed. By the 1890s, there were essentially two types of agents: those who only bought space for firms who wished to advertise; and those who provided a full line of services.[73] 'In the service agency', one of its most successful practitioners, S. H. Benson, explained, 'the "copy" is drafted, the designs prepared, the media selected, the blocks purchased, the papers contracted with, the insertions checked and all the details of the work

[70] Peter N. Stearns, 'Working-Class Women in Britain, 1890–1914', in *Suffer and Be Still: Women in the Victorian Age*, ed. Martha Vicinus (Bloomington: Indiana University Press, 1972), 104, 108; Patricia Branca, *Silent Sisterhood: Middle-Class Women in the Victorian Home* (London: Croom Helm, 1975), 150–3. On the woman's role in the home, see also Ann Oakley, *Women's Work: The Housewife, Past and Present* (New York: Pantheon, 1974), esp. 50–9; and Jane Lewis, *Women in England, 1870–1950: Sexual Divisions and Social Change* (Sussex: Wheatsheaf Books; Bloomington: Indiana University Press, 1984), 1–141. For a Marxist analysis, see Leonore Davidoff, 'The Rationalization of Housework', in *Dependence and Exploitation in Work and Marriage*, ed. Diana Leonard Barker and Sheila Allen (London: Longman, 1976), 121–51. There is an extensive bibliography on this topic.

[71] Quoted in Clarke, *Northcliffe in History*, 149.

[72] J. Murray Allison, 'The Newspaper as an Advertising Medium', in *Advertising and Publicity*, ed. Thomas Russell (London: Educational Book Company [1911]), 65; Thomas Russell, *A Working Text-Book of Advertising*, 3rd edn. (London: Russell-Hart, 1924), 120.

[73] Terence Richard Nevett, 'The Development of Commercial Advertising in Britain, 1800–1914' (Ph.D. diss., University of London, 1979), 169, 187. A revised version of this thesis was later published: id., *Advertising in Britain: A History* (London: Heinemann, 1982). For the development of advertising in Britain, see also Eric Field, *Advertising: The Forgotten Years* (London: Ernest Benn, 1959); Frank S. Presbrey, *The History and Development of Advertising* (Garden City, NY: Doubleday, Doran, 1929), 91–109; and E. S. Turner, *The Shocking History of Advertising!* (New York: Dutton, 1953). For bibliography, see Richard W. Pollay, ed., *Information Sources in Advertising History* (Westport, CT: Greenwood Press, 1979).

carried through.'[74] From 1888 to 1901, the turnover of the service agency Mather and Crowther rose from £20,000 to over £200,000, a tenfold increase. Though the system of billing remained controversial until after the First World War,[75] the fortunes of modern advertising rose with those of the popular daily press.

Though Northcliffe often complained about the aesthetics of advertising in his newspapers, he hired one of the most aggressive advertising managers in Fleet Street. Wareham Smith joined the *Daily Mail* in 1896. When he took control, he recalled in his autobiography, 'there was no attempt at *creating* advertising. The initiative, such as existed, was still in the *advertiser's* office.' Smith created a 'Special Publicity Branch' whose purpose was to 'extract advertising from topical events'. One such event was the Ideal Home Exhibition. Smith believed that a company's willingness to advertise a particular article was limited by its capacity to supply it. He therefore sought an industry 'with an almost inexhaustible capacity to supply any demand which could be created by advertising'.[76] To Smith, the building industry met this criterion. Each year the *Daily Mail* sponsored an exhibition at Olympia devoted to virtually everything connected with the home. Builders from all over the country sponsored exhibits and tens of thousands of interested citizens attended. The *Daily Mail* covered the event as news, and gladly accepted advertisements from builders eager to promote their products in the sponsoring newspaper. Northcliffe often criticized such complicity between newspapers and advertisers, arguing that 'the "Daily Mail" does not need these artificial supports.'[77] Nevertheless, Smith prospered with the organization and became something of a legend among British advertisers.

One of the largest advertisers in the national daily press and the one most directly connected to the women's page needed no encouragement from an aggressive advertising director. Department stores helped transform British retailing in the late nineteenth century. By 1910, there were over 150 department stores in Britain, with an estimated turnover of twenty million pounds.[78] These establishments offered a number of

[74] S. H. Benson, 'The Advertising Agent', in Russell, *Advertising and Publicity*, 247.

[75] David S. Dunbar, 'The Agency Commission System in Britain: A First Sketch of its History to 1941', *Journal of Advertising History* 2 (1979): 19–28. For an excellent discussion of the development of advertising agencies in America, see Daniel Pope, *The Making of Modern Advertising* (New York: Basic Books, 1983), 112–83.

[76] Pound and Harmsworth, *Northcliffe*, 258–9; Wareham Smith, *Spilt Ink* (London: Ernest Benn, 1932), 29, 66; Wareham Smith to A. Butes, 29 Apr. 1908, Northcliffe MSS, British Library Deposit 4890, vol. 60.

[77] Northcliffe to Wareham Smith, 5 June 1911, Northcliffe MSS, British Library Deposit 4890, vol. 60.

[78] Winstanley, *Shopkeeper's World*, 34–7; James B. Jefferys, *Retail Trading in Britain, 1850–1950* (Cambridge: Cambridge University Press, 1954), 6–21. For histories of specific stores, see, among others, Richard S. Lambert, *The Universal Provider: A Study of*

advantages over their smaller competitors. Their central location made them easily accessible to an increasingly mobile female population; they offered a wide selection of products, particularly in women's clothing; they flattered their status-conscious customers with tasteful amenities; and, above all, they provided good value. Economies of scale permitted lower mark-ups and the sheer volume of goods allowed substantial discounts to be cost-efficient. Unlike many Victorian retailers, department stores refused to haggle with customers. They offered one price for everybody, countess and clerk.[79]

In the early twentieth century, the most innovative department store in London was Selfridge's, whose American owner became famed for his publicity stunts.[80] In particular, Gordon Selfridge became the master of the advertising campaign directed at women. To advertise his January clearance sale in 1910, for example, Selfridge placed a major display advertisement in the *Daily Express* every working day for two weeks. Each advertisement was organized round a central theme. On Wednesday 19 January, the Selfridge advertisement emphasized the amenities of the store:

Thousands are visiting us every day and experiencing for themselves the reality of the advantages of shopping here. Here to spend the day—to begin in the morning—lunch comfortably and extremely well at moderate prices in our Luncheon Hall—shop or rest awhile—write a note or two—skim through a magazine—see the latest Election results come through the 'tic-tac' in the Reception Hall—chat with friends, buy of course if you feel so disposed . . . or home again, postponing purchasing until to-morrow. Do what you will, come when you please, and oftener the better . . . [81]

Selfridge's liked to emphasize the dignity of shopping at their store. In 1912, Selfridge himself began to write short articles and ruminations which he inserted into selected newspapers under the name 'Callisthenes'. These

William Whiteley and the Rise of the London Department Store (London: George G. Harrap, 1938); Asa Briggs, *Friends of the People: The Centenary History of Lewis's* (London: B. T. Batsford, 1956); and, for the model store in France, Michael B. Miller, *The Bon Marché: Bourgeois Culture and the Department Store, 1869–1920* (Princeton: Princeton University Press, 1981).

[79] Jefferys, op. cit., 328–31; H. Pasdermadjian, *The Department Store: Its Origins, Evolution, and Economics* (London: Newman Books, 1954), 10–18. See also Gunther Barth, *City People: The Rise of Modern City Culture in Nineteenth-Century America* (New York and Oxford: Oxford University Press, 1980), 110–47; and Daniel J. Boorstein, *The Americans: The Democratic Experience* (New York: Random House, 1973), 106–9.

[80] John William Ferry, *A History of the Department Store* (New York: Macmillan, 1960), 227; A. H. Williams, *No Name on the Door: A Memoir of Gordon Selfridge* (London: W. H. Allen, 1956), 174–5; Reginald Pound, *Selfridge: A Biography* (London: Heinemann, 1960), 58–9.

[81] *Daily Express*, 19 Jan. 1910.

articles celebrated the virtues of capitalism and praised the art of tasteful consumption.[82] Like many American business men, Selfridge considered the business of retailing a high moral calling in which department stores provided the good life for people of all social classes.

Since the popular daily newspapers such as the *Daily Mail* and *Daily Express* relied on department stores for a substantial proportion of their advertising revenue, there was always a danger of turning newspaper articles into encomiums for advertisers. 'I plead guilty to, on occasions, having persuaded the Editor into giving "puffs",' Wareham Smith admitted in a letter to Northcliffe. Northcliffe objected 'strenuously' to such practices. He wrote to Smith that Selfridge's name, for example, should not be in the *Daily Mail* unless 'it comes under general news—in a case of fire or similar event'.[83] The *Daily Express* was often less scrupulous. Articles on its women's page often extolled the virtues of the stores whose display advertisements supported the paper. On 4 January 1915, the *Daily Express* ran an article on the women's page entitled 'Best Bargains of the Year . . . Hints to Shoppers':

The most wonderful winter sales in the history of the great London drapery and other establishments will be in full swing all over the metropolis this week. Never before have such astonishing bargains awaited the clever woman shopper. . . . Every woman who wishes to replenish her wardrobe should seize the unrivalled opportunities now presented to secure the best at the price of the second best. . . . A few among the millions of marvellous bargains at the sales which begin to-day are as follows . . .

This complicity between newspapers and advertisers represents an obvious, and atypical, example of a larger, more important phenomenon. It was in the mutual economic interest of department stores, the advertising business, and popular daily newspapers to persuade women to become frequent consumers. By making shopping fashionable among a wider public, department stores increased sales and newspapers gained reliable, predictable advertisers..Frequent changes in fashions for clothing perpetuated this close relationship between the press and the drapers. Each season began a new fashion cycle with articles and advertisements about a new look in clothing. By encouraging shopping to become a social obligation, newspapers and advertisers hoped to link the personal identities of women with a variety of products.[84]

Yet it is important not to exaggerate the power of newspapers and advertisers to impose their tastes on a female audience. 'Good advertising creates demand,' Thomas Russell declared flatly in an early book on

[82] Pound, op. cit., 96. The feature eventually became exclusive to *The Times*.
[83] Northcliffe to Wareham Smith, 24 and 29 May 1912, Northcliffe MSS, British Library Deposit 4890, vol. 60.   [84] Barth, *City People*, 140–8.

commercial advetising.[85] Such claims were common among professional advertisers in the early twentieth century. In order to generate more business, they needed to promote their own skills, to advertise advertising. In recent times, a number of commentators have taken such claims at face value. Some have argued that the growing economic power of advertisers corrupted editorial freedom, turning newspapers and other mass media into the pawns of advertisers.[86] Others have advanced more subtle arguments. While denying that advertisers exercise editorial control over newspapers, they claim that advertisers and the mass media impose an ethic of materialism and consumption inimical to the authentic interests of the general public. 'There is little covert advertising pressure, no conspiracy, no conscious suppression of information,' James Curran wrote in an article on the contemporary British press. Instead, such things as women's features 'define the interests and horizons of women primarily in terms of consumption, and tacitly portray the roles of women as that of mother, mannequin, and housekeeper.'[87]

When applied to the early twentieth century, these arguments should not be ignored. Popular newspapers did give advertisers editorial favours, and the women's page did reinforce an ethos of consumption. But the power of advertisers and the press to manipulate tastes was also limited by those who purchased popular dailies. Though exceptions can be found, most advertisers sought out papers with large circulations[88] and large circulations depended upon the market-place decisions of tens of thousands and eventually millions of individuals. The women's pages must be evaluated not only by the criterion of how they served the interests of advertisers and newspaper magnates; they must also be examined to see how they served the self-interest of women who read them. Such an examination involves a number of considerations. First, it assumes that British women knew their own self-interest, and that a more 'authentic' interest, defined patronizingly by others, ought not shape the analysis. Second and related, it remains disinterested in the normative problem of materialism. Critiques of advertising often veil a spartan or puritanical

[85] Thomas Russell, *Commercial Advertising* (London: G. P. Putnam, 1919), 12.

[86] See, for example, Frank Whitehead, 'Advertising', in *Discrimination and Popular Culture*, ed. Denys Thompson, 2nd edn. (Harmondsworth: Penguin Books, 1973), 68–9.

[87] James Curran, 'Advertising and the Press', in *British Press Manifesto*, ed. Curran, 244–5. See also id., 'The Impact of Advertising on the British Mass Media', *Media, Culture and Society* 3, 1 (1981): 43–69.

[88] Two exceptions, often cited by Marxists and worth pondering, are the *Daily Herald* and the *News Chronicle*, both of which died with substantial circulations. See Curran, 'Advertising and the Press', in *British Press Manifesto*, ed. Curran, 252–62; and id., 'Capitalism and Control of the Press, 1800–1975', in *Mass Communication*, ed. Curran *et al.*, 224–6. These examples deserve further study.

outlook toward consumption generally.[89] Finally, discussion about demand, particularly for a historical period, involves obvious uncertainties. No one can ever know the thinking behind millions of individual economic decisions.

Women might have been interested in the women's page because the women's page was interested in them. Newspapers sought to identify with female readers and to respond to their needs. Initially, Northcliffe believed that this identification required women journalists. Though a few existed in Fleet Street when the *Daily Mail* first appeared in 1896, Northcliffe gave women more editorial responsibility.[90] Prejudices against female journalists remained strong. In his pioneering *Journalism for Women: A Practical Guide*, published in 1898, Arnold Bennett listed the faults usually attributed to women journalists. They failed to meet deadlines; they overlooked details; they lacked restraint in their prose and overwrote articles. Bennett found such prejudices old-fashioned. 'Is there any sexual reason why a woman should be a less accomplished journalist than a man? I can find none.'[91] In November 1903 Northcliffe founded the *Daily Mirror* as a daily newspaper written for women, by women. An experienced female editor from the *Daily Mail* assembled 'a large staff of cultivated, able and experienced women' to write for the newspaper. After an encouraging beginning, the experiment failed. Circulation dropped from over 200,000 to less than 25,000 copies. Many woman journalists were dismissed, and the *Daily Mirror* was reorganized as a daily illustrated paper.[92] Women journalists were not the only key to the women's market.

The women's page reflected the variety and complexity of women's roles. Articles on the home included practical suggestions on virtually all aspects of domestic life. There were articles on food: 'A Good Oyster Pie', 'The Unsuspected Virtues of Orange Sauce', and 'How to Tell the Age of an Egg'.[93] There were suggestions about child care, sewing, gardening, and home care: 'Hairdressing for Children', 'Beautiful Ideas in Needlework Applied to Dress', 'How to Get Rid of Ants', and 'Damp House Dangers'. Frequently articles offered advice about health and

[89] See Michael Schudson, 'Criticizing the Critics of Advertising: Towards a Sociological View of Marketing', *Media, Culture and Society* 3, 1 (1981): 3–12.

[90] Pound and Harmsworth, *Northcliffe*, 260–1.

[91] E. A. Bennett [Arnold Bennett], *Journalism for Women: A Practical Guide* (London: John Lane, Bodley Head, 1898), 10, 12–18.

[92] Pound and Harmsworth, op. cit. 278–9. See also Hamilton Fyfe, *Sixty Years of Fleet Street* (London: W. H. Allen, 1949), 113–16.

[93] 'A Good Oyster Pie', *Daily Mail*, 1 Oct. 1910; 'The Unsuspected Virtues of Orange Sauce', *Daily Mail*, 20 Oct. 1910; 'How to Tell the Age of an Egg', *Daily Express* 12 Jan. 1905.

beauty: 'How I Kept Well Without a Doctor'.[94] These articles offered practical guidance about aspects of life central to millions of women. By running items previously considered beneath the dignity of a daily newspaper, the popular press acknowledged and reinforced the legitimacy of a woman's domestic role. News expanded to encompass the concerns of a neglected audience.

If the women's page could be practical, it also appealed to fantasy and imagination. Before the First World War, the women's pages often contained an excerpt from a romantic novel. Drawing upon the formulas of nineteenth-century melodrama and romance, these serialized novels chronicled the ordeals of romantic love. 'But it was at the thought of Claude that her heart beat the fastest. From the first moment she had seen him she had loved him, and it seemed incredible to think that she had so completely missed the way to his heart.'[95] Against great odds, love triumphed in *A Creature of Circumstance*, and it was not the only place on the women's page where fantasy predominated. Both the *Daily Mail* and the *Daily Express* ran articles such as 'Riding Costumes: Which do you Favour?' and 'How to Succeed at a Charity Bazaar' which allowed the reader to participate in the social dilemmas of the upper classes. 'Dull-Weather Amusements' lamented the absence of novel indoor games for country weekends and 'Shopping in Paris' suggested that 'the woman who is buying frocks for Ascot and a Court ball will wear quite different things from the woman who is shopping with a view to political receptions and a constituency.'[96] Northcliffe believed that such articles flattered the readers and raised their self-esteem.

---

[94] 'Hairdressing for Children', *Daily Mail*, 21 Oct. 1910; 'Beautiful Ideas in Needlework Applied to Dress', *Daily Express* 10 Jan. 1905; 'How to Get Rid of Ants', *Daily Mail*, 1 Oct. 1896; 'Damp House Dangers', *Daily Mail*, 4 Oct. 1910; 'How I Kept Well Without a Doctor', *Daily Mail*, 22 Oct. 1910.

[95] Quoted from Lady Troubridge, 'A Creature of Circumstance', in *Daily Mail* 4 Oct. 1910. On fiction for women, see Patricia Stubbs, *Women and Fiction: Feminism and the Novel, 1880–1920* (Sussex: Harvester; New York: Barnes and Noble, 1979); and Nicola Beauman, *A Very Great Profession: The Woman's Novel, 1914–39* (London: Virago, 1983). See also Janice A. Radway, *Reading the Romance: Women, Patriarchy, and Popular Literature* (Chapel Hill: University of North Carolina Press, 1984). On fiction for girls, see Mary Cadogan and Patricia Craig, *You're a Brick Angela! A New Look at Girl's Fiction from 1839–1975* (London: Victor Gollancz, 1976); Wendy Forrester, *Great-Grandmama's Weekly: A Celebration of the* Girl's Own Paper *1880–1901* (Guildford and London: Lutterworth Press, 1980); and Kirsten Drotner, 'Schoolgirls, Madcaps, and Air Aces: English Girls and their Magazine Reading Between the Wars', *Feminist Studies* 9, 1 (1983): 33–52. See also Mary Cadogan and Patricia Craig, *Women and Children First: The Fiction of Two World Wars* (London: Victor Gollancz, 1978).

[96] 'Riding Costumes: Which do you Favour?', *Daily Mail*, 1 Oct. 1896; 'How to Succeed at a Charity Bazaar', *Daily Mail*, 18 Oct. 1910; 'Dull-Weather Amusements', *Daily Mail*, 15 Oct. 1910; 'Shopping in Paris', *Daily Mail*, 5 Oct. 1910.

Women of all social classes could now imagine themselves among the prominent.[97]

Though the women's page in the popular daily press clearly reinforced traditional domestic roles, it also suggested paths to greater independence and self-reliance. 'English Girls in Paris: The Pay and Prospects of Typists' was one of many articles in the *Daily Mail* which explored the role of women in the workplace. An article in the *Daily Express* in January 1910 praised American women for their intelligence and independence and another article in the *Express* criticized the sorry state of 'Women's Rights in France'.[98] Articles warned women against spoiling their husbands and, in early 1905, the *Daily Express* ran a leader against 'The Criminal Cult of the Wife-Beater'.[99] Though it is important to avoid anachronism, these articles indicate that the women's page of the popular press acknowledged a diversity of experiences for women.

The First World War transformed the roles of British women. They joined the work-force in record numbers and at home learned to live with wartime economies.[1] The women's page reflected these changes. Women wrote about the difficulties and frustrations of working in positions previously held only by males. 'One is open to derision from the men who, having failed to answer the call to fight, are ever-ready to jeer and laugh at a woman who is helping at home,' one woman related in 'Women Chauffeurs', published in 1915. 'As long as a woman retains her femininity she will always find men ready to help her,' she assured her readers. The war, she concluded happily, brought women 'a unique opportunity in many professions in which they have been hitherto barred'.[2] At home, women confronted new austerities. 'Frocks or Food?' 'How to be Happy with a Smaller Income', 'Cheap but Tasty Cookery', and 'My War-time Economies' were some of the articles which taught women how to adjust to reduced circumstances.[3] For the first time, many women needed to

---

[97] Clarke, *Northcliffe in History*, 153. In discussing flattery, Northcliffe was referring to the 'Man-in-the-Street'.

[98] 'English Girls in Paris: The Pay and Prospects of Typists', *Daily Mail*, 3 Oct. 1905; 'Impressions of New York', *Daily Express*, 6 Jan. 1910; 'Women's Rights in France', *Daily Express*, 26 Apr. 1900.

[99] 'Spoiling a Husband', *Daily Mail*, 29 Oct. 1910; 'The Criminal Cult of the Wife-Beater', *Daily Express*, 14 Jan. 1905.

[1] Arthur Marwick, *The Deluge: British Society and the First World War* (1965; reprint, New York: Norton, 1970), 87–122; Gail Braydon, *Women Workers in the First World War: The British Experience* (London: Croom Helm; Totowa, NJ: Barnes and Noble, 1981); Dame Anne Godwin, 'Early Years in the Trade Unions', in *Women in the Labour Movement: The British Experience*, ed. Lucy Middleton (London: Croom Helm; Totowa, NJ: Rowman and Littlefield, 1977), 104–6.

[2] G. Ivy Saunders, 'Women Chauffeurs', *Daily Mail*, 9 Oct. 1915.

[3] 'Frocks or Food?', *Daily Mail*, 20 Oct. 1915; 'How to be Happy with a Smaller Income', *Daily Mail*, 13 Oct. 1915; 'Cheap but Tasty Cookery', *Daily Mail*, 29 Oct. 1915; 'My War-time Economies', *Daily Mail*, 5 Oct. 1915.

raise children without their fathers. 'The war mother will have to banish self-consciousness and gain the absolute confidence of her children,' one mother advised in 'Educating the War Child'. 'We are all struggling with war problems.'[4] These articles and hundreds like them demonstrate how the women's page identified with the needs of its readers and adapted to changing circumstances.

After the war, as women lost their jobs to returning veterans and the economy slumped, the market for women's weekly and monthly magazines expanded enormously.[5] In the national daily press, the *Daily Mail* lost ground to the *Daily Express*, which became the most innovative popular newspaper of the 1920s. Beaverbrook had acquired the *Daily Express* during the war and after the armistice devoted his considerable energies to revamping the paper. When Northcliffe died insane in 1922, Beaverbrook faced no comparable rival on Fleet Street.[6] He gained the confidence of advertisers and in 1924 negotiated a lucrative deal with Barker's, the department store, who agreed to run a full page of display advertisements every day. Beaverbrook claimed that this transaction represented 'the largest space contract ever made with a single newspaper in Great Britain'. Whatever the truth of this boast, the contract reflected the growing prosperity of large department stores, which during the decade continued to increase their market share.[7] The deal also reflected Beaverbrook's capacity to attract female readers to his paper. The *Daily Express* expanded the number of stories on the regular news pages that might appeal to women readers. It covered extensively developments in Hollywood, often featuring stories about film stars. It continued to offer features which advised women about domestic life, without foreclosing the possibilities of work outside the home. 'Many women who are hopeless housewives and mediocre mothers', an article proclaimed early in 1920, 'are thoroughly efficient in office or factory, and it should not be the penalty of marriage to keep them tied down domestically whether they like it or not.'[8]

Like Northcliffe, Beaverbrook sought female readers because they attracted key advertisers to his newspaper. Yet, the importance of the women's page should not be measured strictly in economic terms. By providing stories and features specifically directed towards females, the

---

[4] 'Educating the War Child', *Daily Mail*, 10 Dec. 1915.

[5] White, *Women's Magazines*, 93–114. On women in the 1920s, see Branson, *Britain in the Nineteen-Twenties*, 203–19.

[6] For Beaverbrook's control over his editors, see Beverley Baxter, *Strange Street* (London: Hutchinson, 1935), 147–9. Some of Beaverbrook's correspondence with his editors can be found in the Beaverbrook Papers, H Series, House of Lords Record Office.

[7] Lord Beaverbrook, *Politicians and the Press* (London: Hutchinson, n.d.), [pages unnumbered]; Jefferys, *Retail Trading*, 60–1.

[8] 'Should Married Women Work?', *Daily Express*, 9 Jan. 1920.

popular daily press gave women a voice in a medium previously dominated almost exclusively by men. This recognition meant that the notion of 'news' underwent yet another redefinition. Like the human-interest story, the women's page undermined the orthodox view that only politics and business mattered. In this sense, the journalists of the women's page prefigured the emergence of the 'new social history' in the 1960s. For different reasons, both broadened the scope of enquiry to include the common, everyday lives of average individuals. Then too, the women's page contributed to the social homogenization of the post-war era. The attention which the popular daily press devoted to fashion, for example, meant that a larger portion of the community might participate in an area of social life previously restricted by income and class. The notion of fashion itself became less élitist.[9] Finally, and perhaps most important, the women's page succeeded because it spoke to the perceived needs of a large section of the population. It offered practical guidance and romantic diversion. It sought to mould fashions, while at the same time reflecting the tastes of its diverse audience. The women's page did not deliver revolutionary prescriptions for the emergence of women from their subordinate position in British society. In 1920, few women were social revolutionaries. What the women's page did provide was a forum, a platform, a place, where the self-esteem of women might be enhanced.

3. *Public Personalities: Chaplin and Stardom*

In the early twentieth century, the newspaper and film industries in both Britain and America discovered an important paradox of mass communication. As new technologies helped create audiences of phenomenal size, the most effective strategy of communication was personal, intimate, and subjective. The mass media often created strong bonds between a communicator and millions of individual consumers. In daily newspapers, columnists approached readers as if they were valued acquaintances. Writers brought the public into their confidence, often revealing details about themselves or others usually confided only among close friends. In the cinema, movie moguls discovered that certain actors and actresses engendered intense loyalty among the general public. Stars transcended the fictional roles which initially defined them and became international celebrities. In both cinema and the press, audiences often showed more interest in the messenger than they did in the message.

For some celebrities, however, the strong identification between mass audiences and specific individuals accentuated the differences between their public persons and their actual personalities. Perhaps more than any

---

[9] Briggs, *Friends of the People*, 186.

other early film star, Charlie Chaplin experienced the conflicts between a fictional public character, beloved by millions, and the individual who created him. A figure of unprecedented fame, Chaplin embodied the often ambiguous nature of what might be called, for lack of a more elegant phrase, the personalization of the mass media. For purposes here, this phenomenon, crucial to understanding modern commercial culture, will be discussed by first examining its early development in the press and cinema, and then exploring in some detail the extraordinary career of the young Chaplin.

In the newspaper industry, an emphasis on the personal and the subjective was not without parallel in the reading habits of the upper classes. The personal essay was a well-established literary genre in the magazines and journals of the middle classes, and, in the élite press, journalists often filed reports which contained the first person singular. *The Times*'s coverage of foreign affairs in the early twentieth century, for example, routinely contained the personal impressions of its correspondents. The leader page occasionally ran light pieces which took readers into the editor's confidence. Yet it was not these practices of élite culture which laid the groundwork for the personal journalism of the popular press. During the 1880s, the 'New Journalism' outraged traditionalists on Fleet Street by imitating the techniques of American newspapers. As one early historian of the British press wrote disapprovingly in 1914, 'the new journalism under Mr. Stead in the *Pall Mall Gazette* introduced what is known as the "personal note". . . . It began with the interview and the personal paragraph. It remained in its fullest expression chiefly in the signed authoritative article. In the introduction of the personal note is Nemesis.'[10]

Columnists became one of the dominant manifestations of personal journalism. Though never as prevalent in Britain as in America, they wrote on a variety of topics, from drama criticism to motor racing. Columns might be occasional inserts, or regular features. Some were serious, others more amusing. Most columnists signed their real name, as in America, but the actual identity of the most popular columnist of the *Daily Express* remained virtually unknown to the public. The readers of 'Beachcomber' never needed to fear that one of their favourites would depart the paper. By writing an amusing personal column under a pen-name, J. B. Morton protected his privacy and Beaverbrook assured himself of retaining a popular feature when Morton retired or left the paper.

Most columnists wrote conversational, informal prose. They approached readers as if talking to friends. 'I really believe I shall be in fashion this year,' 'Beachcomber' wrote in 'By the Way' in 1925. 'I read that

---

[10] J. D. Symon quoted in Schults, *Crusader in Babylon*, 62.

men's trousers are to be baggier. This is cheering.' Sometimes this style approached the grammatical patterns of oral speech. 'In cornering, as I previously told you,' Woolf Barnato wrote in a guest column on 'Skids, Brakes and the "Ham Foot"', 'the accelerator can help you a lot.'[11] Over time, regular columnists created an identity which need not correspond with the writer's actual personality. Establishing a relationship with the reader might involve more artifice than authenticity.[12] Still, as the American journalist C. L. Edson wrote in his pioneering book on the subject, 'the successful Columnist puts his own personality into his column. . . . The reader likes the column because it reveals a daily insight into another man's soul—and he finds this other soul likeable. . . . The Columnist and his readers are comrades.'[13]

This comradeship extended to one of the most widely-read columns in any popular newspaper. 'A gossip-writer is often the only man on the newspaper staff who is able to impart the personal touch,' George Nichols of the *News Chronicle* wrote in 1932. Writing under the pen-name 'Qnex', Nichols sought to create a unique style which separated him from his competitors. Castlerose, whom many observers regarded as Fleet Street's most accomplished practitioner, borrowed his snappy approach from American gossip columnists. Tom Driberg, 'Dragoman' of the *Daily Express*, claimed that his satiric barbs at high society rendered him a 'descendant of Aristophanes, Juvenal and Pepys'.[14] Whatever their style, gossip columnists sought to provide inside information which allowed the reader to participate vicariously in the news and controversies of the social élite. Travels, dress balls, fashions, marriages, births, country weekends, and other bulletins from the prominent became staples of the daily newspaper. Predictably, the popular press tried to create the impression that it knew royalty intimately. An article on Queen Victoria in one of the earliest editions of the *Daily Express*, for example, not only described a typical day, but conveyed her private feelings as well.[15] Such revelations allowed popular newspapers and their readers to consider themselves part of the social universe. Élites received their gossip from private contacts, as part of a restricted oral culture. 'If they had a taste for gossip,' Northcliffe said of high society, 'they got it at their clubs, at their dinner-tables. Their "talking-points" were made for them in social

---

[11] 'Beachcomber', 'By the Way', *Daily Express*, 21 Jan. 1925; Woolf Barnato, 'Skids, Brakes and the "Ham Foot"', *Daily Mail*, 4 Oct. 1930.

[12] On the creation of 'William Hickey' of the *Daily Express*, for example, see Tom Driberg, *Ruling Passions* (New York: Stein and Day, A Scarborough Book, 1979), 103–4.

[13] C. L. Edson, *The Gentle Art of Columning: A Treatise on Comic Journalism* (New York: Brentano's, 1920), 125.

[14] Nichols and Driberg quoted in 'Is a Title Needed for Gossip-Writing?', *World's Press News*, 11 Aug. 1932.

[15] 'The Queen! God Bless Her', *Daily Express*, 24 May 1900.

intercourse.' The popular press made selected and often heavily censored portions of this oral culture part of the public domain, thus helping relieve the isolation of living in a large urban society.[16]

With the rise of the cinema, a new group of individuals began to receive extensive attention. Film stars became international celebrities, whose public personae and private lives fascinated a wide range of audiences. The fame of film stars dwarfed in scope and intensity their predecessors in other arts during the nineteenth century. The reputation of actors and actresses from the theatre, for example, rarely extended beyond national boundaries. Moreover, compared to the box-office statistics of the cinema, relatively few people actually attended the theatre. The cinema, with its capacity to record a performance on film, replicate it endlessly, and distribute it around the world, created a much more potent form of celebrity. Stars helped redefine the meaning of fame.

Film scholars have offered a number of reasons for the rapid ascendancy of the star system. The economic explanation focuses on the ability of some stars to attract an audience even for films with weak scripts. 'Movie stars', one scholar has claimed, 'seemed to represent one of the best means of reducing product uncertainty and effectively differentiating competitive movie products.'[17] Yet, as others have maintained, stars could not guarantee a good box office and often faded from popularity. 'The rise and fall of the stars', Richard Dyer argued in his book on the subject, 'indicates that economics alone cannot explain the phenomenon of stardom.'[18] Another explanation centres on the technology of film. As early as 1914, Robert Grau attributed the success of Mabel Normand to the close-up. More recently, Alexander Walker pointed out the importance of film music and signature tunes in catapulting film actors into stardom.[19] These and similar technological explanations provide a necessary though not sufficient cause for the rise of film stars.

The intense interest of audiences in certain players was not anticipated by Hollywood. In the early years of the cinema, the names of the actors rarely appeared on the screen, a blessing to those who believed that the poor reputation of films might ruin their stage careers. The public, however, found such discreet anonymity annoying. In Britain, the distributor

---

[16] Northcliffe quoted in Fyfe, *Northcliffe*, 81. On the social function of gossip columns, see Robert E. Park, 'The Natural History of the Newspaper' (1923), in *Mass Communications: A Book of Selected Readings*, 2nd edn., ed. Wilber Schramm (Urbana: University of Illinois Press, 1975), 12–13. On gossip, see also Patricia Meyer Spacks, *Gossip* (New York: Alfred A. Knopf, 1985).

[17] Gorham Kindem, 'Hollywood's Movie Star System: A Historical Overview', in Kindem, ed., *American Movie Industry*, 82.

[18] Richard Dyer, *Stars* (London: BFI, 1982), 12.

[19] Robert Grau, *The Theatre of Science* (New York: Broadway, 1914), 136; Alexander Walker, *Stardom: The Hollywood Phenomenon* (London: Michael Joseph, 1970), 21.

of Biograph's films responded to their public by inventing names for the players. Blanche Sweet became Daphne Wayne. In America, Carl Laemmle, the head of an independent studio in a fierce struggle with Edison's powerful trust, decided that the public's clamouring for films with certain favourite players could be turned to his advantage. Florence Lawrence became the first publicized film star.[20] Though Hollywood eventually became synonymous with elaborate schemes to promote the careers of its young prospects, the star system did not wholly originate with the movie moguls. 'The fact is that the almost hysterical acceptance of personality exploitation by movie goers was a startling surprise to all . . . factions in the screen world,' Jamin Hampton observed in an early history of film, published in 1931. '. . . The star system in films was in reality created by the public.'[21]

With stars came fan magazines. In America, an early weekly magazine devoted exclusively to film news was *Moving Picture World*, first published in 1910. Within a year, it spawned a number of imitators.[22] In Britain, one of the first film magazines was *The Pictures*, an illustrated weekly first published in 1911. Like early film magazines in America, *The Pictures* initially devoted more space to film plots, though early issues contained advertisements for photographic postcards which could be used to identify actors on the screen. 'Your enjoyment of motion-pictures will be doubled', one such promotion claimed, 'when you know the identities of the chief artistes.'[23] Within a year, *The Pictures* began to devote more space to film players, including interviews with actors and a feature column 'Photoplay Gossip'. The *Picturegoer*, first published in 1913 and soon to merge with *The Pictures*, obtained an article in early 1914 claiming to be by Florence Lawrence herself, and written specifically 'for my British screen friends'.[24] The *Picture Show*, published from 1919 to 1960, included among its features a 'Cinema Chat' written in a highly conversational style and 'exclusive' interviews with the stars in their Hollywood homes. By 1920, fan magazines attracted an audience substantial enough for the popular press to adopt some of their features, including gossip columns such as 'Cinema Notes' in the *Daily Express*.

Why British audiences displayed such intense interest in film stars remains an open question. Unlike the élites who formed the subjects of earlier gossip columns, film stars exercised no real social or political

[20] Anthony Slide, 'The Evolution of the Film Star', *Films in Review* 25 (1974): Garth Jowett, *Film: The Democratic Art* (Boston: Little, Brown, 1976), 54–7.

[21] Jamin B. Hampton, *A History of the Movies* (New York: Vici Friede, 1931), 89.

[22] Grau, op. cit., 246–56.

[23] *The Pictures: An Illustrated Weekly Magazine of Fiction for Lovers of Moving Pictures*, 20 June 1912.

[24] Florence Lawrence, 'Just About Myself', *Pictures and the Picturegoer*, 18 Apr. 1914.

power over their admirers. They were a status group separate from the traditional hierarchies of British life. Perhaps in this absence of threatening authority lay some of their accessibility and appeal.[25] Then too, film stars often emerged from the humblest of backgrounds, exhibiting an upward mobility which their publicists never ceased to emphasize. For most people, it was easier to imagine becoming a film star than an aristocrat. Yet, realistic ambitions may not have been the key to a star's appeal. As many film scholars have noted, stars embodied fantasies of youth, sex, beauty, wealth, and fame. They lived in fabulous houses, commanded unbelievable salaries, and spent enormous sums entertaining themselves. Young and beautiful, they attracted publicity when they worked, played, married, and divorced. Everyone knew their names.[26]

Yet, as personalities whose business involved calling attention to themselves, film stars faced a problem not shared by most other celebrities. Stars were actors, and it was as fictional characters on the screen that they attracted the loyalty of the audience. Their survival depended upon a screen persona which may not have corresponded to their actual personalities. This potential conflict between their roles on the screen and their lives as individuals became the subject of intense curiosity. Audiences identified most strongly with the fictional persona; they felt betrayed when, as in the case of Fatty Arbuckle, the disparity between the persona and the man became too great.[27] Fan magazines and gossip about the stars in popular newspapers represented an ongoing, often deceptive attempt to reveal the relationship between an individual and, quite literally, an image. Though it is important not to exaggerate the distinction between actor and individual, the split reveals the often complex nature of identification between a communicator and a public.

One of the first movie stars to experience and comment upon this duality was Charlie Chaplin. 'He was the most famous man in the world when I met him in 1919,' Max Eastman wrote in a memoir. 'I am known in parts of the world by people who have never heard of Jesus Christ,'

[25] On this point concerning American audiences, see Lary May, *Screening Out the Past: The Birth of Mass Culture and the Motion-Picture Industry* (New York: Oxford University Press, 1980), 196–7.

[26] Ibid., 96–146; Walker, *Stardom*, 124–5; Leo C. Rosten, *Hollywood: The Movie Colony, the Movie Makers* (New York: Harcourt, Brace, 1941), 110–11, 125–6; Edgar Morin, *The Stars* (New York: Grove Press, 1960), 38–48. On the sociology of such role models, see Orrin E. Klapp, *Heroes, Villains and Fools: The Changing American Character* (Englewood Cliffs: Prentice-Hall, 1962). For a history of fame, see Leo Braudy, *The Frenzy of Renown: Fame and its History* (New York and Oxford: Oxford University Press, 1986).

[27] On the Arbuckle scandal, see David A. Yallop, *The Day the Laughter Stopped: The True Story of Fatty Arbuckle* (New York: St Martin's Press, 1976).

Chaplin boasted to Lita Grey.[28] Chaplin first became a celebrity late in 1914. Within a year there were Chaplin books, toys, dolls, ties, shirts, cocktails, and scores of Chaplin imitators. 'There are only two things which fill the public mind nowadays,' Langford Reed wrote in an English magazine in 1915, 'the War and Charlie Chaplin, or, perhaps I should say, Charlie Chaplin and the War.'[29] From the beginning, commentators acknowledged the key contribution of technology in spawning such phenomenal popularity. 'He is the most celebrated man the world has ever known,' A. G. Gardiner wrote in 1926. 'He is the first man who has realized for us the magnitude of the agency that has projected his personality over the globe. . . . If there had been no film he would have probably lived and died relatively unknown.'[30] Yet, it was not simply that film allowed Chaplin's work to penetrate all parts of the globe. Cinema forced Chaplin to develop constantly as a comedian. 'In the theater I had been confined to a rigid, nondeviating routine of repeating the same thing night after night,' Chaplin wrote in his autobiography. '. . . Films were freer. They gave me a sense of adventure.'[31] Cinema allowed Chaplin to mature as a performer. Particularly after he gained control over his own material, Chaplin sought to improve his characterization and timing. To Chaplin, fame continually needed to be justified.

Yet, technology only created the conditions for Chaplin's enormous popularity. Why audiences identified with his unique screen character remains a more elusive question and the subject of extensive analysis.[32] Certain aspects, however, of his appeal as a film performer should be stressed. First, from his earliest days in the movies, Chaplin grasped the centrality of vivid characterization in comic routines. When he worked for Mack Sennett, he was distressed by the number of mechanical gags, especially chase scenes. 'Personally, I hated a chase,' he recalled later. 'It dissipates one's personality; little as I knew about movies, I knew that nothing transcended personality.'[33] Gradually, Chaplin evolved for himself the character of the Tramp, whose complex origins included music-hall performers such as Dan Leno, and *commedia dell'arte* which

[28] Max Eastman, *Great Companions* (New York: Farrar, Strauss, and Cudahy, 1959), 208; Lita Grey Chaplin and Morton Cooper, *My Life with Chaplin: An Intimate Memoir* (n.p.: Bernard Geis Associates, 1966), 2. For the details of Chaplin's life, see David Robinson, *Chaplin: His Life and Art* (New York: McGraw-Hill, 1985).
[29] Quoted in David Robinson, *Chaplin: The Mirror of Opinion* (London: Secker and Warburg; Bloomington: Indiana University Press, 1984), 37, 35.
[30] A. G. Gardiner, *Portraits and Portents* (New York and London: Harper and Brothers, 1926), 225. I have rearranged the order of these quotations.
[31] Charles Chaplin, *My Autobiography* (New York: Simon and Schuster, 1964), 153.
[32] For a useful though not always accurate compilation of writings on Chaplin, see Timothy J. Lyons, *Charles Chaplin: A Guide to References and Resources* (Boston: G. K. Hall, 1979). Lyons's 'Chronological Biography' lists his birthplace as 'London (Kensington)' rather than Kennington. [33] Chaplin, *Autobiography*, 141–2.

Chaplin perfected as a member of Fred Karno's touring company.[34] The famous costume allowed Chaplin to assume many poses. 'I wanted everything a contradiction,' he wrote in his autobiography; 'the pants baggy, the coat tight, the hat small and the shoes large.' As he explained to Sennett, 'You know this fellow is many-sided, a tramp, a gentleman, a poet, a dreamer, a lonely fellow, always hopeful of romance and adventure. He would have you believe he is a scientist, a musician, a duke, a polo player. However, he is not above picking up cigarette butts or robbing a baby of its candy.'[35] The notion of combining contradictory traits, such as the gentleman and the tramp, in a single character drew from a long tradition of working-class comedy in Britain.[36] Chaplin applied them to a new medium dominated by simple gags and one-dimensional characters.

It was easy for audiences to identify with a charming, marginal character. 'Everyone knows that the little fellow in trouble always gets the sympathy of the mob,' he admitted frankly in 1918. 'Knowing that it is part of human nature to sympathize with the "under dog", I always accentuate my helplessness.'[37]. As janitor, waiter, house-painter, police man, or clerk, Charlie assumed jobs familiar to a mass audience. Often the comedy revolved around his character undermining social hierarchies. In the opening scene of *Work*, for example, Charlie must pull a cart burdened with both supplies and his hefty boss, who shouts orders and remains indifferent to the plight of his subordinate. Later, however, the boss suffers from the comic incompetence of his abused employee. He is tripped, slammed with a board, covered with paste, and doused with water by the solicitous Charlie. In another scene from the same film, the mistress of the house hides her silver after admitting Charlie and his boss to her home. Immediately they respond by hiding their wallets and other valuables. In both scenes, it is the figure of authority who gets mocked.[38] Yet Charlie was not a true underdog. When placed in impossible situations, he displayed a natural dignity, grace, and chivalry which transcended his

---

[34] On the origins of Chaplin's comic persona, see the perceptive but idiosyncratic Robert Payne, *The Great God Pan: A Biography of the Tramp Played by Charles Chaplin* (New York: Hermitage House, 1952), esp. 42–73. On Karno, see J. P. Gallagher, *Fred Karno: Master of Mirth and Tears* (London: Robert Hale, 1971).

[35] Chaplin, *Autobiography*, 144.

[36] On the 'Gent' see Peter Bailey, 'Ally Sloper's Half-Holiday: Comic Art in the 1880s', *History Workshop* 16 (1983): 4–31. On Chaplin's use of contradictions, see Gerard Molyneaux, *Charles Chaplin's* City Lights: *The Production and Dialectical Structure* (New York: Garland, 1983).

[37] Charlie Chaplin, 'What People Laugh At', *American Magazine* 86, 5 (1918), 136. The article was ghost-written by Rob Wagner.

[38] There are many unauthorized versions of Chaplin's films. The films I viewed were from the collection of the University of Chicago.

apparent degradation.[39] In film after film, it was Charlie who rescued the girl, captured the robbers, or rid the street of bullies. Rarely rewarded properly, he embodied a natural decency which the conventionally pious lacked. As a screen character, he thus fulfilled the fantasy of ordinary individuals who imagined themselves possessing extraordinary skills and unacknowledged greatness of character.

Character alone cannot explain Chaplin's hold on his audience. His appeal was also obviously enhanced by his uncanny timing and craft as a film-maker. Chaplin was a perfectionist. He achieved his effortlessly superior comic turns by constantly retaking the same scenes. For some films, he shot on average one hundred feet of film for every foot that eventually made the screen, one of the highest shooting ratios in the history of Hollywood.[40] Early in his career he attended public showings of his films to observe audience reactions. 'Anyone who caters to the public has got to keep his knowledge of "what people like" fresh and up to date,' he wrote in 1918. As he matured as an artist, however, he relied more and more upon his own inspiration. 'I prefer my taste as a truer expression of what the public wants of me than anything . . . I can observe,' he claimed in 1924. Chaplin particularly excelled at creating gags with inanimate things. At Keystone he learned the humour of a serious man confronted by a recalcitrant object.[41] Stairs, mechanical dummies, and retractable beds became formidable opponents. In *The Pawnshop*, released in 1916, Charlie gradually destroys a customer's alarm clock by treating it like a sick child, a can of food, a decayed tooth, and other things rather than a clock. In one of the most famous scenes from *The Gold Rush*, Charlie entertains some female acquaintances by transforming biscuits on a fork into dancing chorus girls. Performed without the benefit of trick photography, and sometimes shot in a single take that required weeks of filming, Chaplin's sight gags astonished audiences by infusing life into everyday objects.

Finally, Chaplin gained the loyalty of an enormous audience because he added a dimension to comedy which many of his rivals ignored. Especially in the later, longer, and more complex films, he constructed plots around surprisingly serious themes. *Easy Street*, released in 1917, was set in a slum and contained a scene of drug addiction. Four years

[39] Walter Kerr, *The Silent Clowns* (New York: Alfred A. Knopf, 1979) 84–5. I have learned much from this valuable study.

[40] Gerald Mast, *The Comic Mind: Comedy and the Movies* (Indianapolis: Bobbs-Merrill, 1973), 67. On the recent discovery of some of Chaplin's out-takes, see Gavin Miller, 'The Unknown Chaplin', *Sight and Sound* 52, 2 (1983): 98–9. Some of these out-takes were used in a series of television programmes, *Unknown Chaplin* (Thames in UK, and PBS in USA).

[41] Chaplin, 'What People Laugh At', 135; id., 'Does the Public Know What it Wants?', *Adelphi* 1 (1924): 705. This article was ghost-written; Mast, *Comic Mind*, 68–9.

later, *The Kid* dealt with illegitimate children, the corruption of marriage, and rampant social hypocrisy. *The Gold Rush*, issued in 1925, involved hunger, fear, loneliness, and greed. From these settings, Chaplin created extraordinary comic effects, such as the celebrated scene where a starved and emaciated Charlie in a remote Alaskan cabin serves boiled shoes for dinner. As Walter Kerr has observed, 'there is only one way of making comedy richer — and, paradoxically, funnier — and that is by making it more serious.'[42] Though many critics recoiled from what they considered the sentimentality and melodrama of Chaplin's feature films, the blending of tragedy and comedy became central to Chaplin's maturation as a film director. Alert to the danger that bathos might swallow comedy, he often undercut with irony the more sentimental scenes in the films of the 1920s, but he retained the notion that laughter stemmed from the serious predicaments of life. 'In the creation of comedy,' he later observed, 'it is paradoxical that tragedy stimulated the spirit of ridicule, because ridicule, I suppose, is an attitude of defiance.'[43]

Chaplin's creation of a remarkable screen character, his willingness to devote time and resources to achieve superb comic timing, and his ability to mature as a comedian, all contributed to his unprecedented popularity among audiences in Britain and around the world. The Charlie whom audiences adored, however, was often quite distinct from the successful lower-class English *émigré* who created him. Chaplin was one of the first international celebrities to experience the curious duality of film stardom. Unlike his screen persona, Chaplin became the ultimate insider, with enormous wealth and access to the rich, prominent and powerful wherever he travelled. In the early years when he worked for other studios, his astronomical salary increases defied easy assimilation. At a time when an American family might survive nicely on $900 a year, Chaplin left Keystone to work for Essanay in 1915 at $1,250 a week. A year later, Mutual gained his services for $10,000 a week plus a bonus of $150,000, a total of $670,000 for the year. From *The Kid* he cleared an estimated one million dollars in profit.[44] 'He embodies the wish fulfilment of our time,' a biographer later wrote; 'the boy who rose from the rags of Kennington to the riches of Hollywood.'[45]

One of Chaplin's earliest and most vivid experiences of fame occurred during a trip from Los Angeles to New York in 1916. In Amarillo, Texas, an excited crowd surrounded the train, demanding an appearance from

---

[42] Kerr, *Silent Clowns*, 162. On this point, see also Michael Roemer, 'Chaplin: Charles and Charlie', *Yale Review* 64, 2 (1974–5): 168–84.

[43] Chaplin, *Autobiography*, 303.

[44] Theodore Huff, *Charlie Chaplin* (New York: Henry Schuman, 1951), 58–9; Robinson, *Chaplin* (1985), 135, 150, 160.

[45] Roger Manvell, *Chaplin* (Boston: Little, Brown, 1974), 3.

their favourite. In Kansas City, the crowds were even larger and more enthusiastic. On the way to Chicago, people stood in cornfields, just to glimpse the train. Chaplin became 'tense, elated and depressed all at the same time. . . . I had always thought I would like the public's attention, and here it was—paradoxically isolating me with a depressing sense of loneliness.' In New York, he made his way to Times Square and gazed at the sign which announced his phenomenal salary with Mutual. 'I stood and read it objectively as though it were about someone else.' His appearance the same year at a benefit concert in Hollywood created such a sensation that Chaplin resolved to limit severely his personal appearances.[46]

By 1921, however, Chaplin emerged from his self-imposed isolation to visit England, where he wished to be present at the opening of *The Kid*. England had proved to be one of Chaplin's best markets. Already in 1915, the *Bioscope* reported that some cinemas prospered by only showing Chaplin films. His early films proved so popular that Essanay helped devise the restrictive practice of block booking. To show Chaplin films, exhibitors needed to rent less lucrative fare from the same company. In 1921 it cost £500 a week to book *The Idle Class*.[47] When, after much anticipation in the popular press, Chaplin finally arrived at Waterloo station in September 1921, the usually sober *Times* reported that 'the stage might have been set for the homecoming of Julius Caesar, Napoleon and Lord Haig rolled into one.' Crowds pressed against his car. The bodyguards assigned to him by the London police asked for his autograph. Seventy-three thousand letters and cards awaited him at his hotel. A cartoon in the *Daily Express* pictured him displacing Lord Nelson in Trafalgar Square. [48]

Chaplin often felt distant from the crowds who believed they knew him and greeted him by his first name. While travelling on ship, he discovered that even the first-class passengers expected him to act like his film character. 'I have an idea that they think I am "Charlie" performing for them,' he recalled in his memoir of the visit. 'They arouse pride, indignation. I have decided to become very exclusive on board. That's the way to treat them.' Chaplin remained ambivalent towards his admirers throughout the visit. Sitting alone in his hotel after his tumultuous welcome

[46] Chaplin, *Autobiography*, 177, 179; Huff, op. cit., 58.

[47] John Montgomery, 'A Brief Overview', in *Focus on Chaplin*, ed. Donald W. McCaffrey (Englewood Cliffs NJ: Prentice-Hall, 1971), 17; Rachael Low, *The History of the British Film, 1914–1918* (London: British Film Institute, 1948), 44–5; id., *The History of the British Film, 1918–1929*, 52.

[48] *The Times*, 12 Sept. 1921; *Daily Express*, 10 Sept. 1921; Charles Chaplin, *My Wonderful Visit* (London: Hurst and Blackett [1922]), 112. The book was ghost-written. On Chaplin's police guards, see J. M. Barrie, *Letters of J. M. Barrie*, ed. Viola Meynell, (New York: Charles Scribner's Sons, 1947), 194.

at Waterloo, he thought: 'Once more I am a private citizen. I am just a bit sad at this. Being a celebrity has its nice points.'[49] He worried that his appearances might only draw small crowds, yet claimed that huge crowds frightened him. Whether meeting the people of impoverished Kennington or the élites whose names he listed with such pride in his book about the visit, Chaplin continually reflected on the problem of his own identity. In personal appearances, he resented acting as 'Charlie' yet he also felt detached from his wealth and fame. On his second visit to London in 1931, a journalist for the *Daily Express* wrote a feature article entitled 'The Two Mr. Chaplins Come to London', in which he contrasted 'Charles the Man and Celluloid Charlie'. Chaplin the man, the journalist argued, was a charming 'wealthy property owner from California', not the 'chap in baggy trousers'.[50] Yet perhaps the contrast missed the mark. As many readers have noted, Chaplin's autobiography, published in 1964, excelled as a vivid depiction of childhood poverty in a London slum. His years as a film star and controversial international celebrity are often described as if they happened to someone else. Perhaps the man who wrote the autobiography remained closest in identity to the talented outsider on the screen after all.

In 1921, Chaplin's difficulties with the press concerning his involvements with young women and his radical political opinions still lay in the future. His early personal appearances as a film star in America and Britain illustrated that the public's attachment to celebrities involved both intimacy and distance. Chaplin's audience identified closely with the patiently crafted figure on the screen. It was the persona they appreciated. They expressed great curiosity, but remained apart, save in their fantasies, from the person of wealth and fame. The emotional identification that existed between a creator of commercial culture and a member of the public created a new élite of heroes, whose success distanced them from their audience. Though mass communication often succeeded best when it emphasized the subjective and the personal, such intimacy remained a compelling, convenient fiction.

When for their own economic benefit the producers of the mass media identified with the preferences of their audience, they created an enormously popular and increasingly pervasive standard of cultural judgement. Commercial culture was at once both materialist and egalitarian. It was materialist because the profit motive lay at its heart. The producers of commercial culture were in the business of providing entertainment and

---

[49] Chaplin, *Wonderful Visit*, 46–7, 76.
[50] Gordon Beckles, 'The Two Mr. Chaplins Come to London', *Daily Express*, 20 Feb. 1931.

information. As business men, they tried to minimize their risk. Both the film and newspaper industries sought to concentrate their power and to practise economies of scale. Both faced competition not only from within their own industries, but from other media as well. Commercial culture served the self-interest of its producers.

Yet it also served the self-determined interests of the audience who supported it with their pocket-books. For shrewd business reasons, commercial culture could not afford to alienate its intended public. It could not afford to treat them like subordinates, pupils, or 'masses'. It could not afford to ignore or patronize the average individual. Commercial culture was fundamentally egalitarian because it collapsed the distance between a communicator and a public. The simple, direct, vivid language of the British popular press in the early decades of the twentieth century levelled the relationship between producer and consumer. The printed word gradually became analogous to a conversation among friends. Millions of readers discovered that a daily newspaper need not be as intimidating as *The Times*. The women's page allowed a huge, neglected audience to participate in a medium previously devoted to male concerns. The popular daily press boosted both circulation and advertising revenue by identifying with the interests of its female readers. Film stars emerged from the demands of audiences, who identified strongly with certain screen personalities. Cinema enabled actors such as Charlie Chaplin to attain a measure of fame unprecedented in the nineteenth century.

The rapid rise and tremendous popularity of the commercial mass media in the early twentieth century provoked the cultivated élites into defining and reasserting their own cultural standards. As we shall see in Part Two, the response varied enormously, but it centred on the conviction that the market-place ought not decide a nation's culture. To many intellectuals, 'commercial culture' was a contradiction in terms. Culture existed apart from economic self-interest. Aesthetic standards, it was argued, could not be democratized. Excellence could not be put to a vote. The conflict was an old one. Once again, a privileged and self-confident minority asserted the values of hierarchy against a majority who threatened to level such distinctions.

2

Technology and Tradition

THE impact of technological innovations has long been a subject of controversy. Writers such as Lewis Mumford, Jacques Ellul, and Harold Innis have arrived at widely disparate conclusions about the relationship between technology and culture.[1] This intellectual diversity, often punctuated by heated controversy, also marks the study of mass communications. Historians, sociologists, philosophers, and literary figures in both Europe and America have debated the effects of mass media upon social and cultural traditions. Among a variety of carefully argued positions, three schools of thought have predominated. First, a number of writers claimed that the new technologies of communication in the twentieth century destroyed, displaced, or otherwise profoundly undermined existing, more authentic traditions of popular culture. These critics maintained that the commercial mass media, in particular, levelled distinctions, homogenized diversity, trivialized complexity, and mechanized the organic, more 'natural' pursuits of traditional culture. Elements of this pessimistic argument often united both Left and Right, binding political adversaries in a common front. Yet despite its modern points of reference, the position descends from an ancient pedigree[2] and, as we shall see in Part Two where the argument will be examined in detail, attracted forceful advocates among the cultivated élites in Britain during the inter-war period.

In the 1950s and 1960s, Marshall McLuhan challenged the derisive attitude of most intellectuals to mass communications. Borrowing from his Canadian colleague Harold Innis and others, McLuhan argued that the introduction of any new technology of communication vitally altered the configuration of sense data whereby humans come to know each other and the outside world. To McLuhan, the printing press radically transformed Western thought and society. Gutenberg initiated a technology that converted words into detached, uniform, infinitely repeatable images

---

[1] Lewis Mumford, *Technics and Civilization* (New York: Harcourt, Brace, 1934); Jacques Ellul, *The Technological Society*, trans. John Wilkinson (New York: Knopf, 1964); H. A. Innis, *The Bias of Communication* (Toronto: University of Toronto Press, 1951). See also William Kuhns, *The Post-Industrial Prophets: Interpretations of Technology* (New York: Weybridge and Talley, 1971).

[2] Patrick Brantlinger, *Bread and Circuses: Theories of Mass Culture as Social Decay* (Ithaca: Cornell University Press, 1983), 53–81.

which demanded a trained visual sense for interpretation. By forcing knowledge into the linear and sequential segments of words on a page, the printing press changed communication into a solitary, private experience. The rise of mass media in the twentieth century, however, recreated an environment of communications not unlike that of primitive societies. To McLuhan, the capacity to transmit sight and sound electronically restored the ability of audiences to grasp messages as a whole, and not from a linear, fixed point of view. The mass media resurrected the sensual richness of oral communication.[3]

This notion that the introduction of new technologies of communication helped transform human consciousness has often met with serious reservations. 'Claims that print revolutionized European society,' Robert Pattison wrote in his book on literacy, 'altered the nature of memory, reorganized perspective, and rang the death knell of oral culture must be examined with great care. Similar claims advanced on behalf of the new technologies of the modern age . . . should be met with equal restraint.' Critics have long been sensitive to the reductive arguments of technological determinism. They point out that innovative techniques prosper only in certain social contexts, and they question any model which elevates inanimate objects into primary agents of historical change.[4] Such caution helps avoid mechanistic interpretations in which a separate entity called 'technology' acts independently upon another phenomenon, 'culture'. More sophisticated analyses emphasize the continuities and adaptations between generations of technology. In a number of recent studies, Walter Ong, Elizabeth Eisenstein, and Jack Goody and Ian Watt have all borrowed from McLuhan's central ideas, but dissented from his technological determinism. Thus, for example, in *The Printing Press as an Agent of Change*, Elizabeth Eisenstein emphasized that the title of her book 'refers to *an* agent not to *the* agent, let alone *the only* agent of change in Western Europe'. Like a number of other scholars, Eisenstein

---

[3] Marshall McLuhan, *The Gutenberg Galaxy: The Making of Typographic Man* (Toronto: University of Toronto Press, 1962); id., *Understanding Media: The Extensions of Man* (New York: McGraw-Hill, 1964; McGraw Paperback, 1965). On McLuhan, see, among others, Gerald E. Stearns, ed., *McLuhan: Hot and Cool* (New York: Dial Press, 1967); Raymond Rosenthal, ed., *McLuhan: Pro and Con* (New York: Funk and Wagnalls, 1967); Jonathan Miller, *Marshall McLuhan* (London: Fontana, 1971); and D. L. LeMahieu, 'McLuhan', in *Thinkers of the Twentieth Century: A Biographical, Bibliographical and Critical Dictionary*, ed. Elizabeth Devine *et al.* (Detroit: Gale Research, 1983), 377–9.

[4] Robert Pattison, *On Literacy: The Politics of the Word from Homer to the Age of Rock* (New York: Oxford University Press, 1982), 99. See also Robert L. Heilbroner, 'Do Machines Make History?', in *Technology and Culture: An Anthology*, ed. Melvin Kranzberg and William H. Davenport (New York: Schocken Books, 1972), 28–40; and Anthony Smith, 'Information Technology and the Myth of Abundance', *Daedalus* 111, 4 (1982): 1–16.

lamented that 'exploring the effects produced by any particular innovation arouses suspicion that one favours a monocausal interpretation, or that one is prone to reductionism and technological determinism.'[5]

This willingness to examine the impact of new forms of communication while steering clear of determinism sets an admirably high standard for evaluating the complex interrelationship between technology and tradition. For, in the late nineteenth and early twentieth centuries, a series of inventions transformed communications in Britain. In the newspaper industry, the development of the Linotype machine in the 1880s allowed a single skilled worker to set type four times faster than the previous system, which required three workers. By 1900, most London daily newspapers and over 250 provincial and other British publications employed Linotype, the latest in a sequence of inventions which permitted the British press to reach a mass audience.[6] The desire to capture motion on film contributed to the development of cinema, a medium which helped define the new century. Eadweard Muybridge's experiments photographing galloping horses in California and the invention of the 'chronophotographic gun' in 1882 by Étienne-Jules Marey to record birds in flight contributed significantly to the development of the first motion-picture camera. By the mid-1890s, films began to be projected for profit in both Europe and America.[7] Though he claimed to be the inventor of cinema, Edison deserved more credit for the phonograph, which he developed in 1877 while attempting to improve telegraphy. In the 1880s, Émile Berliner invented the 'gramophone', which employed lateral-cut discs rather than the vertical-cut cylinders of Edison's machine. Other variations followed, soon commercially exploited.[8] By the turn of the century, sights and sounds could be recorded, produced in quantity, and widely distributed.

[5] Elizabeth L. Eisenstein, *The Printing Press As An Agent of Change: Communications and Cultural Transformations in Early Modern Europe*, (Cambridge: Cambridge University Press, 2 vols., 1979; paperback in one volume, 1980), p. xv. See also Jack Goody and Ian Watt, 'The Consequences of Literacy', in *Literacy in Traditional Societies*, ed. Jack Goody (Cambridge: Cambridge University Press, 1968), 27–68; and Walter J. Ong, *Orality and Literacy: The Technologizing of the Word* (New York: Methuen, 1982).

[6] T. K. Derry and Trevor I. Williams, *A Short History of Technology* (Oxford: Clarendon Press, 1960), 637–51.

[7] On the development of film technology, see Ray Fielding, *A Technological History of Motion Pictures and Television* (Berkeley: University of California Press, 1967); C. W. Ceram, *Archeology of the Cinema* (New York: Harcourt, Brace, 1967); Robert Bartlett Haas, *Muybridge: Man in Motion* (Berkeley: University of California Press, 1976); Gordon Hendricks, *The Edison Motion Picture Myth* (Berkeley: University of California Press, 1961); and John Barnes, *The Beginnings of the Cinema in England* (Newton Abbot: David and Charles; New York: Barnes and Noble, 1976).

[8] Gelatt, *Fabulous Phonograph*, 17–113; Read and Welch, *Tin-Foil to Stereo*, 1–217.

What was the relationship of these new or improved technologies of communications to the established traditions of popular culture in Britain? How did commercial interests adapt proven methods to the newer media in order to engage their audience? These and related questions could be approached in a number of ways. Some might stress how the newer media, such as the cinema and the gramophone, affected established forms of entertainment such as the music-hall, choral societies, or piano playing in the home.[9] Others might emphasize the complex interactions between a national 'mass' culture facilitated by the new technologies, and the diverse regional and local cultures which played such a central and sometimes neglected role in British history.[10] I have no quarrel with these approaches. For purposes here, however, two examples will illustrate the complex, often elusive interrelationship of technology and tradition. First, in the late nineteenth and early twentieth centuries, a series of technological innovations allowed commercial culture to reach its audience through often novel and more ubiquitous visual means. Though images traditionally played an important role in popular culture, the cinema, news photography, and other graphics in the popular press buttressed and widely extended the role of visual information and entertainment. Second, recorded sound and the mechanization of music affected culture in surprising, often heterogeneous ways. Both as commodity and as promising technology, the gramophone sometimes reinforced opposing strands within British musical tradition. These two examples, involving sight and sound, hardly exhaust the general topic. But they illustrate the limitations of simple, one-dimensional statements about the nature and influence of new technologies of communications.

A. IMAGES: COMMERCIAL CULTURE AND THE VISUAL IMAGINATION

Technical developments in photography, film, and other visual media in the late nineteenth and early twentieth centuries paved the way for

[9] There is no comprehensive scholarly history on the music-hall or its decline, though there are a number of useful accounts. See, among others, Raymond Mander and Joe Mitcheson, *British Music Hall*, revised edn. (London: Gentry Books, 1974); D. F. Cheshire, *Music Hall in Britain* (Rutherford, NJ: Fairleigh Dickenson University Press, 1974); Colin Macinnes, *Sweet Saturday Night* (London: MacGibbon and Kee, 1967); Diana Howard, *London Theatres and Music Halls, 1850–1950* (London: Library Association, 1970); and Felix Barker, *The House That Stoll Built: The Story of the Coliseum Theatre* (London: Frederick Muller, 1957).
[10] For examples of the interplay between regional and national cultures, see G. J. Mellor, *The Northern Music Hall: A Century of Popular Entertainment* (Newcastle: Frank Graham, 1970).

new forms of mass communication through images. Cinema evolved from a novelty into a major source of entertainment in a remarkably brief period of time. Borrowing from a number of popular traditions, the directors and producers of commercial cinema sought to develop a film grammar which captured and held the attention of their expanding public. By the end of the First World War, most elements of this grammar were well established. During the same decades in which cinema became entertainment for millions, popular daily newspapers began to communicate extensively through images as well as words. Display advertising, cartoons, bolder headlines, and news photography transformed the appearance of the press. Although the notion of an illustrated paper involved precedents extending deep into British history, the popular daily press took longer than cinema to develop a studied and systematic visual grammar. Words, not images, retained greater respectability.

The early development of cinema as a visual medium of communication has attracted extensive research in recent years. In particular, scholars have explored how directors established a visual narrative in their films. Here examples of continuity with Victorian cultural traditions have been especially well documented. In Britain and America, spectacle and pictorial realism dominated popular theatre in the late nineteenth century. Theatre directors designed elaborate sets for their melodramas which included, for example, live horses who appeared to be racing on stage, violent storms with floods of water, and other spectacular displays. The cinema, it has been argued, was a natural descendant of the pictorial theatre.[11] Yet theatrical spectacle was not the only precursor to the narrative tradition in film. Novels, cartoon strips, optical toys, and other less obvious aspects of nineteenth-century popular culture embodied methods of telling stories which early film may have borrowed.[12] Still, despite these precursors, early film-makers explored camera angles and editing principles which eventually established cinema as a unique visual medium. Some film scholars and enthusiasts have been interested in who first employed a particular technique. Others have asked who first used the technique to best advantage.[13]

---

[11] A. Nicholas Vardac, *Stage to Screen: Theatrical Method from Garrick to Griffith* (1949; reprint, New York: Benjamin Blom, 1968), 12. See also Allandyce Nicoll, *A History of English Drama, 1660–1900, vol. 5: Late Nineteenth-Century Drama, 1850–1900* (Cambridge: Cambridge University Press, 1959), 34–7.

[12] John L. Fell, *Film and the Narrative Tradition* (Norman: University of Oklahoma Press, 1974).

[13] Georges Sadoul, *British Creators of Film Technique* (London: BFI, 1948); Barry Salt, 'The Early Development of Film Form', in *Film Before Griffith*, ed. John L. Fell (Berkeley: University of California Press, 1983), 284–98; Burnes St Patrick Hollyman, 'Alexander Black's Picture Plays, 1893–1894', ibid., 236–43; Jon Gartenberg, 'Camera Movement in Edison and Biograph Films, 1900–1906', *Cinema Journal* 19, 2 (1980):

The ways film-makers integrated technology and tradition to engage their audiences changed as directors gained experience, the demands of the public shifted, and an array of inventions created new opportunities for resourceful producers. Early films luxuriated in the novelty of moving images. A train arriving at a station, fire engines answering an emergency, waves breaking against rocks, women leaving a factory, and other early 'actualities' were the moving snapshots of amateurs exploring the potentialities of a new medium. By the late 1890s, producers discovered the visual appeal of news and sports. In England, the Derby, Henley Regatta, boxing matches, motor races, the Queen's Jubilee, and other similar events became staples of films exhibited in fairgrounds, music-halls, and rented rooms. Trick films often involved more technical manipulation of the medium. Though Méliès became widely acknowledged as the most accomplished film magician,[14] British directors also discovered the excitement of film illusion. Cecil Hepworth's *How it Feels to be Run Over* (1900) contained the image of a car driving straight toward the camera until the film went out of focus, and James Williamson's *The Big Swallow* (1901) involved a man approaching the camera, opening his mouth until it filled the entire screen, and swallowing the camera and cameraman, who appear to be falling through a void. The short film ended with the original subject walking away, chewing.[15]

Yet topical events and short, witty trick films could not sustain the interest of audiences year after year. Films needed plots to engage and maintain the public's attention. Though technology at the turn of the century limited film-makers to brief productions, films did possess crude narrative structures. Some of these narratives drew upon the traditions of the magic lantern. Like the Thaumatrope, Phasmatrope, and other fancifully named inventions, the magic lantern was one of many nineteenth-century optical devices that amused audiences of all classes. Often employed by religious and temperance societies to uplift the poor to moral virtue, the slide shows of the magic lantern also embraced historical and literary subjects.[16] A number of early British film-makers

1–16. Though the distinction remains somewhat artificial, a good example of making the aesthetic criterion more essential is William K. Everson, *American Silent Film* (New York: Oxford University Press, 1978), 30–53.

[14] Rachael Low and Roger Manvell, *The History of the British Film, 1896–1906* (London: George Allen and Unwin, 1948), 36, 62–3. On Méliès, see Paul Hammond, *Marvellous Méliès* (London: Gordon Fraser, 1974); Georges Sadoul, *Georges Méliès* (Paris: Éditions Seghers, 1961); and John Fraser, *Artificially Arranged Scenes: The Films of Georges Méliès* (Boston: G. K. Hall, 1979). On the role of magic in early cinema, see Erik Barnouw, *The Magician and the Cinema* (New York: Oxford University Press, 1981).

[15] Barry Salt, 'Film Form, 1900–1906', *Sight and Sound* 47, 3 (1978): 152.

[16] Olive Cook, *Movement in Two Dimensions: A Study of the Animated and Projected Pictures Which Preceded the Invention of Cinematography* (London: Hutchinson,

entered cinema from magic lantern, and, not surprisingly, photographed and structured their films according to its conventions. James Williamson, for example, produced films which, like the magic lantern, depended upon commentary by the projectionist to connect the narrative. Without this commentary, films such as *Attack on a China Mission* (1900), dealing with an episode in the Boxer Rebellion, appears disjointed and lacking narrative sense. As he gained experience, Williamson began to make films in which the pictures carried more of the story. *Stop Thief!* (1901) contained one of the earliest known chase scenes and *Fire!*, released the same year, linked scenes together with even greater pictorial sophistication.[17] Still, despite this maturation, Williamson remained dependent upon spoken commentary, and well within the narrative traditions of magic lantern.

For a long time, film scholars credited Edwin Porter with a number of cinematic innovations.[18] Yet like his contemporaries, this American director also employed the conventions of magic lantern to construct narratives. For instance, his use of the dissolve as a transition from one scene to another was a common technique among slide projectionists. Moreover, his early time-lapse photography derived from the stereopticon, where pictures of a scene in daylight immediately preceded the same shot at night. Even *Life of an American Fireman* (1903), usually considered a central document in the evolution of film technique, represented an imaginative consolidation of narrative strategies, rather than a sharp break from the past.[19] Porter created films to attract audiences; setting precedents moved him not at all.

Porter's highly successful film at the box office, *The Great Train Robbery* (1903), taught a number of film-makers the value of a good story, efficiently told. Its narrative structure influenced Cecil Hepworth's *Rescued by Rover* (1905), the most famous British dramatic film of the period. The film, which told the story of how a faithful collie saved a small child from an evil gypsy woman, moved rapidly from scene to scene, and employed low-angle camera shots to heighten the drama of the dog's rapid movements.[20] Like Porter, Hepworth invoked the conventions of

1963), 105–16. There are some useful illustrations of these devices in John L. Fell, *A History of Films* (New York: Holt, Rinehart and Winston, 1979), 8–9. On early narrative, see, for example, Marshall Deutelbaum, 'Structural Patterning in the Lumière Films', in *Film Before Griffith*, ed. Fell, 299–310.

[17] Martin Sopocy, 'A Narrated Cinema: The Pioneer Story Films of James A. Williamson', *Cinema Journal* 18, 1 (1978): 1–28.

[18] Lewis Jacobs, 'Edwin S. Porter and the Editing Principle', in *The Emergence of Film Art: The Evolution and Development of the Motion Picture as an Art Since 1900*, ed. Lewis Jacobs, 2nd edn. (New York: W. W. Norton, 1979): 20–35.

[19] Charles Musser, 'The Early Cinema of Edwin Porter', *Cinema Journal* 19, 1 (1979): 1–38.

[20] For a good description of this film, see Low and Manvell, *British Film 1896–1906*, 108–10.

magic lantern and nineteenth-century melodrama. Then too, like Porter, Hepworth began to rely more heavily on images, rather than words, to narrate his story. 'Always . . . ', he recalled later, 'I have striven for . . . *pictorial* meaning and effect in every case where it is obtainable.' With the rise of nickelodeon, inserted titles rather than spoken commentary often became the most convenient way of providing dialogue or linking scenes. Hepworth argued that titles 'should never be used unless it is practically impossible to tell some part of the story without them'. By 1907, films had become something more than magic-lantern shows in motion.[21]

As virtually every film historian acknowledges, however, it was D. W. Griffith who established the cinema as a unique medium. Griffith's style developed gradually. Some of his early films at Biograph, completed often in days, could have been made by a score of other directors. Moreover, he pioneered few of the cinematic techniques which he later claimed, though recent attempts to strip him of all innovations may be overstated.[22] Griffith's real achievement lay in two areas. First, more than any previous director, he employed the unique potentialities of the motion picture camera to heighten the emotional impact of traditional melodrama. He made films calculated to affect and move audiences. 'For Griffith depended absolutely, even slavishly, upon audience reactions,' one of his assistants, Karl Brown, later recalled. 'Whatever audiences responded to was right, no matter how wrong it might seem from any other consideration, and anything audiences did not respond to was wrong, regardless of how finely acted or how beautifully photographed.'[23] Griffith began his career as an actor, steeped in the conventions of nineteenth-century melodrama. He knew that audiences responded viscerally to the stark moral contrasts of the genre. In melodrama, characters embodied good and evil and the fundamental antagonism between the two could not be compromised.[24] Overt villains persecuted

---

[21] Cecil M. Hepworth, *Came the Dawn: Memories of a Film Pioneer* (London: Phoenix House, 1951), 123-4; John L. Fell, 'Motive, Mischief, and Melodrama: The State of Film Narrative in 1907', in *Film Before Griffith*, ed. Fell, 272-83.

[22] William Johnson, 'Early Griffith: A Wider View', *Film Quarterly* 29, 2 (1975-6): 2-3. On Griffith and innovation, see David A. Cook, *A History of Narrative Film* (New York: W. W. Norton, 1981), 63 n.

[23] Karl Brown, *Adventures with D. W. Griffith* (New York: Farrar, Strauss, and Giroux, 1973), 59. Brown was an assistant to Billy Bitzer, Griffith's superb cameraman.

[24] Peter Brooks, *The Melodramatic Imagination: Balzac, Henry James, Melodrama, and the Mode of Excess* (New Haven: Yale University Press, 1976); see also Robert Bechtold Heilman, *Tragedy and Melodrama: Versions of Experience* (Seattle: University of Washington Press, 1968), 79-83; and Michael R. Booth, *English Melodrama* (London: Herbert Jenkins, 1965), 13-39. On Griffith's life and career before joining film, see Richard Schickel, *D. W. Griffith: An American Life* (New York: Simon and Schuster, 1984), 15-93.

the blameless and the innocent. Suspense heightened as evil threatened to prevail. The climax came at the moment of villainy's apparent triumph, when suddenly the hero saved the day, and restored moral order.

Griffith constructed many of his plots around this tested formula. What differentiated his early films from the more pedestrian efforts of other directors was his ability to intensify the moral contrasts of melodrama through the manipulation of images. For example, previous directors occasionally employed cross-cutting to establish parallel action. Griffith used the technique to quicken the pace and increase substantially the tension of the plot. In a famous sequence from *The Lonedale Operator* (1911), he alternated sixty-six different shots of varying length to dramatize the fear of the endangered heroine, the attempt by wicked men to attack her, and efforts to rescue her. 'It is this switching from one scene to another that gives the motion picture its breadth, speed, and variety,' he later observed.[25] The climactic rescue, however, was not the only convention of melodrama which Griffith enhanced visually by taking advantage of the unique technological capacities of film. He also photographed his actors at medium, rather than long, distance from the camera. This shot allowed the players to convey their benign or malicious emotions through facial expressions, rather than the exaggerated gestures of the stage. Griffith's editing was not without flaws. Careful, repeated viewing by film critics has revealed errors of continuity in background, actors' clothing, and other editing lapses from scene to scene. As one of his assistants put it, 'Griffith just never gave a damn about matching.'[26] He did not create films for aesthetes. Concentration on his 'texts' ought not omit the context of his work. Griffith preoccupied himself with the problem of how to affect an audience emotionally by manipulating plot, character, and image.

Griffith's other major achievement concerned the length of his films. He made the transition from short films of one or two reels to longer feature-length productions without sacrificing the pace and dramatic tension of his earlier efforts. The sheer spectacle of *Judith of Bethulia* (1913) impressed audiences and compared favourably with the ponderous Italian epics which had helped inaugurate the trend for longer pictures. It was, of course, *The Birth of a Nation* (1915) which signalled a new era in commercial film. With twelve reels and a running time of over three hours, this epic of the Civil War and Reconstruction originally contained

[25] D. W. Griffith, *The Man Who Invented Hollywood: The Autobiography of D. W. Griffith*, ed. James Hart (Louisville: Touchstone, 1972), 85; Robert M. Henderson, *D. W. Griffith: The Years at Biograph* (New York: Farrar, Strauss, and Giroux, 1970), 175–6.

[26] Andrew Stone quoted in Kevin Brownlow, *The Parade's Gone By* (New York: Alfred A. Knopf, 1968), 282; Cook, *Narrative Film*, 64.

more than fifteen hundred separate shots. Griffith helped maintain the pace of the drama by brilliant editing. He cut between shots photographed at long, medium, and close distances. He varied the amount of time which individual shots occupied the screen. He inserted iris shots to link scenes and focus the attention of the spectator. He employed a split screen to portray simultaneous action. He used carefully paced cross-cutting to heighten climactic moments, such as the assassination of President Lincoln. He established connections between characters by panning the camera, dissolves, and other visual means.[27] Using these and similar devices, *Birth of a Nation* established new standards for film art. 'I was chastened and humbled, conscious of the mediocrity of my own efforts,' the British director George Pearson wrote of his first viewing of the film. 'Griffith had shown to what heights the silent film could rise; a young art had found its artist.'[28]

Griffith's commercial success as a film-maker depended upon more than technical virtuosity. In his early films, he rarely allowed his visual imagination to overwhlem his melodramatic stories and unambiguous characters. Popular melodrama derived much of its emotional impact from its moral clarity. In *Birth of a Nation* that clarity was compromised for some viewers by the film's overt racism. It was one thing to root for the rescuers who were about to save Blanche Sweet from potential rapists in *The Lonedale Operator*; it was quite another to cheer on the Ku Klux Klan as the saviours of American White supremacy. Despite the unprecedented box-office success of the film, protests against its lurid portrayal of Blacks hurt Griffith's pride.[29] He sank all the profits of the film into an even more elaborate production, *Intolerance*, released in 1916. Though he never grasped the irony, Griffith intended his new production to be a veiled attack on those who failed to tolerate *Birth of a Nation*, a racist film. In its technical grasp of the medium, *Intolerance* was a masterpiece. The film contained shots and visual sequences that have astonished film professionals from Eisenstein to the present day.[30] But the film failed at the box office, perhaps because its complicated plot, which involved four separate stories and scores of characters, departed too radically from the moral certitudes and structural simplifications of popular melodrama. Griffith's success as a director sprang from his ability to integrate cinematic technique with the dramatic traditions of popular

---

[27] A. R. Fulton, 'Editing in *The Birth of a Nation*', in *Focus on* The Birth of a Nation, ed. Fred Silva (Englewood Cliffs, NJ: Prentice-Hall, 1971), 144–53.

[28] George Pearson, *Flashback: The Autobiography of a Film Pioneer* (London: George Allen and Unwin, 1957), 58.

[29] Schickel, *Griffith*, 267–302.

[30] Gerald Mast, *A Short History of the Movies* (Indianapolis: Bobbs-Merrill, 1976), 82–4.

threatre. Despite its technical virtuosity, *Intolerance* may have been too great a departure from those traditions.

Between 1908 and 1916, Griffith helped establish the visual grammar of film. During these same years, however, most British cinema remained wedded to static and visually unimaginative forms of presentation. The inability to see cinema as anything more than filmed theatre became a melancholy motif and contributing cause to the decline of British film in the early decades of the century. This visual inertness has been well chronicled in Rachael Low's histories of the British cinema. From 1906 until 1914, the vast majority of British films were adaptations from stage plays, filmed with virtually no movement of the camera. During the First World War, British producers learned little, save the flashback, from Griffith's techniques, and 'the run-of-the mill English film of the early twenties', Low records, 'showed this practical, unimaginative approach with very little variety of camera angle within the set, painfully emphasizing its stage-like construction.'[31] American films gained dominance in Britain for a variety of reasons. With a larger guaranteed market, better financing, and a willingness to impose restrictive practices, Hollywood operated from a number of economic advantages over its British competitors. When the First World War forced many British studios to close or curtail production, American films could penetrate Britain with virtually no competition. Yet, these explanations remain only partially satisfying. 'American films, in particular, have won the hearts of appreciative British audiences,' Davidson Boughey wrote in 1921.[32] Unlike its British competition, Hollywood exploited the unique visual potentialities of the medium. The Americans understood that the 'movies', a name which originated in Hollywood, moved.

The evolution of film narrative shows how a new technology could enhance, rather than replace, existing traditions. For this reason, assertions that 'mass culture' obliterated a more authentic 'popular culture' in the early decades of the twentieth century ought to be treated with caution.[33] In film, popular tradition provided a crucial frame of reference for the early development of the medium. Magic lantern and other optical

[31] Low, *British Film, 1918–29*, 256. See also id., *The History of the British Film, 1906–1914* (London: George Allen and Unwin, 1949), 188–9; and id., *British Film, 1914–1918*, 232–3. On the comparatively poor quality of British films in this period, see also George Perry, *The Great British Picture Show: From the Nineties to the Seventies* (Frogmore: Paladin, 1975), 45–6; and Roy Armes, *A Critical History of British Cinema* (New York: Oxford University Press, 1978), 50–3.

[32] Davidson Boughey, *The Film Industry* (London: Sir Isaac Pitman, 1921), p. xv.

[33] This notion of displacement became an important part of the Frankfurt School's critique of mass culture. See Martin Jay, *The Dialectical Imagination: A History of the Frankfurt School and the Institute of Social Research, 1923–1950* (Boston: Little, Brown, 1973), 173–218.

entertainments of the nineteenth century offered young directors a context for shaping their early efforts. As they gained more experience, directors experimented with the unique capacities of the motion-picture camera to create exciting stories. Griffith integrated these and other experiments into the fabric of melodrama. Although this synthesis of technology and tradition failed to influence British producers for some time, the establishment of film narrative was achieved in less than twenty years. In the British newspaper industry, on the other hand, the successful integration of visual and more traditional modes of communication took considerably longer.

Nineteenth-century newspapers communicated with their readers through words, not images. Illustrated newspapers existed, but most editors paid little attention to visual considerations in the layout of their papers. A page consisted of orderly arranged columns of print. In the élite press, in particular, editors made few compromises with their public. 'The theory of *The Times*', Stanley Morison wrote in his history of the English newspaper, 'was that, as every reader knew by experience that every word in the paper was indispensable, he worked his way through the entire solid and black print, from the first page to the last.'[34] *The Times* could not be scanned quickly by an individual of minimal literacy. To read the élite press demanded leisure time, concentration, and formal education. Even the popular Sunday newspapers of the nineteenth century, whose circulations easily dwarfed the élite press, made relatively few visual concessions to their readers. Papers such as *Lloyd's Weekly Newspaper* contained lengthy articles, few headlines, and a minimum of illustrations.[35] Journalists communicated with their public within the respected traditions of the printing press. Word after word, sentence after sentence, paragraph after paragraph, readers absorbed information and entertainment in a sequential, linear pattern.

In the late nineteenth and early twentieth centuries, this method of communication began to change. Bolder headlines and cross-heads broke up the uniform columns of close print that characterized earlier Victorian newspapers. Maps, diagrams, and other line drawings more frequently supplemented the presentation of news. Display advertising became more prominent, and news photographs occupied space previously reserved

---

[34] Stanley Morison, *The English Newspaper: Some Account of the Physical Development of Journals Printed in London Between 1622 and the Present Day* (Cambridge: Cambridge University Press, 1932), 279.

[35] H. J. Perkin, 'The Origins of the Popular Press', *History Today* 7, 7 (1957): 430. For the social composition of the reading public for popular Sunday newspapers, see Virginia Stewart Berridge, 'Popular Journalism and Working-Class Attitudes, 1854–1886: A Study of *Reynolds' Newspaper*, *Lloyd's Weekly Newspaper* and the *Weekly Times*' (Ph.D diss., University of London, 1976), 376–9.

for verbal descriptions. Images, not words, conveyed essential messages. Less studied by scholars than the emergence of film narrative during the same period, this visual reorientation of the press took place for a variety of reasons. First, images attracted a larger potential circulation than words alone. 'It was easier to look at pictures than to read print,' one of Northcliffe's associates observed. 'The news was displayed and worded in a manner that made assimilation simple.'[36] Unlike columns of print, most images did not demand years of formal training to decipher, but could be grasped almost instantly. 'One of the most useful short cuts to the mind of a reader is illustration,' a British advertiser wrote in 1911. 'Pictures have a more direct appeal to the human intelligence than words.'[37] Editors who cleverly used visual appeals might attract that immense majority of readers who lacked the time, inclination, and background to trudge through long fields of print. The vast new audience for newspapers in the twentieth century were not all 'readers' in the traditional sense. Many simply 'looked' at a paper.

Second, the typography and layout of a daily newspaper differentiated it from other papers, defining its style and journalistic personality. Format became an important means of self-characterization and self-advertisement. 'Comparatively few English journalists have appreciated the fact', W. T. Stead complained about his more staid colleagues in 1901, 'that good journalism consists much more in the proper labelling and displaying of your goods than in the writing of leading articles.' How a paper looked became itself a message, providing a number of often unconscious signals about the paper's audience, politics, and social status.[38] When in 1908 Robert Donald told Northcliffe of his intentions to run the *Daily Chronicle* 'on sound lines, no modern journalism, but good solid stuff,' Northcliffe replied wryly, 'my dear fellow, why not print it in Gothic type?'[39] In the early twentieth century, the conflict between tradition and modernity in Fleet Street often expressed itself typographically. Though the interpretation of images remains subjective and historically conditioned, the editors of *The Times* evidently believed that undisturbed columns of print conveyed a sense of dignity, respectability, tradition, and cultivation. To the editors of the *Daily Express*,

[36] Hamilton Fyfe, *My Seven Selves* (London: George Allen and Unwin, 1935), 98.

[37] Thomas Russell, 'The Preparation of Advertisements', in *Advertising and Publicity*, ed. Russell, 98.

[38] W. T. Stead, *The Americanization of the World, or the Trend of the Twentieth Century* (New York and London: Horace Markley, 1901), 292. For this same point concerning the nineteenth century, see Louis James, 'The Trouble with Betsy: Periodicals and the Common Reader in Mid-Nineteenth-Century England', in *The Victorian Periodical Press: Samplings and Soundings*, ed. Joanne Shattock and Michael Wolff (Leicester: Leicester University Press; Toronto: University of Toronto Press, 1982), 350–1.

[39] Quoted in Koss, *British Press, vol. 2: Twentieth Century*, 93.

on the other hand, headlines, cross-heads, and other visual events pro-jected a sense of modernity, readability, liveliness, and accessibility. *The Times* distanced itself visually from its readers, while the *Express* invited participation. *The Times* self-consciously excluded readers by its layout, while the *Express* opened its pages to a larger audience. Moreover, by placing its main stories on the front page, the *Express* offered its visual invitation to a larger public immediately and without inconvenience.

Other mass media also made newspapers more alert to visual appeals. The rise of cinema, comic strips, and a variety of illustrated magazines helped condition the public to communication through images. The gradual establishment of narrative in cinema meant that audiences became accustomed to increasingly sophisticated visual presentations. As directors moved away from the static cinema of filmed theatre and developed editing procedures which heightened the impact of melodrama, so too newspaper editors began experimenting with techniques which intensified the inherent drama of the news. In film, directors sought means of creating visually a linear narrative, a story in which events connected sequentially. In newspapers, the printed word already provided such a sequence; images broke the page into a mosaic of different visual events. As we shall see in Part Three, only in the 1930s did journalists discover adequate principles of visual integration. Like film directors, editors worked with developing technologies which imposed boundaries limiting their efforts. Unlike film directors, they could draw upon fewer established traditions to guide their development. It took time to appreciate that newspapers might be a visual medium different from books.

Editors began their experiments with novel methods of presenting news and features in the decades immediately preceding the First World War. The 'New Journalism' of the late nineteenth century defined its modernity in part by its unapologetic imitation of the American popular press, where the size and layout of headlines indicated the importance of the news underneath. In the 1880s, for example, the *Star* used multi-column headlines and cross-heads, or centred sub-headings, in the text. In 1888, this same politically radical paper piled a deck of headlines in upper-case letters on top of a second deck of headlines in both upper- and lower-case letters. In 1895, the *Evening News* decorated its main news page with one of London's first banner headlines, a headline which extended across the full width of the page. The *Daily Mail* reported the opening of the Spanish-American War in 1898 with a double-column, five-decker headline, though it recorded most of the Boer War with more restrained single-column headlines. R. D. Blumenfeld, the editor of the *Daily Express*, founded in 1900, helped introduce to English journalism the streamer, a headline which stretched across a number of columns, but not the width of the page.[40] These and other innovations in news headlines became easy to mass-produce because of improvements in the printing press. Stereotyped plates, for example, permitted the breaking of column rules and moreover, as their design became perfected, allowed rotary presses to print at high rates of speed. By 1890, the Hoe press could produce 48,000 papers of twelve pages each in one hour.[41]

Headlines were not the only device to enliven a newspaper. Line drawings took many forms in the British press before the First World War. Borrowing from the Americans once again, the 'New Journalists' of the 1880s inserted maps and diagrams to illustrate their stories, a technique used frequently in the *Daily Mail* and eventually, under Northcliffe, even in *The Times*. Cartoons and caricatures also appeared in the daily national press. Long an element of British political life, satiric drawings became a central feature of such nineteenth-century magazines as *Punch* and *Vanity Fair*.[42] With the gradual development of photomechanical reproduction in the 1870s and 1880s, it became less difficult technically to include cartoons in daily newspapers. In 1888 Francis Carruthers Gould joined the *Pall Mall Gazette* as staff cartoonist, transferring his talent five years later to the *Westminster Gazette*. By the turn of the century, political cartoons appeared in a number of newspapers.[43] One of the most celebrated of these cartoonists was W. K. Haselden, who joined the *Daily Mirror* in 1904. Haselden rarely chose political subjects for his drawings, preferring instead to concentrate on the small ironies and amusing reversals of middle-class life. Many of his cartoons contained more than one frame, thus creating a narrative analogous to that of comic strips. In 'Bilious Music', for example, he demonstrated in five frames how the lugubrious music of 'Slowpang's Burial Symphony' transformed a happy, contented audience into suicidal victims. In this and other cartoons, Haselden attempted to make his images, rather than words, convey the humour. As he wrote in 1908, 'The "Daily Mirror" in its cartoons tries to make pictures that are intrinsically funny even without the lines underneath them. A good cartoon should be so comical in its drawing as to provoke the laughter of even a foreigner who cannot

[40] Allen Hutt, *The Changing Newspaper: Typographic Trends in Britain and America, 1622-1972* (London: George Fraser, 1973), 69–73, 217–19; R. D. Blumenfeld, *The Press in My Time* (London: Rich and Cowan, 1937), 218; Morison, *English Newspaper*, 305.

[41] Edwin Emery, *The Press and America: An Interpretative History of the Mass Media*, 3rd edn. (Englewood Cliffs, NJ: Prentice-Hall, 1972), 338–9.

[42] A number of books contain selections of illustrations from *Punch*. For the history of the magazine, see R. G. G. Price, *A History of* Punch (London: Collins, 1957). On *Vanity Fair*, see Roy T. Matthews and Peter Mellina, *In* Vanity Fair (Berkeley: University of California Press, 1982).

[43] Ann Gould, 'The Newspaper Cartoon', *Penrose Annual*, 64 (1971): 65–8.

translate the wording underneath.'[44] Though he did not always succeed in this undertaking, Haselden confronted the same problem as film comedians in the silent era. Like Chaplin and Keaton, he tried to create sight gags without the help of words. Cartoon captions, like film titles, might establish setting or link scenes, but became a poor substitute for a lively visual imagination.

Although headlines, maps, and cartoons contributed visual interest to innovative late-nineteenth-century newspapers, it was display advertising which most disturbed the landscape of print. In the 1880s the *Daily News* allowed display advertising to spread over more than one column. In August 1896, the year it was founded, the *Daily Mail* ran the first full-page display advertisement on its back page. Six years later, Mellin's Food advertised its goods in the first full front-page advertisement in the *Mail*.[45] With the exception of the *Daily Express*, which devoted its front page to news, and a few others, most national daily newspapers devoted their front page to classified advertisements. After 1900 the amount of display advertising increased substantially. Between 1900 and 1910, the number of column inches of display advertising increased from 156 to 424 in the *Daily Express* and from 450 to 714 in the *Daily Telegraph*. As a percentage of total advertising in the paper, these figures meant that, in the *Daily Express* for example, display advertising increased from 50 to over 75 per cent of available advertising space.[46] By 1910, display advertising had become the most prominent visual feature of many daily newspapers.

It was a visual feature with a controversial pedigree. Display advertising in the early twentieth century derived its techniques from Victorian advertisers who believed that repetition, not artistry, sold goods and services. In 1885, over five hundred different firms in Britain produced posters which zealous promoters posted on virtually every available wall and open space. Attempts by some advertisers to check abuses proved only partially successful. After an advertisement was projected by magic lantern on to the exterior walls of the National Gallery and one company raised a hoarding in Trafalgar Square, Parliament passed a bill in 1894 which gave county councils the power to regulate displays. Yet, it was not simply the ubiquity of advertisements which offended some sensibilities. Promoters crammed their advertisements with an

---

[44] W. K. Haselden, Daily Mirror *Reflections* (London: Pictorial Newspapers [1908]), 5. The 'Slowpang' cartoon is on p. 84.

[45] W. Hamish Fraser, *The Coming of the Mass Market, 1850–1914* (London: Macmillan, 1981), 138; F. A. McKenzie, *The Mystery of the* Daily Mail (London: Associated Newspapers, 1921), 106; Field, *Advertising*, 123–5.

[46] Nevett, 'Advertising in Britain', 218. Nevett based his statistics on a comparison of one day in June 1900, and June 1910.

extraordinary amount of printed information, relieved only by crude illustrations.[47] Like the drawing rooms of the middle class, Victorian advertisements displayed as much as possible.

This tradition shaped the appearance of much display advertising in British newspapers before the First World War. 'If you are going to let bludgeoning advertisements kill your news,' Northcliffe warned one of his editors, 'you are going to kill your newspaper.' Northcliffe understood the dignity and respectability conveyed by an unadorned page of symmetrically arranged print. Despite his crucial role in commercializing the daily press, he complained frequently about the ugliness and intrusiveness of advertising. 'I am sorry to see they are using such shocking type in many of the *Daily Mail* advertisements,' he told one of his editors.[48] Display advertisements deprived the newspaper of valuable space. They cluttered the landscape of print as hoardings ruined the countryside. 'The advertisements are beginning to spoil the paper', he once lamented. 'The leading article now begins below the fold, which robs it of its importance. There is an increasingly large advertisement at the bottom right-hand corner of the editorial page.' In 1907, a little over a decade after the *Daily Mail* accepted its first full-page display advertisement, Northcliffe acknowledged the result of his policies. 'As far as appearance goes,' he told Wareham Smith, 'the advertiser commands the paper.'[49]

Not all advertising in newspapers lacked visual sophistication. Gordon Selfridge stunned the newspaper business in 1909 by publishing over a hundred full-page advertisements in a number of different national newspapers. Many of these advertisements were adorned with striking illustrations symbolizing 'Liberality', 'Confidence', 'Sincerity', 'Courtesy', 'Value', and other qualities presumably embodied in Selfridge's department store. The line drawings in this campaign involved little attempt to create art specifically for the unique visual landscape of a newspaper. Selfridge borrowed from the traditions of nineteenth-century academic art and, at great expense, adapted it to the pages of the daily press. Other advertisers could not afford such extravagance and continued to overcrowd their messages with information. A few, however, sought means to distinguish their advertising from the visual environment which surrounded it. A display for Country Life Cigarettes, for example, which appeared in the *Daily Mail* in early October 1910, illustrated how some advertisers recognized the visual significance of white space. When placed next to a number of typical nineteenth-century advertisements, the simple and

[47] Leonard De Vries, *Victorian Advertisements* (London: John Murray, 1968), 6; Fraser, op. cit., 135–7; Edward S. Lautenbach, 'Victorian Advertising and Magazine Stripping', *Victorian Studies* 10, 4 (1967): 431–4.
[48] Quoted in Clarke, *Northcliffe Diary*, 9; and in Smith, *Spilt Ink*, 37.
[49] Quoted in Fyfe, *Northcliffe*, 294; and in Smith, op. cit., 37.

uncluttered cigarette advertisement dominated the surrounding environment of tiny print and other competing commercial messages.[50] Though before 1914 most advertisers remained tied to the Victorian traditions of crowded display, others began to appreciate the visual boldness of minimalism. They began to 'see' the page of a newspaper in its totality, rather than read each column individually.

A crucial part of that totality was news photography. In the nineteenth century the *Illustrated London News*, founded in 1842, and a number of its imitators included drawings to illustrate news and features.[51] Drawn by special artists and usually engraved by hand on pieces of boxwood, these illustrations often took days to complete. Although developments in photography in the nineteenth century, such as photogravure, allowed photographs to be reproduced in large quantities, these pictures could not be printed reliably alongside regular type on existing presses.[52] The gradual development of the half-tone process in the late nineteenth century made possible the mechanical reproduction of a facsimile relief block, though similar technological improvements in different countries make it difficult to sort out competing claims for priority. It was probably the *Daily Graphic* of New York which first used primitive half-tone illustrations extensively on a separate picture page, though it was not until the 1890s that high-speed presses in America could print half-tones.[53] In 1890, the *Daily Graphic* of London became the first daily illustrated newspaper in Britain although, as one pioneer in the field derisively remarked, it was 'not a recognized newspaper from the point of view of the man in the street'. By the late 1890s, a number of small agencies such as the Illustrated Press Bureau specialized in providing pictures for the national press.[54]

A key event in the development of both news photography and popular journalism came in response to a commercial failure. The *Daily Mirror*, founded by Northcliffe in 1903 as a newspaper written for and by women,

[50] On the Selfridge advertisement, see Pound, *Selfridge*, 58. For Country Life Cigarettes, see *Daily Mail*, 12 Oct. 1910 and plate II.

[51] Mason Jackson, *The Pictorial Press: Its Origins and Progress* (London: Hurst and Blackett, 1885), 284–311; R. H. Smith, 'All the Firsts of *The London Illustrated News*', *Penrose Annual*, 67 (1974): 101–12.

[52] Beaumont Newhall, *The History of Photography from 1839 to the Present Day* (New York: Museum of Modern Art, 1964), 175; Otto M. Lilien, *History of Industrial Gravure Printing up to 1920* (London: Lund Humphries, 1972), 17–43.

[53] Newhall, *History*, 176–7; R. Smith Schuneman, 'Art or Photography: A Question for Newspaper Editors of the 1890's', *Journalism Quarterly* 42, 1 (1965): 43–52; Roger Butterfield, 'Pictures in the Papers', *American Heritage* 13, 14 (1962): 32–55.

[54] William Hartley, ' "News" Photography: The Beginning and Development of the Photographic "News" Pictures in the London Daily Press', *Penrose's Annual*, 22 (1920): 30; Helmut and Alison Gernsheim, *The History of Photography From the Camera Obscura to the Beginning of the Modern Era* (London: Thames and Hudson, 1969), 454–5.

proved to be a circulation disaster. After dismissing some female journalists, Northcliffe made two crucial changes in his reorganization of the *Mirror*. The first concerned the physical dimensions of the paper. On a visit to America in late 1900, Northcliffe had been asked by Joseph Pulitzer to assume control of the *World* for a single day, 1 January 1901. Eager to impress his American mentor, Northcliffe astonished American journalists by reducing the size of the newspaper to that of a magazine. In many of its essentials the experiment had been tried before, but Northcliffe coined a new term for it; he called it 'tabloid journalism'. It was this principle of a conveniently proportioned newspaper, easy to handle and to read, that Northcliffe now applied to the *Daily Mirror*.[55]

Northcliffe also decided to increase substantially the number of illustrations. In the *World* adventure, he had diminished the usual number of pictures which Americans expected. Now in 1904 he was beginning to appreciate their utility for a British audience. 'Till our appearance', the new *Daily Illustrated Mirror* proclaimed in its inaugural issue, 'the occasional illustrations which were to be found in daily newspapers were only a kind of "makeshift", and were only used when it was found necessary to supplement verbal explanations. . . . Our illustrations are themselves "news". They give news which was formerly told only in words.' What distinguished the *Mirror* from its predecessors such as the *Daily Graphic*, was the greater number, larger size, and improved quality of its photographs. 'This is the first paper to produce photographic half-tone pictures on a rotary printing machine,' its editors boasted in the opening leader.[56] Though others could claim credit, this achievement resulted from the ingenuity of one of the paper's editors, Arkas Sapt, who through careful retouching of the original prints and other methods never properly documented, provided the *Mirror* with the technique to reproduce news photographs at high speed for a daily newspaper. Other technical improvements followed. In 1907 the first picture was telegraphed from Paris. Six years later, Harry Bartholomew of the *Daily Mirror* devised a system to wire pictures across the Atlantic, though it would be some time before wire photos sufficiently improved in quality to become routine.[57] It was not until after the First World War that an American newspaper, the New York *Daily News*, imitated Northcliffe's ideas of a compactly proportioned newspaper devoted to news photos. Tabloid photo-journalism was pioneered in Britain.

---

[55] Pound and Harmsworth, *Northcliffe*, 266–8.

[56] *Daily Illustrated Mirror*, 29 Jan. 1904, 3. The name was later changed back to the *Daily Mirror*.

[57] Hutt, *Changing Newspaper*, 87; id., 'Design', in *Scoop, Scandal and Strife: A Study of Photography in Newspapers*, ed. Ken Baynes (London: Lund Humphries, 1971), 60; Derrick Knight, 'Development', ibid., 26, 28.

Press photographers confronted a number of early problems. More than other journalists, their success depended upon timing, initiative, and luck. 'A reporter can pick up his news afterward,' an early editor of the *Mirror* recalled. 'If a photographer is a minute late, he cannot get anything.' The memoirs of James Jarché, one of the earliest and best press photographers, provide an anecdotal account of how he overcame adversities to capture 'good shots'—the term itself suggests the hunt and may help explain the discomfort of the prey. Initially, Royalty frustrated photographers by their elusiveness, except for official pictures. Politicians, on the other hand, were 'as easy to shoot as a sitting pheasant. They want all the publicity they can get.'[58] Though news photographers suffered from low esteem in their profession, their initiative became famous in Fleet Street. One *Mirror* photographer descended 650 feet into the main crater of Vesuvius; another photographed a charging lion from less than thirty feet. In 1908 Arthur Barrett cut a hole in his hat, concealed his camera, and illegally photographed a suffragette in the dock.[59]

Editors faced problems concerning the authenticity and display of photographs. In 1907 the *Mirror* assigned a staff member to photograph a famous rural mystic in Italy. The photographer failed to locate the woman and, keen to satisfy his superiors, sent to London instead the likeness of a photogenic peasant. When the editor discovered the substitution, he was appalled. 'Any member of the photographic staff caught "faking" is at once discharged,' he assured Northcliffe in a letter, 'and I think we have no fakers now.'[60] Few editors, however, condemned the retouching of photographs to enhance the quality of reproduction. Retouching only became fraudulent when, as in the case of a New York paper, a dramatic photograph of San Francisco in flames after the earthquake of 1906 contained the phrase 'Copyright 1900' in the bottom left-hand corner.[61] As the quality of reproduction improved, genuine photographs gradually replaced enhancements and other more technologically primitive ways of illustrating the news. 'Line drawings mixed up with photographs have always been a failure,' Northcliffe told the editor of the *Daily Mirror* in 1912. '. . . Line drawings are killed by photographs.'[62]

[58] Hannen Swaffer, 'Foreward', in James Jarché, *People I Have Shot* (London: Methuen, 1934), p. viii; Jarché, ibid., 98. On Swaffer's career as an editor of news photography during this period, see Tom Driberg, *'Swaff': The Life and Times of Hannen Swaffer* (London: MacDonald, 1974), 46–57.

[59] *Daily Mirror, The Romance of the* Daily Mirror, *1903–1924* (London: Daily Mirror Newspapers [1924]), 62–3; Tom Hopkinson, 'Introduction', in *Scoop*, ed. Baynes, 9.

[60] Alex Kenealy to Northcliffe, 23 Sept. 1907, Northcliffe MSS, British Library, Deposit 4890, vol. 82.

[61] Raymond Smith Schuneman, 'The Photograph in Print: An Examination of New York Daily Newspapers, 1890–1937' (Ph.D. diss., University of Minnesota, 1966), 256.

[62] Northcliffe to Alex Kenealy, 4 July 1912, Northcliffe MSS, British Library, Deposit 4890, vol. 82.

How to display photographs challenged the skills of editors, who only gradually learned what types of photographs riveted the reader's attention. Journalists quickly discovered that people, not places, made photographs interesting. By 1910, editors routinely included small, tightly cropped single-column photographs of the personalities involved in news stories. Sometimes events made even commonplace portraits newsworthy. Since no photographs existed of the sinking Titanic, for example, the *Daily Mirror* devoted its entire front page to a posed photograph of the captain's widow and young child.[63] A human-interest portrait thus replaced an unavailable action shot as the focus of visual attention. Though some newspapers, such as the *Daily Express*, experimented with layouts combining printing types, cropped photographs, white space, and diagonal line drawings, these imaginative designs proved difficult, expensive, and time-consuming.[64] For a variety of technical reasons, it was easier to group photographs on a single sheet rather than intersperse them throughout the newspaper. Eventually the 'picture page' became a standard feature of the popular press. Usually it consisted of unconnected individual photographs illustrating topics from various sections of the paper, but editors also ran a series of photographs on a single theme. In either case, the picture page proved a mixed blessing. It attracted virtually every sort of reader, but it also forced photographs to compete with one another, depriving the rest of the newspaper of an important visual asset.[65]

By 1914, headlines, cartoons, display advertising, and news photography had all contributed to the visual transformation of the popular press. The First World War accelerated this process in two important ways. First, bolder headlines reflected the intensified passions of the war. The *Daily Express* began to employ banner, streamer, and multi-deck headlines as a matter of routine, and experimented with typographical patterns unknown in more tranquil times. The news of an air raid in February 1915, for example, appeared in a multi-deck, three-column announcement in which the body of the story itself became headlines. Other newspapers also displayed their news more dramatically. *The Times* launched a few special editions in which, like the *Daily Express*, news appeared on the front page. The *Daily Mail* employed multiple decks of double-column headlines in a heavy Doric type, though it remained typographically conservative by eschewing both banners and streamers. Unlike some American newspapers during this period, however, the editors

[63] *Daily Mirror*, 22 Apr. 1912. The photograph is reproduced in Baynes, ed., op. cit., 46.

[64] See, for example, 'Diplomacy Exposed', *Daily Express*, 6 Jan. 1905.

[65] Arthur Rothstein, *Photojournalism*, 3rd edn. (Garden City, NJ: American Photographic Book Publishing, 1974), 145.

of the British press never considered their headlines part of an overall plan.[66]

Second, press photography gained new legitimacy during the war. Both amateur and professional photographers captured shots which often supplemented the news in a dramatic manner. On 18 February 1915, for example, the *Daily Mail* devoted its entire back page to a photograph of the sinking German cruiser, the *Bluecher*. The legend underneath the picture instructed readers how to interpret the image:

Here the world sees for the first time the most dramatic moment of history's first Battle of Dreadnoughts. The wounded and broken *Bluecher* lies dying, and hundreds of her men are seen facing death. Some of them against their will are slipping into the sea: some are jumping in. . . . One man, it will be seen, has clambered down to the bilge-keel, from which water is pouring in sheets. Others are sliding down toward the water; one has taken a jump into the sea and in the water several heads appear as black dots. Some of the men on the side stripped and are wearing only swimming jackets. The dense black group astern is perhaps the line of officers, linked arm in arm, who were seen there as the warship sank. . . .[67]

Here the legend provided a running commentary which forced the reader to examine the photograph with great care. Together, words and image created on the page of a newspaper a visual event which combined human interest, nationalism, and the photographic novelty of dramatic action frozen in time. The 'Sinking Bluecher' may not have been, as the editors claimed, 'The Most Wonderful Photograph of the War', but it demonstrated how the best news photography might focus the attention and stimulate the imagination of the reading public.

News photography also portrayed the devastation of the First World War. It is a commonplace of British historiography that throughout the conflict the home front knew little about the horrors of trench warfare. Yet this generalization might be qualified by examining the picture pages of the popular press. Again and again, newspapers ran photographs which portrayed the destructiveness and human misery of the Western Front. On 20 January 1915 the *Daily Express* contained a picture of a 'hole made by a big German shell in Flanders, which the rain and floods have converted into a miniature lake.' In October of the same year, the *Daily Mail* ran a series of photos on the battleground at Loos. One picture showed a British soldier with a heavily bandaged head; two others compared a village before and after heavy bombing; another showed a trench full of dead Germans. A week later, the *Mail* ran six photos about

[66] *Daily Express*, 13 Feb. 1915 and plate III. Hutt, *Changing Newspaper*, 88, 95.
[67] *Daily Mail*, 18 Feb. 1915.

the daily routines of two British officers in Flanders. The legend to this feature concluded by saying that 'one, alas, met a gallant death while leading his men in a recent attack.'[68] Under a heading 'A Pageant of War—and the Reality', the *Daily Mail* of 10 November 1915 visually contrasted four small photos of soldiers and equipment parading in the Lord Mayor's Show in London with a large centred photo of a trench full of dead German soldiers, 'each one riddled by bullets'.[69] Although the popular press avoided photographs of British dead, and although many pictures clearly served the purposes of propaganda, the picture page graphically portrayed the dangers and destructiveness of the war. Some readers may not have made the connection between photos of German casualties and the similar fate of British soldiers. Some readers may not have fully grasped the terrible realities behind these and similar photographs. But it is difficult to argue that British citizens knew nothing about the horrors of the Western Front.

In the 1920s, the British press consolidated the changes in headlines and news photography occasioned by the First World War. Better inks and improved printing processes allowed more flexibility in typography and permitted higher quality photographs. The lighter, more portable Ermanox and Leica cameras made candid shots easier to capture, and both the flash bulb, invented in the 1920s, and the telephoto lens gave photographers more flexibility.[70] In March 1922 *The Times* considered news photography legitimate enough to include its first picture page. Employing a layout similar to that of the *Daily Mirror*, *The Times* once again borrowed a technique from the popular press.[71] Five years later in 1927, Bell R. Bell published the first British textbook on the subject of news pictures. *The Complete Press Photographer* contained detailed sections on every important aspect of the young profession. Bell discussed various cameras, lighting techniques, and methods of processing. He provided shrewd guidelines about how to shoot pictures which editors accepted, and he listed the pictorial biases of various newspapers. He advised beginners how to capture on film such features as beauty contests, sports, and the social events of high society. Above all, he tried to instill a sense of how news could be communicated visually. 'This would-be Press photographer', he advised, 'must train himself to visualize a picture in every bit of news he reads or hears.'[72]

[68] *Daily Express*, 20 Jan. 1915; *Daily Mail*, 14 Oct. 1915; *Daily Mail*, 23 Oct. 1915.
[69] *Daily Mail*, 10 Nov. 1915 and plate IV.
[70] John Young, 'Post-War Progress in Newspaper Production', *Printing News*, 8 Sept. 1932; Knight, 'Development', in Baynes, ed., *Scoop*, 29–30.
[71] Hutt, 'Design', ibid., 61–2; Pound and Harmsworth, *Northcliffe*, 455, 852.
[72] Bell R. Bell, *The Complete Press Photographer* (London: Sir Isaac Pitman, 1927), 7.

Although in the 1920s, the British press mostly refined the innovations pioneered during the war, there were two important changes in the visual appearance of national daily newspapers. The first, which will be treated in detail in Part Two, concerned the rise of commercial art in Britain and the transformation of display advertising. The second involved the comic strip, a feature which, despite its lengthy past, came relatively late to modern British newspapers.[73] In the 1890s, Northcliffe scored some of his earliest commercial successes by launching a series of inexpensive comic papers. *Comic Cuts* and a dozen other titles were intended primarily for an adult audience, though eventually children's comic papers also became a staple of commercial culture.[74] In America the popular press of Pulitzer and Hearst began including comic strips in the 1890s, the era when the term 'Yellow Journalism' derived, it was said, from the special coloured paper upon which one strip appeared. By the first decade of the twentieth century, comic strips became syndicated features of newspapers throughout America.[75] In Britain, however, the popular press initially resisted this American custom. Although, as in the case of early cinema, it becomes difficult to determine precedents accurately, a children's comic strip, 'Mrs. Hippo's Kindergarten', appeared in the *Daily Mirror* as early as 1904. Other children's comic-strip features included 'Teddy Tail', first appearing in the *Daily Mail* in 1915, and 'Pip, Squeak and Wilfred', which the *Mirror* began in 1919. Not all comic strips were for children. In 1920 the *Daily Express* included 'Mutt and Jeff', a much-imitated American strip which began in 1907. The *Express* also ran comic drawings on sporting events.[76] Despite these and other precedents, however, the British popular press in the 1920s remained less enthusiastic about comic strips than their American counterparts. Strips ran only occasionally in most British papers and rarely could be found together, grouped on a

[73] On the early history of comic strips, see David Kunzle, *The Early Comic Strip: Narrative Strips and Picture Stories in the European Broadsheet From c.1450 to 1825* (Berkeley: University of California Press, 1973). There is an extensive bibliography on the history of caricature.

[74] Denis Gifford, 'A Golden Age of Comics', *Penrose Annual*, 65 (1972): 69–92; id., *Discovering Comics* (Tring: Shire Publications, 1971), 4–17; id., *The British Comic Catalogue, 1874–1974* (London: Mansell, 1975), pp. ix–x.

[75] Stephen Becker, *Comic Art in America: A Social History of the Funnies, the Political Cartoons, Magazine Humor, Sporting Cartoons, and Animated Cartoons* (New York: Simon and Schuster, 1959), 9–21; Carlton Waugh, *The Comics* (New York: Macmillan, 1947), 2–14.

[76] Gifford, 'Golden Age', *Penrose*, 73; George Perry and Alan Aldridge, *The Penguin Book of Comics: A Slight History* (Harmondsworth: Penguin Books, 1967), 191. Contrary to Gifford, Perry and Aldridge claim that 'Pip, Squeak and Wilfred' was the first to appear in a British newspaper. For information on Bud Fisher, the originator of 'Mutt and Jeff', see Judith O'Sullivan, *The Art of the Comic Strip* (n.p.: University of Maryland Department of Art, 1971), 70; and Waugh, op. cit., 25–33. For a comic on a sporting event, see, for example, 'Chelsea vs. Swindon at Stamford Bridge', *Daily Express*, 2 Feb. 1920.

single page. For a paper such as the *Daily Mail*, the low reputation of comic strips may have violated the fragile proprieties of one of their targeted publics, the socially conscious readers of the lower middle class.

By the end of the 1920s, pictorial journalism had become an important component of a larger cultural transformation. With the simultaneous rise of both cinema and the popular national daily press, mass-produced images became a central part of cultural life in Britain. 'For many thousands of men and women today', a British popular writer reflected in 1910, 'the picture is as real a means of communicating knowledge and information as it was among the people conquered by Pizarro.'[77] Though overdrawn, the analogy reflected the growing awareness of an often elusive ongoing process. Images—moving and static, photographed and drawn—supplemented and sometimes replaced the written word as the most effective means of informing and entertaining a growing public. Spurred by economic incentives and simple curiosity, inventors in both Europe and America developed technologies which permitted the mass replication of images. Professional communicators, often young and usually inexperienced, framed these images according to existing cultural traditions and their own increasingly sophisticated visual imagination. The development of this imagination was not without paradox. In the new medium of cinema, the creation of a visual narrative was well in place by the First World War, in part because directors such as D. W. Griffith borrowed freely from the theatrical conventions of nineteenth-century melodrama. In the more venerable medium of print journalism, it would take until the 1930s for editors to appreciate how images might be successfully integrated into a coherent layout. In cinema and newspaper, the lines of development varied, but the implication was the same. Technology, commerce, and the visual imagination created a cultural environment where images, as well as words, told the story.

B. SOUND: THE GRAMOPHONE AND RECORDED MUSIC

For almost twenty years after its introduction to England in the late 1870s, the gramophone developed with surprising lethargy both technically and commercially. Edison initially conceived of his invention as a tool for business, but a variety of technical limitations made it easy for commerce to ignore the device. Other inventors and entrepreneurs, however, recognized that a much larger market could be exploited for entertainment, and by the turn of the century the gramophone, like the

---

[77] 'Picture Theatres as an Educational Force', *Picture Theatre News*, 12 July 1910. The author linked cinema and pictorial journalism together in the article.

cinema, began to transform patterns of leisure. Although the fortunes of the gramophone industry varied substantially from year to year in the early decades of the century, the overall trend was unmistakable. In 1907, for example, gramophone sales represented about 4 per cent of the total value of musical instruments produced in Britain. By 1924, this share had risen to over 26 per cent.[78] The recording industry boomed in the 1920s. During a particularly brisk month in 1926, one of the more prosperous English firms, Columbia, sold two million records. Even smaller companies, such as J. E. Hough, produced an average of 6 million records a year.[79] Between 1922 and 1923, the profits of the Gramophone Company, one of the leaders of the industry, soared from £140,307 to over £283,000. This same company reported net profits of over a million pounds in 1928, one of the last great years for the recording business before the slump. 'In every street, in every block of flats,' *The Times* reported in 1929, 'it is usual now to hear half-a-dozen or more gramophones all making different noises at once.'[80]

Just as it is difficult to recapture how audiences first reacted to the flickering images of early cinema, so too the impact of the gramophone on the experience of music must remain, to some degree, speculative. On the one hand, our own expectations about the fidelity of recorded music make it easy to underestimate the sense of wonder which scratchy discs and inconvenient cylinders provoked in early listeners. The short playing time and relatively poor quality of early recordings, which in some circles made the gramophone an intrusive, contemptible novelty, rarely bothered a far greater audience for whom the music transcended the imperfections of its reproduction. Listening to Caruso for two minutes through surface noise was better than no Caruso at all. On the other hand, it is also possible to overestimate the psychological impact of the gramophone on its expanding audience. In the early twentieth century, recorded sound was one of a score of new technologies thrust upon a population increasingly accustomed to mechanical miracles. In a decade when men learned to fly, the clock-sprung motor of a portable gramophone or the extended playing time of a double-sided disc hardly provoked astonishment. Indeed, what may be most remarkable was the rapidity with which technological innovations became absorbed into everyday, commonplace experience.

Although the impact of the cinema on British culture has attracted much scholarly attention, few historians have explored how the gramophone

---

[78] *The Times*, 28 Apr. 1927.
[79] 'Louis S. Sterling, Chairman of the Board, Columbia Co., Discusses World Trade', *Talking Machine World*, 27 Mar. 1927, 3; Mitchell, *Talking Machine Industry*, 82.
[80] *The Times*, 5 Sept. 1929, 17 Oct. 1923, 12 Oct. 1928.

affected British music. One excellent study analyses how the rise of recorded sound altered the economics of both musical composition and performance. A number of general works contain brief discussions of the gramophone.[81] Yet for the most part, the relationship between the new technology of recorded sound and the traditions of British popular culture remains largely unexplored territory. For purposes here, two related aspects of the problem will be discussed. First, the success of the gramophone as a source of musical entertainment depended upon a number of interdependent, constantly evolving factors. The mechanization of music was a complex, ongoing, often ambiguous process. Second, the gramophone often affected the experience of music in paradoxical, even contradictory ways. The wide dissemination of recorded sound reinforced diverse tendencies. For example, the 'Americanization' of British music, which the gramophone clearly accelerated, rarely involved a straightforward process of cultural displacement or substitution. Tradition complicated the pattern of assimilation. Americanization became something recognizably British.

In the early decades of the century, the commercial success and consequently the role of the gramophone in British musical life depended upon a number of constantly evolving factors. The cost of both gramophone and records directly affected the elasticity of demand, but the competitive pressure to cut prices proved to be only one of many variables which contributed to success in the market-place. The length, availability, choice, and durability of records, the fidelity and convenience of a particular gramophone, and a variety of other considerations also affected the selling strategies of manufacturers and the market decisions of consumers. At any given time, the complex relationship among these various factors helped determine the commercial success of individual producers, not only against their competition within the industry, but also against competing forms of entertainment and leisure.

The elasticity of demand for recorded sound was always intimately connected to cost. The early gramophones of the late nineteenth century proved too expensive for most consumers, but by practising economies of scale, the industry gradually lowered the price of both machines and records. In 1900 an Edison Standard Phonograph sold for around £7, an expensive item for, say, a railway clerk whose income averaged less than £76 a year. By the 1920s, both Columbia and Decca produced table

[81] Alan Peacock and Ronald Weir, *The Composer in the Market Place* (London: Faber Music, 1975). For brief discussions of the gramophone, see, among others, E. D. Mackerness, *A Social History of English Music* (London: Routledge and Kegan Paul; Toronto: University of Toronto Press, 1964), 243–6; and Ronald Pearsall, *Popular Music of the Twenties* (Newton Abbot: David and Charles; Totowa: Rowman and Littlefield, 1976), 93–107.

models for slightly over £4 at a time when the income for a railway clerk averaged over £221 a year.[82] For the clerk, then, the relative cost of a gramophone dropped from about one-tenth to less than one-fiftieth of annual income. Higher-priced gramophones offered a number of features which made them attractive to less cost-conscious buyers. Larger sound horns produced greater amplitude, and manufacturers attempted to make expensive gramophones resemble fine furniture. Still, in a decade when the least expensive piano cost about £60, the gramophone proved a cheap alternative source of music in both middle- and working-class homes. Record prices also dropped, though less dramatically. In 1903 it was possible to purchase a seven-inch disc for 2s. 6d. but the longer and better quality ten-inch records usually were priced at 5s. In the 1920s, companies sold durable, good quality ten- and twelve-inch records for 2s. 6d. or 3s.[83]

Lower costs alone cannot explain the success of the gramophone. From the beginning, the fidelity of recorded sound played a key role in the public's acceptance of this new technology. Edison's tin-foil contrivance made the human voice recognizable, but gramophones could become little more than fairground novelties as long as the quality of reproduction remained abysmal. Even after the introduction of electric recording in the mid-1920s, fidelity varied enormously from machine to machine. In general, however, the lengthy struggle to improve the quality of sound centred on three interconnected areas. First, the recording process of the master cylinder or disc strongly influenced the quality of recorded music. Engineers discovered that the recording of sound demanded a studio free of extraneous noise. These dead studios assured a reasonably faithful rendering of the music, but they limited the mobility of recording and produced a sound unlike that of live performances, where the vagaries of acoustics and other background sound created a unique aural setting. Then too, acoustic recording drastically limited the number of musicians who could participate in any given session. Engineers bargained with performers on where instruments should be placed while musicians jockeyed for position nearest the recording horn. In an attempt to capture the sound of an entire orchestra, Edison experimented with a brass recording horn 200 feet long, but the results proved disappointing.[84] Some instruments recorded far better than others. The human voice

[82] Gelatt, *Fabulous Phonograph*, 101; John Stevenson, *British Society, 1914–45* (Harmondsworth: Penguin Books, 1984), 122; Christopher Stone, 'Round and Round', *The Gramophone* 4, 7 (1926): 311.

[83] Cyril Ehrlich, *The Piano: A History* (London: J. M. Dent, 1976), 185–6; Gelatt, op. cit., 119; Mitchell, op. cit., 82.

[84] Read and Welch, *Tin Foil to Stereo*, 205–9; 'Gramophone Societies' Reports', *The Gramophone* 6, 63 (1928): 127.

survived the recording process well, though the vocal nuances of many famous singers failed to register properly. Bands recorded better than orchestras, and as Fred Gaisberg discovered early in the century, military groups such as the Band of the Coldstream Guards came through especially well.[85] Jazz musicians needed to substitute the tuba for the string base, and it was a long time before the piano ceased to sound like a banjo.[86]

The records themselves also played a crucial role in the clarity of reproduction. Edison's tinfoil soon gave way to more sophisticated media for storing sound. The first time Émile Berliner listened to a recording on a disc composed mainly of shellac, he 'danced with joy around the machine'. Such discs, Fred Gaisberg later recalled, revealed 'tones hitherto mute to us'.[87] The reproduction of reasonably accurate copies of a master disc improved quality even further, but difficulties continued to plague the industry throughout the first quarter of the century. The fidelity of a record improved the faster it revolved on the gramophone, but more rapid revolutions per minute diminished playing time. Above all, surface noise proved a virtually intractable problem. Columbia introduced a quieter disc after the First World War, but as H. T. Barnett observed in 1924, surface noise remained 'the most objectionable of all the faults of the ordinary gramophone' because it destroyed 'the illusion of the "instrument in the room" '.[88]

The gramophone machines themselves also directly affected the fidelity of recorded sound. Here a number of variables distinguished one machine from another. Large, heavy soundboxes produced greater amplitude but caused more wear on the records. Companies experimented with diaphragms made of metal, wood, ivory, cardboard, mica, and glass. Tone arms came in a variety of shapes. Many consumers liked gramophones with concealed horns, but purists in England generally preferred this vital component on the outside of the machine. Manufacturers in Redditch and Sheffield produced steel needles by the million, but the quality of sound diminished if the consumer failed to change the needle 'with every disc placed upon the turntable'.[89] In 1908 an American introduced bamboo needles which produced a softer, more even sound, but they too demanded attention after every playing. No one machine or component

[85] F. W. Gaisberg, *The Music Goes Round* (New York: Macmillan, 1942), 83–5. On Gaisberg, see Jerrold Northrop Moore, *A Voice in Time: The Gramophone of Fred Gaisberg, 1873–1951* (London: Hamish Hamilton, 1976).

[86] David Baker, 'The Phonograph in Jazz History and Its Influence on the Emergent Jazz Performer', in *The Phonograph and Our Musical Life*, ed. H. Wiley Hitchcock (New York: Institute for Studies in American Music, 1980), 45–6. See also William H. Talmadge, 'Equipment Failure and Audio Distortion in the Acoustical Recording and Remastering of Early Jazz', *Journal of Jazz Studies* 5, 2 (1979): 61–75.

[87] Gaisberg, op. cit., 12.

[88] H. T. Barnett, 'Surface Vibration', *The Gramophone* 2, 7 (1924): 249.

[89] Mitchell, op. cit., 56; 42–61.

clearly triumphed over all others. Each embodied weaknesses which compromised its advantages.

The introduction of electronic recording in the mid-1920s overcame a number of the disadvantages of the more primitive acoustic method. The new process vastly extended the range of sounds which gramophones could record. The richness and detail of bass and treble frequencies previously irretrievable in recordings suddenly became audible. Then too, because the recording process captured sound electronically rather than acoustically, the number of musicians who might be recorded at one time increased enormously. The music of entire symphony orchestras could be captured without difficulty. Recording shed many of its previous restrictions and became more mobile, ambitious, and authentic. Finally, the electronic process increased the amplitude and minimized the distortion of the records themselves. Volume need not be gained at the expense of increased record wear. 'The result overwhelmed me,' H. T. Barnett wrote of *Adeste Fideles*, one of the first records which Columbia recorded with the new process. 'It was just as if the doors of my machine were a window opening on to the great hall in which the concert was held.'[90]

If the fidelity of recorded music improved, the length of any selection remained relatively fixed. Previously, composers and musicians established the duration of any single piece of music. In concerts and recitals, conductors and musicians rarely abbreviated the often lengthy work of established, serious composers. Popular songs, of course, often contained stanzas and choruses which performers might choose to ignore. The gramophone, however, imposed strict time-limits on musical performance. Depending upon the company and type of gramophone, most discs and cylinders played selections of disappointingly brief duration. Victor's twelve-inch discs provided three and a half minutes of recorded sound, while Edison's Blue Amberol cylinders ran up to four minutes. Efforts to extend playing time proved of limited efficacy. Neophone produced a twenty-inch disc which lasted ten to twelve minutes, but these records demanded an unusually large gramophone to be played. Worse, as recent scholars have explained, the slightest vibration 'would send the tone-arm and sound-box skittering across the record, alarming the listeners'.[91]

These limitations on playing time meant that some music adapted to the gramophone better than others. For devotees of serious composition, German lieder fitted well into the allotted time-period and, as Caruso demonstrated, brief selections from well-known operas became successful

---

[90] Gelatt, op. cit., 223; H. T. Barnett, 'Record Selection', *The Gramophone* 3, 8 (1926): 365.
[91] Read and Welch, op. cit, 193. Neophone went out of business in 1908.

throughout the world. For the most part, however, the music of established composers could not be played on the gramophone without distressing compromises. By the second decade of the century, some companies began recording longer works of favoured composers, but to enjoy these pieces, listeners needed to change discs with annoying frequency. Popular music, on the other hand, adapted well to the new technology. The songs of music-hall, for example, often possessed strong, memorable themes; and many popular favourites of the nineteenth century rapidly found their way on to shellac. More important, commercial song-writers in Tin Pan Alley and Charing Cross Road wrote material specifically designed for recording. Other popular music underwent more drastic change. Accustomed to lengthy improvisations during live performances, American jazz musicians needed to pare their material down to central themes, much repeated, if they hoped to record successfully. Often the jazz pieces which the gramophone helped disseminate world-wide bore little resemblance to the longer, improvised, and continually changing original.[92] Like the telegraph, the gramophone made brevity a virtue. Popular music became a three-minute event.

Yet lowered cost and improved fidelity alone cannot explain the acceptance and rapid dissemination of recorded sound in the early twentieth century. Like many new technologies, the gramophone needed to possess clear advantages over its earlier and more established competitors. Moreover, the cost and bother of owning the new technology must not detract substantially from these advantages. To the prospective buyer in Britain from 1900 to 1930, the gramophone embodied a number of attractive features. First, unlike the piano and other popular instruments, it required no individual talent to produce music. To become proficient in piano required years of practice, whereas the gramophone demanded little effort and no special abilities. Now anyone could 'play' music.

Moreover, most gramophones were portable. Individuals could choose to listen to music where and when they pleased. It was possible to make the experience of music an entirely isolated encounter, like reading a book. Although people often read books and listened to the gramophone to relieve their loneliness, both experiences separated the audience from the originating source of communication. The location of music now became greatly expanded. Rather than the parlour or music room in middle-class dwellings, any room in the house might become the site of music. Choirs sang in bedrooms and Alexander's Ragtime Band played in the parlour. Music could also be carried outdoors. In the era of acoustic gramophones, machines could be driven by hand and carried virtually anywhere. During the First World War, recorded sound helped relieve the terror

---

[92] Baker, op. cit., 45–6.

and monotony of the trenches. Lively selections from favourite musical revues wafted through the battlefields of Ypres and the Somme. Then too, the gramophone helped diminish the isolation of country life. Long before wireless claimed this function, cylinders and discs brought the music of the city to the hearths of the country. Centre and periphery became less distinct. The gramophone became one of a series of modern technologies which helped transform more remote geographic areas into centres of activity.

If the gramophone allowed individuals to decide where to listen to music, it also provided new freedom of choice in what to hear. The audience at a concert or the patrons in a music-hall could not select the programme. Though public taste affected what musicians played, the individuals within an audience exercised no direct control over musical selections. The gramophone, Percy Scholes wrote in 1924, 'allows every man to decide for himself'.[93] The list of choices expanded enormously over time. In the first decade of the century, when the gramophone still remained something of a novelty, only a few tastes in music could be satisfied. By the end of the 1920s, however, virtually every musical preference could find some degree of satisfaction in the catalogues of the large record companies. Though popular music, particularly from America, predominated, Biederdieck did not exclude Bach. Indeed, it was the massive sales of popular records which often permitted companies to record, stock, and distribute music which only a minority preferred.[94]

The advantages which the technology of recorded sound provided over more traditional forms of musical entertainment do not explain, however, why certain gramophones triumphed over others in a rapidly expanding, intensely competitive, and often unforgiving market. Consumers faced an often bewildering series of choices when they decided to buy a gramophone. Why they selected one brand over another depended upon factors which the industry sometimes found difficult to anticipate. One major controversy affected the market virtually from the beginning. Consumers faced the choice of purchasing machines which played cylinders, Edison's original design, or discs, Berliner's innovation. Few experts denied that cylinders produced a better sound. With less surface noise, they withstood greater weight from the stylus and could be played at a constant groove speed. As late as 1924, Edison's machines trounced their competition in a comparison sound-test held in London.[95] Fidelity, however, was not

[93] Percy Scholes, 'Music and Musicians', *Observer*, 14 Dec. 1924, 10.
[94] J. Batten to Compton Mackenzie, 27 Jan. 1931, Compton Mackenzie Papers, Humanities Research Center, University of Texas. On Batten's overall view of the industry, see Joe Batten, *Joe Batten's Book: The Story of Sound Recording* (London: Rockcliff, 1956).
[95] Read and Welch, op. cit., 153; 'The Gramophone Tests at Steinway Hall', *The Gramophone* 2, 2 (1924): 34.

the only reason that consumers purchased a particular gramophone. Disc recordings and machines possessed a number of advantages over their older rival. Discs listed the title of the music on the record, whereas Edison identified the selection on the sleeve, or even more distressing, announced it before the music began. Discs, moreover, could be handled and placed on the machine with greater ease than cylinders. Storage took less space. Around 1900, fifty of Berliner's smaller discs could be stacked in virtually the same area as only one of Edison's cumbersome cylinder boxes.[96] Convenience proved a decisive factor in the eventual triumph of the disc.

Cost, fidelity, convenience—all of these interrelated factors contributed to the decisions of individual consumers when they decided to purchase a gramophone. The complex relationship among these various factors was constantly changing in the early twentieth century. Initially, the inconvenience, high cost, poor fidelity, and other disadvantages of the gramophone restricted sales to those for whom the novelty of recorded sound overcame its obvious limitations. Later, lowered costs, higher fidelity, and improved convenience assured the success of the new technology. The relationship among these various considerations was not always obvious. For example, manufacturers enclosed the sound horn in the expensive gramophones made to resemble 'fine furniture'. Less costly models where the horn remained exposed produced both more amplitude and better fidelity. A higher price did not always guarantee a better sound. In the early years of the gramophone, as with most new technologies, consumers faced a number of confusing trade-offs. Yet the overall trend within the industry was clear. By the 1920s, the experience of recorded sound was made available to major sections of the English population. What one generation considered novelty became commonplace in another.

The gramophone affected the traditions of British music in complex, often paradoxical ways. The capacity of the new technology to record, preserve, and disseminate previously ephemeral moments helped transform British musical habits, but sometimes the gramophone reinforced two quite distinct or even opposing trends. Recorded sound transcended time, and yet in another sense, this modern, technological form of permanence contributed to the transience of music. Recorded sound also transcended space, and yet national boundaries and traditions could be reaffirmed when confronted by a massive influx of American musical culture. Both of these developments merit further attention.

Until Edison made his discovery in 1877, no sound survived the moment of its passing. The gramophone allowed music to transcend the boundaries of time, thereby offering the performer a new promise of immortality.

---

[96] Read and Welch, op. cit., 152–8.

'Formerly, the artist was haunted by the knowledge that with him his music must also vanish into the unknown,' Sergei Rachmaninov observed in 1931. 'Yet, today, he can leave behind him a faithful reproduction of his art.'[97] This hope for immortality on shellac often became lost, however, in the continual and often extraordinarily rapid turnover of records. For commercial culture, the wonder of this new technology lay not in historic preservation, but in mass production. The economies of scale practised in the industry, combined with the unpredictability of demand, impelled most commercial interests to create as many products as possible at the lowest possible price. Alfred Clarke, the Managing Director of the Gramophone Company, admitted that 85 per cent of his company's recordings lasted a year or less.[98] Popular records became almost as transitory in the market-place as the ephemeral sounds which they preserved. Moreover, high turnover in a perpetually changing market led to an indifference, even contempt for earlier, more primitive technologies and the often less sophisticated products they created. Within a few generations, records produced by the thousands and millions became rare items. Many were lost altogether. The promise of immortality, so thrilling to Rachmaninov, was often broken by the realities of commerce.

The industry alone was not responsible for the often transitory nature of sound recordings in this century. The gramophone permitted individual consumers to hear their favourite songs as many times as they liked. This capacity to repeat the same music at will contributed to the high turnover of popular music. Certainly the nineteenth century experienced fashions in music. In the concluding decades of the century, in particular, the rapid sales of popular sheet music meant that favourite songs enjoyed a briefer vogue than in earlier times.[99] The gramophone simply buttressed this trend. Repeatability accelerated the life cycle of popular music. Though this phenomenon awaits more intensive study, the ability to play the same song repeatedly helped music attain popularity more quickly, but also hastened its decline. Few songs could withstand endless repetition. Songs which a few generations before might have remained popular for decades now rose and fell within a year, or even months. On the other hand, the rapid turnover of records meant that many popular songs could be associated in memory more precisely with specific periods of time. Individuals associated certain music with key moments of their own maturation. A once-popular record became emblematic of a long-departed

---

[97] Sergei Rachmaninov, 'The Artist and the Gramophone', *The Gramophone* 8, 95 (1931): 526.

[98] Peacock and Weir, *Composer in Market Place*, 90.

[99] James Walvin, *Leisure and Society, 1850–1950* (London: Longman, 1978), 106–8.

acquaintance, mood, or event. Recorded music became a fixed landmark in time, helping define the identity of an individual or, as in the case of jazz in the 1920s, an entire generation.

The technology of recorded sound permitted music to transcend the boundaries of space as well as time. Once again, national and regional cultures confronted and needed to assimilate alien musical traditions. The mass distribution of sheet music and other printed materials before the twentieth century had long exposed audiences to the music of other cultures. Touring groups and returning travellers from other countries also disseminated foreign music. Yet these and other means of cross-fertilization could not compare in scope or intensity to the impact of recorded sound. By the 1920s, the gramophone was an instrument families could afford and anyone could use. The music of New York, Chicago, and New Orleans could be heard, not interpreted through the musical skills and prejudices of a local musician or family member, but as recorded by its original artists. The gramophone accelerated the controversial process of 'Americanization', an inelegant but unavoidable word.

Three general comments about the Americanization of the mass media help place the gramophone's role in historical context. First, American music rose to prominence at the same time that American films dominated the British market. In 1910 about 15 per cent of the films shown in Britain were American. Five years later, during the First World War, the proportion had increased to about 60 per cent. By 1926, the year before Parliament passed stiff quota restrictions, Hollywood produced a phenomenal 95 per cent of all films distributed in Britain.[1] 'The cinema today is almost wholly an appendage of the United States,' the *Daily Mail* lamented in 1926. '. . . The whole world is surfeited with an exclusive diet of American pictures.'[2] Second, American influence in film and other mass media often remained masked or unnoticed altogether. With the obvious exception of genres such as the Western, silent films produced in America did not always betray their place of origin and, perhaps even more important, as one researcher discovered in the 1930s, many film-goers believed that 'the story and the action are the most important things on the screen, and the American origin is not much thought of.'[3] In popular journalism, press lords rarely disclosed their considerable debt to American newspapers. Few English readers of the *Daily Mail* knew that Northcliffe had appropriated many of his journalistic innovations

[1] Low, *British Film, 1906–1914*, 134; C. J. North, 'Our Foreign Trade in Motion Pictures', *Annals of the American Academy of Political and Social Science* 128 (1926): 102.
[2] Quoted in William Marston Seebury, *The Public and the Motion Picture Industry* (New York: Macmillan, 1926), 201.
[3] Richard Heathcote Heindel, 'American Attitudes of British School Children', *School and Society*, 25 Dec. 1937, 839.

from Pulitzer and Hearst. Few readers of the *Daily Express* were aware that its editor and some of its leading personnel came from America, where they had served their apprenticeships. British daily newspapers were printed on presses imported from Chicago. They were written in the clipped language favoured by the American press. They included interviews, contests, crusades, features, graphics, layouts, and other aspects of popular journalism pioneered by American editors. Few English readers knew that Northcliffe self-consciously retained certain English journalistic customs because, as he told one contemporary, he was 'afraid of alarming the British public, which . . . objected to being Americanized'.[4] Third, cultural influences flowed in both directions. British popular culture affected American life as well. In journalism, Northcliffe developed the tabloid, and in popular theatre, musical productions from the London stage, especially those of Gilbert and Sullivan, became major American successes in the late nineteenth century. Harry Lauder and other British music-hall favourites supplemented their incomes with lucrative tours of American vaudeville circuits. Although Marie Lloyd unexpectedly flopped in America, Charlie Chaplin came to the attention of Hollywood while touring with a British troupe. His comic technique in cinema owed much to his early training in music-hall and other forms of British entertainment. The process of Americanization involved a number of such cross-currents.[5]

As a technology which permitted music to transcend the boundaries of space and time, the gramophone became an important agent of cultural transmission. In particular, music which originated from American Blacks made an enormous impression on British entertainment in the early decades of the twentieth century. Ragtime and jazz offered lively and often exotic alternatives to the conventions of British popular music. Both transcended racial barriers that in other circumstances might have proved insur-mountable. Both became a sound enjoyed by all classes, thus circumventing one of the key boundaries of British society. West End flappers and Lancashire shop-girls became enraptured by the same records, and danced to the same tunes.

The gramophone was certainly not the sole agent of this transformation. Sheet music played a key role in the diffusion of ragtime, especially since the piano, so important to the compositions of Scott Joplin and others,

[4] William Carson, *Northcliffe: Britain's Man of Power* (New York: Dodge, 1918), 154–5.

[5] Ronald Pearsall, *Edwardian Popular Music* (Rutherford, NJ: Farleigh Dickenson University Press, 1975), 19–25, 66; Walvin, *Leisure and Society*, 114; Ian Whitcomb, *After the Ball* (Harmondsworth: Penguin, 1972), 157. For a general history of American popular arts during this period, see Russell Lynes, *The Lively Audience: A Social History of the Visual and Performing Arts in America, 1890–1950* (New York: Harper and Row, 1985).

did not record well. Musical theatre and other forms of live performance also contributed to the dissemination of ragtime. An estimated 400,000 people saw the musical revue *Hullo Ragtime*, which introduced such popular hits as 'Waiting for the Robert E. Lee' and the controversial 'Hitchy Koo'.[6] Tours by American groups also added to the success of both ragtime and jazz. The Original American Ragtime Octette astonished audiences in the London Hippodrome in 1912, and contemporaries universally agreed that the sensationally successful visit of the Original Dixieland Jazz Band from April 1919 to July 1920 inaugurated the jazz age in Britain. Yet, it was the gramophone that helped transform what might have been a London fashion into a national phenomenon. While in England, the Original Dixieland Jazz Band recorded seventeen sides of their most popular numbers for Columbia Graphophone and, although no reliable sales figures have survived, 'At the Jazz Band Ball', 'Sensation Rag', and other numbers became widely popular.[7] More telling, perhaps, the success of this American group spawned a number of British imitators. The Manhattan Jazz Band, a British group, recorded for Zonophone, and the Continental Five, another recording group, carefully followed American trends. The Savoy Orpheans and Savoy Havana Band, both of which included American musicians, recorded over three hundred records in the 1920s.[8]

As an important source of Americanization, recorded sound affected British musical tradition in a variety of ways. First, like the cinema and later wireless, the gramophone contributed to the mechanization of British entertainment. Among intellectuals, as we shall see in Part Two, it was a commonplace to associate mechanization with American life. The gramophone and its popular musical fare became yet another component of a trend which some perceived as dehumanizing. In a famous episode from *The Waste Land*, for example, Eliot associated recorded music with mechanical, devitalized sex. After the bored typist makes indifferent love to 'the young man carbuncular', she 'smoothes her hair with automatic hand, / And puts a record on the gramophone.'[9] Yet at the same time

[6] Terry Waldo, *This is Ragtime* (New York: Hawthorn Books, 1976), 82; Edward A. Berlin, *Ragtime: A Musical and Cultural History* (Berkeley: University of California Press, 1980), 8–9; Pearsall, op. cit., 185.

[7] David Boulton, *Jazz in Britain* (London: W. H. Allen, 1958), 32, 36–39; H. O. Brunn, *The Story of the Original Dixieland Jazz Band* (Baton Rouge: Louisiana State University Press, 1960), 128–34. On the relationship of this band to ragtime, see William J. Schafer and Johannes Reidel, *The Art of Ragtime: Form and Meaning of an Original Black American Art* (Baton Rouge: Louisiana State University Press, 1973), 138–9.

[8] Albert McCarthy, *The Dance-Band Era: The Dancing Decades From Ragtime to Swing, 1910–1950* (London: Studio Vista, 1971), 44; Edwin S. Walker, 'Early English Jazz', *Jazz Journal* 22, 9 (1969): 24. For the best recent history of jazz in Britain, see Jim Godbolt, *A History of Jazz in Britain, 1919–50* (London: Paladin, 1986).

[9] T. S. Eliot, *The Waste Land*, ll. 231, 255–6.

that the gramophone buttressed a trend toward the mechanization of music, it also contributed to a renascence of live performances. Both ragtime and jazz rejuvenated social dancing. The 'dance craze' before the First World War, combined with the rapid growth of dance palaces after the war, meant that men and women from all social classes danced socially to the same music which they learned to enjoy in the privacy of their own homes. Indeed, the gramophone formed the basis of private dance parties, and it was not unknown for individuals to practise new dance steps with recorded music before displaying their talent in public. 'Wherever you look there is a new *Palais de Danse*,' one writer in the *Daily Mail* observed in 1925. 'Everywhere strange music throbs.'[10] That same year a dance floor was constructed over the stalls and stage of Covent Garden, and for a time opera and ballet alternated with the popular dance bands of the day. This intimate relationship between mechanization and live performance extended to the misnamed 'silent film'. In the 1920s, 75–80 per cent of all musicians in Britain were employed in cinema orchestras.[11] Both the cinema and the gramophone thus formed a symbiotic relationship with more traditional sources of entertainment.

To the degree that it helped disseminate ragtime and jazz throughout Britain, the gramophone reinforced opposing musical tendencies in a second, potentially more threatening way. Both ragtime and jazz became part of the early twentieth-century revolt against Victorian social conventions and middle-class gentility. With its syncopated rhythms and strong bass melodies, ragtime displayed an exuberance that challenged the traditional moral emphasis on restraint and self-control. The names and steps of the dances which emerged during the ragtime era reflected this preoccupation with one's fundamental animal nature. The Turkey Trot, Grizzly Bear, Monkey Glide, Bunny Hug, and other whimsically named dance routines allowed the respectable classes to liberate themselves temporarily from the demanding conventions of social propriety. Freer, more spontaneous body movements replaced the precisely ordered, carefully prescribed steps of earlier ballroom dancing. Bodies swayed to the rhythm naturally and unselfconsciously. Jazz was even more overtly sexual and suggestive. To the consternation of the staid and the delight of the young, this music of Black American culture celebrated the sexual instinct at a time when the Great War had already undermined social inhibitions and Freudian psychology began to change the vocabulary of

---

[10] Anna Pavlova, 'The Dancing Age', *Daily Mail*, 2 Oct. 1925; A. H. Franks, *Social Dance: A Short History* (London: Routledge and Kegan Paul, 1963), 159–195; Francis Rust, *Dance in Society* (London: Routledge and Kegan Paul, 1969), 83–7; Edward Lee, *Music of the People: A Study of Popular Music in Great Britain* (London: Barrie and Jenkins, 1970), 134–6.

[11] Rust, op. cit., 93; Pearsall, *Popular Music of the Twenties*, 8.

self-understanding. To both the critics and apologists of jazz in Britain, the Black race epitomized sensuality as opposed to 'civilization'. Dances that began in American Black culture such as the Charleston and the Black Bottom contained movements that exalted the versatility of the human body.[12]

Ragtime and jazz undermined Victorian conventions in another manner as well. Both mocked the social and cultural pretensions of the respectable classes. In America, the popular early ragtime dance, the Cakewalk, called for dancers to move in an exaggerated stroll originally intended to satirize the ostentatious perambulations of the *nouveaux riches*.[13] Ragtime pianists created syncopated versions of great European music, thus 'ragging' the preferred composers of the social élites. The fourth movement of Beethoven's Ninth Symphony, for example, became a honky-tonk favourite and even the most solemn religious music could not escape drastic revision. Jazz buttressed this trend: 'Yes, We Have No Bananas', popular in the early 1920s, took its opening melodic line from a chorus in Handel. Such impertinence extended to other aspects of jazz performance as well. Most of the early jazz groups in England performed in full evening dress, but some also wore funny hats, blew loud, raucous whistles at random points in the music, and occasionally paused to engage in a mock sword fight using their clarinets as weapons.[14] These antics and similar behaviour in both ragtime and jazz manifested an often neglected facet of this music. Both derived their humour and much of their infectious liveliness from an irreverence towards established hierarchies. Both profaned the sacred by puncturing its solemnities, by levelling its social distances. The anarchic elements of ragtime and jazz overturned customary distinctions and, while the music lasted, often allowed nonsense to triumph over reason and spontaneity to reign over social discipline. The music which originated from a distant, oppressed minority helped compensate and liberate, if only temporarily, a more privileged majority.

Not surprisingly, the White majority sanitized and constantly sought to contain the more threatening elements of Black American music and culture. In England, some of the most popular ragtime imported from America bore little resemblance to the original product. Many commercially successful ragtime songs were composed by Whites. Irving Berlin's compositions, such as the immensely popular 'Alexander's Ragtime Band', toned down or eliminated altogether the sexual and other controversial

---

[12] Lewis A. Erenberg, *Steppin' Out: New York Nightlife and the Transformation of American Culture, 1890–1930* (Westport: Greenwood Press, 1981), 148–54, 249–50. I have learned much from this pioneering study.

[13] James Lincoln Collier, *The Making of Jazz: A Comprehensive History* (New York: Delta, 1978), 29.

[14] Pearsall, op. cit., 63.

elements of ragtime.[15] The Original Dixieland Jazz Band may have aroused fears in some quarters, but other observers sought to reassure their audience. 'In view of the unkind and disrespectful things which have been said about Red Indians and Negroids and West African savages,' the *Daily News* reported in 1919, 'it should be said that the players are all white—as white as they can possibly be.'[16] After the First World War, American Blacks recorded their own, uncompromised music on so-called 'race records' that the vast majority of British enthusiasts never knew existed.[17] In Britain, those who professed a love of jazz usually meant the slick, melodic arrangements of such band-leaders as Paul Whiteman, who first toured England in 1923. '[He] came to us with a reputation as a jazz conductor,' the *Dancing Times* wrote. 'He will leave us with a reputation considerably enhanced.'[18] Whiteman underplayed or omitted the blues notes in the American jazz of New Orleans and Chicago, and substituted instead more conventional, symphonic tonality. His records and first tour influenced a number of British bands, though in his memoirs, published in 1926, Whiteman patronized their talents as jazz musicians. He lauded the ability of British musicians to imitate his music, 'but when it came to originating, they fell down. Jazz was simply not in their blood. They lacked the spontaneity, the exuberance, the courage, . . . the indefinable something that is jazz.'[19]

British bands who experimented with hotter, more authentic jazz catered to a minority taste in the 1920s. The most intelligent and influential British jazz magazine, *Melody Maker*, founded in 1926, constantly advocated hot, aggressive jazz, and a number of talented American musicians penetrated the British market. In 1927, the records and music of Fletcher Henderson, Duke Ellington, and 'Jelly Roll' Morton made their début and by the end of the decade some of the extraordinary early recordings of Louis Armstrong could be found in the larger or more specialized retail record shops in London.[20] Yet for the most part, jazz purists paid a price at the box office. Fred Elizalde, a Spanish-born pianist who came to Britain in 1926, quickly became acknowledged by critics as the most talented and original jazz musician playing in Britain. Early in 1928, the Savoy

---

[15] Alexander Woolcott, *The Story of Irving Berlin* (New York: G. P. Putnam's Sons, 1925), 85–7.   [16] Quoted in Brunn, *Original Dixieland Jazz Band*, 125.

[17] Ronald Clifford Foreman, jun., 'Jazz and Race Records, 1920–32: Their Origins and their Significance for the Record Industry and Society' (Ph.D. diss., University of Illinois, 1968); Robert M. W. Dixon and John Godrich, *Recording the Blues* (New York: Stein and Day, 1970).

[18] *Dancing Times* (May 1923) quoted in Boulton, *Jazz in Britain*, 45.

[19] Paul Whiteman and Mary Margaret McBride, *Jazz* (New York: J. H. Sears, 1926), 74. See also Neil Leonard, *Jazz and White Americans: The Acceptance of a New Art Form* (Chicago: University of Chicago Press, 1962), 73–82.

[20] Boulton, op. cit., 52–3, 170–1.

Hotel in London gambled by appointing him as leader of their house band, one of the most popular in Britain and a staple of broadcasts on the BBC. Elizalde bewildered and annoyed his audience by playing music that lacked a clear melodic line and that dance couples found difficult to follow. Though some attempts at compromise proved temporarily successful, Elizalde was dropped by the BBC and the Savoy terminated his contract.[21]

The British defused the threatening elements of Black American music in another way. Though ragtime and jazz freed dance from a number of traditional constraints, new rules quickly emerged. The spontaneous elements of dance rapidly became formalized. During the First World War, Vernon and Irene Castle taught a generation the proper way to dance the Turkey Trot, Lame Duck, and other ragtime steps. The Vernon Castle School of Dancing demonstrated to both American and English élites the appropriate ways to respond to the music's infectious rhythms.[22] After Vernon Castle was killed in an aeroplane accident and Irene retired, others took their place. The teachers of ballroom dancing in England, though initially caught off guard by the new music from America, quickly adapted to changing realities. In 1920, as jazz ascended in popularity, professional dance instructors gathered in London in an attempt to organize their ranks and reassert their authority over the world of social dancing. Philip S. J. Richardson, the chairman of the conference, warned that 'in the ballroom there had been a tendency towards an artistic bolshevism' which 'would end in chaos if fundamental technique be entirely jettisoned'. These attempts at standardization continued throughout the decade, culminating in the Great Conference of 1929 and establishment of British Championships a year later.[23] In many circles, the spontaneous and idiosyncratic now conformed to prescribed standards. The passions of jazz had become ritualized, the revolt contained.

As an instrument of Americanization, the gramophone helped buttress apparently opposing trends in a third way. The men and women who enjoyed 'Hitchy Koo' and the Charleston came from Bradford and Oxford, from Hampstead and Battersea. Ragtime and jazz drew its public from all classes and regions. 'Jazz has secured and still retains a more widespread vogue among its contemporary listeners than any other form of music ever known,' R. W. S. Mendl wrote in the first British book about the

[21] McCarthy, *Dance-Band Era*, 48.

[22] David Ewen, *All the Years of American Popular Music* (Englewood Cliffs: Prentice-Hall, 1977), 173–4. See also Irene Castle, *Castles in the Air* (New York: De Capo Paperback, 1980), 1–142.

[23] Philip S. J. Richardson, *A History of English Ballroom Dancing (1910–45): The Story of the Development of the Modern English Style* (London: Herbert Jenkins, n.d.), 42, 70–89.

subject, *The Appeal of Jazz*, published in 1927.[24] The regional and class distinctions of nineteenth-century popular culture became supplemented by different, more novel allegiances. Both ragtime and jazz attracted a wide audience among youth, who found in the music a reflection of their own restlessness and impatience with tradition. The renewed interest in public dancing created regular, predictable opportunities for young men and women to meet members of the opposite sex. The vigorous, sometimes sensual nature of the dance steps favoured the young and added to the excitement.[25] Since youth culture was itself rarely monolithic, those who shared the same specific tastes in music became themselves a distinct, if not always easily traced, subculture. Musical preference helped define personal identity. What jazz one liked made a statement about who one was.

Despite their wide appeal, ragtime and jazz never completely transcended entrenched social boundaries. Individuals of all classes might enjoy the same gramophone recordings, but where they listened to live public performances varied according to social class. Though as always significant exceptions qualify the general rule, the upper classes danced to ragtime and jazz in night-clubs, cabarets, and in the more exclusive hotels. The wealthy and influential also arranged for the better bands to play for private parties, hunt balls, and other similarly exclusive engagements. The lower-middle and working classes patronized the dance palaces and road-houses that became such a characteristic feature of inter-war Britain. Some restaurants installed large dance floors that catered to all classes, but in general the night-club could be distinguished from the dance palace in at least two important respects. First, night-clubs excluded all but the affluent by exacting heavy entrance fees. Murray's in London charged a fee of three guineas to join, plus five guineas more a year to retain membership. For every guest they charged an additional five shillings, and, as the *Daily Mail* reported in 1915, 'For supper you pay Savoy prices and get Savoy food.'[26] Depending on their size, location, and programme, dance palaces charged a far more modest entrance fee and profited from high volume and turnover. In Rochdale during the 1920s, for example, entrance fees to various public dances ranged from 6*d.* to 2*s.* Second, most night-clubs offered their patrons a more intimate, refined setting than the often huge dance palaces. Though some hotels in London constructed spacious dance floors, they could not match the enormous rooms of the dance palaces of Lancashire and the popular seaside resorts. 'The great

[24] R. W. S. Mendl, *The Appeal of Jazz* (London: Philip Allan [1927]), 80.
[25] Pearsall, *Edwardian Popular Music*, 191; Mackerness, *Social History of English Music*, 249; Erenberg, *Steppin' Out*, 156.
[26] 'What a Nightclub Is', *Daily Mail*, 2 Oct. 1915.

"barn" we patronized as apprentices held at least a thousand,' one participant recalled of Roberts's in Salford. 'Almost every evening . . . it was jammed with a mass of young men and women . . . youth at every level of the manual working class.'[27] In the dance palace, intimacy was sacrificed to cost; jazz became a community experience that mixed the intricate gradations of the same class.

Thus, recorded sound affected the traditions of British music in complex, often unpredictable ways. The gramophone allowed music to transcend time, but this gift of permanence often became lost in the rapid, relentless turnover of musical recordings. The gramophone permitted music to transcend space, but Americanization rarely proved a straightforward process. Some believed that American music on the gramophone helped mechanize British music; and yet recorded sound and live performances reinforced each other's popularity. Ragtime and jazz embodied an important revolt against the traditions of order and propriety, and yet new standards of conformity quickly emerged. American music attracted a wide following among all classes, and yet social distinctions never entirely disappeared from the enjoyment of ragtime and jazz. The mechanization of music by the gramophone and other new technologies reconfigured rather than displaced the diversity of British musical culture.

The challenge of the commercialized mass media was twofold. First, by permitting the market-place to dictate success or failure, commercial interests allowed economic rather than aesthetic factors determine cultural worth. Buttressing a trend that began long before in Britain, the commercial mass media in the early twentieth century placed the profit motive at the heart of cultural activity. Second, by developing and exploiting new technologies of communication, these same commercial interests threatened to undermine valued cultural traditions. The cinema and graphics in the popular daily press eroded the primacy of the written word while, at the same time, the gramophone and music from America rapidly altered patterns of leisure in ways traditionalists often found bewildering. Foreign sounds, like foreign images, threatened the integrity of a national culture.

This analysis has stressed that these challenges involved complexities often ignored, both then and now. First, if the market-place determined success, who determined the market admits of no simple answer. Commercial culture served the interests of its producers, but it also served the needs of its consumers. The women's page in the popular daily press,

---

[27] Quoted in Paul Wild, 'Recreation in Rochdale, 1900–40', in *Working-Class Culture: Studies in History and Theory*, ed. J. Clarke, C. Critchen, and R. Johnson (New York: St Martin's Press, 1979), 148.

for example, attracted key advertisers to newspapers who needed the revenue to remain competitive, but it also allowed women to enjoy a medium previously devoted exclusively to male concerns. Supply and demand were closely intertwined, both economically and culturally. Commercial culture involved a complex interrelationship between producer and consumer. Second, and in an analogous manner, technology and tradition ought not be viewed as isolated causal phenomena. Film narrative developed within the context of traditional popular culture. D. W. Griffith helped pioneer film grammar by translating the conventions of melodrama into cinematic images. Then too, the gramophone changed British musical habits, but rarely in a straightforward manner. The wide dissemination of recorded sound often reinforced diverse trends. Innovation and continuity were closely intertwined. Commercial culture also involved an intricate web of relationships between technology and tradition.

These challenges to authority and to tradition shared another, more significant trait. Both collapsed social and cultural distances. For sound economic reasons, the cultural relationship between a communicator and the public involved a form of pragmatic identification. The popular daily press wrote in a style and vocabulary its public could recognize and appreciate. Language was not employed as a direct weapon of social hierarchy. The women's page devoted itself to concerns that élite papers considered trivial, irrelevant, or contemptible. Half the population was no longer excluded from the regular experience of a daily newspaper. Audiences identified strongly with certain personalities, though, as Chaplin discovered, the nature of this identification involved an amalgam of fantasy and reality. Technological innovations contributed to this collapsing of social and cultural distances. Unlike the written word which demanded years of training to understand properly, images could be grasped immediately by virtually everyone. With its low admission prices, often pleasant surroundings, and ease of access, the cinema excluded few citizens from participation in the medium. Drawing upon a series of technological innovations, the popular press included news photos and other graphics that help make daily newspapers appealing to all classes. Technology also recorded and eased the wide dissemination of sound as well as of images. As a device that anyone could master and most could afford, the gramophone made the music of professional musicians, popular and serious, available to all, at will, virtually anywhere. Technology thus reinforced the central thrust of commercial culture. In a country that by 1930 could claim to be democratic politically, the commercialized mass media, for self-serving economic reasons, offered Britain a more egalitarian culture.

PART TWO
The Response of the Cultivated Élites

3

The Reassertion of Cultural Hierarchy

THE 'cultivated élites'—a deliberately ambiguous, fluid category embracing writers, artists, musicians, academics, and a variety of other educated individuals—responded to the commercialized mass media with a wide range of emotions, prejudices, and opinions. Some remained ignorant of the emerging technologies or reacted with studied indifference. The newer forms of communication, so pervasive among the lower middle and working classes in the first two decades of the twentieth century, often took time to penetrate refined sensibilities. To some, the cinema was not only silent but invisible. Others, more alert to the potential dangers of these new technologies, responded with hostility to the levelling tendencies of a culture based upon market forces. These critics, pessimists drawn from both sides of the political spectrum, believed in the fundamental incompatibility of equality and excellence. Still others, while deeply suspicious of commercialism, welcomed the newer media as future liberators of a poorly educated British public. Astonished by the capacity of mass media to reach an enormous public, they strove to enlighten and uplift the tastes of their countrymen. Among all these groups, attitudes often changed over time. Cynics occasionally came to acknowledge the aesthetic possibilities of a technically improving medium, while enthusiasts became disillusioned with audiences recalcitrant to the pleasures of self-improvement. Moreover, many intellectuals held contradictory or unconsciously ambivalent views about commercial culture. T. S. Eliot loathed the democratization of culture, but enjoyed comic strips as an undergraduate, venerated Marie Lloyd, owned a substantial collection of recorded jazz, and became addicted to detective novels.[1] The response of the cultivated élites to the mass media resists easy characterization. It was an intricate mosaic of shifting opinions among complicated individuals who could not agree among themselves.

For all the differences among them, however, the cultivated élites in early twentieth-century Britain shared a fundamental allegiance to the notion of cultural hierarchy. Arguments about the nature and intricate ordering of this hierarchy preoccupied discourse, both formal and informal,

---

[1] Peter Ackroyd, *T. S. Eliot: A Life* (New York: Simon and Schuster, 1984), 31, 105, 162, 167.

heated and urbane, in a number of disciplines, but few intellectuals challenged the centrality of such a concept. Standards existed and needed to be maintained. These standards, often asserted to be objective realities, served as impersonal measures to evaluate the quality of a single performance, collected works, or individuals themselves. Like artistic creation, aesthetic judgement demanded a combination of talent, training, discrimination, and taste. Since these qualities were not universally shared, those who possessed them, as critics and creators, constituted an élite, though the precise composition of this élite remained another contentious topic. Sometimes, as with an avant-garde, it was self-declared, while in other cases it became identified by more formal, institutionalized mechanisms.

This notion of cultural hierarchy embodied within it a spatial metaphor of crucial significance for understanding one of the fundamental differences between commercial and élite culture. Élite culture conceptualized, and then usually treated as concrete, hierarchies in which, according to the metaphor, vertical distance separated high and low.[2] These vertical distances could not be measured in any literal sense, of course, but they did help serve figuratively to distinguish one cultural product from another. Critics measured the value of a work by its distance, either near or far, from implicit cultural standards. They sought to separate themselves, both in their imaginations and practical life, from anything that compromised or rejected those standards. Commercial culture, as we have seen, sought to maximize its audience by collapsing cultural distances. Through a complex and constantly evolving identification between producer and consumer, it eroded the cultural boundaries between, say, a popular newspaper and its female readership. The new technologies of communication directly contributed to this process by preserving, replicating, and distributing messages which, at low cost to the consumer, brought Hollywood to Birmingham and Harlem to Hartlepool. In its restless search for profitability, commercial culture diminished the distance between producer and consumer. Élite culture, on the other hand, measured itself by the distances it constantly reaffirmed.

Two aspects of the reaffirmation merit special comment. First, the ambiguous process of defining cultural taste involved rejection and negation as well as establishing positive values. Aversions to certain phenomena often became as important a barometer of cultural refinement

[2] For the spatial metaphor and the notion of cultural distancing, see Karl Mannheim, 'The Democratization of Culture', in *Essays on the Sociology of Culture* (London: Routledge and Kegan Paul, 1956), 171–246. This essay has greatly influenced my thinking. I have also learned much from Edward Shils, *The Intellectuals and the Powers and Other Essays* (Chicago: University of Chicago Press, 1972); and Pierre Bourdieu, *Distinction: A Social Critique of the Judgement of Taste*, trans. Richard Nice (Cambridge: Harvard University Press, 1984).

as preferences. What one disliked narrowed the field of choices and helped establish what one preferred. Among writers, artists, and intellectuals, agreement on what to exclude often proved less controversial than concord about acceptability. The concept of aesthetic illegitimacy derived from a number of considerations, most of them rarely made explicit. Tradition, historical context, social class, intelligence, and personal psychology all played a role in forging an informal, yet powerful consensus among an influential minority. In 1910, few cultivated individuals admitted reading *Tit-Bits*, and though actors from the legitimate stage participated in the medium, few in Britain appreciated the aesthetic potential of the cinema. During the same year, however, whether Van Gogh painted well proved a much more controversial proposition. Second, an individual's myriad cultural preferences, if examined singly, might represent only a small, even trivial facet of a complex personality. Yet, together they embodied a fundamental component of individual identity. Vociferous disputes over some apparently minor personal preference often struck outsiders as amusing and absurd. If viewed as significant emblems of personal identity, however, these same disputes might assume greater importance. The depth of passion and bitterness with which some British critics attacked jazz, for example, involved much more than an exaggerated dislike of such music. Jazz, like much else in commercial culture, embodied a system of personal values which some of its critics found profoundly threatening. To those who looked to music not for casual diversion but spiritual renewal, jazz desecrated that which helped define them as persons. In some cultivated circles, taste was not an aspect of personal autonomy but identity itself. Style was the individual.

This individuality became defined within the framework of social class, region, and nation. Though social class did not determine cultural preference, it established parameters which even self-consciously detached observers found extremely difficult to surmount. Class acted as a reasonably accurate predictor of educational level, leisure time, and cultural exposure, among other crucial variables. Despite important changes in patterns of social mobility in the early decades of this century, the working class never came close to producing the number of creative writers, artists, musicians, and critics commensurate with their proportion of the population.[3] At the same time, the critique of commercial culture by middle-class literary figures and intellectuals almost always involved thinly masked elements of class snobbery. These social forces became complicated by regional and national factors. Though London, Oxford, Cambridge, and the South

[3] See the statistics in Richard D. Altick, 'The Sociology of Authorship: The Social Origins, Education and Occupations of 1,100 British Writers, 1800–1935', *Bulletin of the New York Public Library* (June 1962): 389–404.

in general established the tone of élite culture in Britain, other areas contributed their voices, accents, and regional preoccupations. Yeats and Joyce wrote when Ireland remained part of the United Kingdom, and Thomas Hardy, D. H. Lawrence, Compton Mackenzie, and others explored distinctive regional themes. National prejudices became interwoven with class and regional concerns in the long, often ambivalent struggle to combat Americanization. That T. S. Eliot, Ezra Pound, and other Americans helped lead this effort underscores the peculiarities of such allegiances. Class, region, and nation shaped tastes in ways that individuals, wedded to the comfortable notion of their own autonomy, often ignored.

In the early twentieth century, intellectuals based their reassertion of cultural supremacy upon a traditional and enormously influential view of human nature that was itself hierarchical. This hierarchy was described in language that drew upon a wide spectrum of analogous dichotomies. To express it in simplified, generic form, human nature involved an ongoing conflict between the lower instincts—emotions, drives, material needs—and the higher faculties—reason, spirit, and imagination, among others. For both the individual and society, civility depended upon the triumph of the reason over emotion just as, in some religions, the victory of spirit over matter helped assure eternal salvation. Plato described human nature with his famous metaphor of horses and reins, while Christian theologians constructed a sophisticated theology based upon the conflict of the 'Outer' and 'Inner Man'. Some later thinkers analysed the entire hierarchical chain of human capabilities; others explored the strengths and limitations of one particular faculty. Freud, steeped in the classics of the European tradition, reconstructed the metaphor for modern audiences. The history of Western thought could be written on how each generation and epoch adapted this view of human nature for its own purposes.

For most British intellectuals in the late nineteenth and early twentieth centuries, as for so many of their predecessors, the traditional cultural hierarchies reflected either directly or by implication the gradations from lower instincts to higher faculties intrinsic to human nature. These intellectuals believed that low, vulgar, common culture played upon the baser instincts, whereas superior culture emanated, in its creation and appreciation, from the higher, more subtle, complex, and integrative faculties. Commercial culture played to the crowd, the mass, the benighted many. It elevated common individuals beyond their station, flattered them with democratic slogans, and proclaimed that everyone's cultural taste, like everyone's vote in politics, ought to be weighted equally. Though these notions had British defenders, it was claimed they prospered best in the United States, which with alarming efficiency and ruthlessness, disseminated them world-wide. Like the lower emotions it exploited, commercial culture possessed a certain vitality, but it ought not to swamp authentic, enduring culture. This more permanent culture, it was argued, penetrated beneath the surface of things and required superior insight, often genius, to create. These minorities deserved special respect in a civilized society and ought not be judged by the crude standard of ephemeral popularity. Élite culture represented the best in civilization in part because it originated within the higher, more transcendent faculties of human nature.

The reassertion of cultural hierarchy in Britain involved two interrelated discourses. The first centred on a critique of commercial culture that permitted intellectuals to distance themselves from the crowd and what was widely perceived as its generally debased instincts. Here taste was affirmed through negation and rejection; élite culture became more clearly delineated by determining what it did not include. The second discourse proved more contentious. Here intellectuals attempted to establish the boundaries of the culture which they defended. This process of definition, like the critique of commercial culture, involved a number of tensions, ambiguities, cross-currents, and paradoxes. Claims to cultural superiority were based upon a peculiar mixture of penetrating insight and quite extraordinary blindness.

A. CROWDS AND THE BASER INSTINCTS

The identification of the crowd with the lower instincts, emotions, and sensations, though of ancient lineage, became particularly insistent in the later nineteenth and early twentieth centuries. Though 'mobs', 'multitudes', and 'dangerous classes' had frequently exerted an ominous presence among British élites, the extension of the franchise, the rise of mass retailing, the growth of Socialism, and the emergence of mass entertainment, all contributed to a heightened sense of the 'masses' and their potential manipulators.[4] The development of social psychology in France and England provided an enhanced respectability to the notion of collective behaviour. 'The age we are about to enter', Gustave Le Bon wrote in 1896, 'will be in truth the ERA OF CROWDS'.[5] In its English

[4] See Asa Briggs, 'The Language of "Class" in Early Nineteenth-Century England' and 'The Language of "Mass" and "Masses" in Nineteenth-Century England', in Asa Briggs, *The Collected Essays of Asa Briggs, vol. 1: Words, Numbers, Places, People* (Urbana: University of Illinois Press, 1985), 3–33, 34–54. See also id., *Mass Entertainment: The Origins of a Modern Industry*, The 29th Joseph Fisher Lecture in Commerce (Adelaide: Griffin Press, 1960).

[5] Gustave Le Bon, *The Crowd: A Study of the Popular Mind* (London: T. Fisher Unwin, 1896) 15. On Le Bon, see Robert A. Nye, *The Origins of Crowd Psychology:*

translation Le Bon's *The Crowd* went through twelve printings by 1920, and found its kindred spirit in the writings of William McDougall and Wilfred Trotter. Trotter's *Instincts of the Herd in Peace and War*, first published in 1916, criticized Social Darwinism for its 'obvious subservience to prejudice', but found no problem in establishing the scientific validity of its own, analogous portrayal of the human aggregate.[6] Though the influence of Trotter and other social psychologists remains difficult to measure, suspicions about the crowd's gullibility were widespread in early twentieth-century Britain and, in the 1920s, influenced the leadership of the major political parties, including Labour.[7]

Three interwoven aspects of this distrust became particularly important in formulating the critique of commercial culture. First, élites often described crowd behaviour in language calculated to strip people of their full humanity. In its extreme but by no means atypical form, writers portrayed majorities as animals, children, or physical objects. The brutality of these comparisons has not lost its intended shock value. 'The democratic man is a species of ape,' William Inge wrote in the *Evening Standard* in 1928. '. . . The art of success in a democracy is to know how to play upon the ape in humanity.'[8] Wyndham Lewis placed hatred of the general public near the centre of his works. 'He is permanently and for ever an infant', he complained in *The Art of Being Ruled*; 'the Infants' Class always absorbs eighty per cent. of the personnel . . . which we call "mankind".'[9] If the crowd behaved like animals or children, it also, secondly, lacked individuality and personal distinctiveness. Members of the general public acted all alike or, as Trotter put it, 'the cardinal quality of the herd is homogeneity.'[10] This perceived lack of differentiation, a

---

Gustave Le Bon and the Crisis of Mass Democracy in the Third Republic (London and Beverly Hills: Sage Publications, 1975); and Susanna Barrows, *Distorting Mirrors: Visions of the Crowd in Late Nineteenth-Century France* (New Haven: Yale University Press, 1981).

[6] W. Trotter, *Instincts of the Herd in Peace and War*, 2nd edn. (London: T. Fisher Unwin, 1923), 99–100. On Trotter and McDougall, see Reba N. Soffer, *Ethics and Society in England: The Revolution in the Social Sciences, 1870–1914* (Berkeley and Los Angeles: University of California Press, 1978), 217–51.

[7] Stuart Macintyre, 'British Labour, Marxism and Working-Class Apathy in the Nineteen-Twenties', *Historical Journal* 20, 2 (1977): 484; David H. Close, 'The Collapse of Resistance to Democracy: Conservatives, Adult Suffrage, and the Second Chamber Reform, 1911–1928', ibid. 20, 4 (1977): 908.

[8] *Evening Standard*, 6 June 1928.

[9] Wyndham Lewis, *The Art of Being Ruled* (London and New York: Harper Brothers, 1926), 90. For three good recent studies of Lewis, see Frederick Jameson, *Fables of Aggression: Wyndham Lewis, the Modernist as Fascist* (Berkeley and Los Angeles: University of California Press, 1979); Jeffrey Meyers, *The Enemy: A Biography of Wyndham Lewis* (London: Routledge and Kegan Paul, 1980); and id., ed., *Wyndham Lewis: A Revaluation* (Montreal: McGill and Queen's University Press, 1980). Some of Lewis's books are being reprinted by the Black Sparrow Press.

[10] Trotter, op. cit., 29.

stock response among intellectuals, may have originated, in part, from a commonplace visual occurrence. From a distance, the eye grasps a large group of people as a whole, an organic unit, rather than a composition of distinct individuals. T. S. Eliot's chilling description in *The Waste Land* of Londoners' daily journey to work, with its imagery of crowds flowing like water, embodied this visually distant, abstract view of the public.[11]

Third, and most important, the public could be easily manipulated, both politically and culturally. The notion that demagogues might sway multitudes dated from the Greeks, and in the inter-war period assumed a particularly sinister relevance. The fear of cultural manipulation, however, though anticipated in earlier thought, became prominent in the late nineteenth century. The emergence of behaviourist psychology, with its central mechanism of stimulus and response, buttressed the equation between the will of the producer and the action of the consumer. 'The modern, democratic world contains so many newly enfranchised and very slightly educated minds,' *The Times* wrote in 1927, 'that it is more important than ever before to prevent their being led astray by ill-chosen ideas of entertainment and interest which only bore and offend those who know more about life.'[12] Since crowds lacked maturity and individuality, it became difficult to imagine them possessing selective judgement. The public became a *tabula rasa* upon which advertisers, press lords, and movie moguls imposed their messages. The notion that supply created demand underlay much of the critique of commercial culture in the early twentieth century and, as we have seen, retains its adherents in some circles today.

Pessimism about the mental life and social behaviour of the British populace helped affirm the uniqueness, autonomy, and cultural centrality of the pessimists themselves. Even for those like the Fabians who sought to defend the working class, the 'masses' never seemed to include intellectuals or other socially prominent allies.[13] This deliberate distancing from the crowd by many writers bespoke a social isolation from the everyday life of average individuals that may not be perplexing in a society segregated by class. It meant, however, that the critique of commercial culture often lacked the open-mindedness and sympathetic understanding which refined individuals claimed as one product of a privileged background: for some people, education narrowed the mind. At the same time, however, critiques of a single medium by many writers often embodied far greater subtlety, complexity, and ambiguity than the general attitude towards commercialism usually permitted. In the process of focusing their attention

---

[11] T. S. Eliot, *The Waste Land*, ll. 60–8.
[12] 'False Values', *The Times*, 22 Mar. 1927.
[13] On Fabian culture, see Ian Brittain, *Fabianism and Culture: A Study of British Socialism and the Arts, c.1884–1918* (Cambridge: Cambridge University Press, 1982).

on a single medium or manifestation of commercial culture, analysts of the popular press, cinema, and jazz occasionally came to surprising conclusions.

The popular press attracted considerable attention in the early twentieth century and retained its defenders, especially among those who enunciated the ideals of classical Liberalism. One of the most eloquent of these was R. A. Scott-James, an Oxford-educated journalist and literary critic who in 1913 published *The Influence of the Press*. This complex, balanced book argued that 'the task of the popular Press—no matter what the motives with which it was founded—was that of bringing the mass of the people into the corporate, conscious life of the community.' Unlike some nineteenth-century Liberals, whose fear of democracy tempered their faith in individual freedom and autonomy, Scott-James extended the range of his assumptions beyond the safe confines of the middle-class. Though disturbed by the monopolistic impulses of the press lords, he rejected the notion of the popular reading public as passive, inert receptacles of manipulative commercialism. The press, he argued, 'communicates only what people are willing to receive. So far as it is expressive, it is expressive of the reader no less than the writer.' He also refused to sentimentalize the decline of the traditional political editor, whose long leaders and willingness to reprint uncut parliamentary speeches lost circulation in the early twentieth century. Quoting Lord Rosebery, he asked, 'Did any reader of the last twenty years ever read the speeches that were reported?'[14] Scott-James complimented the popular press for creating a wider definition of news, and though wary of its excesses, refused to judge it by the standards of a tiny minority.

Yet disillusion with the press was much more typical than Liberal optimism. This pessimism reflected in part the complex transformation and eventual decline of Liberalism in the late nineteenth and early twentieth centuries.[15] Writers from a wide range of backgrounds lamented the emergence of newspapers which no longer instructed the public in an appropriate manner. In a pamphlet for the National Labour Press published in 1919, F. H. Hayward and B. N. Langdon-Davis complained that the popular press was 'not the educational institution it should be'. Herbert Read claimed that 'an intelligent man ought to be ashamed of

---

[14] R. A. Scott-James, *The Influence of the Press* (London: S. W. Partridge [1913]), 287, 28, 276.

[15] On the decline of Liberalism in Britain, see, among others, D. A. Hamer, *Liberal Politics in the Age of Gladstone and Rosebery* (Oxford: Clarendon Press, 1972); H. V. Emy, *Liberals, Radicals and Social Politics, 1892–1914* (Cambridge: Cambridge University Press, 1973); and Trevor Wilson, *The Downfall of the Liberal Party, 1914–1935* (London: Collins, 1966). See also Michael Freeden, *Liberalism Divided: A Study in British Political Thought, 1914–1939* (Oxford: Clarendon Press, 1986).

devoting more than ten minutes a day to his newspaper,' and in his autobiography, R. G. Collingwood recalled that his alienation from democracy began with the founding of the *Daily Mail*, 'the first English newspaper for which the word "news" lost its old meaning of facts which a reader ought to know if he was to vote intelligently'.[16]

The popular press, its critics reiterated, appealed to the lower instincts and sensations. 'What does the public want?' Wickham Stead asked rhetorically. 'As a rule, it wants emotions.'[17] This sensationalism assumed many forms. It meant, for some, that women's concerns became elevated out of proportion to their objective merit. 'How womanized the popular Press has become,' St John Ervine observed unhappily.[18] Others shared the concern. 'Her slightest and most inconsequential doings', David Ockham wrote in 1927, 'are regarded as of the most compelling interest.' This trivialization, he continued, became compounded by the press's increasing reliance on images, rather than words, to convey its information. The camera invaded privacy and press photographs, like the cinema, played 'largely to a class which is easier to reach through the eye than through an appeal to the intellect'.[19] Northcliffe epitomized the unscrupulous forces which gained control of Fleet Street. Though Arnold Bennett tried to draw a three-dimensional portrait of the press baron in his drama *What the Public Wants*, others sought no such balance in their assessments. J. Middleton Murry in an essay entitled 'Northcliffe as Symbol' accused his subject of democratic tyranny and 'the total rejection of all notion of moral value'. In *Caliban*, published in 1920, W. L. George created a fictional character similar to Northcliffe who pandered to the public's taste for sensation, bullied his subordinates, despised culture, and said of the avant-garde: 'Give me the yellow press rather than the *Yellow Book*.' A. G. Gardiner called Northcliffe 'the most sinister influence that has ever corrupted the soul of English journalism'.[20]

The tension between a residual Liberal optimism and an emergent pessimism about the daily press became manifest in the writings of Norman Angell, the controversial author of *The Great Illusion* and winner in 1933 of the Nobel Peace Prize. Born in Lincolnshire in 1872, Angell began

[16] F. H. Hayward and B. N. Langdon-Davis, *Democracy and the Press* (London: National Labour Press [1919]), 16–17; Herbert Read, review of *The Truth Behind Publishing* by Stanley Unwin, *Monthly Criterion* 6, 1 (1927): 83; R. G. Collingwood, *An Autobiography* (London: Oxford University Press, 1939), 155.

[17] Wickham Stead, *Journalism* (London: Ernest Benn, 1928), 10.

[18] St John Ervine, *The Future of the Press* (London: World's Press News [1933]), 15.

[19] David Ockham, *Stentor, or the Press of To-Day and Tomorrow* (London: Kegan Paul, Trench, Trubner [1927]), 54–5, 80.

[20] John Middleton Murry, 'Northcliffe as Symbol', *Adelphi* NS 1 (1930): 15; W. L. George, *Caliban* (New York and London: Harper Brothers, 1920), 243; A. G. G [ardiner], *The Daily Mail and the Liberal Press* (London: Daily News [1914]), 16.

writing for newspapers at the age of fifteen. A few years later, restless and in search of adventure, he travelled to America where he worked as a cowboy before returning to England and a career in journalism and social reform. In 1904, Northcliffe offered him the editorship of the Continental edition of the *Daily Mail*, a post he held for eight years and one which confirmed his distrust of popular journalism.[21] In his youth an acolyte of John Stuart Mill, Angell became a prolific, stinging critic of Fleet Street. Popular daily newspapers, he wrote in *The Press and the Organization of Society*, published in 1922, 'pander to the instincts and emotions that can be most rapidly excited'. They represent ' a progressive debasement of the public mind and judgement'. Four years later, in a book that decried the exploitation of the public, he argued that the 'supreme paradox' of Northcliffe's career was that his political influence derived from publishing newspapers which eschewed politics. 'It was because of his sports or his fashion page,' he complained, '. . . that Northcliffe was an enormous force in deciding the issues of Free Trade and Protection, peace and war.'[22] Yet for Angell, this attack on sensationalism and its ironic consequences could not shake his abiding faith in human rationality, the assumption which buttressed his efforts to prevent war in *The Great Illusion*, published in 1910, and in the 1920s to reform journalism. As he recalled in his autobiography:

If any progress . . . was to be made against the prevailing disorders of the public mind, that mind had to be reached largely through the Press. How could this be done? How could sense and rationalism be made as attractive as the Hearsts and Harmsworths seemed to make nonsense and irrationalism? . . . In seeking some solution of that problem it did not help very much merely to abuse the Press lords—which the highbrows and intelligentsia did so plentifully. If the 'big' public, as distinct from the small minority, simply would not read the better type of newspaper, it became an impossibility to reach that public through that kind of paper. This was the dilemma.[23]

Angell's continuing adherence to Liberal freedoms prohibited him from recommending authoritarian or paternalistic solutions. Instead he believed, although with diminishing enthusiasm, that better education would

---

[21] See his autobiography: Norman Angell, *After All* (London: Hamish Hamilton, 1951). Angell's personal papers are stored at Ball State University, Muncie, IN.

[22] Id., *The Press and the Organization of Society* (London: Labour Publishing, 1922), 23; id., *The Public Mind: Its Disorders, Its Exploitation* (London: Noel Douglas, 1926), 157.

[23] Id., *After All*, 108. Angell's early optimism and idealism about the popular press manifested itself in a letter to Northcliffe, probably written around 1910: 'your business could, as part of its ordinary commercial enterprise, re-cast the education of Great Britain and place the coming generation indubitably at the head of European civilization.' Ralph Lane to Northcliffe, n.d., Northcliffe Papers, British Library, Deposit 4890, vol. 64. Angell's original name was Ralph Lane.

inoculate the public against appeals to their lower instincts. The press freedoms, which to Liberals in the nineteenth century so triumphantly assured an informed citizenry, became in the early twentieth century a licence to sensationalism which Angell and others felt virtually powerless to combat. So they raged bitterly against the dying of the light.

Unlike the press, the neoteric cinema lacked a tradition of upper-class involvement. Nevertheless, complaints against its sensationalism frequently paralleled those directed at popular journalism and, like those aimed at the press, emanated from a variety of sources. In 1923, General Booth of the Salvation Army called the cinema 'most disgusting and absolutely unfit for public exhibition' and there were similar objections from other professional moral guardians and their sympathizers.[24] Film censorship took many forms, but Britain never experienced the intensity of moral concern and provincial resistance to film endured in the United States.[25] In Britain, rejection of the cinema, like its gradual acceptance, centred on aesthetic, not moral grounds. As Arnold Bennett, who himself wrote for film, observed, 'The screen has laid hands on some of the greatest stories in the world, and has cheapened, soiled, ravaged, and poisoned them by the crudest fatuities.'[26] Writing in the *Daily Mail* in 1930, a young and by then only recently successful Evelyn Waugh reiterated this conventional theme. 'There is hardly a single film', he claimed, 'for which one does not have to make allowances. One has to make a deliberate effort to put oneself into the state of mind to accept and enjoy the second-rate.'[27]

A number of significant literary figures, however, held more complex views. 'I am very fond of the movies,' Bernard Shaw acknowledged in 1927. 'I am what they call in America a "movie fan".'[28] As early as 1914, Shaw defended film against unnamed moral critics by arguing, with his customary adroitness, that cinema adopted a bland morality because it courted a world-wide, ethically heterogeneous audience.[29] Yet, perhaps Shaw never completely understood the special nature of the medium. In 1920 he refused a million dollars for the film rights to his entire corpus

---

[24] Quoted in Low, *British Film, 1918–1929*, 18. For a more sustained attack on the morality of cinema, see R. G. Burnett and E. D. Martell, *The Devil's Camera: Menace of a Film-ridden World* (London: Epworth Press, 1932).

[25] On the United States, see Sklar, *Movie-Made America*, 122–40.

[26] Quoted in Low, op. cit., 19.

[27] Evelyn Waugh, 'For Adult Audiences', *Daily Mail*, 25 July 1930. For an earlier example of the popular press criticizing the intellectual standards of the cinema, see 'Stupid Film Incidents', *Daily Mail*, 2 Oct. 1920.

[28] Quoted in Donald P. Costello, 'George Bernard Shaw and the Motion Picture: His Theory and Practice' (Ph.D. diss., University of Chicago, 1962), 1.

[29] G[eorge] B[ernard] S[haw], 'The Cinema as a Moral Leveller', *New Statesman*, Special Supplement on the Modern Theatre, 27 June 1914, 1–2.

because, as he explained later, 'a play with the words left out is a play spoiled.' In 1924, he predicted that 'the film play of the future will have no pictures and will consist exclusively of sub-titles.' With the arrival of sound, he equated drama and film, and became much more enthusiastic about selling his work to Hollywood. 'I am extremely anxious to have all my plays filmed before I die,' he acknowledged in 1933. With the exception of *Pygmalion*, however, few of his plays became successful films, in part because Shaw tenaciously resisted any alteration of his work to fit the constraints of the medium.[30] Throughout his career, he considered cinema to be filmed theatre and missed almost entirely its capacity to narrate events and move audiences through a succession of images. Like a number of his contemporaries, Shaw apprehended brilliantly the power, range, beauty, and subtlety of aural communication, but remained unimaginative, even inert, to visual appeals.

Virginia Woolf grasped the visual essence of film intuitively, and like one of her more memorable characters, from A to Z. In an essay 'The Movies and Reality', published in 1926, she wondered why films so rarely explored their unrealized potentialities. Here was a medium that in an instant permitted the eye to transcend time and space and thereby enter a world 'with a different reality from that which we perceive in daily life'. Cinema ought not be confused with theatre, she claimed, and proved disastrous when it sought to transcribe literature to the screen. Characters and situations which in novels evoked rich, infinitely varied imaginative representations in the different minds of individual readers were reduced to crude semiotic representations by literal-minded film-makers. 'A kiss is love. A broken cup is jealousy. A grin is happiness. Death is a hearse.' Eventually, Woolf conjectured, cinema would discover an appropriate visual language which transformed the medium into something approaching its technological promise: 'Something abstract, something which moves with controlled and conscious art, something which calls for the very slightest help from words or music to make itself intelligible, yet justly uses them subserviently — of such movements and abstractions the films may, in time to come, be composed.' In the mean time, the cinema would remain an extraordinary anomaly among the arts; a medium which could say everything 'before it has anything to say'.[31]

Woolf's imaginative excursion into film criticism demonstrated that literary figures could transcend their own aesthetic traditions. Yet, while

---

[30] George Bernard Shaw, *The Collected Screenplays of Bernard Shaw*, ed. Bernard F. DuKore (Athens: University of Georgia Press, 1980), 7; George Bernard Shaw and Archibald Henderson, 'The Drama, the Theatre, and the Films', *Fortnightly Review* 122 (1924): 294; Costello, 'Shaw', 62, (and see p. 96 for *Pygmalion*).
[31] Virginia Woolf, 'The Movies and Reality' (1926), in *Authors on Film*, ed. Harry M. Geduld (Bloomington: Indiana University Press, 1972), 87, 88, 90, 91.

granting a glorious future to the cinema, Woolf denied it a past and present. One film star who gained wide admiration among intellectuals in the 1920s, both in Britain and on the Continent, was Charlie Chaplin, 'the only genius the cinema has produced'.[32] It was not simply that Chaplin's extraordinary comic talent impressed even the most obstinate critics of film. Writers also recognized that he vaulted boundaries between popular and élite culture that increasingly seemed insurmountable. He acted as a bridge, Bertram Higgens argued in the *Spectator* in 1923, between a minority art which lacked flexibility and the majority's entertainment which needed more self-control.[33] Moreover, Chaplin protested in his films against many of the same social trends which intellectuals feared and rejected. 'This figure of "Charlie"', John Middleton Murry wrote in 1924, '. . . represents an attitude of rebellion against the mechanism of life. . . . He is the under-dog, who wages his incessant and spontaneous warfare against institutions and the lie of moribund ideals.'[34] Chaplin's ability to universalize the protest against subordination thus encompassed alienated intellectuals who, like so many other members of the public, saw in his work the embodiment of their own frustrations.

Chaplin began making longer, more carefully crafted films after the First World War, a time in Britain when film commentary and criticism became more extensive and legitimate. Both the quality and popular national press hired critics whose film reviews indicated that the cinema, like the theatre, deserved serious notice. C. A. Lejeune became a film critic for the *Manchester Guardian* in 1922 and six years later joined the *Observer*, where she became an established figure. Macer Wright reviewed for the *Westminster Gazette*, and Ivor Montagu, one of the founders of the Film Society, wrote for a number of papers before joining the *Sunday Times* as its regular critic in 1927. The *Fortnightly Review*, *New Statesman*, *London Mercury*, and *English Review*, among others, also included occasional critiques in their pages.[35] Of the regular film critics during the 1920s, however, Iris Barry probably enjoyed the most respect. A reviewer for both the *Spectator* and the *Daily Mail*, Barry published in 1926 *Let's Go to the Pictures*, one of the earliest books in Britain to discuss film seriously. Acting as analyst, critic, and advocate of the popular cinema, Barry alerted her readers to the visual literacy

---

[32] [John Middleton Murry] ['Henry King', pseud.], 'Chaplin and the Hicks', *Adelphi* 3, 5 (1925): 335.

[33] Bertram Higgens, 'Charles Chaplin's Comedy of Shyness', *Spectator*, 8 Sept. 1923, 318.

[34] John Middleton Murry, *To the Unknown God: Essays Towards a Religion* (London: Jonathan Cape, 1924), 110–11. See also Desmond MacCarthy, 'Charlie's Cane', *New Statesman*, 8 Sept. 1923, 618–19. For an unfavourable view of Chaplin, see Wyndham Lewis, *Time and Western Man* (Boston: Beacon Press, 1957), 66–7.

[35] Low, *British Film, 1918–29*, 20.

which film unconsciously inculcated among its enthusiasts. 'Every habitual cinema-goer must have been struck at some time or another by the comparative slowness of perception and understanding of a person not accustomed to the pictures: the newcomer nearly always misses half of what occurs.' Film was not theatre, she reiterated: it was not 'drama with the words left out'. Rather it developed according to its own rules, which needed sympathetic understanding for the medium to be enjoyed. Though often intensely critical of individual films, Barry accepted their formulaic nature as central to their popularity. The cinema, she declared, fulfilled Tolstoy's dictum that art should be intelligible to the simplest people.[36]

Barry's book, like Woolf's imaginative essay, Shaw's skewed advocacy, and the general acclaim for Chaplin, illustrates the range of favourable opinion about film among intellectuals in the 1920s. Jazz attracted less extensive, but more impassioned written comment during this period. Critics levelled three interrelated accusations against the new music. First, jazz represented a particularly offensive triumph of the lower instincts over the higher faculties. It was 'sensual, noisy and incredibly stupid', Sir Hamilton Harty told the National Union of Organists' Associations in 1926. It was, G. K. Chesterton added somewhat later, 'the expression of the pessimistic idea that nature never gets beyond nature, that life never rises above life, that man always finds himself back where he was at the beginning.'[37] In some quarters, jazz became the focus of attacks against the ongoing sexual revolution after the First World War. It became emblematic of the freedoms from Victorian restraints which many found so troubling. Second, critics alleged that jazz lacked musical originality, one of its most widely claimed virtues. Ernest Newman, the influential music critic for the *Sunday Times*, took this tack on a number of occasions. 'Your typical jazz composer', he wrote in 1926, '. . . is merely a musical illiterate who is absurdly pleased with little things because he does not know how little they are.'[38] Third and finally, the critique of jazz often involved overt racial slurs, intended to discredit the music by associating it with its presumed savage origins. 'We may be thankful', a regular contributor to the *Musical Times* wrote in 1926, 'that the "artistic" ascendancy of the nigger is far less marked here than in America.'[39] Clive Bell, writing in the *New Republic* in 1921, spoke bitterly of the impudence of 'those who sat drinking their cocktails and listening to nigger bands. . . . Niggers can be admired artists without any gift more singular than

---

[36] Iris Barry, *Let's Go to the Pictures* (London: Chatto and Windus, 1926), 13, 28, ix.

[37] Harty quoted in 'Accursed Jazz: An English View', *Literary Digest*, 2 Oct. 1926, 28; G. K. Chesterton, *Avowals and Denials* (New York: Dodd, Mead, 1935), 103. See also Cecil Austin, 'Jazz', *Music and Letters* 6, 3 (1925): 256–68.

[38] Quoted in *New York Times*, 12 Sept. 1926.

[39] 'Ad Libitum', *Musical Times* 67, 1002 (1926): 697.

high spirits: so why drag in the intellect?'[40] Jazz represented a rebellion not only of the lower instincts, but of an 'inferior' race against European 'civilization'.

Yet as Bell acknowledged sadly, jazz also attracted its defenders among the young and the sophisticated. In *The Appeal of Jazz*, published in 1927, R. W. S. Mendl provided the same kind of pioneering advocacy for jazz that Iris Barry offered for the cinema. Mendl's analysis, while far from brilliant, answered systematically the charges against the new music. It was, he argued, no more sensual than many waltzes, no louder than an orchestra playing *forte*. This 'folk music of the present generation' permeated all classes, transcended national boundaries, and appealed to all races. It drew upon a number of precedents in European music, but derived its powerful rhythmic patterns from Africa and America. The ephemerality of its individual tunes, Mendl claimed, could be explained in part by the technology that reproduced it. 'No music in the world has had to stand such constant repetition.'[41] Eminent musicians rejected jazz because it lacked tradition, he concluded, but it represented the post-war discontent with the nineteenth century and this rebellion itself would some day become a commonplace.

Mendl's recognition that what some considered illegitimate contemporary music would eventually coalesce into a respectable tradition linked his defence of jazz with some of the other, more favourable analyses of cinema and the popular press in the early twentieth century. The apprehension that commercial culture stimulated the lower, more dangerous instincts became less fearful when placed in historical context. Scott-James's defence of the popular press involved granting the same cultural autonomy to the lower-middle and working classes which the upper classes claimed for themselves in the nineteenth century. Virginia Woolf's analysis of the cinema turned on her perception that film needed time to fulfil the potential which its technology always promised. Time cushioned the shock of the new; tradition conveyed legitimacy.

It was this allegiance to an appropriate tradition that helped shape the discourse concerning the Americanization of the crowd and its culture in Britain. The relationship between America and Britain first became a sub-theme of British writing in the nineteenth century, when a number of travellers recorded their often caustic impressions of the New World. Mrs Trollope, Dickens, and others shared a patronizing disdain for the externals of American behaviour and converted this snobbery into lucrative sources of income. Matthew Arnold departed American shores, the *New York Tribune* remarked sardonically, with '$6,000 of the Philistines'

---

[40] Clive Bell, 'Plus De Jazz', *New Republic*, 21 Sept. 1921, 94, 93.
[41] Mendl, *Appeal of Jazz*, 76, 118.

money in his pockets'.[42] Other nineteenth-century Englishmen expressed more enthusiasm for American values. As one recent historian has carefully calculated, it was an unrepresentative sample of the English who travelled to the United States and who influenced opinion among the cultivated classes. The poor stayed at home or, in numbers that far dwarfed those of its critics, emigrated to America.[43]

Two recurring themes within the critique of America and Americanization dovetailed into the attack on commercial culture and the mass media. First, some argued that, as the British press, cinema, and popular music became increasingly Americanized, rampant materialism and obsessive attention to economic self-interest would triumph over concern for the higher pleasures in life. Secondly, it was claimed that American egalitarianism threatened to undermine the traditional social and culture hierarchies which had nourished European civilization since antiquity. Neither of these criticisms was unique to British commentators. Indeed, some of the most searing observations about American life in the early twentieth century came from American intellectuals, whose ideas British writers appropriated freely and occasionally without acknowledgement. Robert Lynd's *Middletown*, Sinclair Lewis's *Babbitt*, and the essays of H. L. Mencken became authoritative sources about American life in some British circles.[44] Complaints by American intellectuals about their own marginal status and eloquent denunciations of the superficial, empty lives of their compatriots became an awful warning to British writers about what the future might bring.

[42] Quoted in Richard L. Rapson, *Britons View America: Travel Commentary, 1860–1935* (Seattle: University of Washington Press, 1971), 13. On Britain and America, see also, among others, Allan Nevins, *America Through British Eyes* (New York: Oxford University Press, 1948); H. A. Tulloch, 'Changing British Attitudes Towards the United States in the 1880s', *Historical Journal* 20, 4 (1977): 825–40; Bradford Perkins, *The Great Rapprochement: England and the United States, 1895–1914* (New York: Atheneum, 1968), 144–55; Richard Heathcote Heindel, *The American Impact on Great Britain, 1898–1914: A Study of the United States in World History* (Philadelphia: University of Pennsylvania Press, 1940); George Harmon Knoles, *The Jazz Age Revisited: British Criticism of American Civilization During the 1920s* (Stanford: Stanford University Press; Oxford: Oxford University Press, 1955); and Henry Pelling, *America and the British Left: From Bright to Bevan* (London: Adam and Charles Black, 1956).

[43] For statistics on the background of British travellers, see Rapson, op. cit., 198–200. See also Bruce M. Russett, *Community and Contention: Britain and America in the Twentieth Century* (Cambridge: MIT Press, 1963), 101–2; and, for a contemporary comment on what type of English citizens visited America, see Douglas Woodruff, *Plato's American Republic* (New York: E. P. Dutton, 1926), 100–1.

[44] For the reactions of American intellectuals to mass media, see Daniel J. Czitrom, *Media and the American Mind: From Morse to McLuhan* (Chapel Hill: University of North Carolina Press, 1982). See also Catherine L. Covert and John D. Stevens, eds., *Mass Media Between the Wars: Perceptions of Cultural Tension, 1918–1941* (Syracuse: Syracuse University Press, 1984); and David A. Richards, 'America Conquers Britain: Anglo-American Conflict in the Popular Media During the 1920s', *Journal of American Culture* 3, 1 (1980): 95–104.

The concern over American materialism involved a cluster of related concepts. By associating materialism with a foreign country, writers uncoupled the pursuit of wealth from what some presumed to be the more unworldly character of the 'authentic' Englishman. In the early and mid-nineteenth century, the urban industrial North of England had been the symbol and geographical focus of material, bourgeois pursuits which, some maintained, clashed with the more genuinely English, rural, and aristocratic values of the South. In the late nineteenth and early twentieth centuries, the geographic representative of commercial values shifted from the North of England to rapidly industrializing America and, as Martin Wiener has argued, the distrust of materialism became symptomatic of an important cultural transformation in Britain.[45] The equation between materialism and the United States allowed predominantly middle-class writers in England to appropriate for themselves aristocratic loathing of pecuniary gain, while at the same time assuming the heroic role of embattled defenders of authentic English values.

Although some writers acknowledged that the pursuit of wealth imbued Americans with great energy and vitality, the Americanization of English culture provoked especially pained outbursts after the First World War.[46] No area of English life, it seemed, escaped American influences. In an often-cited passage from his book *This American World*, Edgar Ansel Mowrer traced in vivid detail how American products and culture permeated the daily life of an average European.[47] Daphne du Maurier recalled in her memoir on the English theatre that 'to make money, more money, and yet more money, was the only goal in mind. . . . The American invasion began, and the English stage was swamped. . . . Box-office returns were of sole importance in this trade that was no longer an art or a profession.'[48] Despite its English roots, advertising became the embodiment of American materialism. 'Never shall you forget', G. Lowes Dickinson wrote in parody of an advertiser, 'that nothing matters — nothing in the whole universe — except the maintenance and extension of industry.'[49] Advertisers ruined whatever they touched. Their hoardings destroyed the tranquillity of the countryside and cluttered urban vistas. Their insistent demands trivialized the press and eroded its editorial

---

[45] Martin J. Wiener, *English Culture and the Decline of the Industrial Spirit, 1850–1980* (Cambridge: Cambridge University Press, 1981).

[46] Rapson, op. cit., 67–8.

[47] Edgar Ansel Mowrer, *This American World* (London: Faber and Gwyer, n.d.), 136–8.

[48] Daphne du Maurier, *Gerald: A Portrait* (Garden City: Doubleday, Doran, 1935), 202.

[49] G. Lowes Dickinson, *Appearances: Notes on Travel, East and West* (Garden City: Doubleday, Page, 1915), 188–9.

independence. Dishonest appeals promised a happiness their products could not deliver.[50]

It was not just the corrosive solvent of American materialism which threatened the integrity of English culture. America also imported notions of equality which some observers claimed to be profoundly antithetical to English tradition. In the nineteenth century, Tocqueville's analysis of the egalitarian impulse in American character influenced British observers such as James Bryce, who in *The American Commonwealth* asserted that 'the belief in the rights of the majority lies very near to the belief that the majority must be right.'[51] Although British writers employed the term 'equality' ambiguously, applying it in different ways to politics, social relations, and other topics,[52] many considered egalitarianism, like materialism, an alien, regrettable, and increasingly dominant trend in British life. Of the major states in the modern world, Hilaire Belloc argued in *The Contrast*, America was 'by far the most egalitarian' and England 'still by far the most aristocratic. And though it appears that this aristocratic tradition of England is to-day sinking, it will only so sink at the expense of English strength and greatness.'[53] In *Jesting Pilate*, first published in 1926, Aldous Huxley denounced egalitarian doctrine, enunciated confidently in America and with increasing shrillness in England, as 'a most elaborate system of humbug'. D. H. Lawrence observed in his *Studies in Classic American Literature* that 'somewhere deep in every American heart lies a rebellion against the old parenthood of Europe. . . . Democracy in America is just the tool with which the old mastery of Europe, the European spirit, is undermined.' T. S. Eliot, Wyndham Lewis, and a number of other writers agreed.[54]

Egalitarianism threatened culture, it was argued, because in matters of taste not all individuals are equal. The creation and appreciation of art required talent, training, and experience none of which the general population shared in equal proportions. Indeed, it was the scarcity of artistic genius which made it so valuable. Any mechanism, and especially

---

[50] C. E. M. Joad, *The Babbitt Warren* (London: Kegan Paul, Trench, Trubner, 1926), 124-8; Clough Williams-Ellis, *England and the Octopus* (London: Geoffrey Bles, 1928), 127-30; C. E. M. Joad, *The Horrors of the Countryside* (London: Hogarth Press, 1931); J. A. Spender, *Through English Eyes* (New York: Frederick A. Stokes, 1928), 204-5.
    [51] James Bryce, *The American Commonwealth*, vol. 3 (London: Macmillan, 1888), 124.   [52] Rapson, op. cit., 56-7.
    [53] Hilaire Belloc, *The Contrast* (London: J. W. Arrowsmith, 1923), 276-77. For Belloc and America, see A. N. Wilson, *Hilaire Belloc* (London: Hamish Hamilton, 1984), 75-6, 273-4.
    [54] Aldous Huxley, *Jesting Pilate: The Diary of a Journey* (New York: George H. Doran, 1926), 310; D. H. Lawrence, *Studies in Classic American Literature* (New York: Thomas Selzer, 1923), 6, 12; John R. Harrison, *The Reactionaries: Yeats, Lewis, Pound, Eliot, Lawrence: A Study of the Anti-Democratic Intelligentsia* (New York: Schocken Books, 1967).

the market-place, which permitted a vast majority of mediocre, untutored, and naïve voices to dictate taste doomed genuine art to the margins, perhaps even to extinction. Élitism was as intrinsic to culture, the argument suggested, as majority rule was to political democracy. This defence of élite culture echoed many of the same arguments against the Reform Bills of 1832 and 1867. Those who feared political democracy in the nineteenth century shared much in common with those who struggled against cultural egalitarianism in the twentieth. Both pointed to the inherent superiority of some individuals over others; both invoked the binding role of tradition; both acknowledged and considered tragic the inevitable defeat of their own positions.

There was much in modernity that Modernists despised. For many, the culture of the crowd, with its appeals to the lower instincts and sensations, promised a bleak, Americanized future. Even intelligent supporters of the cinema admitted that, despite its revolutionary potential, film usually delivered much less than met the eye. Intellectuals on the Right, such as T. S. Eliot and Wyndham Lewis, condemned both the public and its manipulators, while writers on the Left such as the Fabians, who often hoped to lead the triumph of the common individual, rejected the ascendancy of its commercial culture. Yet, it was one thing to distance oneself from the flat, American plains of the crowd and its banal tastes. It was quite another to chart the heights which offered salvation from the wasteland below.

B. ART AND THE DEFENCE OF CULTURAL ÉLITISM

If, as a number of British intellectuals asserted, commercial culture proved sensational, materialistic, and ominously egalitarian, it did possess one enviable trait. The market-place provided the producers of commercial culture with a yardstick of success or failure that involved few ambiguities or uncertainties. Box-office receipts, circulation statistics, advertising revenue, and profit margins could all be measured in precise, mathematical terms. Élite culture, on the other hand, possessed no such convenient, reasonably certain mechanism to determine the aesthetic merit and, more important, future endurance of its contemporary artefacts. 'When once this question of Beauty comes in,' Roger Fry observed in one of his last lectures, 'we find ourselves in a world of strong convictions based on no demonstrable reasons, of feelings vehement in proportion to their insecurity —a world where intensity of conviction, force of character and eloquence of expression sway opinion in default of more solid arguments.'[55] In aesthetics, virtually everything became debatable.

[55] Roger Fry, *Last Lectures* (1939; reprinted Boston: Beacon Press, 1962), 4.

Intellectuals separated themselves from the crowd and from each other by asserting individualistic, endlessly negotiable hierarchies in which distinctions flowed from acts of the imagination and could not be objectively verified. These imagined distances between high and low, success and failure, acceptable and objectionable, became particularly significant in literary discourse, the focus of cultural criticism in Britain during the nineteenth and early twentieth centuries. For purposes here, three aspects of this discourse will be discussed in greater detail; first, the pervasive notion of the autonomy of art and the artist, asserted with particular clarity within the Bloomsbury coterie; second, the tensions and contradictions that emerged from this assertion; and finally, how the advent of 'practical criticism' at Cambridge University in the 1920s resolved some of these contradictions, while creating new problems of its own.

Despite their many fractious disagreements, most British intellectuals in the early twentieth century agreed that authentic art transcended the conventional limitations of time, place, social class, and individual psychology. Though the descriptions of this autonomy varied enormously, Edwardian realists and Bloomsbury aesthetes acquiesced in the central premiss of the argument.[56] Unlike worldly, transient commercial culture, a great painting or piece of literature embodied insights that survived over generations. 'Art is identical with the idea of permanence,' one character remarked in Wyndham Lewis's *Tarr*, published in 1918. 'It is a continuity and not an individual spasm.'[57] This timelessness, a theme with a lengthy pedigree in the Western tradition but especially prominent among the British Romantic poets,[58] gave to art an aura of immortality that defied historical necessity. Novels, poems, and paintings might be created in a particular time and place, and depict a highly specific social setting, but they also embodied fundamental truths about the essence of human nature and the human condition that went beyond the boundaries of the mundane, phenomenal world.

This notion of permanence affected how some viewed the role of tradition in art. T. S. Eliot conceived of the relationship between past and present in a way that at once both invoked and expelled history from the act of creation. In 'Tradition and the Individual Talent', one of the most influential essays of literary criticism in the inter-war period, Eliot argued that the genuine artist contributed towards and subtly altered the overall configuration of artistic tradition. 'The historical sense compels a man to write not merely with his own generation in his bones, but with

---

[56] See Stephen Spender, *The Struggle of the Modern* (Berkeley and Los Angeles: University of California Press, 1963), 51.

[57] Wyndham Lewis, *Tarr* (New York: Alfred A. Knopf, 1918), 353.

[58] See David Perkins, *The Quest for Permanence: The Symbolism of Wordsworth, Shelley and Keats* (Cambridge: Harvard University Press, 1965).

a feeling that the whole of the literature of Europe from Homer and within it the whole of the literature of his own country has a simultaneous existence and composes a simultaneous order. This historical sense,' Eliot continued, 'which is a sense of the timeless as well as of the temporal and of the timeless and of the temporal together, is what makes a writer traditional.'[59] Eliot thus managed to transform 'history' and 'tradition' into virtually static, ahistorical categories in which all artists suddenly became recognizable, if not always congenial, contemporaries. Art contributed to an order that transcended the exigencies and petty social conflicts of any given time and place.

It was also argued that art transcended the personal limitations and often annoying idiosyncrasies of the artists who created it. Eliot insisted upon the 'impersonality' of the poet and became exasperated by attempts in his later life to discover the personal origins of his most famous poems. For Eliot, as for many others in the period, it was inappropriate to reduce the ineffable to the biographical. If commercial culture profited by the identification between audience and creator, the avant-garde loathed such familiarity. Art transcended both artist and audience, although as at least some acknowledged, it was not always possible to separate the dancer from the dance. The Romantics and other nineteenth-century writers never tired of emphasizing how aesthetic creation involved a heroic struggle to overcome the economic hardship, rejection, and discouragement which inevitably blocked the path of the true artistic genius. For many of its practitioners, the very immortality of great art redeemed and sanctified the bitterness, self-doubt, and deprivation which often lay at the core of its creation.

If few denied the permanence of art, the nature of the aesthetic experience often became the subject of controversy. How did one experience the 'immortality' of art? Was the event a subjective or an objective one? What was the relationship of art and aesthetic experience to mortality? These and other questions arose, in part, because the moment of engagement between a finite, limited individual and a lasting work of art proved difficult to capture in words and, like religious conversion, almost impossible to convey to someone who had never undergone such a transforming experience. 'It gives us the *feeling* of being beyond life or death,' D. H. Lawrence explained in 1925. 'We say an Assyrian lion or an Egyptian hawk's head "lives". What we really mean is that it is beyond life, and, therefore, beyond death. It gives us that feeling. And there is

---

[59] T. S. Eliot, *The Sacred Wood: Essays on Poetry and Criticism*, 2nd edn. (London: Methuen, 1928), 49. See also Allen Austin, *T. S. Eliot: The Literary and Social Criticism* (Bloomington: Indiana University Press, 1971), 1–3. Laura Riding called 'snobbism' 'a useful refuge from historical necessity' (Laura Riding, *Contemporaries and Snobs* (London: Jonathan Cape, 1928), 110).

something inside us which must also be beyond life and beyond death, since that "feeling" is so infinitely precious to us.'[60] It was, in part, this 'feeling' which made art so valuable to both the creator and the connoisseur. 'The whole purpose of culture', John Cowper Powys claimed in 1929, 'is to enable us to live out our days in a perpetual under-tide of ecstasy.'[61]

Bloomsbury reinforced the claims of artistic autonomy in at least two important ways. First, for many figures within this over-scrutinized yet undeniably significant coterie, G. E. Moore's moral philosophy sanctioned the belief in the objective goodness of aesthetic contemplation as an end in itself. Moore's famous assertion that 'the most valuable things, which we know or can imagine, are certain states of consciousness' provided a philosophic legitimacy to the existing preoccupations of the young Cambridge Apostles who eventually shaped Bloomsbury's thinking.[62] Clive Bell and Roger Fry developed the idea that a special 'aesthetic emotion' contemplated an 'objective' though vaguely defined 'significant form' which differentiated individual works within the visual arts. Perhaps more important, Moore's disciples interpreted his definition of aesthetics to include not only art, but love and friendship. 'The appropriate subjects of passionate contemplation and communion', John Maynard Keynes later recalled, 'were a beloved person, beauty and truth, and one's prime objects in life were love, the creation and enjoyment of aesthetic experience and the pursuit of knowledge.'[63] For many Bloomsbury figures, the objective Good conveniently encompassed the overtly sexual. Aesthetics united the transcendent and the sensual, the spiritual and the homoerotic. Secondly and closely related, Bloomsbury detached art from conventional notions of ethics and social responsibility. 'Agreeing that aesthetic apprehension is a pre-eminently spiritual function', Roger Fry argued in 1924, 'does not imply for me any connection with morals.'[64] Like Oscar Wilde's belief in Art for Art's sake, Bloomsbury converted the social isolation of the aesthete into a positive value. 'Why should artists bother about

[60] D. H. Lawrence, 'Morality and the Novel', *The Calendar of Modern Letters* 2, 10 (1925): 270.
[61] John Cowper Powys, *The Meaning of Culture* (1929; reprinted New York: Garden City Publishers, 1941), 200. On this element in his work, see Morine Krissdottir, *John Cowper Powys and the Magical Quest* (London: Macdonald and Jane's, 1980).
[62] George Edward Moore, *Principia Ethica* (1903; reprinted Cambridge: Cambridge University Press, 1959), 188. The literature on the Bloomsbury circle is enormous. For a good, brief, recent discussion, see Michael Rosenthal, *Virginia Woolf* (London: Routledge and Kegan Paul, 1979), 19–34.
[63] Quoted in Robert Skidelsky, *John Maynard Keynes, vol. 1: Hopes Betrayed, 1883–1920* (London: Macmillan, 1983), 141.
[64] Quoted in Virginia Woolf, *Roger Fry: A Biography* (New York: Harcourt, Brace, 1940), 230. For a more recent biography, see Frances Spalding, *Roger Fry: Art and Life* (Berkeley and Los Angeles: University of California Press, 1980).

the fate of humanity?' Clive Bell asked in 1914. 'If art does not justify itself, aesthetic rapture does.'[65] The artist lived apart from society and owed nothing to it, other than the creation or individual contemplation of Beauty.

Scholars have frequently explored the parallels between art and religion and argued that, beginning with the decline of traditional faith in the nineteenth century, art became analogous to a surrogate religion for a variety of influential British intellectuals.[66] In the early twentieth century, this analogy between two phenomena that claimed transcendent, sacred, visionary powers became common among British writers, especially within the Bloomsbury set, where Clive Bell asserted the equation between the two activities with unabashed directness. 'For art is a religion,' he wrote in 1914. 'It is an expression of and a means to states of mind as holy as any that men are capable of experiencing; and it is towards art that modern minds turn, not only for the most perfect expression of transcendent emotion, but for an inspiration by which to live.'[67] Though Bell later acknowledged that he overstated the argument, the analogy also became the centrepiece of J. Middleton Murry's aesthetic philosophy. In a number of articles written in the 1920s, Murry declared that creative expression originated in religious experience and he even claimed to discover 'the complete congruity, nay, the perfect identity, between the morality of great literature and of the essential teachings of Jesus'.[68] These and other statements by British writers and intellectuals would seem to confirm the intimate, perhaps even causal relationship between the decline of traditional religion and the often impassioned insistence on art as a sacred, transcending reality.

Yet, it is also useful to indicate at least some of the easily ignored if obvious differences between the two activities. First, among high Anglicans, Evangelicals, and Nonconformists, the Church promised that the faithful would experience immortality as 'eternal life', a state that although rarely described concretely by serious theologians, cheated death of its certainty for all those who believed. The experience of immortality portrayed in complex, often symbolic terms by British writers since the

---

[65] Clive Bell, *Art* (1914; reprinted London: Chatto and Windus, 1947), 241.

[66] See, among many others, Graham Hough, *The Last Romantics* (London: Gerald Duckworth, 1949), 24 and *passim*; T. W. Heyck, *The Transformation of Intellectual Life in Victorian England* (London: Croom Helm, 1982), 197; and Joseph Carroll, *The Cultural Theory of Matthew Arnold* (Berkeley and Los Angeles: University of California Press, 1982), 105–23. On the issue of surrogate religions in Victorian life, see Noel Annan, *Leslie Stephen: The Godless Victorian* (London: Wiedenfeld and Nicolson, 1984). For American developments, see James Turner, *Without God, Without Creed: The Origins of Unbelief in America* (Baltimore: Johns Hopkins University Press, 1985).

[67] Bell, op. cit., 277.

[68] John Middleton Murry, *Things To Come* (New York: Macmillan, 1928), 157.

Romantics, involved an intense, visionary episode, experienced only fleetingly by a select few. The feeling of transcendence enunciated by D. H. Lawrence and others shared most with the religious mystics, a small and by no means typical minority among English religious circles. Second, the religion of art involved virtually none of the institutions, rituals, and organized activities that differentiated, solidified, and disciplined the more traditional community of believers. The companionship among artists and other devotees of significant expression bears little resemblance to the planned, predictably structured gatherings of the Christian Church. Third, unlike the prescriptive ethical systems of organized religion, the values imbibed by immersion in the creation or appreciation of great art could rarely be expressed precisely and never involved formal procedures for enforcement. Indeed, any attempt to prescribe lessons culled from masterworks would itself manifest a *naïveté* antithetical to genuine appreciation. In these and other ways then, religion and art occupied quite different terrain. Though artists themselves frequently made direct comparisons between the two, the analogy obscured as much as it revealed. Claims for the transcendence and autonomy of art, so crucial for distinguishing élite culture from its more commercial rivals, acted less as a surrogate for religion than a powerful affirmation of superiority in their own right.

This affirmation was not without its ironies. If genuine art transcended the exigencies of time, space, social class, and individual psychology, it removed itself from the very realities it claimed to illuminate. It deliberately and self-consciously alienated itself from the world over which it announced its universal domain. For a number of intellectuals in the early twentieth century, and for Bloomsbury in particular, art became a sophisticated form of escapism and vicarious self-fulfilment less far removed from the darkened cinemas and noisy dance palaces than it liked to admit. The life of aesthetic contemplation compensated its adherents for the disappointments of everyday life no less directly than commercial culture relieved the monotonies of existence for the average individual. Both temporarily removed its participants from the uncertainties and numbing banalities of daily routine and thrust them into a more ordered, less threatening world, recognizable yet wholly distinct.

The compensations of art, however, often proved difficult to sustain. For the artist in particular, the belief in the transcendence of art collided with a number of uncomfortable realities. The self-image of autonomy created tensions and contradictions which each artist needed to resolve. The first of these tensions attracted the most comment, and itself became an important literary theme in the nineteenth century. Artists needed money and leisure time to develop their talent and create a body of mature work. Ever since the collapse of the patronage system in the eighteenth century, a system which embodied its own threats to artistic integrity, material necessities created temptations among artists to compromise their aesthetic principles. George Gissing's *New Grub Street* became the *locus classicus* of this predicament. Torn between the desire to support a family and create works of enduring value, the central character, Reardon, writes novels that satisfy neither the market nor the critics. Friends who share his artistic integrity become anonymous failures while more cynical writers achieve commercial success and critical influence. In literature, Gissing makes clear, the market corrupts; but he also demonstrates how the self-pity of his main character paralyses his will and assures the collapse of his worthy ambitions.[69]

What Reardon needed was five hundred pounds a year and a room of his own. Virginia Woolf's now famous explanation for the paucity of canonized female writers expressed in specific terms the material requirements of aesthetic creativity. As her husband later recalled, Woolf reached the age of forty before she became capable of supporting herself from the income derived from her writing.[70] Her privileged background diminished the urgent need for such income. One historian calculated that since 1800 97 per cent of all writers came from social strata representing less than 25 per cent of the population.[71] Birth into the middle and upper classes unlatched the gate to more income, education, and leisure time—conditions which unquestionably eased the production of art and reinforced its aristocratic notions of culture. Many respected professional writers, like H. G. Wells and Bernard Shaw, supported themselves handsomely through their writing. Younger, less established and more daring artists, however, confronted formidable economic problems if they chose to ignore the market completely. The letters, memoirs, and other accounts of the more original and artistically influential writers early in the century offer a familiar litany of deprivation and indignity, both real and imagined, endured by the committed author. 'It is true I have no money save what comes from my books—and that is exceedingly little now . . .', D. H. Lawrence wrote an acquaintance in June 1918. 'Since last August I have had considerably less than £100. There is no prospect of my receiving anything worth mention. . . . So I am at a loss.'[72] These struggles produced their understandable share of bitterness, envy, and

---

[69] On *New Grub Street*, see John Halperin, *Gissing: A Life in Books* (Oxford: Oxford University Press, 1982), 141–51; and John Allen Goode, *George Gissing: Ideology and Fiction* (London: Vision Press, 1978), 109–41.

[70] Leonard Woolf, *Downhill All the Way: An Autobiography of the Years 1919–1939* (London: Hogarth Press, 1967), 17.

[71] Altick, 'Sociology of Authorship', in *Bulletin*, 394.

[72] D. H. Lawrence to Arthur Llewelyn Roberts, 14 June 1918, in *The Letters of D. H. Lawrence, vol. 3: October, 1916–June, 1921*, ed. James T. Boulton and Andrew Robertson (Cambridge: Cambridge University Press, 1984), 249.

anxiety. 'I do not think that anyone realized how I *just* managed to live before . . .', Wyndham Lewis recalled in a letter to a friend. 'It is a bad joke I have had enough of—to watch every smooth little clown occupying a fat job, well-paid by state or city, and I wasting 90 per cent of my time trying to scrape a dangerous living.'[73]

Artists and writers devised a number of strategies to cope with the often dreary economic realities of their profession. The Romantics made a virtue of necessity by idealizing the Bohemian existence of the creative artist. Though some modern authors such as Lewis eventually became disillusioned with the callow innocence of this asceticism, the rejection of bourgeois materialism cushioned the lives of those whose dedication most likely precluded such comforts. Eric Gill dressed in peasant clothes and did not expect to live in a suburban villa. Others muddled through with less purity of heart. T. S. Eliot worked in a bank and, to the amusement of his friends and astonishment of his admirers, dressed like a banker. Huxley, Waugh, and Auden briefly taught in schools. Many wrote or painted for money in order to support their more ambitious creations. 'I've been engaged in a great wrangle with an old American called Pearsall Smith on the ethics of writing articles at high rates for the fashion papers like Vogue . . .', Virginia Woolf wrote to a friend in 1925. 'Oh these Americans! How they always muddle everything up! What he wants is prestige: what I want, money.'[74] Such ironic frankness was not universally shared. Arnold Bennett attracted bitter criticism for relishing with boyish enthusiasm the comforts of the *haute bourgeoisie* and aristocratic friendships of his literary success.[75]

Money and leisure not only affected the creation of art, they also significantly influenced its appreciation. 'The man who has been heaving clay out of a ditch, or driving an express train against the north wind all night,' Ruskin once wrote, '. . . is not the same man at the end of his day, or night, as one who has been sitting in a quiet room, with everything comfortable about him.'[76] Civilization, it was widely assumed, demanded a class released from financial anxiety and the deadening effects of physical labour. 'Wherefore the existence of a leisured class, absolutely independent and without obligations,' Clive Bell concluded in 1928, 'is the prime condition, not of civilization only, but of any sort of decent

---

[73] Wyndham Lewis to Eric Kennington, 31 Mar. 1943, in *The Letters of Wyndham Lewis*, ed. W. K. Rose (London: Methuen, 1963), 351.

[74] Virginia Woolf to Jacques Raverat, 25 Jan. 1925, in *The Letters of Virginia Woolf, vol. 3: 1923–1928*, ed. Nigel Nicolson and Joanne Trautmann (New York: Harcourt, Brace, Jovanovich, 1978), 154.

[75] John Gross, *The Rise and Fall of the Man of Letters: A Study of the Idiosyncratic and the Humane in Modern Literature* (New York: Collier Books, 1969), 214–16.

[76] Quoted in J. W. Saunders, *The Profession of English Letters* (London: Routledge and Kegan Paul; Toronto: University of Toronto Press, 1964), 204.

society.'[77] Yet money and leisure could also corrupt taste. Roger Fry warned against the dangers of what he deemed 'Philistinism', 'Culture', and 'Snobbism'. For Fry, as for Matthew Arnold, the 'Philistines' possessed money, but not taste. Like Dickens's Mr Podsnap, they knew nothing about art, but they maintained strong allegiance to their own untutored preferences. 'Culture', on the other hand, involved a highly refined sensibility which dwelt in museums, reverently worshipped established traditions, and hated most contemporary art. Within this universe of discourse, no one could be considered a serious artist 'until a learned monograph has been consecrated to his life work'. 'Snobs' eagerly embraced the most recent artistic trends, but only because they hoped to gain tangible social advantages. They accepted new artistic movements uncritically and remained blind to the deeper values which aesthetic excellence conveyed. In a world of ignorant enemies and dubious friends, Fry concluded, the genuine artist must constantly protest 'against the materialism of Mr. Podsnap, against the pontifical authority of the high priests of Culture, and against the capricious interferences of Snobbism.'[78]

Fry's essay hinted at the complexities ignored by those who complacently accepted the cultural role of social inequality. He provided an insider's perspective on an enclave which outsiders often perceived monolithically. Yet, what Fry diagnosed as infecting the leisured audience, some claimed debilitated artistic creation as well. In *The Apes of God*, first published in 1930, Wyndham Lewis blasted the fashionably Bohemian children of the privileged classes who posed as artists and flirted with its risks. In Paris and London, 'these masses of Gossip-mad, vulgar, pseudo-artist, *good-timers*—the very freedom and excess usually of whose life implies a considerable total of money, concentrated in the upkeep of this costly "bohemian" life—are the last people, as every artist will tell you, from whom support for any art can be expected.' It was in Bloomsbury, however, that the worst excesses occurred. 'Its foundation-members consisted of moneyed middleclass descendants of victorian literary splendour,' Lewis revealed contemptuously. '. . . In their discouragement of too much unconservative originality they are very strong. The tone of "society" (of a spurious donnish social elegance) prevails among them.'[79] In his catholic abhorrence of both mass culture and the cultivated élites, both the moguls of Hollywood and the literary lions of Bloomsbury, Lewis prefigured the more famous, though no less impassioned, strictures of F. R. Leavis. Both discovered enemies outside and within the gates.

---

[77] Clive Bell, *Civilization: An Essay* (New York: Harcourt, Brace, 1928), 219.

[78] Roger Fry, *Transformations: Critical and Speculative Essays on Art* (New York: Brentano's [1926]), 61, 64.

[79] Wyndham Lewis, *The Apes of God* (1930; reprinted Santa Barbara: Black Sparrow Press, 1981), 121, 123.

The animadversions of Wyndham Lewis manifest a second and related tension between the transcending qualities of art and the less exalted realities of the mundane world. Despite their often persuasive claims to disinterestedness and the skilfully nurtured self-image of autonomy, writers, artists, and intellectuals found themselves intimately engaged in an ongoing, often demeaning struggle for greater reputation, status, and legitimacy. These internecine rivalries, characteristic of intellectual coteries since ancient times, became exacerbated in the late nineteenth and early twentieth centuries by the dramatic increase in the number of individuals in Britain who considered themselves authors, artists, and other makers of cultural artefacts. In 1881, for example, the census recorded slightly more than six thousand authors, editors, and journalists; forty years later, in 1931, over twenty thousand individuals claimed that status. Among the higher professions, 'writing' recorded the second largest increase in the 1920s.[80] In 1919, publishers announced 8,622 new books, 1,217 of which were fiction. Five years later, in 1924, over twelve thousand new books were published in Great Britain, a figure which represented a virtual doubling of book production over a twenty-year period.[81] Even factoring in the growth of the population and allowing for the characteristic vagaries of statistics, these figures marked a staggering increase in cultural supply. Add to these the unrecorded number of individuals who associated themselves with film, gramophone, the BBC, and other emerging forms of culture, and the problem becomes clear. More and more people claimed the ground once occupied by a small minority.

Although overcrowding affected literary politics in a variety of ways, one result attracted particular attention. As the number of books multiplied, the process of selection became more important, but also more problematic. Formal mechanisms of evaluation, such as book reviews, lost their credibility in some circles as the number of reviewers increased and critical standards declined. Virginia Woolf claimed that in the nineteenth century critics enunciated literary standards which helped writers improve, but contemporary reviewers merely flattered egos, settled personal scores, and generally cancelled each other out because of their vast number.[82] Too many reviewers, it was argued, lacked the tough-mindedness to attack their peers. In *Point Counter Point*, Aldous Huxley portrayed a character who sought to redress the balance:

[80] Altick, 'Sociology of Authorship', in *Bulletin*, 400 n; Guy Routh, *Occupation and Pay in Great Britain, 1906–60* (Cambridge: Cambridge University Press, 1965), 14–15.

[81] John Middleton Murry ['M', pseud.], 'Intimations of Mortality', *The Athenaeum*, 30 January 1920, 133–4; Michael Joseph, *The Commercial Side of Literature* (London: Hutchinson [1925]), 3.

[82] Virginia Woolf, *Collected Essays*, vol. 2 (New York: Harcourt, Brace and World, 1967), 207. On this problem see also, among many others, A. Wyatt Tilby, 'The Best-Seller Problem', *Edinburgh Review* 236, 481 (1922): 88–98.

On paper Walter was all he failed to be in life. His reviews were epigrammatically ruthless. Poor earnest spinsters, when they read what he had written of their heartfelt poems about God and Passion and the Beauties of Nature, were cut to the quick by his brutal contempt. The big game shooters who had so much enjoyed their African trip would wonder how the account of anything so interesting could be called tedious. The young novelists who had modeled their styles and their epical conceptions on those of the best authors . . . were amazed, were indignant to learn that their writing was stilted, their construction non-existent, their psychology unreal, their drama stagey and melodramatic. . . . Nature is monstrously unjust. There is no substitute for talent. Industry and all the virtues are of no avail. Immersed in his Tripe, Walter ferociously commented on lack of talent. Conscious of their industry, sincerity, and good artistic intentions, the authors of Tripe felt themselves outrageously and unfairly treated.[83]

If, as Woolf, Huxley, and others claimed, the rapid increase in authors and reviewers threatened to dilute the overall quality of British writing, it also forced some critics to define the standards which separated the talented from the merely industrious. Contemporary reputation often proved a faulty guide to enduring worth. Keen interest and success in literary politics could not redeem literary mediocrity, as Hugh Walpole discovered to his dismay.[84]

This perceived decline of literary standards helps explain the ascendancy of 'practical criticism' after the First World War. As one traditional forum of evaluation declined, another emerged in a quite different setting. In recent years, scholars from a variety of fields have explored in detail the history of literary criticism at academic institutions, particularly, of course, Cambridge University.[85] This discourse, in part an attempt to assimilate or perhaps exorcize the looming spirit of F. R. Leavis, has been especially illuminating in two closely related areas. First, despite its claims to novelty, the formal study of English literature elaborated upon a rich nineteenth-century tradition of cultural criticism. Coleridge, Carlyle, Ruskin, Arnold, and others established literature as the preferred site for cultural comment and provided the categories which I. A. Richards,

---

[83] Aldous Huxley, *Point Counter Point* (1928; reprinted New York: Harper and Row, 1965), 167.

[84] Hugh Walpole's crushed reaction to the satirical portrait of him in Somerset Maugham's *Cakes and Ale* is recounted in a letter: Virginia Woolf to Vanessa Bell, 8 Nov. [1930], *The Letters of Virginia Woolf, vol. 4: 1929–1931*, ed. Nigel Nicolson and Joanne Trautmann (New York: Harcourt Brace Jovanovich, 1979), 250–1. See also Rupert Hart-Davis, *Hugh Walpole: A Biography* (London: Macmillan, 1952), 316–19.

[85] For the period before 1932, see, among others, George Watson, *The Literary Critics: A Study of English Descriptive Criticism* (London: Chatto and Windus, 1964); Ben Knights, *The Idea of the Clerisy in the Nineteenth Century* (Cambridge: Cambridge University Press, 1978); and especially Chris Baldick, *The Social Mission of English Criticism, 1848–1932* (Oxford: Clarendon Press, 1983).

Leavis, and their disciples appropriated for their own use. Only in recent years has sociology replaced literature as the most innovative area of radical cultural analysis.[86] Second, despite its claims to universality, literary criticism at Cambridge existed within a specifically English social context which defined its boundaries and helped determine its tone. In some educational circles in the late nineteenth century, English studies functioned as the 'poor man's classics', refining both workers and women at home, and helping train civil servants for the growing Empire. After the anti-German hysteria of the First World War, English literature helped throw off from literary studies what Basil Willey called the 'alien yoke of Teutonic philology'.[87] Nationalism imbued literary criticism with an urgency it might otherwise have lacked.

The academic study of literature at Cambridge, while on the surface separating itself self-consciously from earlier aesthetic preoccupations, reinvigorated the traditional cultural hierarchies threatened by the expansion of cultural supply. This transformation was not without tensions and ambiguities of its own, but it maintained the distance between commercial and élite culture in two important ways. First, practical criticism grounded the critique of commercial culture in a solid institutional setting, the university, where it could thrive without some of the distractions which hounded men of letters. Second, the English tripos at Cambridge expanded the social base of those whose mission it became to protect civilization from the scourge of commercialism. I. A. Richards and his disciples in the 1920s may have carefully distinguished themselves from their Cambridge predecessors in Bloomsbury, but they retained and reinforced an obsession with enduring standards which made them spiritual allies.

Although Matthew Arnold warned that an institutional setting might corrupt an intellectual clerisy, the transformation of literary criticism into an academic profession carried with it certain advantages over the amateur tradition. Academics and teachers at all levels of education received a steady, if low, income which innoculated them against the more devastating financial anxieties which often plagued the most creative and ambitious authors. The £400 a year which G. G. Coulton received shortly after his appointment to the English faculty at Cambridge in 1919 may not have satisfied every middle-class need, but it offered a level of support which, when combined with its minimal duties, many writers would have envied.[88] The university provided that money and leisure whose lack,

[86] Perry Anderson, 'Components of the National Culture', in *Student Power: Problems, Diagnoses, Action*, ed. Alexander Cockburn and Robin Blackburn (Harmondsworth: Penguin in association with New Left Review, 1969), 214–84.

[87] Quoted in Baldick, op. cit., 87.

[88] G. G. Coulton, *Fourscore Years: An Autobiography* (Cambridge: Cambridge University Press, 1944), 313.

Woolf argued, prevented women from reaching their creative potential and made the contemplation of the timeless a virtual impossibility among the working classes. Moreover, Cambridge, like Oxford, provided a physical setting and other facilities for cultural pursuits which most independent artists found difficult to match. Even the lowest ranks among instructors enjoyed privileges reserved for gentlemen in earlier generations. Though taken for granted and sometimes the fountain-head of complacency, these privileges made life at the university less altruistic than the yearly stipend might suggest.

The status of the new discipline was more of a problem. Within the university, the formal study of literature struggled for recognition. At Oxford in the 1920s, Helen Gardner later recalled, 'the subject was suspected of being a very soft option, unlikely to demand any great powers of mind from its students, and unlikely to impose on them any very strict intellectual discipline.'[89] In the debate over the founding of the tripos at Cambridge in 1917, one sceptic questioned the need to teach English to the English, and when the course first became established, the subject was 'heartily despised' and mocked as the 'Novel-Reading Tripos'.[90] This professional insecurity, common to any new discipline integrating itself into an established curriculum, probably contributed to the exaggerated claims which I. A. Richards and others made for the subject. To counter the charges of softness and frivolity, Richards transformed literary criticism into a 'scientific' discipline with a worthy social mission.

In *Principles of Literary Criticism* (1924) and *Science and Poetry* (1926), Richards grounded his claims to scientific objectivity on experimental psychology, also a newer discipline embroiled with problems of status, this time among the natural sciences. As modern commentators acknowledge, Richards's appropriation of this field lacked originality and consistency. His theory of 'appetencies' appeared to be a bold excursion into behavioural psychology but actually drew upon mainstream traditions of British empiricism and utilitarianism.[91] Richards's philosophic conservatism in radical dress became most apparent in his hostility towards Freud, whose theories a number of other English literary figures in the 1920s dismissed

[89] Helen Gardner, 'The Academic Study of English Literature', *Critical Quarterly* 1, 2 (1959): 106.

[90] 'Discussion of a Report', *Cambridge University Reporter*, No. 2139, 20 Mar. 1917, 622; E. M. W. Tillyard, *The Muse Unchained: An Intimate Account of the Revolution in English Studies at Cambridge* (London: Bowes and Bowes, 1958), 71–2.

[91] John Paul Russo, 'Richards and the Search for Critical Instruments', in *Twentieth-Century Literature in Retrospect*, ed. Reuben A. Brower (Cambridge: Harvard University Press, 1971), 133–54; John Paul Russo, 'I. A. Richards in Retrospect', *Critical Inquiry* 8, 1 (1982): 743–60.

too easily.[92] Yet whatever its shortcomings, Richards's embrace of science proved a brilliant strategy to attract bright, sensitive students to a seductive though not yet respectable field of study. As Christopher Isherwood recalled, 'poetry wasn't a holy flame, a fire-bird from the moon; it was a group of interrelated stimuli acting upon the ocular nerves, the semi-circular canals, the brain, the solar plexus, the digestive and sexual organs. . . . We became behaviourists, materialists, atheists.'[93] Like theologians of earlier generations who confronted the same spectre, Richards discovered that science proved a better ally than adversary. By integrating its categories and vocabulary into his own thinking, he appended an attractive explanatory procedure to his own agenda.

It was not only through appeals to science that Richards assuaged the insecurities of a young field in an ancient university. Practical criticism enunciated a social mission which older, more prosaic academic disciplines could not match and did not try. In his *Principles of Literary Criticism* and in other works of the 1920s, Richards warned against the dangers of commercialism, and argued that only a trained understanding of literature would 'habilitate the critic', 'defend accepted standards' against their detractors, and 'narrow the interval between these standards and popular taste'. In this emphasis on literature as a 'storehouse of recorded values'[94] and on the uplifting role of a trained intellectual élite in a period of cultural crisis, Richards drew upon well-established traditions in British intellectual history. Like his science, Richards's social conscience masked a familiar face. Yet this mission also achieved at least two other inter-related objectives. First, by restoring a moral purpose to art, Richards distinguished himself from Bloomsbury theorists such as Roger Fry and Clive Bell, whose belief in the refined, morally aloof isolation of the artist became spattered with the mud of Passchendaele and the Somme. To Richards, the destructiveness of war made social conscience an imperative; Art could no longer be separated from Life. In at least one area then, the First World War confirmed rather than shattered a characteristic Victorian attitude. Second, this social mission helped bind its adherents into a community willing to accept its place on the academic margins

---

[92] I. A. Richards, *Principles of Literary Criticism* (1924; reprinted New York: Harcourt Brace, A Harvest Book, n.d.), 29–30. On the English literary reception to Freud, see Frederick J. Hoffman, *Freudianism and the Literary Mind* (Baton Rouge: Louisiana State University Press, 1945), 64–9. For examples of negative reactions, see Gilbert K. Chesterton, 'The Game of Psychoanalysis', *Century Magazine* 106, 1 (1923): 34–43; Aldous Huxley, 'Our Contemporary Hocus-Pocus', *Forum* 73, 3 (1925): 313–20; and Owen Barfield, 'Psychology and Reason', *Criterion* 9, 37 (1930): 606–17. One of the more reflective responses can be found in D. H. Lawrence, *Psychoanalysis and the Unconscious and Fantasia of the Unconscious*, ed. Philip Rieff (New York: Viking Press, 1960).
[93] Quoted in W. W. Robson, *The Definition of Literature and other Essays* (Cambridge: Cambridge University Press, 1982), 237.   [94] Richards, op. cit., 37, 32.

as a badge of its originality. 'We felt ourselves to be a happy band of pioneers', Basil Willey recalled, 'united by common faith, despised perhaps by the older academics, but sure of triumph in a glorious future.'[95]

This community expanded the social base and invigorated the thinking of post-war cultural élitism. Richards and his colleagues both represented and attracted disciples from a new generation, acutely conscious of its own uniqueness and eager to separate itself from the shibboleths of the past. When Mansfield Forbes helped assemble the English faculty shortly after the war, youth became a prime criterion of appointment.[96] In his mid-twenties when first selected, Richards published his seminal *Principles of Literary Criticism* at the age of thirty-one. To those reared amidst the disillusionment of the First World War, he became a youthful prophet of tough-minded realism. 'Many of us were just back from the 1914–1918 war,' Willey recalled, 'and we were unsatisfied with the woolly generalities and the vague mysticism of the accepted schools of criticism.'[97] Richards offered an approach to literature which retained an appreciation of beauty while shedding its Georgian preciosity. He set an agenda which, after his departure from Cambridge, Leavis refined, expanded, and proclaimed as his own.

Moreover, Richards's aesthetics created opportunities for more people to become discriminating cultural critics. Unlike Roger Fry and Clive Bell, Richards rejected the notion of a special aesthetic emotion which restricted the appreciation of beauty to a gifted few. Art was not a mystical encounter. 'The value of the experiences which we seek from the arts', Richards insisted, 'does not lie . . . in the exquisiteness of the moment of consciousness; a set of isolated ecstasies is not a sufficient explanation.' The artist and discriminating critic shared the same basic psychology with all humankind; in this sense, the artist was 'normal'. What distinguished artists from untutored sensibilities was the efficiency and quality of their mental states, 'what is called imagination'.[98] More important, perhaps, such refinement could be attained with persistent effort and vigorous training by any number of committed individuals. In *Practical Criticism*, first published in 1929, Richards developed his famous 'protocols' as models of such training. Pedagogy became wedded to art. The cultivated élites now might easily encompass those members of the middle and lower-middle class dedicated enough to master a rigorous programme of technical

---

[95] Basil Willey, *Cambridge and Other Memories, 1920–1953* (London: Chatto and Windus, 1968), 14.

[96] Hugh Carey, *Mansfield Forbes and his Cambridge* (Cambridge: Cambridge University Press, 1984), 67.

[97] Basil Willey, 'I. A. Richards and Coleridge', in *I. A. Richards: Essays in His Honor*, ed. Reuben Brower, Helen Vendler, and John Hollander (New York: Oxford University Press, 1973), 232. [98] Richards, op. cit, 228, 191.

training. Aesthetics moved from the overstuffed Victorian couch to the wooden classroom chair.[99]

Although Cambridge created a new élite of trained critics hostile to the aesthetics of an earlier generation and impatient with the hollow reviewing of London journalism, this new, younger, and more socially diverse coterie departed less radically from their targeted adversaries than their rhetoric suggested. For Richards, artists may have been 'normal' in one sense, but their superior imaginations and enhanced appreciation of life separated them no less drastically from common humanity than the studied and bemused snobberies of a Bloomsbury aesthete. Indeed, Richards's attack on the 'stock attitudes and stereo-typed ideas' of the popular cinema was itself a stock response, far less imaginative than Virginia Woolf's ruminations on the medium. For Richards and for Woolf, as for Eliot and Lawrence and the whole school of Modernism, art may have explored the human condition but the artist barely tolerated humanity. Moreover, although practical criticism undermined G. E. Moore's aesthetics, it shared with him and his disciples in Bloomsbury a faith in the timelessness of art and the personal value of its sustained contemplation. Richards's protocols wrenched poetry from its social and historical context. Students analysed poems without any knowledge of their date or place of composition. Like Eliot's vision of an overarching aesthetic order in 'Tradition and the Individual Talent', practical criticism assumed that art transcended time and space. It also claimed that in artistic appreciation lay a form of personal redemption. As Basil Willey once pointed out, despite their differences Moore and Richards both believed that 'what mattered most was valuable states of mind'.[1]

The defence of cultural élitism involved a paradox which both confirmed the fears and enhanced the value of life as an intellectual. In their attempt to reassert leadership in a culture increasingly dominated by alien, commercial interests, artists and writers often invoked categories and reinforced attitudes which only affirmed their social marginality. Art, particularly that of the avant-garde, defined itself by standards which assured its remoteness from the vast majority of humanity who judged themselves in quite different terms. Artists despised a public they refused to court, and asserted their superiority over a human aggregate under-standably indifferent to their leadership. For some, this alienation became itself a mark of distinction, an 'otherness' central to their personal identity. To Wyndham Lewis, D. H. Lawrence, T. S. Eliot, and most

[99] Baldick, *Social Mission*, 142–3; I. A. Richards, *Practical Criticism: A Study of Literary Judgement* ([1929], reprinted New York: Harcourt, Brace and World, A Harvest Book, n.d.).   [1] Willey, *Cambridge*, 21.

of the Bloomsbury circle, art could only thrive quarantined from the vulgarities of common taste. Even Richards, who believed that literature embodied an important social mission, confined his message to a tiny minority of enthusiasts. The imagined distances between aesthetic excellence and mediocrity, so contentious and yet so central to the reassertion of cultural hierarchy, may have preserved an important and evolving discourse from outside contamination, but it also erected boundaries which effectively isolated some of the most creative elements of the nation's intelligentsia. The pure admire the pure, Theodore Roethke once wrote, and live alone.

4

Regaining Authority:
Approaches to Cultural Reform

THE reassertion of cultural hierarchy in early twentieth-century Britain not only involved an extensive critique of commercial culture by intellectuals and other professional writers. A number of individuals also pursued a policy of active intervention to raise aesthetic standards among the general public. These figures, here deemed 'progressives', sought patrons or created institutions and organizations which offered cultural alternatives to the commercialized mass media. Since it was widely assumed that the market-place inevitably depressed standards, these alternatives only flourished, many believed, when shielded from the powerful downdraughts of commercialism. Raising standards demanded circumvention or manipulation of the market mechanism, a task laden with risks and disappointments. Cultural reform sometimes struggled to locate a reliable constituency. The producers of commercial culture found it difficult to reconcile patronage with profit. Government contributed only a tiny percentage of its resources to artistic endeavours. The public remained hostile or indifferent to alien schemes of self-improvement. Artists and intellectuals frequently rejected the mission and despised the missionaries who claimed them as allies.

The nineteenth century witnessed similar, if not altogether equivalent, attempts at cultural reform. Efforts to regulate working-class amusements and provide more 'rational recreation' demonstrate that the improvement of cultural standards long occupied an important place on the nineteenth-century agenda.[1] Unlike their Victorian predecessors, however, twentieth-century reformers confronted a far more commercialized and ubiquitous leisure industry. The rise of the mass market after 1870, combined with the introduction and rapid dissemination of new technologies of communication around the turn of the century, not only provided new urgency to reform, but also contributed to the ongoing and complex reconsideration of classical Liberalism in the late nineteenth century. Traditionally, most classical Liberals accepted the paradox that individuals who pursued

---

[1] Peter Bailey, *Leisure and Class in Victorian England: Rational Recreation and the Contest for Control, 1830–1885* (London: Routledge and Kegan Paul; Toronto: University of Toronto Press, 1978).

their narrow economic self-interest within a free and open market-place also contributed to the well-being of the general society. As an abstract argument, this natural identity of interests between private gain and public welfare helped buttress the lengthy political struggle for *laissez-faire* in economic and social policy. Despite some notable victories, this struggle never proved wholly successful, in part because a powerful and often paternalistic land-owning aristocracy rarely venerated an unfettered market-place with the same zeal as its middle-class apologists. In the late nineteenth century, a number of converging forces, including heightened foreign economic competition, some particularly severe business cycles, the continuing social and cultural amalgamation of the aristocracy and upper middle classes, and a growing awareness and disapproval of the social costs of unregulated capitalism, contributed to pervasive doubts within many influential circles about the efficiency, fairness, and social utility of *laissez-faire*.[2] Disgust with the vulgarities and sensationalism of commercial culture became part of this revaluation. To many observers, the natural identity of interests ought not apply to the arts. In matters of culture, an open, free market-place did not contribute to the well-being of society. English press lords and American movie moguls undermined faith in the market mechanism which they so successfully exploited.

Since the diverse group of individuals who sought to uplift cultural taste in the early decades of the twentieth century formed no central organization or unified movement, scholars have usually treated them in isolation from one another. Yet despite their obvious differences in personalities, interests, strategies, and effectiveness, they shared a number of traits in common. First, most were relatively young: John Reith was 33 when asked to lead the BBC in 1922; Stanley Morison was the same age when appointed Typographic Adviser to the Monotype Corporation; John Grierson formed the documentary-film group when still in his twenties. These and others surrounded themselves with men and women of their own age. The BBC, for example, recruited heavily among the young in the 1920s, and in its personnel, if not in its policy, retained a youthful image for much of the inter-war period. Exceptions to this generalization, of course, can easily be found. As a patron of modern design, Frank Pick was middle-aged when he commissioned artists for London Transport. Yet as might be expected, the attempt to reform or shape modern technologies

---

[2] Among a vast literature on these themes, see Derek H. Aldcroft and Harry W. Richardson, *The British Economy, 1870–1939* (London: Macmillan, 1969), 101–89; Roderick Floud and Donald McCloskey, eds., *The Economic History of Britain Since 1700, vol. 2: 1860 to the 1970s* (Cambridge: Cambridge University Press, 1981), 1–238; Helen Merrell Lynd, *England in the Eighteen-Eighties: Toward a Social Basis For Freedom* (1945; reprinted New Brunswick: Transaction Books, 1984); and Wiener, *English Culture and Decline*.

of communication attracted young, energetic individuals, responsive to new ideas and willing to accept financial sacrifices in pursuit of their ideals.

Second, in its social origins, cultural assumptions, and organizational tactics, the attempt to raise standards proved overwhelmingly middle class. Although definition of this ambiguous category depends upon the vagaries and cross-currents of family background, education, occupation, salary, and cultural preference, most progressives willingly acknowledged and even celebrated their bourgeois status. Virtually none came from recognizably working-class backgrounds, though a few rose from the margins of middle-class respectability. Stanley Morison, the son of a commercial clerk who later abandoned the family, spent his youth in poverty and left school at fourteen. Frank Pick's father was a draper. Others came from more comfortable, socially assured middle-class backgrounds. Stephen Tallents, head of the Empire Marketing Board and a key patron of documentary film, was the son of an influential barrister. The middle-class origin of these and similar figures manifested itself most obviously in the conviction that the general public aspired to be culturally uplifted. Not only did most progressives reject the legitimacy of commercial appeals, they adopted tactics whose success among the vast majority of the population hinged upon its unequivocal ambition for upward social mobility. They emphasized the practical utility of culture and stressed the personal and social impact of aesthetic appreciation. They assumed their own tastes should appeal universally.

Third, among both the artists and patrons of cultural reform, few could claim to be genuinely original thinkers. Most borrowed their central ideas from others or demonstrated talents not usually associated with artistic breakthroughs. The skills of many progressives, especially the bureaucrats, lay in the not inconsiderable tasks of organization and implementation. John Reith not only guided the BBC through its difficult early years, he commanded and inspired a generation of its functionaries to believe in his ideals. Even among those who viewed themselves primarily as artists, such as the documentary film-makers, none left a legacy of work commensurate with their early ambitions. For many traditional painters and sculptors in the early twentieth century, all commercial artists and designers doomed themselves to marginal status among their contemporaries and utter obscurity after their deaths. Yet even when judging themselves by their own professional standards, none of the commercial artists discussed here believed themselves to be a transforming genius. Most acknowledged their artistic limitations and satisfied themselves with more modest achievements.

The quest to raise standards took many forms, not all of which will be discussed here. The film industry in Britain, for example, protected itself against outside interference by appointing a British Board of Film

Censors, whose standards of propriety disarmed even the most vigilant moral guardians.[3] There were efforts to improve the training of journalists, and the adult education movement shared many traits with the progressives.[4] Rather than discuss these and other manifestations of intervention, however, this chapter will concentrate on three related strategies of cultural reform. First, by gaining control of an entire medium and thereby monopolizing supply, the BBC intended to offer a powerful alternative to the cinema and popular press. Collectivism prospered in radio, in part because it served the interests of the cultivated élites. Second, by working within certain segments of the market system, commercial artists and their patrons sought to enlighten and improve the visual literacy of the British public. Commercial artists hoped to resolve the contradiction at the heart of their profession. Third, a few committed advocates created organizations and institutions which, although they appealed to only a small number of enthusiasts, pressured the film and gramophone industries to respond to the tastes of cultivated minorities. Each of these approaches involved its own predicaments, and all encountered the problem of circumventing a system that, in its economic resources and audience popularity, proved difficult to manipulate, even for noble purposes. Whether the standards of traditional élite culture would be accepted by the producers and consumers of mass communications remained a central issue, and often the elusive link between ideal and reality.

A. MONOPOLIZING SUPPLY: JOHN REITH AND THE RISE OF THE BBC

In a society that prided itself on free speech the BBC gained a monopoly over an entire medium of communication, a feat difficult to imagine in the press or any other major source of information and entertainment. Certainly business men within the competitive sector of mass communications

[3] See Neville March Hunnings, *Film Censors and the Law* (London: George Allen and Unwin, 1967); Low, *British Film, 1918-1929*, 55-70; Nicholas Pronay, 'The First Reality: Film Censorship in Liberal England', in *Feature Films as History*, ed. K. R. M. Short (Knoxville: University of Tennessee Press, 1981), 113-37; and Nicholas Pronay, 'The Political Censorship of Films in Britain Between the Wars', in *Propaganda, Politics and Film, 1918-45*, ed. Nicholas Pronay and D. W. Spring (London: Macmillan, 1982), 98-125.

[4] On the improving of British journalism see, for example, Political and Economic Planning, *Report on British Press*, 268-301. For adult education, see J. F. C. Harrison, *Learning and Living, 1790-1960: A Study of the English Adult Education Movement* (London: Routledge and Kegan Paul, 1961), 249-363; Thomas Kelly, *A History of Adult Education in Great Britain* (Liverpool: Liverpool University Press, 1970), 267-320; and John A. Blyth, *English University Adult Education, 1908-1958: The Unique Tradition* (Manchester: Manchester University Press, 1983), 1-140.

constantly sought to minimize risk by undercutting and eliminating their competitors. In the United States early in the century, for example, Edison's Motion Picture Patents Company dominated American film until independent producers helped shatter the monopoly, only to form their own restrictive oligopoly.[5] In Britain, as we have seen, the tendency towards concentration of ownership and control characterized the press, film, and gramophone industries. Yet only the BBC achieved, quickly and with relative ease, the unified and centralized authority which, in the hands of a press lord or movie mogul, would have provoked outcries of indignation and organized efforts at reform. In Britain, and for varying reasons in other European countries as well, what became natural in one medium remained impermissible for all others.[6] In the private sector, it was argued, monopoly allowed producers to raise prices; as a public service, it was claimed, monopoly raised cultural standards.

The rise of the BBC cannot be separated from the personality of John Reith, who directed it from late in 1922, when radio barely penetrated national consciousness, to 1938 when the Corporation boasted around nine million licence-holders and competed with film for public attention. 'Reith did not make broadcasting,' Asa Briggs wrote in his monumental history of the medium in Great Britain, 'but he did make the BBC.'[7] Reith's ideal of public service and his authoritarian manner cast a long shadow over the corporation. Years after he departed in bitterness, his presence invoked a spirit and mission which BBC officials could emulate or mock, but not ignore. 'I have heard Caruso sing; I have seen Pavlova dance; I have now heard Reith on the BBC,' one staff member rejoiced after hearing a speech by the retired Director General.[8] Such encomiums were not uncommon in the early decades after Reith's retirement. Among the progressives of the inter-war era, Reith was the most influential and he occupies an important place in the social and cultural history of twentieth-century Britain.

---

[5] Sklar, *Movie-Made America*, 33–47; Cassady, 'Monopoly in Motion Picture Production', in *American Movie Industry*, ed. Kindem, 25–68.

[6] For example, on broadcasting in Germany, see, among others: W. B. Lerg, *Die Entstehung des Rundfunks in Deutschland: Herkunft und Entwicklung eines publizistischen Mediums* (Frankfurt: Josef Knecht: 1965): I. Fessman, *Rundfunk und Rundfunkrecht in der Weimarer Republik* (Frankfurt: Josef Knecht, 1973); Robert E. Peck, 'Policy and Control—a Case Study: German Broadcasting 1923–1933', *Media, Culture and Society* 5 (1983): 349–72.

[7] Asa Briggs, *The History of Broadcasting in the United Kingdom, vol. 1: The Birth of Broadcasting* (London: Oxford University Press, 1961), 4. For a condensed one-volume history of the BBC, see Asa Briggs, *The BBC: The First Fifty Years* (Oxford: Oxford University Press, 1985).

[8] Quoted in Robert Lasty, in his Foreword to John Reith, *Wearing Spurs* (London: Hutchinson, 1966), 11.

Reconsideration of Reith's life and legacy began shortly after his death in 1971. Andrew Boyle's biography, published a year later, revealed a dark side to Reith's personality, known to his acquaintances but obscured from public view by his extraordinary self-assurance. 'His ambition for worldly fame', Boyle observed, 'was off-set by the dead-weight of a progressive and almost pathological despair.'[9] The publication of Reith's diaries in 1975, tactfully edited by Charles Stuart, stunned devotees of the Reith legacy with its revelations of Reith's pettiness, self-hatred, and intellectual banality. 'These diaries are bound to come as a shock to many people who have revered Reith as a great Christian figure, who stood for all that was good in public life,' Hugh Greene, Director General of the BBC during the 1960s, wrote in the *TLS*. 'That image is destroyed for ever. Indeed, after this act of self-destruction nothing is left of the Reith legend but a handful of ashes.'[10] An unflattering portrait of Reith's personality and work soon made its way into the secondary literature.[11]

The early legend and the later, more complex view of Reith need not contradict each other. One theme which united his personal and professional life centred upon his ongoing, often problematic quest for control. Reith's psychological struggle to channel his destructive instincts into constructive activities shaped not only his rigid view of character, but also his vision of culture and the institutions which sustained it. He believed that only strong authority could assure the triumph of good. Within his Manichaean view of the world, he rarely underestimated the strength of his enemies, both psychological and social. He simply insisted that the countervailing forces be made as strong. This insistence meant that, for the individual, the will must be disciplined, and that in government, culture, and society, authority should be centralized and worthy élites ought to prevail. Reith constructed a theory and practice of cultural paternalism contingent upon the coercive strength of these principles, and he became an effective, charismatic spokesman for such leadership. This section will focus on Reith and his notion of public service; part of the following chapter, within the context of a related question, will show how the BBC as an institution implemented this ideal during the 1920s.

Reith's understanding of modern psychology reinforced his Calvinist conviction that an individual's inner life was composed of lower instincts and higher drives competing for dominance. 'The personality is made up of two distinct and often warring elements—one conscious and the other

[9] Andrew Boyle, *Only the Wind Will Listen: Reith of the BBC* (London: Hutchinson, 1972), 27.
[10] *The Reith Diaries*, ed. Charles Stuart (London: Collins, 1975); Hugh Greene, 'The Saddest Story', review of *The Reith Diaries*, ed. Charles Stuart, *TLS*, 19 Sept. 1975, 1061.
[11] See, for example, Seaton's description of Reith in Curran and Seaton, *Power Without Responsibility*, 136–8.

sub-conscious', he told the students at Gresham's School in 1922. 'We surely want to wipe out as much as we can of the barbarian in case it may get control over us, in a weak moment, with results of a disastrous kind.' He recommended that the students 'sublimate' their baser instincts 'so that the energies which are now wrongly used may be diverted into useful channels'.[12] Despite early failures and some intense episodes with the problem of authority, Reith constructed some notable achievements from the raw materials of his own self-described 'horrid character and disposition'. After a lonely and isolated childhood, he became an 'undistinguished and unsatisfactory' student who, at the age of fifteen, was withdrawn from Glasgow Academy by his father for bullying his peers.[13] Though he performed far better at Gresham's, he departed from school prematurely and unhappily at his father's request to become an apprentice engineer, a profession which suited his practical intelligence, but denied him the place at Oxford or Cambridge he so much desired. Although Reith loved military life, first as a school cadet and then during the First World War, he often quarrelled bitterly and self-destructively with his superiors.[14] Only when Reith achieved complete authority over a situation did he demonstrate considerable skills at organization, management, and the inspiration of his subordinates. After suffering his distinctive facial wound in 1915—a badge of courage which subsequently only enhanced his imposing physical presence—he proved an effective agent of British interests in America and, after the armistice, an efficient and respected factory manager. The First World War energized Reith and gave him self-confidence just as surely as it destroyed so many of his generation. 'War is not all ruthless perversion and degradation', he later wrote. 'Characteristics unrealized and unimagined are revealed, and decidedly not all of them are such as had better be left unprovoked.'[15] The BBC post suited his background, skills, and ambitions perfectly. He was given virtually complete authority over a rapidly expanding organization that demanded both managerial experience and technical training, but also benefited immeasurably from an outsider's exaggerated respect for the arts.

Reith defined his notion of public service in testimony before the Sykes Committee, which granted the BBC its first charter in 1923, and in scores of subsequent articles, speeches, and, most comprehensively, in the book *Broadcast Over Britain* published in 1924. Two interrelated elements of this ideal illustrate Reith's preoccupation with authority and control. First,

[12] Quoted in Garry Allighan, *Sir John Reith* (London: Stanley Paul, 1938), 113.
[13] *Reith Diaries*, 322; J. C. W. Reith, 'The Body Scholastic and the Body Politic', *Glasgow Academy Chronicle* (October 1933): 3; Boyle, op. cit., 37.
[14] Charles Stuart in his 'Introduction' to *Reith Diaries*, 26–7.
[15] J. C. W. Reith, 'Why Libel the Soldier?', *John O'London's Weekly*, 15 Mar. 1930.

he viewed culture as a form of self-improvement, a means of personal and social discipline. 'Enjoyment may be sought, not with a view of returning refreshed to the day's work, but as a mere means of passing the time, and therefore of wasting it. . .', he wrote in his book. 'On the other hand, it may be part of a systematic and sustained endeavour to re-create, to build up knowledge, experience and character, perhaps even in the face of obstacles.' Reith's 'high moral standard' involved an intense suspicion of amusements which served no didactic purpose. He shared with the Victorian middle classes a public distrust of the frivolous, the spontaneous, the sensual. In a revealing choice of words, he argued that it would be a 'prostitution of its powers' if the BBC only entertained its audience.[16] This view of culture as moral governor and healthy agent of repression separated Reith not only from the commercial culture which he loathed, but also from many of the leading writers and artists of his day. Reith would not have understood the feelings of ecstasy which absorbed such figures as Clive Bell when he encountered a work of genius. Indeed, Reith embodied a nineteenth-century tradition which Bloomsbury and other Modernists self-consciously mocked, though perhaps never completely escaped. Like Thomas Arnold and other Victorian reformers, Reith placed culture within the context of character rather than, as so many aesthetes insisted, the other way around.

Perhaps the most characteristic feature of Reith's vision of public service, however, lay not in its Victorian morality, but its self-assured paternalism. Here Reith clearly separated himself from the frequent boast of commercial culture that it fulfilled public demands. 'It is occasionally indicated to us', Reith observed with casual understatement, 'that we are apparently setting out to give the public what we think they need—and not what they want, but few know what they want, and very few what they need. There is often no difference.' He put it more bluntly in a speech at Cambridge. 'The best way to give the public what it wants is to reject the express policy of giving the public what it wants.'[17] This startling paradox meant that the BBC demanded not only unity of control—the essentially private monopoly which the Sykes Committee first granted, and which the Crawford Committee transformed into a public corporation in 1926—it also favoured centrality of control in London. The regional scheme of broadcasting developed in the 1920s may seem to contradict this impulse to centralize, but it replaced a system permitting far more local control. Throughout the inter-war period, the regional stations of

---

[16] J. C. W. Reith, *Broadcast Over Britain* (London: Hodder and Stoughton [1924]), 17–18.
[17] Ibid., 34; Cambridge speech quoted in *The Times*, 29 July 1930, 12.

the BBC complained about their inadequate funding, limited authority, and low prestige.[18].

This unity and centrality of administrative control formed the institutional base for the benign rule by experts and trained élites which Reith advocated so strongly. He was one of many influential individuals in Britain who believed in the efficacy of 'planning', a key word not simply of the 1930s, as A. J. P. Taylor has argued, but of most decades after 1914.[19] Drawing its adherents from both sides of the political spectrum and often infused with moral idealism, this middle-class paternalism replaced its more aristocratic and agrarian predecessor of earlier centuries. Alert to the exciting potentials of new technologies and either urban or suburban in cultural orientation, middle-class paternalists reversed the Liberal bias of their grandfathers by arguing that centralized power proved more, not less, efficient than competing authorities. The BBC, like other experiments in public ownership and control such as the Central Electricity Board and the London Passenger Transport Board, gave to planners added momentum and further buttressed their conviction that the future belonged to them.[20]

Reith's paternalist conception of public service assumed that supply created demand. 'It is not insistent autocracy but wisdom', he wrote in his autobiography, 'that suggests a policy of broadcasting carefully and persistently on the basis of giving people what one believes they should like *and will come to like*. . . . The supply of good things will create the demand for more.'[21] At least in his role as public advocate, Reith argued that high culture need only be made available for most people to embrace it. Despite private moments of profound disillusion, he retained in public the rationalist faith in the liberating potential of great ideas. Hostility could usually be explained by ignorance, and ignorance, in turn, might be banished by repeated exposure to 'everything that is best in every department of human knowledge, endeavour and achievement'.[22] Reith conceived of the BBC, in part, as a vital new institution of public education,

---

[18] Paddy Scannell and David Cardiff, 'Serving the Nation: Public Service Broadcasting Before the War', in *Popular Culture: Past and Present*, ed. Bernard Waites, Tony Bennett, and Graham Martin (London: Croom Helm, 1982), 165–7; on regional broadcasting, see Asa Briggs, *The History of Broadcasting in the United Kingdom, vol. 2: The Golden Age of Wireless* (London: Oxford University Press, 1965), 293–339.

[19] A. J. P. Taylor, *English History, 1914–1945* (Oxford: Clarendon Press, 1965), 299.

[20] William A. Robson, ed., *Public Enterprises: Developments in Social Ownership and Control in Great Britain* (London: George Allen and Unwin, 1937), 73–104; Terence H. O'Brien, *British Experiments in Public Ownership and Control* (London: George Allen and Unwin, 1937), 96–201; Lincoln Gordon, *The Public Corporation in Great Britain* (London: Oxford University Press, 1938), 156–244.

[21] J. C. W. Reith, *Into the Wind* (London: Hodder and Stoughton, 1949), 133.

[22] Reith, *Broadcast Over Britain*, 34.

and the institution's paternalism was animated by a genuine idealism often associated with young pedagogues. It presumed that the lower classes eagerly sought the cultivation of the privileged. 'Every man wants in his heart to be a highbrow', one official asserted confidently, and in its various publications the BBC often pointed to the errand boy who now whistled Bach, or the shepherd who relaxed to Beethoven.[23] This belief that an abundant supply of middle-class culture would generate its own demand also presumed, but rarely made explicit, the view that the poor lacked a legitimate culture of their own. Working-class culture occupied a silent space in Reith's writings, and when in the BBC *Handbook* of 1928 an author discussed the regional culture of 'The Industrial North', he wrote about the Hallé Orchestra and the *Manchester Guardian*.[24]

The definition of democracy which flowed from Reith's paternalism necessarily excluded the notion of popular choice. 'A man may be as good a democrat as another', he proclaimed in a speech at Manchester University, 'and yet reject, in the light of philosophy, history, or experience, democratic process to accomplish democratic ends.'[25] Reith believed that democracy meant equal access, not choice. Broadcasting allowed every social group to hear the same programmes in harmony. 'It is the perquisite of no particular class or faction,' he wrote of the BBC in *Broadcast over Britain*. 'The same music rings as sweetly in mansion as in cottage. It is no respecter of persons. The genius and the fool, the wealthy and the poor listen simultaneously. . . . The wisdom of the wise and the amenities of culture are available without discrimination.'[26] This emphasis on access rather than free choice allowed Reith to reconcile his insistence on monopoly and control with the prevailing ethos of his time. Unlike some paternalists in earlier centuries, Reith never equated his notion of leadership with that of a father over his children, or invoked the organic metaphor of a head ruling the body. Rather, his élitism resembled that of radicals who believed 'false consciousness' separated the working classes from their political salvation. To Reith, the vulgarities and inefficiencies of democracy could be eliminated once individuals parted with the shibboleth that they best understood their own self-interest.

The arrogance of this paternalism has often been noted. Yet what may be most interesting about Reith's paternalism was not its invocation of

---

[23] 'Are Talks Too Highbrow?', in *B.B.C. Yearbook: 1931* (London: BBC, 1931), 215; 'And Old Damoetas Loved to Hear Our Song', in *B.B.C. Handbook, 1929* (London: BBC, 1929), 60.

[24] 'The Industrial North', in *B.B.C. Handbook, 1928* (London: BBC, 1928), 165–71.

[25] John Reith, typescript of speech to Manchester University, 17 May 1933, BBC Written Archives Centre, Reading.

[26] Reith, *Broadcast Over Britain*, 217–18. See also C. A. Lewis, *Broadcasting From Within* (London: George Newnes, n.d.), 47; and Walter T. Rault, 'Masts for the Millions', *Radio Times*, 4 Jan. 1929, 11.

cultural standards, but its relationship to the practical necessities of consent. In commercial culture, it has been argued, producers served their own economic self-interest by identifying with their targeted audience whose consent expressed itself in sales, the crucial measure of success. Reith, however, rejected popularity as the arbiter of culture and argued that only a monopoly run by experts assured high moral standards. Yet unlike some authoritarian institutions, the BBC could not ascend to its privileged position of authority or maintain it through force or coercion. To acquire power, it gained the consent of key brokers in British society and to maintain it, the BBC needed to confront the problem of building an audience who deferred to its leadership. If monopoly appeared to solve the problem of supply, the role of demand remained much more ambiguous. Paternalism could not ignore the role of audience consent and yet, according to Reith, dared not capitulate to it.

Although the origins of the BBC's monopoly have been recounted in brilliant detail by Asa Briggs in *The Birth of Broadcasting*, one aspect of the story should be highlighted. The technical and cultural arguments for monopoly which Reith championed in public and before government committees were only partially responsible for the formation and continuance of the monopoly in the early 1920s. Unified control served the perceived self-interests of virtually every powerful group concerned with mass communications in Britain, with the possible exception, cynics later suggested, of ordinary listeners. Despite the often heroic self-portrayal of his early struggles at the BBC, Reith pushed against an opened door when he levelled his arguments against competition. Neither the government nor (perhaps more surprisingly) the producers of commercial culture objected to a service whose organization, financing, and programming often unintentionally served their own agendas. If, as Briggs noted, no one constructed an effective case against monopoly,[27] it was not because no reasonable arguments existed.

The producers of commercial culture welcomed a broadcasting monopoly shaped in the Reithian mould for a variety of reasons. First, among most wireless manufacturers in Britain, the opportunity to choke off foreign competition and share an expanding market for their goods proved extraordinarily attractive. Although the documents recording the negotiations between the radio industry and the Post Office have been lost, manufacturers feared an open market and accepted a number of compromises to assure their exclusive production of receiving sets. Even in America, where business men most loudly proclaimed their allegiance to free enterprise, elaborate collusion between government

---

[27] Briggs, *Birth of Broadcasting*, 9.

and the radio interests characterized the period immediately following the First World War.[28]

Second, while fearful of broadcasting generally, organizations representing music-hall performers and other popular artists reinforced Reith's natural inclinations when they sought restrictions on the amount of popular music broadcast. In a major if understandable miscalculation of the impact of broadcasting, A. V. Broadhurst of the Music Publishers' Association reported to the Crawford Committee in 1925 that 'it is the firm opinion of owners of musical copyrights that broadcasting has a deleterious effect upon the sale of music and consequently upon the earnings of composers and authors.' Radio, he argued, shortened the life of songs, undermined the quality of performances through poor reception, and discouraged attendance at live concerts. Walter Payne spoke for three different organizations when he proclaimed that variety shows sacrificed much of their appeal when, for example, the 'make-up, costume, personality and gestures of comedians' became lost in an aural medium. 'We consider that not more than ten per cent of entertainment of the kind usually given in theatres or Music Halls should be broadcast.'[29] These arguments underscore the unpredictable impact of new technologies, and also demonstrate why, at least initially, a broadcast service whose programming openly sought to uplift tastes met little opposition from the forces which presumably debased it. Indeed, it was one of the ironies of the early BBC that Reith needed to persuade entertainers from the commercial sector to perform on the radio.[30]

Third, although the press initially regarded broadcast technology as a potentially serious rival, they soon learned that it was easier to deal with a regulated monopoly that encouraged their support, rather than a competitive system which might have ignored it. Through their trade organizations, the press successfully negotiated restrictive arrangements on news broadcasts, which though temporary, persuaded Fleet Street that the BBC would not replace the newspaper as the major source of news. Perhaps more important, the press embraced a broadcast system which prohibited advertising, their major source of revenue and one they believed did not increase its expenditures proportionately to cover new media. Although elements of the newspaper industry observed with considerable discomfort the vigour with which the *Radio Times* solicited advertisements, and also opposed the creation of *The Listener*, it took

[28] Ibid., 119–20; R. H. Coase, *British Broadcasting: A Study in Monopoly* (London: Longmans, Green, 1950), 12–15; Hugh G. J. Aitken, *The Continuous Wave: Technology and American Radio, 1900–1932* (Princeton: Princeton University Press, 1985), 302–479.
[29] Testimony Before the Crawford Committee, GPO Archives, London, Minute 15796/26, File 7.
[30] Briggs, *Golden Age of Wireless*, 76–9.

no great leap of imagination to see what would happen if the BBC itself became commercialized, like American radio. In testimony before the Crawford Committee in 1926 the Newspaper Proprietors' Association, the Newspaper Society, and the Scottish Newspaper Society all accepted the essential arguments for unified control.[31]

The case for monopoly by government and politicians proved less ambiguous, particularly for the Post Office, charged by various statutes with overseeing wireless transmissions. Unity of control simplified their administrative duties, though initially the Post Office did not oppose granting authority to more than one broadcasting organization. The technical argument that Britain lacked authorization and capacity for enough wavelengths to sustain a competitive system—an argument which Reith invoked to clinch his case for unified control on more than one occasion—ignored conveniently the myriad technological possibilities for a more pluralistic system. By the mid-1920s, the idea that a limited number of wavelengths prohibited competition in radio became a spent force.[32]

Unlike the Post Office, politicians supported monopoly for ideological, not bureaucratic reasons. In the nineteenth century, politicians usually resisted government involvement in the arts, but the ascendancy of collectivist thought in the late nineteenth and early twentieth centuries, combined with the practical successes of centralized control during the First World War, diminished this traditional antipathy.[33] The Labour Party and diverse elements of the Left considered the monopoly, as Leonard Woolf put it somewhat hyperbolically, 'one of the biggest experiments in socialism that the world has so far watched'.[34] Despite his humble origins or perhaps because of them, Ramsay MacDonald enthusiastically supported Reith's cultural élitism. 'Keep up the standard of your service,' he wrote to his fellow Scotsman in 1923. 'Do not play down. Remember that the great mass of our people really want good things.'[35] On the Right, the paternalist tradition, repeated assurances of the monopoly's political neutrality, and the BBC's skilful cultivation of social respectability muted any reservations which back-benchers might

---

[31] Ibid., 286–92; Coase, op. cit., 58–60.

[32] Briggs, *Birth of Broadcasting*, 95, 112–14; Coase, op. cit., 12.

[33] Janet Minihan, *The Nationalization of Culture: The Development of State Subsidies to the Arts in Great Britain* (New York: New York University Press, 1977), 138–71.

[34] Leonard Woolf, 'Radio Has Revolutionized Entertainment', *Radio Times*, 11 Dec. 1931, 833–4. See also *Beatrice Webb Diaries, 1924–1932*, ed. Margaret Cole (London: Longmans, Green, 1956), 81.

[35] Quoted in 'What We Think of Broadcasting', *Radio Times*, 21 Dec. 1923, 452. See also Ramsay MacDonald to John Reith, 27 Dec. 1933, Photostats of Lord Reith's Papers, BBC Written Archives Centre, Reading; and Stuart Macintyre, *A Proletarian Science: Marxism in Britain, 1917–1933* (Cambridge: Cambridge University Press, 1980), 202–5.

have harboured about unified control. Only a handful of politicians, drawing upon the traditions of Liberal thought, offered serious reservations to the Crawford Report's recommendation for a new Charter. 'There is not a single argument that can be used in favour of the liberty of the Press', one MP declared before a thin House of Commons, 'that is not equally applicable to the liberty of wireless.'[36] This reasoning garnered scant support. Like the Central Electricity Board and the London Passenger Transport Board, the BBC proved an experiment in public ownership and control which drew support from both sides of the political spectrum.

If the BBC's monopoly served the interests and obtained the consent of both government and the producers of commercial culture, its relationship with the audience proved more problematic. Almost from the beginning a tension developed between Reith's official view that supply would ultimately create demand and the growing recognition, acknowledged by Reith in deeds if not always in words, that the public's wishes could not entirely be ignored. Consistent with the notion of public service, the BBC in the 1920s developed programmes based more upon the audience it hoped to discover, than the one it feared actually existed. Reith preferred to draw his knowledge of audience response from panels of experts, advisory committees, the BBC's own personnel, and individuals specifically appointed to represent the average listener, rather than from sources which might contradict official optimism.[37] 'Nobody knew what listeners liked, or even which programmes they listened to . . .', one high official later recalled. 'In programme-planning circles they talked easily about contrasts and alternatives, successes and failures, good programmes and bad; and it was all based on what the BBC officials themselves thought, plus various odd impressions gathered from correspondence . . . , Press comment that nobody in the BBC was supposed to read or at least to take seriously, and occasional *obiter dicta* from friends, charwomen, and people met in the train.'[38] In its official publications, the BBC often portrayed the 'average listener' in highly selective terms. For example, in an article 'Finding the Listener—in Wales', published in 1929, a

---

[36] E. A. Harney, speech to the House of Commons, 15 Nov. 1926, *Parliamentary Debates*, House of Commons, 5th ser., vol. 199 (London: HMSO, 1927), col. 1611. For a similar sentiment, see Chesterton's statement in Maisie Ward, *Gilbert Keith Chesterton* (New York: Sheed and Ward, 1943), 630–1. Crawford saw the BBC as a weapon against the popular press, which he detested. See David Lindsay, *The Crawford Papers: The Journals of David Lindsay, Twenty-seventh Earl of Crawford and Tenth Earl of Balcarnes, 1871–1940, during the years 1892 to 1940*, ed. John Vincent (Manchester: Manchester University Press, 1984), 505–6.

[37] Mark Pegg, *Broadcasting and Society, 1918–1939* (London: Croom Helm, 1983), 92–8.

[38] Maurice Gorham, *Sound and Fury: Twenty-One Years in the BBC* (London: Percival Marshall, 1948), 59. See also Roger Eckersley, *The BBC and All That* (London: Sampson, Low, Marston, 1946), 73.

'typical' licence-holder in a tiny Welsh village delivered this opinion of radio drama:

On the air there is no straining for realistic scenic effects, that bugbear of the intelligent producer. The greater the expanse of canvas to be filled, the greater the opportunity for the mind of the listener to supply mentally the scenic effects regained, to visualize the picture that the spoken word is conveying.[39]

Officially, Reith and other BBC functionaries tended to discount evidence that the average listener might not be so articulate or share in the upper-class tastes and eccentricities which so many foreigners equated with authentic British character. When newspaper polls consistently indicated that the vast majority of the audience overwhelmingly endorsed variety performances and other popular forms of commercial entertainment, the BBC argued that 'in time listeners will adjust'.[40] Although Reith recognized very early in his broadcasting career that letters to the BBC represented the opinions of only a tiny minority of listeners, others used such evidence when it suited their purposes. 'Does the public want broadcast adult education?' the Vice-Chairman of the Central Council for Broadcast Adult Education asked in 1932: 'Newspapers which have taken straw ballots sometimes announce that talks rank near the bottom of the list of preferences expressed. This is, of course, no sure guide to what the public wants. Letters written by listeners to the BBC are safer evidence.'[41] Privately, however, officials knew that their audience was not like the errand boy who whistled Bach. Reith often spoke of the appalling ignorance of the common man and most people, Lionel Fielden wrote bitterly in his memoir, enjoyed 'the red-nosed comedian and the Wurlitzer organ'.[42] As Fielden's and other BBC memoirs disarmingly admitted, however, the cultural tastes of high officials within the BBC itself often fell below the standards proclaimed by the Corporation. Indeed, though he may have glimpsed the moral promised land of an enlightened culture, Reith once acknowledged that his favourite music came from Vincent Youman's *Hit the Deck*.[43]

The continuing tension within the BBC between giving the public 'what it ought to have', and yet not ignoring 'what it wanted', became most evident during the 1920s in the *Radio Times*. First published in 1923,

---

[39] 'Finding the Listener—in Wales', *Radio Times*, 3 May 1929, 226.

[40] *Radio Times*, 16 Jan. 1931, 108.

[41] John H. Nicholson, 'Four Years of Educational Broadcasting', *Sight and Sound*, 1, 3 (1932): 79.

[42] Lionel Fielden, *The Natural Bent* (London: André Deutsch, 1970), 109.

[43] Henry Hall, *Here's To The Next Time* (London: Odhams Press, 1955), 126. Maurice Gorham said of Reith: 'He had no background of culture, no knowledge of literature or music or drama or show business or any of the things in which we dealt.' See Gorham, *Sound and Fury*, 78–9.

the *Radio Times* became an immediate circulation phenomenon, in part because it was the only reliable source for the changing and unpredictable times of programmes. As later statistics of listening patterns confirmed, the *Radio Times* bequeathed to listeners the freedom to select their favourite type of programmes and often to ignore precisely what the BBC most wanted them to hear. The magazine also became immediately popular in part because one of its joint editors was Leonard Crocombe, the experienced editor of *Titbits*. Written in a breezy style and containing cartoons, jokes, competitions, and other similar features, the *Radio Times* engaged its audience in ways reminiscent of the popular press. By the autumn of 1925, however, one official reflected Reith's dissatisfaction with the magazine when he wrote in a memorandum that 'no doubt the "Radio Times" must be "popular" in order to appeal to a very large audience, but it need not be filled with the spirit of vulgarity and cheapness which at present distinguishes it among all wireless periodicals.'[44] The BBC hired a new editor and within the year, as one official wrote, the paper became 'undoubtedly much worthier of the tradition of the service than it ever was before'.[45] Yet as a lucrative source of advertising revenue for the BBC and one of the best-selling weekly magazines in Great Britain, the *Radio Times* could not afford to become too sober. In 1927, a new editor, Eric Maschwitz, brought to the publication a renewed popular flavour. Maschwitz wanted the weekly to have a 'definite personality'. He introduced a gossip column entitled 'Both Sides of the Microphone'. He changed the paper's typography and layout, and included more illustrations. He planned special issues and sponsored competitions which invited the reader's participation.[46] By the end of 1929, the *Radio Times* enjoyed a circulation of over 1,300,000.

The experience of the *Radio Times* during the 1920s indicated that the BBC was not immune to popular appeals and strategies. Monopoly, Reith argued, protected the BBC against commercial pressures to lower its standards, but what precisely did the term 'commercial pressures' mean? Middle-class cultural paternalism, like its aristocratic predecessor, was not a unilateral relationship. The BBC needed not only the consent of crucial power brokers in British society to acquire its monopoly; it also

[44] Director of Education to Director of Publicity, 21 Sept. 1925, *Radio Times* File 1, BBC Written Archives Centre, Reading. For Reith's attitude, see John Reith to Gladstone Murray, 9 Sept. 1925, *Radio Times* File 1, BBC Written Archives Centre, Reading.

[45] A.C.(I) to Managing Director, 5 Nov. 1926, *Radio Times* File 2, BBC Written Archives Centre, Reading.

[46] Eric Maschwitz, Memorandum on 'Radio Times' News Page, 27 Sept. 1927; 'Publications: The Radio Times', n.d.; and Maschwitz to Nicolls, 16 Jan. 1928, BBC Written Archives Centre, Reading. See also Briggs, *Golden Age*, 282–6. For a general history of the magazine, see Susan Briggs, *Those Radio Times* (London: Weidenfeld and Nicholson, 1981).

could not afford to ignore the mass audience it claimed to uplift. How much power this public might command remained a question which Reith preferred to answer forthrightly in his official pronouncements, but more equivocally in practice; especially, as we shall see, when the audience for radio exploded in size.

B. MANIPULATING DEMAND: ENLIGHTENED PATRONS AND COMMERCIAL ART

If the BBC sought to raise standards by monopolizing supply, others pursued the same goal by working more directly within the market system. Among visual artists, in particular, commercial culture provided opportunities for steady employment which many found irresistible, though artistically troubling. 'Of the twenty thousand students in art schools in England at this moment,' Wyndham Lewis wrote in 1929, 'nineteen thousand should be destined to design nothing but smart advertisements for arc-lamps, stomach belts, jumpers, brilliants, the Smoke with the Ivory tip, fire extinguishers, cosmetics [and] beautifully curved house-drains.'[47] These students faced restrictions on their work which, for Lewis and others, an assured salary could never adequately compensate. Commercial artists could not select their own subject-matter, and needed to subordinate their art to the demands of commerce. They usually worked in an ephemeral medium, such as newspaper advertisements, which at best captured the momentary gaze of a preoccupied reader before disappearing altogether. They needed to work rapidly to meet implacable deadlines, and the visual symbolism of their work could not offend the limited tastes of their audience. It was, as one put it, a 'Despotic Art', which served masters outside the artist's control.[48]

Untroubled by these and other restrictions, the vast majority of commercial artists satisfied themselves with mediocre work, routinely performed. In the late nineteenth and early twentieth centuries, however, a small but influential minority of commercial artists and designers set higher standards for themselves and their profession. These individuals not only sought legitimacy and respect among traditional artists, a topic discussed later in a related context, but also more urgently required the financial support and encouragement of commerce and government. Such patronage

---

[47] Wyndham Lewis, *Wyndham Lewis on Art: Collected Writings, 1913–1956* (New York: Funk and Wagnalls, 1969), 256.

[48] H. C. Ferraby, 'Some Characteristics of Despotic Art', *Advertising Display* 1, 2 (1926): 47; Mason Griff, 'The Commercial Artist: A Study in Role Conflict and Career Development' (Ph.D. diss., University of Chicago, 1958), 120; Paul Parker, 'An Analysis of the Style of Advertising Art', (Ph.D. diss., University of Chicago, 1937), 20–4.

did not come easily. 'Art is a word that business men distrust,' the publicist Charles Higham wrote in 1916, 'and an artist has a viewpoint that often they do not understand.' Five years later the Principal of the Royal College of Art, William Rothenstein, observed that 'the breach between creative people and the great manufacturers of the world is now a wide one.'[49] The struggle to bridge this chasm included not only commercial artists but also key individuals within a number of closely related fields, such as book typography and industrial design. Moreover, the attempt to raise the standards of 'art beyond the gallery'[50] gained momentum when, concurrently, the advertising industry sought greater legitimacy for itself, and the British government became directly involved in publicity campaigns. Advertising, propaganda, and public relations formed a nexus of overlapping functions and techniques which complicates efforts to define each sphere separately.[51] Support for better art within commerce, well established by the mid-1920s, depended upon a number of converging financial and political interests, each worthy of further consideration.

Before the First World War, few in Britain considered advertising a business worthy of respect. It was, as the advertising manager of the *Financial Times* admitted, 'diametrically opposed, and consequently repugnant to, the instincts of a gentleman'.[52] Some of the objections were moral. Patent medicines, in particular, relied upon advertising which exploited the credulity of the sick and infirm. 'For all practical purposes', a Select Committee of the House of Commons reported in 1914, 'British law is powerless to prevent any person from procuring any drug, or making any mixture, . . . advertising in any decent terms as a cure for any disease or ailment, recommending it by bogus testimonials . . . and selling it . . . for any price he can persuade a credulous public to pay.'[53] As one character in Wells's novel about the bogus patent medicine *Tono-Bungay* remarked, 'It's advertisement has—done it. . . . He takes something that isn't worth anything . . . and he makes it worth something.'[54] Despite attempts to control the worst abuses, advertising remained unregulated early in the century and, as one of its

[49] Charles Frederick Higham, *Scientific Distribution* (London: Nisbet, 1916), 70; William Rothenstein, 'Possibilities for the Improvement of Industrial Art in England', *Journal of the Royal Society of Arts* 69, 3565 (1921): 269.

[50] See Richard Cork, *Art Beyond the Gallery in Early 20th-Century England* (New Haven: Yale University Press, 1985).

[51] For an attempt at individual definitions, see Philip M. Taylor, *The Projection of Britain: British Overseas Publicity and Propaganda, 1919–39* (Cambridge: Cambridge University Press, 1981), 1–6.

[52] Howard Bridgewater, *Advertising or the Art of Making Known* (London: Sir Isaac Pitman, n.d.), 1.

[53] *Report from the Select Committee on Patent Medicines Together With Proceedings of the Committee, Minutes of Evidence, and Appendices* (London: HMSO, 1914), p. ix.

[54] H. G. Wells, *Tono-Bungay* (London: Macmillan, 1909), 194.

most enthusiastic boosters lamented in 1919, 'suffers from the prejudices created by earlier misconduct'.[55]

Yet some of the objections were also aesthetic. Selfridge's campaign of striking full-page illustrations to launch his store proved exceptional. Most newspaper advertisements suffered from crude illustrations and murky seas of unattractive copy. Even Northcliffe, whose policies made the industry prosper, loathed many of the specific advertisements in his papers.[56] Poster advertisements before the First World War ranged widely in quality, though by modern standards most lacked aesthetic appeal and sophistication.[57] Some of the most memorable posters in the late nineteenth century, illustrating the virtues of products from Bovril, Lipton's, and other companies which sought a national market for their goods, were adaptations from the work of academic artists. After Millais sold one of his paintings to the *Illustrated London News*, he was initially shocked when Pears Soap subsequently purchased the work and used *Bubbles* in one of its most extensive advertising campaigns.[58] When Henry Stacy Marks, a member of the Royal Academy, gladly sold some occasional drawings to a soap manufacturer, he became known in some circles as 'Trade Marks'. Still, Hubert von Herkomer, Edwin Landseer, Maurice Grieffenhagen, and other Academicians permitted their work to be used by insurance companies, shipping firms, and other organizations.[59] Most observers agreed that the French, not the British, pioneered the art of the poster. 'For it is in France', Charles Matlack Price wrote in 1913, 'that poster making was first recognized as an art, and it is France that has characterized it as an art of which the keynote is audacity, *chic*, abandon and sheer cleverness.'[60] Although in Britain posters by Frederick Walker, the Beggerstaffs (James Pryde and William Nicholson), Aubrey Beardsley, and others became noted for their original, evocative designs, their commissions were few and their reproduction limited, in part because the work came from West End theatrical productions, small publishers, and other enterprises restricted to a small area of London.

[55] Russell, *Commercial Advertising*, 3.
[56] Northcliffe to Wareham Smith, 14 June 1909 and 24 May 1912, Northcliffe Papers, British Library, Deposit 4890, vol. 60.
[57] Lautenbach, 'Victorian Advertising', *Victorian Studies* (1967): 431–4; de Vries, *Victorian Advertisements*, 6–7.
[58] For conflicting accounts of this episode, see John Guille Millais, *The Life and Letters of Sir John Everett Millais*, vol. 2 (New York: Frederick A. Stokes, 1899), 189–91; and Diana and Geoffrey Hindley, *Advertising in Victorian England 1837–1901* (London: Wayland Publishers, 1972), 43–4.
[59] Harold F. Hutchinson, *The Poster: An Illustrated History from 1860* (New York: Viking, 1968), 34–5.
[60] Charles Matlack Price, *Posters: A Critical Study of the Development of Poster Design in Continental Europe, England and America* (New York: George W. Bricker, 1913), 47.

Only posters by John Hassall and a relatively few others suggested that commercial art for a mass audience in Britain might be artistically interesting, as well as commercially viable.[61]

The gradual emergence of more sophisticated, aesthetically self-conscious commercial art cannot be separated from developments in related fields. Efforts to raise the level of other 'applied arts' and to find patrons who would support them began in the late nineteenth century, and inspired similar movements, with revised agendas, for a number of decades to come. Many of these movements and individual advocates for better design have been discussed in detail by others. William Morris and the Arts and Crafts Movement in the 1880s, the Design and Industries Association founded in 1915, and the efforts beginning in the 1890s to improve the typography of the book have all found their commentators. Less emphasized has been how all these movements together fostered better aesthetic design and created opportunities for art to thrive within commerce.

William Morris and the various organizations which comprised the Arts and Crafts Movement in the 1880s helped transcend the boundaries which too easily compartmentalized various artistic pursuits. One of Morris's deepest instincts was to discover unifying elements, both conceptual and practical, among the disparate range of activities which compelled his interest. He not only grasped the intimate connections between art and politics, he also recognized the relationship between someone making a kitchen pot and another painting the Ascension. The outside world was the art gallery for the majority of men and women, and that world suffered to the degree that a social and economic system divided and alienated the labour of its industrial workers. This emphasis on unity of artistic production and the dangers of specialization also, paradoxically, limited the appeal of his products to the upper middle class, the only group who could afford them. By denying the commercial efficiencies of the division of labour and in his intrinsic suspicion of the machine, Morris priced himself out of the market that, within the framework of his political commitment, most needed to be improved. The legacy of Morris did not consist of his curiously reactionary medievalism, but in the unity of his overall vision and his insistence on high aesthetic standards in the production of everyday objects.[62]

The Design and Industries Association, founded in 1915, patterned itself on the Werkbund in Germany, an organization founded eight years

---

[61] James Cleaver, *A History of Graphic Art* (New York: Philosophical Library, 1963), 180–3; Bevis Hillier, *Posters* (New York: Stein and Day, 1969), 81–127.

[62] The large bibliography on Morris continues to expand. For a good recent discussion of his work on design, see Peter Stansky, *Redesigning the World: William Morris, the 1880s, and the Arts and Crafts* (Princeton: Princeton University Press, 1985).

earlier and influenced by some of Morris's ideas. The DIA encouraged 'a more intelligent demand amongst the public for what is best and soundest in design' and, as we shall see later, distinguished itself from the Arts and Crafts Movement by fully embracing the notion of machine production.[63] Although membership of the DIA numbered 292 in 1916 and expanded only to 602 members twelve years later, it was not the absolute size of the organization which made it important. Rather, the DIA allowed influential manufacturers and creative individuals from a wide range of the applied arts to form a network of enthusiasts who exchanged ideas and supported each other's efforts to raise standards. The original membership, for example, included representatives from Boots, Cadbury's, and Lever's; printers from a variety of publishers; administrators and teachers of the country's major art schools; architects, designers, journalists, and government bureaucrats.[64] As the typographer Herbert Simon later observed: 'A comforting attraction of the Design & Industries Association lay in its ability to bring together a group of artists, craftsmen, business men and industrial producers and give them an opportunity for discussion and exchange of ideas. . . . Pioneers . . . feel isolated and an association gives them the luxury of occasional preaching to the converted. Furthermore, members were inclined to employ the talents of other members when need or opportunity arose.'[65] Indeed, one of the more striking features of British design in the inter-war period was the web of personal relationships and professional favours which linked individuals from disparate fields.

The DIA encouraged typographers to expand their clientele for quality printing. When William Morris founded the Kelmscott Press in 1890, he hoped to revive a profession whose standards declined precipitously in the nineteenth century. With the indispensable assistance of Emery Walker, Morris demonstrated with his *Chaucer* and other magnificently produced books that printing could be an art, as well as a trade. 'I began printing books', he wrote shortly before his death, 'with the hope of producing some which would have a definite claim to beauty . . . and . . . which it would be a pleasure to look upon as pieces of printing and arrangement of type.'[66] Kelmscott printed books whose facing pages of

---

[63] Quoted in Nikolaus Pevsner, *Studies in Art, Architecture and Design, vol. 2: Victorianism and After* (New York: Walker, 1968), 228.

[64] Ibid., 229; Penny Sparke, *An Introduction to Design and Culture in the Twentieth Century* (London: Allen and Unwin, 1986), 63–4; Fiona MacCarthy, *All Things Bright and Beautiful: Design in Britain, 1830 to Today* (Toronto: University of Toronto Press, 1972), 81–3. MacCarthy's study derives heavily from Pevsner.

[65] Herbert Simon, *Song and Words: A History of the Curwen Press* (London: George Allen and Unwin, 1973), 127.

[66] Morris (1895) quoted in H. Halliday Sparling, *The Kelmscott Press and William Morris, Master Craftsman* (London: Macmillan, 1924), 135.

integrated design featured self-consciously archaic types, elegantly wide margins, and the highest quality inks, paper, and binding.[67] The 'private press' movement which followed in Morris's wake carried on this tradition. Essex House, Ashendene, Doves, and other presses designed beautiful books, in limited editions, for restricted audiences. Like other elements of the Arts and Crafts movement, most private presses turned their back on commercialism and mechanized production, exalting the small-scale printing techniques of an earlier era. In general, their expensively produced books appealed to collectors and wealthy connoisseurs, who regarded them as ornaments to be displayed, rather than publications to be read.[68]

If printing could be an art, some reasoned, it could also become more widely appealing. One early attempt to transform high-quality typography into a more popular, commercially viable enterprise came in 1905, when Joseph Dent began publishing the Everyman Library. In an attempt to disseminate great literature at reasonable prices to all classes of readers, Dent practised economies of scale which did not preclude ornately designed end-papers and title-pages clearly reminiscent of Kelmscott and other private presses. The disjunction between Morris's radical ideals and the fashionable bourgeoisie who purchased his limited editions disappeared in the high-speed presses of Joseph Dent.[69] Ten years later, Francis Meynell proved even more instrumental in transferring the aesthetic ideals of the private presses into commercial publishing. Born into a prosperous and literary family, Meynell founded the Pelican Press in 1916 'primarily to produce the finest possible printing for commerce'.[70] Famous for its decorative flowers and excellent type-faces, the Pelican Press not only published books, but also set advertisements for the Midland Bank, Rolls-Royce, Blackwell's, and other major British firms. A Communist, Meynell also set displays for the radical *Daily Herald* and published pamphlets for the Labour Party. In 1923, he founded the Nonesuch Press 'as a trade publisher specializing in finely printed books'. Its greatest success, *The Week-End Book* first published in 1924, briefly headed the best-seller list in *John O'London's Weekly*, sold 50,000 copies within a few years, and eventually achieved sales of a phenomenal half-million copies.[71] Like Morris, Meynell combined radical politics with an appreciation for

[67] Ruari McLean, *Modern Book Design: From William Morris to the Present Day* (London: Faber and Faber, 1958), 10–11. I have learned much from this study.

[68] Frederick Cave, *The Private Press* (London: Faber and Faber; New York: Watson-Guptill, 1971); Colin Franklin, *The Private Presses* (London: Studio Vista, 1969).

[69] McLean, op. cit., 35–7.

[70] Quoted in John Dreyfus, *A History of The Nonesuch Press* (London: Nonesuch Press, 1981), 10. Italics eliminated.

[71] McLean, op. cit., 48–50; Francis Meynell, *My Lives* (London: Bodley Head, 1971), 146, 165; Dreyfus, op. cit., 161, 184.

elegant design; unlike Morris, he served readers, not simply collectors, with his editions.

The 1920s witnessed a renaissance of English typography. The work of Stanley Morison, discussed later, bequeathed to printing a respectable pedigree, while a number of presses and institutions exemplified and encouraged higher standards. In addition to the contributions of the Nonesuch Press, the Curwen Press, for example, used patterned papers and drawings to raise the level of its routine business printing, as well as its editions of books. Convinced that decoration should remain subservient to legibility, Harold Curwen declared in a manifesto that 'printing is intended for our fellow-man to READ.' Lovat Fraser, whose designs typified the Press shortly after the war, 'shared our view that to put "real beauty", sincerely felt and expressed, at the service of advertising, was, because of its wide and varied distribution, no inconsiderable privilege and opportunity.'[72] Other institutions reinforced this growing conviction among influential typographers and their sponsors that commerce and aesthetics might be reconciled. *The Fleuron — A Journal of Typography*, founded in 1923, published articles and provided illustrations of the best typography not only from England, but from America and the Continent as well. It was, Herbert Simon later wrote, 'a declaration of faith in the new approach to printing'.[73] The Double Crown Club, founded in 1924 for those interested in 'the Art of the Book', allowed typographers, publishers, and bibliophiles to gather formally and exchange ideas about recent trends and problems.[74] Although these institutions and their supporters often tended to exaggerate their own importance, they embodied an important transformation in English printing and publishing. What had been private and limited in the 1890s became more public and widely diffused in the 1920s. Aesthetic principles which once distinguished only a tiny minority of enthusiasts in Hammersmith became nationally disseminated, once the prohibition against commercialism had been modified. For typography to emerge fully from the crudities of the nineteenth century, however, key parts of the equation between art and commerce still needed to be solved.

After the First World War, the advertising industry made a concerted effort to publicize itself and enhance its professional status. Advertisers formed organizations which claimed to regulate the industry, and 'Truth in Advertising' and other campaigns sought to convince the public that

[72] Simon, *Song and Words*, 133, 152. On the Curwen Press, see also (Basil H. Healey), *The Curwen Press: A Short History* (London: Curwen Press, 1971); and Pat Gilmour, *Artists at Curwen* (London: Tate Gallery, 1977).

[73] Simon, op. cit., 171.

[74] Oliver Simon, *Printer and Playground: An Autobiography* (London: Faber and Faber, 1956), 32, 38–40.

the worst abuses would no longer occur.[75] Within the profession, self-promotion became a hallmark of the decade. In an attempt to 'spread the gospel of advertising', the industry convened the International Advertising Exhibition in November 1920. The lure of 'free samples' attracted huge crowds; an elaborate 'Pageant of Publicity', which included figures dressed as Little Johnny Home Pride, the Decca Girl, and the vegetables contained in Edwards's Dessicated Soups, sought to drive home the message that 'Advertising Benefits the Buyer'. The King proclaimed on the final day of the exhibition that 'this is one of really big industries. I did not realize it before.'[76] In 1924, two thousand American business men travelled to London for the first World Advertising Convention held outside the United States. The slogan of the gathering was, shamelessly, 'Advertisers of the World Unite!' The Prince of Wales appeared, and when the Convention approved a new code of advertising ethics, Winston Churchill told the group what they longed to hear: 'You have successfully vindicated the reputation of the advertising profession.'[77]

Equally important, the international meeting helped disseminate American ideas among British advertisers, who were well-known for their parochialism. American methods and techniques had already penetrated Britain through other channels. London firms often published the best American textbooks, and trade journals frequently reported developments within the American industry, though not always with an approving eye. Advertising agencies, such as J. Walter Thompson, established branch offices in London which applied the latest American techniques.[78] The Convention accelerated a process set in motion earlier. In twenty-four separate sessions and a variety of social functions delegates exchanged information on behavioural psychology, market research, and other new developments which sought to minimize risk. In 1928, the President of the Advertising Association in Britain claimed, with some exaggeration, that the Convention of 1924 marked 'the commencement of the effective organization of British advertising'.[79]

These developments in British advertising after the war affected commercial art in two crucial ways. First, American advertisers helped teach

---

[75] Turner, *Shocking History*, 173–5.

[76] 'Advertising Booms Itself To Show That It Can Boom Business', *Advertiser's Weekly*, 3 Dec. 1920, 360; 'The Pageant of Publicity', ibid., 30 Nov. 1920, 328, 351; 'Echoes of the Exhibition', ibid., 10 Dec. 1920, 408.

[77] Quoted in 'Convention Report', ibid., 18 July 1924, 236.

[78] For a list of American texts published in London before the First World War, see G. W. Goodall, *Advertising: A Study of Modern Business Power* (London: Constable, 1914), 90–1. For an example of disapproval, see T. B. Lawrence, 'The Transatlantic Plague', *Advertiser's Weekly*, 21 Dec. 1928, 488. On J. Walter Thompson, see James Playsted Wood, *The Story of Advertising* (New York: Ronald Press, 1958), 456–61.

[79] C. A. McCurdy, 'The Birmingham Convention', *Advertiser's Weekly*, 22 June 1928, 535.

their British colleagues the psychological importance and professional advantages of well-conceived illustration in advertising. In one of the earliest American books on the subject, *The Psychology of Advertising in Theory and Practice*, first published in 1908, Walter Dill Scott emphasized the rapidity with which pictures conveyed information.[80] Others in the United States explored the psychological impact of various colours and, influenced by experimental psychology, conducted elaborate if methodologically primitive experiments which compared the value within advertisements of photos over line drawings, and human subjects over inanimate objects.[81] By the 1920s, this reliance on psychology, particularly the revived notion of the association of ideas, began to penetrate the British profession. 'If the announcements of a firm are *habitually* artistic and beautiful,' Thomas Russell wrote in his text on *Commercial Advertising*, '. . . the firm becomes cumulatively associated in the public mind with ideas of refinement and good taste.'[82] Other writers followed Russell's lead. In *Psychology as a Sales Factor*, published in 1927, A. J. Greenly argued that pictures 'suggest ideas by their associations; they do not merely illustrate arguments', and three years later, D. B. Lucas and C. E. Benson offered the arguments of behaviourism to suggest how good illustrations stimulated the desired response.[83] Psychology thus validated the role of illustration in advertising, while at the same time reinforcing the profession's claims to its own effectiveness and legitimacy.

Second and more important, the rise of public relations—a novel, more subtle means of manipulating demand first developed in the United States—created new sources of enlightened patronage within both commerce and government for a wide range of the visual arts. Like its close relative, the word 'propaganda', difficult to define, public relations sought to manipulate opinion 'in such a manner that the public receives

---

[80] Walter Dill Scott, *The Psychology of Advertising in Theory and Practice* (Boston: Small, Maynard, 1921), 13–14. See also A. Michal McMahon, 'An American Courtship: Psychologists and Advertising Theory in the Progressive Era', *American Studies* 13, 2 (1972): 5–18.

[81] George French, *The Art and Science of Advertising* (Boston: Sherman, French, 1909), 50–3, 70–5, 170–80; J. V. Breitwieser, *Psychological Advertising* (Colorado Springs: Apex, 1915), 52–6; Henry Foster Adams, *Advertising and its Mental Laws* (New York: Macmillan, 1921), 300–3; Howard K. Nixon, *Attention and Interest in Advertising* (New York: n.p., 1924), 36–51; Daniel Starch, *Advertising Principles* (Chicago: A. W. Shaw, 1927), 300–4. For England, see Cyril C. Freer, *The Inner Side of Advertising* (London: Library Press, 1921), 75–88; Frank Watts, 'The Psychological Basis of Publicity', in *Modern Advertising*, vol. 2. (London: Sir Isaac Pitman, 1926), 55, 103, 151, 194, 245, 373.

[82] Russell, *Commercial Advertising*, 127.

[83] A. J. Greenly, *Psychology As A Sales Factor* (London: Sir Isaac Pitman, 1927), 151; D. B. Lucas and C. E. Benson, *Psychology for Advertisers* (New York and London: Harper, 1930).

the desired impression, often without being conscious of it'.[84] As part of a counter-offensive by corporate America against the muck-rakers of the Progressive era, public relations developed strategies to improve the image rather than directly sell the products of big business.[85] Ivy Lee, for example, manipulated the press to blunt the violent realities of a miners' strike in Colorado, and Edward Bernays, the nephew of Freud and one of public relations' more articulate boosters, devised a series of stunts to promote his client's products. To expand the market for the tobacco industry, he created events which helped connect women's smoking in public with the idea of equality and, as he proudly related in his memoirs, 'I also hit on the soap-sculpture movement, and as a result millions of school children carved Ivory soap for the next quarter century.'[86]

In Britain before 1930, public relations never attained the autonomous status and, in some quarters, sinister reputation attached to the activity in the United States. Rather, a small number of influential advertising men and corporate managers assimilated its central principle that the overall image of a corporate entity, including the advertising industry itself, might be as important as the individual product it sells. Like Bernays and other experts in public relations, these British publicists believed that some advertising might be classed as a beneficial form of propaganda, and even a public service. Charles Higham, for example, argued in his book *Scientific Distribution*, published in 1916, that both advertisers and corporate administrators should work in concert to create 'a truly enlightened Public Opinion' favourable to British business.[87] During the First World War, Higham served as Director of Publicity of the National War Savings Committee and later became a key figure in the attempts during the 1920s to sell the products of the Empire. He believed that publicity might serve noble causes in any number of areas. 'There is no good habit or lofty idea', he wrote, 'that could not be inculcated in a people in a few short years, if the right methods were used.'[88]

A second figure who conceived of a broader role for British advertising than merely selling specific goods was William Smith Crawford, whose

---

[84] Edward L. Bernays, *Propaganda* (New York: Horace Liveright, 1928), 69.

[85] Alan R. Raucher, *Public Relations and Business, 1900–1929* (Baltimore: Johns Hopkins University Press, 1968), pp. vi–viii; Richard S. Tedlow, *Keeping the Corporate Image: Public Relations and Business, 1900–1950* (Greenwich, CT: Jai Press, 1979), 15–18.

[86] Edward L. Bernays, *Biography of an Idea: Memoirs of Public Relations Counsel Edward L. Bernays* (New York: Simon and Schuster, 1965), 344, 386–7. For a discussion of the impact of advertising in the 1920s on the smoking of cigarettes by American women, see Michael Schudson, *Advertising, the Uneasy Persuasion: Its Dubious Impact on American Society* (New York: Basic Books, 1984), 192–7.

[87] Higham quoted in Raucher, op. cit., 118–19.

[88] Higham quoted in Howard Wadman, 'Looking Forward', *Penrose Annual* 42 (1940): 29–30.

agency sponsored some of the most daring innovations in commercial art during the 1920s and who also became an influential supporter of the Empire Marketing Board. Born in Glasgow in 1878, Crawford set up his London agency in 1914 and quickly rose to prominence within the profession. 'We are handicapped to-day in British advertising', he wrote in 1926, 'by the old Victorian idea that advertising was something to be ashamed of.' Crawford believed that 'advertising is education . . . not merely salesmanship.'[89] He employed some of the most talented artists in his agency, such as Edward McKnight Kauffer, and, like Higham, became an effective spokesman for advertising as a shaping force in public opinion. 'The real power of advertising', he wrote, 'is not to sell goods, but to form habits of thinking.'[90]

But the man who became most famous for employing artists and typographers to help improve the public image of a corporate entity was Frank Pick, long-time administrator with the London Underground and eventually managing director of the London Passenger Transport Board. Born in 1878 the eldest son of a draper, Pick was hired by the North-Eastern Railway Company in 1902, and spent the rest of his life working for the transport industry. Like Reith a man with a mission and a dictatorial style of leadership, Pick became a founding member and driving force in the Design and Industries Association and its chairman in 1921.[91] In an article 'Art in Modern Life', published in 1921, Pick enunciated his view that sound aesthetics ought not be confined to the tiny minority who display their work in galleries. 'Art must be rediscovered in life,' he insisted; '. . . The task is to acquire for it an ever widening sphere so that all life is made a seemly thing and filled with beauty.'[92]

To fulfil this goal, Pick became one of the great patrons of Modernism in commercial art. He hired Edward Johnston to design a new, more modern type-face for the Underground which would replace the serviceable but dated Grotesque type initially favoured by the company. Johnston designed a highly legible, stylistically distinct variation of sanserif, a type crudely employed in the nineteenth century but one which, in its simplicity, rationality, and lack of decoration, eventually became synonymous with Modernism. From Johnston, the Underground acquired a striking visual

---

[89] William S. Crawford, 'The Business Firm's Advertising Expenditure', in *Modern Advertising*, vol. 1 (London: Sir Isaac Pitman, 1926), 162.

[90] Id., *How To Succeed in Advertising* (London: World Press News [1931]), 22. On Crawford, see G. H. Saxon Mills, *There is a Tide* (London: William Heinemann, 1954).

[91] On Pick, see Christian Barman, *The Man Who Built London Transport: A Biography of Frank Pick* (Newton Abbot: David and Charles, 1979); and Pevsner, *Studies*, 190–209.

[92] Frank Pick, 'Art in Modern Life', *Nineteenth Century and After* 91 (1922): 264, 262.

style in its typography which distinguishes it to this day.[93] Pick also hired some of the most imaginative graphic artists to design posters for the company. Some of these posters depicted pleasant locations which the Underground permitted Londoners to reach inexpensively on their days off. Others employed vivid colours and more abstract designs to illustrate the advantages of the system. 'Those who decry posters which require some pains and thought for their understanding', Pick admonished his critics, 'underrate the urge to stretch the mind a bit more than usual, underrate indeed the intellectual level of an urban population.'[94] London Underground posters became collectors' items beginning in the inter-war era, when special shops set up by the company sold thousands to the interested public.[95]

Like Reith, Pick was a realist as well as an idealist. He recognized that the Underground, a uniquely modern form of transportation which combined speed and convenience with a certain subterranean gloom, needed publicity which both reflected its novel status and ameliorated its less desirable features. He employed the best, most creative commercial artists because he hoped to improve the image and increase the trade of his company. Quality advertising, he wrote in 1927, permits 'the establishment of goodwill and good understanding between the passengers and the companies'.[96] In its typography, posters, and, during the 1930s, in the design of its new stations, the Underground created through its publicity and design an image of tasteful modernity which provided a unique corporate identity. Pick helped transform William Morris's ideal of the unity between art and the everyday world to the advantage of commerce. Unified design created a desirable corporate image. One nexus between art and industry lay in cultivating good public relations.

Another link could be found in government. In the United States, Bernays considered 'propaganda' and 'public relations' to be two manifestations of the same phenomenon, while in Britain, experts also used terms such as 'projection' and 'publicity' to describe government attempts to influence public opinion.[97] The British government first became seriously involved with modern propaganda during the First World War but, as a number

[93] Priscilla Johnston, *Edward Johnston* (London: Faber and Faber, 1959), 198–205; Denis Megaw, '20th-Century Sans Serif Types', *Typography* 7 (1938): 28–31; C. G. Dandridge, 'Evolution in Printing of Railway Propaganda', *Penrose Annual* 39 (1937): 50–5.

[94] Quoted in Barman, op. cit., 212.

[95] Christian Barman, 'London Transport Publicity', *Penrose Annual* 42 (1940): 50–4. See also Harold F. Hutchinson, *London Transport Posters* (London: London Transport Board, 1963); and Maurice Rickards, *Posters of the Nineteen-Twenties* (London: Evelyn, Adams, and Mackay, 1968).

[96] Frank Pick, 'Underground Posters', *Commercial Art* 2, 10 (1927): 137.

[97] Bernays, *Propaganda*, 25, 37.

of scholars have recently shown, these efforts sometimes proved disorganized and misconceived. Reflecting the views of many of his contemporaries, one of the advisers to the government on the subject considered propaganda 'utterly repugnant to our feelings and contrary to our traditions'.[98] This cast of mind explains in part why attempts to mount effective campaigns took so much time. To summarize briefly a complex administrative evolution, it was 1917 before the government formed a Department of Information, replacing the earlier and often highly élitist efforts by the Foreign Office. It was not until 1918 that a Ministry of Information, under Lord Beaverbrook, embarked on more professional campaigns of mass propaganda.[99] British official films during the war reflected this often admirable hesitation by officials to manage opinion. Official films about the battlefronts, such as *Ypres — the Shell-Shattered City of Flanders*, released in 1916, made little effort to conceal the horrors of war or rally strong emotional anger against the Germans. Instead, film-makers expected the images to speak for themselves. When the war ended, the government immediately dissolved the Ministry of Information, an indication of the continuing distaste which many civil servants felt for the enterprise.[1]

Although post-war revelations about the excesses of propaganda further discredited it among the general population, political attempts to mould opinion did not entirely cease in the 1920s. Unlike their opposition in the Labour Party, the Conservatives experimented with film propaganda in the inter-war period, and Baldwin, in particular, recognized the importance of electronic media in shaping public taste.[2] More important for purposes here, however, the formation of the Empire Marketing Board provided opportunities and patronage for those interested in raising the level of commercial art. Created in 1926, the Board consisted of a loose structure of business men and government officials who made recommendations and devised promotional strategies to reverse Britain's

---

[98] Quoted in M. L. Sanders and Philip M. Taylor, *British Propaganda During the First World War, 1914–1918* (London: Macmillan, 1982), 249.

[99] For the organization of propaganda, see especially Sanders and Taylor, op. cit.; Cate Haste, *Keep the Home Fires Burning: Propaganda in the First World War* (London: Allen Lane, 1977), 40–5; and M. L. Sanders, 'Wellington House and British Propaganda During the First World War', *Historical Journal* 18, 1 (1975): 119–46.

[1] Nicholas Reeves, 'Film Propaganda and its Audience: The Example of Britain's Official Films during the First World War', *Journal of Contemporary History* 18 (1983): 466–7; Taylor, *Projection of Britain*, 13. See also Nicholas Reeves, *Official British Film Propaganda during the First World War* (London: Croom Helm, 1986).

[2] T. J. Hollins, 'The Conservative Party and Film Propaganda Between the Wars', *English Historical Review* 96, 379 (1981): 359–69; J. M. Ramsden, 'Baldwin and Film', in *Propaganda*, eds. Pronay and Spring, 126 ff; and, on radio, see Briggs, *Birth of Broadcasting*, 271.

declining position in international trade.[3] 'What we wanted to sell', Leo Amery later recalled, 'was the idea of Empire production and purchase.'[4] To supervise this ambitious effort on limited resources, Amery recruited Stephen Tallents, a civil servant who would become an important figure in the history of public relations in Britain. Born in 1884 the son of a barrister, Tallents left Oxford in 1907 to pursue a varied and successful career in government. Wounded in the First World War, he was Imperial Secretary in Northern Ireland when Amery recruited him for the EMB. A good administrator and energetic spokesman for the cause, Tallents drew on the expertise of Board members such as Frank Pick and William Crawford to aid him in selling the Empire abroad. 'The official world is coming more and more to realize the importance of advertising,' Crawford wrote happily in 1926.[5]

Tallents recorded his views on government and public relations in *The Projection of England*, a slim, elegantly produced volume of urbane patriotism published in 1932. 'If we are to play our part in the new world order,' he wrote, 'we need to master every means and every art by which we can communicate with other people.' Perhaps not surprisingly, the 'England' which Tallents believed that government ought to 'project' consisted almost exclusively of southern, upper-class institutions, diversions, and attitudes; like many civil servants and members of his class, he believed his own tastes to be the most natural and characteristic of his country. To export the virtues of such a national culture, he argued, the government needed to enlist gifted artists and designers. 'Great art has always served the needs of its time, and England needs—most urgently needs—to master the art of national projection.'[6] At the EMB, Tallents administered a poster campaign which, as one observer put it, self-consciously avoided anything 'crude or cheap in its appeal'. In a public relations campaign which eschewed advertising specific branded goods and sought instead to inculcate 'a general Empire bias to the minds of people in the United Kingdom', the EMB displayed hundreds of thousands

[3] Taylor, op. cit., 102–9; J. M. Lee, 'The Dissolution of the Empire Marketing Board, 1933: Reflections on a Diary', *Journal of Imperial and Commonwealth History* 1, 1 (1972): 49–57. For the context of imperial propaganda, see John M. Mackenzie, *Propaganda and Empire: The Manipulation of British Public Opinion, 1880–1960* (Manchester: Manchester University Press, 1984).

[4] L. S. Amery, *My Political Life*, vol. 2 (London: Hutchinson, 1953), 352. See also id., *The Empire in the New Era* (London: Edward Arnold, 1928), 10–11.

[5] William S. Crawford quoted in *Advertising Weekly*, 25 June 1926, 447. See also id., 'Making the Empire "Come Alive"', *Commercial Art* NS 1, 6 (1926): 241–6. On Tallents, see Taylor, op. cit., 110–13; and entry by A. L. F. Smith in *DNB*, *1951–1960*.

[6] Stephen Tallents, *The Projection of England* (London: Faber and Faber, 1932), 18, 44.

of posters designed by some of the same accomplished commercial artists that Frank Pick commissioned for the Underground.[7]

Yet it was not its patronage of the poster campaign which later attracted so much attention. As a small part of its activities and budget, the EMB also sponsored the making of films; both short, essentially static 'poster films' and also longer, more cinematic portrayals of the Empire and its products. To recruit and supervise these film-makers, who became the core of the documentary film movement in Britain, the EMB hired John Grierson, a young Scot who had studied moral philosophy at Glasgow University before accepting a Rockefeller Fellowship for study in the United States, where he began to cultivate a serious interest in the cinema.[8] 'The main facts of the documentary movement . . . are so well known', Rachael Low complained recently in her history of British film, 'that they are in danger of becoming a modern legend, a sort of "Grierson Story".'[9] Yet, for immediate purposes here, it is precisely this lack of mystery about the movement which may be most relevant. Grierson and other participants in the documentary-film movement were masters of self-promotion. They wrote, Tallents observed with tactful hesitation, 'sometimes, perhaps, a little over-generously of each other's productions'.[10] During the 1930s and later, Grierson and his disciples generated an enormous amount of highly articulate, self-absorbed criticism and evaluation. These writings forwarded the cause and maintained the morale of film-makers who constantly faced the indignities of an economically marginal professional existence. Yet these same writings often vastly exaggerated the aesthetic merit and social impact of the documentary films themselves. Grierson shared with the public-relations men who supported him an ability to make self-interested observations part of the public domain.

For it was primarily as public relations, not cinematic art or engaged social comment, that the documentary-film movement acquired its limited funding and distribution. 'Whatever its pretensions in purely cinematic

[7] 'The Posters of the Empire Marketing Board', *Penrose's Annual* 31 (1929), 151, 150; 'Advertising the Empire's Products', ibid., 32 (1930): 88–9.

[8] Among many books and articles on Grierson, see especially Forsyth Hardy, *John Grierson: A Documentary Biography* (London: Faber and Faber, 1979); and James Beveridge, *John Grierson: Film Master* (New York: Macmillan; London: Collier Macmillan, 1978). On the origins of the documentary movement, see Stephen Tallents, 'The Documentary Film', *Journal of the Royal Society of Arts* 95, 4731 (1946): 68–85. For a slightly different perspective, see Paul Rotha, *Documentary Diary: An Informal History of the British Documentary Film, 1928–1939* (London: Secker and Warburg, 1973), 1–65.

[9] Rachael Low, *The History of the British Film 1929–39: Documentary and Educational Films of the 1930s* (London: George Allen and Unwin, 1979), 48.

[10] Stephen Tallents, 'Cinema', typescript in British Film Institute Library, London, 22. This document became the basis of Tallents's article cited in n. 8 above.

terms,' Grierson wrote of cinema at the EMB, 'it was dedicated and devoted to the usual cold-blooded ends of government.'[11] He argued that such propaganda allowed film-makers more time and freedom to develop, but, like others who supported his ideals, he failed to confront squarely the paradox at the heart of the movement. The documentary movement defined itself as a form of alternative cinema, more liberated than commercial film to express its social concerns and more dedicated to educating rather than merely entertaining the public. 'The basic force behind it was social not aesthetic,' he wrote in 1939. 'It was a desire to make a drama from the ordinary to set against the prevailing drama of the extraordinary: a desire to bring the citizen's eye in from the ends of the earth to the story, his own story, of what was happening under his nose.'[12] Yet it was precisely as aesthetically self-conscious 'factual' films, imbued with noble social and educational purposes, that the documentaries achieved such excellent public relations. Government and, increasingly in the 1930s commercial interests such as Shell Oil and Imperial Airways, could deliver their messages, not as stark advertisements easily discounted by an increasingly sceptical and visually sophisticated public, but as 'documentaries' in a medium traditional advertisers found difficult to penetrate successfully. Unlike most directors in commercial film, who acknowledged that commerce must be served before art could be attained, the documentary film-makers wanted to believe their work transcended the sponsors who commissioned it. From the beginning, however, documentary film in Britain was a commercial art. It was constantly evaluated in such terms by the advertisers of the period, and, if judged as a species of public relations today, might be rehabilitated from easy dismissal as 'social comment' or even 'factual film'.

In the 1920s, resistance to better aesthetics within commercial art still remained strong. 'Judging from the many varieties of publicity,' Percy Bradshaw wrote in his massive compendium *Art in Advertising*, published in 1925, 'one is forced to the conclusion that comparatively few advertisers or their agents, are men of taste.' Two years later, Gilbert Russell complained that 'too many advertisements are crude and ugly and blatant.'[13] Still, within this environment of relative indifference, agitation for better commercial art continued to manifest itself in a spate of publications. In 1922, a new British trade journal, *Commercial Art*, began

[11] John Grierson, *Grierson on Documentary*, rev. edn., ed. Forsyth Hardy (London: Faber and Faber, 1966), 47.

[12] Id., 'The Story of the Documentary Film', *The Fortnightly* NS 146 (1939): 122.

[13] Percy V. Bradshaw, *Art in Advertising: A Study of British and American Pictorial Publicity* (London: Press Art School [1925]), 22; Gilbert Russell, *Advertisement Writing* (London: Ernest Benn, 1927), 122. See also Kenneth M. Goode and Harford Powell, jun., *What About Advertising?* (New York and London: Harper, 1927), 212–13.

publishing articles and illustrations which forwarded the cause of 'better business through better Art'. Books such as Bradshaw's and others offered both examples and a rationale for improvement. In 1924, for example, the Chairman of the British Institute of Industrial Art, Hubert Llewellyn Smith, argued in *The Economic Laws of Art Production* that the 'struggle for future economic leadership will turn more and more on quality rather than on quantity of production'.[14] Perhaps more important, as we have seen, elements within both business and government discovered compelling reasons to act as patrons and supporters of better commercial art. Frank Pick, William Smith Crawford, Stephen Tallents, and others combined genuine idealism with a shrewd knowledge of the market to encourage the cause and provide it with financial support. The new art of public relations formed part of a complicated mosaic, extending at least back to William Morris and the Arts and Crafts Movement, which sought to do for sight what John Reith and the BBC hoped to accomplish in sound.

C.   OUTSIDERS AND ADVOCATES

In the 1920s, a small number of enthusiasts for film and gramophone sponsored organizations and journals that catered to cultivated minorities. These tiny and sometimes economically troubled institutions often enunciated missionary goals reminiscent of other progressives, such as Reith and Pick, but they also frankly recognized their own marginal position within the market system and indeed prided themselves on their cultural distinctiveness. Although to practice economies of scale the film and gramophone industries generally courted the largest possible audience, demand rarely proved monolithic, especially internationally, and market fragmentation created a small but economically viable niche for art films and classical music. For some, this status within the market proved troubling; it was one thing to be a cultural élite which set standards others admired and emulated; it was another simply to be one minority among hundreds of others. Yet precisely because these societies and magazines set for themselves limited goals, they succeeded in ways which institutions such as the BBC, with its more lofty ambitions, could not. For purposes here, not all these groups will be discussed; instead, the Film Society and *Close-Up* will be examined briefly, and the magazine *The Gramophone* in far greater detail.

---

[14] 'Our Common Cause', *Commercial Art* 1, 3 (1922): 41; Hubert Llewellyn Smith, *The Economic Laws of Art Production: An Essay Towards the Construction of a Missing Chapter of Economics* (London: Oxford University Press, 1924), 14.

The Film Society was founded in the mid-1920s to screen films and generate support for cinema which regular exhibitors rejected as commercially unappealing. Earlier in the century the Stage Society provided a similar forum for experimental playwrights, and the Ciné Club in Paris, among others, offered a Continental precedent for the English group. 'We were crusaders, propagandists for something that would otherwise have been neglected and ignored,' one of its founders, Ivor Montagu, later recalled.[15] A Marxist, Montagu contributed to the politically radical image of the society which, in the late 1920s, introduced to a limited British audience both the early documentary films and the great revolutionary cinema of Eisenstein, Pudovkin, and others. Not uniquely, the Film Society combined this apparent political radicalism with a strong dose of intellectual and cultural élitism. 'Half the snobs in London, intellectual and social, were at the opening,' Montagu recalled.[16] Early members of the society included an impressive sampling of London's cultural leaders: H. G. Wells, Roger Fry, J. B. S. Haldane, Julian Huxley, John Maynard Keynes, Edward McKnight Kauffer, Lord David Cecil, Augustus John, George Bernard Shaw, and, from the film and entertainment industry, Sidney Bernstein, Anthony Asquith, and Iris Barry.[17] In part to avoid problems with censorship, the society operated as a private club, which necessarily restricted its appeal and drew the opposition of film critic C. A. Lejeune, who argued that it ought to be more public. Furthermore, in 1928, the best season-tickets for eight presentations cost a hefty £3. 3s.[18] The Film Society offered evidence that, as a medium, the cinema had matured sufficiently by the 1920s to be integrated into the more traditional social and cultural élites.

Close-Up, a pioneering journal of avant-garde film criticism, began its short six-year existence in 1927 on an investment of £60. Published in Switzerland and edited by Kenneth Macpherson, *Close-Up* treated mostly Continental cinema with the seriousness usually reserved for more traditional literary and artistic works. It encouraged younger talent, Basil Wright later remembered, that 'if they wanted to be creative they needn't try to be playwrights or novelists — here was a new medium which was

[15] 'Interview: Ivor Montagu', *Screen* 13, 3 (1972): 84. See also Ivor Montagu, *The Youngest Son* (London: Lawrence and Wishart, 1970), 272–80.

[16] Id., 'Birmingham Sparrow: In Memoriam Iris Barry, 1896–1969', *Sight and Sound* 39, 2 (1970): 107. For a more contemporary description, see id., 'The Film Society, London', *Cinema Quarterly* 1, 1 (1932): 42–6.

[17] Low, *British Film, 1919–1929*, 34.

[18] Caroline Moorehead, *Sidney Bernstein: A Biography* (London: Jonathan Cape, 1984), 23; The Film Society, Third Annual Report (1928), Paul Rotha Collection, National Film Archive, London.

still virtually untouched.'[19] Begun as a quarterly with a circulation of around 500 readers, the magazine became a monthly in 1930, only to confront economic problems, competition from newer journals, and internal editorial disputes which a peak circulation of 5,000 readers could not resolve.[20] Yet like the Film Society, *Close-Up* discovered a small, dedicated audience which rewarded the experimental in a medium dominated by the conventional. Film criticism need not consist solely of 300-word evaluations in a daily newspaper or weekly magazine.

The Gramophone, established in 1923, was the first magazine in any language to treat recorded music as seriously as the great British literary reviews examined the written word. The magazine reviewed carefully the new releases of the industry and served as a forum for the lively opinions of its founder. It disseminated information on the technical developments of sound reproduction and, above all, it encouraged the record companies to produce and the public to buy serious music. The creator of this still thriving monthly magazine was neither a musician nor a music critic, but a novelist with a flair for the dramatic and a penchant for the whimsical. Compton Mackenzie was born in 1883, the eldest son of a famous theatrical couple. As a student at Oxford, one contemporary recalled, 'he was a dazzling figure . . . the cynosure of every eye—with a romantic cloak over his shoulder and his hair brushed back in Byronic disorder.'[21] Mackenzie published his first work, a book of poems, at the age of twenty-three, and two of his early novels, *Carnival* and *Sinister Street*, were both critically acclaimed and major best-sellers before the First World War.[22] Mackenzie was a man who loved islands, and this idiosyncrasy, later the subject of an eerie short story by his friend D. H. Lawrence, helped solidify his dedication to the gramophone. In 1921, Mackenzie had a gramophone and a few records sent to his home on Herm, in the Channel Islands. Once a childhood toy, the device raised in him few expectations, but when he put on a recording of the Schumann Piano Quartet, he became

---

[19] Quoted in 'The Critical Issue: A Discussion Between Paul Rotha, Basil Wright, Lindsay Anderson, and Penelope Houston', *Sight and Sound* 27, 6 (1958): 271.

[20] Winifred Ellerman ['Bryher'], *The Heart to Artemis: A Writer's Memoirs* (London: Collins, 1963), 247–65.

[21] Douglas Goldring, *Reputations: Essays in Criticism* (London: Chapman and Hall, 1920), 41–2. On *The Gramophone*, see D. L. LeMahieu, '*The Gramophone*: Recorded Music and the Cultivated Mind in Britain Between the Wars', *Technology and Culture* 23, 3 (1982): 372–91.

[22] On Mackenzie's career, see his massive autobiography: Compton Mackenzie, *My Life and Times*, 10 vols. (London: Chatto and Windus, 1963–71). See also Andro Linklater, *Compton Mackenzie: A Life* (London: Chatto and Windus, 1987). For Henry James's favourable evaluation of Mackenzie, see Henry James, 'The Younger Generation', in *Henry James and H. G. Wells: A Record of Their Friendship, Their Debate on the Art of Fiction and Their Quarrel*, ed. Leon Edel and Gordon N. Ray (Urbana: University of Illinois Press, 1958), 178–215.

enraptured, and within weeks ordered every classical selection from all the major companies, a total of 1,200 discs. No longer would the self-imposed isolation which he needed to compose fiction cut him off from music only available at the great concert halls of London. Mackenzie wrote an article for the *Daily Telegraph* about his enthusiasm and, encouraged by the number of letters the article provoked, decided that 'gramophiles' needed their own magazine, different from the trade papers.[23]

The inaugural number of *The Gramophone* contained articles which ranged from 'A Musical Autobiography' to 'How to Start a Gramophone Society'. In the 'Prologue', Mackenzie conceded that 'the critical policy of *The Gramophone* will be largely personal, and as such it will be honest but not infallible.'[24] This approach immediately distinguished the magazine from *Sound Wave* and *The Talking Machine and Wireless Trade News* which ran articles on the music of the gramophone but concentrated on the technical and commercial aspects of the trade. Moreover, Mackenzie's unequivocal status as a musical amateur separated his magazine from more professional publications such as the *Musical Times*. 'It was not . . . the purpose of our magazine to appeal to just the learned and to compete in any way with a few good music journals,' an early contributor later recalled, 'but rather to give palatable guidance and information, devoid of a plethora of technical terms, to the ordinary gramophone listener.'[25]

The early issues of *The Gramophone* sold so rapidly that, paradoxically, the editors were forced to limit sales by doubling the price and restricting the number of issues printed. With fixed advertising rates, every copy produced beyond the initial projection of sales became a dead loss. Precise circulation figures are difficult to obtain since the business records of the magazine were destroyed in the early months of the Second World War. But from surviving correspondence and other sources, it seems that *The Gramophone* sold well over 5,000 copies a month in its first year, and 12,000 copies per issue by the end of the decade.[26] These readers, according to an informal survey conducted in 1931, represented a broad cross-section of the professional middle classes, though the survey also

---

[23] Compton Mackenzie, 'How It All Began', *The Gramophone* 50, 599 (1973): 1821; id., 'The Gramophone, Its Past, Present and Its Future', *Proceedings of the Musical Association*, Session 51 (1925): 101–3; id., *Life and Times*, vol. 5, 218–20, 242–44. See also id., 'The Gramophone', *Daily Telegraph*, 2 Sept. 1922.

[24] Id., 'Prologue', *The Gramophone* 1, 1 (1923): 1.

[25] Alec Robertson, 'Reviewing the Records', *The* Gramophone *Jubilee Book* (London: General Gramophone Publications, 1973), 20–1.

[26] Compton Mackenzie, 'Editorial', *The Gramophone* 7, 73 (1929): 3; id., 'December Records', op. cit. 4, 8 (1927): 344; Christopher Stone to Compton Mackenzie, 25 May 1924, Compton Mackenzie Papers, Harry Ransom Humanities Research Center, University of Texas, Austin.

uncovered 72 'wage earners' and 64 'clerks' among its 460 respondents.[27] *The Gramophone* found a particularly sympathetic audience among the various 'Gramophone Societies' scattered throughout the country. These local organizations, which began in Liverpool and Manchester before the war, sustained their greatest growth between 1924 and 1936 when over thirty new groups were formed. Ranging in membership from a handful to over five hundred, these societies sponsored lectures, discussions, concerts, and social activities. *The Gramophone* encouraged these groups by devoting a considerable number of its pages to their local activities and, later, by helping organize the National Association of Gramophone Societies.[28]

If the magazine tried to develop close relations with its readers, it also sought 'to encourage the recording companies to build up for generations to come a great library of good music'.[29] In 1923, when *The Gramophone* was founded, most classical recordings were annoyingly short excerpts. There was only one complete recording of Beethoven's Fifth Symphony, for example, and selections from three others. Two years later, there were twenty-three complete recordings of Beethoven symphonies, including three of the Third, four of the Seventh, and three of the Ninth. Despite this largesse, the classics remained a distinctly minority taste and, though accurate statistics remain difficult to obtain, it seems that already by the late 1920s dealers found themselves with large surpluses of these records.[30] Mackenzie never really understood the economics of the industry, or if he did, preferred to operate under the bracing illusion that supply generated demand. In the late 1920s he conceived the notion that great music sold poorly because it was titled so impersonally and cynically suggested that Brahms's Quartet in A minor Opus 51, Number 2 would sell a million copies if retitled 'Your Lips are Hot, Honey'.[31]

In the early 1920s *The Gramophone* formed its own organization to record and distribute lesser classics whose demand was predictably slight. Founded in 1924, the National Gramophonic Society enlisted the Spencer Dyke Quartet to record chamber music which members agreed to purchase at an attractive price. In its early announcements, the society made clear that it was not an attempt to rival the industry, rather, 'its only object

[27] Compton Mackenzie, 'Editorial', *The Gramophone* 9, 100 (1931): 109–12.
[28] W. W. Johnson, 'The Gramophone Society Movement', *The Gramophone* 14, 158 (1936): 85–7.
[29] Mackenzie, 'Prologue', *Gramophone* 1, 1 (1923): 1.
[30] Gelatt, *Phonograph*, 237–44; G. S. Davis, 'Service Without Sales: The Dealer's Point of View Again', *The Gramophone* 6, 72 (1929): 526–8.
[31] Compton Mackenzie, 'Editorial', *The Gramophone* 6, 70 (1929): 425–6. On the response of industry to this suggestion, see Herbert C. Ridout to Compton Mackenzie, 27 Feb. 1929, Compton Mackenzie Papers.

is to supplement the normal commercial output of certain kinds of records for the benefit of [a] handful of the buying public.' As record companies increased the size of their classical catalogue, the rationale of the society became less compelling, but it issued 166 records before its dissolution in 1935.[32] *The Gramophone* also supported the various societies generated by the industry in the 1930s. The first of these projects, the Hugo Wolf Society, began in 1931 under the leadership of Walter Legge of His Master's Voice. It was followed soon after by the Beethoven Sonata Society.[33] Like the National Gramophonic Society, these projects produced distinguished recordings that would have been uneconomic without the guarantee of advance subscriptions.

The Gramophone assisted the industry in other ways as well. In 1925 the editors agreed to withhold mention of electrical recording until a company revised its catalogue. In 1929, Mackenzie translated *La Traviata* for Columbia at no charge and that same year assessed for the company some alternative versions of a symphony.[34] One of the editors of the magazine, Christopher Stone, often published highly complimentary statements about the industry, especially in his monthly column 'Trade Winds and Idle Zephyrs'.[35] Such occasional puffery raised a sensitive issue, since the magazine's relationship to the industry was always an area of potential conflict of interest. The magazine relied upon the industry for advertising and records for review. It tried to persuade the companies to produce more classical material and therefore needed to maintain its goodwill. On the other hand, the magazine could not possibly survive as an independent organ of opinion if its readers considered the reviews uncritical and the articles veiled advertisements. 'We are not a paper for the Trade,' Mackenzie stressed emphatically in an early issue. 'We are a paper for the Public'.[36]

If the magazine needed the industry, industry also needed *The Gramophone*. Mackenzie's random survey of his subscribers in 1931 indicated that a vast majority of them examined advertisements with care. The Managing Director of Parlophone told Christopher Stone in 1928 that, for promoting one product line, 'the results of advertising in *The Gramophone*

[32] 'N.G.S. Notes', *The Gramophone* 2, 5 (1924): 158; 'The National Gramophonic Society', *The Gramophone* 2, 3 (1924): 87; 'British Retailers Educated the Public and Profited', *Talking Machine World* 23, 6 (1927): 54; Christopher Stone, 'The National Gramophonic Society', *The Gramophone* 12, 143 (1935): 432.
[33] Gelatt, *Phonograph*, 259–60.
[34] Compton Mackenzie, 'Editorial', *The Gramophone* 6, 81 (1930): 390; Herbert C. Ridout to Compton Mackenzie, 5 Feb. 1929, Compton Mackenzie Papers; W. S. Meadmore, 'Sir Louis Sterling', *The Gramophone* 15, 169 (1937): 6.
[35] See for example, 'Trade Winds and Idle Zephyrs', *The Gramophone* 7, 74 (1929): 83.
[36] Compton Mackenzie, 'Editorial', *The Gramophone* 1, 7 (1923): 121.

are far and away ahead of any other publicity devoted to these instruments.'[37] More important, the men who ran the companies were not all the vulgarians whom critics of the entertainment business revelled in caricaturing. Some, like Louis Sterling, genuinely believed in the value of the classics and took economic risks in recording them. In the boardrooms of the great recording firms, these men could point to the success of *The Gramophone* as proof to their accountants that a market awaited 'serious' music.[38] Then too, in a country where wealth alone could not confer social status, few captains of industry wished to be known solely for their ability to milk profits from dance bands. The kind of music which *The Gramophone* defended was not without its social usefulness.

Like the Film Society and *Close-Up*, *The Gramophone* provides an interesting case-study of how a newer technology of communication was assimilated by some members of a cultural minority. At a time when many genteel people refused to imbibe their culture from mechanical contrivances, *The Gramophone*, like the Film Society and similar institutions, became havens of encouragement and mutual support for those who championed the artistic potential of new technologies. Though small and sometimes short-lived, these institutions could serve their constituencies with fewer of the compromises that larger, more ambitious organizations, such as the BBC, confronted. Magazines such as *The Gramophone* served a speciality market with limited needs, rather than a general audience with broad expectations. Film and gramophone societies, moreover, established personal relationships among their followers that larger, more impersonal media could not match. Yet in their reduced scale, these forms of advocacy reinforced the status of outsider about which artists and intellectuals often felt ambivalent. If such a status indicated distinctiveness, it also confirmed the isolation from the larger public which many progressives hoped the new technologies might alleviate.

Organizations such as the Film Society represented one of several strategies by defenders of the traditional arts towards the problem of commercial culture. In his ideal of public service, John Reith argued that only unified control could assure the high standards that commercial culture necessarily compromised. The BBC embodied a middle-class cultural paternalism which, with the consent of many of its potential adversaries, assured its listeners that monopoly of supply would elevate the level of demand. Commercial artists, on the other hand, worked within the market system and, for those who wanted to improve standards,

---

[37] Quoted in 'Trade Winds and Idle Zephyrs', *The Gramophone* 6, 67 (1928): 327.
[38] Interview with Anthony Pollard, Managing Director of *The Gramophone*, 29 Aug. 1978.

patronage involved complicity with the often conflicting demands of commerce and government. If the experts of public relations allowed artists more freedom, they traded upon the prestige and social distinctiveness of art which many critics believed formed the shell, not the core, of artistic endeavour. Raising standards involved several such predicaments. Yet, finding patrons and supporting institutions proved only one part of the equation. To embrace new technologies also involved coming to terms with established cultural traditions.

5

Technology and the Quest for Aesthetic Tradition

THOSE who sought to improve the aesthetic standards of the mass media not only confronted the difficulty of finding patronage which shielded them from the harsher realities of the market mechanism. The embrace of new or recently upgraded technologies of mass communications also involved two other closely interrelated problems which shaped the agenda of cultural progressives during the inter-war era. First, most reformers felt keenly the need to justify and make legitimate their espousal of technologies which in many circles garnered little social and cultural respectability. New forms of mechanized entertainment lacked fidelity of reproduction and other desirable attributes of technological maturity sufficient to override the deep-seated ambivalence which characterized the upper-class attitude towards machines generally. Although, for example, William Morris may have parted from the Victorian middle classes in his political radicalism, his posture towards modern technology clearly reflected his social origins and cultural allegiances. A fashionable disdain for new technology among the cultivated formed a psychological barrier which few progressives could afford to ignore. Moreover, the long association between new technologies of communication and both commercial producers and lower-class consumers further intensified the need for the progressives to justify themselves among their peers. The cinema and gramophone, for example, suffered from guilt by association which complicated the advocacy of those who pleaded for their artistic potential. Often the progressives seemed to occupy a no man's land between the commercial forces they sought to modify and the cultivated classes they wished to impress.

This desire for legitimacy became intimately linked to a second, intellectually more engaging problem. In their attempt to uplift standards among the general public and, at the same time, attain legitimacy among their social and cultural peers, reformers needed to recapture or invent aesthetic traditions which adapted to the peculiarities of a given technology. Like their counterparts in the commercial sector, the cultural producers among the progressives varied significantly in their willingness, talent, and flexibility to master the constantly evolving potential of modern technologies of communication. Some considered a new medium as simply a more powerful extension of an existing technology and thus imposed with little modification the traditions of one discourse on to another. Others retailored existing aesthetic traditions to fit more comfortably the size and shape of a different mode of communication. Still others quite self-consciously sought to create new aesthetic traditions which celebrated fully the uniqueness of a different technology. Each of these sometimes overlapping strategies involved their own risks and rewards and none fully satisfied the ambitious, often contradictory social and personal goals of their individual proponents.

For purposes here, four case-studies of varying scope and complexity, in media involving both sound and images, will illustrate the means by which the progressives adapted tradition to technology. The first two case-studies deal with broadcasting, the newest medium of communication after the First World War and the technology over which progressives exercised their greatest influence. In the 1920s, the BBC sought not only to uplift the standards of the general population, but also, perhaps more urgently, to justify itself among the middle classes, whose cultural traditions the BBC self-consciously idealized in its programming. Although this process usually involved broadcasting a specific kind of music adopted with few compromises from the concert-halls of London, it also meant the creation of a new form of drama, with conventions different from the legitimate theatre. No single approach characterized the BBC's adaptation of a particular cultural tradition to a new technology of communication. The last two case-studies involve a variety of visual media, including typography, advertising layout, and documentary film. Here men such as Stanley Morison established histories and traditions for art forms made possible by innovative forms of mechanical repro-duction. Here too, images of the machine which shaped the pessimism of Modernists such as Wyndham Lewis became emblems of optimism and progress among commercial artists and designers of the 1920s. Finally, documentary film-makers appropriated the revolutionary myths, images, and traditions of Russian film to the more prosaic tasks of public relations for the Empire.

A. SOUND: THE RESPECTABLE RISKS OF THE BBC

The achievement of unified, centralized control by the BBC in the early 1920s protected the organization from the market forces which undermined cultural hierarchies by shifting authority away from more traditional cultural brokers. Sanctioned by government and supported by influential elements within the entertainment industry, the BBC embodied a paternalistic ideal of public service which promised to restore power to the cultivated élites who, Reith maintained, would gladly broadcast their talent and wisdom to a grateful nation. In the 1920s, broadcast technology remained in its infancy, replete with the problems and annoyances which other mass media experienced in their early years. To attain a position of cultural importance in a society shaped by the complicated cross-currents of tradition and social class, the BBC needed to transform wireless into a respectable medium of cultural exchange. In the 1920s, in particular, the BBC sought to legitimate the idea of radio, and consequently itself, with at least the same fervour and self-serving dedication that the advertising profession sold itself to an often sceptical British public. Indeed, the BBC's commitment to public service, enunciated with such forceful idealism by Reith, should be viewed as part of that campaign. In its programming during the 1920s, particularly in music, the BBC projected an image of bourgeois culture and traditions which was directed as much at the educated middle classes as it was at the nation as a whole. In the process, the BBC created a myth about itself no less powerful and certainly more enduring than the fantasies advertisers spawned about specific products.

In its early years, radio suffered from many of the same problems of inconvenience, cost, and low fidelity that marked the early decades of the gramophone. Though it was possible to purchase or construct a crystal set at a relatively low price—from around £2. 10s. to over £7 depending on the set—headphones and poor reception probably limited the audience of the BBC in its first two years to a rapidly growing number of the curious and to enthusiasts, particularly among the young. Valve sets, which vastly expanded the potential audience for wireless and became the norm by 1930, amplified sound and improved fidelity, but ranged widely in price, quality, and durability.[1] The most persistent complaint among early listeners remained 'oscillation', interference caused by positive feedback which, according to one contemporary, resembled 'a series of loud squeaks or whistles or sounds like the chirping of crickets'.[2] Understandably, these and other technical problems undermined the enjoyment of music, particularly among demanding professional critics who helped shape opinion among the cultivated. 'What the listener-in hears of a big orchestral work', Ernest Newman complained in the *Sunday Times* in 1924, 'is the merest travesty of the original.'[3]

For at least some writers and intellectuals, radio represented yet another mechanical intrusion into national culture. John Middleton Murry wrote in 1925 of his 'instinctive aversion to wireless' and a year earlier the

---

[1] Pegg, *Broadcasting and Society*, 45–8.
[2] J. A. Fleming, 'The Polite Use of the Ether', *Radio Times*, 2 July 1926, 41.
[3] Quoted in M. D. Calvocoressi, 'On Broadcasting New Music', *Musical Times* 65, 976 (1924): 502.

essayist E. V. Lucas considered broadcasting 'the latest manifestation of our deplorable modern tendency to allow machinery to take the place of individual effort. . . . The player-piano and the gramophone made it a waste of time any longer to become musicians; the cinema hypnotized us into . . . inertia, and now broadcasting comes to tickle our ears with trifles and sidetrack our brains.'[4] In 1929 the *Listener* ran a leader on 'The Intellectual and the Wireless' that pointed out the curious hesitation which characterized the literate response to new technologies. 'The intellectual, who is usually ahead of the herd in matters political, artistic and literary,' the anonymous writer observed ruefully, 'appears to be much more cautious and conservative in turning to account those great mechanical inventions which are almost as capable of revolutionizing our mental as our physical life.'[5]

The BBC responded to this hesitation in a variety of ways. First, particularly in its opening three years, it conducted an extensive campaign in both its broadcasts and official publications on the social and cultural benefits of wireless as a novel medium of communication. Radio, it was emphatically asserted, represented a modern 'miracle' of quite breathtaking proportions. 'The churches are beginning to preach from their pulpits that the age of miracles is over, and that all miracles are myths,' the poet Alfred Noyes wrote in 'Radio and the Master-Secret', published in the *Radio Times* in 1925, 'at the very moment when science itself has revealed the whole universe to be an everlasting miracle.' Radio-waves, he averred, were as Wordsworth described, 'a spirit that . . . rolls through all things'.[6] Ramsay MacDonald became 'a believer in magic' after the BBC installed a valve set in his home. 'It gave me a weird, uncanny feeling,' he wrote in 1926. 'There I was sitting at my own fireside under the grey sky of London with a Hampstead thrush whistling at my window, and yet, by the magic of my wireless set, I was again in the Salle de Reformation in Geneva attending a meeting of the Assembly of the League of Nations.'[7] These opinions manifest the often rapidly assimilated sense of wonder which greeted other mass media in the first decades of the century. However, unlike the initial audience response to gramophone and cinema, which remains largely unrecorded, the BBC made certain this childlike enthusiasm would be preserved in more permanent form and widely disseminated by recruiting some articulate and powerful members of British society to write down their first reactions to wireless.

---

[4] John Middleton Murry ['The Journeyman', pseud.], 'On Wireless and Nightingales', *Adelphi* 3, 2 (1925): 138; E. V. Lucas, 'Mixed Thoughts on Broadcasting', *Radio Times*, 5 Sept. 1924, 441.

[5] 'The Intellectual and the Wireless', *Listener*, 30 Oct. 1929, 572.

[6] Alfred Noyes, 'Radio and the Master-Secret', *Radio Times*, 18 Sept. 1925, 550.

[7] J. Ramsay MacDonald, 'As I Listened to Geneva', *Radio Times*, 16 Apr. 1926, 145.

Other arguments ranged widely in originality and persuasiveness. The Historiographer Royal of Scotland, Robert S. Rait, claimed that wireless would revive the oral traditions of lectures and public readings. Lady Alexander believed that radio would relieve the monotony of home life for women. Viscountess Erleigh hoped that broadcasting would have 'a disintegrating effect upon the power of crowd psychology'. Politicians would now be addressing individuals in their homes, she reasoned, not large groups subject to volatile emotions.[8] These arguments, along with many others in a similar vein, appeared most frequently in the *Radio Times* in the years when the BBC was still a 'Company', from 1923 to 1926. By the time of the new charter in 1927, the 'Corporation' produced fewer broadcasts and articles that marvelled at the peculiarities and speculated on the revolutionary benefits of the new technology. The phase when the medium justified itself as a beneficial novelty passed relatively quickly.

The articles by Robert Rait, Lady Alexander, and Viscountess Erleigh were all composed by individuals of recognized social standing or intellectual eminence. What they said may have been less important than who they were. The case for radio never rested exclusively on abstract arguments about its social and cultural utility; as many have recognized, social class played a major role. Yet the BBC enhanced its own respectability and that of the medium it monopolized not simply by making the Corporation a privileged enclave of middle-class officials and social values. More important, it self-consciously invented an idealized version of a fragile, never fully realized, middle-class cultural tradition which it then proclaimed to be the natural and authentic culture of the nation. Although such a policy was not without its own tensions and contradictions, it invited the admiration and brilliantly foreclosed criticism from the social strata that the BBC most needed to persuade in its quest for legitimacy. 'The risks he has taken', Harold Laski shrewdly observed of Reith in 1931, 'are always those which the eminently respectable have no difficulty in approving.'[9]

Both contemporary observers during the inter-war period and recent scholars have often acknowledged the Corporation's preoccupation with social class.[10] The Board of Governors was overwhelmingly upper class

---

[8] Robert S. Rait, 'The Return of the Ear', *Radio Times*, 15 Aug. 1924, 309–10; Lady Alexander, 'What Women Listeners Gain', *Radio Times*, 1 Jan. 1926, 49–50; Viscountess Erleigh, 'New Influences on Crowd Psychology', *Radio Times*, 23 Sept. 1927, 497–8.

[9] Harold Laski, 'Sir John Reith', *Daily Herald*, 21 Mar. 1931.

[10] For the BBC and social class, see Krishan Kumar, 'Holding the Middle Ground: the BBC, the Public and the Professional Broadcaster', in *Mass Communication*, eds. Curran *et al.*, 231–48. For the views of Briggs, see his *Birth of Broadcasting*, 211–12, 234–50, and *Golden Age of Wireless*, 40–1.

and both Reith and Admiral Carpendale, his trusted deputy who retired officially but not psychologically from the British Navy, agonized over the social status of employees hired for important positions. The required interview with Carpendale, one high official later wrote, concentrated on 'the social qualifications of the candidates—whether they came from the right type of Public School, and had influential "connexions" or not'.[11] The BBC was 'a world of busy, loyal, agreeable people,' one recruit told Reith; 'in fact, it was the kind of world that I left behind me at Winchester.'[12] This feeling that the BBC was an extension of the public schools appears frequently in the memoirs of the period. 'It was asked of every applicant for a responsible job in the BBC,' Peter Eckersley later recalled, "Is he a gentleman?"' After summarily rejecting for a minor post a scholarship student from Glasgow, Reith told an aide: 'I sized him up at once as a type of young Scottish nobody.' Reith himself deeply regretted not having a degree from Oxford or Cambridge, and hired a disproportionate number of his lieutenants from those institutions.[13] Announcers were expected to speak with a proper accent, and in the early years of the BBC wore full evening dress while broadcasting.

In their implementation of Reith's ideal of public service, BBC programmers constructed a schedule which reflected the biases and most treasured cultural aspirations of their class. These aspirations manifested themselves in many areas of the broadcast schedule, not all of which can be discussed here. The BBC's religious policy, for example, mirrored the Sabbatarian discipline of the Victorian middle classes, long since eroded by declining church attendance and other social changes.[14] Despite many sincere attempts within the organization to make 'Talks' more lively, official policy reflected the image of middle-class life as one long exercise in self-improvement. In an 'Open Letter to the Listener Who Hates Talks', published in the *Radio Times* in 1930, Douglas Woodruff reminded his readers that broadcast discussions had taught 'how bats sleep, where papier mâché comes from, common faults in humming, secrets of sardine tinning, the evolution of braces', and other useful things. 'No one pretends that

---

[11] Richard S. Lambert, *Ariel and All His Qualities: An Impression of the BBC From Within* (London: Victor Gollancz, 1940), 26–7.

[12] R. A. Rendall quoted in Reith, *Into the Wind*, 167.

[13] P. P. Eckersley, *The Power Behind the Microphone* (London: Jonathan Cape, 1941), 173; Lambert, op. cit., 28; Reith, *Wearing Spurs*, 150. The BBC was criticized by the Ullswater Committee for its disproportionate number of Oxbridge graduates: *Report of the Broadcasting Committee*, Cmd. 5091 (London: HMSO, 1936), 13.

[14] On the BBC's religious policy, see Kenneth Wolfe, *The Churches and the British Broadcasting Corporation, 1922–1956: The Politics of Broadcast Religion* (London: SCM Press, 1984). For background, see John Wigley, *The Rise and Fall of the Victorian Sunday*: (Manchester University Press, 1980).

acquiring information is particularly pleasant,' he continued, 'any more than physical jerks are particularly pleasant.'[15]

It was in its policy towards music that the BBC most self-consciously constructed a flattering image of bourgeois cultural traditions and social identity. Music occupied a large share of BBC programming and thus best exemplified the Corporation's sense of its own mission. Although programmers recognized their obligation to satisfy the diverse tastes of all segments of British society, the BBC defined 'music' in a way which marginalized and sometimes excluded much of what the majority, including many within the middle classes, considered acceptable forms of entertainment. As Paddy Scannell pointed out in a recent article: 'Dance bands, the cinema organ, operetta and musical revues were never officially classified as music. . . . Symphonies, chamber music, opera and contemporary *avant-garde* compositions—these were the forms of true music.'[16] This definition gave concrete expression to what Reith believed constituted the 'best' in culture, and its implementation determined the programming, finances, structure, and official attitudes of the early BBC. Yet to what degree it accurately reflected the day-to-day realities, rather than the hopes, of the classes most impressed by it remains a much more open question.

BBC officials made certain that 'music' as they defined it occupied a privileged place on the broadcast schedule. In its official publications, the BBC stoutly maintained that it offered a 'balanced' selection of programmes, carefully arranged to satisfy the tastes of its diverse audience while at the same time fulfilling its ideal of public service. 'The problem of the programme builder', one official wrote in a special broadcasting issue of *The Times*, 'is to dispose the resources of broadcasting . . . in such a way that the greatest possible number of individual listeners may find programmes to interest and to amuse them at times at which they are most able to listen, and in proportions which reasonably reflect the general purposes of broadcasting.'[17] In the second volume of his history, Asa Briggs produced a chart of 'Programme Constituents' which he, in defence of the BBC, argued exhibited such 'balance'. Thus, for example, during one randomly selected week in each October between 1927 and 1930, 'classical music' was aired from between 15.79 to 20.01 hours,

[15] Douglas Woodruff, 'An Open Letter to the Listener Who Hates Talks', *Radio Times*, 2 May 1930, 253. On talks and BBC policy generally, see Hilda Matheson, *Broadcasting* (London: Thornton Butterworth, 1933).

[16] Paddy Scannell, 'Music for the Multitude? The Dilemmas of the BBC's Music Policy, 1923–1946', *Media, Culture and Society* 3 (1981): 243. I have learned much from this article, though I do not agree with all its conclusions.

[17] 'Programmes: Interests in Conflict', *The Times*, Special Supplement, 14 Aug. 1934, p. xvii.

whereas 'dance music' occupied from 9.92 to 19.76 hours during the same period. 'Light Music', a broad category including such things as musical comedy and cinema organ, occupied from 21.87 to 35.84 hours during the same period.[18] Clearly, these figures reveal some degree of balance in the total number of hours broadcast among various musical tastes. Yet these aggregates conceal a vital factor for evaluating the music policy of the BBC. It was not simply the raw number of broadcast hours which determined the balance of a schedule. As broadcasters grasped quite early, timing proved far more crucial. When something was broadcast vitally affected the size and nature of its audience. Classical music, or as the BBC deemed it, 'music', may have occupied less than a third of the total number of broadcast hours, but it was usually scheduled from between eight and ten o'clock on weekday evenings, prime listening hours. Thus, for example, until 1936 the BBC carried on its National Programme the symphonic music of the Proms six days a week, from 8.00 to 10.30 p.m., for the entire seven weeks of its annual season.[19] After 1927 the BBC usually provided alternative programmes, but even these occasionally 'balanced' such things as symphonic music with, say, the reading of poetry. More popular programming might be found, but not always at the most convenient hours. Depending on what weeks one chooses to compare, a significant percentage of the ten to twenty hours per week of dance music usually did not begin until 10.30 p.m., when most people had already retired.

Other aspects of official policy reflected this programming bias. The BBC always devoted far more of its finances to 'music' than to other forms of entertainment. Although changing accounting techniques and organizational patterns make comparisons difficult, the BBC spent lavishly on orchestras and the production of classical music while pleading financial hardship when it came to more popular programmes. Then too, while approved music enjoyed its own autonomous department within the BBC, which lobbied for its causes, no such department existed for popular entertainment, 'a great organizational weakness', Briggs acknowledged.[20] High officials expressed a hostility towards most popular music which assured its marginal place within the organization. Reith considered jazz 'degrading' and when in 1926 he was asked by someone within the organization about dance music, he replied 'we should indeed be sorry if we are giving any more than the minimum necessary.'[21] Three years later, the Programme Board listened to the internal complaint from one

[18] Briggs, *Golden Age of Wireless*, 34–6.
[19] Scannell, op. cit., 253.
[20] Briggs, op. cit., 44–6, 79.
[21] Managing Director to Professor A. M. Low, 20 Nov. 1926, R34/323, BBC Written Archives Centre, Reading.

official 'that when Dance Music was broadcast at the end of the evening programme it was frequently announced that "this was the end of the programme but there would be Dance Music for those who wanted it", and that this was announced in a manner which made it appear as if dance music was beneath contempt.'[22]

The BBC's definition of music and its implementation in policy reflected less the diverse realities of middle-class musical tastes than a preferred image of its own cultural identity. Since this assertion once again involves the thorny problem of cultural demand, evidence must necessarily remain circumstantial. Certainly there were individuals in the 1920s whose tastes accurately mirrored those of the BBC, but who were they and what proportion of the population did they represent? First, as other scholars have acknowledged, the programmers of the BBC often sought to appease professional musicians and academics with more vigour than they dedicated to uplifting the tastes of the general public. Programmers responded to the requests of 'experts', whose tastes reflected narrow, often esoteric professional interests. In formal testimony, Adrian Boult criticized the Music Advisory Committee for 'trying to bully the Corporation into adopting courses of action which they think would be to the benefit of the music profession, but without due regard for the Corporation's programme standards or the interests of the listening public'.[23] The *Musical Times* frequently praised the BBC lavishly, but it also marvelled at its willingness to broadcast programmes that few would dare to perform in public, for fear of losing their already self-selected audience. Thus, for example, the BBC transmitted a commissioned series of 'Contemporary Music' from a London concert-hall in which, Percy Scholes later recalled, 'the audience attracted was the smallest the present writer, in all his experience as a London music critic, ever observed. . . . He himself . . . constituted one-fourth or one-fifth of the audience.'[24] Talks devoted to music appreciation became more academically oriented during the 1920s and the *Radio Times* published its guides to specific broadcasts without translating the extensive foreign-language notations. 'Heaven knows what the plain man makes of it all,' one writer commented in the *Musical Times*.[25]

Second, the BBC both rescued the Proms from insolvency and heavily subsidized opera companies which could not have survived on their own. The BBC intervened to save the Proms in 1927, protecting Henry Wood

[22] Programme Board Minutes, 11 Oct. 1929, R34/600/4, File 4, BBC Written Archives Centre, Reading.
[23] Quoted in Briggs, op. cit., 183.
[24] Percy Scholes, ed., *The Mirror of Music, 1844–1944: A Century of Musical Life in Britain as Reflected in the Pages of the* Musical Times (London: Novello, 1947), 797 n.
[25] 'Wireless Notes', *Musical Times* 71, 1044 (1930): 131.

from what he called 'the everlasting box-office problem'. At about the same time, the Corporation devoted extensive financial resources to the British National Opera Company, which despite heroic efforts ceased to function in 1928. Two years later, in 1930, the BBC helped create the Covent Garden Opera Syndicate, which the Corporation, in a complicated financial arrangement, assisted by providing a substantial income of £25,000 a year for five years.[26] Although some contemporaries excoriated these efforts as wasteful, particularly during the Slump, sympathetic observers then and now portrayed them as triumphs of enlightened patronage. In the case of the Proms, the BBC unquestionably protected from oblivion a venerable institution with which it shared a common purpose and which, with further subsidies, later prospered. Yet these same efforts also demonstrated the sometimes tenuous hold of such music over the cultivated classes in Britain during this period. If the middle and upper classes genuinely devoted themselves to what the BBC, the Proms, and the Opera defined as music, it was not sufficiently expressed in actual attendance at public concerts. 'Box-office' was not only an abstraction which Henry Wood and opera musicians blamed for financial insolvency; it also reflected the actual musical preferences, or indifference, of tens of thousands of middle-class households.

Third, when in the 1940s sophisticated Listener Research examined the musical tastes of the British public, it revealed that only a tiny minority, even of the middle and upper classes, preferred the kind of music which the BBC most heavily subsidized and broadcast during the 1920s. The Third Programme, instituted after the Second World War, offered the kind of musical and other programming emphasized during the first decade of the BBC's history. Despite twenty years of effort by the BBC to uplift the tastes of the British public, generally less than 1 per cent of the audience, and sometimes a figure too small to measure, tuned in to the Third Programme.[27] No matter how one determines the size of the British middle and upper classes, this statistic indicates that only a small percentage of the better-educated and more economically privileged groups

[26] Briggs, op. cit., 173. On the BBC and the Proms, see also 'The BBC Saves the Proms', *Radio Times*, 10 June 1927, 466; Ateş Orga, *The Proms* (London: David and Charles, 1974), 91–4; Leslie Ayre, *The Proms* (London: Leslie Frewin, 1968); and Jerrold Northrop Moore, ed., *Music and Friends: Letters to Adrian Boult* (London: Hamish Hamilton, 1979), 86–8.

[27] The BBC did not publish most results of its listening research in the 1940s, but the files can be found in the BBC Written Archives Centre. For example, in 1949 the 'Listening Ratios' for evening programming (6.00 p.m.–11.00 p.m.) during Weeks 31–4 for the Home Service, Light Programme, and Third Programme were as follows: Week 31: 37, 62, 01; Week 32: 32, 67, 01; Week 33: 34, 65, 01; and Week 34: 37, 62, 01. During some weeks and in some areas, the Third Programme attracted an audience too small to measure. Source: BBC Memorandum to Broadcasting Committee, 1949, BBC Written Archives Centre, Reading.

within British society preferred what the BBC designated as music. Although those within the BBC committed to the notion of public service sometimes found such statistics discouraging, it did not deter them from their quest to give the public 'what it ought to have', rather than 'what it wanted'. Listener Research revealed, however, that 'what it ought to have' represented an idealized version, rather than an accurate reflection, of middle-class cultural identity. What opera, the symphony, and similar forms of music symbolized for the BBC and for the middle classes overall may have been as important as the genuine allegiance and personal support it actually commanded.

In its policy towards music and in other areas of programming, the BBC portrayed itself as the embodiment of British culture and tradition, and within a remarkably short period of time created a myth about itself that brilliantly foreclosed most criticism not only of radio as a medium in Britain, but also of the BBC as a monopolistic institution. To argue against the programming policies of the BBC often amounted to an admission of one's own philistine tastes. To be sure, some criticized the Corporation for failing to be even more refined and culturally uplifting in its programming. The BBC replied that it needed to serve the entire nation, not simply a small minority.[28] For the most part, however, and in particular among the cultivated classes, the BBC sustained few assaults to the lofty heights it portrayed itself commanding. 'Under its aegis', a leader in the *Listener* said of the BBC in 1930, 'it has been possible to build up in a very few years a tradition of commercial and political disinterestedness, and of service to national culture such as usually requires generations to establish.'[29]

The BBC particularly enjoyed contrasting itself with American broad-casting, whose commercialism, it was argued, encapsulated a national culture antithetical to that embodied by the BBC. Throughout the inter-war period, the official publications of the Corporation carried articles in which various writers and celebrities compared the two systems of broadcasting and the cultures they represented. Chaliapin claimed that he refused to sing on American radio because of its commercial financing. Harry Lauder disliked the 'muddle' of the US system and claimed that 'henceforth, British prestige among the nations will depend largely on how we develop our radio.'[30] In an article 'Should the BBC Sell Your

---

[28] For an example of such criticisms, see 'Wireless Notes', *Musical Times* 66, 990 (1925): 719. There are many other examples from this feature during the late 1920s. For the BBC's position, see Reith, *Broadcast over Britain*, 175–76, among others.

[29] 'What the Public Wants', *Listener*, 5 Feb. 1930, 232.

[30] Feodor Chaliapin, 'To My British Friends', *Radio Times*, 20 Nov. 1925, 385; Harry Lauder, 'I'll be Seein' Ye Wednesday Night', *Radio Times*, 23 Dec. 1927, 645; id. 'I'm Tellin' Ye!' *Radio Times*, 25 June 1926, 2.

Time?' one writer made explicit what might be sacrificed if the BBC adopted American methods. 'If the BBC departed from its present policy, it would not be merely time that it was selling; it would be selling a spiritual reality . . . that cannot be bought and sold without some degree of degradation to all concerned.'[31] Most high officials within the BBC had travelled to America, and many, including Reith, expressed admiration for certain aspects of American character.[32] Like many others, however, they feared the encroachment of American culture on British life. 'The American invasion of the entertainment world is responsible for many things,' one writer lamented in 1931; 'for changes of taste, for the blunting of dialect, . . . for new manners of thinking, for higher pressure of living, for discontent among normally contented people, for big ideas, and for "Oh yeah!" '[33] To these observers, the BBC represented a bulwark of British culture in a world increasingly dominated by American sights, sounds, and ideas. The BBC, one writer concluded in 1932, 'offers a model of correct use of the new medium, beside which American practice must be judged inferior'.[34]

By the early 1930s, the BBC compared itself favourably with other established institutions in Britain, such as the Bank of England, *The Times*, and the Royal Academy.[35] The Corporation's achievement of this elevated status depended in no small measure upon its ability to invent a cultural identity which influential social and political circles found difficult to fault. Confronted with the problem of mastering and making legitimate an unknown and immature medium, the BBC presented to the middle and upper classes an image of itself and its cultural traditions which virtually assured its respectability, though in 1923 few could have predicted how quickly the Corporation would assume the mantle of an entire national culture. Reith's ideal of public service translated itself into programming which uplifted the medium and the Corporation as much as the vast audience it swore to serve. The BBC demonstrated that embracing modern technology need not sacrifice cherished cultural traditions; indeed, given the right conditions, including absolute authority over an entire medium, traditions might be revived which otherwise would

[31] 'Should the BBC Sell Your Time?', *Radio Times*, 14 Dec. 1928, 717–18.

[32] See, for example, Reith's comments in his 28-page typewritten report, 'Visit to Canada and the United States of America', 25 Nov. 1933, E15/178, BBC Written Archives Centre, Reading.

[33] Basil Maine, 'Is America Killing Our Sense of Humour?', *Radio Times*, 3 July 1931, 3. For a particularly alarmed report of American encroachment on British interests, see 'Memorandum on American Control of the Entertainment Industry', (1929), R34/918/1, BBC Written Archives Centre, Reading.

[34] B. H. Haggin, 'The Music That is Broadcast in America: A Study of the American Wireless Mind', *Musical Times* 73, 1070 (1932): 305.

[35] 'Farewell to Savoy Hill', *Listener*, 4 May 1932, 632.

have perished. In the inter-war era, the BBC was the progressives' greatest triumph, though the nature of that triumph may have differed from the admirable intentions of its most forceful advocates.

B.   RADIO DRAMA: PRACTICES AND PROBLEMS OF AN AURAL ART

As part of its mandate, the BBC sought to increase the audience for cultivated drama, as well as serious music. Early in 1923, the Company broadcast selected scenes from Shakespeare and, a year later, it transmitted the first play written specifically for radio, *Danger* by Richard Hughes. By the middle of the decade, the BBC sponsored well over a hundred plays a year, and radio drama, though it usually occupied less than three hours a week of broadcast time, became an important component of the public-service ideal.[36] As BBC officials and other participants quickly recognized, however, radio drama in Britain differed from West-End theatre in at least two important respects. First, unlike traditional theatre and also the cinema, the BBC broadcast plays whose success or failure did not depend upon the box-office. Liberated from the constraints of the market mechanism, radio dramatists could afford to experiment in ways that commercial theatre might not dare. Second, the technology of wireless both imposed limitations and created opportunities for dramatists which transformed radio drama into a distinct art, separate from theatre and yet recognizably within its conventions. Like the cinema, radio drama needed to discover its own identity and create its own traditions, tasks which its supporters embraced eagerly. Unlike cinema, radio plays of the type favoured by BBC officials never became an overwhelming popular success or a major new art-form. What made drama unique on the BBC contributed to its restricted appeal.

Radio dramatists in England appreciated the aesthetic freedom which monopoly conferred. Tyrone Guthrie, one of the earliest and most talented experimenters in the new form, later recalled that 'radio offered a more promising field than the cinema, because, in Great Britain at all events, it is free from the anxieties of commercial competition.'[37] When in the early 1920s Richard Hughes tried to interest American broadcasters in radio drama, 'they rejected the whole idea. That sort of thing might be possible in England, they explained, where broadcasting was a monopoly

---

[36] Briggs, *Birth of Broadcasting*, 280–3; Briggs, *Golden Age of Wireless*, 34.
[37] Tyrone Guthrie, *Squirrel's Cage and Two Other Microphone Plays* (London: Cobden-Sanderson [1931]), 7. See also id., *A Life in the Theatre* (London: Hamish Hamilton, 1961), 48–51.

and a few crackpot highbrows in the racket could impose what they liked on a suffering public. But the American setup was different: it was competitive, so it had to be popular.'[38] Although American broadcasters soon discovered soap operas and other forms of drama well adapted to a commercialized system, their resistance made Hughes luxuriate all the more in the creative atmosphere which the BBC provided. In Britain during the inter-war period, radio dramatists could experiment without inordinate fear of a disapproving audience.

This experimentation began when BBC producers discovered the problems of broadcasting plays directly from West End theatres. Microphones concealed in flower pots and behind footlights distorted the voices of actors projecting from a stage and could never capture the visual elements central to so many plays. As a key figure in radio drama recalled, 'it required no intelligence beyond the ordinary to reach the conclusion that if plays were to be broadcast at all they must be broadcast from studios; that if they were to be successfully broadcast from studios, they must develop a technique of acting and production peculiar to themselves.'[39] Technology forced radio drama to become a purely aural art. As one participant later wrote, 'the radio play is, in fact, a play designed for a blind audience.'[40] Although in an analogous manner silent films might be thought to be designed for a deaf rather than blind audience, piano or symphonic music always accompanied these productions, and provided a crucial aural enhancement to the images on the screen. As we shall see, radio drama was not without its 'images', but they emanated from the diverse imaginations of the audience, and not from the performers. Wireless confined plays within the strict disciplines of sound alone.

As an aural art distinct from the theatre, radio drama evolved its own unique conventions and traditions. For the performer, broadcasting demanded skills that some West End veterans found difficult to master. 'It took a considerable time', Val Gielgud wrote, '. . . to persuade actors that, because the radio audience was a very large one . . . it was unnecessary for them to project their voices and their personalities as if they were playing in some super-equivalent of Olympia.'[41] Despite its audience of millions, radio proved an intimate medium which, as BBC officials recognized, rewarded those who addressed the microphone as an adjacent individual, not a remote crowd. Actors who underplayed their roles proved

---

[38] Richard Hughes, 'The Birth of Radio Drama', *Atlantic Monthly* 200, 6 (1957): 148.

[39] Val Gielgud, *British Radio Drama, 1922–1956* (London: George G. Harnap, 1957), 33.

[40] Cyril Wood, 'The Technique of the Radio Play', *Journal of the Royal Society of Arts* 138, 4487 (1938): 24. Original all in capital letters.

[41] Gielgud, op. cit., 20.

more convincing than those who adopted the more bombastic vocal conventions of nineteenth-century theatre. Radio drama buttressed a 'natural' style of acting, which Gerald du Maurier, the young Laurence Olivier, and others already practised on the stage during the 1920s and which later triumphed in film as well.[42] Moreover, as in cinema, actors in radio dramas addressed an audience which they could neither see, nor hear, nor engage in a manner often critical to performances on the stage. 'He is conscious of . . . being shut off from the world,' one observer wrote of the actor on wireless, 'and the curious acoustic quality of the studio enhances this feeling of complete isolation.'[43]

In turn, the audience found itself separated from the actors. BBC officials believed that listening to serious radio drama required greater concentration than witnessing a theatrical performance. 'If you think that you will get the reaction from a broadcast play that you will get from a theatre, you will not,' Val Gielgud warned in the *Listener* in 1931. He recommended that people turn out their lights while listening to radio drama in part because he believed that darkness allowed the mind to construct images more easily.[44] For Gielgud, as for other theoreticians of radio drama, each person at home provided what wireless technology could not. 'In radio drama the scene is built up in the imagination of the listener, and actual experience goes to the building,' Gordon Lea wrote in his pioneering *Radio Drama and How to Write It* published in 1926. 'Each individual supplies his own idea of the scene, an idea based on reality, and so sees the play in its ideal setting.'[45] Unlike silent film where local accompanists provided an essentially passive audience with the missing sensation of sound, radio drama gained its visual element from the active participation of its listeners, who may have conjured images far more satisfying than any intended by a professional actor.

For the author and producer of a radio play, the creation of an aural narrative became a special challenge. In the commercial cinema, as we have seen, breaking from the narrative conventions of theatre took time and often considerable imagination. Directors such as D. W. Griffith established a grammar for the medium which buttressed visually the formulaic plots adopted from nineteenth-century popular culture. In radio drama, authors discovered a number of narrative strategies which

[42] Laurence Olivier, *Confessions of An Actor: An Autobiography* (New York: Simon and Schuster, 1982), 65.

[43] Wood, op. cit., 33.

[44] Val Gielgud, 'The Play from the Armchair', *Listener*, 14 Jan. 1931, 62. See also Amyas Young, 'Mental Tuning In: Some Hints on How to Listen to a Wireless Play', *Radio Times*, 28 Jan. 1928, 201.

[45] Gordon Lea, *Radio Drama and How to Write It* (London: George Allen and Unwin, 1926), 40. See also Val Gielgud, *How to Write Broadcast Plays* (London: Hurst and Blackett [1932]), 11.

circumvented the unique problems of an aural medium. Initially, for example, dramatists often employed a narrator to 'bridge each episode with suitable description' and provide their stories with continuity.[46] Although the narrator, like the inserted titles in a silent film, proved a convenient mechanism to introduce and describe scenes that within the script often ranged widely over time and space, many playwrights considered the device crude and pedestrian. They sought more sophisticated techniques to create setting and unite complicated plots.

A second means of establishing narrative proved more successful and enduring. Called the 'self-contained method' by Lea in his text on radio drama, this device made the scenes 'self-explanatory in every detail. . . . It will indicate scenery, character, costume, all action— everything in fact which is necessary to the complete mental vision of the play, in the text of the play itself, with such additional help as may be required from music and sound-effects.'[47] The most obvious manifestation of this technique involved a character indicating the time or describing the surroundings; a method not entirely absent from traditional theatre ('Here is the Forest of Arden'). Playwrights quickly discovered, however, that only essential visual details needed to be provided for the drama to be effective. 'Elaborate, wordy, descriptions of landscapes and houses, of people's faces and clothes more often than not defeat their own ends . . . ,' an important figure in radio drama, Lance Sieveking, wrote in 1934. 'The radio dramatist makes no reference in his dialogue to any characteristic or property in his people or his landscape, unless it is absolutely essential for the audience to know a certain specific fact without which the plot would be un-clear.'[48] The limitations of wireless technology thus led radio dramatists to promote the virtues of minimalism at a time when some theatres voluntarily rejected the clutter of Victorian set-design and rediscovered the advantages of a bare stage.

Dramatists also experimented with more abstract modes of presenting their ideas. Although the BBC broadcast only a relatively few of these experimental productions, they frequently captured the attention of commentators, who speculated whether they might be exemplars of a new art form. Lance Sieveking's *Kaleidoscope I*, for example, traced in sound the life of an individual from cradle to grave. Broadcast in 1928, this play contained brief selections meant to convey different moods from a wide variety of music, including the symphonies of Beethoven, Black spirituals, Chopin, and jazz. The play also featured voices representing

---

[46] Lea, op. cit., 47.   [47] Ibid., 54.
[48] Lance Sieveking, *The Stuff of Radio* (London: Cassell, 1934), 76.

'Man', 'Doctor', 'Good', and 'Bad'.[49] Tyrone Guthrie's *Squirrel's Cage*,
first broadcast in 1929, tried to convey how the free spirit of youth could
be crushed by adult preoccupations with obedience and conformity.
The play contained an 'Interlude', for example, in which an abstracted
authority-figure and a chorus of voices repeated a litany of prohibitions
to a small child.

THE ONE. Don't go there.
ALL. Don't go there.
THE ONE. Don't touch that.
ALL. Don't touch that.
THE ONE. Don't listen to that.
ALL. Don't listen to that.

And so on.[50] In their chilly, distanced portrayals of average individuals
and their belief in the sterility of modern urban existence, both plays
adopted themes and techniques from such figures as T. S. Eliot and
Wyndham Lewis. The repetitious and sometimes nightmarish syncopation
of the dialogue in these plays, like the calculated rhythms of *The Waste
Land*, conveyed meaning no less significant than the words themselves.
In these and other experimental radio dramas, 'sound' often proved more
astonishing than 'sense'.

Whatever narrative strategy radio playwrights selected, however, sound
effects played a key role in enhancing the listener's visual imagination.
Producers discovered almost immediately that microphones could not be
relied upon to transmit certain noises and distorted others in curious ways.
A water fountain in the park sounded more like glass breaking on the
floor; a blank shot from a pistol came across like a cork popping from
a bottle of flat champagne. Personnel from a hastily organized sound-
effects group experimented with a variety of substitutes: banging coconut
shells together reproduced the sound of horse hooves on city streets; tilting
a large drum of buckshot suggested waves crashing on to the shore; rapidly
snapped bands of elastic wound around pieces of wood imitated a flock
of noisy sea-gulls; the crumpling of paper and a matchbox transmitted
the awful crash of a large aeroplane. When publicized, these efforts to
create a special, artificial world of sound captured the public attention.
Revelations about technique in the *Radio Times* and other publications
allowed the public to feel like privileged insiders.[51]

---

[49] As Sieveking claims, no script exists for *Kaleidoscope I*. Some excerpts may be
found in his *Stuff of Radio*, 383–5.

[50] Guthrie, *Squirrel's Cage*, 26–7.

[51] Peter Black, *The Biggest Aspidistra in the World* (London: British Broadcasting
Corporation, 1972), 34–42.

The development of the 'Dramatic Control Panel' in 1928 created new opportunities for radio drama. The panel allowed a producer to co-ordinate electronically the dialogue, music, and sound effects from a number of separate studios, thus liberating the radio play from the kind of overcrowding reminiscent of recording sessions during the acoustic era of the gramophone. Lance Sieveking, the panel's most enthusiastic advocate, compared it to a musical instrument and encouraged dramatists to write plays that challenged its technological potential.[52] It became crucial not only for complex experimental plays such as Sieveking's *Kaleidoscope I* and Guthrie's *Squirrel's Cage*, but also for more conventional narrative dramas, such as the adaptation of Compton Mackenzie's *Carnival*, first performed on radio in 1929 and repeated several times during the 1930s. At over two hours and twenty minutes, *Carnival* proved the one of the longest plays broadcast in the inter-war period, but the quick change of scenes, 'sometimes as rapid as that in a cinematograph', and the elaborate manipulation of sound effects kept the play from sagging.[53] 'There were a hundred touches which showed both ingenuity and imagination,' Grace Wyndham Goldie wrote of a production in 1936: 'the sudden uprush of mewing sea-gulls after the shot on the cliffs; the wheels of the train and of Jenny's hansom beating out the words she had heard in trains and in hansoms in the past; the timing of silences and noise at Jenny's birthday party.'[54] *Carnival* convinced many within the BBC that, nurtured by both experience and evolving technology, radio drama might emerge as another unique art-form of the twentieth-century. 'We can only hope', an anonymous critic wrote of the medium in 1929, 'that pure wireless will not be superseded by some superfluous aid to visualization before there has been time to recreate the literature of the spoken word.'[55]

Despite some notable successes, radio drama remained a marginal endeavour in inter-war Britain, both as art and as popular culture. 'I think it must be admitted', a former BBC official wrote in 1938, 'that in spite of fifteen years' broadcasting, the medium has neither attracted nor discovered many dramatists of distinction.'[56] Though the later contributions of Dylan Thomas, Harold Pinter, and others might eventually qualify this judgement, radio drama never achieved the artistic potential

[52] Sieveking, *Stuff of Radio*, 30–4.
[53] Filson Young, 'Broadcast Drama: A Record of Progress', *Radio Times*, 25 Jan. 1929, 187; 'Both Sides of the Microphone', *Radio Times*, 25 Sept. 1931, 710. For background to the adaptation, see Compton Mackenzie, '*Carnival*, 1911–1929', *Vox*, 9 Nov. 1929, 22–3; and id., *Life and Times, vol. 6* (1967), 161–3.
[54] Grace Wyndham Goldie, 'The Triumph of Carnival', *Listener*, 23 Dec. 1936, 1173.
[55] 'The Minstrel and the Microphone', *Listener*, 2 Oct. 1929, 436.
[56] Wood, 'Technique of Radio Play', 28.

its early supporters hoped. Nor in the inter-war period did radio drama ever attain the popularity of cinema and other new forms of popular culture in this century. Certain serials and melodramas introduced in the late 1930s attracted a reasonably large audience, but the 'radio drama' which Gielgud and other officials hoped would elevate British tastes remained largely unappreciated by the listening public.[57]

The wireless play dwelt on the periphery of British culture for a variety of reasons, two of which might be emphasized. First, the technology of radio permitted broadcast plays to reach a potentially enormous audience, but programmers constantly demanded new material and never continuously repeated old performances. As Lance Sieveking noted with chagrin, in radio drama 'your First Night is also your last night.' This 'ghastly impermanence of the medium'[58] meant that, unlike theatre and the cinema, specific plays could not capitalize on either critical praise or public enthusiasm to generate the audiences which created a long-running hit in the West End or a box-office smash at the cinema. As American and then British broadcasters later realized, serials and soap operas overcame this problem because the public became attached to certain characters, much as it loyally patronized films with favourite stars. In British radio drama during the inter-war period, however, no such continuity existed. Individual plays came and went like the wind.

Second and related, wireless technology and its monopolistic organization in Britain isolated radio dramatists from their audience, thus limiting the responses which actors and playwrights needed to be effective. Unable to see or hear their audience and protected from the box-office, radio dramatists performed in a vacuum that even Reith believed undermined their enterprise. Never a cultural democrat, the Director General nevertheless became irritated in the mid-1920s by the self-absorption of radio dramatists in creating their distinctive aural art. 'It seems to me that in many of our productions there is too much striving for theatre effect', Reith complained, 'and too little attempt at actually discovering the actual radio effect when the play is received in distant homes.'[59] In reflecting upon the early development of radio drama, Val Gielgud argued that

---

[57] John Drakakis, ed., *British Radio Drama* (Cambridge: Cambridge University Press, 1981), 11. In determining popularity, much depends on how the category 'drama' was defined. Some 'plays' on the BBC, especially short serials and what the Americans called 'soap operas', eventually proved quite successful with the general public. Though Listener Research often fudged categories, lower ratings in drama usually applied to the type of radio play that BBC officials themselves considered 'serious'. See, for example, Val Gielgud, *Years in a Mirror* (London: Bodley Head, 1965), 89: '1937 must wear a black spot for the introduction of the soap opera into the BBC programmes.' See also Pegg, *Broadcasting and Society*, 108, 113–46.

[58] Sieveking, *Stuff of Radio*, 15, 44–5.

[59] Quoted in Drakakis, op. cit., 2.

playwrights and producers became too fascinated with the technology of their craft:

> Plays were written—and produced on the air—less for their merits in terms of drama than because they offered opportunities for the simultaneous use of more and more studios, more and more ingenious mechanical devices. Producers concentrated more upon knobs and switches than upon actors and acting. The radio play had so far always been among 'minority' programme-items. At this particular stage it tended to grow progressively and self-consciously 'minority'. . . . The overall impression was one of a complicated mechanical toy with which a few odd young men were having a good deal of private fun.[60]

Emancipation from box-office anxieties, which Guthrie and others found so exhilarating, also inoculated radio dramatists from realities that might have improved their art. The freedom to experiment also courted the danger of self-indulgence. Drama could not prosper in a void.

Like the cinema which preceded it, radio drama evolved conventions and traditions which distinguished it from theatre and made it a unique art. Unlike cinema, however, the wireless play in Britain developed within an institutional structure which at once both encouraged experimentation and restricted its appeal. Radio dramatists explored an aural medium with an attention towards theory and a freedom of practice which directors in commercial film only rarely attained. The grammar of a new medium, which took over a generation to achieve in the cinema, fell into place within a decade at the BBC. Yet, exemption from market pressures, combined with the intrinsic limitations of wireless technology, also tempted radio dramatists to convert a public medium into a private indulgence. If during the inter-war period radio drama proved somewhat disappointing, both the medium and the monopoly shared some of the blame.

C. IMAGES: PAST AND PRESENT IN COMMERCIAL ART

The ubiquity of mechanically reproduced images in the early twentieth century marked an important transformation in British culture. The commercial incentives and rapidly improving technologies which contributed to the rise of cinema, the visual transformation of the popular newspaper, and other manifestations of mass communications through images spawned novel techniques and strategies of reaching large audiences. Commercial artists, like film directors, contributed to the evolution of this new visual grammar. Display advertising, for example, not only

---

[60] Gielgud, *British Radio Drama*, 60–1.

buttressed the finance of the popular daily press, but also provided a key source of visual interest on a newspaper page. Advertising helped shape the aesthetic tastes of millions of citizens and consequently, to the small minority committed to improving visual literacy in Britain, the commercial arts provided a special focus of concern. As we have seen, groups such as the Design and Industries Association and patrons such as Frank Pick of the London Underground and Stephen Tallents of the Empire Marketing Board provided the encouragement, finance, and institutional support to uplift the standards of commercial art. Yet the precise nature of those standards became a central question, particularly during the two decades between 1910 and 1930. For purposes here, two aspects of this complex period in the commercial arts will be emphasized. First, Stanley Morison's explorations into the history of typography helped create a pedigree for typesetting by machine which not only made the new technology more legitimate, but also contributed to a particular style of display advertising. Morison resurrected a tradition and made it novel; the past was once again present. Second, a series of artistic movements originating on the Continent, collectively designated Modernism, reconceived the nature of images, and affected commercial artists in Britain in ways that often distinguished them from the avant-garde. A complex movement with few clear aesthetic or chronological boundaries, Modernism often appeared to repudiate the past and redefine the present. Theory and practice, however, often proved at odds.

The hostility towards machines and modern technology which characterized the Arts and Crafts movement persisted among its disciples and many other designers in the early twentieth century. Yet for influential figures within the artistic establishment, particularly in education, it became increasingly difficult to ignore the realities of the new century. 'Modern Civilization rests on Machinery,' C. R. Ashbee, once head of the Guild School of Handicraft wrote in 1911, 'and no system for the endowment, or encouragement, of the teaching of art can be sound that does not recognize this.'[61] Ashbee grew tired of training craftsmen who fabricated handicraft which only the rich could afford; machines fulfilled the ideals of democracy far more efficiently. 'If we want the Arts,' he argued, 'we must enable them to meet the new industrial and economic conditions of our time.'[62] W. R. Lethaby, in his youth an ardent disciple of Morris and later the first Professor of Design at the Royal College of Art, also came grudgingly to terms with mechanization. In an important

---

[61] Quoted in Nicholas Pevsner, *Pioneers of the Modern Movement From William Morris to Walter Gropius* (London: Faber and Faber, 1936), 28.

[62] Quoted in Gillian Naylor, *The Arts and Crafts Movement* (Cambridge: MIT Press, 1971), 176. On Ashbee, see Alan Crawford, *C. R. Ashbee: Architect, Designer and Romantic Socialist* (New Haven: Yale University Press, 1985).

article, 'Art and Workmanship', published in the *Imprint* in 1913, Lethaby denied that anything made by machine could be 'art', but he granted these products qualities not far removed from what he considered more authentic work.[63] Though never entirely comfortable with their own conditional, ambivalent support of modern technology, Ashbee and Lethaby became important transitional figures between the Arts and Crafts movement which usually disdained the machine, and the modern typographers and designers who harnessed mechanization to the high standards of craftsmanship advocated by Morris.

In the printing industry, the Linotype and Monotype machines transformed the laborious process of casting and composing types. To create a new type-face in the nineteenth century, each individual letter or number needed to be cut and cast by hand, an extraordinarily skilled task which limited the introduction of new forms. In the late nineteenth century, a series of technological inventions and innovations, including the introduction of the punch-cutting machine, resulted in two new, far more efficient mechanical systems to perform the same processes. The Linotype permitted a single operator to enter copy on a keyboard which in seconds cast a single line of print into a metal 'slug'. The Monotype employed two separate machines and operators, one with a keyboard which produced a perforated code of paper ribbon, and a second machine which employed this tape to cast type. Though slower and more expensive than the Linotype, the Monotype embodied advantages which the more careful and aesthetically minded typographers preferred.[64] In Britain, the Monotype Corporation began in 1897, and three years later introduced its first new type design. Improvements before the First World War allowed the machine to set letters of virtually any size or shape, though experimentation was limited and prejudices against modern technology remained strong, particularly within the private-press movement.[65]

A central figure in overcoming these prejudices was Stanley Morison, the typographer who provided mechanization with a usable past. He was, a recent biographer wrote, 'the man who put the study of typographical history firmly on the map. He was not the only type historian and certainly not the first, but for continuous attention to the subject and in terms of

---

[63] W. R. Lethaby, 'Art and Workmanship', *Imprint* 1 (1913): 1–4. On Lethaby and the machine, see Thomas Faulkner, *Design, 1900–1960: Studies in Design and Popular Culture in the Twentieth Century* (Newcastle: Petras, 1976), 4–25.

[64] Ruari McLean, *The Thames and Hudson Manual of Typography* (London: Thames and Hudson, 1980), 80–1; Colin Clair, *A History of Printing in Britain* (New York: Oxford University Press, 1966), 286–7.

[65] Nicolas Barker, *Stanley Morison* (Cambridge: Harvard University Press, 1972), 116–20.

output of printed works, he had no rival.'[66] Born in 1889 the son of an alcoholic commercial traveller who later abandoned his family, Morison left school at fourteen to become a clerk, a job he escaped after a printing supplement in *The Times* riveted his interest in the study of letters and type. In 1913, he secured a post at the *Imprint*, a short-lived periodical committed to better typography which gave Morison the opportunity to read or make the acquaintance of the major figures in the field. A Catholic and a political radical, Morison applied for conscientious objection in 1916 and accepted alternative employment for the duration of the war. He served briefly as typographer to the Cloister Press in the early 1920s, but for the remainder of his life never again sought, nor secured, full-time employment. Instead, Morison acted as an adviser or consultant to the Monotype Corporation, Cambridge University Press, *The Times*, and other organizations.[67]

Morison's work on typography drew from a number of sources and in particular owed its inspiration to the work of American scholars. It was the Americans who developed most of the mechanized advances in the casting and composing of type, and it was Americans such as Theodore Low De Vinne, Bruce Rogers, and, above all, Daniel Berkeley Updike, who set standards of inquiry which Morison emulated. 'Just as the music of great masters like Palestrina makes familiar compositions seem thin and trivial,' Updike wrote in his two-volume *Printing Types: Their History, Forms and Use* published in 1922, 'so, by studying the monumental characters of early typography, do we learn to place in true perspective our types today.' In this landmark history and analysis, Updike sought to establish 'a standard of taste in type-forms' and thereby contribute 'to the progress of printing as an art'.[68] Morison later called *Printing Types* 'the most exciting event of the decade. . . . To us at that time the book had a messianic quality'; and in a long correspondence with Updike he acknowledged his debt to the American.[69] Morison thus extended, rather than initiated, an inquiry which began elsewhere; his

[66] James Moran, *Stanley Morison: His Typographic Achievement* (London: Lund Humphries, 1971), 165.

[67] On Morison's life and work, see the two major works (nn. 65, 66 above). See also Nicolas Barker and Douglas Clevendon, *Stanley Morison, 1889–1967: A Radio Portrait* (Ipswich: W. S. Coveli, 1969); and Herbert Jones, *Stanley Morison Displayed: An Examination of his Early Typographic Work* (London: Frederick Muller, 1976).

[68] Daniel Berkeley Updike, *Printing Types: Their History, Forms, and Use*, vol. 1 (Cambridge: Harvard University Press, 1922), pp. xxxi–xxxii. On Updike, see George Parker Winship, *Daniel Berkeley Updike and the Merrymount Press* (Rochester: Leo Hart, 1947).

[69] Stanley Morison and Rudolph Ruzicka, *Recollections of Daniel Berkeley Updike* (Boston: The Club of Odd Volumes, 1943), 2. See also Daniel McKitterick, ed., *Stanley Morison and D. B. Updike: Selected Correspondence* (New York: Moretus Press, 1979), 91, 124.

scholarship on the history of type and his philosophy of good typography borrowed from scholars less willing to press their claims to originality. Like many of the documentary film-makers, Morison tended in later life to exaggerate his own quite substantial contributions to the field.[70]

Although these contributions often proved of a highly technical nature, directed towards specialists and not easily summarized, certain themes emerged from the numerous books and articles which Morison composed during this period. First, he rejected the view favoured by many anti-quarians that the history of type offered its own reward, and served no other practical or utilitarian purpose. 'We must have new types, new ornaments . . . by the living rather than copies from the illustrious dead,' he wrote in the introduction to *Four Centuries of Fine Printing* published in 1924; 'therefore it is proper, indeed necessary, to study the history of printing not as an end in itself, but as a means, an inspiration to the typographical task before us.'[71] Though himself a practitioner of disinterested scholarship, Morison considered the past a repository of useful models, whose diversity and richness modern typographers could appropriate at little cost. History expanded the range of contemporary choices. This view assumed that certain printing types transcended their historical contexts in a manner not unlike that which T. S. Eliot, I. A. Richards, and others assigned to great poetry. At the same time, Morison scorned the slavish copying of the past and insisted that typogra-phers avoid preciousness or anachronism. 'The constant imitation and adaptation of the ancients,' he wrote in a study written in collaboration with Holbrook Jackson published in 1923, 'however lively and good as a beginning, threatens to be carried to a palsied end. In the absence of creative genius the old mines are being worked, and there is great danger of their being soon worked out.'[72] Morison believed that only certain figures and historical periods provided inspiration for modern typography and, in an array of writings, he enunciated what amounted to a great tradition.

Second, Morison favoured highly legible, classically elegant printing types and page arrangements which disdained the antique ostentation or avant-garde novelty that intruded between a reader and the text. 'Every character, every word, every line should register with maximum clearness,' he wrote in his influential article 'First Principles of Typography', published in 1930. '. . . No printer, in safeguarding himself from the charge of monotony in his composition, should admit, against his better judgement,

[70] Moran, op. cit., 67–79.
[71] Stanley Morison, ed., *Four Centuries of Fine Printing* (London: Ernest Benn, 1924), p. xxv.
[72] Stanley Morison and Holbrook Jackson, *A Brief Survey of Printing: History and Practice* (New York: Alfred A. Knopf, 1923), 53.

any typographical distraction doing violence to logic and lucidity in the supposed interests of decoration.'[73] Morison criticized some Arts and Crafts typographers, including William Morris, because their brilliantly decorated books, while pleasant to view, proved difficult to read. Modernist typography, on the other hand, sacrificed legibility to novelty; jazzy arrangements directed attention more to the design than the message and became 'so idiosyncratic as to make all reading an exercise rather than a relaxation'.[74] In his recommendations to various organizations, including *The Times*, Morison often favoured variations of Roman type, because in an understated manner it combined elegance and readability. His emphasis on well-proportioned, symmetrically arranged pages further manifested his essentially classical style in typography. 'Displaying a proportion pleasing to the eye,' he wrote in his 'Principles', 'the depth of the page follows from its width. It seems that the symmetry of the rectangle or oblong is more pleasing than that of the square, and as the oblong drives out the line to an impossible length, . . . the rectangle has become the normal page.'[75]

Third, like many progressives, Morison could not praise a cloistered virtue; he believed that good typography should extend to newspapers, advertising, and other aspects of commercial culture. To this end, in 1932 he published *The English Newspaper: Some Account of the Physical Development of Journals Printed in London Between 1622 and the Present Day*. Written during the period when he reshaped the typography and layout of *The Times*, Morison's history represented 'a first attempt to interest students of bibliography in the history of newspaper development'. The newspaper, he argued, though 'essentially ephemeral . . . yet has a place, though humble, beside the codex and the printed book—the most permanent records of human thought and experience'. Morison described, analysed, and offered numerous illustrations of layout and typography beginning with the news-pamphlets which preceded newspapers in the seventeenth century. Among other topics, he included chapters on weekly journals in the eighteenth century, the early Sunday press, mid-Victorian penny and halfpenny papers, the New Journalism, and the contemporary newspaper. Like his work on the history of book typography, Morison believed that his extensive scholarship served a didactic purpose. The history of such newspapers as *The Times* demonstrated, he argued near the end of his study, 'that no journal . . . can for any length of time isolate itself from the reading habits of prospective readers.'[76] In his recognition

---

[73] Stanley Morison, 'First Principles of Typography', *Fleuron* 7 (1930): 69.

[74] Id., *Modern Fine Printing* (London: Ernest Benn, 1925), p. xv. For his views of Morris, see Stanley Morison, 'Towards an Ideal Type', *Fleuron* 2 (1924): 69.

[75] Id., 'Principles', *Fleuron*, 66. See also id., *On Type Faces* (London: Media Society and Fleuron, 1923), pp. v–xxi.

[76] Id., *The English Newspaper*, pp. xi, 318–19.

that Northcliffe rescued the paper in part by making it more visually alive, Morison helped make legitimate the graphic techniques and experimentation of the popular press. *The English Newspaper*, published by Cambridge University Press, discovered a tradition and historical pedigree for an element of British culture rarely taken seriously. For newspapers, including the popular press, a resurrected past furnished a valuable context to a changing, often deprecated present.

Morison's insistence on balance and symmetry also influenced advertising, whose aesthetic vulgarity he often lamented. While working for Charles Hobson in the early 1920s, he helped create a visual style for advertising similar to the designs of eighteenth-century title-pages. Hobson, whose clients included Buoyant chairs and Lotus shoes, created advertisements which, surrounded by a decorative border contiguous to visually soothing white space, consisted of a picture that resembled a woodcut, balanced over a block of copy and a nameplate set in elegant printing types selected by Morison. This distinctive style exerted enormous influence, not only in Britain, but in America as well.[77] It particularly suited manufacturers of luxury goods and other products for the wealthy, such as Rolls-Royce, who sought a visual style in their publicity that captured their desired self-image of great wealth, unpretentious elegance, and affluent good taste. Hobson and others created advertisements in a style which private presses and other speciality publishers a generation earlier might have printed for connoisseurs. A number of factors, including an improved technology of mechanized typesetting, an expanding advertising industry, and a group of gifted typographers committed to some newly regenerated traditions, thus converged to help disseminate the visual style of the cultivated minority to a broader public.

The adaptation to new technologies of printing by Morison and other progressive typographers during the 1920s extended rather than extinguished the aesthetic ideals of William Morris and the Arts and Crafts movement. 'These inventions can be made the friends, not the enemies, of the artist and the maker of beauty,' *The Times* wrote in its survey of printing in 1929.[78] A machine could reproduce pages of print no less attractive than a private press, and because of its economies of scale, the machine allowed this beauty to reach a much larger audience than the highly restricted and exclusive group which could afford Morris's

---

[77] Ashley Havinden, 'Prologue', in Michael Frostick, *Advertising and the Motor-Car* (London: Lund Humphries, 1970), 11–15; Ashley Havinden, 'Advertising and Commercial Design', *Journal of the Royal Society of Arts* 96, 4761 (1948): 149–51. On American advertising between the wars, see Roland Marchand, *Advertising the American Dream: Making Way for Modernity, 1920–1940* (Berkeley: University of California Press, 1985).

[78] *Printing in the Twentieth Century: A Survey*, a reprint from *The Times*, 29 Oct. 1929 (London: Times Publishing, 1930), p. x.

expensive productions. In his scholarship, Morison provided typographers, including those involved with newspapers and advertising, with a tradition and a legitimacy which earlier generations would not have granted to such efforts. He found a usable past which, in its emphasis on selected classical values, created a distinctive style for modernity. Morison represented an important element in the lengthy effort by progressives to raise the level of the images which increasingly dominated public discourse.

If Morison and his sympathizers confronted the present by discovering the past, Modern artists sought to dispense with tradition in their quest of the contemporary. As a descriptive term Modernism suffers from a number of ambiguities; disagreements persist about the definition, participants, precise dates, and originality of the movement.[79] In general, however, the impact in Britain of artistic movements usually designated as Modernist came in two overlapping waves. First, Cubism, Post-Impressionism, and Futurism exerted a powerful influence among an informally organized avant-garde of artists and literary figures shortly before the First World War. Human nature may not have changed in 1910, but during the socially and politically turbulent years prior to Sarajevo, painters, sculptors, and other creative artists perceived their subject-matter in startling new ways. After the war, a second wave of Modernism, including De Stijl, Constructivism, and the Bauhaus explored further the territory initially sighted by the Cubists and others. Before and after the war, Continental artists initiated what the English avant-garde then tailored to their own needs. Among the visual arts, and perhaps in literature if one considers the birthplaces of Joyce, Pound, and Eliot, Modernism was more an adopted rather than native child of England. For both commercial culture, where American influences proved strong, and among the avant-garde, where Modernism established itself, English culture between 1910 and 1930 underwent fecund challenges to its insularity. In the often difficult attempt to satisfy both commerce and art, commercial artists responded to these challenges in unique ways.

Within the first wave of Modernism, the Futurists most emphatically supported the values frequently associated with new technologies. 'We declare', the first of many manifestos of Futurism proclaimed in 1909, 'that the world's splendour has been enriched by a new beauty; the beauty of speed. . . . A roaring motor-car, which looks as though running on

---

[79] See, for example, Malcolm Bradbury and James McFarlane, 'The Name and Nature of Modernism', in *Modernism, 1890–1930*, eds. Malcolm Bradbury and James McFarlane (Harmondsworth: Penguin, 1976), 19–55; and Mary Gluck, 'Towards a Historical Definition of Modernism: Georg Lukács and the Avant Garde', *Journal of Modern History* 58, 4 (1986): esp. 845–9. See also Michael H. Levenson, *A Genealogy of Modernism: A Study of English Literary Doctrine, 1908–1922* (Cambridge: Cambridge University Press, 1984).

shrapnel, is more beautiful than the *Victory of Samothrace.*'[80] Certain English writers prefigured this fascination with cars and other efficient modes of travel. W. E. Henley's 'A Song of Speed', published in 1908, lavishly praised 'This astonishing device / This amazing Mercedes' and in 'The Testament of Sir Simon Simplex Concerning Automobilism', John Davidson claimed that motor vehicles restored the values of individualism which earlier technologies, such as the railway, undermined.[81] In his early science fiction, H. G. Wells pondered the social and political implications of a wide variety of future inventions.[82] Yet with their prescient understanding of modern publicity, the Futurists most dramatically captured the British public's amused attention as the embodiment of avant-garde Modernism and outrageousness. F. T. Marinetti's visits to London in 1910 and 1912 included a number of events, such as a bizarre performance at a music-hall, which assured that the Futurist agenda, while mocked, would not be ignored.[83]

For the English avant-garde, however, Futurism became something more than publicity stunts by eccentric foreigners. Like Cubism and Post-Impressionism, Futurism contributed to a profound revaluation of the nature of images. In Europe from 1880 to 1918 technological changes such as the telephone, telegraph, cinema, bicycle, aeroplane, and motor car helped transform perceptions about the past, present, future, and about space, form, distance, and direction.[84] In its rethinking of images, Modernism contributed enormously to this fundamental cultural reorientation. The gradual disintegration of traditional notions of time and space powerfully undermined representational art. Although the disengagement from such art began early in the nineteenth century, it was only after 1900 that representational images struck some artists as particularly naïve. Yet

[80] 'Initial Manifesto of Futurism', in Joshua C. Taylor, *Futurism* (New York: Museum of Modern Art, 1961), 124.

[81] W. E. Henley, *The Works of W. E. Henley*, vol. 2 (London: David Nutt, 1908), 193. On Henley and machines, see Jerome Hamilton Buckley, *William Ernest Henley: A Study in the Counter-Decadence of the Nineties* (Princeton: Princeton University Press, 1945), 206–8; and Joseph M. Flora, *William Ernest Henley* (New York: Twayne, 1970), 138–9. For Davidson, see John Davidson, *John Davidson: A Selection of His Poems*, ed. Maurice Lindsay (London: Hutchinson, 1961), 193–9. See also J. Benjamin Townsend, *John Davidson: Poet of Armageddon* (New Haven: Yale University Press, 1961).

[82] See, for example, Rosylin D. Haynes, *H. G. Wells, Discoverer of the Future: The Influence of Science on His Thought* (New York: New York University Press, 1980), 69–81.

[83] William C. Wees, *Vorticism and the English Avant-Garde* (Toronto: University of Toronto Press, 1972), 40–1. See also Marianne W. Martin, *Futurist Art and Theory, 1909–1915* (New York: Hacken Art Book, 1978), 28–42; Jane Rye, *Futurism* (London: Studio Vista, 1972), 144–5; and, for a recent evaluation, Marjorie Perloff, *The Futurist Movement: Avant-Garde, Avant Guerre, and the Language of Rupture* (Chicago: University of Chicago Press, 1986).

[84] See Stephen Kern, *The Culture of Time and Space, 1880–1918* (Cambridge: Harvard University Press, 1983).

if it was one thing to grasp the limitations of an earlier tradition, it was quite another to find a satisfactory replacement. Despite their vast differences in technique, aesthetic intention, and sources of inspiration, the various schools of Modernism shared the desire to displace representational art with a different image of reality. As maddening or amusing as it may have been to some, abstraction became itself a form of representation, and one with unexpected consequences. The virtues, for example, which the Cubists discovered in primitive art indicated how mentalities shaped by profoundly different social forces might fruitfully converge. The notion of simultaneity bridged cultures and their artefacts which the Victorians routinely separated into utterly distinct moral, historical, and aesthetic categories. Modern technology helped inspire artists to link the advanced and the primitive in ways that baffled and provoked traditionalists.

In England, the disengagement from representational art characterized an avant-garde which, despite its shared repudiation of prevailing academic traditions, was bitterly divided. Two of these rival movements became especially influential before the First World War. The votaries of Post-Impressionism, led by such figures as Roger Fry and Clive Bell, took special interest in a painter who often perplexed cultivated sensibilities; 'in so far as one man can be said to inspire a whole age,' Bell wrote, 'Cézanne inspires the contemporary movement.'[85] The Vorticists, on the other hand, found in Wyndham Lewis a controversial theorist and painter who sought to mask his profound debt to Cubism and Futurism with frequent protests of his own uniqueness. Like the Futurists, the Vorticists issued descriptions of their mission which sometimes proved difficult to reconcile persuasively with their actual art. Even sympathetic critics often confused Lewis's paintings—many now, alas, lost—with the Cubists, and his strikingly modernist typography in *Blast*, though often attributed to him, borrowed heavily from the Futurists.[86] Lewis practised cultural politics in ways many sympathizers found disagreeable, and by the end of 1914 the avant-garde often lacerated each other with the same fierceness that uncomprehending traditionalists directed against Modernism.

If the aesthetic doctrines and practices of Post-Impressionism and Vorticism served to distinguish the avant-garde in England not only from their predecessors but also from each other, Modernism also perpetuated at least one cultural tradition which the Arts and Crafts movement fully endorsed. Modernists often bitterly condemned the very modernity which shaped their most distinctive perceptions. Like the Arts and Crafts

[85] Quoted in Richard Cork, *Vorticism and Abstract Art in the First Machine Age*, vol. 1 (Berkeley: University of California Press, 1976), 202.
[86] Cork, op. cit., 131, 225, 239–54.

movement, Modernists in both art and literature disapproved of the civilization based upon the new technologies of production and communication. The Omega Workshops, for example, crafted a number of artefacts inspired by the Post-Impressionists, but, as Roger Fry wrote in the Omega catalogue, the workshop rejected 'the humbug of the machine-made imitation of works of art'.[87] Like Morris, Fry rejected the mechanization and commercialism which he claimed eroded artistic integrity, but which also might have lowered the prices of the workshop's goods. Whatever their political affiliations, Left or Right, the avant-garde in England retained the moral distance, social detachment, and aesthetic superiority characteristic of traditional élite culture. Modernism may have levelled the old hierarchies of time and space, but Modernists remained wedded to other, more traditional standards which distanced them from the mechanized civilization and commercial culture they sometimes appropriated for their art.

It was this detachment which united thematically Wyndham Lewis's Vorticist images and his prolific literary efforts. Unlike the Futurists, who celebrated modern technology, Lewis employed an abstract, dehumanized style in his Vorticist paintings to condemn a sterile, mechanized world.[88] Lewis scorned the Futurists for trying to capture the speed and dynamism of new technology. 'A machine in violent motion ceases to look like a machine,' he wrote. 'It looks, perhaps, like a rose or a sponge. . . . The very spirit of the machine is lost—the hard, cold, the mechanical and the static. And it was these attributes for which Vorticism had a particular partiality.'[89] Visually prominent in many of his paintings, this same preoccupation with the 'cold, the mechanical and the static' also characterized much of Lewis's literary output during this period. In his novels, Lewis rarely identified sympathetically with any of his characters, whose petty ambitions and devitalized routines, he believed, encapsulated the modern predicament. 'Life itself becomes unreal,' Frederick Jameson wrote of Lewis's post-war narratives, 'and human beings are represented as virtual puppets, enjoying a spasmodic and degraded existence, their bodies jerkily obedient to the first principles of positivist physiology, while their minds function as textbook illustrations of the mechanisms of behavioristic and Pavlovian laws.'[90] In both his paintings and his literary work, Lewis

---

[87] Quoted in Isabella Anscombe, *Omega and After: Bloomsbury and the Decorative Arts* (London: Thames and Hudson, 1981), 32. On Omega, see also Judith Collins, *The Omega Workshops* (Chicago: University of Chicago Press, 1984).

[88] Reed Way Dasenbrock, *The Literary Vorticism of Ezra Pound and Wyndham Lewis: Towards the Condition of Painting* (Baltimore: Johns Hopkins University Press, 1985), 46–7.

[89] Quoted in Cork, op. cit., vol. 2, 326.

[90] Jameson, *Fables of Aggression*, 105–6.

reiterated the Romantic notion that the genuine artist remained detached from the mediocrities of contemporary life. An 'enemy' of most humanity in a mechanized world, the artist became a figure of superior insight and moral stature. Modernism for Lewis, as for others, embodied disdain for modernity.[91]

For commercial artists, on the other hand, the abstract images of Modernism became emblems of hope and prosperity, icons of progress. Although Vorticism proved ephemeral, thereby joining in death what it despised in life, its technique influenced the work of Edward McKnight Kauffer, one of the most distinguished and original commercial artists of the inter-war era. 'Kauffer's posters were like a fresh breeze blowing through the stale commercial atmosphere of the time,' Ashley Havinden later recalled, 'and undoubtedly did more to raise the status of poster design than any single influence.'[92] Born in Montana in 1890, Kauffer spent part of his youth in an orphanage and worked at a series of jobs in early adolescence before beginning his formal training at the Art Institute in Chicago. Kauffer came to Europe in 1913, and in 1915 moved to London, where he spent the next 25 years as an artist and designer with an impressive list of commissions, and a circle of acquaintances that included Roger Fry, T. S. Eliot, and Wyndham Lewis.[93] Vorticism influenced a number of his posters after 1916, most notably *Soaring to Success*, adapted from a woodcut and commissioned by his friend Francis Meynell as part of the campaign to launch the new *Daily Herald* in 1919. In this poster, one of his most famed productions, Kauffer translated a flock of birds into an arresting image of streamlined angularity. 'The result', a recent commentator has suggested, 'is a glancing, chequerboard complex of tensely sprung fragments, half bird and half aeroplane, which would not have looked at all out of place as an illustration in *Blast*.'[94] Two years later, *Winter Sales*, commissioned by Frank Pick for the Underground, conveyed in abstract design what Roger Fry described, with characteristic sensitivity, as a 'fascinating silhouette of dark forms . . . and out of these forms gradually disengage themselves the hints of the flutter of mackintoshes blown by a gusty wind, of the straining forms pushing diagonally against the driving rain.' In Kauffer's work, Vorticism became transformed from the pessimism of Lewis into, as Meynell wrote of *Soaring to Success*,

[91] For a somewhat similar equivocal attitude in Germany, see Jeffrey Herf, *Reactionary Modernism: Technology, Culture and Politics in Weimar and the Third Reich* (Cambridge: Cambridge University Press, 1984).

[92] Havinden, 'Advertising', *Journal*, 148–9.

[93] For Kauffer's life, see Mark Haworth-Booth, *E. McKnight Kauffer: A Designer and His Public* (London: Gordon Fraser, 1979); and, an earlier version, id., 'E. McKnight Kauffer', *Penrose Annual* 64 (1971): 83–96.

[94] Cork, op. cit., vol. 2, 539.

'a symbol, in those days of hope, of the unity of useful invention and natural things'.[95]

This optimism was not the only trait which distinguished Kauffer's Modernism from its Vorticist origins. He also committed himself actively to raising the level of commercial art and thereby, he reasoned, public tastes as well. Like other progressives, Kauffer forthrightly rejected the aesthetic of detachment enunciated by Wyndham Lewis and others. At one point, to be sure, Lewis acknowledged that posters might become an effective means of disseminating Vorticist principles, but he argued that 'definite POPULAR acceptance' of 'such abstract works . . . should never be aimed at'.[96] Kauffer, on the other hand, believed that posters and hoardings could become the art galleries of the common man. In 1924 he edited *The Art of the Poster*, an attempt to 'free the art of the Poster from the abuse to which it is so often subjected'. In a collection of essays and reproductions, various authors traced the origins and evolution of the poster, furnishing it with a tradition, legitimacy, and social rationale. 'The specimens selected for this volume', Kauffer wrote in the introduction, 'provide conclusive evidence that, as long as nearly two centuries ago, a standard in advertising prevailed, the excellence of which has in many instances never been surpassed.' In other writings during this period, Kauffer promoted the aesthetics and mission of commercial art. In 'The Poster and Symbolism', for example, he claimed that the 'veracity, brevity and vigour' of some abstract work translated into commercially effective posters.[97] In both theory and practice, Kauffer's advocacy of modern designs impressed a number of influential contemporaries, including Roger Fry who encouraged his efforts. Writing in *The Nation*, Fry said of Kauffer: 'He has insinuated his good taste in colour, his real delicacy of feeling for form, his ingenuity in interpretation, and his coordinating power so gradually and unobtrusively that at last people have got accustomed to genuine works of art on the walls of tubes, trams, and lifts.'[98] Like Stanley Morison, Kauffer gave commercial art an aesthetic tradition and social purpose that helped justify it to sceptics both in business and in art.

Kauffer's eloquent defence of poster art in the mid-1920s occurred during a period when other Modernist schools on the Continent began to influence commercial art in Britain. Such movements as De Stijl in the

---

[95] Quoted in Haworth-Booth, *Kauffer*, 30, 24.

[96] Quoted in Cork, op. cit., vol. 1, 280.

[97] E. McKnight Kauffer, ed., *The Art of the Poster: Its Origin, Evolution and Purpose* (London: Cecil Palmer, 1924), pp. x–xi; id., 'The Poster and Symbolism', *Penrose's Annual* 26 (1924): 43.

[98] Roger Fry, 'Poster Designs and Mr. McKnight Kauffer', *Nation and Athenaeum*, 23 May 1925, 237. See also id., 'The Author and the Artist', *Burlington Magazine* 49, 180 (1926): 9–12; and id., *Letters of Roger Fry*, vol. 2, ed. Denys Sutton (London: Chatto and Windus, 1972), 426–7.

Netherlands, Russian Constructivism, and the Bauhaus in Germany further developed principles of asymmetric typography and abstract design which the Futurists and others initially explored before the war. Each of these groups within this second wave of Modernism evolved theories and practices which distinguished them from both their predecessors and contemporaries among the European avant-garde.[99] Yet among commercial artists in Britain, what these groups shared in common often became as important as each group's legitimate if sometimes ambiguously expressed claim to its own uniqueness. Constructivism and the Bauhaus continued the experimentation and preserved the vitality of Modernism at a time when the Futurists and the Vorticists had long since disappeared. Unlike Edward Kauffer, who derived his Modernism from the English avant-garde, commercial artists in the 1920s often gained their inspiration directly from the Continent. In 1919, Kauffer's Vorticist posters stood out as clearly exceptional; ten years later, Modernism was much more firmly established.

The advertising agency of William Smith Crawford played a crucial role in promoting Modernist designs. In the early 1920s, Crawford's often imitated the symmetrical, elegantly proportioned style of Hobson and other agencies influenced by Stanley Morison. However, by the middle of the decade, as Ashley Havinden later recalled, 'we were increasingly less certain of the suitability as a solution to urgent twentieth-century problems of communication of what was indeed only a pastiche of the eighteenth-century printer's work.'[1] Crawford, who in his youth studied in Berlin, encouraged his designers to study German developments in advertising which the magazine *Gebrauchsgraphik*, founded in 1923 and read by Crawford, helped disseminate. Havinden became particularly impressed by some early Bauhaus books designed by László Moholy-Nagy, who believed that photography dictated radical changes in typography. Unlike paintings and illustrations, Moholy-Nagy argued, photographs were direct, functional, and impersonal reflections of reality whose 'objectivity . . . liberates the receptive reader from the crutches of the author's personal idiosyncrasies'. It followed that typography must correspond to these new optics. 'Form, size, color, and arrangement of the typographical material (letters and signs) contain a strong visual impact,' he wrote. 'The organization of these possible visual effects gives

[99] The bibliography is immense. See, among others, Reyner Banham, *Theory and Design in the First Machine Age*, 2nd edn. (Cambridge: MIT Press, 1960); Paul Overy, *De Stijl* (London: Studio Vista, 1969); Christina Lodder, *Russian Constructivism* (New Haven: Yale University Press, 1983); and Hans Wingler, *Bauhaus: Weimar, Dessau, Berlin, Chicago* (Cambridge: MIT Press, 1978).
[1] Havinden, 'Prologue', in Frostick, *Motor-Car*, 17.

a visual validity to the content of the message as well.'[2] In practice, this emphasis on type as part of the visual experience meant an increased use of new typefaces, type sizes, geometric forms, and colours. This experimentation, anticipated by the Futurists, *Blast*, and the work of El Lissitzky, rapidly became a characteristic feature of German advertising and publishing during the Weimar period, and a hallmark of its cultural renaissance.[3]

William Crawford introduced the new typography to Britain in his advertisements for Chrysler in 1925. 'We decided to put the whole emphasis on *speed* and *performance*', Havinden remembered, 'and to create advertisements which expressed this as dramatically as possible. We proposed to use bold headlines . . . set at angles to the horizontal. Sometimes I used straight lines of lettering, sometimes curved ones, which I drew in heavy block letters with thin serifs applied to help stress the direction of the lines.'[4] Crawford championed the modern graphics for sound commercial reasons. He saw in the new typography an opportunity to distinguish his advertisements, not only from their competitors, but from the total visual environment. 'The advertiser', he wrote in a trade publication, 'is fighting today, not only against other advertisers, but against the counter-attractions of dramatically presented news, the cinema, the theatre, the thriller. . . . Each fascinates by its exaggeration of life.'[5] Crawford believed that business enterprises selling new products, such as cars, would gravitate towards an agency whose advertisements were as modern as the product itself. Modernism became an effective salesman for businesses in quest of a forward-looking corporate image.

Many British advertisers resisted change. 'The Germanic appeals are certainly more aggressive and more compelling in design', one advertiser wrote in 1926, but they '. . . would not work here.' They were too abstract, too experimental.[6] Others condemned such recalcitrance. In an article 'The New Artistic Epoch: Are We Aware of Its Existence?' published in 1926, one commercial artist lamented that 'we are in a backwater. . . . There has been discovered an entirely new world of form, pattern, and colour. The most advanced of our native work is but the distant echo

---

[2] Havinden, 'Advertising', *Journal*, 152; László Moholy-Nagy, 'The New Typography' (1923) and 'Contemporary Typography' (1926), in his *Moholy-Nagy*, ed. Richard Kostelanatz, (New York: Washington Praeger, 1970), 75, 79. See also Sibyl Moholy-Nagy, *Moholy-Nagy: Experiment in Totality* (Cambridge: MIT Press, 1969), 24–6.

[3] Herbert Spencer, *Pioneers of Modern Typography* (London: Lund Humphries, 1969), 14–33; John Willet, *The New Sobriety, 1917–1933: Art and Politics in the Weimar Period* (London: Thames and Hudson, 1978), 134–8; Sophie Lissitzky, *El Lissitzky: Life, Letters, Texts* (London: Thames and Hudson, 1968), 24–5; and L. Leering van Moorsel, 'The Typography of El Lissitzky', *Journal of Typographic Research* 2, 4 (1968): 323–40.

[4] Havinden, 'Prologue', in Frostick, *Motor-Car*, 20–1.

[5] William Crawford, 'Advertising is Education—Not Salesmanship', *World's Press News*, 10 Apr. 1930, 23.

[6] Jack Bride, 'Two Types of Typography', *Advertiser's Weekly*, 28 May 1926, 318.

of a gigantic explosion.'[7] Symptomatic of the growing success of the movement, the most important trade paper of the English advertising profession began to include in its pages in 1926 an elaborate and expensive supplement entitled *Advertising Display*. Printed on glossy paper, this supplement provided scores of examples, often in full colour, of the new typography and the new designs. Accompanying articles explained the logic underlying these layouts.[8] Within three years, these principles were sufficiently widespread to be codified in the advertising textbooks of the period.[9]

What were these principles that in the late 1920s helped transform the appearance of much English advertising? First, there was an increasing emphasis, by both modernists and traditionalists, on the advertisement as a totality, a mosaic in which the disposition of type, illustration, and white space was carefully calculated to form a complete impression. Since 'words and picture will be taken in one glance', both needed to be subordinated to the whole, 'the optical totality'.[10] 'The illustration should never be completely cut off and isolated from the text,' the American Richard Surrey wrote in his textbook published in London; 'it should not look complete without the text.'[11] Words became part of the picture, just as white space contributed to the copy. As a result, the layout man became a more central figure in advertising. He co-ordinated the various elements into a pleasing whole; he directed the eye in its travels through a page. Advertising was now carefully 'designed', not merely written.[12]

Second and related, advertisements became dynamically rather than statically displayed. In *The Typography of Newspaper Advertisements*, published in 1929, an important figure in the typographical renaissance, Francis Meynell, contrasted the two approaches:

[7] Adrian Bernard Klein, 'The New Artistic Epoch: Are We Aware of Its Existence?', *Penrose Year Book and Review of the Graphic Arts* 28 (1926): 37.

[8] See, for example, W. Livingston Larned, 'Balance in Advertising Design', *Advertising Display* 1, 2 (1926): 50–1; and A. S. Wildman, 'TYPE is Part of the Picture', *Advertising Display* 1, 3 (1926): 84–6.

[9] In addition to those cited below, see, among others, W. A. Dwiggins, *Layout in Advertising* (New York and London: Harper and Brothers, 1928). Dwiggins was British. See also Gordon C. Aymer, *An Introduction to Advertising Illustration* (New York and London: Harper and Brothers, 1929); and Reginald H. Cox, *The Lay-Out of Advertisements* (London: Sir Isaac Pitman, 1931).

[10] Otto L. Benjamin, 'The Relationship of Word and Picture: Principles of Photo-Typography', *Penrose's Annual* 34 (1932): 75.

[11] Richard Surrey, *Layout Technique in Advertising* (New York and London: McGraw-Hill, 1929), 68 (italics omitted).

[12] C. Harold Vernon, 'A Review of Press Advertising in 1929', in *Posters and Publicity, 1929: Fine Printing and Design in* Commercial Art *Annual*, ed. F. A. Mercer and W. Gaunt (London: The Studio, 1929), 87–92.

I. Main news page, *The Times*, 10 September 1901. Information conveyed in virtually unbroken columns of print.

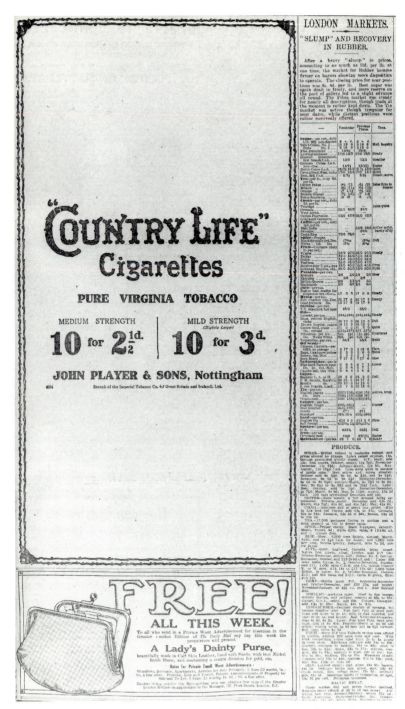

II. 'Country Life Cigarettes' Display Advertisement, the *Daily Mail*, 12 October 1910. An early use of white space to set off message from surrounding print.

Furnished Rooms. Property for Sale and Wanted, and Situations Wanted Advertisers can have a second insertion in French following their advertisement in English inserted at half the price of their original advertisement.

NO. 4,634.

LONDON, SATURDAY, FEBRUARY 13, 1915.

ONE HALFPENNY.

Étant donné le grand nombre de Français et Belges actuellement en Angleterre, les petites annonces (maisons et appartements meublés, pensions et chambres à louer) peuvent, sur demande, gratuitement insérées en français par le personnel du "Daily Express"

Daily Express

WING COMMANDER SAMSON.   SQUADRON COMMANDER PORTE.

NORTH SEA

MAP OF THE SCENE OF THE GREAT AIR RAID.

Wing Commander   Squadron Commander   Squadron Commander   Flight Commander
LONGMORE.   COURTNEY.   RATHBORNE.   GRAHAME-WHITE.

GREATEST AIR RAID OF THE WAR.

FLEET OF THIRTY-FOUR NAVAL AEROPLANES AND SEAPLANES ATTACK GERMAN POSITIONS IN BELGIUM.

COMPLETE TRIUMPH: NO CASUALTIES.

The Secretary of the Admiralty made the following announcement last night:—

During the last twenty-four hours, combined aeroplane and seaplane operations have been carried out by the naval wing in the BRUGES, ZEEBRUGGE, BLANKENBERGHE, and OSTEND districts, with a view to preventing the development of submarine bases and establishments.

Thirty-four naval aeroplanes and seaplanes took part.

Great damage is reported to have been done to OSTEND Railway Station, which according to present information has probably been burnt to the ground; the railway station at BLANKENBERGHE was damaged, and railway lines were torn up in many places.

Bombs were dropped on gun positions at MIDDELKERKE, also on the power station and German mine sweeping vessels at ZEEBRUGGE, but the damage done is unknown.

During the attack the machines encountered heavy banks of snow.

No submarines were seen.

Flight Commander GRAHAME-WHITE fell into the sea off NIEUPORT, and was rescued by a French vessel. Although exposed to heavy gunfire from rifles, anti-aircraft guns, mitrailleuses, etc., all pilots are safe. Two machines were damaged.

The seaplanes and aeroplanes were under the command of Wing Commander SAMSON, assisted by Wing Commander LONGMORE, Squadron Commanders PORTE, COURTNEY, and RATHBORNE.

FLIGHT ACROSS THE CHANNEL.

START FROM DOVER.

THE RAIDERS.

START FROM DOVER.

RAIDER'S PROMOTION.

ZEPPELIN VICTIMS.

PLAN OF STATE COMPENSATION FOR NORFOLK SUFFERERS.

WOMEN TRENCH DIGGERS?

REST AFTER INOCULATION.

THE SUBMARINE ATTACK ON A HOSPITAL SHIP.

OFFICIAL PROOFS OF THE OUTRAGE.

CAPTAIN'S STATEMENT.

SECOND OFFICER'S STATEMENT.

THIRD OFFICER'S STATEMENT.

CADETS' STATEMENTS.

UNPRECEDENTED CLAIM.

AMERICAN VIEW OF THE GERMAN BLUFF.

GRAVE CRISIS BETWEEN THE U.S. AND GERMANY.

"REPARATION WILL BE EXACTED IF YOU TORPEDO ONE OF OUR SHIPS."

IS THE KAISER RIDING FOR A FALL?

By J. W. T. MASON.
"Express" Correspondent.

New York, Friday, Feb. 12.

NO EXCUSE.

MURDER ADDED TO PIRACY.

GERMAN THREAT TO KILL BRITISH WOMEN.

By RENÉ H. FEIBELMAN.
"Express" Special Correspondent.
(Copyright.)

Amsterdam, Friday, Feb. 12.

ANOTHER U.S. PROTEST.

A GERMAN SUBMARINE?

ADMIRAL JELLICOE, G.C.B.

HONOUR FOR MERITORIOUS SERVICES.

KAISER'S FAKED FILMS.

By H. J. GREENWALL.
"Express" Correspondent.
(Copyright.)

Paris, Friday, Feb. 12.

PLAIN LANGUAGE.

AMERICAN PRESS HAS NO DOUBT OF PRESIDENT'S MEANING.

NEW BELGIAN MINISTER.

DR. PAGE AT THE FOREIGN OFFICE.

III. Front page, *Daily Express*, 13 February 1915. Streamer and multi-deck headlines underscore visually the importance of the story.

Daily Mail

WEDNESDAY, NOVEMBER 10, 1915.

A PAGEANT OF WAR—AND THE REALITY.

Members of the City of London National Guard Volunteer Corps who took part in the show.

Indian officers watching the procession from the Mansion House.

THE NARROW WAY OF DEATH.—Here a German communication trench in front of a farm in Champagne looked after one of the deadly French machine guns had been at work. The attackers who rushed forward a terrific enfilading fire into the trench, and above them as they fall where they stood, each one riddled by bullets. Besides detachments from home regiments hundreds of troops from overseas marched in an imposing cavalcade through the City.

A detachment of the anti-aircraft corps, with their guns, in yesterday's procession.

A contingent from the West Indies also took part.

Yesterday's Lord Mayor's Show in London was almost entirely a war pageant.

IV. Picture page, *Daily Mail*, 10 November 1915. Centre picture of German war dead illustrates the realities of war.

V. Edward McKnight Kauffer, 'Soaring to Success', 1919.
Commercial art in Britain assimilates the principles of Modernism.

Daily Express

TODAY'S WEATHER : SQUALLY. RADIO PROGRAMMES : PAGE 33.

NO. 11,418 FRIDAY, DECEMBER 18, 1936 ONE PENNY

M.P.s' Debate On Archbishop "Out Of Order"

Duke Of Windsor Listens In To News Bulletin

THE DUKE OF WINDSOR LISTENED-IN LAST NIGHT WITH HIS HOST AND HOSTESS, BARON AND BARONESS EUGEN ROTHSCHILD, AT THEIR AUSTRIAN CASTLE AT ENZESFELD TO THE REFERENCES IN THE RADIO NEWS BULLETIN FROM ENGLAND TO THE DEBATE IN THE HOUSE OF COMMONS ON THE B.B.C.

Distressed by the attacks on him and his social circle by the Archbishop of Canterbury in his recent broadcast, he had understood that certain M.P.s would speak in his defence.

But there was only a passing reference to the Primate in the course of the debate. This came from Lieut.-Commander Fletcher, Socialist Member for Nuneaton, who said :—

"There has been a certain amount of criticism about the Archbishop of Canterbury's broadcast last Sunday. I have been told that Sir John Reith himself took part in that communication (democratory) service. America has just seen the end of its radio priest."

The reason why no discussion of the archbishop's broadcast on or of the Duke of Windsor's farewell speech took place, writes the Daily Express political correspondent, was that it would have been "out of order."

CRITICISM BARRED

This was made known to M.P.s facing the evening. The decision was apparently based on the ground that it is not permissible to criticise in the Commons members of the Upper House, where the Primate sits as a "Lord Spiritual."

During the debate it was announced that two new governors had been appointed to the B.B.C., increasing their number from five to seven—Sir Ian Fraser, thirty-nine-year-old blind M.P., and Dr. J. J. Mallon, fifty-six-year-old warden of Toynbee Hall. East London's famous university settlement.

A by-election will result in North St. Pancras, where Sir Ian Fraser will resign his seat. His majority over a Socialist in the general election was 5,561.

Mr. Levi-Swift, Postmaster-General under the Socialist Government, launched a bitter attack on the B.B.C. in the debate for their alleged autocratic, dictatorial attitude to Parliament, their public, and their own staff.

William Barkley reports the debate on Page Two.

The King Receives Three Ministers

The King at Buckingham Palace yesterday received in audience Mr. Anthony Eden, Foreign Secretary; Mr. Duff Cooper, Secretary for War; and Sir Samuel Hoare, First Lord of the Admiralty.

The date of the Coronation, May 12, will be promulgated at St. James's Palace tomorrow at 2.30 p.m. The Proclamation will start with a flourish of trumpets. It will be read by Garter King-of-Arms, Sir Gerald Woods Wollaston.

News Summary

NEW 3d. bits to be struck by the Mint in 1937 will have twelve sides.—Page Nine.

Britain will keep five cruisers due to be scrapped under the 1930 London Naval Treaty.—Page Nine.

About 70,000 old "crocks" are to be taken from the roads in the next big safety move.—Page Eleven.

Piat son of A.P. failed three months for smuggling 6s. er. into his native Cork.—Page Seven.

LORD BROWNLOW, friend of the Duke of Windsor—he accompanied Mrs. Simpson on her journey to Cannes—returned to England yesterday from Vienna. He declined to be interviewed.

Duke Plays Golf

Picture below—wire from Berlin—shows the Duke of Windsor playing golf with his host, Baron Eugen Rothschild, at Castle Enzesfeld.

The Duke's Midnight Drive

Daily Express Staff Reporter
VIENNA, Friday morning.
THE Duke of Windsor left Castle Enzesfeld at 10 o'clock last night, returning this morning at one o'clock.

He drove in a black car owned by Baron Eugen Rothschild and followed by a police car.

It is not known where the Duke went, but it has been suggested that he called on a Vienna nerve specialist, coming to the capital at a late hour to avoid attention.

ROYAL INVALIDS

A mild attack of influenza from within the Duke and Duchess of Gloucester are suffering is taking the normal course, it was stated yesterday. Their condition is satisfactory.

Luck—Good And Bad

"But it was too late to catch my Boycott life. So I too made handsome."

We sat together, Beary and I, in the crowded behind Tattersalls, under my roof of good and in cash and "I saw my attentions in Beary's words, since price he had kept silent up...

"I owe my greatest position to a Plancard-Food a few races back, yet I was reduced to 8½d this Appearance of my King Penny II of Jugo Kings I only make mistakes his time. Beautiful..."

One hundred Derwent Ras execudents strike after midnight in overtime dispute.—Page Fourteen.

GANG KINGS SENTENCED

10 Years For Killing Rival

Don Quixote Drama Of 'No Mean City'

Daily Express Staff Reporter
GLASGOW, Thursday.

"IT is a lamentable thing that this great city of Glasgow, whose people are known the world over for their character and worth, should have its good name besmirched by these nefarious and infamous gangs."

So said Lord Aitchison in the High Court here today before sentencing four young men concerned in the death of another to penal servitude for ten, seven, four and three years.

Their victim was George Stankovich, most feared of all gangster chiefs in Glasgow's East End, a Don Quixote of the underworld who always shared with friends the spoils of his crimes and relied solely on his fists against rivals whose favourite weapons were razors.

The imprisonment of the assailants who brought him down closes dramatically a lurid chapter of Glasgow's gang warfare, so vividly described in the famous novel, "No Mean City."

Hundreds of scarred faces in music stores tell of the ferocity with which the razor and broken bottle have been wielded.

But few of the wounded have died ; the razor kings have been skilled in the art of mutilation without killing.

In his quasi-Robinson back on the defiant of the Sacred Heart, in Glasgow's Gorbals, the four players—Dick and Dan McDainness, brothers James Parrell, and Robert Longwalt.

It is those four who were sentenced today for his manslaughter. They attacked him with a bottle, a glass measure, a poker, and a hatchet, stabbed him through the chest.

Stankovitch, a Roman Catholic, under the rules of the underworld as a custom of three-street, and for reason of a religion, he should have seen a function member of the famed Armenian gang.

QUARREL—DEATH

But he was not independent. His greatest friend was a Protestant. For him he would do anything.

Dick McGuinness, his secondary friend, was prominent among those to control of his Armenian family, with whom he would cause enmity to the underworld. That was the way Stankovitch had treated his quarters died.

His father died while he was a boy. His mother, a gentle-spoken woman who knows little English, has three could not control him. Stankovich, growled round began when he was 14 years of age.

Petty thefts, saddle-racketeers, led to a Borstal sentence. This ended and returned him. He is estimated to have spent nearly eight years under detention between the ages of eleven and twenty-three.

He was only fifteen, in height, yet he cut one occasion he threw off a huge attack of policemen with the help of settlement who held everything him until the police arrived.

MICHAEL BEARY SAYS "I HAD A ROUGH DEAL"

Daily Express Staff Reporter
MICHAEL BEARY, the famous jockey, attended yesterday a first meeting of his creditors under a bankruptcy petition filed a fortnight ago.

Last night the five-foot Irishman with seventeen-like magnetic eyes and a bequest made this statement to me :—

"For two years I have been under a cloud. Since 1934 people have been saying. There's something wrong with Beary. Trainers whom I asked for mounts have made excuses, have had a rough deal.

THE POPE Cannot Walk Unaided

VATICAN CITY, Thursday.—The Pope is no longer able to walk without assistance, even for the shortest distance, owing to poor circulation.

A full-length shot chair is stated to have arrived at the Vatican today.

When the Pope receives the Old King of Chashmak on December 24, he will be seated. Hitherto he has always walked until the continual and unusualled and then walked to the papal throne.—B.U.P.

The Pope is seventy-nine years old. He has recently recovered from a serious illness.

Boy King Honours British Writers

BELGRADE, Thursday.—Decorations have been awarded to several distinguished authors and journalists for their representation of boy King Peter II of Jugoslavia.

Among those honoured are the famous writers, Mr. Stephen Graham and Miss Rebecca West.—Reuter.

Richest Christmas

THE Bank of England weekly statement yesterday revealed—Britain has more spending money now than ever before.

Currency notes in circulation have reached the new high record of £467,695,183—average £16 5s. 3d. for every man, woman and child.

Shot Dead In Gold Vault

Daily Express Staff Reporter
MR. G. R. GASH, thirty-four, under-manager of the bullion department of Messrs. Johnson and Matthey, smelters to

LATEST NEWS
Telephone : Central 8000

the Government, in Hatton Garden, was found, shot in the weighing room at 10 o'clock last night, died an hour later.

Gash was found by the

➤ PAGE TWO, COLUMN FIVE

MADRID LEGION RECRUIT BRITONS

Daily Express Staff Reporter
MADRID, Thursday.
STRONG reinforcements have arrived in Spain for the international volunteer corps. Among them is a fresh contingent from Britain.

The three main contingents of the corps are German, French and Italian.

There are also :—
A strong battalion of Poles.
A Jewish platoon.
A Balkan group consisting of Serbs, Croats, Bulgarians, and a few Greeks.

Very few Russians have joined. Despite heavy losses the corps is still about 5,000 strong.

120 'Planes Down, All Were Foreign

Daily Express Staff Reporter
PARIS, Thursday.
Seventeen British airplanes, under Franco's Spanish Government service, thirty-five German, and sixty-nine French have been brought down since the start of the civil war, according to a French newspaper, which quotes statistics said to be issued by Madrid.

M.P.s' report on Madrid—Page Seventeen.

Elizabeth Bankoria, sister-in-law of the murdered man.

Colour gives a new glamour to Marlene Dietrich

Marlene Dietrich, Charles Boyer in
Garden Of Allah
Critical Temperature 65 degrees
LEICESTER SQUARE

HERE is the first of your Christmas film presents, all done up in coloured wrappings, with a £400,000 price ticket on it.

Of course you will all go to see it whatever I say, so why should I worry? It's Dietrich, it's coloured, and it's Christmas.

I am worried because four weeks ago when I spoke after the performance confessed that they had

Tilly Losch dances

Gilding the Lily

DIETRICH
wide-eyed and monosyllabic

Maureen O'Sullivan, Johnny Weissmuller in
Tarzan Escapes
Critical Temperature 56 degrees
EMPIRE

The Rest of the Christmas Films

New Gallery: "The Green Pastures."

Carlton: Hepburn does all the revelling in "A Woman Rebels," sentimental tale of Victorian days, with Herbert Marshall as the man who waits. Very good Hepburn.

Plaza: All the fun of the jungle with Dorothy Lamour and Ray Milland in "The Jungle Princess," and Joe E. Brown to send you home happy in "Earthworm Tractor" (Tuesday).

Regal: That "nice type of man" Marshall pops up again as a schoolmaster in love with his eighteen-year-old pupil in "Girls' Dormitory." You may not weep as much as you are meant to, but Simone Simon, Hollywood's newest star, is well worth looking at.

London Pavilion: Larger than life picture of London theatre world with a lot of hard acting by Miriam Hopkins, Gertrude Lawrence, and Sebastian Shaw in "Men Are Not Gods." Worth while.

Rialto: Mr. Deeds is still in town.

Marble Arch Pavilion: Fredric March again in "Anthony Adverse." A very solid three hours.

His Majesty's: Shakespeare as artistically as Hollywood can do it. Leslie Howard and Norma Shearer and many other familiar faces in a very spacious "Romeo and Juliet."

Curzon: "Mayerling"—Charles Boyer in one of the loveliest and most moving dramas of the year. (French.)

Academy: Vienna brings out its masks, magnums and misunderstandings again in "Confetti." (Austrian.)

Studio One: "La Kermesse Heroïque"—excellent Flemish farce in a very beautiful sixteenth century Flemish setting. (French.)

Just Released

The Bride Walks Out

Will Hay in
Windbag The Sailor
Critical Temperature 28 degrees

Guy Morgan

VII. Features page, *Daily Express*, 18 December 1936.

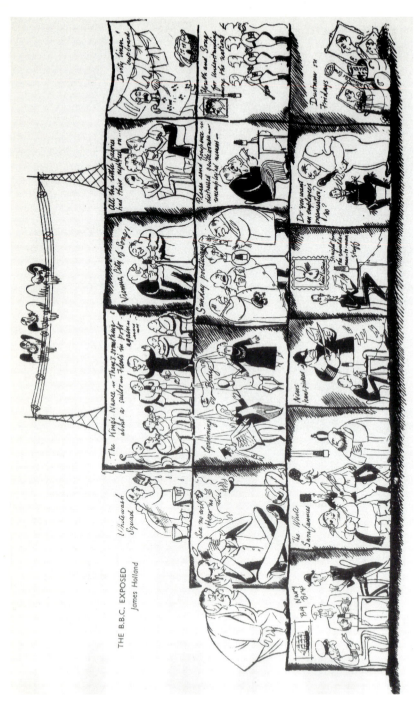

VIII. James Holland, 'The B.B.C. Exposed', *Left Review*, 3, 1 (1937). A cartoonist summarizes visually the Left's dissatisfaction with British broadcasting.

Static display is the familiar classical type of design in which, as on the title-page of the book, a symmetrical pattern centres on a vertical line bisecting the area at the advertiser's disposal. Dynamic display is harder to define. It may roughly be described as an asymmetrical disposition of type, etc., designed to concentrate attention and interest upon the most significant spot on the page. In dynamic display the elements of the pattern are so arranged as to lead the eye toward the focal point, and this gives the reader a sense of movement in the design.

Typography was critical to this movement. Words like 'smooth' might be spaced out to suggest its meaning, or the word 'dropped' would have its letters falling down the page.[13] Copy might be slanted in a specific direction, as in the Chrysler campaign, or typefaces contrasted to emphasize certain words and phrases. Advertisements became streamlined, expressing, as Crawford put it, 'the same simplicity, the same clearness of intention, the same dynamic virility which you will see in the clear lines of an aeroplane, of the latest buildings, of the 1930 motor car.'[14] Dynamic display meant that the typography adapted itself to the sights and sounds of the age. Advertisements became visually syncopated and more 'jazzy'; their dynamism transformed them into a 'moving picture' on a page.

Finally, words talked; their visual representation on the pages suggested a recognizable aural tone. Since most print lacked the inflections of the spoken word, it became necessary to choose typefaces that could 'pulsate with life, talking in the tones of the speaker, modulating his voice to suit both the words and the occasion, sometimes whispering and sometimes rising to a loud crescendo'.[15] Newspapers learned long before that headlines could shout; advertisers now discovered the typographical whisper. White space functioned in a similar aural fashion. 'It never seemed to occur to anybody', Surrey wrote in his text, 'that when a dozen people are all raising a din at one time, the thing that would arouse most curiosity would be a dead silence. . . . White space has much the same effect when it occurs in a medium filled with noisy advertisements made vocal with loud borders and shouting types.'[16] Advertisements were no longer coldly descriptive; they blended sight and sound into a complex image that restored gesture and tone of voice to the printed page.

---

[13] Francis Meynell, *The Typography of Newspaper Advertisements* (London: Ernest Benn 1929), 29, 32.

[14] William Crawford, 'What Gives Our Dreams Their Daring Is That They Can Be Realized', in *Modern Publicity: Commercial Art Annual, 1930*, ed. F. A. Mercer and W. Gaunt (London: The Studio, 1930), 18.

[15] Vincent Steer, *Printing Design and Layout* (1934, reprinted London: Virtue and Company, 1947), 209.

[16] Surrey, op. cit., 126.

By 1929 the editor of *Commercial Art* could proclaim with confidence that most British advertisements were now 'modern'.[17] He meant by the term not the Modernism of the Bauhaus or Constructivism, but the notion that commercial artists designed images which, in a calculated manner, combined words, symbols, and illustrations into a totality intended to be grasped immediately by a reader. Both the symmetrical advertisements influenced by Morison and the asymmetric images of Modernism contributed to the ascendancy of the layout man in British advertising. Both developed an aesthetic which grasped the unity and simultaneity of the visual message. Morison searched the past for typographical models which fulfilled his principles of clarity, balance, and elegance; the Modernists created a self-consciously contemporary look. Yet in his rejection of antiquarianism and his insistence on usable traditions, Morison served modern corporate functions with eighteenth-century designs. Commercial art embraced the present even when it invoked the past, either for inspiration as with Morison, or for legitimacy, as with Kauffer's edition on the history of posters. Past and present often coincided in commercial art.

D. *DRIFTERS* AND *THE FILM TILL NOW*: PROBLEMS OF A DERIVED TRADITION

Modernism on the Continent not only inspired a select group of commercial artists in the late 1920s; the documentary-film movement also assimilated cinematic techniques from abroad, and in particular from the Soviet Union, where film became an important component of a post-revolutionary exuberance in the arts. The early work of two key figures in British documentary reflected both the advantages and problems of a derived tradition. John Grierson's film *Drifters* released in 1929 set the standard for the documentary movement of the 1930s, which, financed by the Empire Marketing Board and later other government agencies and private businesses, considered itself the most creative alternative to the often anaemic British commercial film industry. Paul Rotha's landmark book *The Film Till Now*, published in 1930, discovered a tradition of aesthetic excellence in the recent history of cinema which bolstered its claim to be a legitimate form of art. Young and ambitious, both Grierson and Rotha borrowed heavily from avant-garde figures in other countries, and their early work reflected the difficulties of such appropriation. *Drifters* and *The Film Till Now* provided an alternative tradition for film in Britain, but one not without its own artistic predicaments.

[17] W. Gaunt, 'The Spirit and the Letter of Modern Advertising Design', *Commercial Art* 7, 40 (1929): 142.

First shown at the Film Society in November 1929, *Drifters* recorded the activities of herring fishermen in the Shetland Islands. Financed by the EMB to promote the fishing industry, the film depicted, as Grierson himself summarized it, 'the gathering of the ships for the herring season, the going out, the shooting at evening, the long drift in the night, the hauling of nets by infinite agony of shoulder muscle in the teeth of a storm, the drive home against a head sea, and (for finale) the frenzy of a market in which said agonies are sold.'[18] With a running-time of about an hour, the film preceded on the programme the British première of *Battleship Potemkin*, Eisenstein's stunning tribute to the revolutionary spirit of the Russian people. An invited guest for the special presentation of the two films, Eisenstein complained privately to Ivor Montagu that *Drifters* made in 1929 gave away 'all the best parts in *Potemkin*' filmed four years earlier. Grierson, who did not arrange the programme, also felt humiliated, and expressed his outrage to Sidney Bernstein for screening the two films on the same day and in such an awkward order.[19]

Battleship Potemkin became the best known of a series of works which, late in the decade, convinced Western intellectuals of Soviet dominance in film art during the 1920s. Although this period in Soviet film culture has been well covered by scholars,[20] two aspects of Eisenstein's contribution might be stressed. First, Eisenstein openly acknowledged his debt to D. W. Griffith, whose editing techniques the Soviets borrowed and extended to new subjects. 'I wish to recall what David Wark Griffith himself represented to us, the young Soviet film-makers of the twenties,' Eisenstein later wrote. 'To say it simply and without equivocation: a revelation.' Eisenstein's method of constructing a film, somewhat pompously designated 'montage', took Griffith's cross-cutting techniques, originally employed to heighten visually the tensions of melodramatic plots, and applied them to the intrinsically melodramatic politics of the revolutionary period. Little in *Potemkin* could not be found in *Birth of a Nation*, made ten years earlier; Soviet cinematic techniques rested on 'foundations . . . laid by American film-culture'.[21] Second, despite its reputation among the avant-garde in the West as a new, more enlightened cinema of the Russian 'people', many of the greatest Soviet films attracted

---

[18] Grierson, *Grierson on Documentary*, 135.

[19] Ivor Montagu, *With Eisenstein in Hollywood: A Chapter of Autobiography* (Berlin: Seven Seas Publishers, 1968), 31; Moorehead, *Bernstein*, 28.

[20] See, among others, Jay Leyda, *Kino: A History of the Russian and Soviet Film* (London: George Allen and Unwin, 1960); Richard Taylor, *Film Propaganda: Soviet Russia and Nazi Germany* (London: Croom Helm; New York: Barnes and Noble, 1979); and Peter Kenez, *The Birth of the Propaganda State: Soviet Methods of Mass Mobilization, 1917–1929* (Cambridge: Cambridge University Press, 1985), 195–223.

[21] Sergei Eisenstein, *Film Form: Essays in Film Theory*, ed. and trans. Jay Leyda (New York: Harvest/HBJ, 1977), 201, 204.

little public interest in their own land. For example, after an intense publicity campaign in Moscow, *Potemkin* drew disappointingly small audiences, who continued in vast numbers to prefer Buster Keaton and Douglas Fairbanks. One disgruntled critic sympathetic to Eisenstein's ideals complained that it was easier for Germans to see *Potemkin* than it was for Russians to view the film.[22]

Indeed, Germany proved the launching ground for Soviet cinematic influence among Western intellectuals. In 1928 *Close-Up* ran a series of articles which assured that film enthusiasts unable to travel to Berlin became acquainted with Soviet film. In September the journal devoted its entire issue to Soviet imports, 'because with a rush of new films from Russia into Germany, there was nothing else to write about. Everything else paled into insignificance.' Eisenstein, Pudovkin, Room, and others, the editor wrote, dated previous conceptions of the film. 'The future of pure cinema is safe in their hands.'[23] Pudovkin's *Film Technique* appeared in English translation in 1929, and that same year one of the editors of *Close-Up* published *Film Problems of Soviet Russia* which, among other topics, lamented the British censors' unwillingness to approve Soviet films in England.[24] Yet it was not only censorship which retarded film art in Britain. 'Hollywood has put America on the film map' one critic wrote in *Close-Up* late in 1928; 'certainly Germany has its representatives of giant realism in the film world, and Russia has surpassed everybody. Now where is England?'[25]

Grierson believed that British documentary films would provide the answer. He discovered Eisenstein not from the pages of *Close-Up* in 1928, but earlier while travelling in America and supported initially by a grant from the Rockefeller Foundation. It was in the United States that Grierson may have coined the term 'documentary',[26] and it was in the same country that in 1926 he studied carefully and helped translate the titles for *Battleship Potemkin*. 'With *Potemkin* the Russians Have Gained Film Precedence', Grierson called an article written for the *New York Herald Tribune* and published in December 1926. Grierson offered American readers a detailed synopsis of the plot, but maintained 'the important thing

---

[22] Richard Taylor, *The Politics of the Soviet Cinema, 1917–1929* (Cambridge: Cambridge University Press, 1979), 95–6.

[23] [Kenneth Macpherson], 'As Is', *Close-Up* 3, 3 (1928): 5, 13. See also E. Hellmund-Waldow, 'The Russian Film Industry', *Close-Up*, 2, 5 (1928): 65–70.

[24] Winifred Ellerman ['Bryher', pseud.], *Film Problems of Soviet Russia* (Territet, Switzerland: Pool, 1929), 11–12. On the censorship problem with Soviet film, see especially Ivor Montagu, *The Political Censorship of Films* (London: Victor Gollancz, 1929).

[25] Hilda Doolittle ['H.D.'], 'Russian Films', *Close-Up* 3, 3 (1928): 27.

[26] [John Grierson], 'Flaherty's Poetic *Moana*', *New York Sun*, 8 Feb. 1926, reprinted in Lewis Jacobs, ed., *The Documentary Tradition: From* Nanook *to* Woodstock (New York: W. W. Norton, 1971), 25–6.

is not the story; it is the fact that this variation in the flow, from quiet to intensity and from intensity to quiet, is a visual flow; and this visual flow makes the picture the powerful thing that it is. It is constructed in terms of cinema.'[27] When later asked about the roots of his documentary method Grierson usually played down the Russian influence, and some recent commentators have accepted this explanation at face value.[28]

Yet, as Lewis Jacobs and others recognized, including Eisenstein and Grierson themselves at the Film Society in 1929, the techniques and composition of the two films share much in common. Throughout the film, Grierson constantly cross-cut between images to indicate parallel action and to heighten dramatic effect. During the scene of a storm at sea, for example, shots of turbulent seas rapidly alternated with images of fishermen struggling to maintain control of their nets. 'We took the hand camera', Grierson recalled of the filming, 'and stood to the roll of the ship that we catch [sic] the men as they rose and fell against the horizon.'[29] Moreover, like other film-makers before him, Grierson sought to elevate and make heroic the unacknowledged greatness of the common man. Eisenstein depicted the struggles of working men and women against the oppression of the Czarist State; in *Nanook of the North* (1922), Flaherty dramatized the efforts of an Eskimo family for survival in an extraordinarily hostile environment.[30] Now Grierson sought to 'bring alive' the problems of herring fishermen off the coasts of England. 'I look on cinema as a pulpit,' Grierson declared in one of his most quoted statements, 'and use it as a propagandist.'[31]

For all its easily ignored dangers, however, fishing for herring embodied intrinsically less drama than the events surrounding the Russian Revolution. Eisenstein, like Griffith before him, worked with inherently melodramatic stories that brilliant editing enhanced immeasurably, and in some cases helped transform into visual myths of ineffable power. In and of itself, however, montage could not create powerful stories where, despite noble intentions, none existed. Style could not be separated from content; message could not be entirely subordinated to method. In their demand

---

[27] John Grierson, 'With *Potemkin* the Russians Have Gained Film Precedence', *New York Herald Tribune*, 5 Dec. 1926, reprinted in *The Battleship Potemkin*, ed. Herbert Marshall (New York: Avon Books, 1978), 231–2.

[28] For playing-down of Soviet influence, see interview with Lewis Jacobs in Beveridge, *John Grierson*, 110. For those who accept Grierson's explanation, see Marie Seton, *Sergei M. Eisenstein*, 2nd edn. (London: Dennis Dobson, 1978), 144; and Alan Lovell and Jim Hillier, *Studies in Documentary* (London: Secker and Warburg, 1972), 25.

[29] Quoted in Hardy, *Grierson*, 52.

[30] On Flaherty and *Nanook*, see Robert J. Flaherty, '*Nanook*', in *Emergence of Film Art*, ed. Jacobs, 215–21; and Paul Rotha, *Robert J. Flaherty: A Biography*, ed. Jay Ruby (Philadelphia: University of Pennsylvania Press, 1983), 7–50.

[31] John Grierson, 'Propaganda: A Problem for Educational Theory and for Cinema', *Sight and Sound* 2, 8 (1933–4): 119.

for films about relatively prosaic subjects and themes, the sponsors of the documentary movement undermined the aesthetic hopes and heralded political aspirations of the film-makers. In the final analysis *Drifters* was a public-relations film about the British fishing industry which probably no amount of clever editing could elevate into the high melodrama of *Birth of a Nation* or *Battleship Potemkin*.

Moreover, as some contemporary critics realized, *Drifters* portrayed its fishermen sympathetically but abstractly and at a distance; the men glimpsed working and relaxing in this silent film lacked individual identities and merged into a collective Man Against the Sea. 'Where are the people in his film?' the brilliant American critic Harry Alan Potamkin asked of Grierson. 'He is more engrossed with the *independent graces* of fish in the water — well-done details in themselves, but no part of the human process which the film was to be.'[32] To be sure, Eisenstein also eschewed individual portraits in many of his films during this period, a reason perhaps why *Potemkin* appealed to such a limited audience in Moscow. As many observers have acknowledged then and now, however, the struggle of sympathetic characters against their oppressors in *Potemkin* carries the film far more effectively than Grierson's abstracted, endlessly reiterated conflict between Man and Nature. In an article on 'Making Films for the Empire', published in 1932, Grierson argued that 'the interest of things, after all, is not in the matter but the method of them.'[33] Cinematic method could not, however, at least in Grierson's hands or those of his disciples, rescue their films' content from the essentially prosaic themes which sponsors demanded, or compensate technically for the absence of individual characters that audiences required of commercially successful films. Griffith and Eisenstein developed a film grammar which Grierson learned well and taught effectively, but it was not technique which relegated British documentary of the 1930s to its relatively marginal status in international film culture.

If *Drifters* offered the avant-garde in Britain an alternative to commercial cinema, Paul Rotha's *The Film Till Now* sought to provide its subject with an aesthetic pedigree worthy of a genuine art form. Independent and outspoken, Rotha strove to maintain his autonomy from Grierson, for whom he worked briefly at the EMB. Born in 1907 the son of the museum curator Dr Charles John S. Thompson, Rotha enrolled in the Slade School of Fine Arts in 1924, and a year later won an international award for theatre design at the Paris Exhibition. Prompted by the influential and eccentric Henry Tonks, who informed him that an English name would retard his artistic career, the impressionable young artist

[32] H. A. Potamkin, 'Movie and New York Notes', *Close-Up* 7, 4 (1930): 250.
[33] John Grierson, 'Making Films for the Empire — II', *Listener*, 27 Apr. 1932, 605.

changed his name from Thompson to Rotha and embarked on a varied career in the late 1920s that included reviewing for the *Connoisseur*. In 1929 Rotha conceived the notion of writing a book about cinema, and with a contract and modest advance from Jonathan Cape he finished it in less than a year.[34] 'Mr Paul Rotha's book is undoubtedly the most important contribution which has yet been made to literature dealing with the art of the cinema,' the *Spectator* enthusiastically noted, and others agreed. In 1946, James Agate called it 'easily the best book yet produced on this really quite important subject' and nine years later, after the issue of a revised, expanded edition, Herbert Luft deemed it 'the foremost reference book for the entire industry'.[35]

In *The Film Till Now* Rotha sought to establish the aesthetic legitimacy of cinema in a variety of ways. First, he distanced himself from American film, which he strongly condemned as commercially motivated, 'calculated to appeal to the lowest grade of intelligence', and antithetical to genuine art. Rotha detested the star system, 'a flagrant prostitution of creative intelligence and good film material', and he patronized directors such as D. W. Griffith, whose 'super-spectacles will disappear under the dust of time'. Only Chaplin, 'a genius in the art of suggestion', escaped fully his loathing of Hollywood. Rotha considered American films to be products of industry, not artistry, and he retained this outspoken prejudice against the commercial cinema for much of his career. Second, Rotha argued that Europeans produced the best films, in part because they discovered avenues of escape from market forces. He cautioned against overpraising Russian directors; 'the cult for Soviet films', he wrote, 'has become slightly hysterical and more than a little tedious in its parrot-like cry.' And he acknowledged that State control could bind a Soviet film-maker no less tightly than the profit motive in Hollywood. Still, he showed how Eisenstein, Pudovkin, and other directors, including those in Germany and France, mastered the dynamics of film with far greater understanding than their counterparts in America. These dynamics provided Rotha's third preoccupation; a lengthy section on the theory of film, which concluded the book. Rotha sought to demonstrate among other things how, as fundamentally a visual medium employing such techniques as montage, the art of cinema could never accommodate the new 'dialogue' film. 'No power of speech is comparable to the descriptive value of photographs,' he wrote. 'The attempted combination of speech and pictures is the direct opposition of two separate mediums, which appeal

[34] Rotha, *Documentary Diary*, 1–15; interview with Paul Rotha, 17 Nov. 1978.

[35] 'The Future of the Film', *Spectator*, 6 Dec. 1930, 910; James Agate, *Around Cinemas* (London: Home and Van Thal, 1946), 80; Herbert G. Luft, 'Rotha and the World', *Quarterly of Film, Radio and Television* 10, 1 (1955): 90–1. See also the shrewd review by Penelope Houston in *Sight and Sound* 19, 1 (1950): 40.

in two utterly different ways. If the two are wedded, one must be subordinated to the other, and at once division of appeal will occur.'[36]

Pioneering in its comprehensive approach to world cinema and often lively in its opinions, *The Film Till Now* nevertheless reflected its origins as a rushed composition by an ambitious, essentially unseasoned author in his early twenties. As the critic Harry Potamkin put it in his review of the book for the American publication *Creative Art*, 'Rotha, a young Englishman, has accepted, without accrediting, the points of view of other critics, their observations and even their phraseology.' Potamkin concentrated his attention on Rotha's unacknowledged borrowings from some articles in *Close-Up* written by, in Potamkin's slyly self-referential phrase, 'an American cousin'.[37] Indeed, Rotha's chapter on 'The French Film' followed the general organization and made many of the same points as Potamkin's article 'The French Cinema' published in 1929.[38] Other derivations also went largely unacknowledged. Though Rudolph Messel's *This Film Business* appears in the bibliography, most readers would not know that Rotha's discussion of Griffith's *Intolerance*, for example, sometimes follows Messel's virtually word for word.[39] Then too, Rotha's discussion of film theory leans heavily on Pudovkin's *Film Theory*, translated by Ivor Montagu in 1929, and the pivotal ideas for Rotha's discussion of film 'movement' may be found in Potamkin, who cited Bakshy as the original source of the distinctions.[40]

Rotha understood the dangers of deriving too much from others. In his heavily critical discussion of the British cinema in *The Film Till Now*, he outlined some problems of film-making in his own country. British film, he wrote, too often imitated American or German cinema and failed 'to recognize the value of experiment'. The industry, he observed scornfully, was

filled with persons of moderate intelligence who are inclined to condemn anything that is beyond their range. . . . We are slow to learn from other film-producing countries, but we are always quick to imitate. But the danger lies in the disastrous

---

[36] Paul Rotha, *The Film Till Now: A Survey of the Cinema* (London: Jonathan Cape, 1930), 27, 74, 43, 101, 146, 306.

[37] Quoted in Harry A. Potamkin, *The Compound Cinema: The Film Writings of Harry Alan Potamkin*, ed. Lewis Jacobs (New York: Teachers College Press, 1977), 523.

[38] Compare H. A. Potamkin, 'The French Cinema', *Close-Up* 5, 1 (1929): 11–24, with Rotha, op. cit., 209–25.

[39] Compare Rudolph Messel, *This Film Business* (London: Ernest Benn, 1928), 98–9, with Rotha, op. cit., 91–2.

[40] Compare Harry A. Potamkin, 'The Compound Cinema', *Close-Up* 4, 1 (1929): 32–7, with Rotha, op. cit., 251–2. Compare also the sentence beginning 'The entire film . . .' in H. A. Potamkin, 'Phases of Cinema Unity', *Close-Up* 4, 5 (1929): 28, with the sentence 'It is strictly necessary for an entire film . . .' in Rotha, op. cit., 253. For Pudovkin, see V. I. Pudovkin, *Film Technique*, trans. Ivor Montagu (1929, reprinted London: George Newnes, 1933).

fact that we generally imitate without understanding, without probing to the base of the ideas that we adopt. . . . For this reason there has never been any school of *avant-garde* in England.[41]

These observations, expressed with the author's characteristic bluntness, touched upon difficulties that Rotha and others within British documentary also encountered. For example, Rotha's strong condemnation of 'dialogue' films, shared by Pudovkin, Eisenstein, Chaplin, and others when the sound film first appeared, reflected a conservative attitude towards developing technologies of communication which made many documentaries of the 1930s, including Rotha's *Contact* made in 1932, appear like relics from an earlier era. Although initially restricted in their access to good sound equipment by limited funding, documentary-film makers such as Rotha nevertheless preferred silent films to a technology they mistrusted and whose significance they misunderstood. For much of the early 1930s sound was beyond their range.

Moreover, Rotha's profound dislike of commercialism created tensions and rigidities which other film-makers found less troubling. Eisenstein perceived no difficulty in acknowledging his debt to Griffith and, like many European directors of distinction, learned much from commercial film. Rotha remained hostile during a decade when both technical and aesthetic innovation passed from the avant-garde to directors such as Alfred Hitchcock and John Ford. Then too, a dismissal of commercialism, typical of Rotha but by no means exclusive to him among documentary film-makers, conflicted with the essentially commercial purposes of many of their films. In *Celluloid: The Film Today*, published in 1931, Rotha acknowledged that, for a documentary-film maker, 'his choice between stating the truth or sweetened advertisement will be a dangerous one',[42] but few preferred to view themselves as pioneers of public relations. This tension between the artistic hopes and the realities of sponsorship continued to haunt the documentary movement.

Drifters and *The Film Till Now* illustrated some of the advantages and difficulties of deriving an aesthetic from abroad. In the 1920s, both Grierson and Rotha discovered possibilities in Continental film which they proselytized as socially responsible and artistically superior alternatives to the enfeebled cinematic traditions in British commercial film. *Drifters* and *The Film Till Now* anticipated a movement in the 1930s which applied many of these Continental ideas to making films for the Empire Marketing Board, the Post Office, Imperial Airways, Shell Oil, and other companies interested in better public relations. Yet method could not be separated from message, and imitation was not the equivalent of

---

[41] Rotha, op. cit., 226–7.
[42] Paul Rotha, *Celluloid: The Film Today* (London: Longmans, Green, 1931), 62.

understanding. Despite often heroic efforts, Grierson could not transform advertising for the herring industry into the high melodrama of Griffith or the revolutionary political visions of Eisenstein. Nor could Rotha's admirably conceived but hurried compilation of film theory and criticism create a thoroughly grounded aesthetic tradition flexible enough to adjust to technological and artistic change. *Drifters* and *The Film Till Now* prefigured a movement which made artistic and political claims for itself which later commentators, viewing the films, sometimes found difficult to justify.

The documentary-film movement represented one of many responses to commercial culture. Artists and intellectuals adopted a wide variety of approaches to the challenges posed by the rise of cinema and other contemporary forms of mass entertainment. Although some retreated into scornful isolation from the mass media, others perceived in the newer technologies of communications great opportunities for aesthetic experiment and cultural improvement. These progressives not only needed to discover ways to cope with the often brutal realities of the market mechanism, they also crafted aesthetic traditions which justified their embrace of new technologies. Both quests involved their own problems and predicaments: although, for example, Reith, Pick, and Grierson shared certain goals, their work also differed markedly in scope and practical detail. No single agenda characterized the work of these progressives, just as no single standard can evaluate their successes and failures. The cultivated élites during the 1920s, as before, remained a remarkably diverse group who often defined themselves by their independence from other individuals with whom they shared much.

What they shared can easily be over-simplified, yet should not be ignored. First the cultivated élites retained deep misgivings about the market-place as a mechanism of cultural evaluation. Whatever their differences concerning the relationship between producers and consumers in the mass media, artists, intellectuals, and their sympathetic patrons rejected the box-office as a determining standard of authentic value. Most people, the argument assumed, lacked the intelligence, training, or sensibility to judge artistic worth; the market-place solicited the tutored and untutored without discrimination. In politics, the formal mechanisms of democracy had been extended to virtually every qualified group by 1928; in culture, it was argued, such democracy would only be meaningful if guided by experts. Second and closely related, élites in Britain continued to defend the standards of art which, though difficult to define precisely, embodied a central difference between commercial culture and its more refined alternative. Some intellectuals distanced themselves from new tech-nologies and those who supported them; others, such as the progressives, argued that high standards could be applied to modern communications in order to uplift public taste. Both groups rejected the cultural egalitarianism which the market encouraged and both sought adherence to standards of discrimination which, it was presumed, commercial culture ignored. Yet in the 1920s, conventional distinctions between commercial and élite culture sometimes became blurred, most notably in the films of Charlie Chaplin, but also in other works. In the 1930s these ambiguities would become even more pronounced.

PART THREE

The 1930s: Towards a Common Culture

6

Sight and Sound: Studies in Convergence

THE 1930s marked an important decade for the development of a common culture in Britain. This culture was 'common' not because of its vulgarity or presumed inferiority; rather, it was widely shared by diverse groups within the entire community. Although disciples of Matthew Arnold restricted 'culture' to a limited body of works alien to most citizens, others permitted a more catholic definition of the term. As Raymond Williams pointed out, 'culture' need not be a weapon of social hierarchy; it might also describe the activities of the vast majority.[1] Moreover, a common culture might not be uniform or standardized in ways which both its advocates and critics often imagined. Some prophets on the Left and Right envisaged unified communities linked by a culture of great homogeneity. It became a bond that minimized dissent and eliminated the untidiness of a more open society. In an analogous manner, critics argued that modern communications disseminated an undifferentiated 'mass culture' whose pervasive uniformity threatened to smother traditional humanism. Motivated in part by a powerful sense of their own uniqueness and moral rectitude, these critics perceived in modernity a disastrous variation of the cultural uniformity that visionaries promised for the future. In an age of mechanical reproduction, culture threatened to become as standardized and interchangeable as the machines which replicated it.

Yet a common culture need not be as uniform or dominant as some of its defenders and adversaries claimed. It could exist within the context of great diversity as a shared experience which transcended boundaries without eliminating them or even lessening their social significance. A common culture might be experienced differently by a wide variety of groups and yet retain its value as a mutually acknowledged frame of reference. Though it is troublesome to compare highly complex phenomena, both Christianity and nationalism represented the most obvious and outstanding examples of common cultures in the British past. Both penetrated all strata of society without imposing a flat uniformity or undermining existing social hierarchies. Both provided a storehouse

---

[1] See especially the Conclusion to Raymond Williams, *Culture and Society, 1780–1950* (1958, reprinted New York: Harper Torchbooks, 1966), 295–338. On the word 'culture', see Williams, *Keywords*, 76–82.

of unifying symbols and experiences which helped define communities of intricate and often highly divisive factions. Both acted as powerful components of individual identity and social cohesion. As historical precedents, religion and nationalism embodied obvious differences and clearly dwarfed in longevity the emerging common culture of the twentieth-century in Britain. Yet they provided examples of a culture which might be widely shared and still diversely interpreted in a complex society.

The common culture of the 1930s was not without significant precedents. In the nineteenth century, the works of Charles Dickens embodied qualities and achieved a level of popularity that overcame traditional cultural distinctions. Then too, as we have seen, Charlie Chaplin transcended the boundaries which separated the cultivated élites from the general public. Chaplin's films attracted huge audiences that included intellectuals who otherwise excoriated the cinema. Many other examples might be cited. It was not the historical uniqueness, but the extent and scope of the culture of the 1930s that arguably marked a transformation in British cultural life. Although it should be strongly emphasized that no single decade entirely encompassed this complicated transition, it was during the 1930s that the commercial cinema, the BBC, some nationally distributed newspapers and magazines, and certain literary figures helped create a common culture that became one of many defining features of twentieth-century British society.

This common culture embodied a number of interrelated characteristics. First, it appealed to all classes and regions. Although the entertainment industry compiled circulation and box-office records earlier, it was during the 1930s that statistical profiles of audience tastes became more widespread and sophisticated. Though by current standards these surveys could be easily faulted, they offer valuable insight into the ubiquity of certain cultural forms. The commercial cinema provides the most obvious example. Rowson's survey of the cinema for 1934 revealed that total admissions exceeded 963 millions, or an average of about 22 visits per year for every citizen.[2] To entertain these audiences, the industry increased the number of cinemas from around 3,000 in 1926 to almost 5,000 in 1938; and these numbers do not reflect the vast improvements in the seating quality and general ambience of many houses.[3] The cinema

---

[2] Simon Rowson, 'A Statistical Survey of the Cinema Industry in Great Britain in 1934', *Journal of the Royal Statistical Society* 99, 1 (1936): 70–6.

[3] Jeffrey Richards, *The Age of the Dream Palace: Cinema and Society in Britain, 1930–1939* (London: Routledge and Kegan Paul, 1984), 12. Richards argues that although all classes went to the cinema, it was not 'classless' because 'the classes rarely mixed at the cinema' (p. 17). For the impact of commercial film on the working classes, see also Stephen Craig Shafer, ' "Enter the Dream House": The British Film Industry and the Working Classes in Depression England, 1929–1939' (Ph.D diss., University of Illinois at Urbana-Champaign, 1982).

penetrated every area of the country and, as a remarkably detailed study in 1943 revealed, attracted virtually every sector of the population. Although the vast majority of the audience, like the British population itself, was working-class, over 80 per cent of university-educated participants in the study attended the cinema at least occasionally. Among both the 'middle' and 'higher' economic groups, over 70 per cent of those surveyed went to the movies some of the time. For all groups, the young attended more frequently than the old, and women generally proved more enthusiastic about the medium than did men.[4] As the Moyne Committee Report observed in 1936, 'the cinematograph film is today one of the most widely used means for the amusement of the public at large. It is also undoubtedly a most important factor in the education of all classes of the community.'[5]

Other media also attracted a cross-section of the population. 'Popular' newspapers, defined in 1938 by Political and Economic Planning (PEP) as making 'a general appeal to all classes of people all over the country', continued to grow in circulation, sometimes dramatically. The *Daily Express* increased from slightly less than 1,700,000 copies sold daily in 1930 to over 2,200,000 in 1937, while the *Daily Mail*, which in relative terms endured a difficult decade, still sold an average of over 1,500,000 copies a day in 1937. Both papers appealed to readers from all income groups, with the *Express* ranging from about 8 to over 26 per cent of households in each of five income-classifications. Popular newspapers also attracted readers from various regions. PEP discovered that in an unnamed 'small Wales mining town' the *Express* accounted for over 30 per cent of all newspaper sales while in four villages in Oxfordshire and Gloucestershire over 40 per cent of all households read Beaverbrook's paper. The 1930s proved an important decade for newspapers in Britain. National dailies increased their overall circulation by almost 1,500,000 copies from 1930 to 1936, and in 1934 every hundred families in Britain bought 95 morning and 130 Sunday papers.[6]

Radio experienced even more dramatic growth. Radio licences increased from around 3 million in 1930 to almost 9 million at the end of the decade. In a recent book Mark Pegg warned against the dangers of equating licence holders with the number of listeners, but even by his

[4] J. P. Mayer, *British Cinemas and Their Audiences: Sociological Studies* (London: Dennis Dobson, 1948), 250–75. See also Kathleen Box, 'The Cinema and the Public' (mimeo, London: The Social Survey, 1946) for statistics three years later. For a contemporary account of the cinema habits of one city, see B. Seebown Rowntree, *Poverty and Progress: A Second Social Survey of York* (London: Longmans, Green, 1941), 470–1.

[5] Quoted in Jeffrey Richards and Anthony Aldgate, *British Cinema and Society, 1930–1970* (Totowa, NJ: Barnes and Noble, 1983), 1.

[6] PEP, *Report on British Press*, 3, 125, 232–5; *Royal Commission on the Press, 1947–1949. Report* (London: HMSO, 1949), 190.

own, more sophisticated calculations, growth continued to be extra-ordinarily rapid. Pegg's statistics indicate that the number of listeners, like the number of licences, roughly tripled in the 1930s, from around 12 million listeners at the end of the 1920s to almost 34 million listeners in 1939, a substantial proportion of the total population. The south of England contained the highest percentage of licence holders, with the north of Scotland and Northern Ireland somewhat under-represented.[7] Still, like the cinema and some national daily newspapers, the BBC reached almost all elements of the population in virtually all areas of the country. Although, as we have seen, an important element of this penetration occurred earlier, it was during the 1930s that these media most thoroughly cut across class and regional lines of cultural demarcation.

If this common culture surmounted regional boundaries, however, it was not itself without a 'geography'. This geography involved three specific sites, each with its own unique contribution to the common culture of the whole. First, America maintained its often resented presence in British cultural life. Even government intervention in 1927 could not halt American domination of the British cinema.[8] 'It is perfectly simple, even in these days of protection,' the British film critic C. A. Lejeune wrote in 1935, 'for an Englishman to go regularly once a week to the cinema without ever seeing an English film.'[9] American methods continued to affect British journalists, just as American songs still played on British gramophones. Yet it was not only American products that prevailed. The south of England, and especially London, retained its importance for British culture. The London metropolitan area contained the major publishers, film studios, gramophone companies, national newspapers, as well as the headquarters of the BBC.[10] It was in London and the Home Counties that the most important cultural networks in Britain thrived. Moreover, the rapidly expanding suburbs of London and the major provincial cities also helped set the tone for the emergent culture. The housing revolution of the inter-war era thrust together families from many strata within the class structure. Prosperous but isolated from traditional sources of entertainment in the central city, the suburban population during the 1930s turned during their leisure hours to such forms of entertainment as the cinema, the BBC, and the book clubs.[11] If the

[7] Pegg, *Broadcasting and Society*, 6–22.

[8] See Margaret Dickinson and Sarah Street, *Cinema and State: The Film Industry and the Government, 1927–84* (London: BFI, 1985), 5–75. On American domination, see also (but use with caution) Klingender and Legg, *Money Behind the Screen*.

[9] C. A. Lejeune, 'The British Film and Others', *The Fortnightly* 143 (1935): 287.

[10] On London as a cultural centre for film, see R. A. S. Hennessey, *The Electric Revolution* (London: Oriel Press, 1971), 167–8.

[11] On the growth and cultural role of suburbs during the inter-war era in Britain, see, among others, Alan A. Jackson, *Semi-Detached London: Suburban Development, Life*

common culture of the 1930s transcended regional boundaries, it was America, the south of England, and the rapidly expanding suburbs that provided it with a geographical focus.

A second characteristic of the emerging common culture concerned the nature of its appeal. In commercial culture, as we have seen in Part One, a complex and interactive process of identification between producers and consumers helped determine the content of media such as cinema and the popular press. For example, in popular fiction and commercial cinema a formulaic approach emerged which, while minimizing economic risk, retained enough flexibility to adapt to changing tastes. Directors of unusual talent, such as D. W. Griffith, worked within these formulas to create visually stunning films that many avant-garde figures considered art. During the 1930s, as we shall see, the dividing lines between commercial and élite culture often became blurred when, for example, an increasing number of film directors created widely popular entertainment that many intellectuals also found aesthetically satisfying. Commercial culture appropriated techniques that earlier had been within the domain of the cultivated élites. At the same time, progressives devoted to raising cultural standards became more sensitive to the demands of the public they sought to instruct. Documentary-film makers discovered approaches to their work long standard within the commercial cinema, while the BBC became more responsive to its growing number of listeners. Although by the end of the 1930s intellectuals still distanced themselves from the tastes of the average citizen, bitter attacks on 'mass civilization' by mavericks such as F. R. Leavis testified to the appeal of mass media to all sectors of the population.

The common culture of the 1930s also possessed a third characteristic, more difficult to describe, but intimately related to the technologies and traditions of cultural discourse. The continuing development and maturation of new technologies within mass communications accelerated the trend towards convergence among the various media. This convergence took many forms. Sight and sound, for example, came to be replicated within the same medium. The arrival of the talkies, a watershed in cinema history, meant that recorded sound could be combined with a visual medium. Technology brought together two sensory forms of knowledge that individuals took for granted in everyday oral communications. Moreover, aural and visual appeals combined freely in many forms of

and Transport, 1900–39 (London: George Allen and Unwin, 1973); John Burnett, *A Social History of Housing, 1815–1970* (Newton Abbot: David and Charles, 1978), 244–70; and Anthony D. King, *The Bungalow: The Production of a Global Culture* (London: Routledge and Kegan Paul, 1984), 156–92. For a brief contemporary account of the role of films in suburban life, see Hubert Griffith, 'Films and the British Public', *Nineteenth Century and After* 112 (1932): 197–8.

mass communication. In the early twentieth century, as we have seen, the language of the press began to imitate the rhythms of everyday speech, while at the same time news photography and layout contributed an important visual dimension to information and entertainment. In the 1930s this tendency of one medium to poach upon other media acquired new sophistication. In the *March of Time* the documentary became a dramatized newspaper while, at the end of the decade, *Picture Post* captured the drama of newsreels in a magazine of photographs.[12] Then too, as we shall see, newspapers perfected layouts which shouted their news and attracted an audience of growing visual literacy. Finally, just as one medium borrowed freely from another, so too a number of shrewd individuals discovered the benefits of working within many media. J. B. Priestley wrote best-selling novels, popular newspaper articles, political tracts, and dramas for the West End. He was also involved with Hollywood, the British documentary movement, and two films of Gracie Fields. Early in the Second World War he became one of the most popular broadcasters in the BBC's short history. In many ways Priestley epitomized the common culture of the twentieth century.

Each of these three characteristics represented a form of convergence: among audiences, among standards, and among the media itself. Yet profound differences still separated these same social classes and varied appeals. The common culture did not displace existing arrangements as much as provide a mutual frame of reference among those differences. The animated films of Walt Disney, for example, could be discussed among adults and children of all classes, with widely varying levels of education and intellectual pretension, in all areas of the country, and for that matter throughout much of the industrialized world. Common culture need not have been British in origin, though much of it was. Moreover, it was not the culture that many critics, then and now, hoped to witness. For some intellectuals it remained either too commercialized in its motivation or compromised in its standards. Political radicals despaired of its values, while implicitly acknowledging its hold over the very classes they hoped to redeem. Avant-garde artists and literary figures expressed disdain for the mainstream they needed to know well enough to negate. Critics derived

---

[12] Alan Cameron, 'Gaumont to Launch "Headline" News Reels in Fight With Press', *World's Press News*, 2 Nov. 1933, n.p.; Gerald Sanger, 'News into Entertainment', *World's Press News*, 21 Jan. 1937, 2. For a case-study of British newsreels in this period, see Anthony Aldcroft, *Cinema and History: British Newsreels and the Spanish Civil War* (London: Scolar Press, 1979). On the *March of Time*, see Raymond Fielding, *The* March of Time, *1935–1951* (New York: Oxford University Press, 1978). For *Picture Post*, see the memoirs of an earlier editor: Tom Hopkinson, *Of This Our Time: A Journalist's Story, 1905–50* (London: Hutchinson, 1982). A contemporary account can be found in Edward Hulton, 'The Future of *Picture Post*', *Penrose Annual* 42, (1940): 21–4.

economic benefits and intellectual obligations, often well masked, from the culture they professed to reject.

The 1930s proved especially crucial for the development of this common culture for a number of reasons. First, during this decade the technology of mass communications progressed remarkably, improving quality and lowering costs to attract new enthusiasts while at the same time maintaining the loyalty of the existing audience. The cinema provides a good example of this technical maturation. The talkies initially posed a variety of well-chronicled problems for producers and consumers alike. The installation of sound systems in Britain lagged behind the United States and dictated changes in key aspects of film production. The addition of spoken dialogue affected both narrative strategy and acting style. Lights, camera, and action needed to be adjusted to a system that at first lacked mobility and high-quality sound reproduction. Exhibitors suddenly confronted problems of acoustics and projection that silent cinema, with its live musical accompaniment, had never faced.[13] Intellectuals and film-makers of international distinction found it difficult to accept the intrusion of sound into a supremely visual medium. In 'Why I Prefer Silent Films' written for the *Daily Mail* in 1931, Charlie Chaplin claimed that sound should be an addition, not a substitute, for moving images. 'My screen character remains speechless from choice.'[14] Ernest Betts argued that 'the business of the film is to depict action, not to reproduce sound', and others, such as Paul Rotha, registered their protests.[15]

Yet, only a few years after the introduction of sound, technicians overcame the problems which plagued the early talkies. Western Electric and RCA perfected recording techniques that eliminated the extraneous noise of early recording. Microphones became mobile, and sound engineers developed ingenious techniques to reproduce music and dialogue of good fidelity. Actors adjusted their styles to the intimacy of movie dialogue.[16] Other innovations enhanced the technical quality of films. Improvements in film stock and processing eliminated the graininess of film projected on to the newer, larger screens of giant cinemas. Better cameras and printing techniques improved the appearance of films in a variety of

[13] Rachael Low, *The History of the British Film, 1929–1939. Film Making in 1930s Britain* (London: George Allen and Unwin, 1985), 73–90. See also Alexander Walker, *Shattered Silents: How the Talkies Came to Stay* (London: Elm Tree Books, 1978).

[14] Charles Chaplin, 'Why I Prefer Silent Films', *Daily Mail*, 7 Feb. 1931.

[15] Betts quoted in Harry M. Geduld, *The Birth of the Talkies: From Edison to Jolson* (Bloomington: Indiana University Press, 1975), 271. For Rotha, see Paul Rotha, 'The Cinema To-Day', *Twentieth Century* 1, 1 (1931): 18–21; and id., 'The Lament', *Sight and Sound* 7, 27 (1938): 120–1. As late as 1956 he expressed reservations about sound; see id., 'Sixty Years of Cinema' (1956), in *Rotha on the Film: A Selection of Writings About the Cinema* (London: Faber and Faber, 1958), 37.

[16] Low, op. cit., 89–90.

subtle ways. The development of Technicolor added a dimension to film which, like sound, initially seemed a gimmick but eventually became a commonplace.[17] 'In every material way it has advanced beyond expectations, and technically the film is flawless,' Andrew Buchanan wrote of the medium in 1936. 'The perfection of noiseless recording, of photography, of settings, of projection . . . leave one bewildered. The triumphant technician has been embraced by the showman, and together they have won commercial success.'[18] Already by the mid-1930s the silent cinema of less than a decade earlier struck many as primitive and immature. Masters of the silent screen who refused to adjust to rapidly developing technologies sometimes lost favour. Alistair Cooke wrote that sound and other changes in the cinema made 'the Chaplin talent *look* like a period piece even when his psychology and feeling were subtler than his contemporaries''.[19]

The technology of other media also matured. The 1930s marked an important turning-point in both the technical and economic development of radio. As components became standardized and manufacturers practised new economies of scale, good-quality radio sets became affordable through hire-purchase plans for many working-class families. Automatic volume controls, push-button tuning, multiple wavebands, static reducing devices, better calibration dials, and other innovations during the 1930s also widened the audience for radio and increased its acceptability among the cultivated élites.[20] 'The Modern Set is Radio's Finest Achievement', the heading of a feature proclaimed in 1935. 'High Quality Reproduction, Selectivity and Ease of Control are the Main Points of Appeal', ran the subheading.[21] The newspaper press, on the other hand, enjoyed fewer dramatic improvements in its technology. Better cameras and flashes, the transmission of news photography by wire, and the occasional inclusion of specially printed colour supplements continued the tradition of technical innovation that characterized the popular press earlier in the century.[22]

[17] Barry Salt, 'Film Style and Technology in the Thirties', *Film Quarterly* 30, 1 (1976): 19–32; David Bordwell, 'Technicolor', in Bordwell, Staiger, and Thompson, *The Classical Hollywood Cinema*, 353–7.
[18] Andrew Buchanan, *The Art of Film Production* (London:. Sir Isaac Pitman and Sons, 1936), 32. See also Dallas Bower, *Plan for Cinema* (London: Dent, 1936), 136.
[19] Alistair Cooke, 'Modern Times', in *Garbo and the Night Watchman: A Selection From the Writings of British and American Film Critics*, ed. Alistair Cooke (London: Jonathan Cape, 1937), 332–3.
[20] S. G. Sturmey, *The Economic Development of Radio* (London: Gerald Duckworth, 1958), 171–8.
[21] 'The Modern Set is Radio's Finest Achievement', *Daily Mail*, 31 Oct. 1935, 19. See also E. M. Lee, 'Components', *The Times*, Special Supplement on Radio, 14 Aug. 1934, p. xl.
[22] See Frank Luther Mott, *American Journalism: A History, 1690–1960* (New York: Macmillan, 1962), 682–5. On colour, see G. H. Saxon Mills, 'Colour War', *Penrose Annual* 36 (1934): 8–11.

The 1930s proved important to the development of a common culture for a second reason. Although unemployment, hunger, and severe economic deprivation profoundly affected certain regions of the country and justly dominated contemporary evaluations of the decade, other areas of Britain, particularly the South, experienced marked economic growth and a steady rise in the standard of living. Economic historians have long acknowledged and debated the meaning of this paradox.[23] In Lancashire and the North-East, as well as areas of Scotland, Wales, and Northern Ireland, unemployment and industrial decline reached unprecedented proportions, revealed not only in the chilling statistics of the decade, but in a variety of books that gave suffering a human voice. As Walter Greenwood wrote in *How the Other Man Lives*, 'wherever you go, to any of the depressed areas of these islands you see the same, dreary conditions . . . the same oppression and sense of blank futility which transforms men and women into so much human scrap.' One particular town seemed to represent the entire country. 'Jarrow's plight is not a local problem,' Ellen Wilkinson concluded in *The Town That Was Murdered*. 'It is the symptom of a national evil.'[24]

While some areas underwent well-publicized agony, others quietly prospered. For much of the population in the South and other regions not tied to troubled industries, the standard of living rose substantially. Although statistics from this period involve the usual ambiguities and perplexities, it seems that for most working households the relative price of food, clothing, housing, furniture, and a variety of other goods continued to decline. Some sectors of the economy underwent particularly noticeable growth, though traditional assumptions concerning the split between 'new' and 'old' industries should be treated cautiously.[25] Still,

[23] There is an immense literature on the economics of the 1930s. The elements of prosperity and recovery are emphasized by, among others, H. W. Richardson, *Economic Recovery in Britain 1932–39* (London: Weidenfeld and Nicolson, 1967); John Stevenson, 'Myth and Reality: Britain in the 1930s', in *Crisis and Controversy: Essays in Honour of A. J. P. Taylor*, Alan Sked and Chris Cook, eds. (London: Macmillan, 1976), 90–109; and Derek H. Aldcroft, *The British Economy Between the Wars* (Oxford: Philip Allan, 1983). The more pessimistic case is stated by, among others, B. W. E. Alford, *Depression and Recovery? British Economic Growth, 1918–39* (London: Macmillan, 1972). See also Alan E. Booth and Sean Glynn, 'Unemployment in the Interwar Period: A Multiple Problem', *Journal of Contemporary History* 10, 4 (1975): 611–36.

[24] Walter Greenwood, *How the Other Man Lives* (London: Labour Book Service [1939]), 40; Ellen Wilkinson, *The Town That Was Murdered: The Life Story of Jarrow* (London: Victor Gollancz, 1939), 283.

[25] Neil K. Buxton, 'Introduction', in *British Industry Between the Wars: Instability and Industrial Development, 1919–39*, Neil K. Buxton and Derek H. Aldcroft, eds. (London: Scolar Press, 1979), 15–18; B. W. E. Alford, 'New Industries for Old? British Industry Between the Wars', in *The Economic History of Britain Since 1700, vol. 2: 1860 to the 1970s*, Roderick Floud and Donald McCloskey, eds. (Cambridge: Cambridge University Press, 1981), 308–31.

overall the vehicle, construction, and electrical industries among others contributed to the prosperity of many groups within the population. In towns such as Reading, Slough, and Luton most families experienced an unprecedented level of material comfort during the slump.[26]

This prosperity within the context of visible despair affected the development of a common culture in at least two important ways. First and most obviously, it fuelled both the supply and demand for cinema, radio, gramophone, newspapers, and other leisure activities. To that substantial proportion of the population whose real wages increased and even among some of the unemployed, certain goods became affordable for the first time, thus accelerating demand for those same goods which, through economies of scale, then became cheaper to supply. The rapid electrification of Britain during the 1930s affected demand for radios and gramophones while at the same time providing jobs for men and women who themselves became cultural consumers.[27] Second, as in the 1960s, material comfort provided a secure economic basis for a heightened sense of social responsibility within some circles. Snobbery about the 'masses' persisted but became less fashionable. University students who in 1926 drove buses during the General Strike, now expressed solidarity with the hunger marchers. Poets wrote sonnets about workers. The Left, dwarfed in the House of Commons by the National Government, set the tone among avant-garde artists and intellectuals. Though, as Orwell noted, middle-class assumptions permeated these manifestations of social concern, the culture of the working class became less foreign, less unforgivable, among the governing classes. Depression within the context of prosperity in Britain often bound social groups together rather than split them apart.

A. CINEMA: IMAGE AND IDENTIFICATION

In the 1930s a number of film-makers appealed to both cultivated and popular audiences. Walt Disney, the Marx Brothers, and Frank Capra among others created entertaining cinema that many intellectuals praised and enjoyed. Hollywood dominated international screens in part because it produced films that, in their manipulation of formula and genre, transcended geographical and cultural boundaries. One British director in particular also succeeded in blurring traditional cultural demarcations. 'My policy is to make . . . popular pictures which anybody can understand,'

---

[26] Noreen Branson and Margot Heinemann, *Britain in the Nineteen-Thirties* (London: Weidenfeld and Nicolson, 1971), 68–9.

[27] On the electrical industry in Britain at this period, see R. E. Catterall, 'Electrical Engineering', in *British Industry*, Buxton and Aldcroft, eds., 241–75.

Alfred Hitchcock told the *Daily Herald* in 1933. 'But without being highbrow, I believe in making them in such a way that they will appeal to the most intelligent people as well.'[28] In the late 1920s and throughout the 1930s, Hitchcock made a number of commercially successful films that gained flattering critical attention and loyalty from the cultivated élites. Although in his film criticism Graham Greene remained generally hostile to Hitchcock, others gladly acknowledged the British director's uncanny mastery of a genre of almost universal appeal. 'Some of us are already beginning to say that talkies are an art,' a reviewer for *Close-Up* wrote after seeing *Blackmail*, Hitchcock's first encounter with the new technology.[29] Six years later, a critic for the *Saturday Review* claimed that 'Mr. Hitchcock has not made a dull film.'[30]

The British documentary-film movement, on the other hand, found it difficult to bridge the gap between their own mutual appreciation of each other's works and a less enthusiastic general public, which largely ignored their films. Commercial circuits exhibited very few of their efforts and, until the late 1930s, most of these films were not even registered with the Board of Trade, a procedure which would have qualified them for the mandated quota.[31] Those that did achieve some commercial distribution often encountered an unfriendly public. In an interview, the disarmingly blunt Harry Watt recalled how his documentary *BBC— Droitwich* lasted only one day at the London Pavilion in Piccadilly Circus. Asked by a chagrined director why a Mickey Mouse cartoon supplanted a film on the BBC, the manager replied that 'it got the bird, and we jerked it.'[32] Commercial distributors curtly returned a series of documentaries to Bruce Woolfe with the comment, 'Bored us stiff; no personal appeal.' Defenders of the documentary movement, including John Grierson, argued that their films gained far wider distribution through the school system and in special exhibitions.[33] The statistics of film rentals from the

[28] Quoted in Donald Spoto, *The Dark Side of Genius: The Life of Alfred Hitchcock* (New York: Ballantine Books, 1983), 150. Many of Hitchcock's British films are now available on video cassettes.

[29] Quoted in John Russell Taylor, *Hitch: The Life and Times of Alfred Hitchcock* (1978, reprinted New York: Berkley Books, 1980), 91. See also Buchanan, *Film Production*, 12. For an example of Greene's hostility, see Graham Greene, 'The Middle-brow Film', *The Fortnightly* 145 (1936): 302–7.

[30] Mark Forest, 'A Fine Picture', *Saturday Review*, 22 June 1935, 797.

[31] Low, *Documentary and Educational Films*, 68–9. For a list of films registered, see Paul Swann, 'The British Documentary Film Movement, 1926–1946' (Ph.D. diss., University of Leeds, 1979), 284–6.

[32] Harry Watt quoted in Elizabeth Sussex, *The Rise and Fall of British Documentary: The Story of the Film Movement Founded by John Grierson* (Berkeley: University of California Press, 1975), 48. A slightly different version appears in Harry Watt, *Don't Look at the Camera* (London: Paul Elek, 1974), 69.

[33] H. Bruce Woolfe, 'Commercial Documentary', *Cinema Quarterly* 2, 2 (1933–4): 99; John Grierson, *Grierson on Documentary*, ed. Forsyth Hardy (1966), 68–9; *Report*

Imperial Institute in London indicate that in 1937 an audience estimated
at five million viewed the organization's films, a small minority of which
were documentaries by Grierson's disciples.[34] Still, it is difficult to equate
films shown to a captive audience of often very young schoolchildren
with those exhibited on commercial screens. Though some maintained
that *Night Mail* and a handful of other documentary films achieved
wide distribution—accurate statistics prove hard to obtain—it is more
probable that relatively few adults ever saw a British documentary film
in the 1930s.

Makers of documentary films and their sympathizers offered a variety
of reasons for this lack of popular appeal. Reflecting upon his years at
the EMB, which closed its film division in 1933, John Grierson argued that
insufficient funding for audio equipment forced the documentary directors
to make silent films long after the public expected sound.[35] R. S. Lambert,
editor of the *Listener*, claimed that factual films often failed because of
insufficient advertising. 'I remember a case', he wrote in 1934, 'where
a picture house manager had two films sent down to him—a feature film
with Greta Garbo (a not very good love story) and an interesting film
of Polar exploration. He told me that he was allowed to spend on
advertising the former £50—on advertising the latter 10s. Can you wonder
that "interest" films don't reach the public?' Andrew Buchanan wrote in
1945 that the coming of double features severely retarded the movement
by allowing no room for short subjects.[36] Whatever the fate of their
films, however, few documentary directors underestimated the social and
aesthetic significance of their work. Rotha flatly declared in his memoirs
that 'up till 1940, there was only one real coherent movement . . . which
was destined to have an influence on Western film-making and to attract
world attention among critics and audiences; that was the movement of
documentary film-making in Britain in the 1930s.' Grierson recalled that
'we could all edit well. We could all write well. There was no part of
it we couldn't do.' Basil Wright, viewing a portion of his *Children at School*
decades after directing it in 1937, exclaimed 'My goodness, what genius
I had then!'[37]

From the Select Committee on Estimates (HMSO, 1934), 48–9; Kenneth Clark, 'Broadcast',
Documentary News Letter 1, 1 (1940): 4–5.

[34] Mackenzie, *Propaganda and Empire*, 135.

[35] John Grierson, 'The G.P.O. Gets Sound', *Cinema Quarterly* 2, 4 (1934): 215–16.

[36] Richard S. Lambert, 'How To Get The Films You Want', *Sight and Sound* 3, 9
(1934): 7; Andrew Buchanan, *Film and the Future* (London: George Allen and Unwin,
1945), 30–5. See also the essays in Richard S. Lambert, ed., *For Filmgoers Only: The
Intelligent Filmgoer's Guide to the Film* (London: Faber and Faber and The British Institute
of Adult Education, 1934).

[37] Rotha, *Documentary Diary*, p. xiii; Sussex, op. cit., 39, 99. See also Paul Rotha,
Movie Parade (London: The Studio LD, 1936), p. x.

Yet even though these self-characterizations of artistic merit clearly provided their own consolation, the question remains why directors such as Hitchcock succeeded and the documentary movement failed to attract a broad public of widely divergent backgrounds and tastes. 'Hitchcock was one of our considerable gods . . .', Harry Watt later recalled of his fellow documentary film-makers. 'The early Hitchcocks were the only British pictures worth a damn.'[38] Clearly both Hitchcock and the documentary movement knew how to manipulate images. They all recognized the contributions of D. W. Griffith; and as early members of the Film Society Hitchcock, Grierson, Rotha, and others witnessed the best cinema from the Continent, including the influential Russian experiments with montage and other techniques. Yet Hitchcock possessed a deeper understanding of both the intrinsic ambiguity of cinematic images and, closely related, the crucial role of audience identification in the experience of film. In part because of his films and those of other skilled directors, a number of British intellectuals in the later 1930s shed many of their reservations about the commercial cinema and consistently praised its efforts. At the same time the documentary movement, belatedly and often inadequately, began to imitate commercial techniques that earlier they dismissed contemptuously. Hitchcock epitomized the growing maturation of a commercial medium that eventually established itself as an art.

Hitchcock's cinematic imagination drew from many roots. As a schoolboy he expressed more interest in visual than literary pursuits, and in adolescence his infatuation with American film helped persuade him to join the industry in London shortly after the First World War. Hitchcock designed titles for some silent films, now apparently lost, but, as his biographers make clear, his talent, enthusiasm, thoroughness, and legendary unflappability soon persuaded his superiors to assign him other tasks, including directing. In 1924 he travelled to Germany where, at a critical point in his career, he encountered the Expressionist films that profoundly influenced his later style.[39] Though difficult to define precisely, German Expressionism manifested itself in cinema most characteristically in productions that imaginatively employed symbol, lighting, and camera to create mood or to embody visually an often disturbed state of mind. For example, in *Der letzte Mann* (1924), a film that Hitchcock greatly admired and observed being made, the director F. W. Murnau used low camera angles and special lighting early in the film to accentuate the stature of the protagonist, a doorman who took special pride in a splendid uniform that symbolized his authority. Later, after the doorman

---

[38] Sussex, op. cit., 109.
[39] Taylor, *Hitch*, 39–41; Spoto, *Dark Side of Genius*, 72–8; Ivor Montagu, 'Working With Hitchcock', *Sight and Sound* 49, 3 (1980): 190.

received an undeserved demotion, Murnau employed a mobile camera and a variety of camera angles, including a sequence photographed through a glass pane, to indicate the protagonist's humiliation and despair. Like other directors, Murnau revelled in contrasts between light and dark, and he selected certain objects to act as emblems of character and shifting circumstances.[40]

From German Expressionism, Soviet montage, and his own varied experiences as an apprentice in the industry, Hitchcock developed cinematic techniques that guided him for over half a century. Although not all these methods can be discussed here, two interrelated aspects of his film style during the inter-war period should be emphasized. First, like a number of Continental directors, Hitchcock recognized early in his career the profound ambiguity of moving images. Their meaning depended almost exclusively upon the visual context; as this context altered, so too the significance of the image changed. In a famous experiment from Russia, Kuleshov juxtaposed shots of the blank expression of an actor's face with two vastly different, emotionally charged scenes. Later, spectators of the edited film projected the appropriate feelings on to the actor's face.[41] Although Hitchcock probably discovered this lesson independently, he never abandoned its vital implications for cinema. Like other directors, Hitchcock demonstrated in his early silent films how the meaning of images changed as the viewer's perspective shifted. In *Downhill*, released in 1927, the camera focused on a cheerful protagonist in evening dress, drew back to reveal that he waited tables in a night-club, then moved further to disclose that the entire scene took place on the stage of a musical comedy.[42] Each shift of the camera provided a new interpretation of the scene. This recognition that images possessed no fixed meaning also manifested itself in Hitchcock's studied manipulation of visual symbolism. In *The Ring*, for example, also released in 1927, images involving circles and related geometric configurations became powerful vehicles to convey the inner emotions of lovers in conflict. A complex pun, the title referred to an impressive variety of objects, including a boxing ring and various pieces of jewellery, that unified the film visually and underscored the significance of individual episodes within the emotional dynamics of the story.[43]

[40] John D. Barlow, *German Expressionist Film* (Boston: Twayne, 1982), 15, 137–55; Lotte H. Eisner, *The Haunted Screen: Expressionism in the German Cinema and the Influence of Max Reinhardt* (Berkeley: University of California Press, 1969), 207–21; and id., *Murnau* (Berkeley: University of California Press, 1973), 154–8.

[41] For these and other experiments by Kuleshov, see Leyda, *Kino*, 164–6. On their relationship to Hitchcock, see Robin Wood, *Hitchcock's Films* (New York: A. S. Barnes; London: Tantivy, 1977), 13–18.   [42] Taylor, op. cit., 20–1, 70.

[43] Maurice Yacowar, *Hitchcock's British Films* (Hamden, Conn.: Archon, 1977), 58–64. The notion of 'context' is central to Yacowar's analysis.

With the arrival of the talkies, Hitchcock integrated sound into his fundamentally Expressionist imagination. In a famous scene from *Blackmail*, Hitchcock's first sound feature, the emphasis upon the word 'knife' in the soundtrack, drawn and distorted from everyday conversation, echoed the female protagonist's anxiety over killing a potential rapist. A commonplace object and sound suddenly became sinister within a narrative context shrewdly constructed by the director. In a later film, *The Thirty-Nine Steps*, the fearful sound of a maid screaming at the discovery of a murdered woman dissolved into the high-pitched whistle of a train bearing the accused but innocent central character away. Although in a number of his other British films Hitchcock employed sound as a narrative bridge or to enhance a particular mood, he also recognized that such aural stratagems could become distracting stunts that interrupted rather than punctuated the flow of the story.[44]

Hitchcock never forgot that the experience of film involved as much illusion as reality. What the viewers witnessed in their local cinema need bear little relation to what occurred on the set. 'I want to put my film together on the screen', he wrote in 1937.[45] For Hitchcock, this now commonplace principle of cinematic uniqueness partly involved a preoccupation with the technical wizardry of film production. He enjoyed relating tales of how he fabricated certain illusions in his films. Like a magician, the director fooled an audience who paid to be tricked.[46] This same principle also lay behind Hitchcock's frequent use of montage, the often rapid-paced editing for a predetermined visual effect which the Russians borrowed from the Americans and managed to claim for themselves. 'The screen ought to speak its own language, freshly coined,' Hitchcock observed, 'and it can't do that unless it treats an acted scene as a piece of raw material which must be broken up, taken to bits, before it can be woven into an expressive visual pattern.'[47] One of Hitchcock's most celebrated montage sequences from the inter-war period occurred in *Sabotage*, released in 1936, in a scene once again involving a fatal stabbing. Employing a series of rapidly executed shots involving no dialogue, Hitchcock built the tension between two characters and created the circumstances that made the killing both horrifying and plausible. Had it been filmed at wide angle, as if watching a play, this same scene

---

[44] On Hitchcock's caution about stunts, see Russell Maloney, 'Profile: What Happens After That', *New Yorker*, 10 Sept. 1938, 28.

[45] Alfred Hitchcock, 'Direction', in *Footnotes to the Film*, ed. Charles Davy (New York: Oxford University Press, 1937), 7. The article is reprinted in *Sight and Sound: A Fiftieth-Anniversary Selection*, ed. David Wilson (London: Faber and Faber, 1982), 36–42.

[46] François Truffaut, *Hitchcock* (New York: Simon and Schuster, A Touchstone Book, 1966), 47–8.

[47] Hitchcock in *Footnotes*, ed. Davy, 7.

would have lost most of its power.[48] Silvia Sidney, the female star and an actress accustomed to the stage, found the disjointed filming of the scene utterly frustrating; it was only when she viewed the finished product that she realized the director's intentions.[49]

Hitchcock considered film an artificial construct that demanded consummate skill to appear natural and convincing. Craft, rather than sincerity, usually determined whether a particular sequence carried the desired meaning. To film an entire movie demanded a thoroughgoing understanding of the story's intentions, detailed planning of the individual shots, and a strong, central authority to guide production. In his famous interviews with François Truffaut in the 1960s, Hitchcock drew an analogy between the cinema and a literary form that also demanded special vigour and tautness. 'A film cannot be compared to a play or a novel,' he said. 'It is closer to a short story, which, as a rule, sustains one idea that culminates when the action has reached the highest point of the dramatic curve.'[50] To maintain control over his central idea, Hitchcock outlined his films meticulously before production, using sketch-books to draw each scene. 'I plan out a script very carefully, hoping to follow it exactly, all the way through, when shooting starts,' he wrote in his essay 'Direction' published in 1937. 'In fact, this working on the script is the real making of the film, for me. When I've done it, the film is finished already in my mind.'[51] Powerful images, sequences, and films could not be achieved haphazardly; to master the intrinsic ambiguities of cinema required clarity of vision.

Yet Hitchcock believed that the skilful manipulation of images could not in itself produce great cinema. The effectiveness of his techniques intimately depended upon the participation of the audience; the public needed to identify with the characters for a film to succeed. Like other successful producers of commercial culture, Hitchcock recognized the necessary complicity of the public in his own art. Indeed, the experience of suspense hinged upon the bond between an audience and screen characters. Hitchcock told Truffaut that he disliked mysteries because they generated more curiosity than emotion, 'an essential ingredient of suspense'. An intense emotion such as fear, he continued, could best be generated when the audience identified with an unsuspecting character it knew to be in imminent danger.

A curious person goes into somebody else's room and begins to search through the drawers. Now, you show the person who lives in that room coming up the

---

[48] Alfred Hitchcock, 'A Director's Problems', *Living Age* 354, 4459 (1938): 172. The visual sequence is displayed in Truffaut, op. cit., 78–9.

[49] Taylor, op. cit., 132.   [50] Quoted in Truffaut, op. cit., 50.

[51] Hitchcock in *Footnotes*, ed. Davy, 5.

stairs. Then you go back to the person who is searching, and the public feels like warning him, 'Be careful, watch out. Someone's coming up the stairs.' Therefore, even if the snooper is not a likeable character, the audience will still feel anxiety for him. Of course, when the character is attractive . . . the public's emotion is greatly intensified.

Hitchcock distinguished between 'suspense', in which the audience knew the danger and became sympathetic with the character, and 'surprise', which usually provided only a brief jolt of recognition. He argued that because in 'suspense' the director informed the audience of danger and thereby involved it directly in the action, emotion could be generated, sustained, and magnified far more effectively than in a mystery, where often the 'surprise' ending provided the major thrill.[52] Although necessarily simplified, this distinction nicely revealed Hitchcock's symbiotic relationship with his audience in the production of a film.

During the inter-war era, Hitchcock discovered that this process of identification became closer and more intense if the central characters possessed certain traits. First, 'my hero is the average man to whom bizarre things happen, rather than vice versa.'[53] Although, like other commercial directors, Hitchcock selected physically attractive actors and actresses to portray his protagonists, they usually played individuals—policemen, housewives, a tourist—not hopelessly removed from the experiences of his audience. Hitchcock personally identified with bourgeois values, but the middle-class accents in his films also forestalled pre-emptive closure of a lucrative market. His average men and women usually spoke with accents an American could understand. Second, Hitchcock discovered that his central characters evoked the greatest empathy when they were essentially blameless for the crimes that endangered and isolated them from polite society. 'The theme of the innocent man being accused', he said of *The Lodger* (1927), one of his earliest successes, '. . . provides the audience with a greater sense of danger. It's easier for them to identify with him than with a guilty man on the run. I always take the audience into account.'[54] Here for once Hitchcock may have understated the moral complexity of his films since in *Blackmail* and *Sabotage*, for example, the killings by his female protagonists, while portrayed as justified, nevertheless involved considerable moral ambiguities. Indeed, he excelled at exploring the boundaries between good and evil, moral and immoral.[55]

[52] Quoted in Truffaut, op. cit., 51–2.
[53] Quoted in Gene D. Phillips, *Alfred Hitchcock* (Boston: Twayne, 1984), 20.
[54] Quoted in Truffaut, op. cit., 34.
[55] For an interpretation of Hitchcock that emphasizes the moral elements, see Eric Rohmer and Claude Chabrol, *Hitchcock: The First Forty-Four Films*, trans. Stanley Hochman (New York: Frederick Ungar, 1979). See also John M. Smith, 'Conservative Individualism: A Selection of English Hitchcock', *Screen* 13, 3 (1972): 51–70.

Hitchcock's manipulation of image and identification took many forms in the inter-war period and clearly not all his films proved successful, either with critics or the public. His contracts with various studios obliged him to direct films, such as *Waltzes from Vienna* (1933), outside his range and interests. Only over time in Britain did he gain the reputation and freedom to concentrate on the thriller, the genre he recast and that propelled him to Hollywood. Three of his British films may serve as more detailed illustration of his style during an important period in the evolution of the commercial film. His approach to cinema can then be compared and contrasted with the documentary movement, whose films remained marginal not simply because of their subject-matter or for reasons their directors volunteered.

The silent feature *The Lodger* (1927), analysed in exhaustive detail by William Rothman in his book *The Murderous Gaze*, contains a number of scenes which exemplify Hitchcock's complex manipulation of his camera and his audience. When a stranger portrayed by Ivor Novello first appears in the film asking for a room, Hitchcock deliberately suggests that this character, a major film star in Britain,[56] may be the 'Avenger', a vicious murderer not unlike Jack the Ripper. The camera envelops Novello in shadows, and his ominous behaviour, including mysterious journeys into the night, remains fully consistent with that of the unknown killer. Through imaginative use of special camera angles, contrasts between light and dark, and a careful withholding of material, Hitchcock creates a tension between the audience's prior willingness to identify with Novello and the possibility that he might be the villain of the piece. In a scene involving a chess game between Novello and Daisy, the daughter of the landlord and a beautiful blonde of the type which the Avenger clearly favours, Novello says in a title, 'Be careful, I'll get you', and at one point menacingly reaches for a poker. It turns out that he only wishes to stoke the fire, but Hitchcock has successfully created a mood of highly charged eroticism and violence that sustains the ambiguities of the audience's identification with the central characters. Only much later does the director reveal that Novello seeks to avenge the murder of his blonde sister; he indeed remains an 'Avenger' but not the dreaded killer that Hitchcock skilfully suggested. Throughout the film, the director employs symbols reminiscent of the Kuleshov experiment. A flashing sign 'Tonight Golden Curls' at the beginning of the story silently indicates the murderer's target; at the end, after Novello has been vindicated, the same sign provides an erotic clue of his evening with Daisy. As Rothman comments, 'the film

---

[56] William Rothman, *Hitchcock — The Murderous Gaze* (Cambridge: Harvard University Press, 1982), 6–55. I have learned much from this study. On Novello, see Peter Noble, *Ivor Novello* (London: Falcon Press, 1951).

begins by linking the camera with the mystery of the act of murder and ends by linking it with the mystery of the sexual act.'[57] The flashing sign remains the same; the changed visual context infuses it with a different emotional resonance.

Sabotage illustrated some of the problems of audience identification. In a sequence that Hitchcock later admitted to be a 'grave error', an unsuspecting young boy carries a time bomb through the streets of London. Though instructed to deliver the package promptly, the boy becomes delayed by a crowd and other diversions that threaten his safety. By cross-cutting between the boy's seemingly harmless activities and the rapidly expiring time, Hitchcock heightens the suspense for his audience. In an authentically shocking departure from convention, however, Hitchcock allows the bomb to detonate, killing the child and a bus-load of innocent passengers. 'The boy was involved in a situation that got him too much sympathy from the audience,' Hitchcock later recalled, 'so that when the bomb exploded and he was killed, the public was resentful.'[58] Other problems of identification also affected the film. Hitchcock acknowledged that the male lead John Loder lacked the film presence to be forgiven his adulterous flirtations with Sylvia Sidney, especially since her husband in the story, a foreign saboteur played by Oscar Homulka, proved too amiable a villain. Both contemporary critics, including the usually acerbic Graham Greene, and more recent observers have hailed the film as one of the director's best, in part because of its deviations from accepted formulas.[59] Although Hitchcock's regrets may have been perfunctory, it is also possible that he inadvertently exceeded the audience's tolerance for shock and moral ambiguity. In later films, such as *Psycho*, he killed off central characters with greater skill.

In *The Thirty-Nine Steps* (1935), one of Hitchcock's most popular and critically acclaimed films of the Thirties, the director found an actor and a role which the audience found no difficulty in accepting. Robert Donat offered a screen presence that lesser stars such as Novello and Loder could not match. 'He was as much as anybody responsible for the world-wide success of this picture,' Hitchcock later declared. Writing for the *Observer* in 1935, C. A. Lejeune enthusiastically proclaimed that 'for the first time on our screens we have the British equivalent of a Clark Gable or a Ronald Colman playing in a purely national

---

[57] Rothman, op. cit., 55.

[58] Quoted in Truffaut, op. cit., 76. See also Donald Spoto, *The Art of Alfred Hitchcock: Fifty Years of his Motion Pictures* (New York: Hopkinson and Blake, 1976), 62–3.

[59] Yacowar, *Hitchcock's British Films*, 206; Raymond Durgnat, *The Strange Case of Alfred Hitchcock, or The Plain Man's Hitchcock* (1974, reprinted Cambridge: MIT Press, 1978), 137.

idiom.'[60] Donat portrayed Richard Hannay, an innocent man in flight, entrapped in circumstances that continually force him to outwit the law and the foreign spies who seek his elimination. Intensively analysed by a number of film scholars, the film contains a number of striking visual sequences which exploit the audience's sympathy for Donat/Hannay and his predicament. In one scene, set in a train where Hannay fears other passengers will identify him from his picture in the newspaper, the camera adopts his line of vision and shows the individual faces of men staring at him, one with a slight, ambiguous smile, perhaps of recognition. Once again, as in the Kuleshov experiment, the audience has been invited to project its own emotions on to the essentially neutral image of a human countenance. As before, the director generates suspense through his understanding of the essential link between the camera and the audience. In another scene, Hitchcock creates a characteristically macabre visual pun when the villain, whom Hannay mistakenly considered a sympathetic character, unmasks himself by revealing that he lacks part of a finger. The villain shows his hand by quite literally showing his hand; the tip off becomes a tip-off.[61] Hitchcock also enriched the story that he loosely adapted from a John Buchan novel by creating a romantic interest, played by Madeleine Carroll, for Donat/Hannay. Clearly influenced by Capra's *It Happened One Night* (1934), Hitchcock varied the pace of his story by introducing some romantic comedy into the plot. The two romantic leads must endure a series of misadventures, including a night handcuffed together in a country inn, before their love becomes confirmed. Images of bondage, here understated and played comically, became a motif connecting many of Hitchcock's films.

Hitchcock's manipulation of screen images, combined with his not infallible understanding of the public's need to identify with sympathetic characters, provided his films with a distinct moral and visual texture that audiences quickly appreciated. During the inter-war era, Hitchcock became one of the few directors who, like certain stars, attracted the public to a film simply because of his association with it. His brief personal appearance in each of his films became both a gag and a trademark that attested to the director's astute knowledge of public relations. Hitchcock personalized the usually anonymous role of directing. More important, as master of individual shots and haunting sequences, he attained a status denied his colleagues of more routine abilities. As star and *auteur* Hitchcock transcended the collaborative nature of his medium for both critics and the general public.

---

[60] Hitchcock and Lejeune quoted in Richards, *Age of the Dream Palace*, 228–9; on Donat, see ibid., 225–34. For Donat, see also J. C. Trewin, *Robert Donat* (London: Heinemann, 1968). [61] Phillips, *Hitchcock*, 72.

Like Hitchcock, the documentary movement experimented with the manipulation of images. Borrowing from Russian and other Continental practitioners of the 1920s, Grierson argued that montage best communicated the socially engaged values of the factual film. 'We could create rhythms and tempos, crescendos and diminuendos of energy to help our exposition,' Grierson wrote in 1934. '. . . We could work in images to add atmosphere to our action, or poetry to our description. We could, by the juxtaposition of shots, explode ideas in the heads of our audience.'[62] As in *Drifters*, the British documentaries of the early Thirties relied heavily upon editing to infuse their essentially silent films with dignity and drama. For example, one of the most highly regarded of these works, Basil Wright's *Song of Ceylon*, sought to create a visual tone poem by weaving together striking images of an ancient civilization. In one section of this public-relations film, financed to promote the island's tea, Wright juxtaposed shots of the natives' traditional customs with the sounds of modern commerce. This implied conflict between old and new disappeared, however, in the film's concluding section where Wright once again projected exotic images of stability and social continuity. 'Perfection is not a word one cares to use,' Graham Greene wrote enthusiastically of the film in the *Spectator*; 'but from the opening sequence of the Ceylon forest, the great revolving fans of palms which fill the screen, this film moves with an air of absolute certainty in its object and assurance in its method.'[63]

Yet images might not always mean what film-makers intended. Although documentary directors understood montage and other editing techniques, they occasionally imposed an interpretation upon their films which other, less immediately involved individuals might find arbitrary or incomplete. Not only, as we have seen, did Grierson and his disciples understate the commercial messages both implicit and explicit in their work—an omission many recent scholars have noted—but some directors also extracted social meaning from their work which the films themselves did not always unambiguously support. For example, Paul Rotha often claimed, and his colleagues agreed, that his *Shipyard* (1934–5), made for Vickers Armstrong and the Orient Line, vivified the skill and explored the social impact of British workers in Barrow-in-Furness constructing the ship *Orion*. The film provoked Grierson's comment that Rotha was 'the keeper of our conscience as much as the keeper of our records',[64] and Basil Wright particularly singled out the final scene for praise. This

[62] John Grierson, 'Introduction to a New Art' (1934), in *Sight and Sound: Fiftieth Anniversary*, ed. Wilson, 21–2.
[63] Quoted in Rotha, *Documentary Diary*, 125.
[64] John Grierson, 'Two Paths to Poetry', *Cinema Quarterly* 3, 3 (1935): 194.

sequence cross-cut between some upper-class passengers and a group of workers evidently gazing at the completed ship before gradually departing from the camera's view. 'The pathetic indecision of the workers in the final fade-out is masterly,' Wright observed, and Rotha, later commenting on what he considered his most effective scene from this period, wrote that it showed 'the despair of those men watching her sliding away, hands in their pockets, and then turning off to the Employment Exchange'.[65]

But the scene does not in fact show workers going to the Employment Exchange nor does it reveal their faces at a close enough angle to indicate what emotion they might have been experiencing. Indeed, so much of the film depicts the building of the ship in heroic terms, with dramatic montages of various workers creating abstract geometric shapes, that the final scene might also be one of pride, not despair. 'My theme was . . . not just the building of *Orion*, Rotha observed, 'but its effect on the social life of the town.' Very little of the film, however, depicts this aspect of the worker's existence and even then, it was not without room for an interpretation at variance with Rotha's stated purpose. At one point, a narrator declares of the ship that 'all the time as she grows higher and bigger, the life of the town goes on. Every mouth being fed, every body being clothed, by the work of the men in the yard.'[66] Rotha inserted this passage to establish a contrast between this temporary prosperity and the renewed slump that would engulf the town once the ship has been completed. The passage, however, might also indicate a beneficial and harmonious relationship between business and labour. The shipping company becomes the benefactor, not the betrayer, of the town and its workers.

Shipyard, like the *The Song of Ceylon*, suffered from another problem that might illuminate both their aesthetic limitations, and their marginality among the general public. As David Schrine pointed out:

Documentary films are not concerned with what we clumsily call a 'plot' . . . but with a theme or *motif*. . . . Breaking new ground, it has no individualized human story to offer, no star to present, no vulgar, well-publicized emotional bait to extend. Human beings appearing in documentary pictures are not individuals with insignificant personal emotions, troubles and passions. They are types, types of social groups, symbols of the many.

Grierson profoundly disliked the 'stories' of commercial cinema; 'an unnatural and even childish simplicity determines both theme and treatment,'

---

[65] Basil Wright, review of *Shipyard* by Paul Rotha, *Cinema Quarterly* 3, 3 (1935): 178; Rotha, *Documentary Diary*, 101; Eva Orbanz, *Journey to a Legend and Back: The British Realistic Film* (Berlin: Edition Volker Spiess, 1977), 29; interview with Paul Rotha, 17 Nov. 1978.

[66] Rotha, *Documentary Diary*, 100; title from *Shipyard*, National Film Archive, London.

he complained in an article for the *Spectator* in 1935.[67] *Drifters, Song of Ceylon, Shipyard*, and most other documentaries from the early Thirties offered the viewer no individual protagonists or characters with whom to identify. Instead, these films depicted 'workers' or 'natives' engaged in activities which presumably ennobled them. 'There is a detachment in much of its work,' C. A. Lejeune wrote later of the movement, 'an almost scandalized mistrust of showmanship, an effort, it would seem, to avoid, not only melodramatic, but any form of human appeal or persuasion.'[68] The documentary movement self-consciously distanced itself from the cultural tastes of the very people it claimed to portray in its films and whose political causes it championed. This distancing, as we have seen, was hardly unusual among the cultivated élites, including progressives and other uplifters. But it created a tension between the ideals of the movement and its far more modest realities.

This tension did not pass unnoticed among some documentary directors. In the mid-1930s Paul Rotha began to acknowledge the role of character and story in successful film-making. Earlier in the decade he too believed that 'theme' transcended 'a personal interest in characters or incidents', and his own films such as *Contact* and *Shipyard* manifested this concern.[69] However, in his pioneering book on the movement *Documentary Film*, published in 1936, he asked that the audience be given more attention in the direction of factual film. 'If documentary is going to be significant,' he wrote, 'we must make films which will move the people and not just amuse our fellow-directors. If cinema is a branch of art at all, then it is the most vulgar branch because it is the most popular. And if the masses are interested in seeing individuals and following their emotions on the screen, then documentary must embrace individuals.' Rotha argued that photography should not become a virtue in itself but 'a contributory element to the technique required for an adequate expression of the subject'. Beautiful photography often romanticized the working class and the poor, falsifying their experience and deflecting the social thrust of the movement. 'In the final reckoning,' he observed, 'technique must always come second to content.'[70]

---

[67] David Schrine, 'The Psychology of Film Audiences', *Sight and Sound* 2, 8 (1933–4): 122–3; John Grierson, 'One Hundred Per Cent Cinema', *Spectator*, 23 Aug. 1935, 285.

[68] C. A. Lejeune, *Chestnuts in Her Lap: 1936–1947* (London: Phoenix House, 1947), 83.

[69] Paul Rotha, 'The Function of the Director. 1. The Documentary Director', *Cinema Quarterly* 2, 1 (1933): 79. See also id., 'Approach to a New Cinema', *Cinema Quarterly* 1, 1 (1932): 21; and id., 'The Film: Our Attitude Toward It', *Journal of the Royal Society of British Artists and Art Club* 1, 2 (1932): 15–17. On *Contact*, see '*Contact*: An Interview with Paul Rotha', *Sight and Sound* 2, 5 (1933): 9–10; Paul Rotha, 'Making *Contact*', *Cinema Quarterly* 9, 3 (1933): 156–9; and id., *Documentary Diary*, 66–95.

[70] Paul Rotha, *Documentary Film* (London: Faber and Faber, 1936), 181, 189, 193. See also id., 'Films of Fact and Fiction', *Theatre Arts Monthly* 22, 3 (1938): 186–97;

Rotha's emphasis upon the role of the audience and his admonitions concerning photographic technique occurred at a time when some documentary directors had already begun turning away from a preoccupation with montage and a fastidious eschewal of character. *Housing Problems*, made for the British Commercial Gas Association and released in 1935, contained a number of striking interviews with slum dwellers that, without photographic embellishment, dramatized the plight of the urban poor. Although (not surprisingly) the film's optimistic message about social progress also indirectly served the commercial interests of its sponsors, the film allowed its sympathetic subjects to speak for themselves and to an audience who might identify with their problems. Harry Watt's *The Saving of Bill Blewitt*, released in 1937, adopted a story line and individual characterization with far less circumspection. Financed to promote the Post Office Savings Bank, the short film told the story of how two Cornish fishermen, one portraying himself, saved enough money to replace a lost fishing vessel. 'I found that filming a story was quite different from our usual general sort of atmospheric shooting,' Watt later admitted, somewhat disarmingly. 'Your audience is interested in your principal artists only and, through them, follows the story.'[71] A year later, Watt released *North Sea*, a film which dramatized the advantages of ship-to-shore radio. 'Whereas two years ago it would have been a film primarily about a storm,' Rotha wrote in his review for *The Times*, 'today it is a film primarily about human beings and their reactions in a moment of emergency.'[72]

This growing awareness of story, character, the audience, and other facets of cinema long standard among commercial directors was echoed in other aspects of the documentary movement. In the 1920s, the sober *Close-Up* proved the journal that most reflected avant-garde tastes among cinema enthusiasts. When that journal closed in the early Thirties, an equally serious *Cinema Quarterly* assumed that role, particularly for documentary directors, whose activities and films received extensive coverage in its pages. Based in London, *Cinema Quarterly* lasted only four years however, from 1932 to 1936, when *World Film News and Television Progress* incorporated it. Employing many of the same writers,

---

and id., 'Documentary Has Realism That British Drama Lacks, Says Rotha', *Motion Picture Herald*, 9 Oct. 1937. For Rotha's view of film and the politics of the Left, see id., 'Films and the Labour Party', Address to the Special Labour Conference on Film Propaganda, 30 Oct. 1936 (typescript in British Film Institute, London).

[71] Watt, *Don't Look*, 104. See also Sussex, *Rise and Fall of British Documentary*, 85–8. For background to the public-relations campaigns of the Post Office, see Stephen Tallents, *Post Office Publicity* (London: Post Office Green Paper No. 8, 1935).

[72] *The Times*, 28 June 1938; reprinted in Rotha, *Rotha on the Film*, 214–16. The film is described in Low, *Documentary and Educational Films*, 144–6. For Rotha's attempt to promote the film, see Paul Rotha to 'Mr. Manager', 29 Aug. 1939, The John Grierson Archive, University of Sterling, Sterling, Scotland.

mostly from the documentary movement, *World Film News* adopted a far more popular format, including large photographs, shorter and less intellectual articles, and, perhaps most astonishing, stories about Hollywood stars. 'Our policy is to give information,' an editorial proclaimed in the second issue, 'and concentrate on all creative efforts in the fields of cinema and broadcasting—both high-brow and low-brow.'[73] Though it lasted only two years, *World Film News* exemplified the movement's increasing willingness to embrace commercial methods, including those of the popular press, in pursuit of their social and aesthetic goals. The boundaries separating the commercial and documentary film became less distinct as the decade progressed.

Yet these boundaries still existed. Not all documentary directors accepted Rotha's advice or followed Watt's example. One of the most famous documentaries of the decade, *Night Mail*, made a train its hero, and in the late 1930s and throughout the Second World War, documentaries pursued their own logic of presentation, dictated in part by the genre's inescapable limitations. Though some within the movement continued to denigrate the commercial film, others began to acknowledge its greater sophistication. In his memoirs, Harry Watt remembered his experience working briefly within the commercial film industry during the middle 1930s. 'We looked upon it rather as slumming for a while to earn a bit of extra scratch,' he recalled. It was while slumming that Watt met Alfred Hitchcock, who 'one day gave me a lesson, with drawings, on the use of camera angles, which I never forgot. . . . At its simplest,' Watt continued, 'if you want a man to appear small and insignificant, you shoot down on him, if you want him to look strong and menacing, you shoot up.'[74] One can only speculate upon Hitchcock's detached amusement at teaching such an elementary lesson to a leading representative of a movement that frequently proclaimed its artistic superiority.

Indeed, Hitchcock occasionally included documentary footage within his films. A brief consideration of only one of these sequences might underscore an important difference between his films and those of Grierson's movement.[75] The opening shots of *Blackmail* detailed the procedure of a police arrest; police with a wireless van track a suspect, then apprehend, fingerprint, and photograph him, and place him in a cell. This entire episode well might have been part of a documentary film

---

[73] *World Film News and Television Progress* 1, 2 (1936): 17.

[74] Watt, op. cit., 122.

[75] In a footnote in his *Murderous Gaze*, William Rothman argues that 'a major element' of Hitchcock's films in the 1930s was 'their critique of the British documentary movement' (p. 349). Though I believe this statement an exaggeration, Rothman's suggestion has been a valuable one to me.

on Scotland Yard, a concise visual re-creation of modern police operations. For Hitchcock, however, the sequence provided the dramatic context for understanding the character of a detective, played by John Loder, whose relationship with Alice White, played by Anny Ondra, lay at the heart of the film. Originally, Hitchcock wanted to end the film with the same sequence; but this time the detective would be booking Alice, a character with whom the audience clearly identified. At the urging of producers, he later abandoned this idea: but one contrast between Hitchcock and the documentary movement can at least be suggested. Hitchcock's understanding of story and character instilled his documentary sequences with an inner human context, replete with pathos and irony, that even the often well-constructed abstract images of the documentary movement could not capture. The documentary movement photographed the façade that Hitchcock penetrated. His understanding of the ambiguities and complexities of cinematic images and audience identification provided his films with a moral and visual depth that the documentary movement could not approach.

Hitchcock and other gifted directors helped commercial film mature and become more palatable even to its sternest critics. In the late 1930s, as at least one other scholar has noted, a number of British writers and intellectuals declared their allegiance to an industry that, even a decade earlier, brought a far more mixed response.[76] 'See how that daring young man leaps from his aeroplane in mid air,' Rose Macaulay wrote in an essay on cinema, 'sailing in his parachute so as to alight on the roof of the house in Chinatown where the gangsters have the girl tied up. Can you beat it? Certainly not on the stage; probably not in life.'[77] Writing in *World Film News* in 1938, Norman Wilson claimed that film societies in Britain had lost membership because 'of the steadily improving quality of ordinary commercial films and the lack of any noticeable advance in the continental films which have been shown'.[78] Robert Herring, an important contributor to *Close-Up* and a stringent critic of Hollywood in the late 1920s, argued a decade later that art and entertainment could not be neatly separated. It was the function of art 'to hold, to engage', he wrote, and by this criterion, many commercial films could be classified as art.[79]

Yet it was not simply because commercial films became more artistic in the 1930s that they attracted the cultivated élites to cinemas across

[76] See Peter Stead, 'Hollywood's Message for the World: The British Response in the Nineteen-Thirties', *Historical Journal of Film, Radio and Television* 1, 1 (1981): 29–31.
[77] Rose Macaulay, *Personal Pleasures* (New York: Macmillan, 1936), 136.
[78] Norman Wilson, 'Film Societies, What Now?' *World Film News* 2, 10 (1938): 47.
[79] Robert Herring, 'Film as Entertainment', in *Cinema Survey* (London: Blue Moon Press, n.d.), 21–3.

the country. Intellectuals often went to the pictures for the same reasons as everyone else. In 'Why I Go to the Cinema' published in 1937 Elizabeth Bowen listed the varied, often contradictory reasons that attracted her to film and she went on to connect her motivation with that of the vast audience she joined. 'Cinemas draw all sorts,' she wrote. 'In factory towns they are packed with factory workers, in university cities with dons, at the seaside with trippers, . . . in the West End with more or less moneyed people with time to kill, in country towns and villages with small tradespeople and with workers scrubbed and hard from the fields. Taste, with these different audiences, differs widely, but the degree of pleasure sought is the same.'[80] The commercial cinema became an important part of the common culture in the 1930s, a culture both entertaining and, among its best practitioners, engagingly complex.

B. THE PRESS AND THE ASSIMILATION OF MODERN DESIGN

During the 1930s virtually every major national newspaper in Britain significantly reformed its layout and typography. This transformation, considered by one prominent historian of the field to be 'the Great Divide in the history of newspaper typography',[81] reflected not only market pressures within the industry but also competition from other media. In a culture increasingly saturated with images both moving and static, the press re-created itself to attract a more visually literate audience. Although, as we have seen in Part One, popular daily newspapers had included display advertising, news photography, and other visually prominent material in their pages since the turn of the century, editors possessed few coherent theories concerning the layout of their papers. The press communicated with its readers in a visual language that, unlike the cinema, lacked a formal grammar. During the 1930s newspapers more self-consciously formulated such a grammar, based in part upon the progressive agenda of the decade before. Fleet Street appropriated for its own purposes the lessons of both traditionalists, such as Stanley Morison, and Modernists inspired by the Bauhaus and other Continental movements.

This process of assimilation, never complete and often criticized by the individuals who influenced it, occurred at the same time that many artists, intellectuals, and other cultural brokers more willingly embraced commercial art and industrial design. Motivated by both economic need

---

[80] Elizabeth Bowen, 'Why I Go to the Cinema' in *Footnotes to Film*, ed. Davy, 207.
[81] Hutt, *Changing Newspaper*, 107.

and social idealism, artists jettisoned some of their prejudices against art in commerce and offered their services to a select group of industrial patrons eager to attract an affluent clientele impressed by tasteful appearances. Established institutions and galleries mounted exhibitions of posters extravagantly praised by their sponsors and favourably evaluated by critics who previously equated art with religion. The Royal Society created a special honour for gifted designers, and commercial art became a more legitimate means to communicate with a mass audience. As both a profession and a practice, design became fashionable among the cultivated élites. The streamlining of newspapers thus echoed developments in a number of related areas. A culture of 'Modernism', distinct from its avant-garde predecessors yet recognizably its heir, provided a common frame of reference in the 1930s, a trademark of the decade.

Newspapers experienced intense pressure to increase circulation in the inter-war era. For the popular press in particular, advertising revenue depended upon a readership measured with increasing statistical accuracy by the Audit Bureau of Circulations, established in 1931.[82] With high fixed costs in relation to variable expenses, the press needed to sharpen its economies of scale to lower costs, bolster circulation, and attract the advertising revenue that reduced the price of an average paper for the consumer by as much as 40 per cent. Viewed from one angle, newspapers delivered readers to advertisers who, in 1935 for example, devoted over 54 per cent of their total expenditure to the press, an amount exceeding £48,000,000.[83] Traditionally newspapers acquired these readers by adopting the strategies that Northcliffe helped pioneer early in the century. Early in 1930, however, a new and far more serious circulation war erupted from an unexpected corner of Fleet Street. The *Daily Herald* was purchased by the Trades Union Congress and the Labour Party in 1922, and for the remainder of the decade continued to articulate the politics of the working man. Comparatively few people, however, actually read the paper; it lacked the features and journalistic approach which captured large circulations. In the late 1920s Ernest Bevin and others decided that the *Herald* needed to be changed. After some complicated manoeuvres, they contracted Odhams Press to publish a daily paper that would compete successfully in the crowded national market.[84] The chairman of Odhams, J. B. Elias, was a proven master of commercial journalism. He revived

[82] Turner, *Shocking History of Advertising*, 194.

[83] Nicholas Kaldor and Rodney Silverman, *A Statistical Analysis of Advertising Expenditure and of the Revenue of the Press* (Cambridge: Cambridge University Press, 1948), 6–7, 41.

[84] Francis Williams, *Ernest Bevin: Portrait of a Great Englishman* (London: Hutchinson, 1952), 160–3; Alan Bullock, *The Life and Times of Ernest Bevin*, vol. 1 (London: Heinemann, 1960), 419–25.

the controversial and immensely popular *John Bull*, and in the late 1920s boosted the failing *People* to a circulation of two million. Elias was no crusader; one prominent editor bitterly described him as 'a salesman of journalism, not a journalist'.[85] When Bevin offered Elias a daily paper with a mandate to increase circulation, he seized the opportunity because the modern printing plant he constructed to publish the *People* on Sunday lay idle the remainder of the week. The TUC retained editorial control over the politics of the *Herald*, while Elias acquired 51 per cent of the shares. Bevin wrote: 'We are going to challenge the *Mail* and the *Express* and fight them in every town and village. Just as we have fought the Tories all over the country at every election so now we are going to fight their newspapers.'[86] Thus, perhaps surprisingly, the greatest circulation battle of the inter-war period began with the blessing and enthusiastic support of a key figure within the labour movement.

The expensive and ultimately self-defeating circulation wars of the early 1930s revolved around extensive door-to-door canvassing, elaborate insurance schemes, and an astonishing variety of free gifts. Late in 1931 the *Daily Express* made a concerted public effort to halt the struggle claiming that no paper gained from the campaigns, but within a few months four separate dailies, including the *Express*, doubled their railway benefits. The *News Chronicle* offered fire insurance, and both the *Mail* and the *Herald* provided cash for the birth of twins 'provided that both twins survive for not less than 48 hours'.[87] A short time later the Newspaper Proprietors' Association signed an agreement that limited such inducements. 'It is now frankly recognized', one observer wrote, 'that canvassing, either with free gifts or insurance, is not a permanent circulation builder.'[88] Yet for a brief period in 1933 gift schemes returned, as an estimated fifty thousand canvassers offered encyclopaedias and sets of Dickens to prospective customers. In one ten-week period alone such gifts cost the *Express* over £55,000. Only in January 1934 could the *World's Press News* announce with confidence that peace was at hand.[89]

[85] Francis Williams, *Nothing So Strange* (New York: American Heritage Press, 1970), 131.

[86] Quoted in R. J. Minney, *Viscount Southwood* (London: Odhams Press, 1954), 233.

[87] 'The Truth About the *Mail–Express* Fight', *World's Press News*, 1 Oct. 1931, 1, 19–20; 'Five Dailies Offer £20,000 Death Benefit', ibid., 7 Jan. 1932, 5.

[88] 'Why Gift and Insurance Canvassing Stopped', ibid., 18 Feb. 1932, 25. For an earlier statement of this same conclusion, see 'Publicity', *Gaumont British News* (Feb. 1930): 10–13.

[89] 'Fifty Thousand Canvassers Begging for Readers', *World's Press News*, 24 Aug. 1933, 1, 16; 'Encyclopedias As Circulation Builders', ibid., 29 June 1933, 1; E. J. Robertson to Lord Beaverbrook, 9 Sept. 1933, Beaverbrook Papers, H. Series, House of Lords Record Office, London; '*Daily Express* Stops Gifts', *World's Press News*, 18 Jan. 1934, 1.

Free gifts might persuade readers to subscribe for a few months; the contents and presentation of the newspaper ultimately determined whether circulation increased permanently. The complex and easily misunderstood process of identification between producer and consumer also helped decide which newspapers prospered and which succumbed to their rivals. In the 1930s editors confronted a public increasingly accustomed to sophisticated forms of visual communication. This visual literacy remains, of course, almost impossible to measure objectively and difficult to evaluate historically. Visual media undoubtedly affected different people in different ways and those who usually left behind the most extensive written records of their experiences, the highly educated, often proved most impervious or indifferent to images. Still, two aspects of the cultural environment of the 1930s help provide a context for changes in newspaper design. First and most obviously, the cinema continued to expose millions of British citizens to a fast-paced, sometimes exhilarating panorama of sights and sounds. The adolescent film enthusiasts of earlier decades became the newspaper readers of the 1930s and, as Hitchcock's popularity demonstrated, film audiences absorbed editing techniques once considered avant-garde and experimental. 'The *Sketch* and the *Mirror* are daily organs whose *raison d'être* are their illustrations,' a German writer observed in his book *The Press in England*, published in 1934, 'and the success which these two papers have had shows to what extent the modern mind has become a cinema mind.'[90] Although it is important not to overestimate the epistemological impact of one medium upon the stylistic conventions of another, the popular press during the 1930s sought to attract a mass audience which, upon average, went to films twice a week and devoted at least four hours of its limited free time to viewing images in darkened surroundings.

Display advertising was a second, much more immediate component of the visual environment which helped shape the physical appearance of the press during the 1930s. As before, advertisers often, though certainly not always, proved adept at manipulating images for commercial purposes by anticipating the public's need to comprehend messages visually. In 1932 one expert on advertising wrote that 'the daily paper, morning or evening, wherever it is read . . . is glanced at rather than studied.'[91] It followed that display advertising needed to be carefully planned to capture the ephemeral glance of the popular reader, an insight reinforced by the work of professional psychologists, who continued to produce tracts that advertisers found useful in determining the nature of their

---

[90] Kurt von Stutterheim, *The Press in England* (London: George Allen and Unwin, 1934), 157.
[91] Howard Eley, *Advertising Media* (London: Butterworth, 1932), 83.

various commercial appeals. 'A picture touches our primitive tastes,' A. P. Braddock wrote in *Applied Psychology for Advertisers*. 'It can arouse a direct quasi-percept, which words cannot do without the intervention of concepts. The picture probably arouses the largest number of ideas in the least time.'[92] Images conveyed information quickly and efficiently; the glance of the reader became the target of the knowledgeable advertiser.

In the *Daily Mail* for 10 October 1930, for example, a number of display advertisements manifested the visual astuteness, even daring, of advertisers on Fleet Street. In a line-drawn display entitled 'Three Knots British Hosiery', the legs of a chic lady not only suggested the product, but also directed the reader's eye to the advertiser's corporate name. Interested parties might pause to read the attached copy, while the busy reader grasped in a moment the company, the nature of the product, and the implicit suggestion that both conveyed an aura of fashionable sleekness. A display advertisement for 'Reckitt's Bath Cubes' also featured a line drawing which skilfully directed the eye away from the surrounding news text, visually busy and difficult to absorb quickly, and towards a little pictorial drama that the copy explained. The top half of the display, containing among other images the suggestion of arrested motion in the swinging ends of a bathrobe's rope belt, became the visual hook for a product intrinsically difficult to dramatize visually. In another advertisement, the free-form handwriting within a display for 'Craven "A" Cigarettes', while sometimes difficult to read, nevertheless intruded dramatically on a newspaper page mainly devoted to brief stories in very small print. Here, as in the other displays, white space diverted attention away from the surrounding text, allowing advertisers to highlight their messages without distraction. Each of these advertisements, appearing in a popular national newspaper on a date chosen at random, indicates that already by 1930 advertisers had begun to assimilate principles of design that, only a few years earlier, many considered daring and modernistic.[93] Like the cinema, display advertising contributed to an increasingly sophisticated visual environment that editors needed to confront in order to be competitive.

Early in 1930 both the *Daily Chronicle* and the *Daily Telegraph* changed their layouts. The *Chronicle*, in economic difficulty and soon to be absorbed by the *Daily News*, employed a new typography for its headlines and, like the *Daily Express*, adopted the American custom of placing its main news stories on the front page. The *Telegraph* increased the size of its headlines and improved the reproduction of photographs. 'It is much more attractive and handy in short skirts!' Augustus John exclaimed in

[92] A. P. Braddock, *Applied Psychology for Advertisers* (London: Butterworth, 1933), 79. [93] *Daily Mail*, 1 Oct. 1930.

a congratulatory note.[94] Yet these developments represented only minor changes compared to those of the *Daily Herald*, which drastically revamped its layout in March 1930. J. B. Elias transformed the *Herald* beyond recognition. He reduced the proportions of the paper to that of the *People*, eliminating in a stroke a thousand words of copy per page. He radically increased the number of illustrations, including not simply a picture page—standard in the British press by 1930—but photographs on every page.[95] More important, he provided the paper with a consistency of overall design that made earlier changes in other papers appear *ad hoc* and haphazard. 'The production of the "new" *Daily Herald* by Odhams Press on 17 March 1930 caused an immense sensation in the London newspaper trade,' the typographer Alan Hutt later wrote. 'Fleet Street's backwardness in make-up, text and machining was put to shame by a "popular" paper—which immediately quadrupled circulation to about a million—with a consistently planned typography in the bold variants of one type family only (Cheltenham), with a strong-coloured text in the American Ionic . . . and with rotary presswork of a quality comparable only with that of *The Times*.'[96]

In its campaign to boost circulation, the *Daily Herald* began by making itself more physically attractive to readers. Layout became a means of acquiring a unique visual identity, a corporate trademark, in a market thronged with competition. During the remainder of the decade, other major papers followed the *Herald*'s lead by revamping systematically their layout and embracing a more contemporary mood. Some of these national newspapers borrowed ideas or became directly influenced by the progressive typographers and commercial artists of the decade before. Others became more visually integrated on their own initiative and under their own agendas. Virtually all, however, became more alert to the centrality of design in the presentation of news and other information. Not all of these papers can be discussed in detail, but three in particular, each with different readerships, illustrated the diversity of approaches within the shared commitment to more integrated design.

The Times first began to reconsider its typography after Stanley Morison forcefully criticized it to a senior member of staff in the summer of 1929.[97] Engaged as an adviser shortly thereafter, Morison encapsulated his objections and proposals in a characteristically substantial 'Memorandum'

---

[94] Advertisements for the *Daily Chronicle* in *World's Press News*, 10 March 1930, 20–1; and for the *Daily Telegraph* in ibid., 6 Feb. 1930, 19, and 27 Feb. 1930, 17–18.
[95] Minney, *Viscount Southwood*, 234–7.
[96] Hutt, *Changing Newspaper*, 109. See also his earlier book *Newspaper Design* (London: Oxford University Press, 1960), 35.
[97] For the details of Morison's involvement with *The Times*, see Barker, *Stanley Morison*, 268–302; and Moran, *Stanley Morison*, 123–8.

in 1930. This memorandum proves interesting for a number of interrelated reasons. First, Morison argued that the typography of a newspaper ought to reflect its readership. *The Times*, he claimed, appealed to those 'for whom adequate information, enabling them to form an integral opinion on the affairs of the day, is an essential'. It followed, he reasoned, that its typography should be 'masculine, English, direct, simple, not more novel than it behoveth to be novel . . . and absolutely free from faddishness and frivolity'. Morison began by defining his audience and sought a typography that matched its needs. Second, he devoted most of his memorandum to a detailed historical analysis of *The Times* and its presentation. He discovered in the past a tradition and legitimacy for the quite radical changes he proposed. As before, history became an exercise fundamentally centred on the present. Third, Morison selected a type primarily for its legibility, 'a quality hardly possible to define'. As a result, he acknowledged, 'the new types proposed for *The Times* will tend toward the "modern" though the body will be more or less old-form in appearance.'[98] For Morison, as for others of quite different aesthetic temperaments, a 'modern' type could be read easily and absorbed quickly. Its origin became less important than a certain sleekness of style.

The redesigned *Times* first appeared in October 1932. The 'Times New Roman' type that Morison devised bore a close resemblance to a more familiar type, Plantin, that the Monotype Corporation employed in publishing. Though the new type demanded special care in presswork, it quickly became a standard within the industry for a variety of printing tasks. Remarkably legible and elegantly handsome, Times New Roman fulfilled Morison's ambition to produce a type that evoked a venerable tradition and still appeared modern. *The Times* also adopted new typefaces for its headlines, and in December 1932 ran its first double-column heading, another modest acknowledgement that reading habits had changed.[99] Yet for many readers it was probably the mast-head, more than the text, that symbolized *The Times*'s studied embrace of the contemporary. Morison detested the old front-page title and in a supplemental memorandum demonstrated its relatively recent origin. 'This cult of the mock-antique', he wrote dismissively of his nineteenth-century predecessors, 'produced among other essentially unmedieval results, the present paste-and-watery gothick of *The Times*.'[1] Morison's design, while retaining

---

[98] Stanley Morison, 'Memorandum on a Proposal to Revise the Typography of the *The Times*', in Stanley Morison, *Selected Essays on the History of Letter-Forms in Manuscript and Print*, ed. David McKitterick, vol. 2 (Cambridge: Cambridge University Press, 1980), 295, 296, 310, 313.

[99] Hutt, *Changing Newspaper*, 112–17; Philip B. Maggs, *A History of Graphic Design* (New York: Van Nostrand Reinhold, 1983), 349.

[1] Morison, *Selected Essays*, vol. 2, 318.

an emblem, evoked the classical rigour and simplicity of the original mast-head. Once again, Morison skilfully drew on tradition to trump conservative opponents.

The Times's new visual identity, 'not more novel than it behoveth to be novel', marked another important step in an often unnoticed evolution during the twentieth century. The paper that Morison redesigned in the early Thirties shared more with the *Daily Mail* of 1900 than it did with its own ancestor of the same year. *The Times* in the Thirties ran display advertisements as large and as visually diverting as any that appeared in Northcliffe's popular creation. It devoted more attention to sports than the *Mail* of 1900 and almost as much as the *Mail* of 1937. The new *Times* ran articles on fashion, broadcasting, and the cinema. News photography occupied an entire page. Each day it carried a crossword puzzle, a feature whose popularity may be difficult to overestimate. A survey in 1933 revealed that the items most read in the 'quality press', presumably including *The Times*, were stories about crime and divorce, the same topics that attracted the greatest number of readers in the popular press.[2] In the 1930s *The Times* was still a 'class' as opposed to a 'mass' paper; any number of differences separated it from the popular daily national press. Yet in less than thirty years it had moved considerably in a direction that might have distressed its Victorian editors. *The Times* adopted a new format during a period of intense economic competition in Fleet Street and at a time when most other papers rethought their presentation. The paper that Morison redesigned was less distinct from its journalistic neighbours than it sometimes imagined.

One of these neighbours was the *Daily Express*. Since its inception in 1900, when it placed the main news on the front page, the *Express* frequently adopted American conventions in presentation of the news. Under Beaverbrook the paper attracted a readership that, as with many American papers, cut across the conventional boundaries of wealth and social position. As A. J. P. Taylor later observed, 'It was unique . . . in the universality of its readership. . . . Beaverbrook, its Canadian proprietor, was not confined by the English social system. . . . The *Daily Express* was what England would have been without her class system.'[3] Under the editorship of Beverley Baxter in the late 1920s and early Thirties, the paper remained sensitive to developments in other media, particularly cinema. Indeed, Baxter left the *Express* in 1933 to join Gaumont-British newsreels, where he vowed 'to give the public a hundred

---

[2] James Curran, Angus Douglas, and Garry Whannel, 'The Political Economy of the Human-Interest Story', in *Newspapers and Democracy: International Essays on a Changing Medium*, ed. Anthony Smith (Cambridge: MIT Press, 1980), 295 and Appendix Table 13.4.   [3] Taylor, *English History*, 310.

per-cent illustrated sound newspaper'.[4] Beaverbrook replaced him with a visually oriented editor who, perhaps more than any other individual in Fleet Street, carried forward the revolution in layout begun by the *Daily Herald* in 1930. Arthur Christiansen had made his reputation in the *Express* chain as a typographer, illustrator, and writer of headlines. While editor of the Manchester edition, he introduced an eight-page children's comics supplement, a pull-out racing section, and colour half-tone reproductions. Unlike Baxter, he harboured no ambitions for intellectual achievement, portraying himself instead as 'the Common Man, the typical *Express* reader'. Christiansen believed that common men liked their news simple, immediate, personal, and visually astonishing. 'My approach to newspapers was based on the idea', he wrote in his autobiography, 'that when you looked at the front page you said "Good Heavens," when you looked at the middle page you said "Holy smoke," and by the time you got to the back page—well, I'd have to utter a profanity to show how exciting it was.'[5] Baxter had resigned from the *Express* to create in newsreels 'an illustrated sound newspaper'; Christiansen now converted the paper into a vivid, condensed, eye-catching popular daily—a printed newsreel.

First, he increased the number of banner and streamer headlines on the front page, enlarging the print with a more appealing typeface and employing multi-column headings on the lower half of the page, or below the fold. The result was a main news page which directed the eye horizontally across the page rather than vertically up and down the page as in the traditional columned newspapers.[6] No longer as visually prominent, photographs meshed into the larger pattern of horizontal movement. The *Express* now contained fewer words on the front page, but they attracted more attention. Christiansen helped complete the process of transforming the *Express* into a headline newspaper, and the writing of headlines, always important on Fleet Street, now became crucial. Headlines needed to be short, dramatic, and suggestive, like the slogans of advertisers. Although the *Express* rarely indulged in the vivid slang of some American tabloids, Christiansen prided himself in his ability to construct inviting banners ('NO MORE OF THAT HELL FOR ME!').[7]

He also completed the process begun somewhat tentatively by Baxter of making the features more attractive. Baxter commissioned a number of celebrities to write human-interest stories that he highlighted with

---

[4] Quoted in Cameron, 'Gaumont', *World's Press News*, 2 Nov. 1933, 17. See also Baxter, *Strange Street*, 276–80.

[5] Arthur Christiansen, *Headlines All My Life* (London: Heinemann, 1961), 147.

[6] Hutt, op. cit., 117–20. I owe much to Hutt's professional analysis of newspaper typography for this period.

[7] Christiansen, op. cit., 115.

photographs and larger headlines.[8] Christiansen packaged these features in more graphic form. 'On each page there should be a feature that attracts the eye,' he told his staff. 'This does not necessarily mean the use of ever-increasing type size. It means the correct use of white space, the display of pictures, the headline that intrigues the reader.'[9] Christiansen was one of the first editors in Fleet Street to borrow the techniques developed in the late 1920s by the layout men of advertising. Like the advertisers, he saw the page of a newspaper as a totality, a mosaic that blended the dynamics of typography with the magnetic power of photography and the soothing pauses of white space. The page of a newspaper was not simply a space in which print conveyed information, but an image that engaged the eye.

By adopting the layout principles of advertising, Christiansen eliminated an important advantage they previously enjoyed. No longer were display advertisements the optical centre of attention on a newspaper page. Advertisers could still select where on a page to place their messages, but men such as John Rayner, the features editor under Christiansen and a central figure in the graphic transformation of the *Express*, planned their layouts to include displays in the landscape of the page.[10] 'The journalist has learned from the advertiser,' Robert Harling wrote in 'The New Display' published in 1936. 'Increasingly, the brightest thing on the page, visually, is the feature heading or photograph. . . . Any day can be seen the same advertisement leaping out of the grey type of the *Telegraph*, lost in the variegated columns of the *Express*.' Display advertisements, he concluded, must now become 'bright enough, within their own limits, to stand up to editorial competition'.[11] News had become an advertisement for itself, competing on equal terms with the commercial signals that lay alongside it. The *Express* became a more fully integrated series of optical events of varying intensity, skilfully manipulated by editors and advertisers who operated under the same assumptions. Christiansen blended typography and layout into a unified whole; he had helped reinvent the grammar of newspaper design.

Advertisers played an even more direct role in the reshaping of the *Daily Mirror*. While other popular dailies struggled hard to increase circulation and maintain their advertising revenue, the *Mirror*'s audience plummeted

---

[8] Reginald Pound, 'The Leader Comes Into Its Own', *World's Press News*, 1 May 1930, 3. See also Baxter to Beaverbrook, 5 Jan. 1932, Beaverbrook Papers, H Series, House of Lords Record Office, London.

[9] Christiansen, op. cit., 166.

[10] John Rayner, 'Features for Two Millions', *Typography* 2 (1937): 13–15.

[11] Robert Harling, 'The New Display', *Commercial Art and Industry* 20 (1936): 189–90. See also F. J. Mansfield, *The Complete Journalist: A Study of the Principles and Practice of Newspaper-Making* (London: Sir Isaac Pitman, 1935), 269–311.

in 1933 to less than 750,000 readers. To arrest this decline the *Mirror* consulted J. Walter Thompson, the American advertising agency whose London office served an impressive list of major British clients. J. Walter Thompson believed above all in market research, the systematic gathering of statistical data before reaching business decisions. Introduced in the 1920s, these methods initially encountered some resistance from British firms who believed American methods would not apply to their own market.[12] J. Walter Thompson felt no such hesitation; it insisted on facts and research. Between 1927 and 1929, for example, the agency interviewed over 60,000 consumers and 20,000 retailers before devising its advertising for clients that included Lever Brothers and Horlicks. 'Every headline and sub-head, caption and paragraph of text', the agency boasted, 'was based directly on investigation findings.'[13]

These techniques were now applied to reviving a moribund newspaper. In 1935 J. Walter Thompson conducted an extensive survey to determine what features in a newspaper most attracted the *Mirror's* targeted audience, the working class. Other newspapers, of course, commissioned surveys, usually through the London Press Exchange founded in the late 1920s. What distinguished the *Mirror* from other newspapers, whose surveys revealed to advertisers the demographics of readership,[14] was that the *Mirror* completely refashioned its layout and content to fit the audited preferences of its intended audience. J. Walter Thompson asked a specific public what it wanted, and the *Mirror* provided it for them. Moreover, under the leadership of Cecil King, the nephew of Northcliffe, the *Mirror* hired away from the agency a number of individuals who later became influential members of the editorial staff. 'One of the greatest of British journalistic revolutions', Stanley Morison later observed with regret, 'was thus initiated, carried through, and made successful by men who were not journalists.'[15]

Yet what J. Walter Thompson told the *Mirror*, the *Mirror* should have already known. The British working class preferred a newspaper that was convenient to read and easy to assimilate. The tabloid journalism that Northcliffe pioneered needed to be revised for a contemporary audience. The *Mirror* already employed a man to perform this task.

---

[12] George Frederick, 'Business Research As I See It', *Advertiser's Weekly*, 2 Apr. 1926, 4–5; Harold Herd, *Bigger Results From Advertising* (London: Phillip Allan, 1926), 12–26; Percival White, *Advertising Research* (New York and London: D. Appleton, 1927); F. W. Dodge, 'When Advertising Research Becomes a Fetish', *Advertiser's Weekly*, 3 Aug. 1928, 169, 190.

[13] 'The J. Walter Thompson Company', *World's Press News*, 12 Dec. 1929, 31.

[14] *World's Press News*, 3 Oct. 1935, 11; see also *Daily Sketch Blue Book* (London: Daily Sketch and Sunday Graphic, 1933).

[15] Stanley Morison, 'Picture-printing and Word-printing', *Penrose Annual 50* (1956): 24.

Harry Guy Bartholomew joined the paper in 1904 and became a director in 1913. For thirty years he kept abreast of developments in news photography and layout. 'He was barely literate,' Cecil King wrote of him later, but '. . . he was, of course, an expert in display.'[16] Bartholomew became editor and between 1934 and 1937 redesigned the paper. He dramatically increased the size of headlines, sometimes covering an entire page with a few words in the heavy, black type favoured by American tabloids. The *Mirror* screamed its headlines while the *Express* only shouted. Bartholomew also reorganized the photography department. He selected pictures that not only dramatized a story, but sensationalized it—a photograph of a lynched American black, for example, or a smiling beauty queen who accented her cleavage by leaning toward the camera. In other papers readers looked at the photographs; Bartholomew wanted his audience to stare.[17]

A stunning increase in the number of comic strips added to the visual cornucopia. Ever since the days of Northcliffe, the *Mirror* had run cartoons. In the early 1930s, the paper broke with tradition by introducing 'Jane's Journal', the saga of a 'Bright Young Thing' who survived the trials of life in various states of undress. Thus, when Cecil King hired Basil Nicholson from J. Walter Thompson, the *Mirror* already knew the public's love of comic images. As an advertiser, Nicholson helped devise a strip cartoon for Horlicks that exposed the dangers of 'night starvation', and he also collaborated on the idea for a cartoon that sold to the *News Chronicle*.[18] His philosophy of journalism did not embrace idealism. 'What was the point of publishing pompous articles by avaricious bigwigs when figures proved that nobody would read them?' he once asked a colleague. 'Had it ever occurred to Fleet Street that people didn't want to read anything at all?' Inspired by his reading of the New York *Daily News* and other American tabloids, Nicholson tripled the number of comics and adopted the American practice of grouping them together on a page. By 1936, the *Mirror* devoted a page and a half to 'King Sweepea', 'Ruggles', 'Beelzebub Jones', 'Jane's Journal', 'Just Jake', 'Buck Ryan', 'Belinda Blue Eyes', and 'Pip, Squeak and Wilfred'. 'They were given more space than serious news,' the *Mirror*'s Hugh Cudlipp recalled, 'and the readers still asked for encores.'[19]

[16] Cecil King, *The Future of the Press* (London: MacGibbon and Kee, 1967), 34.

[17] Hugh Cudlipp, *Walking on the Water* (London: The Bodley Head, 1976), 54–5; Cecil King, *Strictly Personal* (London: Weidenfeld and Nicolson, 1969), 105–6.

[18] Perry and Aldridge, *Penguin Book of Comics*, 191–3; Robert Connor, *Cassandra: Reflections in a Mirror* (London: Cassell, 1969), 19–24.

[19] Hugh Cudlipp, *Publish and be Damned! The Astonishing Story of the Daily Mirror* (London: Andrew Dakers, 1953), 81, 73; on the popularity of comics as revealed in reader's surveys, see 'What is the Secret of the Comic Strip?' *World's Press News*, 8 Feb. 1934, 32.

These and other changes in the popular press during the 1930s troubled some observers. Most directed their criticisms at the increasing 'sensationalism' which threatened personal privacy and 'debased' the public mind.[20] Others, however, recognized that something historically more unusual and culturally distressing occurred when the popular press borrowed styles of presentation from advertisers. In a seminal article 'The Dictatorship of the Lay-out Man' published in 1938, the author and typographer Holbrook Jackson analysed 'the substitution of a pictorial for a verbal text, and ultimately . . . the subjugation of that text to the control of the lay-out man'. This substitution, Jackson wrote, began with Northcliffe's *Mirror* early in the century and evolved to a point where graphics and layout now transcended the text. 'The newsreel has conquered the newspaper,' Jackson lamented. 'And this ideographic treatment of news has invaded territories hitherto sacred to the printed word. Even the type pages of popular newspapers are typographically pictorialized. . . . It is no longer the editorial copy which counts, but its presentation.' Jackson claimed that illustrations and other graphics 'disintegrated the text until consecutive reading of more than five hundred words is becoming impossible even for those readers with enough concentration for the task.' He attributed this transformation to the increasing influence of women readers and other feminine concerns on newspapers. 'When men think pictorially they unsex themselves,' he wrote, confessing a bias against both images and women not uncommon among Victorians.[21]

Jackson's strictures concerning the 'dictatorship' of the layout man help reveal the thoroughgoing nature of Fleet Street's assimilation of the principles of design. Although each newspaper created its own unique visual identity, from the self-conscious typographical restraint of *The Times* to the exuberant outrageousness of the *Daily Mirror*, these designs existed within a shared commitment to more functional display. By the end of the 1930s, few newspapers, not even *The Times*, could ignore completely the lessons of advertisers and commercial artists. Like a display advertisement, the page of a newspaper presented to the reader an overall image, a mosaic of words and illustrations, that needed to be carefully planned and visually integrated to be successful in a highly competitive market-place. This process of designing word and image represented, in

[20] 'Editors Would Welcome "Privacy" Agreement', *World's Press News*, 28 Jan. 1937, 1–2; Sanger, 'News', ibid., 21 Jan 1937, 2; J. A. Spender, 'Is "Personal" Journalism Destroying Prestige?', ibid., 3 June 1937, 17; 'Bishop of Liverpool Attacks "Certain Daily Illustrated Papers" ', ibid., 9 Sept. 1937, 5; Jane Soames, *The English Press: Newspapers and News* (London: Lindsay Drummond, 1938), 166–73; Peter Hood, *Ourselves and the Press* (London: John Lane, Bodley Head, 1939), 101–25.
[21] Holbrook Jackson, 'The Dictatorship of the Lay-out Man', *Typography* 7 (1938): 2–4. See also Frank Pick, 'Has Publicity Distorted Commercial Printing?', *Penrose Annual* 38 (1936): 26–9.

part, the legacy of the progressive commercial artists of the 1920s, either directly as with Morison's work on *The Times*, or indirectly in Christiansen and Bartholomew's use of white space, cropped photography, and streamlined display for news and features. In a broad sense, Modernism permeated Fleet Street during the 1930s. Although no major national daily paper affected the experimental styles of the Bauhaus and Russian Constructivism, they did imbibe the general principles which commercial artists in Britain learned from the Continent. 'The essentials governing modern typography were brevity, simplicity, readability, and the elimination of everything not essential to the composition,' Frederic Ehrlich wrote in *The New Typography and Modern Layouts*, published in 1934.[22] By this broad definition, many of the major national newspapers became 'modern' in the 1930s. They presented news and features in more streamlined layouts that sought to attract and hold a contemporary audience. The page of a well-designed newspaper embodied a functionalism not entirely distinct from the sleek lines of an Odeon cinema or the newer Underground stations.

This process of assimilation occurred at a time when commercial art and design acquired greater respectability and legitimacy among the cultivated élites. The Slump not only forced artists to take commissions they earlier might have scorned, it also engendered a sense of social responsibility that made commercial art and industrial design attractively democratic. The traditional hierarchies within the arts became less obvious once painters, sculptors, and critics acknowledged the cultural importance of mass-produced goods and sought actively to raise their standards. This advocacy was not without equivocation; artists continued to insist on aesthetic standards and cultural norms that often distanced them from commerce and the public. Yet the progressive agenda of the 1920s scored some notable successes in the following decade. Leading commercial artists achieved official recognition and institutional legitimacy that earlier must have seemed unattainable.

Some artists changed their attitude towards commercial art from economic necessity. Financial problems in the early Thirties helped Paul Nash focus his talents on commercial design, and the chronically impoverished John Armstrong accepted numerous assignments in industry to support himself.[23] 'The 1930 slump affected us all very considerably,' William Coldstream recalled at the end of the decade. 'Through making

---

[22] Frederic Ehrlich, *The New Typography and Modern Layout* (New York: Frederick A. Stokes, 1934), 49.

[23] Margot Eates, *Paul Nash: The Master of the Image, 1889–1946* (New York: St Martin's Press, 1973), 49; Mark Glazebrook, 'Introduction' to exhibition catalogue; *John Armstrong, 1893–1973*, Royal Academy of Arts (London: Arts Council of Great Britain, 1975), [pages unnumbered].

money much harder to come by, it caused an immense change in our general outlook. . . . It was no longer the thing to be an artist delighting in isolation.'[24] This enforced liberation from the Romantic notion of self-imposed alienation also served the needs of industry. To companies such as Imperial Airlines, Orient Steam Navigation, and Shell-Mex that catered essentially to an upper-middle class clientele, more aesthetic advertising by leading figures in the art world held a number of advantages. First, it provided their products with a cultural distinctiveness and elevated status that appealed to their intended market. 'The advertising of Imperial Airways presupposes a cultivated public', one observer wrote in 1933 of a company that, like Orient, also sponsored some of the early documentary films of Paul Rotha.[25] Moreover, the patronage of leading artists served as shrewd public relations during a controversial period for commerce generally. 'It is good business for the petrol-peddler to hide his opulence behind the livery of art,' a critic wrote in 1939.[26] When some of these companies hired public relations executives personally and professionally committed to the cultivated arts, economic self-interest dovetailed and intertwined with concerns about social prestige and cultural enrichment.

Shell-Mex proved one of the most active corporate sponsors of talented artists during the 1930s. A subsidiary of a powerful multinational corporation that in 1932 absorbed British Petroleum, Shell-Mex discovered in Jack Beddington, its Publicity Director, an effective spokesman for the values of corporate sponsorship. 'The day of the grand private patron of the arts is over,' he wrote in 1938. 'He has gone the way of the landowner.' In the contemporary world, he argued, artists needed to find either the 'collective patronage' of museums, art galleries, and similar institutions or the 'commercial patronage' of enlightened companies such as Shell.[27] In the 1930s Beddington commissioned many of the country's best painters and designers to create work for various publicity campaigns. Duncan Grant, Paul Nash, John Armstrong, Graham Sutherland, Ben Nicholson, E. McKnight Kauffer, Rex Whistler, and others submitted work that appeared on posters, hoardings, and in the pages of national newspapers. Moreover, in 1931 Shell sponsored an elaborate exhibition of 'Modern Pictorial Advertising' at a fashionable gallery in London.[28]

---

[24] William Coldstream, 'Painting', in *Art in England*, ed. R. S. Lambert (Harmondsworth: Penguin, 1938), 101.

[25] 'Modern Industry and Advertising', *Commercial Art and Industry* 14 (1933): 77.

[26] John Cuff, 'Post Office Publicity', *Penrose Annual* 41 (1939): 22.

[27] Jack Beddington, 'Patronage in Art To-Day', in *Art in England*, ed. Lambert, 82–7.

[28] John Harrison, 'That's Advertising — That Is! Shell-Mex', *Commercial Art* 11 (1931): 40–8. For a representative cross-section of work from Shell, see the exhibition catalogue '*That's Shell — That Is!' An Exhibition of Shell Advertising Art* (London: Barbican Art Gallery, 1983).

These exhibitions soon became annual events that attracted respectful attention and even high praise from influential critics. T. S. Eliot officially opened one exhibition, and Clive Bell used another as the occasion to assess the oil firm's contribution to modern art. 'Shell-Mex, Ltd., is likely to do more for English art in a dozen years than the Royal Academy has done in a hundred,' he began an article for the *New Statesman* in 1934. The company, he continued, 'is becoming one of the centres of what is, perhaps, the most interesting movement in contemporary British art— the formation of a school of applied artists.'[29] Bell, whose writings before the First World War emphasized the intense spiritual bonds between Art and Religion, now joined other established critics and painters who endorsed Art's alliance with Commerce.[30]

Yet economic self-interest was not the only reason artists and industrialists co-operated with each other during the 1930s. As Clive Bell hinted in his article on Shell, such co-operation also fulfilled the heightened sense of social responsibility that the economic conditions of the Thirties aroused. What Frank Pick, McKnight Kauffer, and even Wyndham Lewis claimed in earlier decades now became a more conventional rationale: commercial and industrial art served 'democratic' ends. It brought 'Art' to the 'People'. In his opening address at an exhibition of 'Pictures in Advertising' sponsored by Shell-Mex in 1934, Kenneth Clark delivered a version of this argument when he attempted to place commercial art in historical perspective. During the Renaissance, he argued, painting communicated with a relatively large public. During the past hundred years, however, art became 'a luxury designed to attract a few rich people. And as rich people have grown fewer and more ignorant, so art has declined.' Commercial art fulfilled responsibilities neglected by the Victorians. 'Posters are necessary and popular, and in much the same way that the mural decorations of the Renaissance were necessary and popular. They represent a real effort to communicate an idea or belief in a memorable way to a mass of people.'[31] Even discounting for the hyperbole appropriate for the occasion, this endorsement from the Director of the National Gallery not only provided commercial art with new prestige and an enviable historical pedigree, it also enunciated a mission for artists that, by implication, made commerce the midwife of social responsibility.

[29] Clive Bell, 'Shell-Mex and the Painters', *New Statesman and Nation*, 23 June 1934, 946. For T. S. Eliot's participation, see 'Shell-Mex and B.P. Exhibition, 1938', *Art and Industry* 25 (1938): 103–5.

[30] On this participation, see David Mellor, 'British Art in the 1930s: Some Economic, Political and Cultural Structures', in *Class, Culture and Social Change: A New View of the 1930s*, ed. Frank Gloversmith (Sussex: Harvester Press; New Jersey: Humanities Press, 1980), 194–7.

[31] Kenneth Clark, 'Painters Turn to Posters: The Shell-Mex Exhibition', *Commercial Art and Industry* 17 (1934): 65, 69, 74.

Industry opened the lines of communication severed by privilege and isolation. Paradoxically, an element of society responsible for economic deprivation and exploitation became also a means of enlightenment and uplift. To Clark and other critics, companies such as Shell functioned not unlike the Renaissance Church; they served the community by supporting artists who communicated their patron's message to the general public. 'And the day may not be far off', R. H. Wilenski suggested in 1933, 'when artists with creative power will be as fully employed in covering walls in commercial England as Veronese, Tintoretto and Tiepolo were employed . . . in commercial Venice.'[32]

Yet arguments about the social obligations of artists joining commerce to improve the community sometimes also involved conditions and equivocations that undermined the proposed alliance. In the nineteenth century William Morris and others linked sound principles of design with the spiritual condition of humanity; the aesthetics of everyday goods reflected the inner world of their creators. Mass-produced ugliness resulted from an intricate division of labour that alienated, exploited, and spiritually desolated the work-force. As mechanized production became more widely acceptable among artists, a corollary of this argument developed, especially among Modernists both on the Continent and in Britain: good design actively promoted the spiritual health of a community.[33] By immersing themselves in industrial design, artists moulded social harmony by sharing their integrated visions with a wider public. This essentially self-serving argument permitted artists not to compromise their 'standards' when confronted with 'practical' demands from their less penetrating sponsors; the undiluted vision of the artist fundamentally coincided with the well-being of society. Art embraced commerce but dictated the terms of the encounter.

Two influential figures exemplified the prickly, often equivocal relationship between art and industry during the 1930s. Perhaps more than any other, Paul Nash was an established, gifted painter who sought to eliminate lingering prejudices against commercial art. His articles in the early Thirties for various periodicals championed the cause of industrial design. Early in its history, he accepted leadership of the Society of Industrial Artists, an organization formed in 1930 'to secure a recognized status for artists working for industry and commerce'.[34] When in 1933 Nash announced in *The Times* the formation of Unit One, a short-lived movement of some

---

[32] R. H. Wilenski, 'The Evolution of Transport Mural Paintings', *London Studio* 6 (1933): 74–5.

[33] Charles Harrison, *English Art and Modernism, 1900–1939* (London: Allan Lane; Bloomington: Indiana University Press, 1981), 280–2.

[34] *Thirties: British Art and Design Before the War* (London: Arts Council of Great Britain, 1979), 304.

of Britain's most talented artists and sculptors, he chided his peers for their 'immunity from the responsibility of design'.[35] Nash accepted various commissions from companies, including Shell-Mex, not simply from economic necessity but through conviction of their social worth. Yet, as one of his biographers pointed out, Nash often endured stormy relationships with business men, whose judgements on a variety of matters he rejected and whom he considered subordinate to the artist. 'If the artist is to have the honour of being useful,' he wrote, 'it is likely to be upon his own terms.'[36]

Herbert Read, art critic and an influential proponent of Modernism, also defended industrial design in terms that few artists would find threatening. His seminal *Art and Industry: The Principles of Industrial Design*, first published in 1934, rejected the traditional distinction between 'fine' and 'applied' art and accepted mechanized production as an entrenched feature of contemporary life. 'We are irrevocably committed to a machine age,' he wrote, and, like the Bauhaus whose philosophy he promulgated with the enthusiasm of a convert, Read believed that everyday objects, such as typewriters, petrol pumps, refrigerators, and vacuum cleaners, if designed functionally and with imagination, could be considered works of art. *Art and Industry* consisted mainly of plates and figures illustrating such inspired functionalism. Yet like Nash, Read distanced himself from the stubborn realities and inevitable compromises that practising designers faced as a matter of routine. Read argued that the artist ought to occupy a privileged position in industry with the terms of the alliance profoundly favouring the designer rather than the corporate manager. 'The abstract artist . . . must be given a place in all industries in which he is not already established,' he proposed. '. . . His power must be absolute in all matters of design, and within the limits of functional efficiency, the factory must adapt itself to the artist, not the artist to the factory.'[37] Like many Modernists, Read challenged the hierarchy within the arts that venerated painting and sculpture above all other artistic activities. He never challenged, however, the view that Art itself transcended the mundane realities of human existence.[38]

Despite these reservations, the central arguments of Read and Nash contributed to the wider acceptance of the commercial and industrial arts.

[35] Paul Nash, letter to *The Times*, 12 June 1933, 10.

[36] Quoted in Anthony Bertram, *Paul Nash: The Portrait of An Artist* (London: Faber and Faber, 1955), 186–7.

[37] Herbert Read, *Art and Industry: The Principles of Industrial Design* (London: Faber and Faber, 1934), 33, 39.

[38] See the Preface to Herbert Read, *Art Now: An Introduction to the Theory of Modern Painting and Sculpture* (London: Faber and Faber, 1933); id., *The Meaning of Art* (London: Faber and Faber, 1931), 15; and id., 'A Choice of Extremes', *Penrose Annual* 39 (1937): 21–4.

Indeed, 'design' enjoyed an extraordinary vogue during the decade. A stunning variety of books, journals, institutions, and organizations championed a cause once confined to a small group of enthusiasts. Among books, for example, John Gloag's *Design in Modern Life*, published in 1934, contained articles first broadcast as talks on the BBC, an institution frequently supportive of the modern movement.[39] Another compilation, *The Conquest of Ugliness*, published a year later, enlisted the advocacy of a number of prominent figures, including the Prince of Wales. In 1936, Nicholas Pevsner published *Pioneers of the Modern Movement*, a widely circulated study that among other tasks documented the gradual acceptance of the machine among British artists since the late nineteenth century.[40] That same year *Commercial Art* changed its name to *Art and Industry*, explaining that it was 'symbolic of the evolution of the place of the designer in industry'.[41] The journal *Typography*, founded in 1937, provided a new forum for discussion and debate among typographers from all branches of publishing. Extended stays by Moholy-Nagy, Jan Tschichold, and other figures from the Continent brought British designers in personal contact with some of the most creative proponents of Modernism in typography and design.[42] New organizations promoted the cause through special meetings, publications, exhibitions, and other promotions. The Council for Art and Industry, founded in 1933 in response to a recommendation from the Gorell Commission appointed by the Board of Trade, selected as its first chairman Frank Pick, who for both corporate and aesthetic reasons continued throughout the decade to be a powerful sponsor of modern design at the newly formed London Passenger Transport Board. These and other institutions extended the work begun earlier by the Design and Industries Association.[43]

Support and legitimacy came from other sources as well. In 1935 the Royal Academy sponsored an 'Exhibition of British Art in Industry' which, although Modernists found it disappointing, demonstrated that the movement for better design penetrated one of the most established institutions of British Art. 'By opening their Galleries this year to an

[39] John Gloag, ed., *Design in Modern Life* (London: George Allen and Unwin, 1934). On the BBC and Modernism, see *Thirties*, 205–8.

[40] John De La Valette, *The Conquest of Ugliness* (London: Methuen, 1935); Pevsner, *Pioneers*. See also Percy E. Nobbs, *Design: A Treatise on the Discovery of Form* (London: Oxford University Press, 1937).

[41] 'Art and Industry', *Art and Industry* 21 (1936): 3.

[42] On Moholy-Nagy in England, see Sibyl Moholy-Nagy, *Moholy-Nagy*, 118–35. For Tschichold's visit, see Ruari McLean, 'Jan Tschichold', *Penrose Annual* 63 (1970): 94–5.

[43] On both the economics and aesthetics of Pick's changes in design while at the London Passenger Transport Board, see Adrian Forty, *Objects of Desire* (New York: Pantheon Books, 1986), 222–38. For a general discussion of design in the Thirties, see *Thirties*; and Noel Carrington, *Industrial Design in Britain* (London: George Allen and Unwin, 1976), 112–61.

avowed display of industrial goods and wares,' John Gloag observed, 'the members of our leading fraternity of artists have broken down long-standing prejudices and removed barriers which have contributed to hamper the progress of British industries on an artistic side.'[44] In 1936 the Royal Society of Arts instituted a new honour, 'Designer for Industry', which, as the chairman of the society explained, proved that 'the great industrial designer is not only in himself an artist, but the work he produces is of the utmost good to industry and the community.' Among the first recipients was E. McKnight Kauffer, who two years later formally thanked the society and acknowledged the significance of the award for the growing legitimacy of commercial art.[45]

In the 1930s, the assimilation of new layouts and typography by the national daily press and the enhanced respectability of commercial art and industrial design began to fulfil, at least in part, the progressive agenda of previous decades. Typographers such as Stanley Morison and commercial artists like E. McKnight Kauffer sought to raise the standards of design within the print media, while at the same time justifying their mission among the more traditional arts. Unquestionably, Christiansen's *Daily Express* or especially Bartholomew's *Mirror* clearly fell well below the standards prescribed by the *Fleuron* or championed by the more gifted commercial artists. Yet at the same time, the popular press appropriated principles of design that progressives eagerly supported in the 1920s. The visual unity of a newspaper page, with its often shrewd integration of type, display, and white space, represented in part the legacy of earlier reformers. The outpouring of interest in design among artists and intellectuals meant that commercial artists might practice their craft with less apology. Traditional snobberies died hard, however, and progress remained measured, in part because commerce retained its stigma among partisans of both Left and Right.

That such design might be deemed 'modern' clearly involves a broad definition of the term. By any strict reckoning, the changes in layout among the British press bore only a tangential relationship to the experiments in typography within the Bauhaus and other Continental movements. Yet these changes, like those in many other areas of design, consistently impressed contemporaries as manifestations of the 'modern' movement. In an article 'What does "Modern" mean in Typography?' published in 1936, Beatrice Warde, a typographer and close friend of Stanley Morison, explored some of the ambiguities of the term, arguing that 'functionalism'

[44] John Gloag, untitled introduction to Sir William Llewellyn, 'Art and Daily Life', in *Conquest of Ugliness*, 12.
[45] Henry McMahon, '180 Years of Pioneer Work by the Royal Society of Arts', *Journal of the Royal Society of Arts* 85, 4382 (1936): 20; E. McKnight Kauffer, 'Advertising Art: The Designer and the Public', ibid., 87, 4488 (1938–9): 52–67.

came closest to explaining the 'modern' spirit. Although this term involved ambiguities of its own, Warde believed that a concern for function, combined with a commitment to 'planning the job', united Morison and his more experimental colleagues.[46] For Wyndham Lewis, the ageing Modernist of Vorticism and *Blast*, the 'machine art' at the Royal Academy Exhibition in 1935 embodied qualities he mockingly dismissed as 'slick', 'chic', and 'streamlined'.[47] Clearly, no simple definition captured the similarities in 'look' that contemporaries acknowledged linked the 'modern' designs of the 1930s. Nevertheless, whether it was laid out visually upon the pages of the *Daily Express*, or manifest in the design of a host of everyday objects, including the local cinema, the 'modern', like 'design' itself, become part of the common culture of the decade.

C. THE BBC: LISTENING TO THE AUDIENCE

In the 1920s the BBC acquired a monopoly over an entire medium by gaining the consent of key groups in British society. For reasons of their own self-interest, the press, government, major political parties, radio manufacturers, and the entertainment industry recognized the advantages of a centralized authority licensed by the government to control broadcasting. John Reith reinforced this unique convergence of diverse political and economic interests by enunciating a cultural mission for wireless that isolated commercial alternatives to monopoly as philistine surrenders to the 'mass' mind. In its early years, the BBC broadcast a flattering version of middle-class culture that quickly transformed a new technology into an agent of enlightenment and social respectability. Yet middle-class cultural paternalism, like its aristocratic antecedents, could never completely divorce itself from the groups it sought to control and claimed to serve. Although the BBC presented a 'balanced' programme schedule that clearly gave disproportionate weight to the tastes of highly cultivated minorities, it offered enough concessions to popular taste to escape broadcasting into a void. From the beginning a tension existed within the organization between giving the public 'what it wanted' and 'what it ought to have'.

This tension became exacerbated as the audience rapidly increased in size. Between 1929 and 1933 the number of licence holders doubled, and by 1935 98 per cent of the population had some access to wireless

---

[46] B. L. Warde, 'What does "Modern" mean in Typography?', *Penrose Annual* 38 (1936): 44–7. See also J. R. M. Brumwell, 'Modern Art in Advertising', *Penrose Annual* 41 (1939): 17–21.

[47] Wyndham Lewis, 'What is Industrial Art?', *Commercial Art and Industry* 18 (1935): 83–6.

programmes.[48] This increase reflected in part the ability of the BBC to provide a mass audience with programming sufficiently engaging to justify the cost of licence and equipment, but it also resulted in pressures on the organization, both external and internal, that exposed the contradictions within the Reithian ethos. The popular press, still committed to the notion of monopoly, hired radio critics who often deplored the BBC's cultural élitism. Continental stations, such as Radio Luxembourg and Radio Normandie, beamed a steady stream of popular programming that for many listeners provided an attractive alternative to the BBC's often sober fare. As the BBC grew in size, functionaries within the organization, reflecting the evolving tastes of their social class, began to modify some of the assumptions and attitudes that buttressed Reith's cultural mission. These pressures and the BBC's measured response to them provide a focus for understanding the Corporation's role in the emerging common culture of the 1930s.

In the 1920s, as we have seen, the popular press tended to support the BBC's monopoly over broadcasting. Convinced that a commercialized system would compete for what it considered a limited amount of advertising revenue, popular newspapers only intermittently devoted space to their potential rival. In 1930, a high official of the BBC reported to the Board of Governors that 'the attitude of the newspaper press in general is almost embarrassingly friendly to broadcasting.'[49] The circulation war of the early 1930s, however, placed the press in a more ambivalent relationship to broadcasting. On the one hand, it remained convinced that monopoly protected the newspaper industry from a potentially devastating competitor. 'The unrestricted use on issue by the British Broadcasting Corporation of advertisements', a representative of the Newspaper Society testified before the Ullswater Committee in 1935, 'would be a deadly menace to the financial soundness of the Press.'[50] On the other hand, the popular press needed to compete for readers whose enthusiasm for opera, chamber music, and educational talks remained limited, and who welcomed information and advocacy concerning more popular radio programming. In the early 1930s virtually all newspapers expanded their coverage of broadcasting and hired journalists to become professional radio critics who reviewed programmes, shared gossip about leading radio personalities, and generally acted as advocates for the average listener.[51] Although usually dependent upon the Corporation for their

[48] Briggs, *Golden Age of Wireless*, 253.
[49] Gladstone Murray, Report to the Board of Governors, Jan. 1930, BBC Written Archives Centre.
[50] James Owen, Minutes of Evidence (unpublished), 19 June 1935, Broadcasting Committee (Ullswater), BBC Written Archives Centre.
[51] For a list of these critics, see *Newspaper World*, 2 May 1931, 12.

material and often complimentary in their attitude, radio critics never-theless provided a source of information about broadcasting outside the BBC's considerable public relations apparatus. Despite heroic efforts the BBC, like Hollywood, could never completely control the flow of information about its activities.

One of the most outspoken radio critics, and the first to be granted a regular daily column, was Collie Knox of the *Daily Mail*. Educated at Rugby and Sandhurst, Knox miraculously survived a First-World-War plane crash that severely disfigured his face and required eight months of reconstructive surgery. Often painfully shy and hampered by a stutter, Knox applied for a job with the BBC in 1926. Interviewed by Admiral Carpendale, Reith's second-in-command and a man famed for his military bearing if not his sensitivity, Knox was told 'We have a vacancy for an Announcer, as it happens . . . but that would be no good for you. Why, *you can't even talk properly.* '[52] Knox found a job with the *Daily Express* where his duties included covering the BBC. In 1931 he began an occasional column called 'Your Wireless and Mine' which mixed gossip with muted criticisms. Two years later, he crossed the street to the *Daily Mail* where he graduated to a daily column and, more important, gained the freedom to express his often strong reservations about the Corporation and its policies. 'Collie Knox Calling' began appearing in July 1933 as a newspaper column very much in the American style—brief, chatty, informal, populist, and strident. His critiques of broadcasting were variations on a single theme; the BBC catered to a minority, ignoring the tastes of the majority.

Picture yourself as a man who has returned home this evening after a worrying day at the office or factory where everything has consistently gone wrong. You turn on your radio to the National. And what greets you? First, an 'interlude' which may lead you to expect something bright. But you then get 'Foundations of Music' . . . Beethoven this time. . . . By now, if you have not duly given your radio to the dog to play with, you can listen to a sparkling discussion on 'How Do We Evolve?' . . . Then the BBC Orchestra starts to play at 9.20 pm for more than an hour, followed by a Strauss opera 'Arabella'. And all this on the National wavelength. What fun we do have.[53]

BBC announcers spoke 'in the bored, listless manner of a dying duck'. Talks appealed only 'to pseudo-highbrows living around the London district'. Sunday was 'not necessarily meant to be a day of gloom and mortification for our hard-working countrymen'. And finally there was the music. 'Why in the name of Beecham does the BBC expect listeners

---

[52] Collie Knox, *It Might Have Been You* (London: Chapman and Hall, 1938), 288.
[53] Collie Knox, 'Collie Knox Calling', *Daily Mail*, 29 May 1934, 16.

to sit through more than two hours of symphonic music?'[54] Knox's columns remain one of the relatively few inter-war sources on the BBC not written by a Corporation employee, apologist, or sympathizer. Though it proves difficult to determine precisely the representative nature of these opinions, they bear out what later statistical research overwhelmingly confirmed. The general public was not like the errand boy who whistled Bach.

The BBC's immediate reaction to criticism depended upon its source and its compatibility with existing policy. When in 1931 the *Daily Herald* hired Sydney Moseley as its radio critic, Reith sent a message of acknowledgement that included the sentence: 'The B.B.C.'s interest in and respect for the feature depends naturally on Mr. Moseley's attitude to this responsibility and his treatment of it.' As one BBC official confided privately, this statement was worded 'in the proverbially double-edged way, that is, combining a welcome with an element of menace appropriately concealed'.[55] In a series of articles two years later, the *Radio Times* clarified the official position of the Corporation. The BBC would reply to criticism, the anonymously composed first article stated, under three conditions: the critic was 'worthy of respect'; the facts were accurate; and the critique was 'without prejudice or bias'. In the estimation of the BBC only a few publications satisfied these criteria, among them *The Times*, the *Daily Telegraph*, the *Observer*, and the *Musical Times*. This strategy had a double advantage. First, it implicitly wrote off the popular press as unworthy, inaccurate, or biased, and second, it could cast the BBC in a new, disarming role. The *Musical Times*, for example, scolded the BBC for broadcasting dance music too frequently while limiting the number of lectures on classical music. By replying that dance music, not lectures, gratified the majority of listeners, the BBC became the populist champion.[56]

A far more potent challenge to the Reithian ethos emanated from the commercial stations in Europe, particularly Radio Luxembourg and Radio Normandie. From modest beginnings in the late 1920s, these stations rapidly expanded their operations early in the next decade after acquiring powerful transmitters. Revenue from advertisers eager to penetrate a medium denied them in Britain shot up from around £600,000 in 1936

[54] Collie Knox, 'Collie Knox Calling', *Daily Mail*, 20 Oct. 1933, 20; 16 May 1935, 21; 9 Jan. 1934, 8; 13 Nov. 1934, 21.
[55] *Daily Herald*, 5 Jan. 1931; Assistant Controller of Information to Miss Nash, 1 Jan. 1931, BBC Written Archives Centre. See also Sydney A. Moseley, *Broadcasting in My Time* (London: Rich and Lowan, 1935), 66–8; and id., *The Private Diaries of Sydney Moseley* (London: Max Parrish, 1960), 310–19.
[56] 'The Broadcasting of Music: the B.B.C. Replies to Recent Criticism. 1. Administrative Policy', *Radio Times*, 14 July 1933, 67; and 'The Broadcasting of Music: the B.B.C. Replies to Recent Criticism. 2. Artistic Policy', *Radio Times*, 21 July 1933, 123.

to over £1,000,000 in 1939.[57] Philco, Horlicks, Vernon's football pools, and other sponsors poured substantial amounts into a form of advertising that in America proved astonishingly successful.[58] Although the quality and range of transmission varied enormously among Continental stations, Radio Luxembourg claimed in 1935 that it could reach virtually all the United Kingdom. Others could be heard best in the South and, as in the case of Radio Lyon, only after dark.[59] Reception often improved dramatically, however, if listeners subscribed to a relay exchange which received transmissions from either the BBC or Continental stations on a master set equipped with a powerful antenna and then rediffused programmes by cable. This system appealed especially to lower-income families since it provided high quality reception at an economical price. From June 1930 to March 1935 the number of subscribers increased substantially, from 12,000 to 205,000 with an estimated total audience of over a million listeners.[60] Although this number represented only a small percentage of the audience for radio in Britain, it nevertheless disturbed supporters of the BBC. 'The persons in charge of wireless exchanges have power,' Filson Young wrote in 1933, 'by replacing selected items of the Corporation's programmes with transmissions from abroad, to alter entirely the general drift of the B.B.C.'s programme policy.' Three years later *The Times* noted that relay exchanges attracted mainly 'the poorer classes' and warned that 'while the broadcasting is controlled with enlightenment and impartiality by a responsible public corporation, the listening is controlled by Tom, Dick, and Harry.'[61]

Radio Luxembourg, Radio Normandie, and their somewhat less vigorous English-language counterparts in Europe harboured no illusions about popular taste. On any given Sunday in the 1930s, while the BBC broadcast a religious service followed by a string quartet or a dignified silence, Continental stations entertained their audience with 'Your Cinema

---

[57] Igor Vinogradoff, 'History of English Advertising Programmes Broadcast to the United Kingdom From Foreign Stations Down to the Outbreak of War', (1945) File R 34/961, BBC Written Archives Centre, 3, 58–60. See also Briggs, *Golden Age of Wireless*, 339–69; Donald R. Browne, 'Radio Normandie and the IBC Challenge to the BBC Monopoly', *Historical Journal of Film, Radio and Television* 5, 1 (1985): 3–18; and Richard Nichols, *Radio Luxembourg: The Station of the Stars* (London: W. H. Allen, 1983).

[58] See Herman S. Hettinger, *A Decade of Radio Advertising* (Chicago: University of Chicago Press, 1933), for an early account. See Charles Hull Wolfe, *Modern Radio Advertising*, 2nd edn. (New York: Funk and Wagnalls, 1953), 43–64, for a later reckoning.

[59] Vinogradoff, op. cit., 63.

[60] Briggs, *Golden Age of Broadcasting*, 350–69; Coase, *British Broadcasting*, 69–126; Ralph M. Negrine, 'From Radio Relay to Cable Television: The British Experience', *Historical Journal of Film, Radio and Television* 4, 1 (1984): 31–5.

[61] Filson Young, 'Broadcasting and Advertising', in *B.B.C. Yearbook: 1933* (London: British Broadcasting Corporation, 1933), 72; *The Times*, 30 Apr. 1936, 15.

Organ Favourites', the 'Rinso Radio Revue', and 'The O.K. Sauce Band with Bette Bucknelle'.[62] Surveys indicated that these programmes attracted over 50 per cent of the audience on Sundays, though this percentage dropped substantially during the week. Statistics may again be deceptive, however, since the most sophisticated study of the decade, conducted by Arnold Plant of the University of London, omitted asking its respondents about their listening habits in the prime hours from seven to ten o'clock on weekday evenings, and also compiled its aggregate percentages without discounting statistically for the areas of Britain where Continental reception remained poor. Still, Radio Luxembourg, Radio Normandie, and others like them attracted more female than male listeners and made their greatest impact on lower-income groups.[63] Commercial radio penetrated the same market that made Northcliffe a press lord. Indeed, in their programming and general approach to broadcasting, Radio Luxembourg stood in an analogous relationship with the BBC to that between the *Daily Mail* and *The Times* at the turn of the century. In both cases, the élite institution casually presumed it embodied 'standards' that its commercially motivated rival ignored. In both cases, this same rival helped establish trends that the élite institution eventually accommodated.

Popular newspapers, however, envisaged their commercial cousins in radio as 'a great menace to press advertising'. They excluded from their pages any reference to the programmes broadcast from the Continent. When the *Sunday Referee* broke ranks and published the schedules of commercial stations, the Newspaper Proprietors' Association drummed them out of the organization.[64] After the *Referee* finally decided to comply with Fleet Street's wishes in 1934, the threepenny weekly *Radio Pictorial* began publishing the schedules of Continental broadcasts, a tactic that helped increase its circulation to over 200,000 copies per week in 1938. Perhaps more surprising, beginning in 1935 the *Daily Worker* included the weekend schedules of the commercial stations.[65] In general, advertisers decried the strained relationship between newspapers and commercial radio. 'Press boycotting will be as successful as was King Canute with those other waves,' one agent wrote; '. . . air-advertising

---

[62] A typical programme schedule can be found in Vinogradoff, op. cit., Appendix E.

[63] See Arnold Plant, comp., *Survey of Listening to Sponsored Radio Programmes* (London: Joint Committee of the Incorporated Society of British Advertisers and the Institute of Incorporated Practitioners of Advertising, 1938).

[64] E. O. Norton to Kingsley Wood, 19 Oct. 1934, Minute 19,692/35, GPO Archives; 'Memorandum of Case Presented by Representatives of the Newspaper Proprietors' Association, the Newspaper Society, and the Scottish Daily Newspaper Society', Paper No. 55 (unpublished), Broadcasting Committee, 1935, BBC Written Archives Centre.

[65] Vinogradoff, op. cit., 39.

need not be at the expense of white-space advertising.' The Incorporated Society of British Advertisers lamented the united opposition of the Press and the BBC against commercial radio. 'How can it matter one iota,' one advertiser asked, '. . . whether a foreign station mixes up Beethoven with Bovril or Mendelssohn with mustard?'[66] Ultimately, however, newspapers turned out to be an unreliable ally of the BBC. When the Corporation asked the Newspaper Proprietors' Association to refuse advertising from anyone who used Radio Luxembourg, the press was, as one official remarked, 'unable to help us as of 90 Luxembourg advertisers, 50 were big advertisers on which the Press depended, and they could not afford to lose their support'.[67]

The BBC attempted to suppress commercial radio by other means as well. They presented their case to the International Broadcasting Union which passed resolutions against the stations. They asked the Post Office to prohibit relay exchanges from carrying commercial broadcasts. Beginning in 1931, they undertook a lengthy correspondence with the Foreign Office requesting information about the stations and seeking diplomatic action against the competition. By 1937 the Foreign Office commented wearily that 'this question has formed the subject of fruitless negotiations for a number of years', and that further protests were useless. The BBC also conducted a public-relations campaign against the stations and lobbied politicians to nationalize the relay exchanges. Success greeted none of these efforts.[68] Commercial broadcasting eluded the BBC, the press, and the government. The 'O.K. Sauce Band' continued to be heard in British homes.

Continental stations offered popular alternatives to BBC programming that radio critics such as Collie Knox implicitly supported. The BBC demonstrated that it could be not only extraordinarily sensitive to such competition and unflattering appraisal, but relentless in its efforts to maintain its privileged position among the mass media in Britain. As we have seen, however, relations among the popular press, commercial radio, and the BBC involved a number of cross-currents and complexities. Fear of losing advertising revenue, for example, often made the popular press an unlikely ally of the BBC and an equivocal representative of the readership whose culture it claimed to embrace. Yet domestic criticism

---

[66] An Advertising Agent, 'Clearing the Air About Radio Advertising', *World's Press News*, 4 Aug. 1932; W. A. Bristow in *Reports of Speeches Stating the View of British Advertisers* (London: Incorporated Society of British Advertisers, 1935), 10.

[67] Director General's Meeting, 30 Oct. 1934, BBC Written Archives Centre.

[68] Briggs, *Golden Age of Wireless*, 354–63; 'Advertisement Broadcasting in English From Foreign Stations: Summary of Correspondence with Foreign Office', Minute 19,563/1938, GPO Archives; Foreign Office to General Post Office, 9 Aug. 1937, Minute 19,562/1938, ibid.; S. Tallents' Report of Telephone Conversation with C. Powell on Relay Exchanges, 3 Apr. 1936, BBC Written Archives Centre.

from the popular press and foreign competition from European stations represented only two sources of revolt against the theory of cultural deference that buttressed Reith's notion of public service. The forces that converged in the 1930s to make the BBC a more integral part of an emerging common culture in Britain emanated not only from the commercial sector. Both outside the Corporation and from within, a number of influential and articulate individuals argued that the BBC needed to become more responsive to changing tastes. If 'giving the public what it wanted' directly challenged the paternalism of the Reithian ethos and heightened the ongoing tension between the rhetoric of cultural uplift and the often less trumpeted practice of accommodation, competition and criticism also roused the Corporation from the lethargy and complacency that might have undermined a monopoly entering its second decade.

Certainly, throughout the 1930s Reith's conception of public service retained its forceful defenders among the cultivated élites. 'The Public has been treated like a gentleman . . . by the B.B.C.,' Wyndham Lewis wrote in 1935 as the Ullswater Committee met to review the Charter, 'and by its response to such treatment the Public will show whether it deserves to be treated like a gentleman, or prefers to be approached as if it were some sort of half-wit sub-man . . . preferred by most of the popular Press.' The same occasion also prompted the artist C. R. W. Nevinson to warn against capitulating to market pressures. 'The B.B.C. next year may be handed over to commerce and get entirely out of control of men of discrimination in the arts,' he argued; 'monotony will rule; sentimentality will croon and croak. . . . The public, willy-nilly, will be once again compelled to have nothing else but 'what it wants' . . . All thinking people . . . realize, in spite of the talk of art and industry, that where commerce, as now instituted, walks in, the artist of necessity walks out.'[69] These and similar pronouncements from other writers represented the kind of support that, beginning in the early 1920s, Reith and his lieutenants counted upon to legitimate the medium among the social and cultural élites. The equation between 'public service' and the tastes of a cultivated minority quite naturally retained a powerful attraction for the social groups most served by it.

Yet Reith's assumptions about culture also found detractors within these same circles. C. Henry Warren, the radio critic for the *Spectator*, devoted a number of articles in various journals to the BBC's unwillingness to

[69] Wyndham Lewis, 'Art and Patronage (1)', in *B.B.C. Annual* (London: British Broadcasting Corporation, 1935), 187; C. R. W. Nevinson, 'Art and Patronage (2)', ibid., 191. For Nevinson's fears about radio, see also id., *Paint and Prejudice* (London: Methuen, 1937), 204–5. See also Basil Maine, *The B.B.C. And Its Audience* (London: Thames and Hudson, 1939), 116–20; and Malcolm Muggeridge, *The Thirties: 1930–1940 in Great Britain* (London: Hamish Hamilton, 1940), 43–6.

adjust its programming to the tastes of a mass audience. 'No amount of preparatory talks', he complained, for example, 'can ever make opera broadcasts intelligible to the great majority of listeners. It remains for them just a bore.'[70] In a radio talk in 1935, William Beveridge lamented 'that the B.B.C. cares nothing for its listeners. . . . Nobody in this audience today, nobody in the B.B.C., knows how many listeners are listening, or if any listeners are listening. . . . The B.B.C. is the most devoted believer in one-way conversation that the world has ever seen.' The author and critic Frank Swinnerton argued that the Corporation was 'one of the least democratic institutions in the country', in part because many of its broadcasts were 'addressed solely to middle-class persons who have been educated at public schools.'[71] These and similar reflections by other writers indicated that the BBC's implementation of the public service ideal sustained attack not simply from spokesmen for commercial culture. At least some intellectuals recognized the futility of broadcasting programmes that the public ignored, or, like Beveridge, stressed the reciprocity involved in any paternalistic relationship. The pressure to concede to popular demands, these writers implied, need not be capitulation to the forces of darkness.

This tension between the desire to maintain standards and the need to accommodate shifting public demand also affected an institution closely intertwined with the BBC and one also strongly committed to the goals of cultural uplift. *The Gramophone*, as we have seen earlier, sought to raise the musical standards of an industry heavily dependent upon popular music for its profits. Compton Mackenzie's monthly magazine served the needs of thousands of individuals eager for advice and information about classical recordings. The economic slump of the early 1930s took its toll, however, on both the industry and the magazine. In 1931 Columbia and The Gramophone Company merged into Electrical and Musical Industries, which two years later lost over £374,000—the most ever. *The Gramophone*'s pages reflected these financial set-backs as circulation dropped and advertisers faded away. For a period in the early 1930s the magazine gave free copies to lapsed subscribers who no longer could afford to pay. One year it lost over £1,300. In a dark mood, Mackenzie hinted that the magazine, like the industry, might be finished.[72]

---

[70] C. Henry Warren, 'Opera and the B.B.C.', *Bookman* 86, 509 (1934): 105. See also id., 'Broadcast Talks: Are They Too Highbrow?', *Radio Times*, 6 Jan. 1930, 11; and id., 'Who Listens to the B.B.C. Talks?', *Bookman* 85, 508 (1934): 440.

[71] William Beveridge quoted in 'Does the B.B.C. Care for its Listeners?', *Listener*, 3 July 1935, 1; Frank Swinnerton, 'The B.B.C.—Candid Criticism', *Nash's Pall Mall Magazine* (June 1932): 82.

[72] *The Times*, 30 Nov. 1931 and 30 Oct. 1933; Compton Mackenzie, 'Editorial', *The Gramophone* 11, 132 (1934): 464.

The slump fuelled within the magazine a debate that began in the late 1920s and involved a number of interrelated issues. One of these concerned the BBC, whose monopoly *The Gramophone* often defended in the 1920s and which employed as broadcasters both Mackenzie and Christopher Stone, the London editor of the magazine.[73] Mackenzie delivered talks on a variety of subjects, including Siamese cats, wrote for the *Radio Times* and the *Listener*, and in 1929 participated in a highly successful radio drama based upon his best-selling novel *Carnival*.[74] Stone began his career in broadcasting in the summer of 1927 as the host of a record programme. He proved an instant huge success and became something of a celebrity. He appeared at the Palladium and Madame Tussaud's cut a wax figure of him. Newspapers asked him to write articles and the BBC featured him in a documentary film.[75] The popularity attracted commercial interests. Stone became a spokesman for Bush Radio and in 1934 began regular broadcasts from Radio Luxembourg. The BBC asked him to abandon these programmes but he refused, dismayed that 'a perfectly honest and demonstrably efficient medium for advertising should be boycotted, cold-shouldered and generally treated as if it were a criminal'. Never a haven for rebels, the BBC dismissed one of its most effective broadcasters.[76]

Stone's popularity and his defence of commercial interests often conflicted with Mackenzie's more critical attitude toward mass culture. They clashed over the contents of both *Vox*, a short-lived magazine of radio criticism founded by Mackenzie in 1929,[77] and the struggling *Gramophone*. To combat declining circulation and diminished advertising revenue, Stone believed that the magazine should adapt itself more aggressively to modern tastes. As the simple rhythms of 'Yes, We Have No Bananas' evolved into the more complex sounds of Duke Ellington, jazz attracted a number of influential defenders, including Constant Lambert, who integrated the music into his own compositions and whose book *Music Ho!*, published in 1934, argued that jazz represented an

[73] For Mackenzie's defence of the BBC, see Compton Mackenzie, 'The B.B.C.', *The Gramophone* 4, 9 (1927): 359; and id., 'Can Wireless Aid the Art of Drama?', *Radio Times*, 27 Sept. 1929, 667.

[74] Goldie, 'Triumph of *Carnival*', *Listener*, 23 Dec. 1936, 1173. On Mackenzie as broadcaster, see Compton Mackenzie File, BBC Written Archives Centre.

[75] Christopher Stone, *Christopher Stone Speaking* (London: Elkin Mathews and Marnot, 1933), 69–98, 178–88, 225.

[76] Christopher Stone, 'Radio Luxembourg', *The Gramophone* 12, 139 (1934): 269; id. to Compton Mackenzie, 29 May 1932, Compton Mackenzie Papers, Harry Ransom Humanities Research Center, The University of Texas at Austin; 'Copy of Note by B.B.C. Discussed at Meeting at Post Office on 20 September 1934', Minute 17,013/34, GPO Archives, London.

[77] On *Vox*, see LeMahieu, '*The Gramophone*', *Technology and Culture*, (1982): 387–90.

important element of twentieth-century music.[78] Stone argued that *The Gramophone* ought to become more responsive to this music, thereby attracting a new audience to the magazine. With Mackenzie's tentative approval, he hired an expert on the subject, Edgar Jackson, whose enthusiastic comments on Louis Armstrong and Benny Goodman in the back of the magazine often contradicted Mackenzie's hostile opinions in the editorials. Moreover, as a former editor of *Melody Maker*, the most prominent jazz magazine in Britain, Jackson persuaded Stone to brighten *The Gramophone*'s layout. By the end of 1934, the magazine contained more photographs, snappier graphics, and a more dynamic typography— all an effort to adapt to the new realities of the 1930s.

Mackenzie greeted these changes with mixed emotions. He hated vapid populism but he also knew that a fussy purity could lead to bankruptcy. In an editorial for August 1934 he frankly acknowledged his ambivalence. *The Gramophone*, he wrote, had always experimented with new features and though he sometimes disagreed with them, he did not want an 'insensitive conservatism to stand in the way of serviceable change'. He admitted that he disliked the space devoted to popular records, but wondered if the magazine could afford to alienate readers and advertisers.[79] The conflict was partially resolved when Stone agreed to diminish his involvement in the magazine and transfer some of his responsibilities to Mackenzie's wife Faith. Jackson's reviews continued but occupied less space: the more exuberant aspects of the modern layout gradually became modified. One reason for these changes involved the gramophone industry, which by the mid-1930s began to rebound economically: EMI registered handsome profits, and Decca revitalized the market by cutting its prices for recordings.[80] Advertising picked up dramatically and subscribers began to return to *The Gramophone*. The magazine survived in part for reasons outside its control, but also because it proved flexible enough to adapt to developments within the subculture it served.

The tensions within *The Gramophone* mirrored those of the BBC during the same period. Unlike the relationship between Mackenzie and Stone, however, the conflict between popularization and unwavering loyalty to élite culture occurred within a much more complex institutional context. The staff of the BBC doubled in size between 1931 and 1935, and doubled once again in the following four years.[81] This rapid increase in the number of BBC officials and support staff, combined with both

[78] Constant Lambert, *Music Ho! A Study of Music in Decline* (London: Faber and Faber, 1934). See also Richard Shead, *Constant Lambert* (London: Simon, 1973), 102–8.
[79] Compton Mackenzie, 'Editorial', *The Gramophone* 12, 135 (1934): 81.
[80] Gelatt, *Fabulous Phonograph*, 257–77.
[81] Tom Burns, *The BBC: Public Institution and Private World* (London: Macmillan, 1977), 22–3.

a major reorganization of the internal bureaucracy and the transfer of the Corporation to a new, larger headquarters made unity of purpose a more elusive goal. Unlike the decade before, Reith found it difficult to impose his convictions at every level of the organization. 'There is much less of personal direction than in the early days,' he told the Ullswater Committee in 1935. 'I regard myself as being of increasingly less importance in the B.B.C.' A year earlier he confided to Lord Beaverbrook that as Director General 'one has often to suppress one's own opinion and have done (or not done) what one personally doesn't like (or does).'[82] In his writings, speeches, and appearances, Reith continued to maintain his forceful advocacy of public service, but within the organization there is evidence that he began to lose touch with the rapidly changing realities of the medium. In 1935, for example, in the midst of a continuing boom for radio, he proposed curtailing the hours of broadcasting, acknowledging that the change might be 'putting the clock back' but arguing that 'we should do what we feel to be right.' With the exception of one unnamed individual, he found no support for this proposal among his major subordinates, who tactfully informed him of their overwhelming dissent.[83]

As the BBC mushroomed into a complex bureaucracy and Reith became increasingly detached from control over the organization, the Corporation became more subject to cross-currents of opinion, some of which argued vigorously for more popular programming. In the mid-1930s two committees examined the schedule and proposed change: the first, led by a recently appointed Controller of Programmes, advocated only minor changes but the second, written two years later by a more aggressive official, offered far more sweeping proposals to attract and hold a growing number of listeners.[84] These recommendations probably more accurately reflected the actual tastes of the middle-class personnel who directed the BBC than did the official version of bourgeois culture dominant in programming during the 1920s. Indeed, as anyone who has read the numerous anecdotal memoirs and breezy autobiographies of BBC functionaries from the inter-war period can testify, these officials often shared more patterns of leisure with their friends on the golf course than they did with the composers and intellectuals whose work they patronized. Even one of the most ardent supporters of the Reithian ethos could

[82] John Reith, Minutes of Evidence (unpublished), Broadcasting Committee, 1935, Public Record Office T162/371/E41413/04/1; J. C. W. Reith to Lord Beaverbrook, 30 May 1934, Beaverbrook Papers, File C/273, House of Lords Record Office.

[83] See D.G. to [main officials], 7 Mar. 1935, and 'Reply by Dawnay after discussion with all', 14 May 1935, Policy: Programme Planning, R34/609, BBC Written Archives Centre.

[84] Briggs, *Golden Age of Wireless*, 48–55.

be surprisingly unpredictable in his own tastes. Both in internal BBC memoranda and in his published reflections Val Gielgud, the head of radio drama, constantly mocked commercial culture and the benighted individuals who supported it. 'Is it too pessimistic a viewpoint to note with gloom', he asked in a memoir, 'a pretty general acceptance of decay of a sense of real values? A pretty general tendency to replace the good by the glittering, the tasteful by the noisy?' Gielgud attacked the popular press, worried about the legitimate theatre's embrace of commercialism, and doubted that film could 'ever be called art'. Yet in the same book, this central figure in developing British radio drama and vociferous opponent of popularizing BBC programming admitted that in his own leisure hours he enjoyed 'the writing of sensational fiction' and that 'most of all, I like going to the cinema. Indeed, if put into a corner over it, I would confess that by and large I prefer going to the cinema to going to the theatre. I find, as a rule, that I get more fun out of it.'[85] This ambivalence need not undermine the sincerity of Gielgud's defence of élite culture; it indicates, however, that as with T. S. Eliot's love of the Marx Brothers, the commercialized mass media sometimes entranced its most staunch adversaries.

Thus, a number of converging factors, both within the BBC and external to it, help explain the quiet accommodation of the Corporation during the 1930s to the tastes of its rapidly expanding audience, an accommodation often attributed to a later period in its history.[86] This reorientation manifested itself in many areas, not all of which can be discussed here. Yet in several different though interconnected ways, the BBC proved itself more responsive to public demand than its official rhetoric sometimes indicated. First, the number of variety and related programmes increased dramatically. As early as 1927 a poll of its readers by the *Daily Mail* demonstrated that variety hours were by far the most popular item in the BBC schedule.[87] In 1930 the Corporation created a special 'Revue and Vaudeville Section' and in a crucial development three years later Variety became a separate department, thus acquiring more bureaucratic power within the often complex politics of the expanding organization. Headed by Eric Maschwitz, who acted as a vigorous force for popularization while editor of the *Radio Times*, the Variety Department quickly gained more money, staff, freedom, and time for broadcasts than ever remotely

---

[85] Val Gielgud, *Years of the Locust* (London: Nicholson and Watson, 1947), 105, 112, 127.

[86] See, for example, Kumar, 'Holding the Middle Ground', in *Mass Communication*, ed. Curran, 231–48. This notion that the BBC adapted to popular tastes in the 1930s can also be found in the two articles of David Cardiff cited below.

[87] *Daily Mail*, 28 Feb. 1927. The three most popular items were 'Variety and Concert Parties', 'Light Orchestral Music', and 'Military Bands'.

possible under earlier arrangements. Before 1933 there were only 4 weekly variety programmes broadcast from London; by the winter of 1936 there were 25 such weekly programmes. Between 1930 and 1933 there were only 3 musical comedies adapted for radio; in 1934 alone the BBC broadcast 24 musical comedies.[88] Other light entertainment also prospered. Although between 1934 and 1937 the overall proportion of time devoted to 'dance music' and 'light music' declined—the BBC's definitions of each type involved some ambiguity—the actual amount of broadcast time devoted to such music increased by over 200 hours.[89] More important, the BBC scheduled such music at more convenient hours, eliminating the need, for example, to stay up past 10.30 p.m. on week-nights to listen to favourite bands. 'Dance music is the entertainment of millions,' Maschwitz declared in an article in the *Radio Times*, 'and if it is to reach the millions, it seems to us that it must be broadcast at hours when they are awake and listening.' Even jazz, which Reith abhorred and in some forms continued to prohibit, found its place in the schedule. 'We may be slaves to Jazz but we will at least make our master show his paces!' Maschwitz promised enthusiastically in 1936.[90]

Other areas of programming reflected these changing priorities. In the autumn of 1934, the BBC extended its broadcast hours, reduced its weekly talks of adult education from five to three, and eliminated public chamber concerts.[91] More important, the Corporation began to abandon gradually its Sabbatarianism and respond to the inroads of European commercial competition. Late in 1933, the BBC provided alternative programmes from six to eight p.m. on Sunday, a time period that, shortly before listening research confirmed it, officials conceded to their Continental rivals. Even Reith acknowledged this and other minor concessions to be inadequate. Early in 1934 he reported to a meeting of his subordinates that 'Sunday programmes were too highbrow in spite of the remodelling of last autumn.'[92] Over the next four years, continuing alterations and the general lightening of Sunday programming indicated the vulnerability of the Corporation to competition from abroad. Programmers filled virtually all 'silent periods' during key listening hours

[88] Eric Maschwitz, 'Radio Variety in 1935', *Radio Times*, 13 Sept. 1935, 4–5; Briggs, *Golden Age of Wireless*, 89–94. See also Eric Maschwitz, *No Chip on My Shoulder* (London: Herbert Jenkins, 1957), 55–80.

[89] David Cardiff, 'Time, Money and Culture: BBC Programme Finances, 1927-1939', *Media, Culture and Society* 5 (1983): 379–80.

[90] Eric Maschwitz, 'New BBC Plans for Dance Music', *Radio Times*, 6 Mar. 1936, 4–5, 10. On the dance bands of the Thirties, see McCarthy, *Dance Band Era*, 75–120.

[91] 'Programme Changes in Autumn, 1934', Policy: Programme Planning, BBC Written Archives Centre.

[92] 'D.G.' [Reith] reported in Minutes, D.G.'s Meetings, 23 Jan. 1934, BBC Written Archives Centre.

on Sunday. The Corporation removed its informal prohibition on its dance bands playing Sunday concerts anywhere outside the BBC.[93] Alternative programmes became available throughout the afternoon and their content became noticeably less forbidding for the general public. Sunday morning, the cornerstone of Reith's commitment to religious broadcasting, also experienced change. On 3 July 1938, for example, the last day of Reith's tenure as Director General, the BBC's National Programme broadcast a religious service at 9.25 a.m., followed at 10.45 by Fred Hartley and his Sextet, who opened the programme with 'Who's Afraid of the Big Bad Wolf?'[94]

Second and closely related, the Corporation not only devoted more prime listening hours to popular programming, but also spent a disproportionate amount of money to finance these broadcasts. Here again, statistics must be regarded with the usual caution since the BBC's accounting procedures and classifications changed over time. Still, the financial resources devoted to 'serious music' decreased by about £1,000 between 1934 and 1937, while in the same period the money spent on variety and closely related areas of programming increased by over £30,000. As Director of Variety, Eric Maschwitz invested heavily in star performers and, rather than continue the practice of remote broadcasts from well-known venues, he originated shows from the BBC that demanded their own often expensive scripts and rehearsals. Moreover, in addition to these new costs, expenditure for both 'light music' and 'dance music' also increased considerably, in part because copyright costs increased once the BBC aggressively stalked the most popular material. By the end of the 1930s, individuals with ambitious plans for expensive broadcasts of serious music such as opera found it increasingly difficult to attract bureaucratic support and gain Corporation funding. It was argued that the size of the listening audience for such broadcasts could not justify the expense.[95]

Third, if the BBC devoted more time and money to popular programming, in selected areas it also increasingly adopted an approach to its listeners not unlike that of commercial culture. Some radio talks, for example, continued to be delivered in the formal, impersonal style that characterized the BBC's National Lectures. More and more in the 1930s, however, the officials who supervised the spoken word popularized the

---

[93] Jack Payne, *Signature Tune* (London: Stanley Payne, n.d.), 37–8. On Payne, see also id., '*This is Jack Payne*' (London: Sampson, Low, Marston [1932]).

[94] *Radio Times*, 1 July 1938. On changes in Sunday broadcasting, see also, among others, 'Sunday Broadcasting Programmes: Memorandum by Director of Telecommunications', 5 Mar. 1937, 5297, Minute 20,095/38, GPO Archives; and the testimony of Donald Banks to the Broadcasting Committee, 1935, Minutes of Evidence, T162/371/E41413/04/2, Public Record Office, Kew.

[95] Cardiff, 'Time, Money and Culture', *Media, Culture and Society* 5 (1983): 373–93.

format of such broadcasts and introduced audience-participation programmes that American commercial radio had discovered to be enormously
successful. Magazine and certain feature programmes such as 'In Town
Tonight' included a great deal of material that in the press would have
been considered human-interest stories. A programme broadcast from
the North Region called 'Owt About Owt' focused upon character types
and unusual situations long familiar to journalists within the popular
daily press.[96] Moreover, BBC publicity about its schedule reflected this
willingness to engage readers in a manner pioneered by Northcliffe and
other press lords early in the century. The launching of a serious weekly,
the *Listener*, in 1929 gave the *Radio Times* a clearer identity; continuing
a trend begun in the late 1920s, the magazine further lightened its format.
It dropped its editorials. Popular articles devoted to dance music, well-
known radio personalities, humorous incidents, and similar topics far
outweighed the educational and other uplifting items that once filled the
magazine.[97] A regular feature 'What Is Your Choice This Week?' initiated
early in 1938 indicated the orientation of the magazine and, increasingly,
of the Corporation itself.

Fourth and finally, it was in the 1930s that the BBC accepted the
notion of systematic listener research and hired an expert from advertising
to discover what the public wanted. This step represented the culmination
of a long debate within the Corporation. In 1930, for example, the call
for better information on listening habits came from an unexpected
source. Val Gielgud, in a memorandum often quoted by later scholars,
argued against relying on correspondence from the general public since
'the plain listener is not a person who ever writes a letter, except under
very startling circumstances.' He wondered about 'the true reactions of
our programme public', and he feared 'that a very great deal of our money
and time and effort may be expended on broadcasting into a void.' Three
years later, after no action by the BBC, Gielgud made the same request:
'I am still entirely in the dark as whether five thousand, ten thousand,
a million, or twenty, people listen to the average play broadcast.' There
is nothing in radio, he wrote, that corresponds with the box-office in

[96] David Cardiff, 'The Serious and the Popular: Aspects of the Evolution of Style in
the Radio Talk, 1928–1939', *Media, Culture and Society* 2 (1980): 29–47. On *In Town
Tonight*, see the heavily anecdotal Peter Duncan, '*In Town Tonight*' (London: Werner
Laurie, 1951). On changing attitudes towards radio and education, see *Wireless Discussion
Groups: What They Are and How to Run Them* (London: British Broadcasting Corporation, 1935), 8–10. On the evolution of feature programmes, see D. G. Bridson,
Prospero and Ariel: The Rise and Fall of Radio: A Personal Recollection (London: Victor
Gollancz, 1971), 30–71.
[97] On the *Listener*, see 'A New Venture', *Listener*, 16 Jan. 1929, 14; Lambert, *Ariel*,
98–112; Briggs, *Golden Age*, 280–92; and the special anniversary issue: *Listener*, 18 Jan.
1979.

theatre.[98] Opposition to listener research centred, predictably enough, on the belief that 'what the public wants' may not be 'what the public ought to have'. In 1934 the Programme Board discussed whether or not to include a questionnaire on listeners' preferences in the *Radio Times*. The scheme met defeat because 'if the results of the questionnaire were not published, the Corporation would be pressed to publish them. On the other hand, if they were published, the Corporation would be pressed to modify its programmes in the light of the information received.'[99] Listener research, it was claimed, might compromise standards of programming; it represented to some BBC officials a transfer of responsibility to the consumer, the focus of commercial culture. Opposition to listener research became as much an acknowledgement of élite culture's fragility as it was a conviction of its superiority.

Yet by 1936 such arguments became more difficult to sustain and thus, as before, what the BBC could not ignore, it learned to accommodate. Listener research confronted a number of problems in its early years. Officials needed to define the specific purposes of their research and to discover the means whereby these findings might be considered reasonably accurate. It took time to evolve from inexpensive, relatively primitive, and statistically unreliable methods of probing listening habits to more costly, accurate, and methodologically sophisticated protocols. Moreover, some officials insisted that elaborate studies only confirmed what experienced personnel already knew; listener research became for these cynics an overblown exercise in measuring the obvious. Some departments ignored the findings of listener surveys; others took them more seriously.[1] Yet the results of the early surveys usually prefigured what later studies revealed with less doubt. Regional differences in listening habits proved far less distinct than expected and, although men and women often preferred different specific programmes, their tastes shared much in common. Age and class offered far sharper divergences, but not without qualifications. Differences in age, for example, clearly and predictably affected the enjoyment of contemporary dance music, but in a number of other programme categories age rarely proved 'at variance with that of the listening public as a whole'. Class affiliation also measurably affected programme choice, but once again statistical differences often proved less dramatic than expected. 'While there may have been people who fitted

[98] Val Gielgud to Director Programmes, 12 May 1930 and 18 Nov. 1933, BBC Written Archives Centre.

[99] Programme Board Minutes: Policy, 26 Apr. 1934, R34/600/06, BBC Written Archives Centre.

[1] Briggs, op. cit., 256–80; Pegg, *Broadcasting and Society*, 113–46. On the BBC and its audience, see also Burton Paulu, *British Broadcasting: Radio and Television in the United Kingdom* (Minneapolis: University of Minnesota Press, 1956), 242–80.

the highbrow–lowbrow stereotypes,' Robert Silvey recalled of his pioneering role in the BBC's efforts at audience research, 'there was in fact widespread catholicity in listening. A liking for light music, comedy shows and football commentaries tended to be common to all levels of brow. What usually distinguished the so-called highbrow from the lowbrow was not that he disliked easy fare but that he also liked other kinds.'[2]

The adoption of listener research meant that the BBC institutionalized a mechanism of audience response as certain though economically less unforgiving as the net circulation statistics of the popular press. In its role as a chartered monopoly formally committed to Reith's notion of public service, the BBC concealed these figures from the public and, especially in the early years, could choose to disregard the implications of its findings on audience preferences. It was not listener research alone that forced the Corporation to become more sensitive to the public it claimed to serve: yet after 1936 it became increasingly difficult to evaluate programmes and devise schedules solely on the basis of the opinions and anecdotal evidence of privileged insiders. Statistics provided a level of certainty about the tastes of listeners that the self-assured opinions of windy pontificators could not match. It was no longer enough to assert that opera would gradually build a significant audience of committed enthusiasts from all classes. The proof or disproof was in the surveys. The BBC still launched expensive operatic productions and continued to finance experimental dramas, but these and similar decisions could not involve a rationale that listener research flatly contradicted. Even a monopoly committed to sustaining the arts could not ignore completely the sometimes subtle, sometimes brutal pressure of statistics. Listener research gradually became the box-office of the BBC.

In a statement of policy in 1939, the *BBC Handbook* reported that 'no one whose business it is to supply things to people—least of all those who supply entertainment—can afford to be ignorant about what people want.'[3] This statement, virtually inconceivable a decade before, illustrated how far the Corporation had travelled during the 1930s. The cultural paternalism defined by John Reith and sustained by the BBC in the 1920s always depended upon the consent of key interest groups, including the press, the government, and the radio manufacturers. As the number of listeners first expanded and then exploded, they too became an interest group, informal and disorganized to be sure, but with self-proclaimed and articulate spokesmen who represented their opinions both

    [2] Robert Silvey, *Who's Listening? The Story of BBC Audience Research* (London: George Allen and Unwin, 1974), 125, 68–70.
    [3] 'Listener Research in 1938', in *BBC Handbook, 1939* (London: British Broadcasting Corporation, 1939), 55.

outside and within the Corporation. Commercial stations in Europe testified to the economic importance of this interest group by vigorously competing for their attention. The BBC, in turn, also responded. The popularization of BBC programming in the 1930s could be viewed as fitting comfortably within the rubric of cultural paternalism, since such a hierarchical relationship always involved some degree of reciprocity. Yet, something else was also happening. The BBC not only increasingly gave the public what it wanted, it gradually established in some of its programming a more sympathetic, egalitarian relationship with its diverse listeners. The Reithian ethos always remained in tension with this trend, long after its central spokesman departed for an extended, bitter, and self-imposed exile from broadcasting. The experience of the BBC during the 1930s demonstrated that even a government-chartered monopoly could not be immune from competition and from market forces. Indeed, the BBC gradually became part of the common culture of British life in part because it could adjust to changing circumstances. Listener research confirmed that certain programmes that were initially anathema to Reith in the 1920s appealed to virtually all classes, ages, and regions of the country. As the Corporation increased the number of such programmes and broadcast them at accessible times, it became both as an organization and as a medium of communication part of an emerging common culture. By listening to its audience, the BBC helped confirm its place in the daily lives of the British public.

The cinema, the graphics of the daily popular press, and wireless all contributed to a common culture of sights and sounds during the 1930s. These often closely interrelated visual and aural media communicated experiences and cultural references that transcended the customary boundaries of age, sex, region, and social class. As a number of statistical surveys demonstrated, young and old, male and female, North and South, and individuals from all classes enjoyed popular films, newspapers such as the *Daily Express*, and radio programmes from the BBC. Together these media contributed to a shared frame of reference within the rich diversity and intricate stratifications of British cultural life. Moreover, as we have seen, the internal mechanisms of this common culture often borrowed from both commercial sources and the artistic élites. Hitchcock's films merged Expressionist visual imagery with a sensitivity towards audience identification that the documentary-film movement only belatedly recognized as crucial to successful cinema. The popular daily press, locked in a ruthless quest for higher circulation, borrowed visual techniques from progressive commercial artists and typographers who a decade before lamented their lack of influence. The BBC, committed to uplifting tastes, provided listeners with information and entertainment that assured the

Corporation would not dwell self-righteously on the margins of British life. These case-studies, by no means exhaustive, illustrate some of the cultural convergences of the 1930s. They also embody cultural trends that were not without their critics and parallels among the literary intelligentsia.

7

Literature: The Strategies and Paradoxes
of Cultural Dissent

DURING the Thirties, writers and literary intellectuals remained central figures of cultural dissent in Britain. Building upon traditions that extended deep into the nineteenth century and encompassed work by Coleridge, Carlyle, Ruskin, Arnold, and Morris, authors and critics responded to the economic and political crises of the Thirties by committing themselves to a broad agenda of reform. Profoundly alienated by the complacencies of the National Government and galvanized by political developments on the Continent, some writers embraced radical political ideologies that promised sweeping, fundamental change; others quietly aligned themselves with less revolutionary causes. In either case it became increasingly difficult to justify artistic endeavour that self-consciously removed itself from contemporary life. Though it retained its influential spokesmen, the view that art transcended all social and political realities struck many, particularly young writers, as a self-indulgent, grossly inappropriate creed. Engagement rather than detachment became an imperative obligation; literature, it was widely argued, should both reflect and help ameliorate a social system in crisis.

For some authors and critics, part of this political crisis involved the increasing dominance of the mass media in the cultural life of the nation. By the 1930s, cinema, the popular press, and radio had long since passed from novelties into necessities among a vast cross-section of the population, including key elements of the intelligentsia. Writers might decry the banalities of Hollywood, for example, but like millions of their fellow citizens they too sat in darkened cinemas. Unlike some of their predecessors in earlier decades, critics of mass media and commercial culture in the 1930s often revealed a knowledge of these media that unconsciously paid tribute to the universality of its reach. Contempt often betrayed familiarity. More important for purposes here, the widespread commitment to social engagement and reform meant that many authors and poets sought to influence the level of taste among the general population. In the 1930s, a surprising number of the most gifted and influential poets, novelists, and critics adopted some version of what this essay has called the progressive agenda. Literary figures might be alienated from the culture of the majority, but their social idealism impelled them towards strategies of intervention that often reflected the practices of the dominant culture they deplored. Not all these critics can be considered here. Instead this chapter will focus on three cases of cultural dissent, each with its own advantages and predicaments. First, the Leavises formulated an extensive critique of 'mass civilization' and 'minority culture' that, beginning with only a few adherents in the early Thirties eventually captured national attention, in part because of the couple's uncanny ability to personalize every issue. Second, the diverse elements of the Left in the Thirties engaged in an extensive debate over the role of art and mass culture in revolutionary politics that reflected tensions in the larger culture they sought unsuccessfully to displace. Finally, unlike either the Leavises or the Left in the 1930s, J. B. Priestley became an integral part of the common culture of the decade by shrewdly mastering the very media he so often criticized.

A. THE LEAVISES: CULTURE AND PERSONALITY

Unlike their colleagues and professional peers, the Leavises often attracted more attention than the creative authors they championed. Few academic critics could make such a claim, in part because of the evolving nature of literary criticism. In the late eighteenth and early nineteenth centuries, writers such as Johnson and Coleridge contributed substantially to the literary heritage they evaluated in their essays and, in more recent times, T. S. Eliot's reputation as a poet markedly enhanced his standing as a commentator. Other professional critics commanded attention, but rarely for as long or in such intensity as the Leavises. For example, I. A. Richards, who pioneered many of the reading techniques that the Leavises adapted and disseminated, became a less dominating figure among the cultivated once he focused his attention on a universal language and international problems of illiteracy. The Leavises helped establish the imposing presence of literary criticism in modern cultural life. Their method of analysing texts deeply influenced a generation of intellectuals that included Raymond Williams, Richard Hoggart, Marshall McLuhan, and a number of American scholars. Moreover, their radical critique of modern culture, which daringly encompassed the privileged literary élites of London as exemplars of the ongoing crisis, attracted disciples from across the political spectrum and reinforced the academic standing of literary studies in universities. In the 1930s the Leavises began to consolidate a significant place for themselves in twentieth-century British cultural life.

Yet, as many commentators acknowledge, the literary criticism of F. R. and Q. D. Leavis was not without its curious anomalies. Neither their literary method of close reading nor their general cultural analysis embodied a level of originality that might explain fully their extraordinary influence and reputation. Their method of explicating texts was clearly derived from I. A. Richards, and their general cultural criticism, enunciated most forcefully in F. R. Leavis's *Mass Civilization and Minority Culture* and Q. D. Leavis's *Fiction and the Reading Public*, borrowed heavily from T. S. Eliot, D. H. Lawrence, Wyndham Lewis, and the crowd psychologists of the late nineteenth and early twentieth centuries. Their criticism of the United States and of Americanization echoed the works of American critics.[1] Though the Leavises often composed individual essays of great penetration and analytic power, it was not primarily their intellectual originality which thrust them into prominence. Moreover, as some observers pointed out already in the early 1930s, the Leavises' belief in an 'organic community' that industrialism gradually destroyed, while not without foundation, enormously simplified British social development. 'The theory that there was ever a golden age of culture this side of prehistory will hardly hold water,' a commentator for the *Cambridge Review* wrote dismissively of *Fiction and the Reading Public* in 1932. More recently, Raymond Williams demonstrated how such nostalgia for pastoral harmony has been a persistent theme within British culture for hundreds of years.[2] The Leavises adhered to the useful fiction of a disappearing organic community, in part because they derived their historicism uncritically from a few, mainly literary, sources. From the 1930s onward, no amount of challenge, backed by generations of careful historical scholarship, could shake them from their fundamental convictions about the superiority of English culture and society in the pre-industrial era. Their view of the past remained as Utopian as the vision of the future enunciated by the revolutionaries they mistrusted. Finally, the literary criticism of the Leavises always involved the anomaly of their refusal to define precisely the 'standards' they so passionately defended. Although in 1937 René Wellek directly challenged F. R. Leavis to declare his principles, Leavis refused to commit himself to 'such a theoretical statement' because he considered it 'too clumsy to be of any use'.[3] For the next forty years, he continued to evaluate writers by standards none could ascertain and to argue from assumptions he refused to examine.

[1] F. R. Leavis, *Mass Civilization and Minority Culture* (Cambridge: The Minority Press, 1930); Q. D. Leavis, *Fiction and the Reading Public* (London: Chatto and Windus, 1932). For an analysis of their often ambivalent attitude towards America, see Francis Mulhearn, *The Moment of* Scrutiny (London: New Left Books, 1979), 125–7.

[2] Geoffrey W. Rossetti ['G.W.R.'], 'Democratic Tastes', *Cambridge Review*, 3 June 1932, 444–5; Raymond Williams, *The Country and the City* (New York: Oxford University Press, 1973). See also Austin Duncan-Jones, 'The Organic Community', *Cambridge Review* 54, 1336 (26 May 1933): 432–3.

[3] F. R. Leavis, 'Literary Criticism and Philosophy: A Reply', *Scrutiny* 6, 1 (1937): 62–3. See also René Wellek, 'Literary Criticism and Philosophy', *Scrutiny* 5, 4 (1937): 375–83.

These anomalies suggest that the Leavises' reputation and their impact on British culture cannot be attributed solely to the force of ideas which even sympathizers acknowledged to be often derivative, simplified, or vague. The controversies they aroused acquired much of their emotive power from the distinctive personalities of the Leavises themselves and from the manner in which they managed to inject themselves into most of their literary and cultural criticism. In both their style of argument and in the heroic self-characterizations that provided the sub-text of their writings, the Leavises used personality in an area of culture accustomed to greater detachment, self-effacement, and formality. The Leavises broke the rules of academic decorum; while proclaiming their own objectivity and fairness, they ridiculed their university colleagues mercilessly, publicly transformed criticism into an *ad hominem* practice, and ceaselessly engaged in self-promotional exercises. In one crucial respect, then, they unconsciously mirrored the 'mass civilization' which they argued threatened enlightened minorities. The Leavises personalized cultural dissent. Commercial culture long recognized the value of personality in generating interest among audiences. Gossip columnists, film stars, and personal endorsements in advertising all reflected this emphasis. Though clear and striking differences existed between the Leavises and such phenomena, it is also worth noting at least one feature they had in common. Both involved the promotion of a public persona that, although sometimes at odds with private behaviour, became the focal point, the centre of gravity, for other issues and concerns. Marginal figures in a newly created university course and often deeply provincial in their assumptions, the Leavises gradually drew national attention to themselves and their ideas by practising a strategy of dissent symbiotic with the culture they resisted.

Two aspects of this strategy may be defined more precisely and evaluated. First, the Leavises infused discourse with an *ad hominem* polemical style that proved difficult either to answer or ignore. Though such argument drew from a rich tradition of historical precedents extending back to antiquity, where it was considered a form of satire, it nevertheless retained its power to shock and outrage opponents. In his very first article for *Scrutiny* in 1932, F. R. Leavis demonstrated this style in an extended review of Max Eastman's *The Literary Mind*. The essay began:

Mr. Max Eastman . . . presents an interesting case. It is of himself that I am thinking. For, while the case he propounds about "the literary mind" is too naïve and muddled in its complacent philistinism to be seriously discussed, he does indeed witness impressively to the decay of literary culture.

Other excerpts convey the characteristic flavour of Leavis's writing.

Mr. Eastman simply cannot see the difference in intellectual status between Mr. Eliot and Miss Sitwell, except that he finds Miss Sitwell more discussable. . . . The late Arnold Bennett, it will be remembered, had a like preference.

What . . . is wrong with Mr. Eastman's *intelligence?* — That he is deficient in taste and sensibility is plain. . . . By a little analysis it should be possible to bring home to him that he is deficient on the side of intelligence.

It is not unrelated to the quality that enables him to discuss the 'thought' of Mr. J. C. Powys seriously.

The author [A. L. Rowse] . . . shows that he cannot read. And to this illiteracy relates, in the ways suggested, the blurred muddle of the writing, a certain unnecessary grossness of manners and a disabling impercipience.[4]

The tactics revealed in these quotations—direct attacks on an individual's character, guilt by association, the use of quotation marks to dismiss a notion without actually confronting its substance, the casual sneer—provide a sample of Leavis's polemical style. The fierceness of these public attacks, moreover, was often matched in private dealings with perceived enemies. The Leavises prided themselves in conveying to students their contempt for many of their colleagues within the university. 'Listen to the Henn—cackling', F. R. told a student as another member of the faculty, Tom Henn, delivered a lecture. 'Ah, yes, Willey,' Leavis said of the famous literary scholar; 'a Methodist . . . cowardly and deceitful.'[5]

This method of dealing with individuals possessed at least one clear advantage over more polite, detached argumentation. It so rapidly elevated the emotive level of a discourse that it virtually forced readers to take sides, to declare themselves about an agenda that Leavis dictated. By constantly reverting to *ad hominem* arguments, he effectively foreclosed indifference to his opinions. He often took opponents and readers outside their experience and, by enraging them with incivility, compelled them to address issues, including that of the Leavises themselves, which otherwise might have quietly disappeared. For his supporters, this style of argument reflected a level of sincerity and personal commitment often absent or skilfully masked in more genteel academic discourse. 'He has planned to fight in desperate earnestness for his principles,' one reviewer wrote admiringly in the *Spectator* in 1932.[6] To his detractors, on the other hand, Leavis and his wife embodied the fanaticism and rude intolerance of zealots. 'Their manner, and sometimes even their manners

---

[4] F. R. Leavis, 'The Literary Mind', *Scrutiny* 1, 1 (1932): 20, 21, 29, 31.
[5] Denys Thompson, ed., *The Leavises: Recollections and Impressions* (Cambridge: Cambridge University Press, 1984), 30. This book provides many other examples of this style, including some directed at admirers. See also Ronald Duncan, *All Men Are Islands: An Autobiography* (London: Rupert Hart-Davis, 1964), 84–5.
[6] Richard Church, 'The Labyrinthine Way', *Spectator*, 26 Mar. 1932, 453.

failed them, almost before they had begun the great cure,' Wyward Browne observed with understated fury in 1933. Arthur Calder-Marshall was less polite. 'The emotions of the dining-room grow big in the servants' hall,' he wrote in 1933 concerning Leavis's appropriation of T. S. Eliot's ideas. 'Whom the master dislikes, the housemaid hates . . . with a venomous bitterness.' 'His propagandism,' he wrote of Leavis, 'his fanatical devotion to sheep and hatred of goats, his own eclecticism and loathing of eclecticism, his evangelical attitude to culture . . . qualify him rather as a prophet of puritanism than a professor of poetry.'[7] Few academics in Britain aroused such passion; in their anger and frustration, detractors of Leavis often found themselves adopting his abrasive polemical techniques, thereby unintentionally testifying to his power. Leavis not only selected the battleground, he chose the weapons as well.

An aggressive polemical style was not the only element in the Leavises' controversial strategy of cultural dissent. Their critique of 'mass civilization' and defence of 'minority culture' clearly functioned as something more than an academic analysis of contemporary trends. It also served to create highly flattering roles for themselves in a self-proclaimed drama between the forces of darkness and light. The Leavises viewed themselves as lonely, heroic figures in a struggle against a corrupt, debilitating commercialism that penetrated even the highest levels of the nation's consciousness. This corruption, they maintained, proved all the more insidious because it prospered among those who falsely considered themselves the literary and artistic élites. Only a discriminating programme of education in English literature, meticulously selected, nurtured, and taught by the Leavises at Cambridge and eventually dispersed more widely, might preserve the vital heritage of the national culture among a new, revitalized minority. The Leavises, in brief, portrayed themselves as both heroic outsiders and redeemers, roles not unlike those found within the conventions of formulaic fiction. Although such kinship should not be exaggerated and certainly would have outraged the Leavises and their disciples, their vigorously promoted self-image helps explain their impact among undergraduates who became persuaded that aesthetic taste embodied the fundamentals of morality, social harmony, and personal identity.

F. R. Leavis explicitly characterized himself as a 'rebel' or 'outlaw' a number of times during his career, though perhaps most vividly in the retrospective essay that he composed for the final volume of the reissue of *Scrutiny* by Cambridge University Press in 1963. 'Our position as outlaws', he wrote of himself and his followers, 'was certainly an advantage

---

[7] Wyward Browne, 'The Culture-Brokers', *London Mercury* 28, 167 (1933): 437; Arthur Calder-Marshall, 'One Must Have Standards', *New Statesman and Nation*, 3 June 1933, 739.

in the matter of maintaining standards; we were less troubled by the anti-critical pressures incidental to "belonging".' As Colin Wilson revealed in a famous book, this notion of the intellectual as 'outsider' drew upon a distinguished pedigree in modern intellectual history.[8] The Leavises cherished and cultivated this role both in their writings and in their private behaviour. They became outsiders not simply because the surrounding culture excluded them, as they persistently claimed, but because they excluded the surrounding culture. 'These are the times', F. R. Leavis wrote in 1932, 'in which the acquiring of taste and discrimination and sensitiveness of intelligence, is probably harder than ever before in the history of civilization.'[9]

The radical and thoroughgoing critique of modernity by the Leavises and their disciples has been ably summarized and evaluated by a number of recent commentators.[10] For purposes here, two more paradoxical aspects of this critique might be stressed. First, F. R. Leavis and his students levelled accusations against the dominant culture that sometimes became ironically echoed in their own approach. It was asserted, for example, that the mass media lacked diversity and complexity; that, like the American society most responsible for its dissemination, commercial culture manifested a uniformity and standardization which threatened to obliterate discrimination and critical 'awareness'. The mass media aroused 'the cheapest emotional responses,' Leavis wrote in *Culture and Environment*, co-authored with Denys Thompson and published in 1933; 'films, newspapers, publicity in all forms, commercially-catered fiction — all offer satisfaction at the lowest level, and inculcate the choosing of the most immediate pleasures, got with the least effort.'[11] The two authors

---

[8] F. R. Leavis, '*Scrutiny*: A Retrospect', in *Scrutiny, vol. 20: A Retrospect, Indexes, Errata* (Cambridge: Cambridge University Press, 1963), 18; Colin Wilson, *The Outsider* (London: Gollancz, 1956).

[9] F. R. Leavis, 'What's Wrong With Criticism?', *Scrutiny* 1, 2 (1932): 144.

[10] See, among others, Williams, *Culture and Society*, 252–63; Gross, *Rise and Fall*, 269–84; Mulhearn, *Moment of* Scrutiny, 45–176; Baldick, *Social Mission*, 162–93; Terry Eagleton, *Literary Theory: An Introduction* (Minneapolis: University of Minnesota Press, 1983), 30–7; Lesley Johnson, *The Cultural Critics: From Matthew Arnold to Raymond Williams* (London: Routledge and Kegan Paul, 1979), 93–115; Pamela McCallum, *Literature and Method: Towards a Critique of I. A. Richards, T. S. Eliot and F. R. Leavis* (London: Gill and Macmillan, Humanities Press, 1983), 151–204. Also useful is 'Leavis at 80 — What Has His Influence Been?', *Listener*, 24 July 1975, 107–10. On Leavis's life, see Ronald Hayman, *Leavis* (London: Heinemann; Totowa, NJ: Rowan and Littlefield, 1976).

[11] F. R. Leavis and Denys Thompson, *Culture and Environment: The Training of Critical Awareness* (London: Chatto and Windus, 1933), 3. Thompson wrote a number of works on the mass media that manifested Leavis's influence. See Denys Thompson, *Reading and Discrimination* (London: Chatto and Windus, 1934); id., *Between the Lines, or How to Read a Newspaper* (London: Frederick Muller, 1939); and id., *Voice of Civilization: An Enquiry into Advertising* (London: Frederick Muller, 1943). *Scrutiny* contained a number of articles on the mass media, particularly during its first three years.

devised exercises that trained students to discriminate among and resist the cultural messages which they encountered daily. Leavis and Thompson hoped that a reformed system of secondary education would instruct students how to make critical distinctions and avoid stock responses. Yet, if there was one trait that most characterized the analysis of mass media in *Culture and Environment*, it was precisely an inability to discriminate. Leavis and Thompson lumped together virtually the entire mass media and charged that 'all offer satisfaction at the lowest level'. Were all films from all countries in all periods the same? Were all popular newspapers alike? Did all best-sellers, written on a variety of subjects and composed by hundreds of authors, always engender the same response? The 'uniformity' may not have been in the mass media but in Leavis's perception of them. Of course, he may have been exaggerating for rhetorical or persuasive purposes, thus unconsciously employing a familiar tactic of the advertising industry he despised. Certainly such exaggeration often proved effective since Leavis's appraisal of advertising's social impact accepted uncritically the industry's self-serving boasts concerning its own importance. He failed to recognize that advertising often advertised itself.[12] Once again he echoed what he sought to resist. Stock responses were not confined simply to those deprived of a university education.

The critique of commercial culture also involved a second paradoxical feature. The Leavises established their professional careers as analysts, even apologists, of the culture they later became famous for dismissing out of hand. F. R. Leavis received his Ph.D. for a dissertation on 'The Relationship of Journalism to Literature', a topic that, despite its focus on early modern Britain, must have struck academics in more established fields as slightly disreputable, like the new field of English Literature itself. In this dissertation, submitted in 1924, Leavis stressed the close relationship in journalism between the writer and the public, or what he called that 'intimate relation between supply and demand'. 'Presumably all writers, even the most ecstatic, write to be read,' he argued, 'but the journalist has the reader most directly and frankly in view.' Leavis claimed that journalism served literature by 'keeping it on terms of intimacy with the life of the day', and though his own descriptive analysis ended in the eighteenth century, he concluded by quoting Arnold Bennett favourably and observing that 'journalism still gives writers a start and an introduction to the public.'[13] As a graduate student, then, Leavis acknowledged the continuities and complexities between early journalism and the

---

[12] Baldick, op. cit., 189–90.

[13] F. R. Leavis, 'The Relationship of Journalism to Literature: Studied in the Rise and Earlier Development of the Press in England' (Ph.D. diss., Cambridge University, 1924), [unnumbered page], 141, 337–8.

contemporary popular press. Only later would he claim that a radical disjuncture occurred between modern and pre-industrial times. This rupture lay at the core of Q. D. Leavis's dissertation, later published as *Fiction and the Reading Public*. Like her husband, Q.D. devoted her early professional career to an area of research that others found distasteful. 'When my book appeared in 1932,' she later recalled, 'a leading senior academic of the Cambridge "English" School . . . held it and me up to opprobrium, since, he said, to read "bestsellers" (as popular fiction was then contemptuously labelled) showed a depraved taste and was quite outside the literary field.' Such guilt by association provides yet another cross-current to any evaluation of the Leavises. Famed for their profound alienation from the commercial and the profane, they began their careers closely and not always favourably linked to popular culture. Indeed, the Leavises considered this connection one aspect of their heroic rebellion against 'a largely hostile academic world' and the basis, in part, of what Q.D. called her 'concentrated seminal work—throwing off fruitful ideas and suggestions that have been followed up by research students, doing exemplary pieces of criticism in new fields, opening up new lines of interest and finding fresh relations between writers and subjects'.[14]

Whatever the cross-currents and ironies of their critical stance, however, it was as resisters to the dominant culture, not reflections of it, that the Leavises defined their mission. This position was not without its advantages. Many students found it easy to identify sympathetically with a vigorous rebel whose literary criticism involved a deep seriousness of purpose not always evident in academic study. 'He associated literature with the hunger for ultimate meaning without which we would not be human,' one student later recalled. 'He came upon a world where the enjoyment of literature was confined to an "aesthetic" sphere . . . and said a resounding No to its division of labour and consequent emasculation of the spirit.'[15] Like earlier protesters, Leavis made his role as 'outlaw' all the more attractive to potential disciples by claiming that an unconventional 'outsider' was, from another perspective, really an 'insider' guided by superior standards. As he later wrote, 'the research students and under-graduates who used, in the early 'thirties, to meet at my house, which was very much a centre, did not suppose that they were meeting at an official centre of "Cambridge English", or one that was favoured by the official powers. They gravitated there because it had become known as a place where the essential nature . . . had an intensified conscious

---

[14] Q. D. Leavis, 'A Glance Backward, 1965', in id., *Collected Essays, vol. 1: The Englishness of the English Novel*, ed. G. Singh (Cambridge: Cambridge University Press, 1983), 10, 17, 25.
[15] Sebastion Moore, 'F. R. Leavis: A Memoir' in Thompson, ed., *Leavises*, 60–1.

life.'[16] In their frequent assessments of their own cultural significance, the Leavises transformed the marginal into the central, the peripheral into the fundamental. On the fringes of a newer academic course that itself fought for status within the university, they claimed to embody the essence of both the department and the larger institution. As editors of a journal which in the 1930s never printed more than 750 copies, they believed that *Scrutiny* rescued 'culture' from the 'civilization' which surrounded it. Parochial in their assumptions, they deemed their values truly 'English'.

Thus, it was not simply as 'outsiders' that the Leavises personally assumed the mantle of literary criticism. They also viewed themselves as redeemers of a cultural legacy muddled by false literary authorities. Leavis took upon himself the task of 're-evaluating' the central figures in English literature and, by measuring them against certain 'standards', determining their relative merits. Like their cultural criticism, these studies have been well summarized by a number of commentators.[17] Two aspects of this role might be underlined. First, as many of Leavis's critics pointed out, the task of revaluation sometimes became arbitrary and authoritarian, with Leavis dictating what British authors currently deserved special attention and which ones might be profitably ignored. 'Dr. Leavis', Stephen Spender wrote in the *Criterion* in 1937, 'nearly always is primarily concerned not with a poet, but with a position in which criticism has "placed" him. . . . Poetry, one would gather, exists simply in the minds of the critics, and poets become "dislodged" or "unreadable" (Shelley) if Dr. Leavis and his colleagues think badly about them.'[18] The revivified cultural hierarchy with which Leavis opposed the levelling tendencies of mass civilization threatened to become a kind of literary stock-market, with Leavis personally determining the rising or declining value of specific authors on the exchange. Or, to alter the metaphor, taste in books became curiously similar, Lionel Trilling slyly hinted, to fashions in clothes.[19]

---

[16] Leavis, 'Scrutiny: A Retrospect', 1. For a brief contemporary account of English literature at Cambridge during this period, see Stephen Potter, *The Muse in Chains: A Study in Education* (London: Jonathan Cape, 1937), 241–54.

[17] In addition to comments in the relevant works cited above, see, among others, Vincent Buckley, *Poetry and Morality: Studies in the Criticism of Matthew Arnold, T. S. Eliot, and F. R. Leavis* (London: Chatto and Windus, 1959), 158–213; the essay on Leavis in Watson, *Literary Critics*; Robert Boyers, *F. R. Leavis: Judgement and the Discipline of Thought* (Columbia: University of Missouri Press, 1978); R. P. Bilan, *The Literary Criticism of F. R. Leavis* (Cambridge: Cambridge University Press, 1979); P. J. M. Robertson, *The Leavises on Fiction: An Historic Partnership* (New York St Martin's Press, 1981); and William Walsh, *F. R. Leavis* (Bloomington: Indiana University Press, 1980). Bilan, Robertson, and Walsh are especially sympathetic to the Leavises.

[18] Stephen Spender, review of *Revaluation, Tradition and Development in English Poetry* by F. R. Leavis, *Criterion* 16, 63 (1937): 351.

[19] Lionel Trilling, 'Science, Literature and Culture: A Comment on the Leavis–Snow Controversy', *Universities Quarterly* 17, 1 (1962): 31. The comparison to the stock-market has also been made by others.

Second, Leavis's role as literary arbiter also involved a more positive function. If the critique of commercialism and the mass media in the early 1930s indicated the depth of the crisis, literary criticism might restore affairs to health. 'The essential discipline of an English School is the literary-critical,' Leavis wrote in 1940; 'it is a true discipline, only in an English School if anywhere will it be fostered, and it is of inestimable value. It trains, in a way no other discipline can, intelligence and sensibility together.'[20] Like Richards before him, Leavis sought to improve perceptions of the formal study of English literature. What some considered a pleasant though frivolous irrelevancy he championed as a demanding, socially responsible necessity. Literary criticism helped re-create the 'common reader' that industrialism destroyed. This 'common reader', it should be stressed, bore little resemblance to the 'common culture' of the 1930s; by 'common' Leavis seemed to mean a reader who embraced Leavis's own undefined but highly sophisticated 'standards', though he issued contradictory pronouncements on the precise relationship between cultural values and an educated public.[21] Nevertheless, the mandate of literary criticism involved goals not that far removed from figures such as Reith, Grierson, and Morison. In 1933, Arthur Calder-Marshall called Leavis and his disciples 'popularizers of criticism', a charge that Leavis might have qualified, but one that nevertheless captured the missionary elements of his work.[22] Despite his cultural pessimism and unapologetic élitism, Leavis always remained an uplifter.

As both 'outlaw' and 'redeemer', Leavis exposed himself to charges of self-aggrandizement and hypocrisy. What some praised as a rebel, others endured as a crank; what some venerated as a crusading humanist, others derided as a misanthrope. Leavis argued that great literature enhanced life; others, such as F. L. Lucas, wondered whether the Leavises substituted books for more authentic experience. The Leavises praised qualities in literature that even their friends acknowledged the couple often lacked in life.[23] Yet, however both admirers and detractors interpreted their behaviour, the Leavises managed to draw attention to themselves and to infuse their work with their controversial personalities. They adopted a strategy of cultural dissent that in a variety of ways echoed what they sought to criticize. Although never part of the 'mass civilization' of the 1930s, they bore witness to its potency. As early as 1934 a London writer observed: 'If there is one name in the literary world to-day the mention

---

[20] F. R. Leavis, 'Education and the University: Sketch for an English School', *Scrutiny* 9, 2 (1940): 98–9.
[21] Bilan, op. cit., 50.
[22] Calder-Marshall, 'Standards', *New Statesman*, 739.
[23] T. E. B. Howarth, *Cambridge Between Two Wars* (London: Collins, 1978), 195–6; Thompson, *Leavises*, 49.

of which is likely to cause acrimonious discussion, that name is Leavis. It has become a red rag to all sorts and conditions of bulls.' Forty years later, as the pages of the *TLS* demonstrated, little had changed.[24] By skilfully drawing attention to themselves and by linking their own professional status to the fate of the cause they championed, the Leavises transformed themselves into the celebrities of minority culture.

B. THE LEFT: CULTURE AND THE PREDICAMENTS OF CLASS

The literary Left in Britain during the 1930s shared much with the Leavises and their disciples. For differing reasons, both formulated a radical cultural critique that encompassed the aesthetic élites as well as the commercialized mass media. Underlying this critique lay a profound hostility towards an economic system that corrupted human values and warped artistic expression. This aversion to contemporary realities drew some of its strength from idealized notions of the past and the future. For the Leavises, the 'organic community' once found among villages in the English country-side provided a model of harmony and integrated cultural diversity that industrialism displaced with a mechanized uniformity most distressingly evident in the United States. For the Left in the 1930s, the revolutionary society of the future, like that evolving in the Soviet Union, would eliminate the vicious inequities and cultural impoverishment of class conflict. For both the Leavises and the Left, the crisis of modern times impelled a personal commitment either to gradual or to revolutionary change. The Leavises believed that a new élite, carefully trained to be discriminating in literature, might preserve culture from the civilization which engulfed it. The Left, often fragmented by sectarian disputes, sought means to expose the contradictions of capitalist society and thereby assist in its disintegration. These similarities between the Leavises and the Left should not obscure, however, the numerous differences among them. F. R. Leavis considered the Marxist preoccupation with economic categories to be a mirror image of the bankrupt values which animated capitalist society and, as we have seen, critics on the Left exposed the limitations and pretensions of Leavis's agenda.[25]

---

[24] H. R. Williamson, 'Notes at Random', *Bookman* 86, 511 (1934): 1; for the *TLS*, see the remarkable exchange of letters in the following issues: 28 Nov., 5, 12, 19, and 26 Dec. 1975; and 2 and 9 Jan. 1976.

[25] See Mulhearn, *Moment of* Scrutiny, 85–9. For a good general work on British literature and politics during the Thirties, see Samuel Hynes, *The Auden Generation: Literature and Politics in England in the 1930s* (New York: Viking, 1977).

Above all, the Left in Britain confronted the predicaments of class affiliation. By birth, education, income, taste, and other crucial indicators of social allegiance, many prominent members of the literary Left during the Thirties were undeniably middle class. Their political commitment, like that of other radicals in the British past, placed them in conflict with their own social background and often their deepest personal instincts. Persuaded that 'culture'—itself a problematic word among radicals— should play a substantial role in political change, they needed to resolve the contradictions of their own heritage. How should Marxists regard élite culture? What should be the Left's relationship to the mass media that dominated the attention of the working class? In matters of culture, how might the barriers of social class be overcome? Although these and related questions generated a variety of complex answers that belie patronizing dismissals of the decade for its political simplifications and *naïveté*, the debate over class, culture, and the strategies of literary dissent exposed at least one key division within the literary Left in Britain. In general, writers divided themselves among those who remained attached to certain elements of Liberalism and those who believed in enforcing more strict Marxist categories. This split between the 'Liberal Left' and the 'Orthodox Left' should not be exaggerated; the sectarian disputes and shifting alliances of the decade tended to undermine broad categorizations. Still, on a number of central issues, writers with marked Leftist sympathies such as Stephen Spender and C. Day Lewis adopted notably different positions from more orthodox Marxists such as Christopher Caudwell and Alick West. These differences became apparent not only in their critique of élite, progressive, and commercial culture, but also in their plans to overcome the barriers of class in building a new society. On major issues, Orthodox Marxism and commercial culture found itself in curious agreement.

The notion of 'culture' itself involved problems of definition. C. Day Lewis defended Matthew Arnold's narrow conception of the word, and asked 'how then shall we make "sweetness and light" prevail?' 'Culture' became something that, although previously restricted to privileged élites and always subject to vulgarization by the bourgeoisie, could be more widely diffused among the general population. 'Everyone should be enabled', Day Lewis argued, 'to share in the cultural heritage to the utmost of (his) potentiality.'[26] Others found this prescription too sterile and confining. Searching for a definition more compatible with the materialism of Marxist philosophy, Derek Kahn borrowed the notion from anthropology that culture embraced 'all the facts of social life' and therefore remained 'co-extensive with the whole method of living of a

---

[26] C. Day Lewis, 'Sword and Pen', *Left Review* 2, 15 (1936): 795.

given society'.[27] This more catholic definition, it was claimed, not only facilitated analysis of the economic and technological forces that shaped culture, it also revoked the privileges of a minority who assumed its tastes transcended space and time. Culture could no longer escape from history.

The Liberal Left felt particularly ambivalent about élite culture. Though they acknowledged its passive complicity in maintaining a corrupt social order, they also refused to jettison a rich cultural heritage for purely ideological reasons. The traditional aesthetic hierarchies, they argued, offered revolutionary socialism more than its partisans recognized. 'Good architecture is a criticism of slums,' Spender wrote in *The Destructive Element* published in 1935. 'Good painting is a criticism of the pictures we have, the clothes we wear, all the appearances with which we surround ourselves. Good poetry is a criticism of language. . . . Art has been resisted . . . but no system can afford to be without the criticism of art.'[28] Spender believed that aesthetic excellence and social equality need not be incompatible; élite culture embodied values that enriched the entire society. Assimilated over generations, these values proved too ingrained to be dismissed at will. In poems such as 'In Me Two Worlds', C. Day Lewis expressed the conflict between his commitment to radical political doctrine and his instinctual fidelity to more traditional cultural standards. 'I have never ceased to be aware', he wrote in his autobiography, 'of the forces in myself which kept pulling me towards the past, the status quo, the traditions and assumptions in which I had been brought up.'[29] For Spender and Day Lewis, it became impossible to reject completely the prejudices of their youth and education. Radical politics became the occasion of an inner conflict and turmoil that could not be resolved by ideological formulas. The best art transcended contemporary politics.

Orthodox Marxism found such lingering allegiance to bourgeois culture difficult to tolerate. 'They announce themselves as prepared to merge with the proletariat, to accept its theory and its organization, in every field of concrete living except that of art,' Christopher Caudwell wrote of Spender and Day Lewis in *Illusion and Reality*. 'Now this reservation . . . is absolutely disastrous for the artist. It leads to a gradual separation between his living and his art—his living as a proletarian diverging increasingly from his art as a bourgeois.'[30] In a series of essays published

---

[27] Derek Kahn, 'What is Culture?', *Left Review* 2, 16 (1937): 891.

[28] Stephen Spender, *The Destructive Element* (London: Jonathan Cape, 1935), 229.

[29] C. Day Lewis, *The Buried Day* (London: Chatto and Windus, 1960), 212. For 'In Me Two Worlds', see C. Day Lewis, *A Time to Dance and Other Poems* (London: Hogarth Press, 1935), 15–16. On Day Lewis, see also Sean Day-Lewis, *C. Day-Lewis: An English Literary Life* (London: Weidenfeld and Nicolson, 1981); and Joseph N. Riddel, *C. Day Lewis* (New York: Twayne, 1971).

[30] Christopher Caudwell, *Illusion and Reality: A Study of the Sources of Poetry* (New York: International Publishers, 1947), 285.

posthumously, Caudwell analysed the political limitations of writers such as George Bernard Shaw, D. H. Lawrence, and H. G. Wells and argued for a culture that distanced itself from the persistent 'illusions' of middle-class aesthetic expression.[31] With similar impatience, Edward Upward announced that 'no book written *at the present time* can be "good" unless it is written from a Marxist or near-Marxist viewpoint.' Upward's own novel, *Journey to the Border*, offered a narrative of such political commitment.[32] John Cornford, who like Caudwell would perish in the Spanish Civil War, wrote 'Keep Culture Out of Cambridge' as a protest against the irrelevance of élitist aesthetic concerns.

> There's none of these fashions have come to stay,
> And there's nobody here got time to play.
> All we've brought are our party cards
> Which are no bloody good for your bloody charades.[33]

Cornford, Caudwell, and Upward recognized in varying degrees the limitations of their own ideological purity. Yet, they believed that revolutionary politics could not be compromised by granting artists their traditional privileges. Art could not remain immune from sacrifice.

Elements of the Left also found fault with the progressives and others who sought to uplift the tastes of the general public. Articles in the *Left Review*, for example, criticized the BBC for its social aloofness and reactionary political tendencies. 'You have to be in the B.B.C. to appreciate its feeling of superiority to ordinary mortals,' Raymond East wrote in 1935. '. . . Broadcasting House . . . is remote from reality, knowing nothing of the masses, and caring less.'[34] James Holland, one of three talented cartoonists for the *Left Review*, summarized visually the Left's political dissatisfaction with British broadcasting. In a drawing entitled

---

[31] Id., *Studies and Further Studies in a Dying Culture* (New York: Monthly Press, 1971). On Caudwell, see David Margolis, *The Function of Literature: A Study of Christopher Caudwell's Aesthetics* (New York: International Publishers, 1969); Francis Mulhern, 'The Marxist Aesthetics of Christopher Caudwell', *New Left Review* 85 (1974): 37–58; and E. P. Thompson, 'Caudwell', in *The Socialist Register, 1977*, ed. Ralph Miliband and John Saville (New York and London: Monthly Press, 1977), 228–76.

[32] Edward Upward, 'Sketch for a Marxist Interpretation of Literature', in C. Day Lewis, ed. *The Mind in Chains: Socialism and the Cultural Revolution* (London: Frederick Muller, 1937), 41; Edward Upward, *Journey to the Border* (London: Hogarth Press, 1938). At the end of the novel the central character, a tutor, becomes politically committed and decides to leave the house of a wealthy patron.

[33] Quoted in Peter Stansky and William Abrahams, *Journey to the Frontier: Two Roads to the Spanish Civil War* (1966, reprinted New York: W. W. Norton, 1970), 218. On Cornford, see also Margot Heinemann, 'Louis MacNeice, John Cornford and Clive Branson: Three Left-Wing Poets', in *Culture and Crisis in Britain in the Thirties*, ed. Jon Clark *et al.*, (London: Lawrence and Wishart, 1979), 103–32.

[34] Raymond East, 'B.B.C.', *Left Review* 1, 12 (1935): 523. See also Alan D. Bush, 'Music and the Working-Class Struggle', *Left Review* 2, 12, (1936): 646–51.

'The B.B.C. Exposed', obsequious subordinates bow before a Director General who sees or hears no evil, while at the same time within the drawing the police censor news, Fascists appeal to youth, thugs suppress union organizers, the Navy, Church, and Industry exert undue influence, and a band plays on.[35] To Holland and other members of the Left, culture could not be divorced from politics. Though it proclaimed neutrality, the BBC buttressed the forces of complacency and reaction.

This emphasis on the political implications of cultural messages also informed the Left's extensive and in some ways surprising analysis of the commercialized mass media. Here the split between 'Liberal' and 'Orthodox' became less obvious; all elements on the Left objected to the growing control of the media by fewer and fewer capitalists. In *Money Behind the Screen*, for example, F. D. Klingender and Stuart Legg exposed the closely linked financial interests which increasingly dominated the international production of films. Similar concerns regarding the economic control of British newspapers were not dispelled when Political and Economic Planning published its massive study of the national press. As the veteran editor Hamilton Fyfe put it, 'the British press is now almost entirely under the control of very rich men.'[36] For some commentators, the emphasis became how supply controlled demand, how commercial interests in Britain and America manipulated a passive public. 'The mind is really in chains to-day,' C. Day Lewis wrote in the introduction to a collection of essays on mass culture, and 'these chains have been forged by a dying social system.'[37] This type of analysis tended to accept uncritically the direct causal relationship between 'base' and 'superstructure' that many Marxists considered a simplification of their philosophy. By controlling the means of production, press lords and movie moguls forged a culture that directly reflected their own economic interests.

Yet, although the Left never abandoned its preoccupation with the economics of cultural production, other writers presented broader, more sophisticated analyses of the media. In an essay on the film industry, for example, Arthur Calder-Marshall began with the commonplace assertion that cinema mirrored 'powerful financial interests in the capitalist state', but he also provided specific and often illuminating examples of how the cinema reinforced the status quo. He argued that although Frank Capra's films such as *Mr. Deeds Goes to Town* sometimes dramatized the human

---

[35] James Holland, 'The B.B.C. Exposed', *Left Review* 3, 1 (1937): 29. For the work of another of the talented cartoonists who worked for the *Left Review*, see 'James Boswell: An Introductory Note to the Work of the 1930's', in *The 1930s: A Challenge to Orthodoxy*, ed. John Lucas (Sussex: Harvester; New York: Barnes and Noble, 1978), 265–8.

[36] Klingender and Legg, *Money*; PEP, *Report on the British Press*; Hamilton Fyfe, 'The Press and the People's Front', *Left Review* 2, 15 (1936): 806.

[37] C. Day Lewis, 'Introduction', in *Mind in Chains*, 17.

suffering of the Depression, the characters and plots of these films led audiences to believe that 'the difficulties of our time are not economic but moral.' Capra transformed the Depression into an optimistic moral fable. Calder-Marshall also claimed that newsreels, which might easily document national and regional problems, chose instead to cover events of marginal significance: garden parties, not hunger marches, dominated the screen. Even the British version of the *March of Time*, which employed members of the documentary movement, accentuated positive developments in Britain. 'In the films, as elsewhere, progressive tendencies are muzzled, not by complete suppression, but by semi-expression.'[38] Other writers developed variations of this theme. Elizabeth Coxhead observed that Chaplin's *Modern Times* 'will shake the world, but only with laughter. . . . He thinks things are unfair and upside-down and wrong. But he has no idea what is to be done about it.' Willy Goldman, on the other hand, claimed that the Marx Brothers reacted to the social system far less passively than Chaplin. 'The Marx Brothers are the satirists of the screen,' he wrote. 'They are the free, untrammelled spirit of mankind playing havoc with its would-be oppressors.'[39] In all these commentaries, both critical and celebratory, what may be most striking is how much these writers understood about the cinema. In the 1930s, the Left displayed a knowledge of films difficult to imagine among political radicals of a generation before. Although they believed that the cinema remained deeply implicated in the contemporary crisis, their analysis betrayed an intimacy with the medium that forms a notable sub-text of their arguments. Commercial film provided a shared frame of reference that encompassed its most implacable political opponents.

Like film, the popular daily press attracted critics on the Left who went beyond the more facile versions of economic determinism. Charles Madge, for example, rejected simple-minded models of the relationship between supply and demand. 'The literate mass demands newspapers,' he wrote. 'The newspaper proprietors seek to satisfy the demand. . . . They therefore try to sell the mass a newspaper which satisfies their own requirements as well as the requirements of the mass. Every newspaper is a compromise between these two aims.' Though he acknowledged that the public could be manipulated by advertisers, he also emphasized how the popular press served the needs of its reading public and how, consequently, it 'brought a remarkable change in the intellectual life of the people by giving them some common basis of opinion'. Once a reporter for the *Daily Mirror*,

---

[38] Arthur Calder-Marshall, 'The Film Industry', in *Mind in Chains*, 59, 67, 74.
[39] Elizabeth Coxhead, 'Charlie Chaplin', *Left Review* 2, 6 (1936): 274; Willy Goldman, 'The Marx Brothers too!', *Left Review* 2, 15 (1936): 830–1. On film and the Left during this period, see Bert Hogenkamp, *Deadly Parallels: Film and the Left in Britain, 1929–39* (London: Lawrence and Wishart, 1986).

Madge objected to the unthinking dismissal of the popular press by the cultivated élites. 'Many critics of these things are critics only because they are snobs,' he observed. Madge, whose employment as a popular journalist inspired him to help originate Mass Observation,[40] refused to condescend to the working-class public which his politics intended to serve.

The Liberal Left found it especially difficult to overcome class barriers. 'It is useless to pretend that there is no gulf between us at present,' Spender admitted. '. . . The attitude of the bourgeois communist or socialist to his proletarian ally is inevitably self-conscious.'[41] Goodwill could not erase a lifetime of social distance; class shaped personal identity in ways political commitment suddenly exposed. W. H. Auden, for example, could not shed his essentially aesthetic distaste for urban workers.

> A digit of the crowd, would like to know
> Them better whom the shops and trams are full of,
> The little men and their mothers, not plain but
> Dreadfully ugly.[42]

Ignorance compounded the problem. In an essay for *Fact*, Storm Jameson chronicled the difficulty of a middle-class writer who decided to write about the lower classes. 'He discovers that he does not even know what the wife of a man earning two pounds a week wears, where she buys her food, what her kitchen looks like to her when she comes into it at six or seven in the morning.' Even if these rudimentary details become available, Jameson continued, middle-class writers emphasized their own personal reactions to the discovery. 'What things I am seeing for the first time! what smells I am enduring!'[43] Individualism remained strangely triumphant; workers became the occasion for documenting the feelings of a middle-class mind.

Among the literary Left it was George Orwell, of course, who ruminated most deeply on the issue of class. A complex individual whose life and work continue to attract enormous attention,[44] Orwell transformed his documentary explorations of lower- and working-class life into a series of

---

[40] Charles Madge, 'The Press and Social Consciousness', *Left Review* 3, 5 (1937): 283, 282, 285. A version of this essay was also reprinted in *Mind in Chains*, 147–63. For what Madge learned as a reporter on a popular daily newspaper, see Charles Madge, 'Viewpoint', *TLS*, 14 Dec. 1979, 119.

[41] Stephen Spender, *Forward From Liberalism* (London: Victor Gollancz, 1937), 192, 193.

[42] W. H. Auden, Poem XVII from *Look Stranger*, quoted in A. T. Tolley, *The Poetry of the Thirties* (New York: St Martin's Press, 1975), 158.

[43] Quoted in Jack Lindsay, *After the Thirties: The Novel in Britain and Its Future* (London: Lawrence and Wishart, 1956), 35.

[44] Among many good works on Orwell, see: George Woodcock, *The Crystal Spirit: A Study of George Orwell* (Boston: Little, Brown, 1966); Alex Zwerdling, *Orwell and the Left* (New Haven: Yale University Press, 1974); Peter Stansky and William Abrahams, *The Unknown Orwell* (New York: Alfred A. Knopf, 1972); eid., *Orwell: The Transformation*

extended reflections on bourgeois perception. Unlike many middle-class radicals, Orwell actually lived among the people his politics sought to help. It can be argued, however, that the working classes and the unemployed were never really the main subjects of his books. Despite his pronounced sympathies for the working class and his admirable egalitarian instincts, Orwell wrote fundamentally about himself, or in his novels about figures not unlike himself, who embodied the characteristics and sometimes vague dissatisfactions of his class. Orwell charted the complicated ways in which social class became a prism that determined the shape of reality. As he put it in *The Road to Wigan Pier*, 'all my notions — notions of good and evil, of pleasant and unpleasant, of funny and serious, of ugly and beautiful — are essentially *middle-class* notions; my taste in books and food and clothes, my sense of honour, my table manners, my turns of speech, my accent, even the characteristic movements of my body, are the products of a special kind of upbringing and a special niche about half-way up the social hierarchy.'[45]

This bias, no less powerful because Orwell disarmingly admitted it, informed his view of working-class culture. 'The movies are probably a very unsafe guide to popular taste,' he once observed, 'because the film industry is virtually a monopoly. . . . The same applies to some extent to the daily papers, and most of all to the radio.' Sensitive to the unreconstructed prejudices of other politically committed middle-class intellectuals, Orwell here dismissed the wide appeal of modern forms of communication. Instead, in an essay such as 'Boys' Weeklies', he focused his attention on a type of literature most popular before the First World War. 'A good many boys now regard them as old-fashioned and "slow",' he acknowledged. Though Orwell disapproved of the themes that animated the distinctively English adventure stories, he also clearly regretted the rapidly increasing popularity of faster-paced American substitutes. Nostalgia for disappearing forms of working-class culture, themselves thoroughly commercialized, became implicitly equated with greater social authenticity and a generalized feeling of cultural decline. Yet at the same time, Orwell recognized that the Left needed to provide a popular alternative. 'There is no clear reason why every adventure story should necessarily be mixed up with snobbishness and gutter patriotism.' Britain, Orwell argued, needed a left-wing boys' paper.[46]

(New York: Alfred A. Knopf, 1979); Bernard Crick, *George Orwell: A Life* (Boston: Little, Brown, 1980); and Christopher Norris, ed., *Inside the Myth: Orwell: Views from the Left* (London: Lawrence and Wishart, 1984).

[45] George Orwell, *The Road to Wigan Pier* (1937, reprinted New York: Harcourt Brace Jovanovich, A Harvest Book, 1958), 161.

[46] George Orwell, 'Boys' Weeklies', in *The Collected Essays, Journalism and Letters of George Orwell, vol. 1: An Age Like This, 1920–1940*, ed. Sonia Orwell and Ian Angus (New York: Harcourt, Brace and World, 1968), 461, 462, 483.

This concern for establishing a politically more attractive popular culture emerged as an issue among other writers during the decade. How might entrenched social barriers be overcome to create a new, revolutionary culture that appealed to all classes? What would be the role of traditional élite culture in such a scheme? These and related questions once again revealed divisions among the literary Left. For some the prospects of art became enhanced by the possibility of revolution; Matthew Arnold's culture flourished in Karl Marx's state. The artist, Stephen Spender wrote, 'will fight on the side of the workers . . . because a new age of creative activity can only exist in an environment of peace and social justice . . . [and] because his final goal is an unpolitical age, in which great works of art may be produced.'[47] English writers could point towards the Soviet Union in the 1920s when revolutionary politics allied with experimental art to express the spirit of the times. In England, it was assumed, socialism would permit the wider dissemination of traditional élite culture that commercialism, with its emphasis on the box-office, excluded. 'They come to communism not because they care for the interests of the workers,' Dmitri Mirsky wrote cynically of these authors, 'but because they come to a belief in communism as an organized and disciplined force which can save civilization—which is strong enough to prevent its destruction and to put it on the right path again.'[48]

The more orthodox Left and their allies maintained that it was not the point of revolutionary politics to expand the literary influence of Oxford poets. Though Marxists disagreed on specific tactics, many looked for ways to engage the working class in terms it understood. A revolutionary culture, it was argued, needed to be democratized. Writers should respect the tastes of the working-class public they served. 'So the author must know his people,' Ralph Fox wrote in 1937, 'be as familiar with them as though the men were his constant tavern companions, the women his loving doxies and the children his own brats.'[49] If writers shed their airy preconceptions about art, they might understand what entertained workers. Victor Glenville, for example, praised the films of Frank Capra 'because he has a strong sense of kinship with his audience . . . and a vital sense of common life.'[50] This notion of sympathetic identification was clearly not shared by all orthodox Marxists; cultural prejudices died hard and the notion of a vanguard retained its influential

---

[47] Spender, *Forward From Liberalism*, 37.

[48] Dmitri Mirsky, *The Intelligentsia of Great Britain*, trans. Alec Brown (New York: Covici, Friede, 1935), 133.

[49] Ralph Fox, *The Novel and the People* (1937, reprinted New York: International Publishers, 1945), 115.

[50] Victor Glenville, 'Film Production: A Survey of New Films and Books', *Left Review* 2, 3 (1936): 708.

followers. Yet, for some writers at least, it was the author who needed to pay attention to the reader, not the other way round.

The attempt to simplify language in political literature represented one manifestation of this more populist attitude. 'A great deal of what we write *is* unintelligible jargon to our worker readers,' J. M. Hay admitted in 1935. 'The proletarianization of our language is an imperative task of craftsmanship and should result in the enrichment of written English.'[51] Though Hay's diction undermined his admonition, other Leftists also sought to engage their audience on more egalitarian terms. In an exchange of letters to *Vanguard*, for example, Julian Bell and John Cornford debated the role of art and language in revolutionary politics. This exchange, full of misunderstandings on both sides, involved a number of ironies. Bell, the son of Bloomsbury, accused Cornford, the orthodox Marxist, of overestimating the role of poetry in revolution, and Bell, accused by Cornford of cultural élitism, called for greater clarity in political literature to reach larger audiences: 'At present the propaganda of the Left is conducted in a technical and incomprehensible language: it should be possible for the intellectuals to produce a persuasive prose that would be understood by, and that would affect, anyone able to read.'[52] Echoing Bell's demand, Alec Brown wanted politically committed writers to adopt the slogan 'LITERARY ENGLISH FROM CAXTON TO US IS AN ARTIFICIAL JARGON OF THE RULING CLASS: WRITTEN ENGLISH BEGINS WITH US.' Brown claimed that his novel *Daughters of Albion*, published in 1935, represented such an attempt to reform literary prose.[53]

In an analogous manner, Marxists also argued that the visual arts should be accessible to workers. The arrival of Surrealism in Britain provided a focus for this debate. In 1936 Herbert Read, one of the movement's most articulate defenders, claimed in the *Left Review* that the Surrealists challenged 'not only all bourgeois conceptions of art, but also the official Soviet doctrine of socialist realism. In this matter of art the Surrealists claim, in no uncertain terms, to be more marxist than the Marxians.'[54] This attempt to equate abstract, experimental art with revolutionary politics drew its inspiration from an important period in Soviet development, but it struck fewer responsive chords in the altered political climate of the 1930s. Imitating the bluff language and no-nonsense outlook of

---

[51] J. M. Hay in 'Writers' International', *Left Review* 1, 6 (1935): 221.

[52] Quoted in Stansky and Abrahams, *Journey to the Frontier*, 221.

[53] Quoted in David Smith, *Socialist Propaganda in the Twentieth-Century British Novel* (Totowa, NJ: Rowman and Littlefield, 1978), 81. See also Alec Brown, *Daughters of Albion: A Novel* (London; Boriswood, 1935); and id., *The Fate of the Middle Classes* (London: Victor Gollancz, 1936), esp. 269–71.

[54] Herbert Read, 'Surrealism—the Dialectic of Art', *Left Review* 2, 10 (1936): pp. ii–iii.

a proletarian, the *Daily Worker* dismissed the Surrealist Exhibition in London as élitist frivolity: 'The general impression one gets is that there is a group of young people who just haven't got the guts to tackle anything seriously.'[55] Anthony Blunt took another, less abrasive approach. Within the enclosed world of painting, he argued, Surrealism made an important contribution, but it failed to ground itself in social reality and consequently added little to the workers' struggle. 'Abstract art and, above all, Surrealism . . . serve their purpose in destroying the old standards of Capitalist culture, but they have no roots at all in the proletariat, and therefore their contribution cannot lead up to the new culture which will come with the Socialist state.'[56]

This defence of Socialist Realism followed the Party line, of course, and it might be tempting to view the Orthodox Left as merely the British voice of the Soviet Union. Certainly Soviet developments profoundly affected thinking and action among some Marxists in Britain. Yet, the attempt to engage workers in familiar language and with recognizable images might be something more than a 'revolution from above'. It might also reflect, as has been argued for the Soviets themselves,[57] the desires of intellectuals to reach a larger audience with their revolutionary message. On a variety of issues, it was the Orthodox Marxists, not the Liberal Left, who most consistently distanced themselves from traditional cultural élitism. The tensions and ambiguities that resulted from this process should not be ignored; the self-deception and contradictions of the literary Left in the 1930s have often been noted. Yet, it remains significant the degree to which Orthodox Marxism and commercial culture converged in the 1930s. Some Marxists began to realize the limits of cultural paternalism and embraced methods that press lords and movie moguls long before took for granted. The willingness to identify sympathetically with the public, the use of more colloquial English, and the defence of representational images can be viewed as part of that process.

The mass marketing of Leftist ideology also mirrored this populist impulse. During the first half of the decade, the *Daily Worker* delivered the Party line to the faithful in long, earnest articles reminiscent of nineteenth-century journalism. With the triumph of the Popular Front in France and other changes in official Party policy during the mid-Thirties, however, the *Daily Worker* adopted a less forbidding, more accessible format. The number of illustrations increased; articles became shorter, more concise, and openly colloquial in tone; the women's page concentrated

---

[55] Quoted in Paul C. Ray, *The Surrealist Movement in England* (Ithaca: Cornell University Press, 1971), 151.

[56] Anthony Blunt, 'The "Realism" Quarrel', *Left Review* 3, 3 (1937): 170.

[57] See John Barber, 'The Establishment of Intellectual Orthodoxy in the U.S.S.R., 1928–1934', *Past and Present* 83 (1979): 141–64.

less on ideological and more on domestic concerns. Columns such as 'Alice O'Neal's Home Beauty Parlour' appeared, and there were patterns for serviettes embossed with a hammer and sickle. The editors proclaimed their intention to distribute a 'popular workers' paper'.[58] Though overall circulation remained small, the *Daily Worker* in the late 1930s flattered its more popular rivals with such imitation.

Like the Book-of-the-Month Club in America and the Book Society in England, the Left Book Club discovered a means of wide distribution that cut the prices of individual titles by eliminating the retailer and selling directly to subscribers. In a business noted for the unpredictability of its sales, the publisher gained an assured market while the reader acquired ideologically compatible works at a bargain price. The Left Book Club became a phenomenon of the decade, astonishing Victor Gollancz and other founders by its rapid success. Launched in 1936, the club enrolled over 40,000 members during its first year and could list 57,000 subscribers at its peak in 1939. Like the Book Society, the Left Book Club appealed predominantly to the middle class, though it went beyond its less ideological progenitors in Britain and America by sponsoring a range of activities. Over twelve hundred separate discussion circles met to debate the issues and events that formed the subject of its publications. The monthly paper of the organization, *Left News*, became itself an important political journal. The Left Book Club discovered and solidified a politically committed readership that, although in absolute numbers relatively small, matched the sales of many 'best-selling' novels.[59]

Though never formally committed to a specific ideology, Penguin Books published titles that reflected the Left-wing politics of its major editors. Founded by Allen Lane, whose commitment to the Labour Party did not preclude opposition to trade unions in his own company, Penguin Books followed a long tradition in Britain of publishing popular works, including reprints, at cheap prices. Early in the century, for example, Nelson's Classics, Collins' Pocket Classics, and Dent's Everyman Library all demonstrated the advantages of practising economies of scale in the industry. Then too, various Continental publishers, and in particular Tauchnitz, contributed to the development of the modern paperback.

[58] Alan Howkins, 'Class Against Class: The Political Culture of the Communist Party of Great Britain, 1930–35', in *Class Culture and Social Change*, ed. Gloversmith, 254.

[59] Stuart Samuels, 'The Left Book Club', *Journal of Contemporary History* 1, 2 (1966): 65–86; John Lewis, *The Left Book Club: An Historical Record* (London: Gollancz, 1970); Betty Reid, 'The Left Book Club in the Thirties', in *Culture and Crisis*, ed. Clark *et al.*, 193–207; James Jupp, *The Radical Left in Britain, 1931–1941* (London: Frank Cass, 1982), 96–9; 128–9. On Gollancz, see Ruth Dudley Edwards, *Victor Gollancz: A Biography* (London: Gollancz, 1987).

Penguin Books did not arrive upon the scene unanticipated.[60] The company did, however, vastly accelerate the process whereby individuals could acquire an extensive personal library for a fraction of the cost of traditionally bound volumes. Books became a more accessible commodity. Moreover, Lane claimed that, unlike his competitors, he sought to uplift tastes. '"GOOD BOOKS CHEAP",' he declared in the *Left Review*. 'The clue to the success of the Pelicans and Penguins resides in the first word of the slogan. There are many who despair at what they regard as the low level of the people's intelligence. We, however, believed in the existence in this country of a vast reading public for *intelligent* books at a low price, and staked everything upon it.'[61] This process often involved political education; three of the four major editors for Lane in the late Thirties espoused Left-wing politics and chose titles accordingly. Distinctive in appearance and design, the paperback volumes from Penguin and its subsidiaries addressed many of the same issues, such as unemployment at home and fascism abroad, that preoccupied the Left Book Club. With sales often exceeding 100,000 copies, the Penguin Specials in particular demonstrated once again that in the charged political climate of the 1930s radicalism itself could be successfully commercialized.[62]

In a variety of ways, then, the literary Left in Britain reflected both the thinking and methods of the dominant culture it sought to resist. Distressed by the barriers of class privilege, politically committed writers could no longer retreat into a complacent isolation that constantly validated its own cultural superiority. The Left called upon the social élites within its own ranks to reflect upon its relationship to the vast audience of the working class. Some responded by forwarding an agenda of cultural paternalism not unfamiliar to the partisans of documentary film, the BBC, and other manifestations of cultural uplift in the 1920s. Others recognized the advantages of closely identifying with the tastes of the general public. Still others marketed the ideas of the Left in ways fully consistent with the profit motive. The Left often found itself swimming in the same water as its ideological opponents. To the extent that 'mass' might oppose 'class' culture, commercialism and orthodoxy became different means of attaining similar ends. As the Marxists discovered, however, the version of 'mass' culture that ultimately prevailed

[60] See, among others, Kurt Enoch, 'The Paper-Bound Book: Twentieth-Century Publishing Phenomenon', *Library Quarterly* 24, 3 (1954): 211–25; Robert Escarpit, *The Book Revolution* (London: George G. Harrap; Paris: UNESCO 1966), 26–7; and John Sutherland, 'A Pragmatic Popular Educator', *TLS*, 27 Sept. 1985, 1073–4.

[61] Allen Lane, 'Books for the Millions . . . ', *Left Review* 3, 16 (1938): 969.

[62] J. E. Morpurgo, *Allen Lane. King Penguin: A Biography* (London: Hutchinson, 1979), 120–35. On Lane, see also W. E. Williams, *Allen Lane: A Personal Portrait* (London: The Bodley Head, 1973).

could not be dictated from above. Dissent needed more than good intentions to thrive.

C. J. B. PRIESTLEY: A MAN FOR ALL MEDIA

As an enormously popular novelist and commercially successful playwright in the 1930s, J. B. Priestley might not be considered within the same tradition of cultural criticism as the Leavises and the Left. Yet his view of British society had much in common with these other more isolated and alienated literary contemporaries. Like these other critics, for example, Priestley feared the cultural uniformity and standardization associated with the 'Americanization' of Britain. In his famous conclusion to *English Journey*, he argued that modern developments such as cinema, wireless, Woolworths, cocktail bars, and bungalows embodied 'this new England' that developed rapidly since the First World War and imposed itself uneasily upon the older aristocratic and industrial landscapes. Though fundamentally democratic, this more contemporary England lacked character, individuality, and redeeming idiosyncrasy: 'there is about it a rather depressing monotony,' he lamented.[63] Moreover, like the Leavises and the Left, Priestley formulated a cultural critique that encompassed both the mass media and the cultivated élites. He warned against press lords and movie moguls, but also censured the self-imposed isolation and unforgiving individualism of élitist intellectuals. Finally, Priestley based his critique of inter-war Britain in part upon his pleasant memories of the Edwardian age; nostalgia for an idealized past shaped his vision of modernity. 'The England of 1914', he wrote in 1939 and often reaffirmed thereafter, 'was superior, in every important department of national life, to the England of to-day.'[64] The country of his childhood became the lost national ideal of his maturity.

Yet Priestley's cultural criticism differed from that of many other writers during the Thirties in at least two important respects. First, he presented

---

[63] J. B. Priestley, *English Journey* (1934, reprinted London: William Heinemann in association with Victor Gollancz, 1937), 405, 403.

[64] Id., *Rain Upon Godshill: More Chapters of Autobiography* (1939, reprinted London: Readers' Union and William Heinemann, 1941), 223. See also id., *Margin Released: A Writer's Reminiscences and Reflections* (London: Heinemann, 1962), 87–8; and id., *The Edwardians* (London: Heinemann, 1970), 288–9. For some critical works on Priestley, see Ivor Brown, *J. B. Priestley* (London: Longmans, Green and Company, 1957); Alick West, *The Mountain in the Sunlight: Studies in Conflict and Unity* (London: Lawrence and Wishart, 1958), 155–83; Ladislaus Löb, *Mensch und Gesellschaft Bei J. B. Priestley* (Francke Verlag Bern, 1962); Susan Cooper, *J. B. Priestley: Portrait of an Author* (London: Heinemann, 1970); and John Braine, *J. B. Priestley* (New York: Barnes and Noble, 1979).

himself to his audience as an instinctive egalitarian and democrat who, within the context of English tradition, mistrusted entrenched social and cultural élites. Priestley constantly reaffirmed values that many sophisticated observers deemed commonplace but that, in their very simplicity and deep sincerity, linked a diverse public from all regions and social classes. Such virtues as love of family, sympathy for others, and decency provided a common bond, if not always with critics, among audiences of varying backgrounds and cultural tastes. These universal values shaped both Priestley's literature and his progressive politics. He considered himself a humanist who actually liked common humanity and who described it in all its diversity. Second, unlike Leavis and at least some elements of the Left, Priestley gained a wide following in Britain in the 1930s by embracing and shrewdly exploiting the very media he often criticized. He disseminated his work and made a handsome living by participating in virtually every form of modern communication. He composed poems and essays for cultivated weeklies and quarterlies. He contributed a staggering number of articles to popular newspapers and magazines. He was a best-selling novelist whose books sold hundreds of thousands of copies. He wrote successful plays for the fashionable West End and screenplays for Gracie Fields, the popular film star of the British working classes. In Hollywood he contributed dialogue to films. He appeared in British documentaries and published a documentary account of Britain during the Thirties. The BBC engaged him as a broadcaster and, early in the Second World War, his talks attracted huge audiences. Priestley not only involved himself in a variety of media, he also knew how to adapt a single work for many purposes. A number of his novels and plays became films. Indeed, *The Good Companions* began as a novel, then was transformed into a play, and finally became a film. The BBC broadcast some of his plays, and he composed the first novel for radio, that later also became a film and a book. Priestley was one of the first, for lack of a more elegant term, 'multi-media' personalities. Mass communications helped him establish a national presence and then, in a variety of ways, constantly reinforced it. In the culture of 1930s Britain, it was hard to avoid J. B. Priestley.

Perhaps more than any other single British figure, he represented the common culture of the decade. He appealed to all classes and regions; his work penetrated virtually all the mass media; his ideas and approach drew from both commercial and élite culture. Priestley demonstrated that cultural dissent need not be restricted to the margins of society; it could also serve to reaffirm traditional moral values for a vast public during a period of economic dislocation and rapid technological change. Two aspects of his cultural critique might be examined in more detail. First, as a best-selling author, Priestley confronted a literary culture that often regarded commercial success as an emblem of inferior aesthetic standards. He responded to these critics by vigorously attacking their élitism and by turning his own supposed deficiencies into democratic virtues. Second, Priestley devoted considerable attention to the limitations and cultural dangers of the mass media he so successfully mastered. Here he reiterated many of the stock complaints against the press, cinema, and radio, while at the same time affirming the egalitarian possibilities of modern technology. In both his critique of élite and of commercial culture, Priestley assumed the mantle of the English Everyman, bluff and commonsensical yet not without idealism, wary of change yet susceptible to its exciting possibilities. Though critics often found this persona sentimental and wearying, it proved not without its affecting moments and genuine triumphs.

Priestley's critique of literary culture, like so much else in his work, drew from the peculiarities of his own personal background. Born in Bradford in 1894 the son of a schoolmaster, Priestley spent his childhood and youth in the North, whose prejudices and sensitivities on a wide range of subjects he chose never completely to forget. In September 1914 he enlisted in the Army, where over the next four years he was commissioned as an officer and twice wounded, including by gas. Demobilized in 1919, Priestley studied the recently approved course of English Literature at Cambridge University, where he solidified his commitment to become a professional writer. He married, began a family, and published poems and personal essays that impressed some commentators, but failed to sell. In the mid-1920s his wife died of cancer and his personal affairs reached a crisis. Soon, however, remarriage and the publication of some moderately successful novels allowed him to rebound.[65] In 1929 he published *The Good Companions* and his life changed for ever. The book became an immediate best-seller. Five thousand copies were sold in one day, tens of thousands during the first year, eventually a million copies found their way into print. A new novel published in 1930, *Angel Pavement*, confirmed the success of a year earlier and initially sold almost as many copies.[66] 'His rise and progress have been almost sensationally swift,' the *Bookman* commented. He became a selector for the newly formed Book Society; the *Evening Standard* asked him to contribute their

---

[65] J. B. Priestley to Hugh Walpole, 31 May 1925, J. B. Priestley Papers, Harry Ransom Humanities Research Center, University of Texas at Austin; Priestley, *Margin Released*, 245–84.

[66] Accurate statistics on book sales prove difficult to obtain. For *Good Companions* and *Angel Pavement*, however, see 'J. B. Priestley', Reference Biography Series, Reference Division, Central Office of Information, which can be found in the British Film Institute. See also J. B. Priestley to Hugh Walpole, 22 Dec. 1931, J. B. Priestley Papers, Ransom Research Center.

literary column, once written by Arnold Bennett; American publishers invited him on lucrative promotional tours.[67] Priestley became a wealthy man, whose house in Hampstead attested to his success as a best-selling literary author. He had conquered Grub Street during a difficult period for men of letters.[68]

Yet if literature provided him with money, it did not assure him status within some intellectual circles. Priestley often received flattering reviews in the élite press, but he also sustained withering criticism from respected writers and professional critics. The short-lived but highly influential *Criterion*, edited by T. S. Eliot, referred to 'his roast-beef and beer attitude towards literature' and connected him with other writers who were 'never carried away by the agonies of a great imagination'. *Scrutiny* dismissed him out of hand: 'there could be no serious discussion of modern literature', F. R. Leavis wrote, 'that should not be an implicit condemnation of Mr. Walpole and Mr. Priestley.' Graham Greene also linked Priestley with Walpole, calling them 'rather crude minds representing no more of contemporary life than is to be got in a holiday snapshot'.[69] Priestley's hearty attitude towards literature and his frequent defences of the 'common man' struck some observers as humbug, an artificial pose repugnant to refined sensibilities. 'I see Priestley consolidating his idea of himself,' Virginia Woolf wrote in her diary concerning one of his articles in the *News Chronicle*. '. . . Begins his article, Helping to receive refugees &c . . . thus bringing before himself P. the active, the helper in the cause of common life: & so doubtless releasing his rush of ideas. But I dont [*sic*] like P's figment, necessary as it may be.'[70]

Priestley's reaction to such criticism was complicated. Naturally, he dreaded accusations that suggested he was an intellectual fraud, not only because such charges proved impossible to answer but also, more important, because they confirmed his personal doubts about his own limitations. In his autobiography, he reflected upon the feelings of professional writers 'who have talent but not genius'. 'We may come to

---

[67] On Priestley and the Book Society, see J. B. Priestley to Hugh Walpole, 11 Mar. 1932, J. B. Priestley Papers. See also *The Times*, 18 Oct. 1929, 23; and 3 Dec. 1932, 8; and 'Mr. Priestley—*and* Mr. Walpole', *Bookman* 76, 451 (1929): 49.

[68] For contemporary comments on the profession of letters in this period, see Joseph, *Commercial Side of Literature*; Stanley Unwin, *The Truth About Publishing*, 3rd edn. (London: George Allen and Unwin, 1929); Sydney Horler, *Writing For Money* (London: Ivor Nicholson and Watson, 1932); Frank Swinnerton, *Authors and the Book Trade* (New York: Alfred A. Knopf, 1932); and Arthur Waugh, 'Authors, Publishers and the Public', *Quarterly Review* 259, 514 (1932): 129–44.

[69] Anonymous review of J. B. Priestley, *Thomas Love Peacock*, in *Monthly Criterion* 7, 3 (1928): 287–8; F. R. Leavis, 'What's Wrong With Criticism?', *Scrutiny* 1, 2 (1932): 144; Graham Greene, 'Subjects and Stories', in *Footnotes to Film*, ed. Davy, 58.

[70] Virginia Woolf, *The Diary of Virginia Woolf, vol. 5: 1936–1941*, ed. Anne Olivier Bell (San Diego: Harcourt Brace Jovanovich, 1984), 235.

have some pride in our ideas and skill, industry and experience—and great genius may never stoop to consider such matters—but from first to last we are never really proud of our *selves*.'[71] Behind the studied mask of heartiness and resilience, Priestley occasionally revealed great vulnerability to hostile criticism. To friends and admirers, he talked about how 'They'—certain unnamed detractors—never forgave him his enormous popularity and fame. 'If you are "popular",' he wrote in 1933, '. . . you may depend upon it that in certain circles, supposed to consist of people who are interested in literature, your last chance is gone.'[72]

Priestley was not without defences, however, against his intellectual antagonists. He argued that élite literary culture, for all its claims to superior insight, lacked the basic humanity and brotherhood which great art ought to confer. He pointed out that F. R. Leavis, for example, sought to restrict the understanding of literature to a tiny and privileged minority, rather than the broader audience which the most penetrating artists often affected. 'They behave more like members of a very small and terribly exclusive club', he wrote of Leavis and his followers, 'than ardent disciples of a great new artist. They do not address us like men and brothers. In high, mincing, disdainful voices they suggest their own invincible superiority.'[73] Priestley spoke of the 'strange, enduring malevolence' of intellectual novelists such as Aldous Huxley: 'He belongs to the melancholy school of Swift, the haters of life. His grievance grows like a malignant tumour.'[74] Priestley argued that such novelists and critics drained literature of all humaneness and vitality, replacing it with arid puzzles that briefly amused the cultivated but deliberately alienated everyone else. In *The Good Companions*, he created a character who embodied the pretensions and affected speech of the modern aesthete. 'We Statics—that's what we call ourselves—awfully good name, isn't it?—believe that Art has got to be beyond emotion. Life and Art have got absolutely choked up with filthy emotion, and we say the time has come for them to be—what shall I say?—feelingless, all calm and clear.'[75] Priestley attacked élitist writers and intellectuals for the same fundamental reason that, in a different forum, he disparaged Tories and other conservative political apologists. He argued that democracy ought to be inclusive, not exclusive. Artists ought to embrace, not abjure humanity.

---

[71] Priestley, *Margin Released*, 69–70.

[72] Id., 'Some Reflections of a Popular Novelist', in *Essays and Studies by Members of the English Association*, vol. 28 (Oxford: Clarendon Press, 1933), 158; interview with J. B. Priestley, 18 Sept. 1978.

[73] J. B. Priestley, 'Men, Women and Books', *Evening Standard*, 10 Mar. 1932, 11.

[74] Id., *I For One* (London: John Lane, The Bodley Head, 1923), 119; id., 'Men, Women and Books', *Evening Standard*, 4 Feb. 1932, 7. See also id., *Talking* (London: Jarrolds, 1926), 15.

[75] Id., *The Good Companions* (London: William Heinemann, 1929), 58–9.

Priestley also defended himself against his critics by transforming his perceived limitations as an artist and individual into literary advantages and personal strengths. His regional and class background became a source of defensive pride whenever he encountered patronizing attitudes about the North or about the working and lower-middle classes. In some revealing letters to Hugh Walpole he acknowledged that he suffered from 'a social inferiority complex', but he claimed that his background gave him access to social classes and situations that vastly enriched his experience and contributed to his range as a novelist. 'Provincial life—working and lower-middle class stuff . . . is my matter obviously,' he wrote in 1928. '. . . I really do know about these people because I've spent a lot of time in pubs and low music halls and at football matches—especially the early impressionable years. . . . One of the weaknesses of fiction today is that most of the novelists who can write have not an extensive acquaintance with the people and life of this country.'[76] Unlike some Marxists in the Thirties who struggled to comprehend working-class habits, Priestley claimed to understand the mentality of workers. He took pride in his portrait of Jess Oakroyd from *The Good Companions* and he could argue with some justification that *Angel Pavement*, published in 1930, provided one of the first searching examinations of the precarious working conditions during the Thirties.[77] Some Marxists experimented with works which they hoped workers might understand; Priestley wrote scripts for Gracie Fields that became box-office hits in working-class districts.

Priestley's personal history also served as a bridge to middle-class life. He set many of his novels and virtually all of his plays during the Thirties in landscapes familiar to the British middle classes. The drama *Laburnum Grove*, for example, unfolded in one of the suburban bungalows developed in the inter-war period. Written for the theatre and later successfully adapted as a film, the play explored the anxieties and preoccupations of middle-class respectability. When the father of a typical suburban household laconically revealed that he obtained his assets illegally, each member of his family must come to terms with their own social identity. Other plays by Priestley such as *Dangerous Corner*, *Time and the Conways*, and *Eden End* also took place in settings easily recognizable to West End audiences.[78] As a prosperous London author with roots in

[76] J. B. Priestley to Hugh Walpole, 12 Apr. and 29 Mar. 1928, J. B. Priestley Papers, Ransom Research Center.

[77] J. B. Priestley to Hugh Walpole, 15 Aug. 1928; J. B. Priestley to Eugene Sexton, 6 Oct. ?1934, J. B. Priestley Papers, Ransom Research Center.

[78] On Priestley and the theatre, see Priestley, *Margin Released*, 200–12; Morton Eustis, 'On Time and the Theatre: Priestley Talks About Playwriting', *Theatre Arts Monthly* 22, 1 (1938): 46–55; Aubrey Williamson, *Theatre and Two Decades* (London: Rockliff, 1951), 63–71; and Gareth Lloyd Evans, *J. B. Priestley—The Dramatist* (London: Heinemann, 1964).

the provincial bourgeoisie, Priestley could draw on experiences from a number of social strata.

Priestley was sometimes accused of targeting his audience, and certainly he excelled on occasion at writing for specific working- or middle-class publics. Still, it was the continuity among his works rather than any class-bound differences that perhaps best explains his wide appeal during the 1930s. In both his novels and his plays, Priestley created characters and developed themes whose appeal, he proudly claimed, transcended class and regional lines. *The Good Companions* brought together individuals from a number of classes, all of whom wanted to escape from the daily routines and numbing predictability of their everyday lives. The novel's gallery of memorable characters, its optimism, and cosy atmosphere helped assure its success as a novel, play, and film during a period of social divisiveness and economic stress in Britain. Even in his more daring and demanding works, Priestley sought a public that went beyond the social confines of a single class. In *Johnson Over Jordan*, for example, perhaps his most experimental play of the decade, he sought to universalize the ambitions and fears of a middle-class business man whom, in an essay on the drama, he described as 'this man of our time, an ordinary citizen of the suburbs', 'an English Everyman'.[79] Like other authors who addressed large themes and sought broad audiences, Priestley was often only partially successful both at the box-office and among critics. Yet his provincial upbringing and his more than casual exposure to different social classes prior to the 1930s helped him discover some common denominators among classes.

An unfashionable background was not the only disadvantage that Priestley converted into an asset. He also made a virtue of necessity whenever he reflected upon his own talents and role as a professional writer. In 1936, he defined himself as 'a professional man of letters on the solid old eighteenth-century plan, prepared to write anything'.[80] However accurate, this self-characterization linked Priestley with a literary tradition that countered the Romantic insistence on genius and on the struggles of artistic creation which still gripped many twentieth-century writers and critics. Priestley identified himself with a century that, in a slightly different context, the Leavises also praised. He deflected sneers about his originality and motivation by invoking a notion of art that antedated the assumptions of his detractors. Moreover, by viewing writing as a craft, Priestley grouped himself with artisans and craftsmen in other

---

[79] J. B. Priestley, *Johnson over Jordan: The Play and All About It* (London: William Heinemann, 1939), 119, 122.

[80] J. B. Priestley, 'Self-Portrait', typescript for George Schreiber's Portraits and Self-Portraits, [pages unnumbered], 1936, J. B. Priestley Papers, Ransom Research Center.

trades rather than with aesthetes whose pretensions he often satirized but whose impulses he sometimes shared. Unlike some writers who acknowledged residence in Grub Street, Priestley was neither an anti-intellectual nor a cynic. He appreciated and described in print the often mystical feelings of transcendence which great art conveyed.[81] He also enjoyed and defended pleasures which some artists found vulgar. Priestley considered himself a cultural pluralist. He rejected the label 'middlebrow' which he found imprecise and substituted instead another term that described his eclectic tastes. 'If you can carry with you your sense of values,' he wrote in 1927, 'your appreciation of the human scene, your critical faculty, to Russian dramas, variety shows, football matches, epic poems, grand opera, race meetings, old churches, new town halls, musical comedies, picture galleries, boxing booths, portfolios of etchings, bar parlours, film shows, symphony concerts, billiard matches, dance halls, detective stories, tragedies in blank verse, farces, and even studio teas and literary parties . . . than you are a Broadbrow.'[82]

Priestley's evaluation of literary culture in Britain, then, involved a number of cross-currents. He repudiated the anti-democratic elements within élite culture, and rejected its narrow definition of acceptable pleasures. Yet he also appreciated the claims of art to transcendence and proved himself personally vulnerable to criticism from those who defended high aesthetic standards. Priestley justified his own status as a best-selling writer both within the terms of the English literary tradition and by virtue of his personal insight into the predicaments of individuals from all classes. In his defence of the common man and cultural pluralism, Priestley saw himself as distinct from many other writers. 'Unlike most of my intellectual contemporaries,' he wrote in 1933, 'I still retain some belief in democracy.'[83] This faith did not always extend, however, to the commercialized mass media which, like Priestley, claimed to speak for democracy. If when confronted with élitism Priestley sometimes became a militant commoner, he was not an uncritical defender of the popular press, film, and radio. In each case, he expressed reservations about the media that helped establish his national credentials.

Though he wrote extensively for the popular press, Priestley instinctively distrusted press lords and their brand of news. One of his earliest published essays ridiculed a 'Newspaper King' and in the 1930s he devoted an entire

---

[81] See, for example, J. B. Priestley, *The Balconniny and Other Essays* (London: Methuen, 1929), 82–8; and id., *Midnight on the Desert: An Excursion into Auto-biography During a Winter in America, 1935–36* (New York: Harper and Brothers, 1937), 159–61.

[82] Id., *Open House: A Book of Essays* (London: William Heinemann, 1927), 166–7. See also id., *Margin Released*, 188–9.

[83] Id., 'About Myself', *Listener*, 21 June 1933, 991.

novel to satirizing the excesses of popular journalism.[84] *Wonder Hero* narrated the tale of a working-class individual from the North whom the popular daily press in London mistakenly elevated into a heroic national figure. In their insatiable desire for larger circulations, the popular newspapers in the novel manufactured human-interest stories that distorted the realities of working-class life. 'We're not a newspaper in the old-fashioned sense of the word,' a journalist tells the bewildered 'Wonder Hero'. 'There are still one or two of them left, and they sell about one copy for every ten of ours. No, we're not really a newspaper, we're a circus in print, a vaudeville show, a Fun City, a daily comic.' Like most other critics of the popular press who championed the political causes of Labour and the Left, Priestley distanced working-class readers from the commercialized newspapers they purchased by the millions.

He opened the *Daily Tribune*. . . . His attitude toward it was typical. To begin with, he had no particular respect for it. Gone was that reverence which his father and his grandfather had had for the news-sheet, the printed page. He did not believe every statement it made, nor did he disbelieve. He read it in a curious state of suspended belief or disbelief, the mood of a man at a conjuring entertainment. It . . . was not life and the world as he knew them . . . but of course it might easily be life and the world as they existed anywhere else. And he could not help being flattered by the endless attentions of the *Tribune*, which was only too willing to do everything for him on earth. . . . He felt it was a grand pennyworth, no matter whether it lied or told the truth.[85]

Priestley rejected the notion that the popular press embodied authentic working-class consciousness, though he acknowledged that it entertained its readers. He preferred the Liberal press of his Edwardian youth and tried to make his fictional protagonist a representative figure of working-class scepticism and cultural independence. Ramsay MacDonald praised *Wonder Hero*; a trade paper of the newspaper industry called it 'a good laugh rather than a good book'.[86] Priestley understood the appeal of the modern press, but he feared and denied its cultural influence.

Though troubled by the excesses of popular journalism, Priestley devoted considerably more of his attention to the cinema. He often included observations on film in his novels and essays; he wrote original

[84] For the essay, see id., 'The Room of Lost Souls', in *Brief Diversions: being Tales, Travesties and Epigrams* (Cambridge: Bowes and Bowes, 1922), 28. For a listing of press and other articles by Priestley, see Alan Edwin Day, *J. B. Priestley: An Annotated Bibliography* (New York: Garland Publishing, 1980).

[85] J. B. Priestley, *Wonder Hero* (London: William Heinemann, 1933), 288, 7. For Priestley's intentions in writing this novel, see J. B. Priestley to Hugh Walpole, 9 Aug. 1933, J. B. Priestley Papers, Ransom Research Center.

[86] Ramsay MacDonald to J. B. Priestley, 24 Aug. 1933, J. B. Priestley Papers, Ransom Research Center; 'Building a Newspaper Hero by "Ballyhoo:" J. B. Priestley's New Novel', *World's Press News*, 31 Aug. 1933, 9.

scripts and adaptations for both the British and American industries; he appeared in documentaries. The commercial cinema provoked in him the ambivalence he felt towards virtually any new technology or modern development that appealed to the mass audience, but which threatened to undermine cherished British traditions. Certainly he acknowledged the democratic tendencies of the medium and sympathized with those who gained enjoyment at the great cinema palaces. In the late 1920s he published an essay on a 'Super-super Kinema' which described sympathetically the unaccustomed pleasures that these American-inspired institutions conferred upon average individuals. 'I began to feel that I had wandered into the Arabian Nights,' he exclaimed.[87] A character in one of his later novels elaborated upon why it was an 'age of celluloid', and in *Angel Pavement* Priestley recounted in detail the experiences of a lonely young clerk attending a film on a Saturday evening in London. 'He arrived at his second destination, the Sovereign Picture Theatre, which towered at the corner like a vast spangled wedding-cake in stone. It might have been a twin of that great teashop he had just left; and indeed it was; another frontier outpost of the new age.'[88] Though the images on the screen could not entirely compensate for the character's loneliness, he had survived another weekend with his hopes for romantic love unextinguished.

Yet if for Priestley the great cinema palaces surrounded ordinary individuals with luxury, the films engulfed them in aesthetic poverty. With an insider's knowledge of its workings, Priestley joined a legion of writers who declared that Hollywood was not for real. It preoccupied itself with fantasies and superficial glamour that he thought should be resisted, not indulged. Its films, he wrote in 1936, were 'a triumph of skill and organization, of clever men working together for one end, men with everything at their finger tips but real art, the desire to reveal the vision of life, the honest unfolding of the mind, . . . all of which they had never known or said goodbye to, long ago, on the *Chief* between Chicago and Los Angeles.'[89] Priestley classed the movie moguls of Hollywood with the press lords of England as men obsessed with commercialism at the expense of all other values. They sold films as commodities and treated audiences like customers. They made deals. Any attempt to improve movies needed to surmount the obsession of the industry with financial success.

[87] J. B. Priestley, 'Super-super', in id., *Balconinny*, 173.

[88] Id., *Faraway* (New York: Harper and Brothers, 1932), 285; id., *Angel Pavement* (London: William Heinemann, 1930), 174.

[89] Id., *They Walk in the City* (London: William Heinemann, 1936), 398–9. See also J. B. Priestley to Hugh Walpole, 8 Dec. 1937, J. B. Priestley Papers, Ransom Research Center. On the relationship of Hollywood fantasy and working-class reality, see J. B. Priestley, *Albert Goes Through* (London: William Heinemann, 1933).

Still, film companies paid their writers, including Priestley, very well.[90] Reservations about its blatant materialism did not inhibit him from occasionally joining the industry and adopting its narrative conventions. A professional writer, he often observed, needed to make a living and, moreover, to communicate with the mass audience it became necessary to work within the media that most engaged them. Priestley proved especially adept at integrating his reservations about modern commercialism into popular screenplays for British producers. Although he once claimed that it was easier to write about Americans than about the British working class, his scripts for Gracie Fields became important vehicles in her rise to British stardom.[91] Released in the mid-Thirties, *Sing As We Go* and *Look Up and Laugh* contained portraits of working-class life and attitudes that were remarkable for two, somewhat antithetical reasons. First, in *Sing As We Go* the documentary footage shot in Blackpool as background for the main story captured the Northern working class in ways that the British documentary movement, with its more self-conscious emphasis on such subjects, neglected altogether. The film contained many evocative images of the popular Northern resort: a group of men quietly enjoying their beer; a noisy crowd walking among the various amusements; a policeman leading by the hand two lost and crying children. With its strong working-class accents throughout and its willingness to show workers in settings familiar to them, *Sing As We Go* embodied a realism absent from most British films of the period.

On the other hand and perhaps less surprising, Priestley's two original screenplays for Gracie Fields operated well within a formulaic framework long familiar to Hollywood and increasingly the despair of the Orthodox Left during the Thirties. These films implicitly accepted the inequities of the status quo and affirmed the traditional values which Priestley associated with working-class life. In *Sing As We Go* Gracie Fields led the workers in song, not protest; as a cheerful heroine and combative optimist in the face of unemployment and other crises, she showed no bitterness, only resourcefulness. She lost her man to a prettier rival, but she remained enamoured of romantic love and the personal embodiment of cheeky sentimentality. In *Look Up and Laugh* she rallied small shop-keepers against a large commercial firm that sought to destroy a village

---

[90] Though information is scarce on Priestley's fees for working in the film industry or for having his novels and plays adapted for the screen, see J. B. Priestley to Hugh Walpole, 27 May 1934, J. B. Priestley Papers, Ransom Research Center; and 'Budgets for Films', Basil Dean Papers, British Film Institute, London.

[91] J. B. Priestley, 'English Films and the English People', *World Film News and Television Progress* 1, 8 (1936): 3. On Gracie Fields, see among others Richards, *Dream Palace*, 169–190 and Gracie Fields, *Sing As We Go* (London: Frederick Muller, 1960). See also Basil Dean, *Mind's Eye: An Autobiography, 1927–1972* (London: Hutchinson, 1973), 204–7.

market-place and construct a modern department store that catered to wealthy patrons. A repository of vivid characters, the local market clearly represented an authentic English tradition threatened by the destructive forces of modernity. Despite the sinister machinations of the store owner, the intrusions of the local élite, and the vacillation of incompetent politicians, Fields helped save the village market and reconcile the two opposing sides. Tradition was preserved; the community redeemed itself through the moral integrity and hearty resilience of common men and women.

Among the more popular mass media, however, it was neither in the press nor from the cinema that Priestley attracted widest attention to himself and to his opinions. His involvement in broadcasting, one of his greatest successes during this period, began inauspiciously. In 1929, a BBC official complained that 'Priestley himself has a very unattractive voice on the microphone, and after using him once or twice we have rather ploughed him.'[92] Shortly before a talk in 1932 he somehow mislaid his manuscript and, as *The Times* reported, 'for the whole of that quarter of an hour nothing was heard from the national station of the B.B.C.'[93] Priestley disputed his fees and complained bitterly to BBC officials about the unwillingness to publicize adequately a series of his broadcasts.[94] More important, he often criticized the Corporation in the popular press, in 1929 calling it 'a futile kind of night school'. A few years later in a different newspaper he observed that 'there seems something both amateurish and patronizing about the B.B.C. As if the charitable lady of the manor had got up an entertainment to keep the men of the village out of the public houses.'[95] Like other radio critics for the popular press such as Collie Knox, Priestley considered the middle-class paternalism of the BBC to be an antiquated, insulting, and largely ineffective approach to working-class audiences. To some, he must have seemed a difficult

[92] Hilda Matheson to Director of Programmes, 18 Nov. 1929, BBC Written Archives Centre, Reading.

[93] 'Comedy at Broadcasting House', *The Times*, 11 Oct. 1932, 11. Worse, the broadcast was to have gone to America and, as the *Daily Telegraph* reported the same day, 'the sixty stations of the Columbia Broadcasting Corporation network, to which the talk was to have been relayed, listened to the B.B.C. clock.' See also J. B. Priestley, 'Complaints of B.B.C. Speakers', *World Film News and Television Progress* 1, 9 (1936): 25.

[94] See J. B. Priestley to Ackerley, 7 and 9 Sept. 1932; and J. B. Priestley to Siepmann, 5 Apr. 1933, BBC Written Archives Centre, Reading. On the dispute over inadequate publicity, see also J. B. Priestley to Hugh Walpole, 7 Apr. 1933, J. B. Priestley Papers, Ransom Research Center.

[95] Id., 'Wireless Without Tears: Turning Our Drawing Rooms into Kindergartens—Too Much Talk and Too Little Music', *Daily Mirror*, 28 Jan. 1929; id., 'If I Ran the B.B.C.', *Sunday Dispatch*, 24 July 1938. See also id., 'Cash, Comics and Culture at the B.B.C.', *Star*, 16 Jan. 1935. More favourable comments appear in id., *Apes and Angels: A Book of Essays* (London: Methuen, 1928), 25–31.

individual to please. He criticized the popular press and cinema for its commercialism; he mocked the BBC for its paternalism. It appeared that neither the market nor public control satisfied him.

Yet in broadcasting, as with the popular press and commercial cinema, Priestley managed to master the media he so frequently disparaged. Despite his disagreements with BBC officials, he broadcast a number of successful talks during the Thirties, and late in the decade the Corporation commissioned from him *Let the People Sing*, described as 'the first novel to be written for broadcasting'.[96] It was his 'Postscripts', however, that solidified his reputation as one of the most effective broadcasters in the BBC's young history. Usually scheduled immediately after the nine o'clock News on Sunday evenings, these broadcasts in 1940, followed by a second series in 1941, consisted essentially of brief personal reflections upon a wide variety of topics, many of them deceptively mundane. In late September 1940, for example, he described a trip to his native Bradford where, while looking over the lamentable results of a German bombing raid, he noticed that a favourite eating-house which he recalled from his youth, still exhibited a model of one of its excellent meat and potato pies in its heavily damaged front display. In a subdued, conversational tone, Priestley talked about the shop, its owners, and the enduring model pie. He concluded:

And now, I suppose, all my more severe listeners are asking each other why this fellow has to go on yapping about his pies and nonsense at a time like this when the whole world is in a turmoil, the fate of empires is in the balance, and men, women and children are dying terrible violent deaths; to which I can only reply, that we must keep burnished the bright little thread of our common humanity that still runs through these iron days and black nights; and that we are fighting to preserve and, indeed, I hope to enlarge that private and all-important little world of our own reminiscence and humour and homely poetry in which a pie that steamed for forty-five years and successfully defied an air-raid to steam again has its own proper place.[97]

Unlike the abstract rhetoric of some propagandists and politicians, Priestley's broadcasts focused on highly specific and concrete examples of the humane values which united the British. Delivered in his distinctive Yorkshire accent, once considered inappropriate for broadcasting, Priestley's oral essays quietly reaffirmed commonplace values at a time of national peril. What earlier his critics labelled as banal or sentimental in his social and cultural criticism, now assumed a fresh urgency.

---

[96] *The Times*, 10 Nov. 1939. See also 'Mr. Priestley and the Microphone', *Listener*, 31 Aug. 1939, 414; and J. B. Priestley, *Let the People Sing* (London: Heinemann, 1939).
[97] Id., *All England Listened: The Wartime Broadcasts of J. B. Priestley* (1940–1, reprinted New York: Chilmark Press, 1967), 125.

The 'Postscripts' attained an astonishing level of general popularity and critical acclaim. During some weeks more people listened to Priestley than to 'Music Hall', the BBC's most popular programme other than the News. 'Listeners feel him to be human and kindly and above all, not *remote*,' a survey of opinion reported in 1941. '. . . The average man in the street tacitly recognizes that an immense gulf separates him from the famous. Anyone who can bridge that gulf naturally and easily has a tremendous pull.'[98] People wrote thousands of letters to Priestley, expressing their gratitude in often moving terms.[99] He was stopped in the street and congratulated. The pie shop was photographed and appeared in the national press, which praised him lavishly.[1] The *New Statesman* said that as a broadcaster he was 'the one great discovery in this war'. *The Economist* wrote that 'he captured the mood of the people and put it into the plain words that the people could understand.'[2] Graham Greene, one of his most persistent detractors in the 1930s, wrote in the *Spectator* that before the war he, like many others, 'regarded Mr. Priestley with some venom. We felt that as a novelist he represented a false attitude . . . that he clothed himself in the rags of a Victorian tradition. He was continually speaking for England, and we very much doubted whether *The Good Companions* or *Let the People Sing* represented England at all.' With the coming of the war, Greene continued, this view of Priestley changed dramatically. 'He became in the months that followed Dunkirk a leader second in importance only to Mr. Churchill. And he gave us what our other leaders have always failed to give us—an ideology.'[3]

The 'Postscripts' confirmed Priestley's special place within the common culture of the period. His method and ideas shared much with another prominent figure of the decade. Like the film director Frank Capra in America, Priestley formulated a vision of national character that transcended the usual social and geographic boundaries and, like Capra, he was often accused of sentimentality and pandering to the mass audience. Though understandable, these charges underestimated the craftsmen whose work,

---

[98] Listener Research Report LR/231, 14 Mar. 1941; Listener Research Bulletin Number 27, 24 Mar. 1941; BBC Written Archives Centre, Reading.

[99] See, for example, Ian MacAlister to J. B. Priestley, 16 Oct. 1941, J. B. Priestley Papers, Ransom Research Center.

[1] See, for example, *Daily Mail*, 2 July 1940; *Star*, 18 July 1940; *Yorkshire Post*, 16 July 1940.

[2] 'Critic', 'A London Diary', *New Statesman and Nation* 17 Aug. 1940, 153; 'The Mood of Progress', *The Economist*, 26 Oct. 1940, 509. See also Ian McLaine, *Ministry of Morale: Home Front Morale and the Ministry of Information in World War Two* (London: George Allen and Unwin, 1979), 98.

[3] Graham Greene, 'A Lost Leader', *Spectator*, 13 Dec. 1940, 646. On the controversy surrounding the termination of the 'Postscripts', see Asa Briggs, *The History of Broadcasting in the United Kingdom, vol. 3: The War of Words* (London: Oxford University Press, 1970), 320–3; and Curran and Seaton, *Power Without Responsibility*, 174–7.

many critics acknowledged, went beyond the customary formulas of popular entertainment. Often situating their work in realistic settings with credible protagonists, both Capra and Priestley wove narratives that dramatized the powerful forces opposed to their own democratic visions of community. They pointed to the dangers of concentrated ownership, particularly within the mass media, and they often mocked the pretensions of the cultivated and the socially prominent. To Priestley, the press lords of Fleet Street and the moguls of Hollywood failed to represent English tastes any more than Oxbridge intellectuals embodied authentic English culture. Troubled by the decay of tradition and yet committed to the democratic potential of new technologies, he defended values and sentiments which he associated with ordinary men and women. As with Capra, this defence involved a good deal of calculation and consummate showmanship which detractors found manipulative and hypocritical. Yet both figures serve as useful representatives of the common culture of the period. Their work provided a shared frame of reference for individuals from all social classes and, in the case of Priestley, became an embodiment of national character at a difficult moment in British history.

Priestley established a form of cultural dissent marked by its social inclusiveness and cultural accessibility. In his studied and clearly successful role as an English Everyman, he criticized those elements of commercial and élite culture which excluded, manipulated, or patronized average citizens. He mistrusted those of wealth and economic power who not unlike himself claimed to speak for democracy, but he also warned against the false cultural authorities who with self-conscious disdain transformed the humane arts into a privileged activity. He was, at bottom, a populist and an egalitarian whose roots, paradoxically enough, lay as much in the America that Tocqueville described, as they did in the North of Edwardian England. He spoke for those traditions within both countries that instinctively disliked anyone who asserted a natural superiority over others. Priestley was a leveller in an age when mass communications often rewarded such a philosophy. A master of the media, he reached an enormous audience who shared many of his dissatisfactions and who, when threatened by a grave economic crisis at home or endangered by an enemy abroad, assented to his values.

When Priestley broadcast his 'Postscripts' early in the Second World War, he addressed a nation of great cultural diversity. Intricacies of class, region, generation, and other determinants of cultural taste made it difficult to discern the separate strands that fashioned the overall pattern. Broad differences among classes, for example, sometimes concealed more subtle differences within them. It was not simply that bourgeois tastes differed from those of the working classes. Within the middle classes themselves, preferences on a wide range of subjects varied markedly between the upper and lower ranks within these loosely defined social strata. Isolation among the social classes exacerbated rivalries within them. Moreover, these differences became compounded by regionalism and other variations. Once again, it was not simply that North and South diverged on a variety of issues. Manchester might respond in ways that Newcastle did not. The provinces took pride in distinguishing themselves from London; the suburbs, new and old, amalgamated features from both rural and urban life. Regionalism added complexity to social class, just as generational differences became an increasingly pronounced feature of British cultural life. In the twentieth century, youth carved out its own culture separate from that of its elders. Generational affiliation sometimes superseded class allegiance as a primary constituent of taste. And of course there were always individuals who utterly confounded all these fallible categories. Class, region, generation, and personal idiosyncrasy each contributed to a complex national culture.

It was during the inter-war era and especially in the 1930s, however, that a relatively new element became part of this configuration. The common culture of the Thirties did not displace traditional patterns of taste as much as provide unifying points of reference among them. The continuing maturation of newer technologies of communication was one of many factors that allowed individuals from all social classes, regions, and generations to view the same films, listen to the same radio programmes, sometimes even read the same newspapers. This common culture was not without precedent in the nineteenth century, and clearly no single decade in the twentieth accounted fully for its development. Sometime during the First World War and certainly in the 1920s, for example, Charlie Chaplin became almost universally known. Even those who never attended any of his films recognized an individual who, a generation earlier, might have become a music-hall favourite known only to a fraction of the population. In a similar fashion, few in the 1920s could escape the sound or influence of jazz, which even for its most dedicated opponents became the defining music of the decade. The Thirties, then, accelerated an existing trend. Hitchcock and other film-makers such as Disney and Capra added to the corpus of works that transcended the usual boundaries of class, region, and generation. These directors adopted techniques which succeeded both critically and at the box-office. At the same time, newspapers became more similar to each other in their incorporation of graphics and other visual appeals, often heavily derived from Modernism. Some national daily papers, such as the *Daily Express*, built their circulation on readers from all classes within the population. The BBC, officially a bastion of cultural paternalism, modified its programming and broadened its audience, thereby gradually evolving into the national institution it always claimed to be. Critics and dissenters sometimes appropriated the tactics of the culture they sought to reform.

This common culture helped define the collective identity of a broad cross-section of the British public. Although some analysts might prefer to associate the Thirties with W. H. Auden, most British citizens never heard of this gifted figure or read his poems. To individuals from all social classes and regions, the decade's culture more likely consisted of radio programmes such as 'In Town Tonight' and films like *The Thirty-Nine Steps*. These manifestations of an emerging common culture linked the unemployed labourer in Huddersfield, the Oxford don, the shopkeeper in Leeds, and the typist in Grimsby. Shared cultural experiences became one of many cohesive forces in British society. This unity within the diversity of a complex culture could not be translated into easy agreement on socially divisive issues. Though sometimes politically useful, as Priestley showed, it usually appealed to values and emotions that transcended the controversies of the moment. Moreover, the technology of common culture changed as the century progressed. Later television would largely replace the radio and cinema as the medium of collective experience. Intellectuals, then and now, often found such culture disappointing. Some lamented its political allegiance to the status quo; others recoiled for more aesthetic reasons. The common culture of the 1930s may not have been what everyone wanted, or what some believed the public ought to have, but within a pluralistic society it united individuals of widely divergent tastes.

Works Cited

WORKS CITED

With a few exceptions, anonymous works have been omitted from this bibliography. Books that contain a collection of articles have been listed as a single entry.

Abercrombie, Nicholas, Stephen Hill, and Bryan S. Turner. *The Dominant-Ideology Thesis*. London: George Allen and Unwin, 1980.

Ackroyd, Peter. *T. S. Eliot: A Life*. New York: Simon and Schuster, 1984.

Adams, Henry Foster. *Advertising and its Mental Laws*. New York: Macmillan, 1921.

Agate, James. *Around Cinemas*. London: Home and Van Thal, 1946.

Aitken, Hugh G. J. *The Continuous Wave: Technology and American Radio, 1900–1932*. Princeton: Princeton University Press, 1985.

Aldcroft, Anthony. *Cinema and History: British Newsreels and the Spanish Civil War*. London: Scolar Press, 1979.

Aldcroft, Derek H. *The Inter-War Economy in Britain, 1919–1939*. New York: Columbia University Press, 1970.

—— *The British Economy Between the Wars*. Oxford: Philip Allan, 1983.

—— and Harry W. Richardson. *The British Economy, 1870–1939*. London: Macmillan, 1969.

Alexander, Lady. 'What Women Listeners Gain'. *Radio Times*, 1 Jan. 1926, 49–50.

Alford, B. W. E. *Depression and Recovery? British Economic Growth, 1918–39*. London: Macmillan, 1972.

Altick, Richard D. 'The Sociology of Authorship: The Social Origins, Education and Occupations of 1,100 British Writers, 1800–1935'. *Bulletin of the New York Public Library* (June 1962): 389–404.

—— *Deadly Encounters: Two Victorian Sensations*. Philadelphia: University of Pennsylvania Press, 1986.

Amery, L. S. *The Empire in the New Era*. London: Edward Arnold, 1928.

—— *My Political Life*. 2 vols. London: Hutchinson, 1953.

Andrews, Linton and H. A. Taylor. *Lords and Laborers of the Press: Men Who Fashioned the Modern British Newspaper*. Carbondale: Southern Illinois University Press; London: Feffer and Simons, 1970.

Angell, Norman. *The Press and the Organization of Society*. London: Labour Publishing, 1922.

—— *The Public Mind: Its Disorders, Its Exploitation*. London: Noel Douglas, 1926.

—— *After All*. London: Hamish Hamilton, 1951.

Annan, Noel. *Leslie Stephen: The Godless Victorian*. London: Weidenfeld and Nicolson, 1984.

Anscombe, Isabella. *Omega and After: Bloomsbury and the Decorative Arts*. London: Thames and Hudson, 1981.

Armes, Roy. *A Critical History of British Cinema*. New York: Oxford University Press, 1978.

Austin, Allen. *T. S. Eliot: The Literary and Social Criticism*. Bloomington: Indiana University Press, 1971.

Austin, Cecil. 'Jazz'. *Music and Letters* 6, 3 (1925): 256–68.

Aymer, Gordon C. *An Introduction to Advertising Illustration*. New York and London: Harper and Brothers, 1929.

Ayre, Leslie. *The Proms*. London: Leslie Frewin, 1968.

Bailey, Peter. *Leisure and Class in Victorian England: Rational Recreation and the Contest for Control, 1830–1885*. London: Routledge and Kegan Paul; Toronto: University of Toronto Press, 1978.

—— 'Ally Sloper's Half-Holiday: Comic Art in the 1880s'. *History Workshop* 16 (1983): 4–31.

Baldick, Chris. *The Social Mission of English Criticism, 1848–1932*. Oxford: Clarendon Press, 1983.

Balio, Tino, ed. *The American Film Industry*. Madison: University of Wisconsin Press, 1976.

Banham, Reyner. *Theory and Design in the First Machine Age*. 2nd edn. Cambridge: Massachusetts Institute of Technology Press, 1960.

Barber, John. 'The Establishment of Intellectual Orthodoxy in the U.S.S.R., 1928–1934'. *Past and Present* 83 (1979): 141–64.

Barfield, Owen. 'Psychology and Reason'. *Criterion* 9, 37 (1930): 606–17.

Barker, Diana Leonard and Sheila Allen, eds. *Dependence and Exploitation in Work and Marriage*. London: Longman, 1976.

Barker, Felix. *The House That Stoll Built: The Story of the Coliseum Theatre*. London: Frederick Muller, 1957.

Barker, Nicolas. *Stanley Morison*. Cambridge: Harvard University Press, 1972.

—— and Douglas Clevendon. *Stanley Morison, 1889–1967: A Radio Portrait*. Ipswich: W. S. Coveli, 1969.

Barker, Rodney. *Education and Politics, 1900–1951: A Study of the Labour Party*. Oxford: Clarendon Press, 1972.

Barlow, John D. *German Expressionist Film*. Boston: Twayne, 1982.

Barman, Christian. 'London Transport Publicity'. *Penrose Annual* 42 (1940): 50–4.

—— *The Man Who Built London Transport: A Biography of Frank Pick*. Newton Abbot: David and Charles, 1979.

Barnato, Woolf. 'Skids, Brakes and the "Ham Foot" '. *Daily Mail*, 4 Oct. 1930.

Barnes, John. *The Beginnings of the Cinema in England*. Newton Abbot: David and Charles; New York: Barnes and Noble, 1976.

Barnett, H. T. 'Surface Vibration'. *The Gramophone* 2, 7 (1924): 249.

—— 'Record Selection'. *The Gramophone* 3, 8 (1926): 365.

Barnouw, Erik. *The Magician and the Cinema*. New York: Oxford University Press, 1981.

Barrie, J. M. *Letters of J. M. Barrie*. Viola Meynell, ed. New York: Charles Scribner's Sons, 1947.

Barrows, Susanna. *Distorting Mirrors: Visions of the Crowd in Late Nineteenth-Century France*. New Haven: Yale University Press, 1981.

Barry, Iris. *Let's Go to the Pictures*. London: Chatto and Windus, 1926.

Barth, Gunther. *City People: The Rise of Modern City Culture in Nineteenth-Century America*. New York and Oxford: Oxford University Press, 1980.

Batten, Joe. *Joe Batten's Book: The Story of Sound Recording*. London: Rockcliff, 1956.

Baxter, Beverley. *Strange Street*. London: Hutchinson, 1935.

Baynes, Ken, ed. *Scoop, Scandal and Strife: A Study of Photography in Newspapers*. London: Lund Humphries, 1971.

BBC Handbook(s). (Titles vary with year.) London: British Broadcasting Corporation, 1928–39.

BBC Written Archives Centre, Reading.

Beauman, Nicola. *A Very Great Profession: The Woman's Novel, 1914–39*. London: Virago, 1983.

Beaverbrook, Lord. *Politicians and the Press*. London: Hutchinson, n.d.

—— Beaverbrook Papers. House of Lords Record Office, London.

Becker, Stephen. *Comic Art in America: A Social History of the Funnies, the Political Cartoons, Magazine Humor, Sporting Cartoons, and Animated Cartoons*. New York: Simon and Schuster, 1959.

Beckles, Gordon. 'The Two Mr. Chaplins Come to London'. *Daily Express*, 20 Feb. 1931.

Bell, Bell R. *The Complete Press Photographer*. London: Sir Isaac Pitman, 1927.

Bell, Clive. *Art*. 1914. Reprinted London: Chatto and Windus, 1947.

—— 'Plus De Jazz'. *New Republic*, 21 Sept. 1921.

—— *Civilization: An Essay*. New York: Harcourt, Brace, 1928.

—— 'Shell-Mex and the Painters'. *New Statesman and Nation*, 23 June 1934, 946.

Belloc, Hilaire. *The Contrast*. London: J. W. Arrowsmith, 1923.

Benjamin, Otto L. 'The Relationship of Word and Picture: Principles of Photo-Typography'. *Penrose's Annual* 34 (1932): 75–6.

Bennett, Arnold. *Journalism for Women: a Practical Guide*. London: John Lane, Bodley Head, 1898.

—— *What the Public Wants*. London: Duckworth, 1909.

—— *The Journals of Arnold Bennett, 1896–1910*. Newman Flower, ed. London: Cassell, 1932.

—— *Letters of Arnold Bennett*. James Hepburn, ed. 2 vols. London: Oxford University Press, 1966–8.

Bennett, Michelle, *et. al.*, eds. *Ideology and Cultural Production*. New York: St Martin's Press, 1979.

Berlin, Edward A. *Ragtime: A Musical and Cultural History*. Berkeley: University of California Press, 1980.

Bernays, Edward L. *Propaganda*. New York: Horace Liveright, 1928.

—— *Biography of an Idea: Memoirs of Public Relations Counsel Edward L. Bernays*. New York: Simon and Schuster, 1965.

Bernstein, B. 'Some Sociological Determinants of Perception: An Inquiry into Sub-Cultural Differences'. *British Journal of Sociology* 9 (1958): 159–74.

Berridge, Virginia Stewart. 'Popular Journalism and Working-Class Attitudes, 1854–1886: A Study of *Reynolds' Newspaper, Lloyd's Weekly Newspaper* and the *Weekly Times*'. Ph.D. diss.: University of London, 1976.

Bertram, Anthony. *Paul Nash: The Portrait of An Artist*. London: Faber and Faber, 1955.

Beveridge, James. *John Grierson: Film Master*. New York: Macmillan; London: Collier Macmillan, 1978.

Bienefeld, M. A. *Working Hours in British Industry: An Economic History*. London: Weidenfeld and Nicolson, 1972.

Bigsby, C. W. E., ed. *Approaches to Popular Culture*. Bowling Green, OH: Bowling Green University Press, 1976.

Bilan, R. P. *The Literary Criticism of F. R. Leavis*. Cambridge: Cambridge University Press, 1979.

Black, Peter. *The Biggest Aspidistra in the World*. London: British Broadcasting Corporation, 1972.

Blumenfeld, R. D. *What is a Journalist?* London: World's Press New Library, n.d.

—— *The Press in My Time*. London: Rich and Cowan, 1937.

Blunt, Anthony. 'The "Realism" Quarrel'. *Left Review* 3, 3 (1937): 169–71.

Blyth, John A. *English University Adult Education, 1908–1958: The Unique Tradition*. Manchester: Manchester University Press, 1983.

Board of Trade. *Tendencies to Monopoly in the Cinematograph Film Industry*. London: His Majesty's Stationery Office, 1944.

Bocock, Robert. *Hegemony*. Chichester: Ellis Harwood; London and New York: Tavistock, 1986.

Boorstein, Daniel J. *The Americans: The Democratic Experience*. New York: Random House, 1973.

Booth, Alan E. and Sean Glynn. 'Unemployment in the Interwar Period: A Multiple Problem'. *Journal of Contemporary History* 10, 4 (1975): 611–36.

Booth, Michael R. *English Melodrama*. London: Herbert Jenkins, 1965.

Bordwell, David, Janet Staiger, and Kristin Thompson. *The Classical Hollywood Cinema: Film Style and Mode of Production to 1960*. New York: Columbia University Press, 1985.

Boughey, Davidson. *The Film Industry*. London: Sir Isaac Pitman, 1921.

Boulton, David. *Jazz in Britain*. London: W. H. Allen, 1958.

Bourdieu, Pierre. *Distinction: A Social Critique of the Judgement of Taste*. Richard Nice, trans. Cambridge: Harvard University Press, 1984.

Bower, Dallas. *Plan for Cinema*. London: Dent, 1936.

Box, Kathleen. 'The Cinema and the Public'. Mimeo. London: The Social Survey, 1946.

Boyce, George, James Curran, and Pauline Wingate, eds. *Newspaper History: From the Seventeenth Century to the Present Day*. London: Constable; Beverly Hills: Sage, 1978.

Boyd-Bennett, Oliver, Colin Seymour-Ure, and Jeremy Tunstall. *Studies on the Press*. Royal Commission on the Press. London: HMSO, 1977.

Boyers, Robert. *F. R. Leavis: Judgement and the Discipline of Thought.* Columbia: University of Missouri Press, 1978.

Boyle, Andrew. *Only the Wind Will Listen: Reith of the BBC.* London: Hutchinson, 1972.

Bradbury, Malcolm and James McFarlane, eds. *Modernism, 1890–1930.* Harmondsworth: Penguin, 1976.

Braddock, A. P. *Applied Psychology for Advertisers.* London: Butterworth, 1933.

Bradshaw, Percy V. *Art in Advertising: A Study of British and American Pictorial Publicity.* London: Press Art School [1925].

Braine, John. *J. B. Priestley.* New York: Barnes and Noble, 1979.

Branca, Patricia. *Silent Sisterhood: Middle-Class Women in the Victorian Home.* London: Croom Helm, 1975.

Branson, Noreen. *Britain in the Nineteen-Twenties.* London: Weidenfeld and Nicolson, 1975.

—— and Margot Heinemann. *Britain in the Nineteen-Thirties.* London: Weidenfeld and Nicolson, 1971.

Brantlinger, Patrick. *Bread and Circuses: Theories of Mass Culture as Social Decay.* Ithaca: Cornell University Press, 1983.

Braudy, Leo. *The Frenzy of Renown: Fame and its History.* New York and Oxford: Oxford University Press, 1986.

Braydon, Gail. *Women Workers in the First World War: The British Experience.* London: Croom Helm; Totowa, NJ: Barnes and Noble, 1981.

Breitwieser, J. V. *Psychological Advertising.* Colorado Springs: Apex, 1915.

Bride, Jack. 'Two Types of Typography'. *Advertiser's Weekly,* 28 May 1926, 318.

Bridgewater, Howard. *Advertising or the Art of Making Known.* London: Sir Isaac Pitman, n.d.

Bridson, D. G. *Prospero and Ariel: The Rise and Fall of Radio: A Personal Recollection.* London: Victor Gollancz, 1971.

Briggs, Asa. *Friends of the People: The Centenary History of Lewis's.* London: B. T. Batsford, 1956.

—— *Mass Entertainment: The Origins of a Modern Industry.* The 29th Joseph Fisher Lecture in Commerce. Adelaide: Griffin Press, 1960.

—— *The History of Broadcasting in the United Kingdom. Volume One: The Birth of Broadcasting.* London: Oxford University Press, 1961.

—— *The History of Broadcasting in the United Kingdom. Volume Two: The Golden Age of Wireless.* London: Oxford University Press, 1965.

—— *The History of Broadcasting in the United Kingdom. Volume Three: The War of Words.* London: Oxford University Press, 1970.

—— *The BBC: The First Fifty Years.* Oxford: Oxford University Press, 1985.

—— *The Collected Essays of Asa Briggs. Volume One: Words, Numbers, Places, People.* Urbana: University of Illinois Press, 1985.

Briggs, Susan. *Those Radio Times.* London: Weidenfeld and Nicolson, 1981.

Brittain, Ian. *Fabianism and Culture: A Study of British Socialism and the Arts, c.1884–1918.* Cambridge: Cambridge University Press, 1982.

Brooks, Peter. *The Melodramatic Imagination: Balzac, Henry James, Melodrama, and the Mode of Excess.* New Haven: Yale University Press, 1976.

Brower, Reuben A., ed. *Twentieth-Century Literature in Retrospect*. Cambridge: Harvard University Press, 1971.

—— Helen Vendler, and John Hollander, eds. *I. A. Richards: Essays in His Honor*. New York: Oxford University Press, 1973.

Brown, Alec. *Daughters of Albion: A Novel*. London: Boriswood, 1935.

—— *The Fate of the Middle Classes*. London: Victor Gollancz, 1936.

Brown, Ivor. *J. B. Priestley*. London: Longmans, Green and Company, 1957.

Brown, Karl. *Adventures With D. W. Griffith*. New York: Farrar, Strauss, and Giroux, 1973.

Browne, Donald R. 'Radio Normandie and the IBC Challenge to the BBC Monopoly'. *Historical Journal of Film, Radio and Television* 5, 1 (1985): 3–18.

Browne, Wyward. 'The Culture-Brokers'. *London Mercury* 28, 167 (1933): 436–45.

Brownlow, Kevin. *The Parade's Gone By*. New York: Alfred A. Knopf, 1968.

Brumwell, J. R. M. 'Modern Art in Advertising'. *Penrose Annual* 41 (1939): 17–21.

Brunn, H. O. *The Story of the Original Dixieland Jazz Band*. Baton Rouge: Louisiana State University Press, 1960.

Bryce, James. *The American Commonwealth*. Vol. 3. London: Macmillan, 1888.

Buchanan, Andrew. *The Art of Film Production*. London: Sir Isaac Pitman and Sons, 1936.

—— *Film and the Future*. London: George Allen and Unwin, 1945.

Buckley, Jerome Hamilton. *William Ernest Henley: A Study in the Counter-Decadence of the Nineties*. Princeton: Princeton University Press, 1945.

Buckley, Vincent. *Poetry and Morality: Studies in the Criticism of Matthew Arnold, T. S. Eliot, and F. R. Leavis*. London: Chatto and Windus, 1959.

Bullock, Alan. *The Life and Times of Ernest Bevin*. Vol. 1. London: Heinemann, 1960.

Burnett, John. *A Social History of Housing, 1815–1970*. Newton Abbot: David and Charles, 1978.

Burnett, R. G. and E. D. Martell. *The Devil's Camera: Menace of a Film-ridden World*. London: Epworth Press, 1932.

Burns, Tom. *The BBC: Public Institution and Private World*. London: Macmillan, 1977.

Bush, Alan D. 'Music and the Working-Class Struggle'. *Left Review* 2, 12 (1936): 646–51.

Butterfield, Roger. 'Pictures in the Papers'. *American Heritage* 13, 14 (1962): 32–55.

Buxton, Neil K. and Derek H. Aldcroft, eds. *British Industry Between the Wars: Instability and Industrial Development, 1919–39*. London: Scolar Press, 1979.

Cadogan, Mary and Patricia Craig. *You're a Brick Angela! A New Look at Girls' Fiction from 1839–1975*. London: Victor Gollancz, 1976.

—— *Women and Children First: The Fiction of Two World Wars*. London: Victor Gollancz, 1978.

Calder-Marshall, Arthur. 'One Must Have Standards'. *New Statesman and Nation*, 3 June 1933, 739.

Calvocoressi, M. D. 'On Broadcasting New Music'. *Musical Times* 65, 976 (1924): 500–2.

Cameron, Alan. 'Gaumont to Launch "Headline" News Reels in Fight with Press'. *World's Press News*, 2 Nov. 1933.

Camrose, Viscount. *British Newspapers and Their Controllers*. London: Cassell, 1947.

Cardiff, David. 'The Serious and the Popular: Aspects of the Evolution of Style in the Radio Talk, 1928–1939'. *Media, Culture and Society* 2 (1980): 29–47.

—— 'Time, Money and Culture: BBC Programme Finances, 1927–1939'. *Media, Culture and Society* 5 (1983): 373–93.

Carey, Hugh. *Mansfield Forbes and his Cambridge*. Cambridge: Cambridge University Press, 1984.

Carrington, Noel. *Industrial Design in Britain*. London: George Allen and Unwin, 1976.

Carroll, Joseph. *The Cultural Theory of Matthew Arnold*. Berkeley and Los Angeles: University of California Press, 1982.

Carson, William. *Northcliffe: Britain's Man of Power*. New York: Dodge, 1918.

Castle, Irene. *Castles in the Air*. New York: De Capo Paperback, 1980.

Caudwell, Christopher. *Illusion and Reality: A Study of the Sources of Poetry*. New York: International Publishers, 1947.

—— *Studies and Further Studies in a Dying Culture*. New York: Monthly Press, 1971.

Cave, Frederick. *The Private Press*. London: Faber and Faber; New York: Watson-Guptill, 1971.

Cawelti, John G. *The Six-Gun Mystique*. Bowling Green, OH: Bowling Green University Press, 1971.

—— *Adventure, Mystery and Romance: Formulaic Stories as Art and Popular Culture*. Chicago: University of Chicago Press, 1976.

Ceram, C. W. *Archeology of the Cinema*. New York: Harcourt, Brace, 1967.

Chaliapin, Feodor. 'To My British Friends'. *Radio Times*, 20 Nov. 1925, 385.

Chanan, Michael. *The Dream That Kicks: The Prehistory and Early Years of Cinema in Britain*. London: Routledge and Kegan Paul, 1980.

Chaney, David. *Processes of Mass Communications*. London: Macmillan, 1972.

Chaplin, Charles. 'What People Laugh At'. *American Magazine* 86, 5 (1918): 34, 134–7.

—— *My Wonderful Visit*. London: Hurst and Blackett, [1922].

—— 'Does the Public Know What it Wants?'. *Adelphi* 1 (1924): 702–10.

—— 'Why I Prefer Silent Films'. *Daily Mail*, 7 Feb. 1931.

—— *My Autobiography*. New York: Simon and Schuster, 1964.

Chaplin, Lita Grey, and Morton Cooper. *My Life with Chaplin: An Intimate Memoir*. N.p.: Bernard Geis Associates, 1966.

Chapman, A. L. and Rose Knight. *Wages and Salaries in the United Kingdom, 1920–1938*. Cambridge: Cambridge University Press, 1953.

Cheshire, D. F. *Music Hall in Britain*. Rutherford, NJ: Farleigh Dickenson University Press, 1974.

Chesterton, G. K. 'The Game of Psychoanalysis'. *Century Magazine* 106, 1 (1923): 34–43.

—— *Avowals and Denials*. New York: Dodd, Mead, 1935.

Christiansen, Arthur. *Headlines All My Life*. London: Heinemann, 1961.

Church, Richard. 'The Labyrinthine Way'. *Spectator*, 26 Mar. 1932, 453–4.

Cinema Survey. London: Blue Moon Press, n.d.

Clair, Colin. *A History of Printing in Britain*. New York: Oxford University Press, 1966.

Clark, Carroll Dewitt. 'News: A Sociological Study'. Ph.D. diss.: University of Chicago, 1931.

Clark, Jon, *et al.*, eds. *Culture and Crisis in Britain in the Thirties*. London: Lawrence and Wishart, 1979.

Clark, Kenneth. 'Painters Turn to Posters: The Shell-Mex Exhibition'. *Commercial Art and Industry* 17 (1934): 65–74.

—— 'Broadcast'. *Documentary News Letter* 1, 1 (1940): 4–5.

Clarke, J., C. Critchen, and R. Johnson, eds. *Working-Class Culture: Studies in History and Theory*. New York: St Martin's Press, 1979.

Clarke, Simon, *et al.*, eds. *One-Dimensional Marxism: Althusser and the Politics of Culture*. London and New York: Allison and Busby, 1980.

Clarke, Tom. *My Northcliffe Diary*. New York: Cosmopolitan Book Corporation, 1931.

—— *Northcliffe in History: An Intimate Study of Press Power*. London: Hutchinson, n.d.

Cleaver, James. *A History of Graphic Art*. New York: Philosophical Library, 1963.

Close, David H. 'The Collapse of Resistance to Democracy: Conservatives, Adult Suffrage, and the Second Chamber Reform, 1911–1928'. *Historical Journal* 20, 4 (1977): 893–918.

Coase, R. H. *British Broadcasting: A Study in Monopoly*. London: Longmans, Green, 1950.

Cockburn, Alexander and Robin Blackburn, eds. *Student Power: Problems, Diagnoses, Action*. Harmondsworth: Penguin in association with *New Left Review*, 1969.

Collier, James Lincoln. *The Making of Jazz: A Comprehensive History*. New York: Delta, 1978.

Collingwood, R. G. *An Autobiography*. London: Oxford University Press, 1939.

Collins, Judith. *The Omega Workshops*. Chicago: University of Chicago Press, 1984.

Connor, Robert. *Cassandra: Reflections in a Mirror*. London: Cassell, 1969.

Cook, David A. *A History of Narrative Film*. New York: W. W. Norton, 1981.

Cook, Olive. *Movement in Two Dimensions: A Study of the Animated and Projected Pictures which Preceded the Invention of Cinematography*. London: Hutchinson, 1963.

Cooke, Alistair, ed. *Garbo and the Night Watchman: A Selection from the Writings of British and American Film Critics*. London: Jonathan Cape, 1937.

Cooper, Susan. *J. B. Priestley: Portrait of an Author*. London: Heinemann, 1970.

Cork, Richard. *Art Beyond the Gallery in Early 20th-Century England.* New Haven: Yale University Press, 1985.

—— *Vorticism and Abstract Art in the First Machine Age.* 2 vols. Berkeley: University of California Press, 1976.

Costello, Donald P. 'George Bernard Shaw and the Motion Picture: His Theory and Practice'. Ph.D. diss.: University of Chicago, 1962.

Coulton, G. G. *Fourscore Years: An Autobiography.* Cambridge: Cambridge University Press, 1944.

Covert, Catherine L. and John D. Stevens, eds. *Mass Media Between the Wars: Perceptions of Cultural Tension, 1918–1941.* Syracuse: Syracuse University Press, 1984.

Cox, Reginald H. *The Lay-Out of Advertisements.* London: Sir Isaac Pitman, 1931.

Coxhead, Elizabeth. 'Charlie Chaplin'. *Left Review* 2, 6 (1936): 274.

Crawford, Alan. *C. R. Ashbee: Architect, Designer and Romantic Socialist.* New Haven: Yale University Press, 1985.

Crawford Committee. Testimony. GPO Archives, General Post Office, London.

Crawford, William S. 'Making the Empire "Come Alive"'. *Commercial Art* NS 1, 6 (1926). 241–6.

—— 'Advertising is Education—Not Salesmanship'. *World's Press News*, 10 Apr. 1930.

—— *How to Succeed in Advertising.* London: World's Press News [1931].

Crick, Bernard. *George Orwell: A Life.* Boston: Little, Brown, 1980.

'The Critical Issue: A Discussion between Paul Rotha, Basil Wright, Lindsay Anderson, and Penelope Houston'. *Sight and Sound* 27, 6 (1958): 270–5, 330.

Crossick, Geoffrey, ed. *The Lower Middle Class in Britain, 1870–1914.* New York: St Martin's Press, 1977.

Cudlipp, Hugh. *Publish and be Damned! The Astonishing Story of the Daily Mirror.* London: Andrew Dakers, 1953.

—— *Walking on the Water.* London: The Bodley Head, 1976.

Cuff, John. 'Post Office Publicity'. *Penrose Annual* 41 (1939): 22–4.

Curran, James. 'The Impact of Advertising on the British Mass Media'. *Media, Culture and Society* 3, 1 (1981): 43–69.

—— and Jean Seaton. *Power Without Responsibility: The Press and Broadcasting in Britain.* N.p.: Fontana Paperbacks, 1981.

—— ed. *The British Press: A Manifesto.* London and Basingstoke: Macmillan, 1978.

—— Michael Gurevitch, and Janet Woolacott, eds. *Mass Communication and Society.* London: Edward Arnold, 1977.

—— and Vincent Porter, eds. *British Cinema History.* London: Weidenfeld and Nicolson, 1983.

Curtis, J. J. *Education in Britain Since 1900.* London: Andrew Dakers, 1952.

Czitrom, Daniel J. *Media and the American Mind: From Morse to McLuhan.* Chapel Hill: University of North Carolina Press, 1982.

Daily Mirror. The Romance of the Daily Mirror, *1903–1924.* London: Daily Mirror Newspapers [1924].

Daily Sketch Blue Book. London: *Daily Sketch* and *Sunday Graphic*, 1933.

Dandridge, C. G. 'Evolution in the Printing of Railway Propaganda'. *Penrose Annual* 39 (1937): 50–5.

Dasenbrock, Reed Way. *The Literary Vorticism of Ezra Pound and Wyndham Lewis: Towards the Condition of Painting*. Baltimore: Johns Hopkins University Press, 1985.

Davidson, John. *John Davidson: A Selection of his Poems*. Maurice Lindsay, ed. London: Hutchinson, 1961.

Davis, G. S. 'Service Without Sales: The Dealer's Point of View Again'. *The Gramophone* 6, 72 (1929): 526–8.

Davison, W. Phillips and Frederick T. C. Yu, eds. *Mass Communications Research: Major Issues and Future Directions*. New York: Praeger, 1974.

Davy, Charles, ed. *Footnotes to the Film*. New York: Oxford University Press, 1937.

Day, Alan Edwin. *J. B. Priestley: An Annotated Bibliography*. New York: Garland Publishing, 1980.

Day Lewis, C. *A Time to Dance and Other Poems*. London: Hogarth Press, 1935.

—— 'Sword and Pen'. *Left Review* 2, 15 (1936): 794–6.

—— *The Buried Day*. London: Chatto and Windus, 1960.

—— ed. *The Mind in Chains: Socialism and the Cultural Revolution*. London: Frederick Muller, 1937.

Day-Lewis, Sean. *C. Day-Lewis: An English Literary Life*. London: Weidenfeld and Nicolson, 1981.

Dean, Basil. *Mind's Eye: An Autobiography, 1927–1972*. London: Hutchinson, 1973.

—— Basil Dean Papers. British Film Institute, London.

Dean, D. W. 'Conservatism and the National Education System, 1922–40'. *Journal of Contemporary History* 6, 2 (1971): 150–65.

DeFleur, Melvin L. *Theories of Mass Communication*. New York: David McKay, 1966.

De La Valette, John. *The Conquest of Ugliness*. London: Methuen, 1935.

Devine, Elizabeth, *et al.*, eds. *Thinkers of the Twentieth Century: A Biographical, Bibliographical and Critical Dictionary*. Detroit: Gale Research, 1983.

De Vries, Leonard. *Victorian Advertisements*. London: John Murray, 1968.

Derry, T. K. and Trevor I. Williams. *A Short History of Technology*. Oxford: Clarendon Press, 1960.

Dexter, Lewis Anthony and David Manning White, eds. *People, Society and Mass Communications*. New York: Free Press, 1964.

Dickinson, G. Lowes. *Appearances: Notes of Travel, East and West*. Garden City: Doubleday, Page, 1915.

Dickinson, Margaret and Sarah Street. *Cinema and State: The Film Industry and the Government, 1927–84*. London: British Film Institute, 1985.

Dixon, Robert M. W. and John Godrich. *Recording the Blues*. New York: Stein and Day, 1970.

Dodge, F. W. 'When Advertising Research Becomes A Fetish'. *Advertiser's Weekly*, 3 Aug. 1928.

Doolittle, Hilda ['H.D.']. 'Russian Films'. *Close-Up* 3, 3 (1928): 18–29.

Drabble, Margaret. *Arnold Bennett*. London: Weidenfeld and Nicolson, 1974.

Drakakis, John, ed. *British Radio Drama*. Cambridge: Cambridge University Press, 1981.

Drawbell, James. *The Sun Within Us*. London: Collins, 1963.

Dreyfus, John. *A History of The Nonesuch Press*. London: Nonesuch Press, 1981.

Driberg, Tom. *'Swaff': The Life and Times of Hannen Swaffer*. London: MacDonald, 1974.

—— *Ruling Passions*. New York: Stein and Day, A Scarborough Book, 1979.

Drotner, Kirsten. 'Schoolgirls, Madcaps, and Air Aces: English Girls and their Magazine Reading Between the Wars'. *Feminist Studies* 9, 1 (1983): 33–52.

Dunbar, David S. 'The Agency Commission System in Britain: A First Sketch of its History to 1941'. *Journal of Advertising History* 2 (1979): 19–28.

Duncan, Peter. *'In Town Tonight'*. London: Werner Laurie, 1951.

Duncan, Ronald. *All Men are Islands: An Autobiography*. London: Rupert Hart-Davis, 1964.

Duncan-Jones, Austin. 'The Organic Community'. *Cambridge Review* 54, 1336 (26 May 1933): 432–3.

Durgnat, Raymond. *The Strange Case of Alfred Hitchcock, or The Plain Man's Hitchcock*. 1974. Reprinted Cambridge: Massachusetts Institute of Technology Press, 1978.

Dwiggins, W. A. *Layout in Advertising*. New York and London: Harper and Brothers, 1928.

Dyer, Richard. *Stars*. London: British Film Institute, 1982.

Eagleton, Terry. *Literary Theory: An Introduction*. Minneapolis: University of Minnesota Press, 1983.

East, Raymond. 'B.B.C.' *Left Review* 1, 12 (1935): 522–3.

Eastman, Max. *Great Companions*. New York: Farrar, Strauss, and Cudahy, 1959.

Eates, Margot. *Paul Nash: The Master of the Image, 1889–1946*. New York: St Martin's Press, 1973.

Eckersley, P. P. *The Power Behind the Microphone*. London: Jonathan Cape, 1941.

Eckersley, Roger. *The BBC and All That*. London: Sampson, Low, and Marston, 1946.

Edson, C. L. *The Gentle Art of Columning: A Treatise on Comic Journalism*. New York: Brentano's, 1920.

Edwards, Ruth Dudley. *Victor Gollancz: A Biography*. London: Gollancz, 1987.

Ehrlich, Cyril. *The Piano: A History*. London: J. M. Dent, 1976.

Ehrlich, Frederick. *The New Typography and Modern Layout*. New York: Frederick A. Stokes, 1934.

Eisenstein, Elizabeth L. *The Printing Press As An Agent of Change: Communications and Cultural Transformations in Early Modern Europe*. 2 vols. Cambridge: Cambridge University Press, 1979. Paperback in one volume, 1980.

Eisenstein, Sergei. *Film Form: Essays in Film Theory*. Jay Leyda, ed. and trans. New York: Harvest/HBJ, 1977.

Eisner, Lotte. *The Haunted Screen: Expressionism in the German Cinema and the Influence of Max Reinhardt*. Berkeley: University of California Press, 1969.

—— *Murnau*. Berkeley: University of California Press, 1973.

Eley, Geoff. 'Reading Gramsci in English: Some Observations on the Reception of Antonio Gramsci in the English-Speaking World, 1957–1982'. CRSO Working Paper 314. Center for Research and Social Organization, University of Michigan, 1984.

Eley, Howard. *Advertising Media*. London: Butterworth, 1932.

Eliot, T. S. *The Sacred Wood: Essays on Poetry and Criticism*. 2nd edn. London: Methuen, 1928.

Ellerman, Winifred ['Bryher']. *Film Problems of Soviet Russia*. Territet, Switzerland: Pool, 1929.

—— *The Heart to Artemis: A Writer's Memoirs*. London: Collins, 1963.

Ellul, Jacques. *The Technological Society*. John Wilkinson, trans. New York: Knopf, 1964.

Emery, Edwin. *The Press and America: An Interpretative History of the Mass Media*. 3rd edn. Englewood Cliffs, NJ: Prentice-Hall, 1972.

Emmert, Phillip, and William Donaghy. *Human Communications: Elements and Contexts*. Reading, Mass.: Addison-Wesley, 1981.

Emy, H. V. *Liberals, Radicals and Social Politics, 1892–1914*. Cambridge: Cambridge University Press, 1973.

Enoch, Kurt. 'The Paper-Bound Book: Twentieth-Century Publishing Phenomenon'. *Library Quarterly* 24, 3 (1954): 211–25.

Erenberg, Lewis A. *Steppin' Out: New York Nightlife and the Transformation of American Culture, 1890–1930*. Westport: Greenwood Press, 1981.

Erleigh, Viscountess. 'New Influences on Crowd Psychology'. *Radio Times*, 23 Sept. 1927, 497–8.

Ervine, St John. *The Future of the Press*. London: World's Press News [1933].

Escarpit, Robert. *The Book Revolution*. London: George G. Harrap; Paris: United Nations Educational, Scientific and Cultural Organization, 1966.

Espinosa, Paul. 'The Audience in the Text: Ethnographic Observations of a Hollywood Story Conference'. *Media, Culture and Society* 4 (1982): 77–86.

Essays and Studies by Members of the English Association. Vol. 28. Oxford: Clarendon Press, 1933.

Eustis, Morton. 'On Time and the Theatre: Priestley Talks About Playwrighting'. *Theatre Arts Monthly* 22, 1 (1938): 46–55.

Evans, Gareth Lloyd. *J. B. Priestley—The Dramatist*. London: Heinemann, 1964.

Everson, William K. *American Silent Film*. New York: Oxford University Press, 1978.

Ewen, David. *All the Years of American Popular Music*. Englewood Cliffs: Prentice-Hall, 1977.

Faulkner, Thomas. *Design, 1900–1960: Studies in Design and Popular Culture in the Twentieth Century*. Newcastle: Petras, 1976.

Fell, John L. *Film and the Narrative Tradition*. Norman: University of Oklahoma Press, 1974.

—— *A History of Films*. New York: Holt, Rinehart, and Winston, 1979.

—— ed. *Film Before Griffith*. Berkeley: University of California Press, 1983.

Ferraby, H. C. 'Some Characteristics of Despotic Art'. *Advertising Display* 1, 2 (1926): 47–9.

Ferry, John William. *A History of the Department Store*. New York: Macmillan, 1960.

Fessman, I. *Rundfunk und Rundfunkrecht in der Weimarer Republik*. Frankfurt: Joseph Knecht, 1973.

Field, Audrey. *Picture Palace: A Social History of the Cinema*. London: Gentry Books, 1974.

Field, Eric. *Advertising: The Forgotten Years*. London: Ernest Benn, 1959.

Fielden, Lionel. *The Natural Bent*. London: André Deutsch, 1960.

Fielding, Ray. *A Technological History of Motion Pictures and Television*. Berkeley: University of California Press, 1967.

Fielding, Raymond. *The* March of Time, *1935–1951*. New York: Oxford University Press, 1978.

Fields, Gracie. *Sing As We Go*. London: Frederick Muller, 1960.

Fleming, J. A. 'The Polite Use of the Ether', *Radio Times*, 2 July 1926, 41.

Flora, Joseph M. *William Ernest Henley*. New York: Twayne, 1970.

Floud, Roderick and Donald McCloskey, eds. *The Economic History of Britain Since 1700. Volume Two: 1860 to the 1970s*. Cambridge: Cambridge University Press, 1981.

Folson, James K. *The American Western Novel*. New Haven: College and University Press, 1966.

Foreman, Ronald Clifford, jun. 'Jazz and Race Records, 1920–32: Their Origins and their Significance for the Record Industry and Society'. Ph.D. diss.: University of Illinois, 1968.

Forest, Mark. 'A Fine Picture'. *Saturday Review*, 22 June 1935, 797.

Forrester, Wendy. *Great-Grandmama's Weekly: A Celebration of the* Girl's Own Paper, *1880–1901*. Guildford and London: Lutterworth Press, 1980.

Forty, Adrian. *Objects of Desire*. New York: Pantheon Books, 1986.

Fox, Ralph. *The Novel and the People*. 1937. Reprinted New York: International Publishers, 1945.

Franklin, Colin. *The Private Presses*. London: Studio Vista, 1969.

Franks, A. H. *Social Dance: A Short History*. London: Routledge and Kegan Paul, 1963.

Fraser, John. *Artificially Arranged Scenes: The Films of Georges Méliès*. Boston: G. K. Hall, 1979.

Fraser, W. Hamish. *The Coming of the Mass Market, 1850–1914*. London: Macmillan, 1981.

Frederick, George. 'Business Research As I See It'. *Advertiser's Weekly*, 2 Apr. 1926, 4–5.

Freeden, Michael. *Liberalism Divided: A Study in British Political Thought, 1914–1939*. Oxford: Clarendon Press, 1986.

Freer, Cyril C. *The Inner Side of Advertising*. London: Library Press, 1921.

French, George. *The Art and Science of Advertising*. Boston: Sherman, French, 1909.

French, Phillip. *Westerns*. Bloomington: Indiana University Press, 1973.

Frostick, Michael. *Advertising and the Motor-Car*. London: Lund Humphries, 1970.

Fry, Roger. 'Poster Designs and Mr. McKnight Kauffer'. *Nation and Athenaeum*, 23 May 1925, 236–7.

—— *Transformations: Critical and Speculative Essays on Art*. New York: Brentano's [1926].

—— 'The Author and the Artist'. *Burlington Magazine* 49, 180 (1926): 9–12.

—— *Last Lectures*. 1939. Reprinted Boston: Beacon Press, 1962.

—— *Letters of Roger Fry*. Vol. 2. Denys Sutton, ed. London: Chatto and Windus, 1972.

Fyfe, Hamilton. *Northcliffe: An Intimate Biography*. New York: Macmillan, 1930.

—— *My Seven Selves*. London: George Allen and Unwin, 1935.

—— 'The Press and the People's Front'. *Left Review* 2, 15 (1936): 806–11.

—— *Sixty Years of Fleet Street*. London: W. H. Allen, 1949.

Gaisberg, F. W. *The Music Goes Round*. New York: Macmillan, 1942.

Gallagher, J. P. *Fred Karno: Master of Mirth and Tears*. London: Robert Hale, 1971.

Gans, Herbert J. *Popular Culture and High Culture: An Analysis and Evaluation of Taste*. New York: Basic Books, 1974.

G[ardiner], A. G. *The* Daily Mail *and the Liberal Press*. London: Daily News [1914].

—— *Portraits and Portents*. New York and London: Harper and Brothers, 1926.

Gardner, Helen. 'The Academic Study of English Literature'. *Critical Quarterly* 1, 2 (1959): 106–10.

Garnham, Nicholas. 'Subjectivity, Ideology, Class and Historical Materialism'. *Screen* 20, 1 (1979): 121–34.

Gartenberg, Jon. 'Camera Movement in Edison and Biograph Films, 1900–1906'. *Cinema Journal* 19, 2 (1980): 1–16.

Gaunt, W. 'The Spirit and the Letter of Modern Advertising Design'. *Commercial Art* 7, 40 (1929): 142–6.

Geduld, Harry M. *The Birth of the Talkies: From Edison to Jolson*. Bloomington: Indiana University Press, 1975.

—— ed. *Authors on Film*. Bloomington: Indiana University Press, 1972.

Gelatt, Roland. *The Fabulous Phonograph, 1877–1977*. 2nd rev. edn. London: Cassell, 1977.

George, W. L. *Caliban*. New York and London: Harper Brothers, 1920.

Gernsheim, Helmut and Alison. *The History of Photography From the Camera Obscura to the Beginning of the Modern Era*. London: Thames and Hudson, 1969.

Gielgud, Val. 'The Play from the Armchair'. *Listener*, 14 Jan. 1931.

—— *How to Write Broadcast Plays*. London: Hurst and Blackett [1932].

—— *Years of the Locust*. London: Nicholson and Watson, 1947.

—— *British Radio Drama, 1922–1956*. London: George G. Harnap, 1957.

—— *Years in a Mirror*. London: Bodley Head, 1965.

Gifford, Denis. *Discovering Comics*. Tring: Shire Publications, 1971.

—— 'A Golden Age of Comics'. *Penrose Annual* 65 (1972): 69–92.

—— *The British Comic Catalogue, 1874–1974*. London: Mansell, 1975.

Gilmour, Pat. *Artists at Curwen*. London: Tate Gallery, 1977.

Glasgow University Media Group. *Bad News*. London: Routledge and Kegan Paul, 1976.

—— *More Bad News*. London: Routledge and Kegan Paul, 1980.

Glazebrook, Mark. 'Introduction' to Exhibition Catalogue: *John Armstrong, 1889–1973*. Royal Academy of Arts. London: Arts Council of Great Britain, 1975.

Glenville, Victor. 'Film Production: A Survey of New Films and Books'. *Left Review* 2, 3 (1936): 708–9.

Gloag, John, ed. *Design in Modern Life*. London: George Allen and Unwin, 1934.

Gloversmith, Frank, ed. *Class, Culture and Social Change: A New View of the 1930s*. Sussex: Harvester Press; NJ: Humanities Press, 1980.

Gluck, Mary. 'Towards a Historical Definition of Modernism: Georg Lukács and the Avant Garde'. *Journal of Modern History* 58, 4 (1986): 845–82.

Godbolt, Jim. *A History of Jazz in Britain, 1919–50*. London: Paladin, 1986.

Goldie, Grace Wyndham. 'The Triumph of *Carnival*'. *Listener*, 23 Dec. 1936, 1173.

Goldman, Willy. 'The Marx Brothers too!'. *Left Review* 2, 15 (1936): 830–1.

Goldring, Douglas. *Reputations: Essays in Criticism*. London: Chapman and Hall, 1920.

Gollin, Alfred M. The Observer *and J. L. Garvin, 1908–1914: A Study in a Great Editorship*. London: Oxford University Press, 1960.

Goodall, G. W. *Advertising: A Study of Modern Business Power*. London: Constable, 1914.

Goode, John Allen. *George Gissing: Ideology and Fiction*. London: Vision Press, 1978.

Goode, Kenneth M. and Harford Powell, jun. *What About Advertising?* New York and London: Harper, 1927.

Goody, Jack, ed. *Literacy in Traditional Societies*. Cambridge: Cambridge University Press, 1968.

Gordon, Lincoln. *The Public Corporation in Great Britain*. London: Oxford University Press, 1938.

Gordon, Peter and Denis Lawton. *Curriculum Change in the Nineteenth and Twentieth Centuries*. London: Hodder and Stoughton, 1978.

Gorham, Maurice. *Sound and Fury: Twenty-One Years in the BBC*. London: Percival Marshall, 1948.

Gould, Ann. 'The Newspaper Cartoon'. *Penrose Annual* 64 (1971): 47–68.

GPO Archives, General Post Office, London.

Gramophone *Jubilee Book, The*. London: General Gramophone Publications, 1973.

Grau, Robert. *The Theatre of Science*. New York: Broadway, 1914.

Greene, Graham. 'The Middle-Brow Film'. *The Fortnightly* 145 (1936): 302–7.

Greene, Graham. 'A Lost Leader'. *Spectator*, 13 Dec. 1940, 646.

Greene, Hugh. 'The Saddest Story'. Review of *The Reith Diaries*. Charles Stuart, ed. *TLS*, 19 Sept. 1975, 1061.

Greenly, A. J. *Psychology As A Sales Factor*. London: Sir Isaac Pitman, 1927.

Greenwood, Walter. *How the Other Man Lives*. London: Labour Book Service [1939].

Grierson, John. 'Making Films for the Empire—II'. *Listener*, 27 Apr. 1932, 604–5.

—— 'Propaganda: A Problem for Educational Theory and the Cinema'. *Sight and Sound* 2, 8 (1933–4): 119–21.

—— 'The G.P.O. Gets Sound'. *Cinema Quarterly* 2, 4 (1934): 215–21.

—— 'Two Paths to Poetry'. *Cinema Quarterly* 3, 3 (1935): 194–6.

—— 'One Hundred Per-Cent Cinema'. *Spectator*, 23 Aug. 1935, 285–6.

—— 'The Story of the Documentary Film'. *The Fortnightly* NS 146 (1939): 122–7.

—— *Grierson on Documentary*. Revised edition. Forsyth Hardy, ed. London: Faber and Faber, 1966.

—— The John Grierson Archive. University of Sterling, Sterling, Scotland.

Griff, Mason. 'The Commercial Artist: A Study in Role Conflict and Career Development'. Ph.D. diss.: University of Chicago, 1958.

Griffith, D. W. *The Man Who Invented Hollywood: The Autobiography of D. W. Griffith*. James Hart, ed. Louisville: Touchstone, 1972.

Griffith, Hubert. 'Films and the British Public'. *Nineteenth Century and After* 112 (1932): 190–200.

Gross, John. *The Rise and Fall of the Man of Letters: A Study of the Idiosyncratic and the Humane in Modern Literature*. New York: Collier Books, 1969.

Gussow, Mel. *Don't Say Yes Until I Finish Talking: A Biography of Darryl F. Zanuck*. New York: Doubleday, 1971.

Guthrie, Tyrone. *Squirrel's Cage and Two Other Microphone Plays*. London: Cobden-Sanderson [1931].

—— *A Life in the Theatre*. London: Hamish Hamilton, 1961.

Haas, Robert Bartlett. *Muybridge: Man in Motion*. Berkeley: University of California Press, 1976.

Haggin, B. H. 'The Music That is Broadcast in America: A Study of the American Wireless Mind'. *Musical Times* 73, 1070 (1932): 305–8.

Hall, Henry. *Here's To The Next Time*. London: Odhams Press, 1955.

Hall, Stuart, *et al.*, eds. *Culture, Media, Language: Working Papers in Cultural Studies*. London: Hutchinson in association with the Centre for Contemporary Cultural Studies, University of Birmingham, 1980.

Halperin, John. *Gissing: A Life in Books*. Oxford: Oxford University Press, 1982.

Hamer, D. A. *Liberal Politics in the Age of Gladstone and Rosebery*. Oxford: Clarendon Press, 1972.

Hammerton, J. A. *With Northcliffe in Fleet Street*. London: Hutchinson [1932].

Hammond, Paul. *Marvellous Méliès*. London: Gordon Fraser, 1974.

Hampton, Jamin B. *A History of the Movies*. New York: Vici Friede, 1931.

Hardy, Forsyth. *John Grierson: A Documentary Biography.* London: Faber and Faber, 1979.

Harling, Robert. 'The New Display'. *Commercial Art and Industry* 20 (1936): 183–90.

Harmsworth, Alfred C. *The Romance of the* Daily Mail. London: Carmelite House, 1903.

—— ed. *Motors and Motor-Driving.* London: Longmans, Green and Co., 1902.

—— Northcliffe Manuscripts. British Library, London.

Harrington, H. F. and T. T. Frankenberg. *Essentials in Journalism.* Boston and London: Ginn, 1922.

Harris, Roy. 'The Dialect of Fleet Street'. Review of *Daily Mirror Style*, by Keith Waterhouse. *TLS*, 22 May 1981, 559–60.

Harrison, Charles. *English Art and Modernism, 1900–1939.* London: Allen Lane; Bloomington: Indiana University Press, 1981.

Harrison, J. F. C. *Learning and Living, 1790–1960: A Study of the English Adult Education Movement.* London: Routledge and Kegan Paul, 1961.

Harrison, John. 'That's Advertising—That is!. Shell-Mex'. *Commercial Art* 11 (1931): 40–8.

Harrison, John R. *The Reactionaries: Yeats, Lewis, Pound, Eliot, Lawrence: A Study of the Anti-Democratic Intelligentsia.* New York: Schocken Books, 1967.

Hart-Davis, Rupert. *Hugh Walpole: A Biography.* London: Macmillan, 1952.

Hartley, William. '"News" Photography: The Beginning and Development of the Photographic "News" Pictures in the London Daily Press'. *Penrose's Annual* 22 (1920): 29–33.

Haselden, W. K. Daily Mirror *Reflections.* London: Pictorial Newspaper [1908].

Haste, Cate. *Keep the Home Fires Burning: Propaganda in the First World War.* London: Allen Lane, 1977.

Havinden, Ashley. 'Advertising and Commercial Design'. *Journal of the Royal Society of Arts* 96, 4761 (1948): 145–57.

Haworth-Booth, Mark. 'E. McKnight Kauffer'. *Penrose Annual* 64 (1971): 83–96.

—— *E. McKnight Kauffer: A Designer and His Public.* London: Gordon Fraser, 1979.

Hayman, Ronald. *Leavis.* London: Heinemann; Totowa, NJ: Rowan and Littlefield, 1976.

Haynes, Rosylin D. *H. G. Wells, Discoverer of the Future: The Influence of Science on His Thought.* New York: New York University Press, 1980.

Hayward, F. H. and B. N. Langdon-Davies. *Democracy and the Press.* London: National Labour Press [1919].

Healey, Basil H. *The Curwen Press: A Short History.* London: Curwen Press, 1971.

Heilman, Robert Bechtold. *Tragedy and Melodrama: Versions of Experience.* Seattle: University of Washington Press, 1968.

Heindel, Richard Heathcote. 'American Attitudes of British School Children'. *School and Society*, 25 Dec. 1937.

Heindel, Richard Heathcote. *The American Impact on Great Britain, 1898–1914: A Study of the United States in World History*. Philadelphia: University of Pennsylvania Press, 1940.

Hellmund-Waldow, E. 'The Russian Film Industry'. *Close-Up* 2, 5 (1928): 65–70.

Henderson, Robert M. *D. W. Griffith: The Years at Biograph*. New York: Farrar, Strauss, and Giroux, 1970.

Hendricks, Gordon. *The Edison Motion-Picture Myth*. Berkeley: University of California Press, 1961.

Henley, W. E. *The Works of W. E. Henley*. 2 vols. London: David Nutt, 1908.

Hennessey, R. A. S. *The Electric Revolution*. London: Oriel Press, 1971.

Hepworth, Cecil M. *Came the Dawn: Memories of a Film Pioneer*. London: Phoenix House, 1951.

Herd, Harold. *Bigger Results From Advertising*. London: Phillip Allan, 1926.

Herf, Jeffrey. *Reactionary Modernism: Technology, Culture and Politics in Weimar and the Third Reich*. Cambridge: Cambridge University Press, 1984.

Hettinger, Herman S. *A Decade of Radio Advertising*. Chicago: University of Chicago Press, 1933.

Heyck, T. W. *The Transformation of Intellectual Life in Victorian England*. London: Croom Helm, 1982.

Hicks, J. Cranfeld. *Newspaper Finance*. London: General Press, n.d.

Higgens, Bertram. 'Charles Chaplin's Comedy of Shyness'. *Spectator*, 8 Sept. 1923.

Higham, Charles Frederick. *Scientific Distribution*. London: Nesbet, 1916.

Hillier, Bevis. *Posters*. New York: Stein and Day, 1969.

Hindley, Diana and Geoffrey. *Advertising in Victorian England, 1837–1901*. London: Wayland Publishers, 1972.

Hitchcock, Alfred. 'A Director's Problems'. *Living Age* 354, 4459 (1938): 172–4.

Hitchcock, H. Wiley, ed. *The Phonograph and Our Musical Life*. New York: Institute for Studies in American Music, 1980.

Hoffman, Frederick J. *Freudianism and the Literary Mind*. Baton Rouge: Louisiana State University Press, 1945.

Hogenkamp, Bert. *Deadly Parallels: Film and the Left in Britain, 1929–39*. London: Lawrence and Wishart, 1986.

Holland, James. 'The B.B.C. Exposed'. *Left Review* 3, 1 (1937): 29.

Hollins, T. J. 'The Conservative Party and Film Propaganda Between the Wars'. *English Historical Review* 96, 379 (1981): 359–69.

Hood, Peter. *Ourselves and the Press*. London: John Lane, Bodley Head, 1939.

Hopkinson, Tom. *Of This Our Time: A Journalist's Story, 1905–50*. London: Hutchinson, 1982.

Horler, Sydney. *Writing for Money*. London: Ivor Nicholson and Watson, 1932.

Hough, Graham. *The Last Romantics*. London: Gerald Duckworth, 1949.

Houston, Penelope. Review of *The Film Till Now* in *Sight and Sound* 19, 1 (1950): 40.

Howard, Diana. *London Theatres and Music Halls, 1850–1950*. London: Library Association, 1970.

Howarth, T. E. B. *Cambridge Between Two Wars*. London: Collins, 1978.

Huettig, Mae. *Economic Control of the Motion Picture Industry.* Philadelphia: University of Pennsylvania Press, 1944.

Huff, Theodore. *Charlie Chaplin.* New York: Henry Schuman, 1951.

Hughes, Helen MacGill. *News and the Human-Interest Story.* Chicago: University of Chicago Press, 1940.

Hughes, Richard. 'The Birth of Radio Drama'. *Atlantic Monthly* 200, 6 (1957): 145–8.

Hulton, Edward. 'The Future of *Picture Post*'. *Penrose Annual* 42 (1940): 21–4.

Hunnings, Neville March. *Film Censors and the Law.* London: George Allen and Unwin, 1967.

Hutchinson, Harold F. *London Transport Posters.* London: London Transport Board, 1963.

—— *The Poster: An Illustrated History from 1860.* New York: Viking, 1968.

Hutt, Allen. *Newspaper Design.* London: Oxford University Press, 1960.

—— *The Changing Newspaper: Typographic Trends in Britain and America, 1622–1972.* London: Gordon Fraser, 1973.

Huxley, Aldous. 'Our Contemporary Hocus-Pocus'. *Forum* 73, 3 (1925): 313–20.

—— *Jesting Pilate: The Diary of a Journey.* New York: George H. Doran, 1926.

—— *Point Counter Point.* 1928. Reprinted New York: Harper and Row, 1965.

Hynes, Samuel. *The Auden Generation: Literature and Politics in England in the 1930s.* New York: Viking, 1977.

Innis, H. A. *The Press: A Neglected Factor in the Economic History of the Twentieth Century.* London: Oxford University Press, 1949.

—— *The Bias of Communication.* Toronto: University of Toronto Press, 1951.

Jackson, Alan A. *Semi-Detached London: Suburban Development, Life and Transport, 1900–39.* London: George Allen and Unwin, 1973.

Jackson, Holbrook. 'The Dictatorship of the Lay-out Man'. *Typography* 7 (1938): 2–7.

Jackson, Mason. *The Pictorial Press: Its Origins and Progress.* London: Hurst and Blackett, 1885.

Jacobs, Lewis, ed. *The Documentary Tradition: From* Nanook *to* Woodstock. New York: W. W. Norton, 1971.

—— *The Emergence of Film Art: The Evolution and Development of the Motion Picture as an Art Since 1900.* 2nd edn. New York: W. W. Norton, 1971.

James, Henry and H. G. Wells. *Henry James and H. G. Wells: A Record of Their Friendship, Their Debate on the Art of Fiction and Their Quarrel.* Leon Edel and Gordon N. Ray, eds. Urbana: University of Illinois Press, 1958.

Jameson, Frederick. *Fables of Aggression: Wyndham Lewis, the Modernist as Fascist.* Berkeley and Los Angeles: University of California Press, 1979.

Jarché, James. *People I Have Shot.* London: Methuen, 1934.

Jay, Martin. *The Dialectical Imagination: A History of the Frankfurt School and the Institute of Social Research, 1923–1950.* Boston: Little, Brown, 1973.

Jefferys, James B. *Retail Trading in Britain, 1850–1950.* Cambridge: Cambridge University Press, 1954.

Joad, C. E. M. *The Babbitt Warren.* London: Kegan Paul, Trench, Trubner, 1926.

Joad, C. E. M. *The Horrors of the Countryside*. London: Hogarth Press, 1931.

Johnson, F. Craig, and George R. Klare. 'Feedback: Principles and Analogies'. *Journal of Communication* 12, 1 (1962): 150–9.

Johnson, Lesley. *The Cultural Critics: From Matthew Arnold to Raymond Williams*. London: Routledge and Kegan Paul, 1979.

Johnson, William. 'Early Griffith: A Wider View'. *Film Quarterly* 29, 2 (1975–6): 2–13.

Johnson, W. W. 'The Gramophone Society Movement'. *The Gramophone* 14, 158 (1936): 85–7.

Johnston, Priscilla. *Edward Johnston*. London: Faber and Faber, 1959.

Jones, Geoffrey. 'The Gramophone Company: An Anglo-American Multinational, 1898–1931'. *Business History Review* 59 (1985): 76–100.

Jones, Herbert. *Stanley Morison Displayed: An Examination of his Early Typographic Work*. London: Frederick Muller, 1976.

Jones, Kennedy. *Fleet Street and Downing Street*. London: Hutchinson [1920].

Joseph, Michael. *The Commercial Side of Literature*. London: Hutchinson [1925].

Jowett, Garth. *Film: The Democratic Art*. Boston: Little, Brown, 1976.

Juergens, George. *Joseph Pulitzer and the New York* World. Princeton: Princeton University Press, 1966.

Jupp, James. *The Radical Left in Britain, 1931–1941*. London: Frank Cass, 1982.

Kahn, Derek. 'What is Culture?'. *Left Review* 2, 16 (1937): 891–4.

Kaldor, Nicholas and Rodney Silverman. *A Statistical Analysis of Advertising Expenditure and of the Revenue of the Press*. Cambridge: Cambridge University Press, 1948.

Kauffer, E. McKnight. 'The Poster and Symbolism'. *Penrose's Annual* 26 (1924): 41–5.

—— 'Advertising Art: The Designer and the Public'. *Journal of the Royal Society of Arts* 87, 4488 (1938–9): 52–67.

—— ed. *The Art of the Poster: Its Origin, Evolution and Purpose*. London: Cecil Palmer, 1924.

Kelly, Thomas. *A History of Adult Education in Great Britain*. Liverpool: Liverpool University Press, 1970.

Kenez, Peter. *The Birth of the Propaganda State: Soviet Methods of Mass Mobilization, 1917–1929*. Cambridge: Cambridge University Press, 1985.

Kern, Stephen. *The Culture of Time and Space, 1880–1918*. Cambridge: Harvard University Press, 1983.

Kerr, Walter. *The Silent Clowns*. New York: Alfred A. Knopf, 1979.

Kindem, Gorham, ed. *The American Movie Industry: The Business of Motion Pictures*. Carbondale and Edwardsville: Southern Illinois University Press, 1982.

King, Anthony D. *The Bungalow: The Production of a Global Culture*. London: Routledge and Kegan Paul, 1984.

King, Cecil. *The Future of the Press*. London: MacGibbon and Kee, 1967.

—— *Strictly Personal*. London: Weidenfeld and Nicolson, 1969.

Klapp, Orrin E. *Heroes, Villains and Fools: The Changing American Character.* Englewood Cliffs: Prentice-Hall, 1962.

Klein, Adrian Bernard. 'The New Artistic Epoch: Are We Aware of Its Existence?'. *Penrose Year Book and Review of the Graphic Arts* 28 (1926): 36–8.

Klingender, F. D. and Stuart Legg. *Money Behind the Screen.* London: Lawrence and Wishart, 1937.

Knights, Ben. *The Idea of the Clerisy in the Nineteenth Century.* Cambridge: Cambridge University Press, 1978.

Knoles, George Harmon. *The Jazz Age Revisited: British Criticism of American Civilization During the 1920s.* Stanford: Stanford University Press; Oxford: Oxford University Press, 1955.

Knox, Collie. 'Collie Knox Calling'. *Daily Mail*, 1933–5.

—— *It Might Have Been You.* London: Chapman and Hall, 1938.

Koss, Stephen. *The Rise and Fall of the Political Press in Britain.* 2 vols. Chapel Hill: University of North Carolina Press, 1981, 1984.

Kranzberg, Melvin and William H. Davenport, eds. *Technology and Culture: An Anthology.* New York: Schocken Books, 1972.

Krissdottir, Morine. *John Cowper Powys and the Magical Quest.* London: Macdonald and Jane's, 1980.

Kuhns, William. *The Post-Industrial Prophets: Interpretations of Technology.* New York: Weybridge and Talley, 1971.

Kunzle, David. *The Early Comic Strip: Narrative Strips and Picture Stories in the European Broadsheet From c.1450 to 1825.* Berkeley: University of California Press, 1973.

Lambert, Constant. *Music Ho! A Study of Music in Decline.* London: Faber and Faber, 1934.

Lambert, Richard S. 'How to Get the Films You Want'. *Sight and Sound* 3, 9 (1934): 5–9.

—— *The Universal Provider: A Study of William Whiteley and the Rise of the London Department Store.* London: George S. Harrap, 1938.

—— *Ariel and All His Qualities: An Impression of the BBC From Within.* London: Victor Gollancz, 1940.

—— ed. *For Filmgoers Only: The Intelligent Filmgoer's Guide to the Film.* London: Faber and Faber and The British Institute of Education, 1934.

—— ed. *Art in England.* Harmondsworth: Penguin, 1938.

Lane, Allen. 'Books for the Millions . . . '. *Left Review* 3, 16 (1938): 968–70.

Larned, W. Livingston. 'Balance in Advertising Design'. *Advertising Display* 1, 2 (1926): 50–1.

Laski, Harold. 'Sir John Reith'. *Daily Herald*, 21 Mar. 1931.

Lauder, Harry. 'I'm Tellin Ye!' *Radio Times*, 29 June 1926, 2.

—— 'I'll be Seein' Ye Wednesday Night'. *Radio Times*, 23 Dec. 1927, 645.

Lautenbach, Edward S. 'Victorian Advertising and Magazine Stripping'. *Victorian Studies* 10, 4 (1967): 431–4.

Lawrence, Arthur, ed. *Journalism as a Profession.* London: Hodder and Stoughton, 1903.

Lawrence, D. H. *Studies in Classic American Literature*. New York: Thomas Selzer, 1923.

—— 'Morality and the Novel'. *The Calendar of Modern Letters* 2, 10 (1925): 268–74.

—— *Psychoanalysis and the Unconscious* and *Fantasia of the Unconscious*. Philip Rieff, ed. New York: Viking Press, 1960.

—— *The Letters of D. H. Lawrence. Volume Three: October, 1916–June, 1921*. James T. Boulton and Andrew Robertson, eds. Cambridge: Cambridge University Press, 1984.

Lawrence, Florence. 'Just About Myself'. *Pictures and the Picturegoer*, 18 Apr. 1914.

Lawrence, T. B. 'The Transatlantic Plague'. *Advertiser's Weekly*, 21 Dec. 1928, 488.

Lea, Gordon. *Radio Drama and How to Write It*. London: George Allen and Unwin, 1926.

Lears, T. J. Jackson. 'The Concept of Cultural Hegemony: Problems and Possibilities'. *American Historical Review* 90, 3 (1985): 567–93.

Leavis, F. R. 'The Relationship of Journalism to Literature: Studied in the Rise and Earlier Development of the Press in England'. Ph.D. diss.: Cambridge University, 1924.

—— *Mass Civilization and Minority Culture*. Cambridge: The Minority Press, 1930.

—— 'The Literary Mind'. *Scrutiny* 1, 1 (1932): 20–32.

—— 'What's Wrong With Criticism?'. *Scrutiny* 1, 2 (1932): 132–46.

—— 'Literary Criticism and Philosophy: A Reply'. *Scrutiny* 6, 1 (1937): 59–70.

—— 'Education and the University: Sketch for an English School'. *Scrutiny* 9, 2 (1940): 98–120.

—— '*Scrutiny*: A Retrospect' in *Scrutiny. Volume Twenty: A Retrospect, Indexes, Errata*. Cambridge: Cambridge University Press, 1963.

—— and Denys Thompson. *Culture and Environment: The Training of Critical Awareness*. London: Chatto and Windus, 1933.

Leavis, Q. D. *Fiction and the Reading Public*. London: Chatto and Windus, 1932.

—— *Collected Essays. Volume One: The Englishness of the English Novel*. G. Singh, ed. Cambridge: Cambridge University Press, 1983.

Le Bon, Gustave. *The Crowd: A Study of the Popular Mind*. London: T. Fisher Unwin, 1896.

Lee, Alan. *The Origins of the Popular Press in England, 1855–1914*. London: Croom Helm; Totowa, NJ: Rowman and Littlefield, 1976.

Lee, Edward. *Music of the People: A Study of Popular Music in Great Britain*. London: Barrie and Jenkins, 1970.

Lee, E. M. 'Components'. *The Times*. Special Supplement on Radio. 14 Aug. 1934, p. xl.

Lee, J. M. 'The Dissolution of the Empire Marketing Board, 1933: Reflections on a Diary'. *Journal of Imperial and Commonwealth History* 1, 1 (1972): 49–57.

Lejeune, C. A. 'The British Film and Others'. *The Fortnightly* 143 (1935): 285–94.

—— *Chestnuts in Her Lap: 1936–1947.* London: Phoenix House, 1947.

LeMahieu, D. L. '*The Gramophone*: Recorded Music and the Cultivated Mind in Britain Between the Wars'. *Technology and Culture* 23, 3 (1982): 372–91.

Leonard, Neil. *Jazz and White Americans: The Acceptance of a New Art Form.* Chicago: University of Chicago Press, 1962.

Lerg, W. B. *Die Entstehung des Rundfunks in Deutschland: Herkunft und Entwicklung eines publizistischen Mediums.* Frankfort: Joseph Knecht, 1965.

Lethaby, W. R. 'Art and Workmanship'. *Imprint* 1 (1913): 1–4.

Levenson, Michael H. *A Genealogy of Modernism: A Study of English Literary Doctrine, 1908–1922.* Cambridge: Cambridge University Press, 1984.

Lewis, C. A. *Broadcasting From Within.* London: George Newnes, n.d.

Lewis, Jane. *Women in England, 1870–1950: Sexual Divisions and Social Change.* Sussex: Wheatsheaf Books; Bloomington: Indiana University Press, 1984.

Lewis, John. *The Left Book Club: An Historical Record.* London: Gollancz, 1970.

Lewis, Wyndham. *Tarr.* New York: Alfred A. Knopf, 1918.

—— *The Art of Being Ruled.* London and New York: Harper Brothers, 1926.

—— *The Apes of God.* 1930. Reprinted Santa Barbara: Black Sparrow Press, 1981.

—— 'What is Industrial Art?'. *Commercial Art and Industry* 18 (1935): 83–6.

—— 'Art and Patronage (1)'. In *B.B.C. Annual.* London: British Broadcasting Corporation, 1935.

—— *Time and Western Man.* Boston: Beacon Press, 1957.

—— *The Letters of Wyndham Lewis.* W. K. Rose, ed. London: Methuen, 1963.

—— *Wyndham Lewis on Art: Collected Writings, 1913–1956.* New York: Funk and Wagnalls, 1969.

Leyda, Jay. *Kino: A History of the Russian and Soviet Film.* London: George Allen and Unwin, 1960.

—— ed. *Voices of Film Experience.* New York: Macmillan; London: Collier Macmillan, 1977.

Lilien, Otto M. *History of Industrial Gravure Printing up to 1920.* London: Lund Humphries, 1972.

Lindsay, David. *The Crawford Papers: The Journals of David Lindsay, Twenty-seventh Earl of Crawford and Tenth Earl of Balcarres, 1871–1940, during the years 1892–40.* John Vincent, ed. Manchester: Manchester University Press, 1984.

Lindsay, Jack. *After the Thirties: The Novel in Britain and Its Future.* London: Lawrence and Wishart, 1956.

Lindsay, Kenneth. *Social Progress and Educational Waste.* London: George Routledge and Sons, 1926.

Linklater, Andro. *Compton Mackenzie: A Life.* London: Chatto and Windus, 1987.

Lissitzky, Sophie. *El Lissitzky: Life, Letters, Texts.* London: Thames and Hudson, 1968.

Littlejohn, Stephen. *Theories of Human Communications.* Columbus, OH: Charles E. Merrill, 1978.

Löb, Ladislaus. *Mensch und Gesellschaft Bei J. B. Priestley.* Francke Verlag Bern, 1962.

Lodder, Christina. *Russian Constructivism.* New Haven: Yale University Press, 1983.

Lovell, Alan and Jim Hillier. *Studies in Documentary.* London: Secker and Warburg, 1972.

Low, Rachael. *The History of the British Film, 1914–1918.* London: British Film Institute, 1948.

—— *The History of the British Film, 1906–1914.* London: George Allen and Unwin, 1949.

—— *The History of the British Film, 1918–1929.* London: George Allen and Unwin, 1971.

—— *The History of the British Film, 1929–39: Documentary and Educational Films of the 1930s.* London: George Allen and Unwin, 1979.

—— *The History of the British Film, 1929–1939. Film Making in 1930s Britain.* London: George Allen and Unwin, 1985.

—— and Roger Manvell. *The History of the British Film, 1896–1906.* London: George Allen and Unwin, 1948.

Lucas, D. B. and C. E. Benson. *Psychology for Advertisers.* New York and London: Harper, 1930.

Lucas, E. V. 'Mixed Thoughts on Broadcasting'. *Radio Times*, 5 Sept. 1924, 441.

Lucas, John, ed. *The 1930s: A Challenge to Orthodoxy.* Sussex: Harvester; New York: Barnes and Noble, 1978.

Luft, Herbert G. 'Rotha and the World'. *Quarterly of Film, Radio and Television* 10, 1 (1955): 89–99.

Lynd, Helen Merrell. *England in the Eighteen-Eighties: Toward a Social Basis for Freedom.* 1945. Reprinted New Brunswick: Transaction Books, 1984.

Lynes, Russell. *The Lively Audience: A Social History of the Visual and Performing Arts in America, 1890–1950.* New York: Harper and Row, 1985.

Lyons, Timothy J. *Charles Chaplin: A Guide to References and Resources.* Boston: G. K. Hall, 1979.

MacCabe, Colin, ed. *High Theory/Low Culture: Analysing Popular Television and Film.* New York: St Martin's Press, 1986.

Macaulay, Rose. *Personal Pleasures.* New York: Macmillan, 1936.

McCaffrey, Donald W., ed. *Focus on Chaplin.* Englewood Cliffs, NJ: Prentice-Hall, 1971.

McCallum, Pamela. *Literature and Method: Towards a Critique of I. A. Richards, T. S. Eliot and F. R. Leavis.* London: Gill and Macmillan, Humanities Press, 1983.

McCarthy, Albert. *The Dance-Band Era: The Dancing Decades From Ragtime to Swing, 1910–1950.* London: Studio Vista, 1971.

MacCarthy, Desmond. 'Charlie's Cane'. *New Statesman*, 8 Sept. 1923, 618–9.

MacCarthy, Fiona. *All Things Bright and Beautiful: Design in Britain, 1830 to Today.* Toronto: University of Toronto Press, 1972.

McCurdy, C. A. 'The Birmingham Convention'. *Advertiser's Weekly*, 22 June 1928, 535.

MacDonald, J. Ramsay. 'As I Listened To Geneva'. *Radio Times*, 16 Apr. 1926, 145.

McGarry, K. J., ed. *Mass Communications: Selected Readings for Librarians.* London: Clive Bingley, 1972.

Macinnes, Colin. *Sweet Saturday Night.* London: MacGibbon and Kee, 1967.

Macintyre, Stuart. 'British Labour, Marxism and Working-Class Apathy in the Nineteen-Twenties'. *Historical Journal*, 20, 2 (1977): 479–96.

—— *A Proletarian Science: Marxism in Britain, 1917–1933.* Cambridge: Cambridge University Press, 1980.

Mackenzie, Compton. 'The Gramophone'. *Daily Telegraph*, 2 Sept. 1922.

—— 'Prologue'. *The Gramophone* 1, 1 (1923): 1.

—— 'Editorial'. Various in *The Gramophone*, 1923–38.

—— 'The Gramophone, Its Past, Present and Its Future'. *Proceedings of the Musical Association.* Session 51 (1925): 101–3.

—— 'December Records'. *The Gramophone* 4, 8 (1927): 344.

—— 'The B.B.C.'. *The Gramophone* 4, 9 (1927): 359.

—— 'Can Wireless Aid the Art of Drama?'. *Radio Times*, 27 Sept. 1929, 667.

—— 'Carnival, 1911–1929'. *Vox*, 9 Nov. 1929, 22–3.

—— *My Life and Times.* 10 vols. London: Chatto and Windus, 1963–71.

—— 'How It All Began'. *The Gramophone* 50, 599 (1973): 1821.

—— Compton Mackenzie Papers. Harry Ransom Humanities Research Center, University of Texas at Austin.

McKenzie, F. A. *The Mystery of the* Daily Mail. London: Associated Newspapers, 1921.

Mackenzie, John M. *Propaganda and Empire: The Manipulation of British Public Opinion, 1880–1960.* Manchester: Manchester University Press, 1984.

Mackerness, E. D. *A Social History of English Music.* London: Routledge and Kegan Paul; Toronto: University of Toronto Press, 1964.

McKitterick, Daniel, ed. *Stanley Morison and D. B. Updike: Selected Correspondence.* New York: Moretus Press, 1979.

McLaine, Ian. *Ministry of Morale: Home Front Morale and the Ministry of Information in World War Two.* London: George Allen and Unwin, 1979.

McLean, Ruari. *Modern Book Design: From William Morris to the Present Day.* London: Faber and Faber, 1958.

—— 'Jan Tschichold'. *Penrose Annual* 63 (1970): 89–105.

—— *The Thames and Hudson Manual of Typography.* London: Thames and Hudson, 1980.

McLuhan, Marshall. *The Gutenberg Galaxy: The Making of Typographic Man.* Toronto: University of Toronto Press, 1962.

—— *Understanding Media: The Extensions of Man.* New York: McGraw-Hill, 1964; McGraw Paperback, 1965.

McMahon, A. Michal. 'An American Courtship: Psychologists and Advertising Theory in the Progressive Era'. *American Studies* 13, 2 (1972): 5–18.

McMahon, Henry. '180 Years of Pioneer Work by the Royal Society of Arts'. *Journal of the Royal Society of Arts* 85, 4382 (1936): 10–21.

McQuail, Denis. *Towards a Sociology of Mass Communications.* London: Collier Macmillan, 1969.

[Macpherson, Kenneth]. 'As Is'. *Close-Up* 3, 3 (1928): 5–13.

Madge, Charles. 'The Press and Social Consciousness'. *Left Review* 3, 5 (1937): 278–86.

—— 'Viewpoint'. *TLS*, 14 Dec. 1979, 119.

Maggs, Philip B. *A History of Graphic Design*. New York: Van Norstrand Reinhold, 1983.

Maine, Basil. 'Is America Killing Our Sense of Humour?'. *Radio Times*, 3 July 1931, 3.

—— *The B.B.C. and its Audience*. London: Thames and Hudson, 1939.

Maloney, Russell. 'Profile: What Happens After That'. *New Yorker*, 10 Sept. 1938, 24–8.

Mander, Raymond and Joe Mitcheson. *British Music Hall*. Revised edition. London: Gentry Books, 1974.

Mannheim, Karl. *Essays on the Sociology of Culture*. London: Routledge and Kegan Paul, 1956.

Mansfield, F. J. *The Complete Journalist: A Study of the Principles and Practice of Newspaper-Making*. London: Sir Isaac Pitman, 1935.

Manvell, Roger. *Chaplin*. Boston: Little, Brown, 1974.

Marchand, Roland. *Advertising the American Dream: Making Way for Modernity, 1920–1940*. Berkeley: University of California Press, 1985.

Margolis, David. *The Function of Literature: A Study of Christopher Caudwell's Aesthetics*. New York: International Publishers, 1969.

Marshall, Herbert, ed. *The Battleship Potemkin*. New York: Avon Books, 1978.

Martin, Marianne W. *Futurist Art and Theory, 1909–1915*. New York: Hacken Art Book, 1978.

Marwick, Arthur. *The Deluge: British Society and the First World War*. 1965. Reprinted New York: Norton, 1970.

Maschwitz, Eric. 'Radio Variety in 1935'. *Radio Times*, 13 Sept. 1935, 4–5.

—— 'New BBC Plans for Dance Music'. *Radio Times*, 6 Mar. 1936, 4, 10.

—— *No Chip on My Shoulder*. London: Herbert Jenkins, 1957.

Mast, Gerald. *The Comic Mind: Comedy and the Movies*. Indianapolis: Bobbs-Merrill, 1973.

—— *A Short History of the Movies*. Indianapolis: Bobbs-Merrill, 1976.

Matheson, Hilda. *Broadcasting*. London: Thornton Butterworth, 1933.

Matthews, Roy T. and Peter Mellina. *In Vanity Fair*. Berkeley: University of California Press, 1982.

Maurier, Daphne du. *Gerald: A Portrait*. Garden City: Doubleday, Doran, 1935.

May, Lary. *Screening Out the Past: The Birth of Mass Culture and the Motion-Picture Industry*. New York: Oxford University Press, 1980.

Mayer, J. P. *British Cinemas and Their Audiences: Sociological Studies*. London: Dennis Dobson, 1948.

Meacham, Standish. *A Life Apart: The English Working Class, 1890–1914*. Cambridge: Harvard University Press, 1977.

Meadmore, W. S. 'Sir Louis Sterling'. *The Gramophone* 15, 169 (1937): 6.

Megaw, Denis. '20th-Century Sans Serif Types'. *Typography* 7 (1938): 28–31.

Mellor, G. J. *The Northern Music Hall: A Century of Popular Entertainment*. Newcastle: Frank Graham, 1970.

—— *Picture Pioneers: The Story of the Northern Cinema, 1896–1921.* Newcastle: Frank Graham, 1971.

Mendl, R. W. S. *The Appeal of Jazz.* London: Philip Allan [1927].

Mercer, F. A. and W. Gaunt, eds. *Posters and Publicity, 1929: Fine Printing and Design in* Commercial Art *Annual.* London: The Studio, 1929.

—— eds. *Modern Publicity:* Commercial Art *Annual, 1930.* London: The Studio, 1930.

Messel, Rudolph. *This Film Business.* London: Ernest Benn, 1928.

Meyers, Jeffrey. *The Enemy: A Biography of Wyndham Lewis.* London: Routledge and Kegan Paul, 1980.

—— ed. *Wyndham Lewis: A Revaluation.* Montreal: McGill and Queen's University Press, 1980.

Meynell, Francis. *The Typography of Newspaper Advertisements.* London: Ernest Benn, 1929.

—— *My Lives.* London: Bodley Head, 1971.

Middleton, Lucy, ed. *Women in the Labour Movement: The British Experience.* London: Croom Helm; Totowa, NJ: Rowman and Littlefield, 1977.

Miliband, Ralph and John Saville, eds. *The Socialist Register, 1977.* New York and London: Monthly Press, 1978.

Millais, John Guille. *The Life and Letters of Sir John Everett Millais.* 2 vols. New York: Frederick A. Stokes, 1899.

Miller, Gavin. 'The Unknown Chaplin'. *Sight and Sound* 52, 2 (1983): 98–9.

Miller, Jonathan. *Marshall McLuhan.* London: Fontana, 1971.

Miller, Michael B. *The Bon Marché: Bourgeois Culture and the Department Store, 1869–1920.* Princeton: Princeton University Press, 1981.

Minihan, Janet. *The Nationalization of Culture: The Development of State Subsidies to the Arts in Great Britain.* New York: New York University Press, 1977.

Minney, R. J. *Viscount Southwood.* London: Odhams Press, 1954.

Mirsky, Dmitri. *The Intelligentsia of Great Britain.* Alec Brown, trans. New York: Covici, Friede, 1935.

Mitchell, Ogilvie. *The Talking Machine Industry.* London: Sir Isaac Pitman and Sons [1922].

Modern Advertising. 2 vols. London: Sir Isaac Pitman, 1926.

Moholy-Nagy, László. *Moholy-Nagy.* Richard Kostelanatz, ed. New York: Praeger, 1970.

Moholy-Nagy, Sibyl. *Moholy-Nagy: Experiment in Totality.* Cambridge: Massachusetts Institute of Technology Press, 1969.

Molyneaux, Gerard. *Charles Chaplin's* City Lights*: The Production and Dialectical Structure.* New York: Garland, 1983.

Montagu, Ivor. *The Political Censorship of Films.* London: Victor Gollancz, 1929.

—— 'The Film Society, London'. *Cinema Quarterly* 1, 1 (1932): 42–6.

—— *With Eisenstein in Hollywood: A Chapter of Autobiography.* Berlin: Seven Seas Publishers, 1968.

—— *The Youngest Son.* London: Lawrence and Wishart, 1970.

—— 'Birmingham Sparrow: In Memoriam, Iris Barry 1896–1969'. *Sight and Sound* 39, 2 (1970): 106–8.

Montagu, Ivor. 'Interview: Ivor Montagu'. *Screen* 13, 3 (1972): 71–113.

—— 'Working With Hitchcock'. *Sight and Sound* 49, 3 (1980): 189–93.

Moore, George Edward. *Principia Ethica*. 1903. Reprinted Cambridge: Cambridge University Press, 1959.

Moore, Jerrold Northrop. *A Voice in Time: The Gramophone of Fred Gaisberg, 1873–1951*. London: Hamish Hamilton, 1976.

—— ed. *Music and Friends: Letters to Adrian Boult*. London: Hamish Hamilton, 1979.

Moorehead, Caroline. *Sidney Bernstein: A Biography*. London: Jonathan Cape, 1984.

Moorsel, L. Leering van. 'The Typography of El Lissitzky'. *Journal of Typographic Research* 2, 4 (1968): 323–40.

Moran, James. *Stanley Morison: His Typographic Achievement*. London: Lund Humphries, 1971.

Morin, Edgar. *The Stars*. New York: Grove Press, 1960.

Morison, Stanley. *On Type Faces*. London: Media Society and *Fleuron*, 1923.

—— 'Towards an Ideal Type'. *Fleuron* 2 (1924): 57–75.

—— *Modern Fine Printing*. London: Ernest Benn, 1925.

—— 'First Principles of Typography'. *Fleuron* 7 (1930): 61–72.

—— *The English Newspaper: Some Account of the Physical Development of Journals Printed in London Between 1622 and the Present Day*. Cambridge: Cambridge University Press, 1932.

—— 'Picture-printing and Word-printing'. *Penrose Annual* 50 (1956): 21–6.

—— *Selected Essays on the History of Letter-Forms in Manuscript and Print*. 2 vols. David McKitterick, ed. Cambridge: Cambridge University Press, 1980.

—— ed. *Four Centuries of Fine Printing*. London: Ernest Benn, 1924.

—— and Holbrook Jackson. *A Brief Survey of Printing: History and Practice*. New York: Alfred A. Knopf, 1923.

—— and Rudolph Ruzicka. *Recollections of Daniel Berkeley Updike*. Boston: The Club of Odd Volumes, 1943.

Morpurgo, J. E. *Allen Lane. King Penguin: A Biography*. London: Hutchinson, 1979.

Morris, Derek, ed. *The Economic System in the United Kingdom*. Oxford: Oxford University Press, 1977.

Mortensen, C. David, ed. *Basic Readings in Communication Theory*. New York: Harper and Row, 1973.

Moseley, Sydney A. *Broadcasting in My Time*. London. Rich and Lowan, 1935.

—— *The Private Diaries of Sydney Moseley*. London: Max Parrish, 1960.

Mott, Frank Luther. *American Journalism: A History, 1690–1960*. New York: Macmillan, 1962.

Mowat, Charles Loch. *Britain Between the Wars, 1918–1940*. Chicago: University of Chicago Press, 1955.

Mowrer, Edgar Ansel. *This American World*. London: Faber and Gwyer, n.d.

Muggeridge, Malcolm. *The Thirties: 1930–1940 in Great Britain*. London: Hamish Hamilton, 1940.

Mulhearn, Francis. 'The Marxist Aesthetics of Christopher Caudwell'. *New Left Review* 85 (1974): 37–58.

—— *The Moment of* Scrutiny. London: New Left Books, 1979.

Mumford, Lewis. *Technics and Civilization*. New York: Harcourt, Brace, 1934.

Murry, John Middleton ['M', pseud.]. 'Intimations of Mortality'. *Athenaeum*, 30 Jan. 1920.

—— *To The Unknown God: Essays Towards a Religion*. London: Jonathan Cape, 1924.

—— ['Henry King', pseud.] 'Chaplin and the Hicks'. *Adelphi* 3, 5 (1925): 333–8.

—— ['The Journeyman', pseud.]. 'On Wireless and Nightingales'. *Adelphi* 3, 2 (1925): 138.

—— *Things To Come*. New York: Macmillan, 1928.

—— 'Northcliffe as Symbol'. *Adelphi*, NS 1 (1930): 15–18.

Musser, Charles. 'The Early Cinema of Edwin Porter'. *Cinema Journal* 19, 1 (1979): 1–38.

Nash, Paul. Letter to *The Times*, 12 June 1933, 10.

Naylor, Gillian. *The Arts and Crafts Movement*. Cambridge: Massachusetts Institute of Technology Press, 1971.

Negrine, Ralph M. 'From Radio Relay to Cable Television: The British Experience'. *Historical Journal of Film, Radio and Television* 4, 1 (1984): 29–48.

Nevett, Terence Richard. 'The Development of Commercial Advertising in Britain, 1800–1914'. Ph.D. diss.: University of London, 1979.

—— *Advertising in Britain: A History*. London: Heinemann, 1982.

Nevins, Allan. *America Through British Eyes*. New York: Oxford University Press, 1948.

Nevinson, C. R. W. 'Art and Patronage (2)'. In *B.B.C. Annual*. London: British Broadcasting Corporation, 1935.

—— *Paint and Prejudice*. London: Methuen, 1937.

Newhall, Beaumont. *The History of Photography From 1839 to the Present Day*. New York: Museum of Modern Art, 1964.

Nichols, Richard. *Radio Luxembourg: The Station of the Stars*. London: W. H. Allen, 1983.

Nicholson, John H. 'Four Years of Educational Broadcasting'. *Sight and Sound* 1, 3 (1932): 79.

Nicoll, Allandyce. *A History of English Drama, 1660–1900. Volume Five: Late Nineteenth-Century Drama, 1850–1900*. Cambridge: Cambridge University Press, 1959.

Nixon, Howard K. *Attention and Interest in Advertising*. New York: n.p., 1924.

Nobbs, Percy E. *Design: A Treatise on the Discovery of Form*. London: Oxford University Press, 1937.

Noble, Peter. *Ivor Novello*. London: Falcon Press, 1951.

Norris, Christopher, ed. *Inside the Myth: Orwell: Views From the Left*. London: Lawrence and Wishart, 1984.

North, C. J. 'Our Foregin Trade in Motion Pictures'. *Annals of the American Academy of Political and Social Science* 128 (1926): 100–8.

Noyes, Alfred. 'Radio and the Master-Secret'. *Radio Times*, 18 Sept. 1925, 549–50.

Nye, Robert A. *The Origins of Crowd Psychology: Gustave Le Bon and the Crisis of Mass Democracy in the Third Republic.* London and Beverly Hills: Sage Publications, 1975.

Oakley, Ann. *Women's Work: The Housewife, Past and Present.* New York: Pantheon, 1974.

O'Brien, Terence H. *British Experiments in Public Ownership and Control.* London: George Allen and Unwin, 1937.

Ockham, David. *Stentor, or the Press of To-Day and Tomorrow.* London: Kegan Paul, Trench, Trubner [1927].

Olivier, Laurence. *Confesions of an Actor: An Autobiography.* New York: Simon and Schuster, 1982.

Ong, Walter J. *Orality and Literacy: The Technologizing of the Word.* New York: Methuen, 1982.

Orga, Ateş. *The Proms.* London: David and Charles, 1974.

Orbanz, Eva. *Journey to a Legend and Back: The British Realistic Film.* Berlin: Edition Volker Spiess, 1977.

Orwell, George. *The Road to Wigan Pier.* 1937. Reprinted New York: Harcourt Brace Jovanovich, A Harvest Book, 1958.

—— *The Collected Essays, Journalism and Letters of George Orwell. Volume One: An Age Like This, 1920–1940.* Sonia Orwell and Ian Angus, eds. New York: Harcourt, Brace and World, 1968.

O'Sullivan, Judith. *The Art of the Comic Strip.* N.p.: University of Maryland, Department of Art, 1971.

Overy, Paul. *De Stijl.* London: Studio Vista, 1969.

Palmer, Jerry. *Thrillers: Genesis and Structure of a Popular Genre.* London. Edward Arnold; New York: St Martin's Press, 1979.

Parker, Paul. 'An Analysis of the Style of Advertising Art'. Ph.D. diss.: University of Chicago, 1937.

Parliamentary Debates. House of Commons. Fifth Series. Vol. 199. London: His Majesty's Stationery Office, 1927.

Pasdermadjian, H. *The Department Store: Its Origins, Evolution, and Economics.* London: Newman Books, 1954.

Pattison, Robert. *On Literacy: The Politics of the Word from Homer to the Age of Rock.* New York: Oxford University Press, 1982.

Paulu, Burton. *British Broadcasting: Radio and Television in the United Kingdom.* Minneapolis: University of Minnesota Press, 1956.

Pavlova, Anna. 'The Dancing Age'. *Daily Mail*, 2 Oct. 1925.

Payne, Jack. *Signature Tune.* London: Stanley Payne, n.d.

—— *'This is Jack Payne'.* London: Sampson, Low, Marston [1932].

Payne, Robert. *The Great God Pan: A Biography of the Tramp Played by Charles Chaplin.* New York: Hermitage House, 1952.

Peacock, Alan and Ronald Weir. *The Composer in the Market Place.* London: Faber Music, 1975.

Pearsall, Ronald. *Edwardian Popular Music.* Rutherford, NJ: Farleigh Dickenson University Press, 1975.

—— *Popular Music of the Twenties*. Newton Abbot: David and Charles; Totowa, NJ: Rowman and Littlefield, 1976.

Pearson, George. *Flashback: The Autobiography of a Film Pioneer*. London: George Allen and Unwin, 1957.

Peck, Robert E. 'Policy and Control—A Case Study: German Broadcasting 1923–1933'. *Media, Culture and Society* 5 (1983): 349–72.

Pegg, Mark. *Broadcasting and Society, 1918–1939*. London: Croom Helm, 1983.

Pelling, Henry. *American and the British Left: From Bright to Bevan*. London: Adam and Charles Black, 1956.

Pemberton, Max. *Lord Northcliffe: A Memoir*. London: Hodder and Stoughton, n.d.

Perkin, H. J. 'The Origins of the Popular Press'. *History Today* 7, 7 (1957): 425–35.

Perkins, Bradford. *The Great Rapprochement: England and the United States*. New York: Atheneum, 1968.

Perkins, David. *The Quest for Permanence: The Symbolism of Wordsworth, Shelley and Keats*. Cambridge: Harvard University Press, 1965.

Perloff, Marjorie. *The Futurist Movement: Avant-Garde, Avant Guerre, and the Language of Rupture*. Chicago: University of Chicago Press, 1986.

Perry, George. *The Great British Picture Show: From the Nineties to the Seventies*. Frogmore: Paladin, 1975.

—— and Alan Aldridge. *The Penguin Book of Comics: A Slight History*. Harmondsworth: Penguin Books, 1967.

Pevsner, Nicholas. *Pioneers of the Modern Movement From William Morris to Walter Gropius*. London: Faber and Faber, 1936.

—— *Studies in Art, Architecture and Design. Volume Two: Victorianism and After*. New York: Walker, 1968.

Phillips, Gene D. *Alfred Hitchcock*. Boston: Twayne, 1984.

Phillips, K. C. *Language and Class in Victorian England*. Oxford: Basil Blackwell, 1984.

Philo, Greg *et al. Really Bad News*. London: Writers and Readers, 1982.

Pick, Frank. 'Art in Modern Life'. *Nineteenth Century and After* 91 (1922): 256–64.

—— 'Underground Posters'. *Commercial Art* 2, 10 (1927): 137–44.

—— 'Has Publicity Distorted Commercial Printing?'. *Penrose Annual* 38 (1936): 26–9.

Plant, Arnold, comp. *Survey of Listening to Sponsored Radio Programmes*. London: Joint Committee of the Incorporated Society of British Advertisers and the Institute of Incorporated Practitioners of Advertising, 1938.

Political and Economic Planning. *Report on the British Press: A Survey of its Current Operations and Problems*. London: Political and Economic Planning, 1938.

—— *The British Film Industry*. London: Political and Economic Planning, 1952.

Pollard, Anthony, Managing Editor of *The Gramophone*. Interview. 29 Aug. 1978.

Pollard, Sidney. *The Development of the British Economy, 1914–1950*. London: Edward Arnold, 1962.

Pollay, Richard W., ed. *Information Sources in Advertising History*. Westport, Conn.: Greenwood Press, 1979.

Pope, Daniel. *The Making of Modern Advertising*. New York: Basic Books, 1983.

Potamkin, Harry A. 'The Compound Cinema'. *Close-Up* 4, 1 (1929): 32–7.

—— 'Phases of Cinema Unity'. *Close-Up* 4, 5 (1929): 27–38.

—— 'The French Cinema'. *Close-Up* 5, 1 (1929): 11–24.

—— 'Movie and New York Notes'. *Close-Up* 7, 4 (1930): 235–52.

—— *The Compound Cinema: The Film Writings of Harry Alan Potamkin*. Lewis Jacobs, ed. New York: Teachers College Press, 1977.

Potter, Stephen. *The Muse in Chains: A Study in Education*. London: Jonathan Cape, 1937.

Pound, Reginald. 'The Leader Comes Into Its Own'. *World's Press News*, 1 May 1930, 3.

—— *Selfridge: A Biography*. London: Heinemann, 1960.

—— and Geoffrey Harmsworth. *Northcliffe*. London: Cassell, 1959.

Powys, John Cowper. *The Meaning of Culture*. 1929. Reprinted New York: Garden City Publishers, 1941.

Pratten, C. F. *Economies of Scale in Manufacturing Industry*. Cambridge: Cambridge University Press, 1971.

—— and R. M. Dean. *The Economics of Large-Scale Production in British Industry: An Introductory Study*. Cambridge: Cambridge University Press, 1965.

Presbrey, Frank S. *The History and Development of Advertising*. Garden City, NY: Doubleday, Doran, 1929.

Price, Charles Matlack. *Posters: A Critical Study of the Development of Poster Design in Continental Europe, England and America*. New York: George W. Bricker, 1913.

Price, R. G. G. *A History of* Punch. London: Collins, 1957.

Priestley, J. B. *Brief Diversions: Being Tales, Travesties and Epigrams*. Cambridge: Bowes and Bowes, 1922.

—— *I For One*. London: John Lane, The Bodley Head, 1923.

—— *Talking*. London: Jarrolds, 1926.

—— *Open House: A Book of Essays*. London: William Heinemann, 1927.

—— *Apes and Angels: A Book of Essays*. London: Methuen, 1928.

—— *The Balconinny and Other Essays*. London: Methuen, 1929.

—— *The Good Companions*. London: William Heinemann, 1929.

—— 'Wireless Without Tears: Turning Our Drawing Rooms into Kindergartens— Too Much Talk and Too Little Music'. *Daily Mirror* 28 Jan. 1929.

—— *Angel Pavement*. London: William Heinemann, 1930.

—— 'Men, Women and Books'. *Evening Standard*, [various dates] 1932.

—— *Faraway*. New York: Harper and Brothers, 1932.

—— *Albert Goes Through*. London: William Heinemann, 1933.

—— 'About Myself'. *Listener*, 21 June 1933, 991.

—— *Wonder Hero*. London: William Heinemann, 1933.

—— *English Journey*. 1934. Reprinted London: William Heinemann in association with Victor Gollancz, 1937.

—— 'Cash, Comics and Culture at the B.B.C.'. *Star*, 16 Jan. 1935.

—— *They Walk in the City*. London: William Heinemann, 1936.

—— 'English Films and the English People'. *World Film News and Television Progress* 1, 8 (1936): 3.

—— 'Complaints of B.B.C. Speakers'. *World Film News and Television Progress* 1, 9 (1936): 25.

—— *Midnight on the Desert: An Excursion into Autobiography During a Winter in America, 1935-36*. New York: Harper and Brothers, 1937.

—— 'If I Ran the B.B.C.'. *Sunday Dispatch*, 24 July 1938.

—— *Rain Upon Godshill: More Chapters of Autobiography*. 1939. Reprinted London: Reader's Union and William Heinemann, 1941.

—— *Johnson Over Jordan: The Play and All About It*. London: William Heinemann, 1939.

—— *Let the People Sing*. London: Heinemann, 1939.

—— *All England Listened: the Wartime Broadcasts of J. B. Priestley*. 1940-1. Reprinted New York: Chilmark Press, 1967.

—— *Margin Released: A Writer's Reminiscences and Reflections*. London: Heinemann, 1962.

—— *The Edwardians*. London: Heinemann, 1970.

—— Interview. 18 Sept. 1978.

—— J. B. Priestley Papers. Harry Ransom Humanities Research Center, University of Texas at Austin.

Printing in the Twentieth Century: A Survey. Reprint from *The Times*, 29 Oct. 1929. London: Times Publishing, 1930.

Pronay, Nicholas and D. W. Spring, eds. *Propaganda, Politics and Film, 1918-45*. London: Macmillan, 1982.

Pudovkin, V. I. *Film Technique*. Ivor Montagu, trans. 1929. Reprinted London: George Newnes, 1933.

Rachmaninoff, Sergei. 'The Artist and the Gramophone'. *The Gramophone* 8, 9 (1931): 526.

Radway, Janice A. *Reading the Romance: Women, Patriarchy and Popular Literature*. Chapel Hill: University of North Carolina Press, 1984.

Rait, Robert S. 'The Return of the Ear'. *Radio Times*, 15 Aug. 1924, 309-10.

Rammelkamp, Julian S. *Pulitzer's* Post-Dispatch, *1878-1883*. Princeton: Princeton University Press, 1967.

Rapson, Richard L. *Britons View America: Travel Commentary, 1860-1935*. Seattle: University of Washington Press, 1971.

Raucher, Alan R. *Public Relations and Business, 1900-1929*. Baltimore: Johns Hopkins University Press, 1968.

Rault, Walter T. 'Masts for the Millions'. *Radio Times*, 4 Jan. 1929.

Ray, Paul C. *The Surrealist Movement in England*. Ithaca: Cornell University Press, 1971.

Rayner, John. 'Features for Two Millions'. *Typography* 2 (1937): 13-15.

Read, Herbert. Review of *The Truth Behind Publishing* by Stanley Unwin. *Monthly Criterion* 6, 1 (1927): 83.

—— *The Meaning of Art*. London: Faber and Faber, 1931.

Read, Herbert. *Art Now: An Introduction to the Theory of Modern Painting and Sculpture*. London: Faber and Faber, 1933.

—— *Art and Industry: The Principles of Industrial Design*. London: Faber and Faber, 1934.

—— 'Surrealism—the Dialectic of Art'. *Left Review* 2, 10 (1936): pp. ii–iii.

—— 'A Choice of Extremes'. *Penrose Annual* 39 (1937): 21–4.

Read, Oliver and Walter L. Welch. *From Tin Foil to Stereo: Evolution of the Phonograph*. 2nd edn. Indianapolis: Howard W. Sams, 1977.

Reeves, Nicholas. 'Film Propaganda and its Audience: The Example of Britain's Official Films during the First World War'. *Journal of Contemporary History* 18 (1983): 463–94.

—— *Official British Film Propaganda during the First World War*. London: Croom Helm, 1986.

Reith, J. C. W. *Broadcast Over Britain*. London: Hodder and Stoughton [1924].

—— 'Why Libel the Soldier?'. *John O'London's Weekly*, 15 Mar. 1930.

—— Typescript of speech to Manchester University, 17 May 1933. BBC Written Archives Centre, Reading.

—— 'The Body Scholastic and the Body Politic'. *Glasgow Academy Chronicle* (Oct. 1933): 3–5.

—— *Into the Wind*. London: Hodder and Stoughton, 1949.

—— *Wearing Spurs*. London: Hutchinson, 1966.

—— *The Reith Diaries*. Charles Stuart, ed. London: Collins, 1975.

—— Photostats of Lord Reith's Papers. BBC Written Archives Centre, Reading.

Report From the Select Committee on Estimates. London: His Majesty's Stationery Office, 1934.

Report From the Select Committee on Patent Medicines Together With Proceedings of the Committee, Minutes of Evidence, and Appendices. London: His Majesty's Stationery Office, 1914.

Report of the Broadcasting Committee. Cmd. 5091. London: His Majesty's Stationery Office, 1936.

Reports of Speeches Stating the View of British Advertisers. London: Incorporated Society of British Advertisers, 1935.

Richards, David A. 'America Conquers Britain: Anglo-American Conflict in the Popular Media During the 1920s'. *Journal of American Culture* 3, 1 (1980): 95–104.

Richards, I. A. *Principles of Literary Criticism*. 1924. Reprinted New York: Harcourt Brace, A Harvest Book, n.d.

—— *Practical Criticism: A Study of Literary Judgement*. [1929.] Reprinted New York: Harcourt, Brace and World, A Harvest Book, n.d.

Richards, Jeffrey. *The Age of the Dream Palace: Cinema and Society in Britain, 1930–1939*. London: Routledge and Kegan Paul, 1984.

—— and Anthony Aldgate. *British Cinema and Society, 1930–1970*. Totowa, NJ: Barnes and Noble, 1983.

Richardson, H. W. *Economic Recovery in Britain, 1932–39*. London: Weidenfeld and Nicolson, 1967.

Richardson, Philip S. J. *A History of English Ballroom Dancing (1910–45): The Story of the Development of the Modern English Style*. London: Herbert Jenkins, n.d.

Rickards, Maurice. *Posters of the Nineteen-Twenties*. London: Evelyn, Adams, and Mackay, 1968.

Riddel, Joseph N. *C. Day Lewis*. New York: Twayne, 1971.

Riding, Laura. *Contemporaries and Snobs*. London: Jonathan Cape, 1928.

Robertson, P. J. M. *The Leavises on Fiction: An Historic Partnership*. New York: St Martin's Press, 1981.

Robinson, David. *Chaplin: The Mirror of Opinion*. London: Secker and Warburg; Bloomington: Indiana University Press, 1984.

—— *Chaplin: His Life and Art*. New York: McGraw-Hill, 1985.

Robinson, E. A. G. *The Structure of Competitive Industry.* Cambridge: Cambridge University Press, 1935.

Robson, William A., ed. *Public Enterprises: Developments in Social Ownership and Control in Great Britain*. London: George Allen and Unwin, 1937.

Robson, W. W. *The Definition of Literature and other Essays*. Cambridge: Cambridge University Press, 1982.

Roemer, Michael. 'Chaplin: Charles and Charlie'. *Yale Review* 64, 2 (1974–5): 168–84.

Rohmer, Eric and Claude Chabrol. *Hitchcock: The First Forty-Four Films*. Stanley Hochman, trans. New York: Frederick Ungar, 1979.

Rosenthal, Michael. *Virginia Woolf*. London: Routledge and Kegan Paul, 1979.

Rosenthal, Raymond, ed. *McLuhan: Pro and Con*. New York: Funk and Wagnalls, 1967.

Rossetti, Geoffrey W. ['G.W.R.', pseud.]. 'Democratic Tastes'. *Cambridge Review*, 3 June 1932, 444–5.

Rosten, Leo C. *Hollywood: The Movie Colony, the Movie Makers*. New York: Harcourt, Brace, 1941.

Rotha, Paul. *The Film Till Now: A Survey of the Cinema*. London: Jonathan Cape, 1930.

—— *Celluloid: The Film Today*. London: Longmans, Green, 1931.

—— 'The Cinema To-Day'. *Twentieth Century* 1, 1 (1931): 18–21.

—— 'Approach to a New Cinema'. *Cinema Quarterly* 1, 1 (1932): 18–32.

—— 'The Film: Our Attitude Toward It'. *Journal of the Royal Society of British Artists and Art Club* 1, 2 (1932): 15–17.

—— 'The Function of the Director. 1. The Documentary Director'. *Cinema Quarterly* 2, 1 (1933): 78–9.

—— '*Contact*: An Interview With Paul Rotha'. *Sight and Sound* 2, 5 (1933): 9–10.

—— 'Making *Contact*'. *Cinema Quarterly* 9, 3 (1933): 156–9.

—— *Documentary Film*. London: Faber and Faber, 1936.

—— *Movie Parade*. London: The Studio LD, 1936.

—— 'Films and the Labour Party'. Address to Special Labour Party Conference on Film Propaganda, 30 Oct. 1936. Typescript in British Film Institute, London.

—— 'Documentary Has Realism That British Drama Lacks, Says Rotha'. *Motion Picture Herald*, 9 Oct. 1937, 21.

—— 'Films of Fact and Fiction'. *Theatre Arts Monthly* 22, 3 (1938): 186–97.

—— 'The Lament'. *Sight and Sound* 7, 27 (1938): 120–1.

—— *Rotha on the Film: A Selection of Writings About the Cinema*. London: Faber and Faber, 1958.

Rotha, Paul. *Documentary Diary: An Informal History of the British Documentary Film, 1928–1939*. London: Secker and Warburg, 1973.

—— *Robert J. Flaherty: A Biography*. Jay Ruby, ed. Philadelphia: University of Pennsylvania Press, 1983.

—— Interview. 17 Nov. 1978.

—— Paul Rotha Collection. National Film Archive, London.

Rothenstein, William. 'Possibilities for the Improvement of Industrial Art in England'. *Journal of the Royal Society of Arts* 69, 3565 (1921): 268–77.

Rothman, William. *Hitchcock — The Murderous Gaze*. Cambridge: Harvard University Press, 1982.

Rothstein, Arthur. *Photojournalism*. 3rd edn. Garden City, NJ: American Photographic Book Publishing, 1974.

Routh, Guy. *Occupation and Pay in Great Britain, 1906–60*. Cambridge: Cambridge University Press, 1965.

Rowntree, B. Seebown. *Poverty and Progress: A Second Social Survey of York*. London: Longmans, Green, 1941.

Rowson, Simon. 'A Statistical Survey of the Cinema Industry in Great Britain in 1934'. *Journal of the Royal Statistical Society* 99, 1 (1936): 67–129.

Royal Academy of Arts. *John Armstrong, 1893–1973*. London: Arts Council of Great Britain, 1975.

Royal Commission on the Press, 1947–1949. Report. London: His Majesty's Stationery Office, 1949.

Russell, Gilbert. *Advertisement Writing*. London: Ernest Benn, 1927.

Russell, Thomas. *Commercial Advertising*. London: G. P. Putnam, 1919.

—— *A Working Text-Book of Advertising*. 3rd edn. London: Russell-Hart, 1924.

—— ed. *Advertising and Publicity*. London: Educational Book Company [1911].

Russett, Bruce M. *Community and Contention: Britain and America in the Twentieth Century*. Cambridge: Massachusetts Institute of Technology Press, 1963.

Russo, John Paul. 'I. A. Richards in Retrospect'. *Critical Inquiry* 8, 1 (1982): 743–60.

Rust, Francis. *Dance in Society*. London: Routledge and Kegan Paul, 1969.

Rye, Jane. *Futurism*. London: Studio Vista, 1972.

Sadoul, Georges. *British Creators of Film Technique*. London: British Film Institute, 1948.

—— *Georges Méliès*. Paris: Éditions Seghers, 1961.

Salt, Barry. 'Film Style and Technology in the Thirties'. *Film Quarterly* 30, 1 (1976): 19–32.

—— 'Film Form, 1900–1906'. *Sight and Sound* 47, 3 (1978): 148–53.

Samuels, Stuart. 'The Left Book Club'. *Journal of Contemporary History* 1, 2 (1966): 65–86.

Sanders, M. L. 'Wellington House and British Propaganda During the First World War'. *Historical Journal* 18, 1 (1975): 119–46.

—— and Philip M. Taylor. *British Propaganda During the First World War, 1914–1918*. London: Macmillan, 1982.

Sanger, Gerald. 'News into Entertainment'. *World's Press News*, 21 Jan. 1937.

Saunders, G. Ivy. 'Women Chauffeurs'. *Daily Mail*, 9 Oct. 1915.

Saunders, J. W. *The Profession of English Letters*. London: Routledge and Kegan Paul; Toronto: University of Toronto Press, 1964.

Saxon Mills, G. H. 'Colour War'. *Penrose Annual* 36 (1934): 8–11.

—— *There is a Tide*. London: William Heinemann, 1954.

Scannell, Paddy. 'Music for the Multitude? The Dilemmas of the BBC's Music Policy, 1923–1946'. *Media, Culture and Society* 3 (1981): 243–60.

Schafer, William J. and Johannes Reidel. *The Art of Ragtime: Form and Meaning of an Original Black American Art*. Baton Rouge: Louisiana State University Press, 1973.

Schatz, Thomas. *Hollywood Genres: Formulas, Film-making and the Studio System*. Philadelphia: Temple University Press, 1981.

Schatzman, Leonard and Anselm Strauss. 'Social Class and Modes of Communication'. *American Journal of Sociology* 60, 4 (1955): 329–38.

Schickel, Richard. *D. W. Griffith: An American Life*. New York: Simon and Schuster, 1984.

Scholes, Percy. 'Music and Musicians'. *Observer*, 14 Dec. 1924.

—— ed. *The Mirror of Music, 1844–1944: A Century of Musical Life in Britain as Reflected in the Pages of the* Musical Times. London: Novello, 1947.

Schramm, Wilber, ed. *Mass Communications: A Book of Selected Readings*. 2nd edn. Urbana: University of Illinois Press, 1975.

Schrine, David. 'The Psychology of Film Audiences'. *Sight and Sound* 2, 8 (1933–4): 122–3.

Schudson, Michael. *Discovering the News: A Social History of American Newspapers*. New York: Beacon Books, 1978.

—— 'Criticizing the Critics of Advertising: Towards a Sociological View of Marketing'. *Media, Culture and Society* 3, 1 (1981): 3–12.

—— *Advertising, the Uneasy Persuasion: Its Dubious Impact on American Society*. New York: Basic Books, 1984.

Schults, Raymond L. *Crusader in Babylon: W. T. Stead and the* Pall Mall Gazette. Lincoln: University of Nebraska Press, 1972.

Schuneman, Raymond Smith. 'Art or Photography: A Question for Newspaper Editors of the 1890s'. *Journalism Quarterly* 42, 1 (1965): 43–52.

—— 'The Photograph in Print: An Examination of New York Daily Newspapers, 1890–1937'. Ph.D. diss.: University of Minnesota, 1966.

Scott, Walter Dill. *The Psychology of Advertising in Theory and Practice*. Boston: Small, Maynard, 1921.

Scott-James, R. A. *The Influence of the Press*. London: S. W. Partridge [1913].

Seebury, William Marston. *The Public and the Motion Picture Industry*. New York: Macmillan, 1926.

Seton, Marie. *Sergei M. Eisenstein*. 2nd edn. London: Dennis Dobson, 1978.

Seymour-Ure, Colin. *The Press, Politics and the Public: An Essay on the Role of the National Press in the British Political System*. London: Methuen, 1968.

Shafer, Stephen Craig. ' "Enter the Dream House": The British Film Industry and the Working Classes in Depression England, 1929–1939'. Ph.D.diss.: University of Illinois at Urbana-Champaign, 1982.

Sharp, Denis. *The Picture Palace and Other Buildings for the Movies*. London: Hugh Evelyn, 1969.

Shattock, Joanne and Michael Wolff, eds. *The Victorian Periodical Press: Samplings and Soundings*. Leicester: Leicester University Press; Toronto: University of Toronto Press, 1982.

Shaw, George Bernard ['G.B.S.']. 'The Cinema as a Moral Leveller'. *New Statesman*. Special Supplement on the Modern Theatre. 27 June 1914.

—— *The Collected Screenplays of Bernard Shaw*. Bernard F. Dukore, ed. Athens: University of Georgia Press, 1980.

—— and Archibald Henderson. 'The Drama, the Theatre, and the Films'. *Fortnightly Review* 122 (1924): 289–302.

Shead, Richard. *Constant Lambert*. London: Simon, 1973.

'Shell-Mex and B.P. Exhibition, 1938'. *Art and Industry* 25 (1928): 103–5.

Shils, Edward. *The Intellectuals and the Powers and Other Essays*. Chicago: University of Chicago Press, 1972.

Short, K. R. M., ed. *Feature Films as History*. Knoxville: University of Tennessee Press, 1981.

Sieveking, Lance. *The Stuff of Radio*. London: Cassell, 1934.

Silva, Fred, ed. *Focus on* The Birth of a Nation. Englewood Cliffs, NJ: Prentice-Hall, 1971.

Silvey, Robert. *Who's Listening? The Story of BBC Audience Research*. London: George Allen and Unwin, 1974.

Simon, Brian. *The Politics of Educational Reform, 1920–1940*. London: Lawrence and Wishart, 1974.

Simon, Herbert. *Song and Words: A History of the Curwen Press*. London: George Allen and Unwin, 1973.

Simon, Oliver. *Printer and Playground: An Autobiography*. London: Faber and Faber, 1956.

Sked, Alan and Chris Cook, eds. *Crisis and Controversy: Essays in Honour of A. J. P. Taylor*. London: Macmillan, 1976.

Skidelsky, Robert. *John Maynard Keynes. Volume One: Hopes Betrayed, 1883–1920*. London: Macmillan, 1983.

Sklar, Robert. *Movie-Made America*. New York: Vintage, 1975.

Slide, Anthony. 'The Evolution of the Film Star'. *Films in Review* 25 (1974): 594–6.

Smith, Anthony. 'Information Technology and the Myth of Abundance'. *Daedalus* 111, 4 (1982): 1–16.

—— ed. *Newspapers and Democracy: International Essays on a Changing Medium*. Cambridge: Massachusetts Institute of Technology Press, 1980.

Smith, David. *Socialist Propaganda in the Twentieth-Century British Novel*. Totowa, NJ: Rowman and Littlefield, 1978.

Smith, Hubert Llewellyn. *The Economic Laws of Art Production: An Essay Towards the Construction of a Missing Chapter of Economics*. London: Oxford University Press, 1924.

Smith, John M. 'Conservative Individualism: A Selection of English Hitchcock'. *Screen* 13, 3 (1972): 51–70.

Smith, R. H. 'All the Firsts of *The London Illustrated News*'. *Penrose Annual* 67 (1974): 101–12.

Smith, Wareham. *Spilt Ink.* London: Ernest Benn, 1932.

Soames, Jane. *The English Press: Newspapers and News.* London: Lindsay Drummond, 1938.

Soffer, Reba N. *Ethics and Society in England: The Revolution in the Social Sciences, 1870–1914.* Berkeley and Los Angeles: University of California Press, 1978.

Sopocy, Martin. 'A Narrated Cinema: The Pioneer Story Films of James A. Williamson'. *Cinema Journal* 18, 1 (1978): 1–28.

Spacks, Patricia. *Gossip.* New York: Alfred A. Knopf, 1985.

Spalding, Frances. *Roger Fry: Art and Life.* Berkeley and Los Angeles: University of California Press, 1980.

Sparke, Penny. *An Introduction to Design and Culture in the Twentieth Century.* London: Allen and Unwin, 1986.

Sparling, H. Halliday. *The Kelmscott Press and William Morris, Master Craftsman.* London: Macmillan, 1924.

Spencer, Herbert. *Pioneers of Modern Typography.* London: Lund Humphries, 1969.

Spender, J. A. *Life, Journalism and Politics.* 2 vols. London: Cassell, 1927.

—— *Through English Eyes.* New York; Frederick A. Stokes, 1928.

—— 'Is "Personal" Journalism Destroying Prestige?'. *World's Press News*, 3 June 1937.

Spender, Stephen. *The Destructive Element.* London: Jonathan Cape, 1935.

—— *Forward From Liberalism.* London: Victor Gollancz, 1937.

—— Review of *Revaluation, Tradition and Development in English Poetry* by F. R. Leavis. *Criterion* 16, 63 (1937): 350–1.

—— *The Struggle of the Modern.* Berkeley and Los Angeles: University of California Press, 1963.

Spoto, Donald. *The Art of Alfred Hitchcock: Fifty Years of his Motion Pictures.* New York: Hopkinson and Blake, 1976.

—— *The Dark Side of Genius: The Life of Alfred Hitchcock.* New York: Ballantine Books, 1983.

Stansky, Peter. *Redesigning the World: William Morris, the 1880s, and the Arts and Crafts.* Princeton: Princeton University Press, 1985.

—— and William Abrahams. *Journey to the Frontier: Two Roads to the Spanish Civil War.* 1966. Reprinted New York: W. W. Norton, 1970.

—— and William Abrahams. *The Unknown Orwell.* New York: Alfred A. Knopf, 1972.

—— and William Abrahams. *Orwell: The Transformation.* New York: Alfred A. Knopf, 1979.

Stannard, Russell. *With the Dictators of Fleet Street: The Autobiography of an Ignorant Journalist.* London: Hutchinson, 1934.

Starch, Daniel. *Advertising Principles.* Chicago: A. W. Shaw, 1927.

Stead, Peter. 'Hollywood's Message for the World: The British Response in the Nineteen-Thirties'. *Historical Journal of Film, Radio, and Television* 1, 1 (1981): 19–32.

Stead, Wickham. *Journalism.* London: Ernest Benn, 1928.

Stead, W. T. *The Americanization of the World, or the Trend of the Twentieth Century.* New York and London: Horace Markley, 1901.

Stearns, Gerald E., ed. *McLuhan: Hot and Cool*. New York: Dial Press, 1967.

Steer, Vincent. *Printing Design and Layout*. 1934. Reprinted London: Virtue and Company, 1947.

Stevenson, John. *British Society, 1914–45*. Harmondsworth: Penguin Books, 1984.

Stone, Christopher. 'Round and Round'. *The Gramophone* 4, 7 (1926): 311.

—— *Christopher Stone Speaking*. London: Elkin Mathews and Marnot, 1933.

—— 'Radio Luxembourg'. *The Gramophone* 12, 139 (1934): 269.

—— 'The National Gramophonic Society'. *The Gramophone* 12, 143 (1935): 432.

Straumann, Heinrich. *Newspaper Headlines: A Study in Linguistic Method*. London: George Allen and Unwin, 1935.

Stubbs, Patricia. *Women and Fiction: Feminism and the Novel, 1890–1920*. Sussex: Harvester; New York: Barnes and Noble, 1979.

Sturmey, S. G. *The Economic Development of Radio*. London: Gerald Duckworth, 1958.

Stutterheim, Kurt von. *The Press in England*. London: George Allen and Unwin, 1934.

Surrey, Richard. *Layout Technique in Advertising*. New York and London: McGraw-Hill, 1929.

Sussex, Elizabeth. *The Rise and Fall of British Documentary: The Story of the Film Movement Founded by John Grierson*. Berkeley: University of California Press, 1975.

Sutherland, John. 'A Pragmatic Popular Educator'. *TLS*, 27 Sept. 1985, 1073–4.

Swanberg, W. A. *Citizen Hearst: A Biography of William Randolph Hearst*. New York: Charles Scribner's Sons, 1961.

—— *Pulitzer*. New York: Charles Scribner's Sons, 1967.

Swann, Paul. 'The British Documentary Film Movement, 1926–1946'. Ph.D. diss.: University of Leeds, 1979.

Swinnerton, Frank. 'The B.B.C.—Candid Criticism'. *Nash's Pall Mall Magazine* (June 1932): 82–6.

—— *Authors and the Book Trade*. New York: Alfred A. Knopf, 1932.

Tallents, Stephen. *The Projection of England*. London: Faber and Faber, 1932.

—— *Post Office Publicity*. London: Post Office Green Paper 8, 1935.

—— 'The Documentary Film'. *Journal of the Royal Society of Arts* 95, 4731 (1946): 68–85.

—— 'Cinema'. Typescript in British Film Institute Library, London.

Talmadge, William H. 'Equipment Failure and Audio Distortion in the Acoustical Recording and Remastering of Early Jazz'. *Journal of Jazz Studies* 5, 2 (1979): 61–75.

Tawney, R. H. *Secondary Education for All: A Policy for Labour*. London: George Allen and Unwin [1922].

Taylor, A. J. P. *English History, 1914–1945*. Oxford: Clarendon Press, 1965.

—— *Beaverbrook*. New York: Simon and Schuster, 1972.

Taylor, John Russell. *Hitch: The Life and Times of Alfred Hitchcock*. 1978. Reprinted New York: Berkley Books, 1980.

Taylor, Joshua. *Futurism.* New York: Museum of Modern Art, 1961.

Taylor, Philip M. *The Projection of Britain: British Overseas Publicity and Propaganda, 1919–39.* Cambridge: Cambridge University Press, 1981.

Taylor, Richard. *Film Propaganda: Soviet Russia and Nazi Germany.* London: Croom Helm; New York: Barnes and Noble, 1979.

—— *The Politics of the Soviet Cinema, 1917–1929.* Cambridge: Cambridge University Press, 1979.

Tedlow, Richard S. *Keeping the Corporate Image: Public Relations and Business, 1900–1950.* Greenwich, CT.: Jai Press, 1979.

'That's Shell— That is!': An Exhibition of Shell Advertising Art. London: Barbican Art Gallery, 1983.

Thirties: British Art and Design Before the War. London: Arts Council of Great Britain, 1979.

Thompson, Denys. *Reading and Discrimination.* London: Chatto and Windus, 1934.

—— *Between the Lines, or How to Read a Newspaper.* London: Frederick Muller, 1939.

—— *Voice of Civilization: An Enquiry into Advertising.* London: Frederick Muller, 1943.

—— ed. *Discrimination and Popular Culture.* 2nd edn. Harmondsworth: Penguin Books, 1973.

—— ed. *The Leavises: Recollections and Impressions.* Cambridge: Cambridge University Press, 1984.

Thompson, E. P. *The Poverty of Theory and Other Essays.* New York and London: Monthly Review Press, 1978.

Tilby, A. Wyatt. 'The Best-Seller Problem'. *Edinburgh Review* 236, 481 (1922): 88–98.

Tillyard, E. M. W. *The Muse Unchained: An Intimate Account of the Revolution in English Studies at Cambridge.* London: Bowes and Bowes, 1958.

Tolley, A. T. *The Poetry of the Thirties.* New York: St Martin's Press, 1975.

Tompkins, Jane P., ed. *Reader-Response Criticism: From Formalism to Post-Structuralism.* Baltimore: Johns Hopkins University Press, 1980.

Townsend, J. Benjamin. *John Davidson: Poet of Armageddon.* New Haven: Yale University Press, 1961.

Trewin, J. C. *Robert Donat.* London: Heinemann, 1968.

Trilling, Lionel. 'Science, Literature and Culture: A Comment on the Leavis–Snow Controversy'. *Universities Quarterly* 17, 1 (1962): 9–32.

Trotter, W. *Instincts of the Herd in Peace and War.* 2nd edn. London: T. Fisher Unwin, 1923.

Troubridge, Lady. 'A Creature of Circumstance'. *Daily Mail,* 4 Oct. 1910.

Truffaut, François. *Hitchcock.* New York: Simon and Schuster, A Touchstone Book, 1966.

Tulloch, H. A. 'Changing British Attitudes Towards the United States in the 1880s'. *Historical Journal* 20, 4 (1977): 825–40.

Tunstall, Jeremy, ed. *Media Sociology: A Reader.* Urbana: University of Illinois Press, 1970.

Turner, E. S. *The Shocking History of Advertising!* New York: Dutton, 1953.

Turner, James. *Without God, Without Creed: The Origins of Unbelief in America*. Baltimore: Johns Hopkins University Press, 1985.

Unwin, Stanley. *The Truth About Publishing*. 3rd edn. London: George Allen and Unwin, 1929.

Updike, Daniel Berkeley. *Printing Types: Their History, Forms, and Use*. 2 vols. Cambridge: Harvard University Press, 1922.

Upward, Edward. *Journey to the Border*. London: Hogarth Press, 1938.

Vardac, A. Nicholas. *Stage to Screen: Theatrical Method from Garrick to Griffith*. 1949. Reprinted New York: Benjamin Blom, 1968.

Vicinus, Martha, ed. *Suffer and Be Still: Women in the Victorian Age*. Bloomington: Indiana University Press, 1972.

Vickerman, R. W. *The Economics of Leisure and Recreation*. London: Macmillan, 1975.

Vinogradoff, Igor. 'History of English Advertising Programmes Broadcast to the United Kingdom From Foreign Stations Down to the Outbreak Of War'. 1945. BBC Written Archives Centre, Reading.

Wadman, Howard. 'Looking Forward'. *Penrose Annual* 42 (1940): 29–30.

Waites, Bernard, Tony Bennett, and Graham Martin, eds. *Popular Culture: Past and Present*. London: Croom Helm, 1982.

Waldo, Terry. *This is Ragtime*. New York: Hawthorn Books, 1976.

Walker, Alexander. *Stardom: The Hollywood Phenomenon*. London: Michael Joseph, 1970.

—— *Shattered Silents: How the Talkies Came to Stay*. London: Elm Tree Books, 1978.

Walker, Edwin S. 'Early English Jazz.' *Jazz Journal* 22, 9 (1969): 24–6.

Walsh, William. *F. R. Leavis*. Bloomington: Indiana University Press, 1980.

Walvin, James. *Leisure and Society, 1850–1950*. London: Longman, 1978.

Ward, Maisie. *Gilbert Keith Chesterton*. New York: Sheed and Ward, 1943.

Warde, B. L. 'What does "Modern" mean in Typography?'. *Penrose Annual* 38 (1936): 44–7.

Warner, Jack L. *My First Hundred Years in Hollywood*. New York: Random House, 1964.

Warren, C. Henry. 'Broadcast Talks: Are They Too Highbrow?'. *Radio Times*, 6 Jan. 1930, 11.

—— 'Who Listens to the B.B.C. Talks?'. *Bookman* 85, 508 (1934): 440.

—— 'Opera and the B.B.C.' *Bookman* 86, 509 (1934): 105.

Waterhouse, Keith. Daily Mirror *Style*. London: Mirror Books, 1981.

Watson, George. *The Literary Critics: A Study of English Descriptive Criticism*. London: Chatto and Windus, 1964.

Watt, Harry. *Don't Look at the Camera*. London: Paul Elek, 1974.

Waugh, Arthur. 'Authors, Publishers and the Public'. *Quarterly Review* 259, 514 (1932): 129–44.

Waugh, Carlton. *The Comics*. New York: Macmillan, 1947.

Waugh, Evelyn. 'For Adult Audiences'. *Daily Mail*, 25 July 1930.

Webb, Beatrice, *Beatrice Webb Diaries, 1924–1932*. Margaret Cole, ed. London: Longmans, Green, 1956.

Wees, William C. *Vorticism and the English Avant-Garde*. Toronto: University of Toronto Press, 1972.

Wellek, René. 'Literary Criticism and Philosophy'. *Scrutiny* 5, 4 (1937): 375–83.

Wells, H. G. *Tono-Bungay*. London: Macmillan, 1909.

West, Alick. *The Mountain in the Sunlight: Studies in Conflict and Unity*. London: Lawrence and Wishart, 1958.

Whitcomb, Ian. *After the Ball*. Harmondsworth: Penguin Books, 1972.

White, Cynthia L. *Women's Magazines, 1693–1968*. London: Michael Joseph, 1970.

White, Percival. *Advertising Research*. New York and London: D. Appleton, 1927.

Whiteman, Paul and Mary Margaret McBride. *Jazz*. New York: J. H. Sears, 1926.

Wiener, Martin J. *English Culture and the Decline of the Industrial Spirit, 1850–1980*. Cambridge: Cambridge University Press, 1981.

Wigley, John. *The Rise and Fall of the Victorian Sunday*. Manchester: Manchester University Press, 1980.

Wildman, A. S. 'TYPE is Part of the Picture'. *Advertising Display* 1, 3 (1926): 84–6.

Wilenski, R. H. 'The Evolution of Transport Mural Paintings'. *London Studio* 6 (1933): 73–6.

Wilkinson, Ellen. *The Town That Was Murdered: The Life Story of Jarrow*. London: Victor Gollancz, 1939.

Willet, John. *The New Sobriety, 1917–1933: Art and Politics in the Weimar Period*. London: Thames and Hudson, 1978.

Willey, Basil. *Cambridge and Other Memories, 1920–1953*. London: Chatto and Windus, 1968.

Williams, A. H. *No Name on the Door: A Memoir of Gordon Selfridge*. London: W. H. Allen, 1956.

Williams, Francis. *Ernest Bevin: Portrait of a Great Englishman*. London: Hutchinson, 1952.

—— *Nothing So Strange*. New York: American Heritage Press, 1970.

Williams, Raymond. *Culture and Society, 1780–1950*. 1958. Reprinted New York: Harper Torchbooks, 1966.

—— *The Country and the City*. New York: Oxford University Press, 1973.

—— *Keywords: A Vocabulary of Culture and Society*. N.p.: Fontana/Croom Helm, 1976.

—— *Marxism and Literature*. Oxford: Oxford University Press, 1977.

Williams, W. E. *Allen Lane: A Personal Portrait*. London: Bodley Head, 1973.

Williams-Ellis, Clough. *England and the Octopus*. London: Geoffrey Bles, 1928.

Williamson, Aubrey. *Theatre and Two Decades*. London: Rockcliff, 1951.

Williamson, H. R. 'Notes at Random'. *Bookman* 86, 511 (1934): 1–5.

Wilson, A. N. *Hilaire Belloc*. London: Hamish Hamilton, 1984.

Wilson, Colin. *The Outsider*. London: Gollancz, 1956.

Wilson, David, ed. *Sight and Sound: A Fiftieth- Anniversary Selection*. London: Faber and Faber, 1982.

Wilson, Norman. 'Film Societies, What Now?'. *World Film News* 2, 10 (1938): 47.

Wilson, Trevor. *The Downfall of the Liberal Party, 1914–1935*. London: Collins, 1966.

Wingler, Hans. *Bauhaus: Weimar, Dessau, Berlin, Chicago*. Cambridge: Massachusetts Institute of Technology Press, 1978.

Winkler, Henry R., ed. *Twentieth-Century Britain: National Power and Social Welfare*. New York: New Viewpoints, 1976.

Winship, George Parker. *Daniel Berkeley Updike and the Merrymount Press*. Rochester: Leo Hart, 1947.

Winstanley, Michael J. *The Shopkeeper's World, 1830–1914*. Manchester: Manchester University Press, 1983.

Wireless Discussion Groups: What They Are and How to Run Them. London: British Broadcasting Corporation, 1935.

Wolfe, Charles Hull. *Modern Radio Advertising*. 2nd edn. New York: Funk and Wagnalls, 1953.

Wolfe, Kenneth. *The Churches and the British Broadcasting Corporation, 1922–1956: The Politics of Broadcast Religion*. London: SCM Press, 1984.

Wood, Alan. *Mr. Rank: A Study of J. Arthur Rank and British Films*. London: Hodder and Stoughton, 1952.

Wood, Cyril. 'The Technique of the Radio Play'. *Journal of the Royal Society of Arts* 138, 4487 (1938): 23–43.

Wood, James Playsted. *The Story of Advertising*. New York: Ronald Press, 1958.

Wood, Robin. *Hitchcock's Films*. New York: A. S. Barnes; London: Tantivy, 1977.

Woodcock, George. *The Crystal Spirit: A Study of George Orwell*. Boston: Little, Brown, 1966.

Woodruff, Douglas. *Plato's American Republic*. New York: E. P. Dutton, 1926.

—— 'An Open Letter to the Listener Who Hates Talks'. *Radio Times*, 2 May 1930, 253.

Woolcott, Alexander. *The Story of Irving Berlin*. New York: G. P. Putnam's Sons, 1925.

Woolf, Leonard. 'Radio has Revolutionized Entertainment'. *Radio Times*, 11 Dec. 1931, 833–4.

—— *Downhill All the Way: An Autobiography of the Years 1919–1939*. London: Hogarth Press, 1967.

Woolf, Virginia. *Roger Fry: A Biography*. New York: Harcourt Brace, 1940.

—— *Collected Essays*. vol. 2. New York: Harcourt, Brace and World, 1967.

—— *The Letters of Virginia Woolf. Volume Three: 1923–1928*. Nigel Nicolson and Joanne Trautmann, eds. New York: Harcourt, Brace, Jovanovich, 1978.

—— *The Letters of Virginia Woolf. Volume Four: 1929–1931*. Nigel Nicolson and Joanne Trautmann, eds. New York: Harcourt, Brace, Jovanovich, 1979.

—— *The Diary of Virginia Woolf. Volume Five: 1936–1941*. Anne Olivier Bell, ed. San Diego: Harcourt, Brace, Jovanovich, 1984.

Woolfe, H. Bruce. 'Commercial Documentary'. *Cinema Quarterly* 2, 2 (1933–4): 96–100.

Wright, Basil. Review of *Shipyard*, by Paul Rotha. *Cinema Quarterly* 3, 3 (1935): 177–8.

Yacowar, Maurice. *Hitchcock's British Films*. Hamden, CN: Archon, 1977.

Yallop, David A. *The Day the Laughter Stopped: The True Story of Fatty Arbuckle*. New York: St Martin's Press, 1976.

Young, Amyas. 'Mental Tuning In: Some Hints on How to Listen to a Wireless Play'. *Radio Times*, 28 Jan. 1928.

Young, Filson. 'Broadcast Drama: A Record of Progress'. *Radio Times*, 25 Jan. 1929, 187.

—— 'Broadcasting and Advertising'. In *B.B.C. Yearbook: 1933*. London: British Broadcasting Corporation, 1933.

Young, John. 'Post-War Progress in Newspaper Production'. *Printing News*, 8 Sept. 1932.

Zwerdling, Alex. *Orwell and the Left*. New Haven: Yale University Press, 1974.

INDEX

NOV 21 1988